Philosophical Melancholy and Delirium

Donald W. Livingston

Philosophical Melancholy and Delirium

Hume's Pathology of Philosophy

The University of Chicago Press • Chicago and London

Donald W. Livingston is professor of philosophy at Emory University. He is the author of *Hume's Philosophy of Common Life,* also published by the University of Chicago Press, and the coeditor of three books on Hume.

The University of Chicago Press, Chicago 60637
The University of Chicago Press, Ltd., London
 Published 1998
Printed in the United States of America
07 06 05 04 03 02 01 00 99 98 5 4 3 2 1

ISBN (cloth): 0-226-48716-4
ISBN (paper): 0-226-48717-2

Library of Congress Cataloging-in-Publication Data

Livingston, Donald W.
Philosophical melancholy and delirium : Hume's pathology of philosophy / Donald W. Livingston.
p. cm.
Includes bibliographical references and index.
ISBN 0-226-48716-4. — ISBN 0-226-48717-2 (pbk.)
1. Hume, David, 1711–1776. 2. Philosophy. I. Title.
B1498.L59 1998
192—dc21 97-35175
CIP

∞ The paper used in this publication meets the minimum requirements of the American National Standard for Information Sciences—Permanence of Paper for Printed Library Materials, ANSI Z39.48-1992.

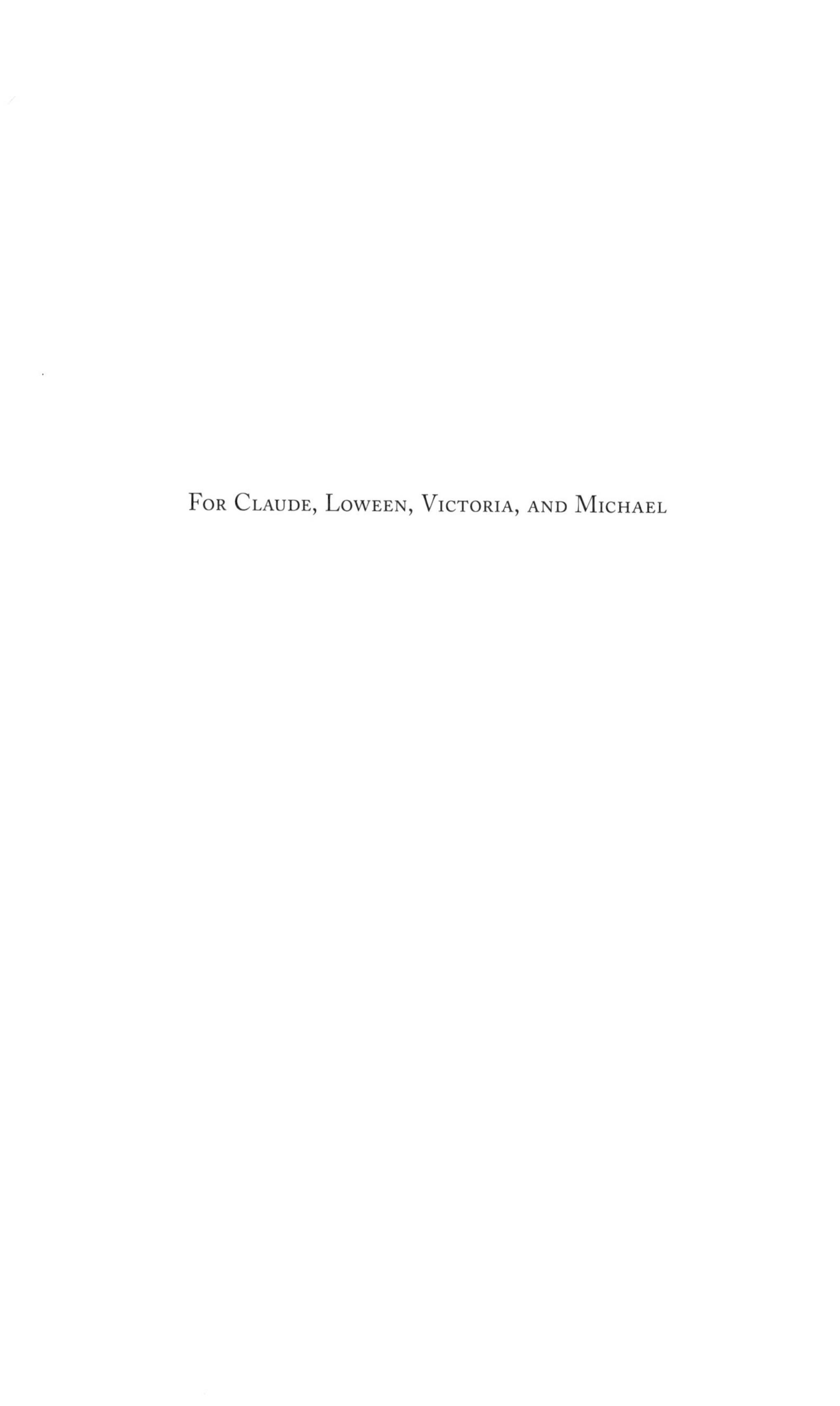

For Claude, Loween, Victoria, and Michael

Metaphysics is the finding of bad reasons for what we believe upon instinct, but to find these reasons is no less an instinct.

F. H. Bradley

To consider the matter aright, reason is nothing but a wonderful and unintelligible instinct in our souls, which carries us along a certain train of ideas, and endows them with particular qualities, according to their particular situations and relations.

David Hume

CONTENTS

PREFACE

What is philosophy? This study seeks to discover Hume's answer to that question. The question is intended to be comprehensive, including in its scope such questions as, What is the philosophical life? What is philosophical truth? What is the proper relation of philosophy to religion, to culture, to its own history? In particular I have tried to understand what Hume meant by a distinction that occurs throughout his writings between what he calls "true philosophy" and "false philosophy." In exploring Hume's answer to these questions, the study ranges over all of his writings, touching a wide variety of topics such as morals, politics, civilization, barbarism, religion, history, literature, and law. But none of these are taken up in their own right; rather, they are considered only insofar as they exemplify or otherwise illuminate Hume's conception of philosophy.

This is a study both in the history of ideas and in philosophy. It is, of course, difficult to combine the two. The former demands the Collingwoodian ideal of rethinking past thoughts as the agent understood them. The latter demands speculative judgment about reality independent of what past thinkers have thought. But in the end, both things must be done, and in the same inquiry, if there is to be such a thing as a tradition of philosophical inquiry. I have written about Hume because I think his criticism of philosophy is insightful and merits further development in ways he could not have fully understood. Historical and philosophical questions, though distinguishable, are therefore united in this study from the beginning. In some chapters, however, the one dominates the other, and I have indicated this by dividing the study into two parts. Part 1 is entitled "Humean Reflections" and is, for the most part, concerned to illuminate Hume's self-understanding about philosophy and its meaning for his own age. Part 2 is entitled "Humean Intimations" and continues the idiom of a Humean philosophy in certain topics into the nineteenth century and into our own time. But even the pursuit of these philosophical intimations has an oblique historical importance, for in viewing Hume's thought retrospectively, in terms of later events, it is possible to bring into focus features of that thought that otherwise might be missing from view.

In chapter 1, I argue against the older understanding of Hume as an empiricist. The fundamental problem of his philosophy is not the epistemologist's problem of establishing an empiricist foundation for knowledge but the skeptic's problem of determining what philosophy is and how to live a philosophical life properly conceived. The distinction between true and false philosophy is a distinction immanent in the activity of philosophizing itself and can be grasped only by a dialectical mode of inquiry. Chapter 2 explores the nature of this all-important dialectic. True philosophy, for Hume, is not only a mode of inquiry but a way of life, a form of wisdom. In this chapter I explore the virtues that inform the character of the true philosopher and the vices that inform the character of a corrupt philosophical consciousness.

Having examined the normative question of what distinguishes true from false philosophy, I turn in chapter 3 to a question in philosophical anthropology, namely, what is the source in human dispositions of philosophical activity? Hume finds that religion and philosophy spring from distinct dispositions; yet it is mythical polytheistic religion that provides men with the first understanding of the world and of themselves. Philosophy first makes its appearance in a world structured by mythical religion, and its subsequent history is largely the story of its self-definition in relation to religion and the struggle to reach a rapprochement with religion. As Hume forges a distinction between true and false philosophy, so he draws a distinction between true and false religion. And, as I argue, he considers true philosophy and true religion to be aspects of the same ideal identity.

It is typical of Hume's philosophy to seek the origins of practices in dispositions of human nature, but such an inquiry provides only a generic understanding of these practices. To have gained even this understanding is not to be disdained, but to obtain a concrete understanding of a practice as it is lived out in the contingent contexts of life and as it is modified by the speculative acts of an inventive species requires an historical narrative of the practice. Hume's *The Natural History of Religion* is a nod in this direction. It is a generic account of the dispositions that give rise to religious practices and a sketch of more concrete narrations of religious practices yet to be written.

In the case of politics, however, Hume provides not only a generic natural history of politics in the *Treatise* and second *Enquiry* but also a concrete narration of an actual practice in *The History of England* and the *Essays,* namely, a narrative of the practice of liberty in Britain. The point of the narrative is to enable the reader to understand the origins of the practice in human nature and in contingent circumstances of Britain and Europe and to discover norms immanent in the practice which can enable a participant in eighteenth-century Britain to correct mistaken conceptions of the practice (especially those generated by corrupt philosophical theories such as rationalism), and to continue the practice in the new context of the present and into the uncertain context of the future. The same could have been done for the practice of causal judgment. Hume locates this practice on the map of human nature as the disposition to form metaphorical ties of necessity between experiences of discrete constant conjunctions. As part of this natural history of causal judgment, Hume explores in the *Treatise* the disposition of human nature to form its causal judgments into a system, and he uncovers the rules for judging causes and effects that are immanent in the practice. The concrete narration of the practice of causal judgment in its developed scientific form would be a history of the practice of science or some part of it on the order, say, of Kuhn's *The Structure of Scientific Revolutions,* but there are only hints in Hume's writings as to what a Humean narration of the practice of science would look like.

Considerably more can be said, however, about a historical narration of the practice of philosophy. In chapters 4 through 7, I piece together Hume's conception of the history of philosophy. In these chapters I ask, How did Hume conceive of his relation to the philosophical tradition he had inherited (i.e., the philosophy of the ancients, of Christendom, and of the moderns)? And more particularly, How did he conceive of his relation to the skeptical tradition of philosophy within which his own distinction between true and false philosophy was forged—a distinction, moreover, which provides canons of interpretation for a Humean history of philosophy.

Having explored the critical distinction between true and false philosophy, the origin of philosophy in human nature, and the idea of its history, I turn to the question of the place of the philosopher in human society. The topic of civilization and barbarism was a lively one for Hume and the Scottish Enlightenment. For us, however, it is a topic that can be recovered only with difficulty. In chapters 8 and 9, I examine the relation of philosophy to civilization and barbarism. Is it speculative philosophy that generates civilization, or is it civilization that gives rise to philosophy? Hume argues that the practice of liberty is prior to philosophy and that philosophy did not arise and could not have arisen prior to the establishment of rudimentary republican government. Just as it is a guiding theme of its history that philosophy establish a proper relation to religion, so it is a guiding theme that it establish a proper relation to liberty. Not only do the practices of civilization generate philosophy, they may generate, indiscriminately, true and false philosophy. As civilization develops, it becomes more self-reflective and philosophical in its character; but should a corrupt philosophical consciousness come to dominate culture, a civilization could subvert itself by its own corrupt self-understanding. Hume calls this condition "barbarism"; albeit a barbarism possible only in an advanced civilization that has widely cultivated a philosophical consciousness. This barbarism arises from what he calls the "false refinements" of the intellect, and as I suggest, it bears fruitful comparison with Vico's "barbarism of reflection" in *The New Science* (1744).

Hume thought the culture of Europe, though still religious, was being progressively shaped by secular philosophical modes of thought and being. He did not greet this with the ritualistic enthusiasm of his Enlightenment colleagues D'Alembert, D'Holbach, Diderot, and Turgot, who did not view human reality through the lens of Hume's subtle distinction between true and false philosophy. It would not be an improvement if false religion were supplanted by corrupt modes of philosophy, but Hume believed that to be happening in Britain as politics, interest, and ambition began to mask themselves in the legitimacy of corrupt philosophical theorizing. Chapters 10 and 11 explore the theme of "English barbarism" prevalent in the letters of the last decade of Hume's life. I have treated the letters (or those that survive) as Hume's publisher William Straham thought they should be treated, namely, as a continuation of Hume's political philosophy. Two forms of English barbarism appear in the letters: the mass movement carried out under the slogan "Wilkes and Liberty!" and the use of military force to secure the colonies as a source of revenue for an emerging British commercial empire. These were *philosophical* English barbarisms because they were legitimated by corrupt forms of the philosophical act.

Chapters 12 through 14 examine the difference between the premodern polities of Europe and the modern unitary state that had been in the making since the emergence of absolute monarchy and appeared in its present form in the republic framed by the French Revolution. Hume's thought was developed during this transition, and it looks both ways. On balance, however, it is cast in a premodern idiom, and it is strongly critical of a number of trends that would eventually lead to the massive destruction of traditional independent social authorities and the attempt to consolidate these into unitary states. The relevance of this to a study of Hume's conception of *philosophy* is that Enlightenment ideologies such as liberalism and Marxism have played a prominent role in legitimating these efforts at destruction and consolidation.

The destruction of independent social authorities for the sake of a consolidated unitary state was met everywhere with resistance. In chapters 13 and 14, I take up a theme in Hume that has been neglected, namely, his doctrine of the right of resistance. It is in the light of this theme that we must understand Hume's solitary and cross-grained support for the secession of the American colonies. In chapter 14, I show that the concept of secession has been strangely neglected by philosophers not only in Hume's time but also in our own. Within the idea of the modern state, secession is not a contingent good or evil to be determined by a judgment of prudence; it is ruled out as a conceptual absurdity. In the two-hundred-year career of the modern state, as it coiled into ever tighter forms of consolidation, there appear to have been only three cases of peaceful secession but a great number of cases in which attempts at peaceful secession were brutally suppressed. Belgium seceded from the Netherlands in 1830; Norway from Sweden in 1905; and Singapore from the Malaysian federation in 1965. After 1990, however, a number of peaceful secessions occurred in Central Europe, including the peaceful dismemberment by referendum of fifteen republics formerly united in the U.S.S.R., the most centralized state in modern times. These, as well as growing secessionist and devolution movements in Europe and elsewhere in the world, raise the question of whether the modern unitary state still has the legitimacy it once had. This question enables us to view Hume's doctrine of resistance, his own resistance to the trends that brought about the modern state, and his defense of American secession in a new light.

Hume saw his own age as the first philosophical age, that is the first age in which a philosophical consciousness was becoming a mass phenomenon and no longer merely the province of elites. Today that process is complete. But if, as Hume teaches, there is a distinction between a true and a corrupt form of philosophical activity, and if the tendency of philosophy is to its corrupt forms, then we may ask, as I do in the last chapter, What guidance can Humean true philosophy provide in an age dominated by a corrupt philosophical consciousness?

Alasdair MacIntyre has said that Hume "constituted himself the philosophical champion of an essentially unphilosophical culture"

(*Whose Justice? Which Rationality?* [Notre Dame: University of Notre Dame Press, 1988], 324). In one form or another this has been a common and understandable reading of Hume, but it is mistaken. Hume's distinction between true and false philosophy enabled him to provide a philosophical defense of one sort of philosophical culture and a criticism of another kind of philosophical culture. On one point at least, MacIntyre and Hume appear to be in agreement. MacIntyre has presented us with the deepest criticism of Enlightenment conceptions of rationality (*After Virtue* [Notre Dame: University of Notre Dame Press, 1984]; *Whose Justice? Which Rationality?;* and *Three Rival Versions of Moral Enquiry* [Notre Dame: University of Notre Dame Press, 1990]). For both Hume and MacIntyre the Enlightenment notion of reason as an act emancipated from an inherited tradition of thought is incoherent and so not fully enlightened. For both, reason is and ought to be rooted in the particularities and historical contingencies of an inherited *sensus communis.* For Hume the task of reason is to "methodize and correct" this inherited culture. In outline the same is true of MacIntyre's reconstruction of reason—what he calls a "tradition of rational inquiry." They differ on what can count as "methodizing and correcting" a tradition, and MacIntyre has had considerably more to say about the nature of tradition-laden critical thought than Hume. And again the philosophies of both require writing a concrete historical narrative of inherited practices which exhibit rational criticism. Hume actually wrote such a narrative in its full character, namely, a narrative of the practice of liberty in *The History of England,* whereas MacIntyre has so far written only sketches of traditions of rational inquiry.

Other thinkers have insisted on the connection between the inherited, the contingent, and the rational. Oakeshott writes, "A man's culture is an historic contingency, but since it is all he has, he would be foolish to ignore it because it is not composed of eternal verities. It is itself a contingent flow of intellectual and emotional adventures, a mixture of old and new where the new is often a backward swerve to pick up what has been temporarily forgotten; a mixture of the emergent and the recessive, of the substandard and the somewhat flimsy, of the common-place, the refined and the magnificent" (*The Voice of Liberal Learning* [New Haven, CT: Yale University Press, 1990], 28). Plato sought out a community of philosophers who were "friends of the Forms." Hume emerges from this study as one of a family-resembling group of thinkers who may be said to be friends of the *sensus communis* and who understand that the beginning of wisdom (though not the end) is to recognize the force of Cicero's rhetorical question, "For what speech of theirs is excellent enough to be preferred to a state well provided with law and custom?"

In *Hume's Philosophy of Common Life* (1984), I argued against the Descartes-Locke-Berkeley reading of Hume as a kind of phenomenalist. In its place I suggested the thesis that common life is the governing idea of Hume's philosophy and is internal to his reformed notion of rationality. Most of the effort was spent exhibiting the historical, narrative structure of Hume's reformed notion of reason. The question of what Hume considered philosophy itself to be was put aside; it is taken up now in this work.

In completing this study I am aware of a great many debts both personal and intellectual. I am especially grateful for over two decades of friendship and conversation with Peter Jones on Hume and every other conceivable topic. His influence runs throughout this study, but I have especially benefited from his insight that Ciceronian humanism is crucial for understanding Hume. From my colleague Donald Verene I have learned much about the importance of rhetoric for philosophy and about a rhetorical tradition of modern philosophy growing out of Renaissance humanism and most clearly expressed in the philosophy of Vico. Hume's Ciceronian humanism invites the question of the extent to which his conception of philosophy can be viewed as a part of this Renaissance humanistic tradition.

Earlier versions of the manuscript were read by Peter Jones, Donald Verene, Ann Hartle, James Gouinlock, Terence Penelhum, and Nicholas Capaldi. Jack Greene read chapters 10–12. I am grateful for their criticisms and suggestions. The errors that remain are entirely my own.

I have learned much from conversations over the years with Ann Hartle, Carl Page, and Nicholas Capaldi about the nature of philosophy, and from John Gray's criticism of liberalism as a form of hubristic philosophy. M. A. Stewart, Roger Emerson, Richard Sher, and David Raynor have enriched my understanding of Hume by the work they have done in recovering its historical context.

The idea of this study was first developed in the Institute for Advanced Studies in the Humanities at the University of Edinburgh, where on two occasions I have had the pleasure of being a Fellow. I am indebted to the Institute for providing an interdisciplinary context for discussion and for its generosity.

Over the past decade, discussion with scholars from many fields in symposia sponsored by Liberty Fund, Inc. have given this study a breadth and scope it otherwise would not have had. I am especially grateful for the work of Charles King in making these gatherings possible. The Dean of Emory College and Emory's University Research Council made possible an uninterrupted year in which the manuscript was put into final form. And I owe much to Pat Redford, who not only typed the manuscript but made thoughtful editorial suggestions.

I have benefited from my wife Marie's deep understanding of the Scottish moral sentiment theory and from conversations with her about each stage in the development of this project. But this is only a small part of a debt that goes quite beyond what words here can express.

ABBREVIATIONS FOR HUME'S WORKS

D	*Dialogues Concerning Natural Religion,* ed. Norman Kemp Smith. Indianapolis: Bobbs-Merrill, 1947.
E	*Essays Moral, Political, and Literary,* ed. Eugene Miller. Indianapolis: Liberty Classics, 1985.
EU/EM	*David Hume's Enquiries Concerning Human Understanding* [*EU*] *and Concerning the Principles of Morals* [*EM*], ed. L. A. Selby-Bigge. 3d ed. revised, ed. P. H. Nidditch. Oxford: Clarendon Press, 1975.
H	*The History of England, From the Invasion of Julius Caesar to The Revolution in 1688,* with the author's last corrections and improvements. 6 vols. Indianapolis: Liberty Classics, 1983.
HEM	"Hume's Early Memoranda, 1729–40: The Complete Text," *Journal of the History of Ideas* 9 (1948): 492–518.
L	*The Letters of David Hume,* ed. J. Y. T. Greig. 2 vols. Oxford: Clarendon Press, 1969.
LG	*A Letter from a Gentleman to His Friend in Edinburgh,* ed. Ernest C. Mossner and John V. Price. Edinburgh: University of Edinburgh Press, 1967.
NHL	*New Letters of David Hume,* ed. R. Klibansky and E. C. Mossner. Oxford: Clarendon Press, 1954.
NHR	*The Natural History of Religion and Dialogues Concerning Natural Religion,* ed. A. Wayne Colver and John Vladimir Price. Oxford: Clarendon Press, 1976.
T	*A Treatise of Human Nature,* ed. L. A. Selby-Bigge. 2d edition with text revised and variant readings by P. H. Nidditch. Oxford: Clarendon Press, 1978.

PART ONE

HUMEAN REFLECTIONS

CHAPTER ONE

Is Hume an Empiricist?

Modern philosophy has been obsessed with epistemology. In surveys of the history of philosophy, it is common to find philosophies identified by epistemological descriptions (empiricist, rationalist, idealist, pragmatist, etc.) as if these descriptions captured their essence. But a philosophy is and must be more than its epistemology. One can always ask what is the value of knowledge, and how it is to be ranked in the wider order of valuable things. This is not an epistemological question, and presupposed in every theory of knowledge, whether recognized or not, is some view of the worth of knowledge and its rank in the order of value. No philosopher has suffered more from the narrowing of vision that comes from the modern habit of epistemological classification than Hume. He is commonly identified as an empiricist and indeed as an especially clear case of what radical empiricism is.

Empiricism as Ideology

But what is empiricism? If we mean the doctrine that all knowledge originates from experience and that nothing is in the intellect that was not first in sense, then Hume is an empiricist. But so are Aristotle, Aquinas, and other philosophers too numerous to mention. If we narrow the definition to mean the doctrine that all knowledge claims are either analytic or synthetic and that all necessary propositions fall in the former class and all scientific propositions fall in the latter, then Hume is not an empiricist because he did not think that necessary propositions are analytic. That is, he did not think that what makes a proposition necessary is that its denial is formally self-contradictory. Indeed, he held a doctrine similar to Kant's that, in addition to analytic propositions, there are propositions which have both empirical content and are necessary.[1] One could go on perhaps indefinitely proposing definitions of empiricism and testing to see whether Hume's philosophy is a counter-example. But this would be a fruitless and even misleading task, because what is at issue in classifying Hume as a radical empiricist is something ideological. Epistemologies are internally connected to a wider view of the whole of experience, including a judgment about the worth of knowledge. The epistemology can, of course, be abstracted from this wider context, but then it loses its life and collapses into an abstraction. Since there are no "radical" abstractions, to think of Hume as a radical empiricist is to think of him as, in some way, participating in a certain sort of ideology either as a hero or villain. What ideology could that be?

It will be helpful to begin with the origin of the word *empiricism*. According to the *Oxford English Dictionary*, the term appears in English around the middle of the seventeenth century and denotes a medical quack who, without scientific knowledge, practices by trial and error. It was largely a term of abuse throughout the eighteenth century. Any science or art could be "debased with empiricism," and an absurd policy in government could be described as "the most sorry juggle of political empiricism." James Mill can say in 1817 that "mere observation and empiricism" are "not even the commencement of science." It is not until the end of the nineteenth century that the term *empiricism* begins to take on the favorable connotations it has today, as when Thomas Huxley says in 1881 that "all true science begins with empiricism." It is the favorable connotations of this essentially Victorian term that are now read back into the history of philosophy to pick out a line of heroes or villains: Bacon, Locke, Berkeley, Hume, Bentham, Mill, Carnap, Ayer, and so on. If Hume was an empiricist, he could not have known that he was, since the favorable connotations of the term were not available to him.

It is true that Locke, Berkeley, and Hume take a position on the epistemological debates of their time that contrasts with that taken by Descartes, Spinoza, and Leibniz. We may call this empiricism if we like, but we must be careful to purge the term of its latter-day ideological connotations—something especially difficult to do in the case of Hume. And we must also take care to show how a common "empiricism" is internal to the natural-law Stoicism of Locke, the Christian Platonism of Berkeley, and the Ciceronian humanism of Hume. Such a generic empiricism contains none of the substantial content and bite usually associated with talk of "Hume's empiricism."

Epistemological theories, I have suggested, move against a deep background of beliefs about the worth of knowledge in a wider scheme of things. As such, epistemologies have an ideological and rhetorical dimension, and may be viewed as speeches embedded in a culture and addressed to that culture. The true home of empiricism is the late nineteenth century and our own time, where it is a theory of knowledge at the service of an ideology of perpetual progress through science, technology, and democracy. It is a militant ideology, resolutely forward-looking and hostile not only to religious tradition but to all traditions. The faint image of this ideology of progress can be found in the theory of history as inevitable progress sketched out by Turgot, Condorcet, and Kant; it appears boldly in the superstitious scientism of Comte's *positivism;* it is found in Bentham, Mill, Thomas Huxley, the manifesto of the Vienna Circle, logical positivism, logical empiricism, and various forms of pragmatism. A. J. Ayer records, in his account of the Vienna Circle, that the positivists found little in the history of philosophy with which to identify and that the two thinkers closest to their own views were Hume and Mach.[2]

Empiricism with its background ideology of progress is very much a speech rooted in the industrial revolution, which provided capital and a vast array of machinery and managerial technology for projects of social transformation. By 1825 the fixed steam engines of Britain were producing the equivalent of the labor of 5,400,000 men. These engines alone represented a capital value of about ten million pounds sterling. A century earlier, when Hume was a university student, the total value of all fixed capital in Britain was around two million pounds. By 1900 the work done by the steam engines of the world equaled the labor of five billion men, more than the entire population of the earth.[3] Watt and Boulton sold their first steam engines in 1775, a year before Hume's death.

The great transformation of the meanings of men and things brought on by the industrial revolution, and in which empiricism finds its natural home, makes no appearance in Hume's philosophy. The controlling images and metaphors of that philosophy derive from societies of family, kinship, and friends rooted in an agrarian order which cultivated commerce and the sort of light manufacturing that was largely under the control of landed gentry. The technology of production had changed little in five thousand years. Nearly everything was made by hand. The sources of power were what they had always been: wind, water, the strength of animals, and above all, human labor. Thoughts of famine and the decline of the national population were always in the background. Hume thought there were physical limits in the nature of human arrangements that prevented the population of a city from growing much beyond six hundred thousand (*E*, 447–48). Almost everywhere, combinations of princes and priests ruled as they had always done. Hume's philosophy encouraged "improvement" and "reform" but was radically ignorant of the industrial notion of a "progressive" society. And its "improvements" were always proposed with an eye first on the stability of society and the hierarchical orders of family, kinship, and the traditional establishment that held them together. It does not teach—because it can scarcely conceive—deliberate projects of total social transformation which are standard in the ideologies of industrial society; it has no notion of the ceaseless destruction and creation that is known today as progress. It is not a philosophy such as liberalism or Marxism that is forward-looking or that looks impatiently at the present from the perspective of a future that it thinks it knows and, in thought, has already occupied. When the theory of history as inevitable progress first made its appearance in the speculations of his friend Turgot, Hume firmly rejected it (*L*, 2: 180). The present is not a disposable launching pad for future adventures in technological progress but a place to dwell, to understand, and to enjoy, and something to pass on with whatever improvements are desirable to one's posterity. The present is understood to be what it is because of the past, because of traditions and customs built into it. And the greatest wisdom is not what an individual following a rational "method" can discern but the knowledge spontaneously collected by many generations, often working in ignorance of each other, and deposited in traditions, customs, and conventions. It is a philosophy whose favorite way of understanding something is to tell a story about its origins.

Its view of the human world is not technological but poetic. Hume teaches that in a world of constant flux and dissolution, the metaphorical imagination forms identities which are housed in habits, customs, and traditions, and which are its only means of resisting the horror of dissolution. Hence the Humean imagination, although it encourages improvement and even radical change when necessary, betrays a prejudice on behalf of what is familiar and long-established just because it is so. Time is a value immanent in human institutions. But because of this prejudice on behalf of the familiar, boredom may set in, or a custom may outlive its utility. And so novelty is valued as a welcome relief, but only as an enrichment of the deeper and wider background of the familiar. The ceaseless pursuit of novelty and creativity for their own sakes makes no appearance in Hume's thought.

The tone, tenor, and style of Hume's philosophy are therefore entirely different from those of empiricism, which is the tip of the ideological iceberg of progress. Here, in philosophy as elsewhere, style and nuance are of the essence. Given the present and backward-looking character of Hume's philosophy and the importance he gives to custom, one might think of it as an *historical* empiricism. This is a better identification, because Hume's conception of experience has more affinity with the notion of historical experience as understood by the English Common Law tradition and the Latin rhetorical tradition in philosophy, as exemplified by Cicero, than with an empiricism which views sense experience as the ahistorical foundation against which scientific theories are tested. But though it is an improvement to think of Hume as a historical empiricist, such violence is done to the conventions governing the use of the term *empiricism* that this phrase is either misleading or paradoxical. To describe Hume as a historical empiricist is rather like describing Hegel's philosophy as historical Aristotelianism. There is a point to such a description, but there must be a better way to think about Hegel's philosophy, and Hume's. The solution is to resist the prejudice of epistemological classification and to look for a broader topic under which to understand Hume's thought.

The "Sceptical System" of Philosophy

I suggest going back to Hume's own description of his philosophy in the *Treatise.* He called it simply the "sceptical" philosophy (*T,* 180). The exploration of what Hume understood this philosophy to be is the task of this study. But we can make a beginning by sketching out the rationale of Pyrrhonian skepticism. As will be shown later, Hume's philosophy is different from Pyrrhonism, but it owes much to the dialectic of philosophical reflection first exposed by the Pyrrhonians, and it is with this dialectic that I would like to begin.

The ancient philosophical sects of Platonism, Epicureanism, Stoicism, Skepticism, Cynicism, and the Peripatetic philosophy conceived of philosophy as the search for wisdom or the best way to live. Each had a theory of what constitutes human happiness and also a theory of the source of human unhappiness. For the Platonist, the source of human misery is philosophical ignorance, which is overcome by philosophical knowledge; for the Epicurean, it is pain, which is overcome by maximizing pleasure; for the Stoic, it is a false will, which is overcome by a will in accord with nature or right reason; for the Cynic, it is the tyranny of convention, which is overcome by an ascetic independence. But the skeptics had an especially interesting theory of the source of human misery; they found it not in philosophical ignorance, pain, a false will, or the grip of convention but in *philosophical theorizing* itself. An act of philosophical theorizing could be overcome only by another act of philosophical reflection which subverted both the first and itself, and so opened the way for a life free of philosophical reflection and guided entirely by the fourfold practical criterion: natural inclination, instinct, the piety of custom, and the practical arts. Sextus Empiricus tells a story of how the skeptics came to discover that the good life is a life free of the oppressions of philosophical reflection.[4]

The skeptics began as philosophers who were determined to live by the dictates of philosophical theory, no matter what those dictates were. Their happiness depended entirely on possessing the correct theory of nature and of the good life. But they soon discovered that for every theory of reality supported by philosophical reasons, they could find a contrary theory equally well supported, and so they were forced to suspend judgment. This led to depression. For being committed to the philosophical life, their happiness depended entirely on philosophical reason, which was leading nowhere. While in the melancholy state of suspending philosophical judgment, they noticed for the first time the radiant world of unreflectively received common life. Here was society, family, friends, the pleasures of the table, the glory of one's city, festive companionship with the gods, the ingenious working of a grist mill, and much else. One could delight in all of these things without the mediation of philosophical theory, without having to answer questions about their ultimate origins, nature, or meaning. Philosophers could say that these things are appearances and wonder about their relation to ultimate reality, but their being appearances would not affect our enjoyment of them. Even if the sweetness of honey were an appearance, that would not affect our enjoyment of it, nor its price in the market, nor the value placed on beekeepers. Of course, in the mode of suspending philosophical judgment, one cannot say that the things of unreflectively received common life are appearances. They might be, but then again they might not. The philosophical distinction between appearance and reality vanishes in the mode of suspending philosophical judgment, and the world of common life can appear in its full radiance, untainted by philosophical reflection. It is in this philosophically unreflective order of common life that the skeptics realize they have enjoyed whatever happiness they have known, and it is in this mode of existence that they are determined to stay. But there is an essential tension within Pyrrhonism which makes the achievement of happiness in philosophically unreflective common life difficult. The Pyrrhonians divided all philosophers into three types: the dogmatists who claim to have discovered ultimate truth, the academics who claim that knowledge of ultimate truth is impossible, and the Pyrrhonians who, not making a dogmatic claim one way or the other, continue the search for ultimate truth. *Skeptikos* means an inquirer. The Pyrrhonians acknowledge that they have no argument capable of showing that philosophical truth about ultimate reality is impossible. But without such a demonstration, the Pyrrhonian is vulnerable to every new philosophical sect that may come along. The new theory could be true, and so the Pyrrhonian is forced out of the peace and self-imposed innocence of common life into the anxieties of philosophical reflection. The old philosophical desire to grasp the real reappears and continues until suspense of judgment and peace of mind are again achieved through argument. The method of Pyrrhonian wisdom is to become proficient at thinking up such arguments so that one will be disturbed as little as possible by the intrusion of new philosophical theory. Since the skeptic can never entirely suppress the desire to philosophize, his happiness is never complete and always exists against a background of philosophical anxiety.

In a sense, the Pyrrhonians were the deepest of the eudaemonistic sects because they were the most philosophically self-aware. Like the other sects, they thought the task of philosophical reflection was to secure happiness and personal well-being. But unlike the other sects, the happiness they discovered required the subversion of philosophical reflection by itself. In undertaking this, the Pyrrhonians threw into question not merely this or that philosophical theory of the good life but the value of philosophical theorizing itself. They thought themselves the most critically reflective of the ancient philosophers, for they could see, whereas the others apparently could not, that philosophical theories contrary to their own were equally well supported by argument. A philosophy that radically questions the nature and value of its own activity is more self-aware than one that does not. In this sense, the Pyrrhonians were the most philosophical of the ancient philosophers. They were not Philistines who opposed custom and the natural inclination to philosophical reflection but, as Sextus Empiricus described them, men of noble nature who, through rigorous philosophical reflection, discovered to their astonishment that philosophical reflection itself was entirely empty.

It should be stressed that the Pyrrhonian questioning of philosophy is itself a philosophical act. Likewise, the insight into the emptiness of philosophical theorizing, the discovery of the domain of common life as the scene for happiness, the recognition of the necessity of the practical criterion (instinct, natural inclination, piety, and the practical arts) as the appropriate guides for living in this domain—all of these are insights won through an act of philosophical reflection. It is of course a paradoxical insight: seeing through to its own vacuity and at the same time recognizing its "other" (the philosophically unreflective domain of custom and inclination) as its authority. But the conclusions reached by philosophers are typically paradoxical, so this in itself is no reason to reject the purported wisdom of Pyrrho. In the meantime, the Pyrrhonians have entirely inverted the Platonic dictum that philosophical knowledge is virtue. It is now *philosophical* ignorance that is virtue. For without the recognition of philosophical ignorance, one would be shut out from the scene of human happiness.

What I have summarized as the Pyrrhonian insight into the nature of philosophy is too strong for what can actually be claimed. The Pyrrhonian cannot make the general claim that philosophical theories about ultimate reality are empty nor that the practical criterion and common life guided by the practical criterion is the true scene of human happiness. This is the conviction of the Pyrrhonian, but he cannot give theoretical expression to it. He must always speak undogmatically. All he can say is that every case of philosophical theorizing examined so far appears empty and that he follows the practical criterion undogmatically. He is and must be open to new philosophical theories, and this openness preserves a certain anxiety, but the ethical (eudaemonistic) goal of Pyrrhonism is to eliminate as much of this anxiety as possible by developing the powers and habits that enable a sure and swift return to suspense of judgment. A Pyrrhonian intellect that was ideally whole and fully developed (one might even say holy) would be able to see through a new philosophical theory immediately and so would be able to preserve, without interruption, the peace that transcends all philosophical understanding.

Hume's philosophy is founded on a philosophical act of self-inquiry like that of the Pyrrhonians, and therefore the structure of Hume's philosophy is quite different from what has come to be understood as empiricism. The central idea of empiricism is that there is an unproblematic foundation of knowledge given in experience and usually identified with sense experience, from which all knowledge is derived and against which all theoretical interpretations must be tested. The threat to scientific progress is due to undisciplined interpretations of the world arising from rationalist intuitions or unreflective dictates of custom and tradition. The given in sense experience, being uninterpreted, or nearly so, is the only standard against which interpretations can be brought to account. There are superficial resemblances to this view in Hume, but they must be seen in perspective. A skeptical philosophy in the Pyrrhonian tradition that finds philosophy itself to be suspect and, by inquiring into its nature, subverts all the received foundations of knowledge is not and cannot be a philosophy aimed at constructing an "epistemology," empiricist or otherwise. The dialectical structure of Hume's radical questioning of philosophy is different from the Pyrrhonian, but it contains a Pyrrhonian "moment" which is sufficient to separate it from the foundational enterprise of empiricism.

Philosophical Self-Understanding

The question "What is the nature and worth of philosophy?" may not be the most important question that can be asked, but it is surely the most *philosophical* question. And it is so because self-knowledge is the goal of philosophy and the standard of philosophical truth. Philosophy is the only inquiry that can throw itself into question and still be what it is. The question "What is the nature and worth of physics?" is a question about physics but not a question *in* physics. That physics is done at all is the object of wonder, and it will not help simply to do more physics. But the question "What is philosophy?" is both a question about philosophy and a question in philosophy. The question itself reveals most clearly the nature of the philosophical enterprise: self-inquiry. Likewise, the question "What is man?" is a question about humanity and a question which manifests an essential human characteristic: self-inquiry. Man just is that being who throws into question the nature and worth of his own existence. In a word, man is a philosophical being, and to philosophize is an essentially human activity. Indeed, it is not too extravagant to suggest that the questions "What is man?" and "What is philosophy?" are isomorphic. In both cases, throwing into question what one is reveals an essential characteristic of one's nature. A science of man is and must be a philosophical science.

A philosopher who presents a philosophical theory of knowledge, or justice, or God, or truth, or whatever, but who has not inquired into the nature and worth of his own philosophizing is not as profound a thinker as one who has. And one who throws philosophy itself into question has plunged into an adventure from which he cannot expect to return unchanged. Having satisfied oneself about the nature of philosophy, one's earlier efforts might appear as not being true exemplifications of philosophy or as poor approximations. Kant, under Hume's influence, went through such a metaphilosophical crisis and viewed his earlier work as dogmatic slumber. But the crisis was original to Hume, who is one of those rare thinkers (Plato, the Pyrrhonians, Hegel, and Wittgenstein being others) for whom the radical questioning of philosophy is the defining moment and the key in which all their thought is played. The radical questioning of philosophy is the master philosophical question.

Whatever answer is given to that question will be seen as having the authority to color and shape our understanding of what counts as an authentic philosophical interpretation of impressions, ideas, beliefs, knowledge, justice, and so on. Hume's science of human nature should be viewed as a philosophical science: an inquiry that emerges as a satisfactory resolution of a philosophical crisis in which the nature and worth of philosophy are thrown into question. This science will have what might in some loose sense be called "empirical" elements, but these will be constrained by a prior act of *autonomous* philosophical thought. The radical questioning of philosophy by itself is not an empirical form of questioning to be answered by confirming or falsifying cases. It requires establishing an *ideal* of philosophizing which a philosophical mind can recognize as its own true nature and which enables it to identify true and false forms of its own activity.

The place where Hume has the philosophical mind turn in on itself to examine its own nature and to judge whether present philosophical acts are true to that nature is part 4, book 1 of the *Treatise.* There, through a series of dialectical maneuvers, he makes a distinction between what he calls "true philosophy" and "false philosophy." Philosophy that is "true" is genuine philosophy (true to its own nature) and yields self-knowledge. Philosophy that is false is alienated from its nature and issues in self-deception. If the language I have used to describe the dialectical act of philosophical self-examination in part 4 sounds Hegelian and unlike what one would expect of an empiricist, that is because Hume is not an empiricist and because, in this part of the *Treatise,* he anticipates something of the logic of *The Phenomenology of Spirit,* which is also an act of philosophical self-inquiry.

Hume's own language can be made to sound Hegelian. The dialectic of philosophical self-understanding is expressed in the metaphor of a voyage of discovery (*T,* 263–64). The mind, though a unity, is presented as divided within itself, struggling with itself, and driven by what Hume calls "contradictions"; the mind "at once denies and establishes" suppositions (*T,* 218); deceives itself with experiences which are founded on "principles, which are contrary to each other, which are both at once embrac'd by the mind, and which are unable mutually to destroy each other" (*T,* 215); the mind's own disguises are exposed and discovered as its "monstrous offspring" (*T,* 215); one self of the mind takes on the role of master only to find itself enslaved in turn (*T,* 186). Hume describes the dialectic of philosophical self-understanding in the idealist language of degrees of understanding: "opinions, that rise above each other, according as the persons, who form them, acquire new degrees of reason and knowledge" (*T,* 222). To speak of "degrees of reason" here is not to speak of quantities of factual knowledge, as an empiricist must, but of thought becoming more coherent with an ideal of true philosophy.

Having established this ideal, Hume hopes to establish a science of human nature, that is, "a system or set of opinions, which if not true (for that, perhaps, is too much to be hop'd for) might at least be *satisfactory to the human mind,* and might stand the test of the most critical examination" (*T,* 272; italics mine). Hume's science of human nature is not "true" in the sense that its propositions *correspond* with ultimate reality or any other "foundation," such as the empiricist foundation in sense experience which is supposedly free of skeptical subversion. Hume taught that there is no such foundation. The science of human nature is true in that it conforms to the mind's own autonomous demands. And these demands are just the demands of what Hume calls true philosophy. I do not wish to make too much of the comparison between Hume and Hegel, but it is important to see that the philosophies of both are given form by a prior act of philosophical self-examination.

Part 4 of book 1 includes ninety-four pages and contains seven sections. Two of these, "Of Scepticism with Regard to the Senses" and "Of Personal Identity" have spawned a considerable literature concerned with what is thought to be Hume's "empiricist" analysis of what it means to perceive physical things and the nature of personal identity. But the overall purpose of part 4 has been largely overlooked. That purpose is to determine the nature of philosophy and to delineate the normative distinction between true and false forms of philosophical reflection. This is evident in the title of part 4: "*Of the Sceptical and Other Systems of Philosophy.*" The point of the exercise is to set forth the nature of the true (skeptical) philosophy and to distinguish it from the "*other systems of philosophy.*"

Hume, of course, does raise questions about what it means to perceive things and what it means to say the self is the same over time. But he treats these questions in a bifocal way: asking the first-order question, How is it possible to perceive physical things? while at the same time keeping his eye on the second-order question, What can count as an adequate *philosophical* theory of perception or, indeed, of anything?

This is suggested by the titles of the two sections where Hume discusses perception of the external world: "Of Scepticism with Regard to the Senses" and "Of the Modern Philosophy." In these sections Hume is not so much interested in framing the correct theory of perception of physical objects (much less an "empiricist" analysis of such perception) as he is in exploring various theories of perception as exemplifications of true and false philosophical theorizing.

We must read part 4, then, with bifocals, viewing answers to first-order questions as exemplifications of philosophical theorizing for the sake of answering the second-order question, What does it mean to philosophize? The final section, "Conclusion," of part 4 is clearly devoted to answering this question. Hume opens this concluding section with the metaphor of having narrowly survived a perilous voyage through the preceding sections. The lessons learned from the exemplifications of various modes of philosophizing in the preceding sections are reviewed and forged into an understanding of what true philosophizing is.

In the preceding sections philosophical thought suffers self-alienation. In section 1, "Scepticism with Regard to Reason," reason is shown to subvert itself. In section 2, "Scepticism with Regard to the Senses," philosophical theories of perception which seek emancipation from vulgar perceptual realism subvert themselves. In section 3, "Of the Antient Philosophy," the ancient philosophical theory of substance is shown to alienate the thinker from the true understanding of substance he possesses; such thinkers suffer "the punishments of Sisyphus and Tantalus" (*T,* 223). In section 4, "Of the Modern Philosophy," causal reasoning, which is the essence of modern scientific philosophizing, is shown to subvert itself and to destroy the possibility of belief in an external world. In section 5, "Of the Immateriality of the Soul," the theological interpretation of the soul as immaterial is shown to support atheism not theism. In section 6, "Of Personal Identity," the philosophical theory of a substantial mind is subverted and replaced with the image of the mind as a "bundle" or "republic" of perceptions. This section is the only one in which the first-order question of what constitutes personal identity is in the foreground and the second-order question about the nature of philosophizing is in the background. The bundle theory of personal identity is one of the best-known examples of "empiricist" analysis in Hume. But he rejected it in the *Appendix* to the *Treatise,* where he welcomed the "opportunity of confessing my errors" (*T,* 623). He did not replace it with another theory, and it is not clear why he rejected it. But the *Treatise* ends with no answer to the first-order question about personal identity, "empiricist" or otherwise. Finally, in section 7, "Conclusion of This Book," philosophical thought comes to rest with a conception of its activity that is coherent with what is thought to be its own nature: a system of thought "satisfactory to the human mind" (*T,* 272). This act of philosophical self-knowledge issues in the distinction between true and false forms of philosophizing and enables the thinker to engage in first-order theorizing which does not issue in the self-alienation, self-deception, or self-subversion so vividly portrayed in the cavalcade of philosophical folly presented in the preceding sections.

This concluding section of part 4, book 1 is the most important section of the *Treatise* and is the key to understanding the special character of Hume's philosophy. In answering the master question about the nature of true philosophizing, Hume brings to a close the story of book 1, "Of the Understanding," which itself is merely a preparation for the investigation of the *Treatise* proper, namely, human conduct in its broadest sense and the passions which are the source of conduct. Since it is the passions that move us to act, they are the central study of the *Treatise* and the special study of Book 2, "Of the Passions" (*T,* 8). Book I, "Of the Understanding," is important because our passions are determined by our understanding of ourselves and the world (*T,* 8). Book 3, "Of Morals," examines the world of culture, which is the public display of the passions determined by the understanding. The highest act of self-understanding is philosophy. Book I examines what it means to understand and so necessarily issues in a story, the dramatic conclusion of which is a dialectical investigation of the philosophical act itself. This critical investigation of philosophy is absolutely crucial for the project of the *Treatise,* for a disorder in philosophical reflection, if taken seriously, yields a disorder in the understanding of ourselves and the world. This in turn generates perverse passions.

The empiricist reading of Hume takes him to be an especially clear case of epistemological "foundationalism." Sense impressions are viewed as the uninterpreted foundation on which knowledge is built and against which it is tested. But it would be more correct to say that the "foundation" of the *Treatise* occurs at the end of book 1, not at the beginning where impressions are introduced. The foundation of the *Treatise* is the distinction explicated at the end of book 1 between true and false philosophical theorizing, and this investigation is not and could not be an empirical one. Empirical investigations yield hypotheses about objects and are confirmed or disconfirmed by objects. The dialectical investigation ending in the distinction between true and false philosophy is not a study of objects but a form of self-inquiry: an act of the speculative intellect seeking to understand its own nature. What we learn at the end of book 1 is that impressions perceived by passionate agents in culture are shaped by general rules, judgments, customs, and conventions. Rules, Hume said, are "able to impose on the very senses" (*T,* 374, 147). For purposes of analysis, we can talk about impressions as being unstained by judgment and custom, but our concrete experience of impressions is always shaped by judgment and custom. Hume is concerned to examine the concrete experience of human conduct as determined by our passions and by the understanding which generates those passions.

Hume, of course, did believe in impressions: objects of awareness which "impress" themselves upon us with "force and vivacity." But he did not present these as foundations of certainty on which a theory of knowledge could be erected.[5] He argued plainly in "Scepticism with Regard to the Senses" that there are no such foundations in sense experience which reflection can discover, and more generally in "Scepticism with Regard to Reason" that there are no foundations of certainty of any kind on which a theory of knowledge could be built. The great topical distinction in the *Treatise* is not the empiricist one between uninterpreted sense impressions and interpretation, but the dialectical distinction between two sorts of interpretation: custom and reflection. The exploration of this dialectical relation is the central theme of all Hume's philosophical writing, and of this study as well.

Whatever may be the fate of empiricism and of epistemological foundationalism, the "foundation" of philosophy is what it has always been: the speculative intellect's inquiry into its own nature. Hume understood this and devoted part 4, which is a full third of book 1, to a dialectical inquiry designed to uncover the distinction between true and false philosophizing. Chapter 2 examines the logic of this dialectic of philosophical self-knowledge.

CHAPTER TWO

The Dialectic of True and False Philosophy

The Philosophical Act

I have said that part 4, book 1 of the *Treatise* should be read with bifocals, enabling one to see that in raising first-order philosophical questions, Hume also has his eye on the second-order question about the nature of philosophy, and he views answers to first-order questions as exemplifications of philosophizing to be ordered by an ideal of what true philosophy is. This means that several dialectical episodes in part 4 are tied to different first-order questions which may appear unrelated, and so the significance of the whole as a critique of philosophy may not appear obvious. This is remedied somewhat by Hume's "Conclusion," for which bifocals are not needed because there philosophy is explicitly the object of inquiry, and Hume gathers the lessons learned from the earlier dialectical episodes into an account of the true condition of philosophical theorizing. Rather than present a detailed commentary on the whole of part 4, I shall draw out the main movements of thought that lead to the ideal distinction between true and false philosophizing. Support for this account is taken mainly from Hume's "Conclusion," but I have also used passages from elsewhere in part 4, from other parts of the *Treatise,* and, in rare instances, from Hume's later writings that clearly bear on the point at issue.

An objection to this approach might be that the dialectic presented is stylized and does not follow, in all respects, Hume's order of presentation. A topical study of this sort can offer no reply to this objection except to present a persuasive case that the dialectic captures Hume's teaching about the nature and limits of philosophy. If the case is persuasive, then the very stylized character of the dialectic can be a virtue, serving as a useful guide to the interpretation of all of Hume's writings; for his critical reflections on philosophy are not limited to the *Treatise.*

In the remainder of this chapter I explore the logic of the philosophical act of reflection considered in abstraction and as a timeless activity. Chapter 3 examines Hume's conception of the origin of philosophical and religious consciousness in human nature and their relation to each other. Chapters 4–7 examine Hume's conception of the evolution of the philosophical tradition and his understanding of his own relation to it. The remaining chapters explore Hume's views on the role of philosophy in the evolution of civilization and on the virtues and vices of philosophical self-display in culture.

Although philosophy has a history, the intentionality of its thought is timeless. Philosophical reflection, as Hume understands it, is structured by three principles which I shall call the principles of ultimacy, autonomy, and dominion. These are taken in turn.

The Principle of Ultimacy. One who philosophizes is trying to understand things as they are ultimately. We are not content with an understanding mediated through custom or experience but, as Hume says, "push on our enquiries, till we arrive at the original and ultimate principle. . . . This is our aim in all our studies and reflections" (*T,* 266). Philosophical thought can never rest until it believes itself to have achieved an understanding that is final, absolute, and unconditioned. And when it does come to rest, it will have such a belief.

The Principle of Autonomy. Philosophical reflection is a radically free and self-justifying inquiry. Philosophy is not the handmaiden of theology, politics, or custom. The radical autonomy of philosophy is a dialectical concept and cannot be understood without contrasting it to its absolute other. That domain is the unreflectively received world of custom, prejudice, convention, and tradition from which the philosopher originated but which he can no longer view as having authority. The autonomy of philosophy demands that the philosopher, at least in thought, cease being a participant in the prejudices of common life and imagine himself the sovereign spectator and arbiter of them. He must occupy, to use Descartes's expression, an Archimedian point outside the prejudices of common life as a whole from which critical principles can be formulated untainted by prejudice. As Hume puts it, "Reason first appears in possession of the throne, prescribing laws, and imposing maxims with an absolute sway and authority" (*T,* 186).

The Principle of Dominion. By the ultimacy principle, philosophical systems that are different are contrary. Philosophical disagreements are and must be ultimate disagreements. By the autonomy principle, the philosopher must consider his own system to be ultimately correct and to be entitled to rule over other systems; failure to do so means that he is not taking his own philosophical thinking seriously and is doing violence to his integrity as a thinker. This sense of a fitness to rule, internal to the philosophical intellect, is transformed into a passion by an original propensity of the mind, which Hume thinks is triggered whenever men reach the level of philosophical reflection. "Such is the nature of the human mind, that it always lays hold on every mind that approaches it; and as it is wonderfully fortified by an unanimity of sentiments, so is it shocked and disturbed by any contrariety. Hence the eagerness which most people discover in a dispute; and hence their impatience of opposition, even in the most speculative and indifferent opinions" (*E*, 60–61). Plato's doctrine that philosophers should be kings is a natural expression of the disposition of the philosophically reflective mind to seek dominion and to imagine itself as entitled to rule. This title is a gift of the autonomy principle; that is, a title the philosophical mind has conferred upon itself.

Anyone, then, who philosophizes engages in an act of reflection guided by the principles of ultimacy, autonomy, and dominion. But what Hume discovered is that these principles do not cohere with other principles of our nature and that, consequently, philosophy so understood is inconsistent with human nature. And since philosophy is supposed to yield human self-understanding, it is inconsistent with *its* own nature. If philosophy is to continue, it must take account of this discovery and reform itself.

This discovery that philosophy is inconsistent with itself and with the critical thinking which achieves the reform that renders philosophy self-coherent is expressed by Hume in a dialectical circle of thought. Philosophers who have passed through this disturbing circle of philosophical self-understanding Hume calls "true philosophers." Those who have not reached the level of self-awareness in which philosophical reflection itself is seen as a problem and so have not themselves instantiated the dialectical circle are "false philosophers." Their "falsity" consists not in asserting propositions that do not correspond to a world of objects, but in a failure of philosophical self-knowledge. The false philosopher's thought is not "true" in the sense that it is not true to what a more coherent philosophical understanding knows to be its real nature. The dialectical circle, first exhibited in the *Treatise,* is in the background of all Hume's philosophical writings, shaping his reflections and giving them their special character. Its full examination is the subject of this study, but it will be helpful at the outset to give a brief sketch of it.

In exposing the massive philosophical ignorance exhibited in the incoherent notion of substance, which for so long had held the ancient philosophers in its grip, Hume has occasion to outline the dialectical circle of philosophical self-knowledge. “In considering this subject we may observe a gradation of three opinions, that rise above each other, according as the persons, who form them, acquire new degrees of reason and knowledge. These opinions are that of the vulgar, that of a false philosophy, and that of the true; where we shall find upon enquiry, that the true philosophy approaches nearer to the sentiments of the vulgar, than to those of a mistaken knowledge” (*T,* 222–23). Philosophical reflection emerges, unexpectedly, out of the primordial habits, customs, and prejudices of common life; imagines itself to be free of these prejudices and to be their law-giver; falls into self-alienation and despair; and through further reflection wins through to a true understanding of itself and to a reconciliation with the prejudices of common life from which it originated. Hume presents this dialectic as a timeless natural history of philosophical consciousness which anyone seeking philosophical self-knowledge can reenact in his own mind.

The central insight of the dialectic is that the autonomy principle must be reformed. Philosophical reflection that is really emancipated from the prejudices of common life is empty and if consistently pursued ends in total skepticism. As Hume put it, “The understanding, when it acts alone, and according to its most general principles, entirely subverts itself, and leaves not the lowest degree of evidence in any proposition, either in philosophy or common life” (*T,* 267–68). Most philosophers are not driven to skepticism—but only because they lack self-knowledge. Unknowingly they smuggle in some favorite prejudice which gives content to and hides what must be the emptiness of philosophical thinking that is truly autonomous. Stocked with this illegitimate content, the philosopher parades, as the work of autonomous reason, untainted by prejudice, what is in reality the “monstrous offspring” of prejudice and reflection (*T,* 215). Emancipated philosophical reflection is inconsistent and arbitrary if it has content, and empty if it is consistent. At this stage in the dialectic, we have “no choice left but betwixt a false reason and none at all” (*T,* 268).

If philosophy is to continue at all, it must reform itself by abandoning the autonomy principle and by affirming the philosophically unmediated authority of the domain of prejudice to command judgment. Hume’s reform brings to awareness a new principle that I shall call the *autonomy of custom,* which places limits on the previously unrestrained autonomy of reflection. Whereas emancipated philosophy had presumed custom to be false unless certified by autonomous reflection, Hume's new principle is that custom is presumed true unless shown to be otherwise, and where showing it to be otherwise presupposes the authority of custom as a whole. In Hume's reform a revised version of the autonomy principle survives: Philosophical reflection may criticize any prejudice of common life by comparison with other prejudices and in the light of abstract principles, ideals, and models (what Hume calls "general rules"). But these critical principles, ideals, and models must themselves be thought of as reflections, abridgments, or stylizations of a particular domain of custom. What we cannot do is form critical principles from some Archimedian point, or what Thomas Nagel has called the "view from nowhere," which throws into question the order of custom as a whole.[1] Critical principles and idealizations do and must bear the imprint of an actual order of custom, so that those who participate in the order criticized can recognize themselves in the critical principles. The false philosopher imagines himself to be the sovereign spectator of and lawgiver to whatever domain of custom he is reflecting upon. By contrast the true philosopher recognizes that he is a critical participant in whatever domain of custom he is reflecting upon and so is not entirely free of its authority.

In Hume's reform in philosophy, the ultimacy principle remains intact. Philosophical questions are still thought of as attempts to understand the way things ultimately are, and philosophical beliefs are beliefs about the real. However, these beliefs are now viewed with some diffidence owing to the restrictions put on the autonomy principle, which is now reduced to critical reflection within the primordial prejudices and customs of common life. This is not to say that true philosophy is merely a study of these customs. Some customs contain judgments which are about reality and not about the customs in which they are lodged. For example, causal judgments, though triggered by the experience of constant conjunctions, are not *about* those experiences. Rather causal judgments purport to be about the invisible powers that produce experiences. The same is true of metaphysical, religious, moral, and aesthetic judgments. They have life only within custom, but they are intentional and can point to realities beyond custom.

The task of true philosophy is to form general rules which can be used to render the customs of common life as coherent as possible. "Philosophical decisions are nothing but the reflections of common life, methodized and corrected" (*EU,* 162). The ideal of truth for true philosophy is correspondence with reality, but the test of truth is the establishment of a coherent "system or set of opinions, which if not true (for that, perhaps, is too much to be hop'd for) might at least be satisfactory to the human mind, and might stand the test of the most critical examination" (*T,* 272). False philosophy emancipated from custom is critical, but not critical enough to recognize that the autonomy principle, cut loose from custom, is either empty or arbitrary; and so it is not a form of critical theorizing "satisfactory to the human mind."

The new principle of the autonomy of custom points out a hitherto unrecognized mode of understanding, namely, understanding that comes not through philosophical reflection, but through primordial *participation* in custom. However, the recognition of the autonomy of participation is available only to those who have passed through the dialectic of the natural history of philosophical consciousness and have become "thoroughly convinced of the force of the Pyrrhonian doubt" (*EU,* 162). That is to say, it is made possible by skeptical arguments that have the power to suspend the authority of all emancipated philosophical reflection. It is only when the entire domain of philosophical speech is reduced to silence that the mute authority of primordial participation can be heard. As Hume put it in the introduction to the *Treatise,* we must be able to see "that we can give no reason for our most general and most refined principles, beside our *experience of their reality;* which is the *reason* of the mere vulgar, and what it required no study at first to have discovered" (*T,* xviii; italics mine). In the mode of philosophical doubt we just find ourselves participating in a world of objects with other people, making causal judgments and judgments of worth that are independent of philosophical theorizing about them. This insight into the primordial authority of custom or the domain of participation, which emerges only against the background of a philosophical reflection that has been brought to bay, is itself a philosophical insight. But this philosophical insight is necessarily higher than the philosophical reflection held in suspension, for that reflection is its object and, indeed, one over which it exercises authority. The philosophical self behind this new insight identifies itself both with the self as participant in primordial custom and with the former philosophical self viewed now as the bearer of exploded reflections.

Finally, with Hume's reform in philosophy, the third principle of philosophical reflection loses its force. Custom is now seen to have a better title to rule than autonomous reason. And custom is always internal to a historic social order which requires, by its very nature, deference to others.

No one is a philosopher at all unless he has instantiated the three principles of ultimacy, autonomy, and dominion. But no one is a *true* philosopher unless he has passed through the dialectic and recognized the necessity of their reform. Hume taught that ideas give rise to passions, or what he called "impressions of reflection." Consequently, philosophical reflection, like any mode of reflection, generates an order of passions peculiar to itself. These philosophical passions differ with each stage of the dialectic and yield a spiritual aviary of philosophical characters. In the next two sections I explore the logic of the philosophical passions and their proper ordering in the modes of true and false philosophical existence.

The Character of the False Philosopher

The act of philosophical reflection occurs when there is a break in what had been the seamless whole of custom brought on by an unexpected experience which is contrary to established belief. This could be almost anything: the experience of double images when pressure is put on the eye, which throws into question the belief that what we directly perceive are objects, not private images; or an encounter with the morality of an alien culture which is contrary to our own. But whatever it is, this experience of contrariety loosens the authority of custom as a guide to the domain of experience in which it occurs. The thinker, alienated from custom as a guide, is thrown back upon himself as the source of rules to guide judgment. In this situation he may borrow from other domains of custom in which he is placed, but little reflection is needed to suggest that if the first domain of custom was a cover for error, any custom may harbor error, since it is the nature of custom to be philosophically unreflective. With this thought, the thinker forms the idea of the *totality of custom* and separates himself from its authority. He is now the spectator of custom, instantiating the view from nowhere. The autonomy of the thinker is radical and absolute. The only acceptable principles of judgment are those he makes for himself and out of his own reason, purged of the authority of custom. Reflection is now fully transformed into the philosophical act. Reflection of a sort had always existed in common life but was shaped and constrained by custom. By following, without restriction, rules embedded in custom (contrary experiences throw into question established judgments), reflection has worked itself out of the entire order of custom, which it now views as a strange and alien object.

This first moment of philosophical reflection is experienced therefore as "heroic" and sublime, for it takes a certain courage to alienate the totality of custom and with it one's former self. The philosopher thinks of himself as "a simple spectator," "a superior being thrust into a human body," and as "a sublime philosopher" (*E,* 175–76). From this heroic and superior position, the philosopher views the totality of custom as "contemptible, and puerile" (*E,* 175), and heroic philosophical experience contains within itself "a certain sullen Pride or Contempt of mankind" (*E,* 539).

Along with disdain, the heroic moment of philosophical reflection generates feelings of resentment. The sublime philosopher cannot entirely forget his former self, and now, in having his consciousness raised, feels resentment toward the unreflective world of custom which had so long held him under its dominion.

The contempt and resentment experienced here are of a peculiar sort. As passions which follow upon the philosophical act in its heroic moment, they are properly thought of as *philosophical* contempt and *philosophical* resentment. The ordinary versions of these philosophical passions operate within custom and are always directed at some particular absurdity for which one has contempt or to a particular wrong which one resents. But *philosophical* contempt and resentment are not directed at any particular absurdity or wrong located in custom; rather, they are triggered by the philosophical act itself, which alienates one from the totality of custom. Philosophical contempt and resentment are not directed at anything in particular but to custom in general. A good example of this is the philosophical passion of the early Marx, whose contempt was directed not against any "wrong in particular" but against "wrong in general." Among philosophers instantiating the heroic moment of philosophical reflection, such totalizing contempt and resentment is "esteemed the greatest Wisdom; tho', in Reality, it be the most egregious Folly of all others" (*E,* 539).

But can the heroic philosopher really preserve himself in "this severe wisdom" (*E,* 151)? The sublime contains, submerged within it, the element of fear. And fear emerges when the heroic philosopher moves from being the alienated spectator of custom and turns within to determine the principles of judgment. The heroic philosopher betrays a certain giddiness when he begins to put questions to himself about his alienated state and so experiences the frightful freedom of radical autonomy. "Where am I, or what? From what causes do I derive my existence, and to what condition shall I return? Whose favour shall I court, and whose anger must I dread? What beings surround me? and on whom have I any influence, or who have any influence on me? I am confounded with all these questions, and begin to fancy myself in the most deplorable condition imaginable, inviron'd with the deepest darkness, and utterly depriv'd of the use of every member and faculty" (*T,* 269). These are thought of as questions about ultimate reality projected from a position unconditioned by custom. The heroic philosopher answers them by constructing a theoretical world out of his own self-determining reason, which is in total opposition to the world of custom, what Hume calls "a world of its own . . . with scenes, and beings, and objects, which are altogether new" (*T,* 271).

The heroic moment of philosophical reflection is only an act of thought. There is no "view from nowhere" which allows a survey of the totality of custom. But although the philosopher is necessarily a being in the world of custom, he need not be *of* the world. Yet how can he conduct himself in a world which, in thought, he does not recognize as having authority to command judgment? What speech can he give to those who dwell in that world? The news of this alternative world, spun out of his own self-determining reason, falls on deaf ears, and the philosopher suffers total isolation. This perception of philosophical loneliness gives rise to passions of fear, rejection, and self-disgust. "I am first affrighted and confounded with that forlorn solitude, in which I am plac'd in my philosophy, and fancy myself some strange uncouth monster, who not being able to mingle and unite in society, has been expell'd all human commerce, and left utterly abandon'd and disconsolate." The obvious remedy is to embrace his fellow participants in custom. "Fain wou'd I run into the crowd for shelter and warmth; but cannot prevail with myself to mix with such deformity."

The next move is to establish a philosophical community. "I call upon others to join me, in order to make a company apart; but no one will harken to me. . . . I have expos'd myself to the enmity of all metaphysicians, logicians, mathematicians, and even theologians; and can I wonder at the insults I must suffer? I have declar'd my dis-approbation of their systems; and can I be surpriz'd, if they shou'd express a hatred of mine and of my person? When I look abroad, I foresee on every side, dispute, contradiction, anger, calumny and detraction" (*T,* 264). There cannot be a community of philosophers each instantiating his own heroic act of total transcendence.

The philosophical passions of contempt, resentment, and loneliness follow the rise and fall of the heroic moment of philosophical reflection. It is worth stressing again that these are peculiarly philosophical passions and are not to be confused with ordinary contempt, resentment, and loneliness. They are, as it were, transcendent passions which alienate from the world of custom. We have now to see that each of these philosophical passions makes possible a special mode of false philosophical existence. Philosophical contempt breeds the *ascetic* philosopher; philosophical resentment, the *revolutionary* philosopher; and philosophical loneliness, the *guilty* philosopher. These are ideal identities designed to illuminate forms of philosophical existence to be found in Hume's writings. As ideal types, no philosophical character can fully satisfy them, and the forms may overlap with each other and with other modes of existence, such as religion and politics, to form a vast display of unique characters. They are natural ways in which human beings who have instantiated the heroic moment of philosophical reflection and who are in a state of self-imposed alienation from custom attempt to come to terms with it. I shall take them in turn.

In the heroic moment of philosophical reflection, the philosopher stands in total alienation from the world of custom, which he views with contempt and disdain. The response of the ascetic philosopher to this condition is to withdraw into the world of his own autonomous reason, where he can maintain his independence. But his withdrawal cannot be physical; he is still a being in custom. His problem is to be in the world but not of it. The solution is to live a life of cynical self-display which expresses contempt for the world of custom and keeps it at bay. The master example here is Diogenes, who was, according to Hume, "the most celebrated model of extravagant philosophy" to be met with in history (*EM,* 342; *T,* 272).

The revolutionary philosopher responds to the heroic alienation from custom with resentment. Here thought is resolved to destroy the entire domain of custom and to replace it with the alternative world of its own self-determining reason. Something of this attitude is expressed in Descartes's conception of methodology. Comparing the totality of custom to an old house, Descartes has Eudoxus say in *The Search After Truth:* "I know no better remedy than absolutely to rase it to the ground, in order to raise a new one in its stead. For I do not wish to be placed amongst the number of these insignificant artisans, who apply themselves only to the restoration of old works, because they feel themselves incapable of achieving new."[2] This conception of reason rejects reform and requires total revolution, and being conservative politically, Descartes insisted that it apply only to natural science, mathematics, and metaphysics. But thinkers in the heroic moment of philosophical reflection can have no reason for such restraint, and although Descartes did not make morals and politics objects of heroic reflection, others could and did. A member of the National Assembly during the French Revolution speaks not with the language of reform but with the Cartesian language of *total* destruction and creation: "All the establishments in France crown the unhappiness of the people: to make them happy they must be renewed, their ideas, their laws, their customs must be changed; . . . men changed, things changed, words changed . . . destroy everything; yes destroy everything; then everything is to be renewed."[3] And for Marx the task of philosophical criticism would not be to reform the society in which one is a loyal participant but to totally transform an alien object. "We are not interested in a change in private property but only in its annihilation, not in conciliation of class antagonisms but in the abolition of classes, not in reforms of present society but in the foundation of a new one."[4]

Existence in the mode of philosophical guilt, like ascetic and revolutionary philosophical existence, is made possible by the heroic moment of philosophical reflection. But the guilty philosopher is not a heroic spirit. Like the others, he exists in the world of custom but is not of it. Unlike the others, his will is weak, and he cannot consistently carry the project of total criticism through to the end of either ascetic or revolutionary existence. Though alienated in thought from the prejudices of common life, Hume says, "I feel all my opinions loosen and fall of themselves, when unsupported by the approbation of others" (*T,* 264–65). He looks with a fascinated and longing eye at heroic philosophical existence, and is the fellow traveler of those who exist in that mode, but he does not have the courage to separate himself from the order of "deformity" (*T,* 264). He participates in the customs of common life, enjoys them, and makes his own contribution, but his reason does not allow him to affirm this participation. He has not yet reached that higher stage in the dialectic that Hume calls "true philosophy," in which the necessity of participation in custom is recognized and the authority of the domain of custom as such is affirmed. The guilt he experiences is not ordinary guilt but a special kind of guilt that follows only upon a certain kind of philosophical reflection. His guilt is not about anything he has done but about what he *is:* a participant in custom.

These three forms of false philosophical existence are instances of an act of thought which, following a suggestion of Hume's, I shall call philosophic superstition. *Superstition* is something of a technical term in Hume's social thought and has a much wider connotation than it does for us. He has much to say about it as a form of thought which expresses itself not only in religion but also in the secular social and political world. Superstition is essentially an act of thought believed to have transformed a natural object and to have endowed it with powers it did not formerly have. Public acts of superstition are constituted by the performative use of language, whereby the words uttered by some authority are thought to transform a natural object. Thus the ritualistic use of words may turn what was before good food into something unclean, or change wine into blood, or transform an ordinary man into a priest having special powers.

One of Hume's most important philosophical insights is this discovery of the performative use of language (*T,* 522–25). Belief in the power of performative utterances to transform natural objects is natural to human beings and has its counterpart in the social and political world. "Had I worn this apparel an hour ago, I had merited the severest punishment; but a man, by pronouncing a few magical syllables, has now rendered it fit for my use and service" (*EM,* 199). Hume says of this power of thought and language to spiritualize natural objects, even in the secular world, that it is "one of the most mysterious and incomprehensible operations that can possibly be imagin'd, . . . where a certain form of words, along with a certain intention, changes entirely the nature of an external object" (*T,* 524). The ritualistic use of language constitutes the non-natural objects of property, contract, marriage, political authority, rank, and status—indeed the very fabric of culture. And at the base of it all is the artificial virtue of justice which, being founded on performative utterances, Hume says, looks and behaves very much like superstition.

But there is a "material difference between superstition and justice": the former is "frivolous, useless, and burdensome," whereas the latter is "absolutely requisite to the well-being of mankind and existence of society" (*EM,* 199). Though there is a difference between justice and superstition, both are the result of a natural human disposition to constitute, through the ritualistic use of language, a non-natural world of its own. The spiritualized objects of this world, such as property, marriages, and political authority, are viewed as having a "sacred" character. Hume often describes the deep determinations of custom as sacred. He speaks of "the most sacred attention to property," of the "sacred authority of the laws," of "the venerable precedents of many ages," and of the "sacred" names of "KING and PARLIAMENT" (*EM,* 200–201; *H,* 5: 431, 386). The sacred here applies only to those secular things which are foundations of the deepest and most established customs and conventions in common life. Deep conventions are always spiritualized by the imagination.

Now something of this "incomprehensible operation" of thought in spiritualizing natural objects occurs also in the heroic moment of philosophical reflection and so yields a form of "superstition," or spiritualization of the natural, peculiar to the philosophical act itself. I would now like to explore how this is so and how philosophic superstition differs from justice and from religious superstition.

In the heroic moment of philosophical reflection, the authority of custom in its totality is suspended. Thought turns inward in the form of autonomous reason to construct a world of its own, unspotted by custom, which it boldly declares to be the real and which magically transforms the world of custom into an order of illusion or appearance having no authority to command judgment. We now enter the dark, inverted world of false philosophical consciousness, where the ordinary objects of common life are magically transformed by an act of thought into their opposites. Thales taught that all is really water; Hobbes, that benevolence is really self love; Berkeley, that to be is to be perceived; Proudhon, that property is theft; Rousseau, that man in civil society is born free but everywhere is in chains; Marx, that all history is the story of class struggle; Quine, that to be is to be the value of a bound variable. These are all cases of what Hume describes as the fundamental error of philosophers. "There is one mistake, to which they seem liable, almost without exception; they confine too much their principles, and make no account of that vast variety, which nature has so much affected in all her operations. When a philosopher has once laid hold of a favourite principle, which perhaps accounts for many natural effects, he extends the same principle over the whole creation, and reduces to it every phaenomenon, though by the most violent and absurd reasoning" (*E,* 159). Philosophical reflection is governed by the ultimacy principle, and this means that its deepest concern is not with good and evil or truth and falsity but with the more fundamental categories of reality and illusion. The good and the true must first be real. It is important to be clear about this, for otherwise the superstition internal to the philosophical act might be missed. When Proudhon says that property is theft, he is not making a moral judgment. Considered as a moral judgment, the statement is contradictory. Theft, by definition, is taking someone's property; so property cannot be theft. The rhetorical force of the statement is due to its apparent philosophical profundity. A distinction is opened up between the established order of property (the world of custom in respect to property) and what autonomous reason has established as the true conditions of property. Since, by the autonomy principle, these conditions cannot be infected with the prejudices of custom, they are not satisfied *anywhere* in the world of custom; so what is ordinarily called property is an illusion and not true property at all.

Further, true property is thought of not merely as an ideal which could serve as a guide for reforming the customary order of property, for that would issue in the thought that the established property order would be *better* if it were closer to the ideal. But this would be to say that the established order of property already has a degree of goodness and legitimacy, and a debate could then ensue about how far (or even whether), given the circumstances, things could be changed to conform more closely to the ideal. But the rhetorical force of Proudhon's statement excludes this possibility. The claim is that *all* so-called property in the order of custom is theft; if so, that order contains no degree of goodness or legitimacy at all. And this can be the case only if the "true" property of autonomous reason is thought of not merely as an ideal but as *reality*. If that were so, then the established order of property, as a totality, would be theft. And this thought generates the passion of philosophical resentment: that one's own has been taken away.

Again it must be stressed that this is not ordinary resentment, which is always determined and constrained by the world of custom and, in principle, can be satisfied within that world. Philosophical resentment follows upon the heroic moment of philosophical reflection, and so it is resentment about the totality of custom (philosophical thought and passions are always about what is thought to be the whole). Consequently, it cannot be satisfied by any adjustment within that world. Unlike ordinary resentment which, if just, is caused by things within the world of custom, philosophical resentment, being a passion attendant upon self-determining reason, is *self-imposed.* The passions produced in the heroic moment of philosophical reflection are formed in what Hume calls a "vacuum"; that is, they are self-imposed by a reason cut free from all custom (*EM,* 343). But as philosophical resentment is self-imposed, so are philosophical contempt and philosophical loneliness. No adjustments within the world of custom can extinguish these melancholy passions that naturally attend the heroic moment of philosophical reflection. Philosophers who seek to guide life by these self-imposed philosophical passions are said to lead "artificial lives," and "no one can answer for what will please or displease them. They are in a different element from the rest of mankind; and the natural principles of their mind play not with the same regularity, as if left to themselves, free from the illusions of religious superstition or *philosophical enthusiasm*" (*EM,* 343, italics mine).

The heroic moment of philosophical reflection is an act of superstition in that it takes a favorite part of the order of custom and, by an act of thought, opens up a distinction between reality and appearance, magically transforming a part of custom into the whole. As King Midas had the power to turn whatever he touched into gold, so the false philosopher has the power to transmute whatever the object of thought might be into the structure of a favorite prejudice. I shall call this philosophical act the Midas touch. Hume describes this act with the language of superstition. In the second *Enquiry,* he calls it "philosophical chymistry," by which he means alchemy, an instance of which is the "Hobbist" attempt "to resolve the elements" of benevolence into self-love (*EM,* 296–97). And in "The Sceptic," he compares it to "magic" and "witchcraft" (*E,* 161).

The philosophic superstition generated by the Midas touch is different from religious superstition and from the sense in which artificial virtues such as justice can be compared to superstition. The spiritualization of a natural object into property, or a wife, or a king has its rationale in social utility and has authority only for those who are loyal participants in a tradition. Religious superstition, Hume thinks, is generally devoid of social utility and is usually even pernicious. This was Hume's view in the *Treatise* and in the second *Enquiry,* but he softened somewhat in his later writings, evincing some appreciation of the humanizing value of religious art, ritual, and ceremony. The transformations wrought by the Midas touch of philosophic superstition have no social utility whatsoever, not even the humanizing value that might attach to religious ritual. Indeed Hume seems to think that there is something especially evil about false philosophy. The "philosophical chymistry" mentioned above is said to be a "malignant philosophy" (*EM,* 302), and the famous injunction, "Be a philosopher; but, amidst all of your philosophy, be still a man," implies that there is a kind of philosophical reflection which subverts one's humanity.

There is another difference between religious and philosophic superstition. The transformation of custom in philosophic superstition is not perceived as the work of a divine power, but as a profound insight into the nature of reality that is due entirely to the thinker's own power and that places him "in a different element from the rest of mankind" (*EM,* 343). In religious superstition, the divine power is thought of as a being limited in some way by custom. This is certainly true of polytheism, but it also true of theism; for, though all powerful, the God of theism intervenes only occasionally in the world of custom, allowing that world to retain its identity. Philosophic superstition, however, works with totalities; its transformations are always world-inversions performed at the expense of custom. It is for this reason that they appear as profound insights.

Instantiating some world-inversion, the false philosopher views the world of custom with the mocking laughter of the alienated. In this he reenacts the career of Democritus, who is known through tradition as the laughing philosopher. The dominion exercised by divine power and by the priests in religious superstition is claimed by the philosopher's own self-determining reason. And though he speaks in the name of universal truth and reason, he is also in it for the power; for the inverted world that has dominion over custom is, in reality, his favorite prejudices transformed into the whole by the Midas touch. The world-inverting paradoxes of the false philosopher always seem profound and serve to keep the world of custom in awe. This self-determining title to dominion over custom is one of the perennial attractions of philosophy, pandering as it does to the human desire for dominion. "Whatever has the air of a paradox, and is contrary to the first and most unprejudic'd notions of mankind is often greedily embrac'd by philosophers, as shewing the superiority of their science, which cou'd discover opinions so remote from vulgar conception" (*T,* 26). Likewise, whatever causes "surprise and admiration" gives such pleasure to the mind that it "will never be persuaded that its pleasure is entirely without foundation" (*T,* 26). "From these dispositions in philosophers and their disciples," Hume continues, "arises that mutual complaisance betwixt them; while the former furnish such plenty of strange and unaccountable opinions, and the latter so readily believe them" (*T,* 26).

The awe that participants in custom have for the heroic philosopher is a fertile breeding ground for hypocrisy and corruption of character. The philosopher cannot really invert the world of custom. And though he may totally transcend it in abstract thought, he is inescapably a participant in it. The most he or anyone can do is reform parts of it by relying on other parts. Hume asks, "Do you come to a philosopher as to a *cunning man,* to learn something by magic or witchcraft, beyond what can be known by common prudence and discretion?" (*E,* 161). But on another turn of reflection, "The philosopher is lost in the man," and we see that he cannot consistently understand the world of custom as inverted. The heroic philosopher speaks with "the voice of PRIDE, not of NATURE," and his title to dominion can be maintained only by hypocrisy: he can regulate only "the *outside;* and with infinite pains and attention compose the language and countenance to a philosophical dignity in order to deceive the ignorant vulgar" (*E,* 140).

So the philosopher must wear a mask of hypocrisy to maintain the wonder of the vulgar. But there is another source of hypocrisy to be found not in the relation between the philosopher and the vulgar, but within the philosophical intellect itself, which forces the philosopher to play the hypocrite with himself. If the heroic moment of philosophical reflection is to have any content, it must seize upon one part of custom which, by the Midas touch, transforms the whole. But what part will be seized upon? Hume's answer is that "almost every one has a predominant inclination, to which his other desires and affections submit, and which governs him, though, perhaps, with some intervals, through the whole course of his life. It is difficult for him to apprehend, that any thing, which appears totally indifferent to him, can ever give enjoyment to any person, or can possess charms, which altogether escape his observation" (*E,* 160). Philosophy greedily feeds upon this disposition in human nature, transforming and projecting what is a psychological compulsion into a metaphysical necessity, thereby deceiving others and itself. "The passion for philosophy, like that for religion, seems liable to this inconvenience, that, though it aims at the correction of our manners, and extirpation of our vices, it may only serve, by imprudent management, to foster a predominant inclination, and push the mind, with more determined resolution, towards that side which already *draws* too much, by the bias and propensity of the natural temper" (*EU,* 40). Hume gives examples of how what appears to be rational in philosophy is really the work of an usurping passion: while seeking the "magnanimous firmness of the philosophic sage" and endeavoring "to confine our pleasures altogether within our minds, we may, at last, render our philosophy like that of Epictetus, and other Stoics, only a more refined system of selfishness, and reason ourselves out of all virtue as well as social enjoyment." And "While we study with attention the vanity of human life, and turn all our thoughts towards the empty and transitory nature of riches and honours, we are, perhaps, all the while flattering our natural indolence, which hating the bustle of the world, and drudgery of business seeks a pretence of reason to give itself a full and uncontrolled indulgence" (*EU,* 40). In the pursuit of virtue, virtue itself is undermined by the "philosophical chymistry" of the Midas touch.

One inclination usurps the competing claims of other inclinations and, taking on philosophical form, "seeks a pretence of reason to give itself a full and uncontrolled indulgence" (*EU,* 40). The indulgence is "uncontrolled" because the heroic philosopher can recognize no authority other than his own self-determining reason, which in this case has become the mask ("a pretence of reason") for the dominant passion. The philosopher is utterly lost in self-deceit, and his belief that he is acting in the name of reason only makes matters worse. Rational autonomy, purged of custom, creates the seamless whole of Lady Philosophy's gown, which is such that any criticism from outside either appears as an attack on reason itself or is magically transmuted into a confirming case. By virtue of the autonomy principle, there is no insularity as impervious as philosophical insularity and no deceit as deep as philosophical self-deceit. Even the religious man has a better route to self-knowledge than the philosopher. The religious mind contains a struggle between faith and reason. The devotee knows that his faith is rooted in a sacred tradition, not in autonomous reason, and that such reason is always a temptation away from faith. One might seek to resist temptation by strengthening faith, or one might take the offensive and seek to show that faith is confirmed by reason, but in either case faith is vulnerable to the call of autonomous reason.

No such conflict exists in the heroic moment of philosophical reflection. The "other" of autonomous reason is custom, viewed as blind and unthinking prejudice. Although Hume teaches that there is in fact a struggle here between autonomous reason and custom, the existence of such a struggle forms no part of the false philosopher's *self-conception.* Within the seamless whole of the heroic moment, "Reason" is "in possession of the throne, prescribing laws, and imposing maxims, with an absolute sway and authority" (*T,* 186). Custom does not threaten reason as reason threatened faith. And there is no temptation at all to abandon reason and allow custom to be the guide of life. This thought does not and cannot enter the heroic philosopher's mind. And so the tension in his own soul between custom and reason cannot be acknowledged, and when felt, it is misinterpreted and twisted by the Midas touch into something that it is not.

The absurdities, self-deceit, and hypocrisy of heroic philosophical consciousness are the result of a radically self-determining reason and so are self-imposed. As long as reason is of this radically self-determining sort, escape from the distortions and constrictions of heroic philosophical existence is impossible. Reason, argument, critical theory are merely self-congratulatory, and serve only to confirm the philosopher in his insular world. The grip can be broken only by the force of the Pyrrhonian doubt which shatters the seamless whole of self-determining reason. But for this very reason it is difficult for the heroic philosopher to pass through the Pyrrhonian door of salvation. Pyrrhonism, though a more refined development of the philosophical intellect, is not only disowned by the heroic philosopher but is considered its greatest threat. The Pyrrhonian doubt is seen not as a moment which liberates thought, leading it to a higher and truer form of critical reflection, but as the subverter of reason and truth. To the heroic philosopher, it is the object of "groundless reproach and obloquy" and of the strongest "hatred and resentment" (*EU,* 41). Hume taught that philosophy (of the true sort) is the "sovereign antidote" to religious superstition. Philosophical reflection alone can bring one lost in religious superstition to self-knowledge. Likewise, only true philosophy can cure one of the philosophic superstitions of false philosophy. Yet liberating self-knowledge is easier for the religious mind than for the philosopher lost in the heroic and self-certifying mode of philosophical reflection.

The Character of the True Philosopher

Hume taught that human passions (impressions of reflection) should be thought of as colors that can be blended together to form new colors (*T,* 366). The philosophical passions of contempt, resentment, and loneliness are second-order passions and so might be thought of as a prism through which the great variety of first-order passions pass in refraction, yielding a brilliant display of colors which are the many forms of false philosophical existence generated by the heroic moment of philosophical reflection. To change the metaphor slightly, we may say that the prism itself may change, since philosophical contempt, resentment, and loneliness may themselves intermingle, yielding still more false philosophical existences, whose variety is even greater when we consider that each first-order passion has a concrete object that varies according to culture and historical time. Thus arise hatred of monarchs, the clergy, the middle class; resentment of the wealthy, the educated and refined; love of security, one's country, one's religion; jealousy of one's inherited rights and liberties; ambition for fame. All of these may pass through the prism of second-order philosophical passions and be transformed into philosophical shape, yielding a spiritual bestiary of false philosophical characters displayed in culture. The master passion of the heroic moment of philosophical reflection is philosophical pride ("the voice of PRIDE, not of NATURE"). And it is the subversion of this pride by the "Pyrrhonian doubt" that enables the philosopher to break free of the grip of a corrupt philosophical consciousness.

This is accomplished by that passion which has all along guided philosophical reflection and which prompted the questioning of vulgar consciousness in the first place. Hume calls this passion "curiosity" or "the love of truth." It is the only passion that "never is, nor can be, carried to too high degree" (*EU,* 41; *T,* 448–54). False philosophy occurs because the passion for truth is not strong enough. The philosophical act begins with an attempt to emancipate itself from the unreflective domain of custom. It is guided by the love of truth and does not seek to "mingle itself with any natural affection or propensity"; nor is it guided by any "disorderly passion of the human mind" (*EU,* 40–41). But this is precisely where the false philosopher fails. He unknowingly gives an "uncontrolled" indulgence to a favorite passion or prejudice. The true philosopher, by contrast, really does push inquiry beyond the determination of custom, and this necessarily leads to the shock of the Pyrrhonian doubt and the consequent recognition that such thinking is entirely empty. Whatever content philosophical reflection has is, in bad faith, borrowed from custom, yet passed off as the work of autonomous reason entirely emancipated from custom and prejudice. One whose passion for truth has carried him this far is a true philosopher. For he now understands his true condition as a thinker. He must affirm the principle of the autonomy of custom and think of himself not as the sovereign spectator and arbiter of custom, but as a critical participant within it.

What philosophical sentiments arise from this reflection? There are six: humility, piety, folly, eloquence, greatness of mind, and extensive benevolence. As settled dispositions, these sentiments are characteristics of the true philosopher. They are implied in the dialectic of philosophy in part 4, book 1 of the *Treatise,* but I have also drawn upon other places in Hume's writings where the nature of philosophy is discussed. These characteristics of the true philosopher arise from sentiments generated by the dialectic, but they will appear in a broader context as the study unfolds.

The first is philosophical *humility.* The philosophical self-discovery that autonomous reason, independent of custom, is empty subverts the pride of heroic philosophical reflection. The "Pyrrhonian doubt" throws the philosopher into the darkest despair. He imagines himself "in the most deplorable condition imaginable, inviron'd with the deepest darkness, and utterly depriv'd of the use of every member and faculty" (*T,* 269). Again this is not ordinary despair prompted by the loss of some object in the world of custom such as a loved one or one's livelihood. It is a peculiar sort of despair prompted by a philosophical reflection that alienates one from the whole of custom. Hume calls it "philosophical melancholy and delirium" (*T,* 269). It is a kind of despair available only to a philosophical intellect which, in the service of truth, has pushed the autonomy principle to the bitter end. Like the prodigal son who could come to himself only after having wasted his inheritance, so the false philosopher must eat away at his own substance (participation in common life) until, through philosophical despair, he discovers that it *is* his substance.

Only in a state of intellect in which all theories, arguments, principles, reasons, and systems are viewed as antinomic and thus empty can the primordial authority of custom be heard. And its authority is known not through the speculation of autonomous reason but through participation. "I dine, I play a game of back-gammon, I converse, and am merry with my friends; and when after three or four hours' amusement, I wou'd return to these speculations, they appear so cold, and strain'd, and ridiculous, that I cannot find in my heart to enter into them any farther" (*T,* 269). But though the principle of the autonomy of custom cannot be known by speculation, prior to completing the dialectical circle, the dialectic itself is nothing but the episodes that speculation passes through in its journey of self-knowledge. The philosopher's recognition that he is a participant in custom is itself a philosophical act. And the principle of the autonomy of custom is a philosophical principle available only to those who have passed through the dialectical circle of philosophical self-inquiry. Consequently, the knowledge of ourselves as participants in custom that Hume exhibits is not to be confused with the "commonsense" school of Thomas Reid. Participation in custom does not provide one with an epistemologically privileged access to truth; nor can it serve as a foundation for knowledge. On the contrary, the recognition of oneself as a participant in custom is revealed only through philosophical ignorance and the philosophical melancholy that follows from it. This recognition of the autonomy of custom may be viewed as a shift of attention within the speculative intellect's field of consciousness. Having recognized the magnificent and radiant order of participation in custom, philosophical speculation can never be the same. Henceforth, any return to the speculative moment must take account of oneself as a participant in custom.

From the perspective of true philosophy, the philosophical pride of the heroic moment of reflection now appears as a vice, as vanity and arrogance. With its subversion, the ground for philosophical contempt, resentment, and loneliness vanishes. The world of custom is no longer viewed with contempt as a "deformity" with which one "cannot bear to mix," for it is now seen as the domain of one's own participation. It cannot be *resented,* because one's identity is tied to it. And philosophical loneliness vanishes because custom is necessarily social and requires deference to and enjoyment of others. With the subversion of philosophical pride, philosophical humility emerges as a virtue, for without it, the cultivation of true philosophy is impossible.

I turn now to the second passion prompted by true philosophical reflection. Recognition of the principle of the autonomy of custom yields the philosophical passion of *piety.* To say that all custom is presumed innocent until proven otherwise (and where to prove otherwise is to criticize one part of custom in the light of the whole) is to say that custom as a totality is sacred. The sacred is, at the very least, some particular thing or order of things, the value of which is not determined by the application of some universal principle, reason, or theory. The sacred is usually associated, directly or indirectly, with the founding of a people. And although it is usually a religious people, it need not be. The founding fathers and documents of a secular regime may also be endowed with the character of the sacred. Hume saw the establishment of property as the founding act of civil society, and as we have seen, he explicitly compares this act to religious ritual and views our regard for property as "sacred" (*EM,* 199; *T,* 524). Since the sacred is the particular spiritualized in an order of custom, there can be no rational justification for it which is available to all right-thinking individuals. The prohibition against questioning the sacred has its source not in reason but in piety. From the point of view of the law, the reason for obeying the law is simply that it is the law. That is, the law is treated as sacred whether or not it contains values recognizable by all rational beings. Of course, if the law contains such values, the reason for obedience would not be the sacred as such, that is, the fact that it is our law or the law of God's people, but its rational necessity.

But again philosophical piety is not the same as ordinary piety. Ordinary piety is respect for things and rituals *within* the world of custom, whereas philosophical piety is respect for the totality of custom as such. And the prohibition against throwing into question the whole of custom involves not simple impiety, as with the ordinary sacred, but the rational insight of an act of self-knowledge, namely, that critical reflection without custom is empty and leads to "philosophical melancholy" or that, if it has content, the content has been illegitimately smuggled in from custom and so is self-deceptive and hypocritical. Though the totality of custom is revealed through an act of philosophical reflection, its authority is not determined by philosophical reflection. Custom is revealed by reflection to be that domain in which we live and move and have our being, independent of any theories about this domain, all of which have been silenced by the shock of the "Pyrrhonian doubt." The authority of custom is known through our participation in it. As the Eucharist is the sacred founding of the Christian people, and as property is the sacred founding of people in civil society, so the totality of custom is the sacred grounding of the human world. It is "*to us,*" as Hume says in another context, "the cement of the universe," and the universe is the ultimate founding particular (*T,* 662). Recognition of the sacred character of custom is necessary if critical thinking that is coherent (true philosophy) is to continue at all. Thus the progress of the dialectic reveals that the false philosopher (one stuck in the heroic moment of philosophical reflection) is not only given to a kind of superstition, self-deception, arrogance, and hypocrisy but is impious as well.

Note that philosophical piety, like all the philosophical passions, presupposes the background dialectic of the philosophical act. The source of philosophical piety is specifically philosophical, not religious. Only those who have instantiated the dialectic can have this sentiment. It does, however, have a connection to what Hume calls "true religion." But "true religion" is itself an attitude attendant upon philosophical reflection and so is not an ordinary religion. The full discussion of philosophical piety must await the discussion of true religion in chapter 3.

Another sentiment of the true philosopher is that of the comic attitude—the philosopher's understanding of himself as playing the *fool.* Hume describes the emergence of the true philosopher from the abyss of "philosophical melancholy" as awakening from a dream where "he will be the first to join in the laugh against himself" (*EU,* 160). What is revealed in this laughter? Recall that the ultimacy principle survived the descent into philosophical despair. The philosophical beliefs of the true philosopher are still about the real; however, the philosopher now knows that these beliefs are and must be mediated through custom. He knows that our deepest beliefs about self, world, causality, society, and the Divine are the work of the imagination. Reflection, through analysis, can take these beliefs apart. When it does so, it discovers to its dismay that they have a metaphorical structure and that they cannot be put back together again in a way that satisfies reason. Autonomous reason is never happy with metaphor and custom. The paradox is that, knowing all this, we still hold to the beliefs. It should be stressed that Humean natural beliefs are *believed,* notwithstanding the embarrassment they may pose to a self-determining reason purged of custom and the workings of the metaphorical imagination.

That our deepest beliefs about the real are mediated through custom and metaphor is a mortifying reflection. Hume describes it as this "whimsical condition of mankind, who must act and reason and believe; though they are not able, by their most diligent inquiry to satisfy themselves concerning the foundations of these operations, or to remove the objections, which may be raised against them" (*EU,* 160). Democritus was the laughing philosopher, but his laughter arose in the heroic moment of philosophical reflection. It was cynical and at the expense of philosophically innocent participants in custom. But the Humean laughter of the true philosopher is directed at himself, for he is in the highly reflective but ridiculous position of believing and at the same time of knowing that he cannot justify the belief to himself. The true philosopher has come to see that the heroic moment of philosophical reflection is a joke at his own expense.

In the *Treatise* Hume describes this post-theoretic posture of the true philosopher as that of the *Fool:* "If I must be a fool, as all those who reason or believe any thing *certainly* are, my follies shall at least be natural and agreeable" (*T,* 270, Hume's italics). Hume is drawing here from the long tradition of Christian Humanism, which celebrates the wisdom of the Fool. Beginning with St. Paul's doctrine of the foolishness of Christianity, Tertullian's maxim *credo quia absurdum est,* the wisdom of the Fool takes on philosophical shape in the *Learned Ignorance* of Nicholas of Cusa and the Christian Pyrrhonism of Montaigne, and receives its classic modern formulation in Erasmus's *The Praise of Folly.* Hume gives this tradition a twist of his own, but he is nonetheless a part of it.

It is the character of the true philosopher as fool that explains what has seemed perplexing to many, namely, the deference to vulgar opinion that is to be found throughout Hume's writings. The *Treatise* begins with an image of all philosophers closed in a room where "even the rabble without doors may judge from the noise and clamour, which they hear, that all goes not well within" (*T,* xiii–xiv). And in book 3 Hume opposes "the sentiments of the rabble to any philosophical reasoning. For it must be observ'd, that the opinions of men, in this case [the nature of political authority], carry with them a peculiar authority, and are, in a great measure, infallible" (*T,* 546). And again, "The general opinion of mankind has some authority in all cases; but in this of morals 'tis perfectly infallible. Nor is it less infallible because men cannot distinctly explain the principles, on which it is founded" (*T,* 552). More generally philosophers themselves "can give no reason for our most general and most refined principles, beside our experience of their reality; which is the reason of the mere vulgar, and what it required no study at first to have discovered for the most particular and most extraordinary phenomenon" (*T,* xviii). And in his statement of the dialectic of true and false philosophy, Hume observes that "true philosophy approaches nearer to the sentiments of the vulgar, than to those of a mistaken knowledge" (*T,* 222–23). The claim that we know *principles* of human nature not by philosophical reflection but by direct "experience of their reality" is what I have called knowledge through participation as opposed to knowledge through reflection.

Finally, observe that in none of the passages just quoted is Hume lapsing into philistinism. The appreciation of the authority of vulgar opinion is possible only for true philosophers who have run the circle of the dialectic. Hume uses the term *vulgar* and related expressions in two senses. One is to symbolize the authority of custom as a totality. Only true philosophers recognize this authority and so recognize that they are no different from the unreflective vulgar in being participants in custom. The second sense symbolizes a philistine attitude that is fearful of and hostile to any kind of critical reflection that would question one's favorite prejudices. The vulgar here are victims of inherited superstition and so come into conflict with true philosophy.

True philosophical criticism goes on within the totality of custom. It supposes all custom innocent until proven otherwise. It is in this sense that the rabble, prejudice, the vulgar, and popular opinion are innocent and are even extolled at the expense of those philosophers stuck in the heroic moment of philosophical reflection. Hume pictures such philosophers as composed of "fiery particles" and much in need of being tempered by "the gross earthy mixture" of the prephilosophical vulgar (*T,* 272). Hume thinks in this way in his celebration of "prejudice" in the essay "Of Moral Prejudices." In this affirmation of and identification with the "rabble," through the mediation of true philosophy, the Humean philosopher embraces the ancient wisdom of the Fool.

But again philosophical folly is not ordinary folly. Folly in ordinary life is destructive and is a vice. Philosophical folly is an attitude arising from the philosophical act which has arrived at a true understanding of its own nature. It is a joyful affirmation of common life in the face of contingency and the despair following the failure of the philosophical act in its heroic forms. Hume called it "the gaiety of MONTAIGNE" (*E,* 179 n). It is far removed from those contemporary philosophers who are stuck at some moment or other of the heroic act of philosophical reflection: the alienated solipsism of Sartrean nausea; the grim self-determining will to power of Nietzsche; the *angst* of Heidegger and the project of waiting for a god to save us; the cynical self-display of Foucault; the alienated ferocity of Marx. In none of these forms of the philosophical life does one find Humean philosophical folly or the gaiety of Montaigne: the disposition to enjoy and to critically explore an inherited culture of conduct and belief in the face of philosophical disillusionment.

Another characteristic of the true philosopher is *eloquence.* In a remarkable essay "Of Eloquence," Hume argues that eloquence is the only art in which the ancients are clearly superior to the moderns. Eloquence accomplishes two tasks. First, it is a form of speech designed to "inflame the passions" and to communicate them through sympathy to the audience. Second, it exercises "the sublimer faculties of the mind"; it attempts to "elevate the imagination," to "elevate the genius," and the sentiments it communicates are "elevated conceptions" (*E,* 101–4). Hume does not explain what he means by the "sublimer faculties," nor in what way eloquence "elevates" sentiments to a noble and sublime level. But being classically educated, he probably had in mind the traditional teaching that eloquence is universalizing in that it elevates the mind to grasp the whole of the subject under consideration. Quintillian says that "the verb *eloqui* means the production and communication to the audience of all that the speaker has conceived in his mind."[5] To have an eloquent mind is to be able to grasp the whole of the topic at hand. It is the ability of the imagination to "include a whole science in a single theorem" (*E,* 254). In eloquence of the "deliberative kind" the whole might be "the liberty, happiness, and honor of the republic" (*E,* 103). But eloquence might also be about wisdom, that is, about a philosophical whole: the nature of man, the nature of philosophy, the nature of custom, the nature of the Divine. It is this that Cicero had in mind when he said that "eloquence is wisdom put into language," and that Vico meant in saying that "eloquence is nothing but wisdom speaking."[6]

Eloquence is necessary because the true philosopher is a critical participant in common life, which is constituted by the passions (impressions of reflection) to satisfy human needs and wants. To understand this passion-constituted world, it is not enough to analyze its conceptual structure; one must either directly have the passions that are to be understood, or indirectly experience them through sympathy with the feelings of others or through eloquent speech. Eloquence is the art whereby passions are not only described but raised in consciousness to the level of feeling and conveyed to an audience. Without eloquence the true philosopher can neither properly understand the spiritualized world of custom nor communicate his understanding to others.

Eloquence is also necessary for philosophical self-knowledge. Human vanity, arrogance, and lust for dominion naturally incline philosophy to its corrupt and self-deceptive forms. Rational autonomy always opens up a scene of reflection at the expense of the totality of custom. Reflection disowns its identity as a participant in custom and divests itself of the sentiments of that identity in favor of a world of its own making. Abstractions formed in the "vacuum" of a custom-purged reason (the concept, the theory, the system, the principle, the rule) are endowed with a life of their own. This yields the speech of the false philosopher, which is not eloquence but the paradoxical language of the inverted world of philosophical alchemy. And it is a language always at the service of the principle of dominion. When false philosophy appears on the scene, it "bends every branch of knowledge to its own purpose, without much regard to the phenomena of nature, or to the unbiased sentiments of the mind, hence reasoning, and even language, have been warped from their natural course" (*EM,* 322). Eloquence can raise to consciousness and to feeling the disowned passions of the false philosopher, thereby reminding him of his identity as a participant in custom. In this way eloquence, in the hands of the true philosopher, conveys the most important sort of philosophical self-knowledge.

Hume refers to the act whereby the false philosopher divests himself of custom and endows his own abstractions with the quality of reality as "refinement." Throughout his writings, he inveighs against "refined precepts of philosophy," and against what is too "refined and philosophical a system" (*E,* 55, 470). "Refinement" is used here not in the sense in which the awkward motions of the body are refined by the art of dance into graceful movements, but in the sense in which refined sugar is unhealthy; or in the sense in which philosophical alchemy can "refine" a custom or practice away into something that it is not, as Proudhon refined property into theft and as Marx refined history into class struggle; or, to use an example of Hume's, in the sense in which "the magnanimous firmness" of the Stoics is transmuted into "only a more refined system of selfishness" (*EU,* 40). More generally, "There is no virtue or moral duty, but what may, with facility, be *refined* away, if we indulge a false philosophy, in sifting and scrutinizing it, by every captious rule of logic, in every light or position, in which it may be placed" (*E,* 482). The false philosopher is an alchemist refining away his own substance. The grip of this self-mutilation is broken by the shock of the Pyrrhonian doubt and by eloquent speech that enlivens the disowned passions of the false philosopher and recalls him to his true condition and identity as a participant in custom.

The true philosopher knows that custom or pre-reflective practice is prior to the abstract artifacts of principle, rule, or theory. These artifacts do not and cannot constitute practice, nor do they guide it in any fundamental way. They are mere abstractions from, or abridgments of, or stylizations of practices spontaneously and successfully carried out without knowledge of these artifacts. The rules of English grammar could be known only after English was first successfully spoken without any awareness of what those rules were. The rules of any practice cannot be known without the skills with which the practice (in ignorance of the rule) has endowed its participants. It is this tacit knowledge, embodied in practical skills, that makes it possible to know what the rules are and, most important, how and in what way they can be applied. The abstract rules, principles, and theories that are abridgments of prereflectively successful practice are always underdetermined and require the skills of the practice to guide their interpretation and application.

One of the greatest philosophic superstitions is to think, as perhaps Kant did, that rules and principles *constitute* a practice or in any fundamental way guide a practice. On the contrary, it is the practice that guides the interpretation and application of the rule. And this raises the question of what it means to follow a rule and what value there is in formulating and promulgating rules. Hume thought there was little value in doing either, and he rarely formulates rules for such fundamental domains of custom as science, morals, and politics. When he does so, it is always with the deflationary recognition that they are merely abridgments of successful practice and that the practice is the thing, not the abridgment. The rules for determining cause and effect would appear to be the most fundamental of all rules—yet Hume sees little value in them. "Here is all the Logic I think proper to employ in my reasoning; and perhaps even this was not very necessary, but might have been supply'd by the natural principles of our understanding" (*T,* 175). Once again Hume defers to the authority of the vulgar at the expense of false philosophy. "Our scholastic headpieces and logicians shew no such superiority above the mere vulgar in their reason and ability, as to give us any inclination to imitate them in delivering a long system of rules and precepts to direct our judgment, in philosophy. All the rules of this nature are very easy in their invention, but extremely difficult in their application" (*T,* 175). And there are no rules for applying the rules. In the end, the application of any rule requires "the utmost of human judgment," that is, skillful participants in custom acting without any awareness of rules and guided by "views and sentiments, which are essential to any action of the mind," but "are so implicit and obscure, that they often escape our strictest attention, and are not only unaccountable in their causes, but even unknown in their existence" (*T,* 175).

This discovery of the underdetermination of rules and the necessity of "tacit" or "implicit" knowledge, operating in custom, for the interpretation and application of rules, is one of Hume's most important doctrines. Its source is the Latin rhetorical tradition of philosophy exemplified especially by Cicero. Its rationale is to be found in Aristotle's doctrine of topics *(topoi),* that the topic, or inherited commonplace, is more fundamental than the syllogism since it is in the commonplaces of common life that the premises have their source.[7] It appears in one form in Hume's maxim that "reason is, and only ought to be the slave of the passions" (*T,* 415). It is to be found in Burke's maxim that tradition is "the happy effect of following nature, which is wisdom without reflection and above it," and in Vico's doctrine that "common sense is judgment without reflection, shared by an entire class, an entire people, an entire nation, or the entire human race."[8]

The insight of this humanistic philosophy—that theoretical, propositional, and explicit knowledge presupposes a background of tacit, practical, and inarticulate knowledge—was eclipsed by Cartesianism and the Enlightenment and the habits and dispositions that have survived today in their wake. But it has also been revived in recent times, and in a variety of ways, by thinkers as diverse as Oakeshott, Gadamer, Heidegger, Michael Polanyi, Wittgenstein, Hayek, and Ryle.

The philosophical importance of eloquence was not developed in the *Treatise.* It first appears in "Of Essay Writing" and "Of Eloquence," both published in 1742, shortly after the *Treatise,* and in the first *Enquiry* (1748). In the *Enquiry* Hume distinguishes between two kinds of philosophy: "the abstruse" or "the profound and abstract philosophy," and the "easy and humane" philosophy. The former is speculative; it seeks to understand the real. Its form is highly abstract, and its conclusions are novel and often repugnant to common ways of thinking. The latter is practical and eloquent: its purpose is "only to represent the common sense of mankind in more beautiful and more engaging colours" (*EU,* 7). Its theories not only mark out the conceptual difference between vice and virtue, they "make us *feel* the difference" (*EU,* 6). Hume grants that "the most durable as well as justest fame, has been acquired by the easy philosophy" (*EU,* 7). Abstruse philosophies, not being disciplined by custom, may yield the wildest theories. One abstraction follows another in any direction that the most whimsical imagination can command, and so there is an element of *fashion* in abstract and profound philosophy. The easy and humane philosophy, however, speaking eloquently to "the natural sentiments of the mind," acquires a stability over time. Thus the "fame of Cicero flourishes at present; but that of Aristotle is utterly decayed," and "the glory of Malebranche is confined to his own nation, and to his own age" (*EU,* 7).

Hume argues that true philosophy is a union of these two forms of philosophical reflection. If philosophy is to be an inquiry into the real (the ultimacy principle), it must partake of the rigor, accuracy, and novelty of the abstruse philosophy. On the other hand, we can think about the real only through the medium of custom and human sentiment, that is, through the humane philosophy. In Hume's proposed union there is "subserviency" of the abstruse to the "easy and humane" philosophy (*EU,* 9).

In "Of Essay Writing" Hume makes the point about the importance of eloquence to true philosophy in a different way. Instead of distinguishing between two forms of philosophy, he distinguishes between two worlds of discourse: the world of learning and the world of conversation. The former cultivates the "more difficult Operations of the Mind, which require Leisure and Solitude, and cannot be brought to Perfection, without long Preparation and severe Labour" (*E,* 533). The latter "join[s] to a sociable Disposition, and a Taste of Pleasure, an Inclination to the easier and more gentle Exercises of the Understanding, to obvious Reflections on human Affairs, and the Duties of common Life, and to the Observation of the Blemishes or Perfections of the particular Objects, that surround them" (*E,* 534). The vice of learning is the desire of "being shut up in Colleges and Cells, and secluded from the World and good Company" (*E,* 534). Compare this with that moment of the dialectic in the *Treatise* which Hume describes as "forlorn solitude." Isolation renders philosophy "as chimerical in her Conclusions," as "unintelligible in her Stile and Manner of Delivery. And indeed, what cou'd be expected from Men who never consulted Experience in any of their Reasonings, or who never search'd for that Experience, where alone it is to be found, in common Life and Conversation?" (*E,* 534–35). Here "experience" is not the ahistorical, asocial phenomenalism of nineteenth- and twentieth-century empiricism but the humanistic conversation of participants in custom. Hume proposes the essay form as a form of literature that can unite the best of these two worlds. "The Materials of this Commerce must chiefly be furnish'd by Conversation and common Life: The manufacturing of them alone belongs to Learning" (*E,* 535). The essay form symbolizes "a League, offensive and defensive, against our common Enemies, against the Enemies of Reason and Beauty, People of dull Heads and cold Hearts" (*E,* 536). The vice of the world of conversation is that it tends to dull heads. The vice of the world of learning is its tendency to false philosophy and to the cold hearts produced by philosophical contempt, resentment, and solitude. True philosophy, as critical participation in custom, unites "those of sound Understandings and delicate Affections; and these Characters, 'tis to be presum'd, we shall always find inseparable" (*E,* 536). If sound understanding and delicate affections really are inseparable, then eloquence must be thought of as internal to philosophical understanding itself and not merely as an ornament of it.

Another ideal characteristic of the true philosopher is *greatness of mind,* or what Hume sometimes calls *magnanimity.* Hume identifies "greatness of mind or dignity of character; with elevation of sentiment, disdain of slavery, and with that noble pride and spirit, which arises from conscious virtue" (*EM,* 252). It is a "generous pride or self-value" which demands recognition of "what is due to one's self, in society and the common intercourse of life" (*EM,* 253). It is of "the same class of virtues with courage," and Hume mentions three characters in which it may appear in the world: the soldier, the patriot, and the philosopher. All of these in their ideal types manifest that noble sense of self-worth which under oppression of any kind displays itself in contempt for life and the adversities of fortune. Hume stresses that although greatness of mind is a virtue which may have social utility, our admiration of it is founded entirely on its intrinsic worth. "To any one who duly considers of the matter, it will appear that this quality has a peculiar lustre, which it derives wholly from itself, and from that noble elevation inseparable from it" (*EM,* 254).

Greatness of mind is an impression of reflection attendant upon consciousness of one's own virtue. Consequently, the magnanimity of the soldier, patriot, and philosopher will differ in quality depending on the different conceptions of reality and the sentiments peculiar to these conceptions. What is the true philosopher's "conscious virtue"? The true philosopher understands the nature and limits of human attempts at self-knowledge. In respect to self-knowledge, the true philosopher, having worked through the dialectic, knows he stands above the vulgar and the false philosopher. This transcendent position is thought of as a kind of absolute moment comprehending the totality of autonomous reflection, the totality of its opposite (custom), and the true philosopher's relation to both. Though conscious of his own superior philosophical self-understanding, the true philosopher is not given to arrogance at the expense of the vulgar or the false philosopher because, having worked through the dialectic, he knows these to be moments in his own intellectual activity. It is part of the self-knowledge of true philosophy to retain a dialectical identity with the prior moments of the dialectic. No one can be a true philosopher unless he has passed through the moments of vulgar consciousness and false philosophical consciousness. And the experience of philosophical humility, piety, and folly mortifies any inclination to arrogance. True philosophy is not something that can be formulated, codified, and passed on to the next generation as a methodology. True philosophy is not the study of *objects* for which there could be a methodology. True philosophy is an achievement of self-inquiry, and so each generation must rediscover the truth of the dialectic for itself.

What is the sentiment of the true philosopher as he instantiates this absolute moment of philosophical reflection? Hume describes it as "that undisturbed philosophical tranquility, superior to pain, sorrow, anxiety, and each assault of adverse fortune" (*EM,* 256). The aspiration to self-command arises from self-knowledge. Hume presents the philosophical sentiment of greatness of mind in its idealized and exaggerated form. "Conscious of his own virtue, say the philosophers, the sage elevates himself above every accident of life; and securely placed in the temple of wisdom, looks down on inferior mortals engaged in pursuit of honours, riches, reputation, and every frivolous enjoyment. These pretensions, no doubt, when stretched to the utmost, are by far too magnificent for human nature. They carry, however, a grandeur with them, which seizes the spectator, and strikes him with admiration" (*EM,* 256). And finally, who "admires not Socrates; his perpetual serenity and contentment, amidst the greatest poverty and domestic vexations; his resolute contempt of riches, and his magnanimous care of preserving liberty, while he refused all assistance from his friends and disciples, and avoided even the dependence of an obligation" (*EM,* 256).

As a species of courage, philosophical magnanimity is capable of expressing the *heroic.* "Among the ancients, the heroes in philosophy, as well as those in war and patriotism, have a grandeur and force of sentiment, which astonishes our narrow souls, and is rashly rejected as extravagant and supernatural" (*EM,* 256). Though they are exaggerated in their pretensions and at times slide into the self-deceit of false philosophy, Hume admires the ancient "heroes in philosophy" and presents them as models for emulation. "And the nearer we can approach in practice to this sublime tranquility and indifference (for we must distinguish it from a stupid insensibility), the more secure enjoyment shall we attain within ourselves, and the more greatness of mind shall we discover to the world. The philosophical tranquility may, indeed, be considered only as a branch of magnanimity" (*EM,* 256).

The philosophical virtue of greatness of mind appears along with humility and folly in Hume's image of the true philosopher who, having narrowly escaped shipwreck in a "leaky weather-beaten vessel" (humility), has the "temerity to put out to sea" (folly), and "even carries his ambition [greatness of mind] so far as to think of compassing the globe under these disadvantageous circumstances" (*T,* 263–64). This image should be compared with Kant's famous image in *The Critique of Pure Reason* of an island surrounded by a stormy sea and of the philosopher as a timid person content to putter about the island of phenomena. When Hume speaks of "compassing the globe" here, he means the traditional notion of philosophy as an attempt to grasp the whole of reality.

Hume's mentor Cicero defined philosophical wisdom as "a knowledge of things human and divine." To appreciate speech of this kind about the whole (the human and the divine), Hume recommended mastering "the sublimity of SHAFTESBURY" (*E,* 179 n).

Kant's image of philosophy can be applied to the later logical positivists who sought to keep philosophy on the island of phenomena by declaring all speech about the real to be meaningless. And perhaps Hume's image of philosophy should be contrasted with Rorty's, since similarities are beginning to be asserted between the two owing to their common antifoundationalism. Having become disillusioned about the image of philosophy as the mirror of nature, Rorty has abandoned inquiry into the real and has declared the "world well lost." Philosophy now shrinks to a matter of "coping" within what Rorty conceives as the unproblematic world of "post-modernist bourgeois liberalism."[9] Whatever is to be said for this liberal provinciality writ large, it should be sharply distinguished from Hume's conception of true philosophy. For Hume, as for Cicero, philosophy is speech about the whole, the human and the divine. It is, to be sure, the speech of a skeptic (in Hume's special sense of that term); and what can be said is limited, but it is nonetheless about the real. Hume's sphere is "compassing the globe," not "coping" in the self-contained world of bourgeois liberalism. The wisdom of Humean true philosophy is in no way self-contained. It is not the self-certifying knowledge of Cartesian ideas, nor the self-certifying sense data of empiricism and positivism, nor the self-determining reason of Hegel. The Humean true philosopher sails the sea of the real in a "leaky weather-beaten vessel" and is placed by the dialectic midway between the prephilosophical human and the divine. Hume's conception of the divine (his notion of "philosophical theism" and "true religion") is the subject of chapter 3. In the meantime, it is important to see that the divine is a category of true philosophy. Without it, Hume's skepticism and the virtues belonging to the character of the true philosopher discussed here are not possible. A profound difference between many contemporary discussions of the limits of philosophy (or even of its end) and Hume's is the absence in the former of any notion of the divine. Rorty declares that a truly "liberal society . . . would be one in which no trace of divinity remained."[10]

The final virtue of the true philosopher is *extensive benevolence.* Benevolence and greatness of mind are the two natural virtues that constitute the Humean moral universe. These have their source, respectively, in two original dispositions of human nature: love of others and love of self. Through long experience and reflection, these dispositions have been shaped into the master virtues of benevolence (humanity) and greatness of mind (honor) (*T,* 592–605; *EM,* 269–70). Of these two, benevolence is superior (*T,* 603–4). The artificial virtue of justice (and its subdivisions, political allegiance, the laws of nations, and chastity) depends for its *moral merit* on its connection to the natural virtues (*T,* book 3, part 2). Commentators, however, have tended to concentrate their attention on the artificial virtue of justice, to the neglect of the natural virtues. One reason for this is that Hume's account of justice is modern. The laws of justice are primarily the stability of possessions, their transference by consent, and the performance of promises. Such a conception of justice is in sharp contrast to the Platonic tradition that thinks of justice as the key to the proper ordering of the virtues in the soul and in the state. Here the excellent soul and the just soul are the same.

Commentators such as Alasdair MacIntyre, who think of justice in a similar way, find in Hume an extremely contracted bourgeois notion of the just soul and of the just state.[11] Hume appears as little more than an early defender of an emerging liberalism that stresses economic freedom and productivity as the highest moral ideal. Although this is a telling criticism of latter-day liberalism, it is a parody of Hume's conception of virtue. It arises from imposing upon his moral theory the format of the Platonic notion that justice is the master virtue. If this were true, the Humean soul would indeed be truncated. But justice for Hume is an artificial virtue and consequently a second-rate virtue. It originates in self-love, and its function is to provide peace and stability in property relations (as well as political, international, and sexual relations). Operating solely within the sphere of self-love, it has no moral merit. The system of justice acquires a moral dimension only by a certain connection with the natural virtue of benevolence (*T,* 484–501). His position is that the peace and stability provided by a system of justice in restraining the inevitable fight over property provides a relatively tranquil scene in which the natural virtue of benevolence is more likely to flourish than not. The end of Humean justice is not to be found within itself; what makes it a morally satisfying engagement is to be found in something outside itself, namely, its service in promoting extensive benevolence. That is why it is said to be an *artificial* virtue. What many have looked for and found missing in Hume's theory of justice is to be found in his theory of what he calls "moral merit." And moral merit has its source in the natural virtues.

In ranking justice as a second-rate virtue, Hume separates himself from the Platonic conception of justice in another way. By treating justice as primarily law regarding property relations and in placing benevolence over justice, Hume's moral thought is more in accord with the Christian tradition than with the classical Greek tradition, for Christianity places benevolence over law. And Hume's understanding of moral merit is Christian in another and deeper way. He holds that the moral merit of an action is to be found in the motive of the act, so benevolence for him is not merely doing good for another (as a utilitarian or even an Epicurean could allow) but doing good for another from the motive of love. Without the motive of charity, a benevolent act has no moral merit. On its face at least, this is a doctrine with which St. Paul would have agreed (1 Corinthians 13). From this it follows that there could be two regimes of justice, exactly the same, except that in one the disposition of charity would be cultivated to a high degree and in the other not. In that case the first would have higher moral merit than the other. That the artificial virtue of justice serves to cultivate and strengthen the disposition of benevolence is a contingent matter.

Hume, of course, did not and perhaps could not acknowledge these Christian roots, and I do not wish to deny the great differences between Humean and Christian ethics. But it is important to realize that we are dealing with a thinker whose moral theory in its basic structure owes more to the Augustinian tradition of Hume's Presbyterian culture than to the classical Greek tradition, and that in evaluating it we should ask the right questions.

Extensive benevolence must be a virtue of the true philosopher because it is a human excellence, and the philosopher is human. But the disposition to benevolence (or any other disposition) may be perverted or enhanced by passing through the philosophical act. The hubris of false philosophy can corrupt the disposition by theorizing it away as self-love, as a power play, or as a weakness, or otherwise transforming it into a philosophic superstition.

In returning to common life, the true philosopher becomes a loyal participant in a social world requiring deference to others. In this new experience, the disposition to charity is free to flourish and develop. There is, of course, no guarantee that it will; selfishness is ubiquitous in common life (and in Hume's view its greatest threat), but at least there will be no barriers to its cultivation that are self-imposed by corrupt forms of the philosophical act.

Philosophical alienation had been from the whole of common life and not merely from the customs of the philosopher's own nation. It was a separation from the human, and it was through this corrupt transcendence that the philosopher was transformed into an "uncouth monster," a "satyr," and became "malignant." In returning to common life, the true philosopher returns as a participant, not merely in the customs of his own country but in the whole of common life, and so becomes a friend of the prephilosophical human. Such a character, if cultivated, may be expected to have more enlarged and generous views of mankind and a more extensive benevolence than ordinary participants in common life whose reflections have not been carried much beyond the local scene. But more will be said about the cultivation of this and the other virtues that shape the character of the true philosopher in later chapters.

CHAPTER THREE

The Origin of the Philosophical Act in Human Nature

There are three ways one might go about understanding philosophical activity. The first is a critical examination of the idea of philosophy, an inquiry that would attempt to determine both what philosophy is and what it ought to be. A critical and normative inquiry of this sort can be carried out only by one who instantiates the ideal identity of philosophy and can recognize his own activity in the explication. That is, such an inquiry is a search for, and yields, philosophical self-knowledge. The understanding gained is timeless—not in the sense that it has always existed but in the sense that the ideal identity internal to philosophical self-understanding is independent of and distinguishable from goings on in the past, present, and future.

The second sort of inquiry is causal and genetic and seeks to understand the origin of philosophical activity in human nature. Its question is about the dispositions in human nature and the circumstances of the world that made possible the origin of that peculiar activity known as philosophical reflection. This may be called the anthropology of philosophy.

The third sort of inquiry is historical and cultural. Here attention shifts to the concrete embeddedness of philosophical activity in culture and in historical time. The thinker conceives of himself as instantiating historical time, and philosophy appears in the form of a custom or tradition of thought. The thinker must somehow come to terms with both the timeless intentionality of philosophy and the historicity of philosophy. He must tell a story about philosophy which reveals his self-understanding of what it means to philosophize in historical time.

Hume seeks to understand philosophy in all three of these ways: critically, anthropologically, and historically. It should be stressed that the critical understanding is prior to the anthropological and historical. For

Hume taught that all cultural artifacts are constituted by "opinion," that is, by *ideas,* yielding impressions of reflection and, in turn, the self-understanding of these in ideas of reflection. A self-reflective and critical idea of philosophy is required to determine what questions an anthropology of philosophy and a history of philosophy may ask and what can count as significant answers. Hume first raises the critical question in book 1, part 4 of the *Treatise.* The anthropological question is first broached in *The Natural History of Religion* as part of Hume's anthropology of those ideas and impressions of reflection that make up the religious mind and passion. Hume's understanding of the historical question is revealed primarily in the *Essays* and *Enquiries.* But most of Hume's writings imply answers in some form or other to all three questions.

I explored Hume's understanding of the critical question in chapter 2. There philosophical thinking appeared as dialectical, and the narrative of philosophical self-understanding is the story of how reflection comes to terms with its pre-reflective other, namely, habit, custom, and tradition. True philosophy is the proper, true, and only reconciliation of these forms of thought, that is, thought as reflection and thought as custom (and where custom is now perceived as wisdom without reflection). Chapters 4–7 explore Hume's understanding of his relation to the philosophical tradition. Hume's anthropology of philosophy is the subject of the present chapter.

Philosophy and Religion

Although philosophy and religion are, for Hume, different and distinguishable experiences, they are so intimately connected and intertwined in the evolution of culture that the one cannot be adequately understood without considering the other. In some cases philosophy has sought to emancipate itself from religion and to be the sole guide of life, as among the Cynics and Epicureans. In others, it has combined with religion. The Stoics, Hume said, "join a philosophical enthusiasm to a religious superstition" (*NHR,* 77). In the thought of Augustine and Aquinas, philosophy not only combined with religion but was entirely captured by it, and was content to play the role of handmaiden to theology. In modern times, philosophy has sought to free itself from religion, and in doing so has left religion, paradoxically, with a certain philosophical shape. Hume thought that the more radical forms of Protestantism which grew out of the Reformation (such as Puritanism) resembled a system of metaphysics more than a religion. By the eighteenth century, modern religion had become so dominated by philosophy as to be virtually a branch of it. And so Hume could say in the first *Enquiry* that "religion . . . is nothing but a species of philosophy" (*EU,* 146).

The changing relations of subservience and dominance which characterize the history of religion and philosophy should not be thought of on the model, say, of two wrestlers who struggle for dominion but whose identities remain unchanged throughout the contest. Hume compares the passions which constitute the cultural artifacts of religion and philosophy to colors which, by being mixed, lose much of their identity in the production of a different hue (*T,* 366). Philosophy and religion, throughout history, have intermingled to form qualitatively different experiences; one of them may be said to dominate in the sense in which blue may be said to dominate in a hue of green mixed with a greater saturation of blue than yellow.

But even this analogy is misleading insofar as colors are thought of as substances that are independent of a historical dimension. We are inclined to speak of cultural artifacts such as religion, philosophy, reason, and science as substances, and to ask whether such and such is in accord with reason, whether religion and philosophy are compatible, and so forth. This is due in part to the nature of ideas. Hume compares ideas to primary qualities (substances), and he compares passions, or impressions of reflection, to secondary qualities (*T,* 366). Our tendency to substantialize the objects of ideas, when indulged in thinking about the natural world, is excusable, for that world may or may not be composed of substances; but when indulged in thinking about the moral world (the world of conventions and cultural artifacts), it is deleterious, for that world is the result of human activity, and so is constituted by passion and opinion. Hume, for instance, warned against the tendency of modern political theorists to treat the British Constitution as one of those "essences of the schools" rather than as an evolving historical, cultural artifact that embodies British political practice (*H,* 5: 127).

Hume's warning about substantializing cultural artifacts should be kept in mind when examining his views on long-standing artifacts such as religion, philosophy, reason, science, and justice. It is common for readers who do not believe in substance metaphysics nor in faculties of the mind to talk of Hume's philosophy as subverting something called *reason.* But Hume is not out either to subvert or certify reason. His task is rather to expose the conditions in human nature which make critical thinking possible. Hume goes about this first by bringing to attention a critical practice such as the practice of making causal judgments; second by finding the origin of the practice in human nature; and third by formulating critical rules, principles, or ideals which seem to reflect the practice. That these are the true critical principles of the practice can be known only by comparing them to the actual critical activity of the practice. The master example here is Hume's famous explication of the practice of causal judgment which finds its origin (1) in the human and even animal tendency to expect constant conjunctions to continue and (2) in the specifically human capacity of reflection and speech that makes possible the recognition and record of failed expectations and thus the correction of judgments. One generation learns from another. Over a long stretch of time a system of "corrected" judgments emerges, and a philosopher such as Hume, having been raised in the tradition of corrected judgments, may reflect on this practice and formulate eight "rules by which to judge of causes and effects" (*T,* 173). Thus the practice of making causal judgments is not the instantiation of a substantial activity called reason. Rather, by *reason* we must mean simply the availability and enjoyment of the inherited practice of making causal judgments (along with other practices which might fall under that name, e.g., the practice of making moral judgments).

For all the conventions and artifacts of the moral world, the Humean strategy is the same: find the origin of the practice in human nature and convention, and formulate the critical rules, principles, or ideals of the practice. Hume does both of these things for causal judgment, moral judgment, religious judgment, political judgment, aesthetic judgment, and even philosophical judgment. To ask whether the critical rules of the convention are not merely true to the practice but true of reality is to step outside not only the convention in question but all conventions. It is to ask a philosophical question, and the practice of asking such questions has itself become, paradoxically, an established convention. Philosophy is a cultural artifact, a convention for critically reflecting on all conventions including itself. Philosophy is the only convention that seeks to ground itself. Its principles, traditionally, are those of ultimacy, autonomy, and dominion. In chapter 1, I showed that when the convention reflects upon itself, it discovers that these are not its true principles; that is, they are not the principles that truly reflect its own practice. Contrary to what the autonomy principle demands, philosophers do not and cannot philosophize independently of pre-reflective custom. Reflection shows that the autonomy principle, purged of custom, entirely subverts itself along with the other principles. This recognition of the true condition of philosophical thought leads to Hume's distinction between true and false forms of philosophical reflection. One might, if one likes, describe this as an absolute moment where philosophy comes to a true understanding of itself, and so, in this new and reformed way, ends up being self-determining after all.

Hume thought of philosophy and religion as overlapping and evolving conventions. The philosophical tradition he inherited was intimately bound up with religion. Consequently, his lifelong study of religion was also at the service of philosophical self-understanding. To fully appreciate Hume's conception of the role of philosophy in culture, one has to understand not only the distinction between its true and false forms but also the distinction between those true and false forms of religion that are intimately bound up with it. In the end, Hume argues that true philosophy and true religion are the same. So the inquiry must begin with Hume's account of the origin of religion.

The Origin of Polytheism and Vulgar Theism

It was an error common in Hume's time to regard the past as an order of greatness and the present as an order of decline. Much of Hume's work is an attempt to correct this historical hallucination. *The History of England* was written largely to combat the Whig doctrine that the modern British constitution of liberty existed in greater perfection in the Anglo-Saxon past. The *Essays* refute a number of such theses. "Of the Populousness of Antient Nations" argues against the theory that the ancient world was more populous than the modern. "Of Refinement of the Arts," "Of Commerce," and other essays argue against the thesis that modern commerce has corrupted morals and that a return is necessary to the virtue and public spirit of the ancient, frugal agrarian republics. Hume exposed the fraud of Ossian's poems. The hoax was made possible by a European public all too ready to believe in a poetic wisdom of ancient Scottish Highlanders which was lost to the moderns (a belief to which, as David Raynor has shown, Hume himself was at first inclined).[1]

The same prejudice about decline from greatness was applied to the question of the origin of religion, but with a rationalistic twist peculiar to the age. The first religion was theism, and it was known by the first men through rational reflection, and in particular through the design argument. This original religious truth has since been corrupted. Sir Isaac Newton puts the view this way: "So then the first religion was the most rational of all others till the nations corrupted it. For there is no way ([without] revelation) to come to [the] knowledge of a Deity but by the frame of nature."[2]

Behind this theory of the origin of religion is the general rationalist prejudice that the principles, ideals, and values we associate with rationality existed in the first men either innately or as achievements of heroic rational reflection. Much of Hume's philosophy is an attempt to show that what we call rationality in science, morals, politics, and religion is the result of a long, gradual, and largely unreflective evolution of conventions, the end of which is the coordination and satisfaction of conflicting human needs and desires. Principles of rationality are achievements of a largely unreflective process of social and historical evolution which Hume calls civilization. To speak in the substantive mode, it was not reason that formed civilization, but civilization that formed reason. Consequently, behind each critical principle there is a strange story to be told; and the present principle bears little resemblance to its original. Whig ideology, in Hume's day, pictured the British constitution as the envy of the world and as a rational solution to the problem of reconciling liberty and authority. The solution was supposed to have been achieved by the conscious and rational design of heroic ancestors and handed down to modern times. Hume thought the British constitution was, indeed, the best system of liberty that had ever existed. But he did not think it was the work of conscious design. Rather, the utilities framed in the constitution were the unintended result of painful and often unwilling adjustments forced by over a century of political chaos. And so Hume could speak of "the wisdom of the constitution, or rather the concurrence of accidents" (*H,* 5: 569). It is not a continuous process of rational decision making, but discontinuity, unexpected novelties, fortune, the unintended result of blind armies clashing by night, and irony that form the links leading to what are later called principles of reason. Looking back, one can see that some principles which inform modes of participation that have been lived through and found good (such as the British constitution of liberty) could not have been established in earlier times and, indeed, were scarcely even conceivable. It is an illusion to read them into the remote past, and worse still to see such a past as an order of greatness from which we have declined.

Against Newton, Clarke, Cudworth, and other "religious philosophers," Hume argues that the first religion was polytheism, not rationalistic theism. A vulgar and nonrationalistic form of theism evolved out of polytheism. Later, with the appearance of philosophical reflection, what Hume calls "true theism," or "philosophical theism," emerged. It is this sort of theism that Hume accepts, and as I shall show later, it is a fundamental part of what Hume understands true philosophy to be. For Hume, philosophical theism is a rational idea (in the sense in which Humean true philosophy explicates "reason," i.e., as "reflections of common life methodized and corrected"), but he differs from the religious philosophers in thinking of it as one of the fruits of the process of civilization and not as an idea that could have existed prior to civilization.

There are three propensities original to human nature that are necessary for Hume's account of the origin of religion. (1) Men have a disposition to believe in "invisible, intelligent power" as the cause of things. This disposition is "diffused over the human race, in all places and in all ages." (*NHR*, 25). I shall call this the principle of transcendence, meaning that human nature does not find the visible world intelligible in its own right but has an original urge to understand it by reference to a dimension of invisible power. (2) "There is an universal tendency amongst mankind to conceive all beings like themselves, and to transfer to every object those qualities, with which they are familiarly acquainted, and of which they are intimately conscious" (*NHR*, 33). I shall, following Hume, call this the principle of "*prosopopeia* . . . where trees, mountains and streams are personified, and the inanimate parts of nature acquire sentiment and passion" (*NHR*, 34). (3) Faced with the flux and contrariety of phenomena, men would despair of understanding the causes of things, "were it not for a propensity in human nature, which leads into a *system*, that gives them some seeming satisfaction" (*NHR*, 33; italics mine). This urge of mankind to organize the parts of its understanding into a whole I shall call the principle of systematic thinking. The system may be a metaphorical one (as, Hume thinks, the first system was), or it may be, as developed later, a conceptual one; but a system there will be.

Though universal, the urge to transcendence, *prosopopeia,* and systematic thinking need not generate a religious system, much less a religious system of a certain kind such as theism. What sort of system is generated depends upon the contingent, historical circumstances in which men find themselves. Therefore, while religious belief of some sort is natural to man, it "may easily be perverted by various accidents and causes, and . . . may by an extraordinary concurrence of circumstances, be altogether prevented" (*NHR*, 25–26).

The first men must be supposed primitive and barbarous. Without the arts and sciences, their condition was that of a "necessitous animal" whose main concern was survival (*NHR*, 28). In this condition, the idea of divinity could not have arisen from "the pure love of truth" or from a motive of "speculative curiosity" about the causes of order and regularity in the world (*NHR*, 32). Rather it was the shock of dreadful and unexpected events which triggered the human disposition to read intelligent power in the world and to assert, by an act of *prosopopeia,* a metaphorical identity between the visible contrary event and the invisible power: Neptune is the stormy sea. The explanation sought was practical not theoretical. The gods alone control events and have to be placated. Thus it was not the design argument but *fear* that led the first men to "scrutinize, with a trembling curiosity, the course of future causes, and examine the various and contrary events of human life. And in this disordered scene, with eyes still more disordered and astonished, they see the first obscure traces of divinity" (*NHR,* 32).

From this primitive beginning, a rudimentary transcendence is opened up between the visible world and an invisible world which is, nonetheless, metaphorically identified with it. Eventually the third propensity is triggered (the disposition to impose a system on experience) and understanding of the gods is made systematic. The god is not only immediately identified with the stormy sea but also with the sea when calm. The god is seen to be related to other gods, and eventually the entire world is populated with gods. But the logic of the entire system is fear, flattery, and the need to placate a terrible power over which one has no control. Thus a local deity is praised for the advantage of the believer. To merit recognition, the praises are magnified. The local god is said to be greater than other gods and free of their limits. These exaggerated praises eventually free the god from all limits of the visible world.

In this way theism evolves out of polytheism. But what emerges is not the "true" or "philosophical" theism Hume accepts. True theism is the belief in a supreme intelligence who created a universe governed by law and who is perfect. Such a notion conforms to "the principles of reason and true philosophy" and inspires men to scientific inquiry into the laws that govern the universe (*NHR,* 52). It should "banish every thing frivolous, unreasonable, or inhuman from religious worship, and set before men the most illustrous example, as well as the most commanding motives of justice and benevolence" (*NHR,* 59). Only a being who could inspire such practice is worthy of what Hume calls "rational worship and adoration" (*NHR,* 52).

True theism entails belief in a "general providence" but not in a "particular providence." The former is the belief that the universe is the result of purposive intelligence which expresses itself in the form of law. The latter is the belief that the creator "disturbs . . . at every turn, the settled order of events, by particular volitions" (*NHR,* 50). Theism as it has appeared in the world nearly always carries with it belief in a particular providence, and so is not fully emancipated from polytheistic roots—the rationale of which is nothing but a strategy for effecting a particular providence. Vulgar theism, then, contains within itself a contradiction. The same being who is represented as perfect and not governed by human passions is, at the same time, viewed as "the particular cause of health or sickness; plenty or want; prosperity or adversity . . ." (*NHR*, 55).

The propensity of the imagination to metaphorically identify invisible, intelligent power with visible things exacerbates the contradiction and generates what Hume calls a "flux and reflux" of polytheism and theism. The abstract conception of a perfect being, independent of space and time and impossible to imagine, renders the "active imagination of men, uneasy" (*NHR*, 57). Soon there appears an order of "inferior mediators or subordinate agents, which interpose betwixt mankind and their supreme deity" (*NHR*, 57–58). These demigods, or middle beings, resemble the human and are seized upon to satisfy the polytheistic need for "a particular providence." Thus theism descends insensibly back to idolatry: "The virgin *Mary*, ere checkt by the reformation, had proceeded, from being merely a good woman to usurp many attributes of the Almighty" (*NHR*, 52–53). Eventually the idolatrous relation to these middle beings can no longer be masked, and the religious mind begins again the painful ascent in the direction of theism, only to fall, in time, back towards polytheism. The "flux and reflux" of polytheism and theism can be restrained and moderated, but it can never be overcome (*NHR*, 58).

The Origin of Philosophy, Atheism, and True Theism

The view of Newton and other religious philosophers that theism (established by the design argument) was the first religion implied also that the first theists were philosophers and that religion and philosophy were coextensive in their origins. Hume argues, to the contrary, that the first philosophers were polytheists and that polytheism (in Hume's special use of the term) is a form of atheism. The first philosophers were atheists.

Polytheism is a world filled with gods and men. The philosophical question of what principle gave rise to this world never arises. What were the circumstances that made philosophical questioning possible? Hume's answer is the cultivation of the arts and the security and leisure brought on by "the institution of order and good government" (*NHR*, 35). The rationale of polytheism is fear brought on by helplessness and the inexplicable and dreadful irregularities of experience. The *regularities* of experience are entirely absorbed into the struggle for survival and never surface as objects of attention. But with the appearance of the arts and good government, security and leisure appear, and a space is opened up in which regularity and order become objects of attention. Superstition flourishes when life is governed by accident (*NHR*, 35). As self-acknowledged *makers* of civil society, men become aware of order in their own works, and this enables them to attend to order and regularity in the world. The security of civil society enables another original disposition of human nature to manifest itself, namely "curiosity" or "the love of truth" (*T*, 448–54; *NHR*, 32). Philosophy has its origin in the *polis* of ancient polytheism.

Hume mentions Thales, Anaximander, Anaximenes, and Heraclitus as the first philosophers. They sought to give an ultimate explanation of the world by fixing on some privileged item in the world, "fire, water, air, or whatever they established to be the ruling element," and metaphorically identifying it with the whole (*NHR*, 43, 44, 44 n, 45). The philosophical explanation of experience differs fundamentally from the polytheistic explanation. (1) The primordial urge to view experience as what Hume calls "a system" is expressed in philosophy as the perception that the visible world is a totality in need of explanation. No such conception existed in polytheism. Stories of gods and men existed, and systems of such stories, but no conception of the visible world as a unity requiring explanation. (2) The first philosophical explanation of the world was speculative not practical. The explanatory entity was not an intelligent invisible agent to be placated but an item within the world itself deemed to be especially significant and metaphorically identified with the whole. Instead of a particular thing having its intelligibility in a particular agent (Neptune is the sea), the visible system as a whole has its intelligibility in being identified with one of its parts (the world is water). (3) The explanation of the visible totality is accepted not because it satisfies a practical need generated by fear but because it satisfies the mind's own demands, which arise from the original disposition of curiosity. The philosophical authority of the explanation is nothing other than the delight and satisfaction the mind takes in its own account of things (*T*, 272).

In these first theories, the philosophical principles of ultimacy, autonomy, and dominion are clearly manifest. The philosophical explanation is ultimate: it transcends the world of experience, grasps the whole, and is unconditioned. The thinking behind it is radically autonomous: it is entirely emancipated from polytheistic custom and tradition, and its authority is self-determining. The theory extends its dominion over everything within its scope, and its scope is total: the gods themselves are generated from the ultimate cause and are subject to its laws (*NHR*, 44).

Hume stresses that the first philosophers were atheists and that, indeed, polytheism itself was atheistic. Neither, however, denied the existence of a supreme author of the universe; they simply had no idea of a "being, that corresponds to our idea of a deity. No first principle of mind or thought: No supreme government and administration: No divine contrivance or intention in the fabric of the world" (*NHR*, 38). Polytheistic religion scarcely thought of the question of the origin of the world: "It was merely by accident, that the question concerning the origin of the world did ever in antient times enter into religious systems, or was treated of by theologers" (*NHR*, 43). And when it did arise, the "ancient mythologists, indeed, seem throughout to have rather embraced the idea of generation than that of creation or formation" (*NHR*, 42). Hume presents it as a paradox to his modern readers that the atheism of the first philosophers did not prevent their being religious. And so "Thales, Anaximander, and the early philosophers, who really were atheists" had no difficulty providing an ultimate explanation of the world based on their own autonomous reason while at the same time being "very orthodox in the pagan creed" (*NHR*, 44 n). Hume calls them "a kind of superstitious atheists" (*NHR*, 38). Here, as elsewhere, Hume understands that philosophy is embedded in the wider culture from which it originates.

The evolution of philosophical theism out of philosophical atheism is different from the evolution of vulgar theism from polytheism. The latter is generated by fear, the former by "speculative curiosity" or "the love of truth" (*NHR*, 32). Philosophical theism emerges out of critical reflection on the first philosophical atheists, and its appearance, Hume thinks, marks a superior achievement in understanding. The reason is that the imagination understands reality by metaphorically identifying its own parts with the real. "The mind rises gradually, from inferior to superior: By abstracting from what is imperfect, it forms an idea of perfection: And slowly distinguishing the nobler parts of its frame from the grosser, it learns to transfer only the former, much elevated and refined, to its divinity" (*NHR*, 27). The great achievement of the first philosophers was to shift polytheistic attention away from the contrarieties of experience to regularity. It was not the horror of a monstrous birth which demanded explanation in the form of a particular providence but the regularities involved in normal birth. However, the first philosophers, being themselves polytheists, were limited by the rationale of polytheism insofar as their thinking was wholly absorbed in a practical involvement with the physical world. The objects of attention were regularities and cycles such as birth and death, and the explanatory entities were such things as water, air, earth, and fire. The polytheistic philosophers metaphorically identified the "secret and unknown causes" of the world with bits and pieces of themselves as passive recipients of nature. They had not yet achieved the deeper understanding of themselves as self-directing agents.

But Hume teaches that after men became accustomed to the leisure and security of the *polis* and established the habit of organizing the regularities of experience into systems, they naturally began to view these systems as a unity that resulted from purposive activity: "A purpose, an intention, a design is evident in every thing; and when our comprehension is so far enlarged as to contemplate the first rise of this visible system, we must adopt, with the strongest conviction, the idea of some intelligent cause or author." And the "uniform maxims . . . which prevail thro' the whole frame of the universe, naturally, if not necessarily, lead us to conceive this intelligence as single and individual." (*NHR*, 92, 30). It is, of course, logically possible, as Hume has Philo suggest in the *Dialogues,* that the universe is the work of a number of intelligent beings (*D*, 167). But this hypothesis, though logically possible, is not, to use the language of the *Treatise,* "satisfactory to the human mind" (*T*, 272). It offends against the mind's original disposition to seek unity in its experience; and so the hypothesis of "different authors . . . serves only to give perplexity to the imagination, without bestowing any satisfaction on the understanding" (*NHR*, 30). One should observe that this language is the same as that of the *Treatise* where, in discussing theories of the external world in opposition to vulgar realism, Hume speaks of how the imagination is confused by these theories without any benefit to the understanding (*T*, 209–18). This is not to say that any unity framed by the imagination must be accepted. The understanding (i.e., reflection and general rules) may correct beliefs spontaneously formed by imagination. What the understanding cannot do, however, is carry this process of correction to the length of emancipating itself entirely from the metaphorical unities of the imagination. It is a theorem of true philosophy that when this is attempted, the understanding entirely subverts itself. What must be accepted, on pain of not being able to engage in critical thinking at all, are those deeply established beliefs which reflection shows are spontaneously formed by the imagination and which constitute the fundamental order of participation in common life: self, a causally ordered world of objects, and sympathetic communication with other selves. To the fundamental orders of participation in common life, self, world, and society, we may add a fourth: divinity.

Hume allows that belief in divinity is not as deeply established nor as fundamental to participation in common life as belief in self, society, and world. Belief in divinity though "very generally diffused over the human race, in all places and in all ages . . . has neither perhaps been so universal as to admit of no exceptions, nor has it been, in any degree, uniform in the ideas, which it has suggested" (*NHR*, 25). It is a belief more vulnerable to reflection than belief in self, world, and society and "may, by an extraordinary concurrence of circumstances, be altogether prevented" (*NHR*, 26). But Hume qualifies even this extraordinary possibility by observing that it is difficult for anyone to know what his religious beliefs or disbeliefs are (*NHR*, 74). With these considerations in mind we may think of belief in divinity not as a natural belief on the order of belief in self, world, and society but as a virtually natural belief deeply embedded in participation in common life but more variable and more vulnerable to reflection.

And, like the more deeply established natural beliefs, the concrete experience of divinity has been mediated by historical and cultural circumstances. Through changing circumstances and the judgments that follow them, the idea of divinity has evolved through the great varieties of polytheism to vulgar theism which, in Europe at least, has come to dominate—though retaining permanently in sublimated form the logic of polytheism. Philosophical theism is rationally the most perfect form of theism. But it should not be thought of as continuous with and as a correction of vulgar theism. It has an entirely different origin and follows a different path in its development. Philosophical theism is continuous with and is a correction of the philosophical atheism of the first philosophers. The passion that motivates it is not fear of unknown causes but the passion that motivated the first philosophers: speculative curiosity, or "the love of truth" (*NHR*, 32).

When Hume says that philosophical theism is rational and cannot be rejected by "any one of good understanding," he does not mean it is rational in being the conclusion of an *a priori* or of an empirical argument. Hume makes it very clear in the first *Enquiry* and in the *Dialogues* that *a priori* arguments cannot establish existence claims and that empirical arguments apply only *within* the world and can afford no inference to the ultimate origin of the world. Philosophical theism is a belief that only philosophers can have and only after they have refined and corrected the activity of philosophizing to the point where they have come to conceive of the visible world as a single system ordered by causal laws. This conception spontaneously gives rise to the metaphysical belief that the whole visible system is the result of purposive activity. This metaphysical belief about the world *as a whole,* that it is ordered by "some consistent plan" and reveals "one single purpose or intention, however inexplicable and incomprehensible," in turn guides scientific activity in its research *within* the world. It is a rational belief roughly in the way in which true philosophy explicates the rationality of natural beliefs about self, public objects and society: they are in fact unavoidable, and their supposed elimination would subvert the understanding and make critical thinking impossible. All of this must, of course, be weakened a bit in the case of philosophical theism. The belief is not a natural belief but a virtually natural one, and its supposed elimination would not make critical thinking about what goes on within the visible world impossible for, before its appearance, a rudimentary sort of critical thinking went on in polytheism and a more sophisticated form in the philosophical atheism of the first philosophers.

But if one really did not believe in philosophical theism, there would be no reason to think of the visible system as a system of laws. For the idea of law is, in the end, tied to the idea of intentionality. Purged of the belief in philosophical theism, there would be no *world* but only a spectacle of constant conjunctions. Without the background belief in philosophical theism there would be no motive to think of these constant conjunctions as forming a coherent system and for searching out the systematic connections between them. And without the notion of an intelligible system, there is no point in attempting to distinguish an accidental constant conjunction from one that is "lawlike." The ultimate system will never be known, but the belief that there is one and that the regularities we observe are and must be coherently related to it encourages and guides scientific inquiry. Without this background belief science would revert to the fanciful and arbitrary cosmologies generated by the innocent atheism of the first philosophers.

The "naturalness" of philosophical theism can be put in another way. Hume describes the artificial virtues as both artificial and as natural. They are artificial in that they do not occur unless a certain sort of society has emerged. But once that society appears the practice of justice occurs spontaneously. Likewise philosophical theism does not and cannot appear until mankind has acquired the habit of making causal judgments and of critically ordering them into systems. Once this disposition is in place, the belief occurs spontaneously, and is regarded, retrospectively, as an essential part of a rational and well-disposed mind.

Philosophical Theism and True Philosophy

Why did Hume see philosophical theism as superior to the atheism of the first philosophers? I will conjecture three reasons. First, he taught that the mind searches in its own nature for metaphors with which to understand reality. It slowly learns to distinguish "the nobler parts of its frame from the grosser" and "to transfer only the former, much elevated and refined, to its divinity" (*NHR*, 27). The metaphor for the real in the case of theism is taken from our being as *agents,* not from our being as passive patients of nature. The first philosophers "readily assented to the grossest theory, and admitted the joint origin of gods and men from night and chaos; from fire, water, air, or whatever they established to be the ruling element" (*NHR*, 44). Hume calls these the "blind, unguided powers of nature" (*NHR*, 44 n). They are brute regularities which we can follow as spectators but of which we can have no understanding of the sort that we can have of the actions of an agent. Philosophical theism, however, conceives of nature as the result of purposive activity and so as an intelligible system open to human understanding, though never completely understood.

Second, philosophical theism is the belief that nature is ordered according to "some consistent plan" and manifests "one single purpose or intention, however inexplicable and incomprehensible" (*NHR*, 92). The transcendence of philosophical theism makes possible an ideal which, as we have seen, encourages inquiry. Further, the radical character of the transcendence rules out as *impious* any claim to have discovered the ultimate system. What regularities we discover must appear to us as brute constant conjunctions, the denials of which are as conceivable *a priori* as the conjunctions themselves. At the same time, these regularities are thought of as part of an ultimately coherent system. Given this belief, we are motivated to look for and are able to recognize contrarieties in our present theories; nor can we rest until the defect is remedied by finding a greater coherence. But it is part of the whimsical condition of inquiry under philosophical theism that we believe beforehand that however complete our present system is, there might always be some "straggling absurdity" left out of the system. It is a requirement of philosophical theism to look for this absurdity and to continue the inquiry. No such motive existed for the first philosophers.

Third, the first philosophers worked with a compacted notion of transcendence, and so were inclined to the illusions and distortions of false philosophy. I have shown that, for Hume, a fundamental error of false philosophy is that it seizes upon one part of the world of custom and reduces all the rest to it. Thales, the first philosopher, is also the first instance of the error: all is water.

All criticism presupposes transcendence: a distance between the thing evaluated and the standard of evaluation. In philosophical theism, transcendence is radical, being the distance between the world of experience as a whole and the divine mind of which the world is an expression. The philosophical atheist, however, seeks a transcendence that is between one part of the world and another while at the same time reducing the whole to the favorite part. Such immanent transcendence, if we may so call it, is arbitrary and distorts experience. The world is not really water; property is not really theft; history is not really the story of class struggle; and benevolence is not really self-love any more than all colors are really red. Or to put the point another way, the philosophical atheist makes a distinction between the surface appearance of custom (experience) and the deep underlying cause, where the deep cause is some privileged item of the surface of custom transformed by the Midas touch of false philosophy into an explanatory entity capable of reducing the rest to the category of appearance. Philosophical theism blocks this move. There is a distinction between the surface of custom and the hidden ultimate cause. But the latter is the mind of God and is, and must remain, a mystery. Since the philosophical demand for ultimacy is met by the philosophical theist in the belief in a mysterious providence, there is no tendency to satisfy this demand by a philosophically superstitious transformation of the surface. The surface of custom is free to be the transparent medium of participation in common life that it is. Skepticism and ignorance about the ultimate cause of the surface clear the way to make the surface itself the object of inquiry; that is, the inquiry of true philosophy which is nothing but "reflections of common life methodized and corrected" (*EU*, 162). For us, the surface (participation in common life) is the reality.

To sum up, philosophical theism is superior to the philosophical atheism of the first philosophers in providing a more adequate account of the transcendence implied in critical inquiry. Theistic transcendence opens up an ideal of endless self-correcting inquiry while freeing the domain of custom to be what it is known to be through participation. Atheistic transcendence is a distance opened up within the domain of custom where inquiry can come to rest, but only at the price of superstitiously transforming the whole of custom into a favorite part. The order of participation then becomes a topsy-turvy world in which nothing ever appears as it is and never is as it appears to be.

Hume's philosophical theism bears some affinity to Kant's notion of God as a regulative idea. But there is an important difference. Kant thinks of a regulative idea as something used in inquiry. As an instrument, it is something about which we can have some distance. From this it is a short distance to the pragmatic notion of a regulative idea as an instrument over which we have some choice, as in William James' *The Will to Believe.* In Hume, however, the stress is on the conditions under which the idea of theism naturally appears, is believed, and becomes an established part of the human world. In short, the emphasis is not on the utility but the fact that philosophical theism is *believed,* and, for Hume, belief is something over which we have little control.

How does Hume understand the relation between vulgar theism and philosophical theism? As I have shown, their origins are different. Vulgar theism evolves out of polytheism and like polytheism is motivated by fear. Philosophical theism evolves out of philosophical atheism and is motivated by speculative curiosity or the love of truth. Although of different origins, they share the same doctrine of a perfect creator. In this way, the vulgar have a notion of transcendence which "coincide[s], by chance, with the principles of reason and true philosophy; tho' they are guided to that notion, not by reason, of which they are in a great measure incapable, but by the adulation and fears of the most vulgar superstition" (*NHR,* 52). Vulgar theism is inescapably tied to the rationale of its polytheistic origins. The radical transcendence it achieves is only the Sisyphean point at which it falls back into the direction of polytheism and superstition.

Although vulgar theism and philosophy have independent origins and rationales, they often appear in culture in a variety of blends: "Where theism forms the fundamental principle of any popular religion, that tenet is so conformable to sound reason, that philosophy is apt to incorporate itself with such a system of theology" (*NHR,* 65). One raised in a theistic culture will naturally be attracted to philosophy, and a philosopher of that culture will be attracted to its theistic religion. In such a union, philosophy, ideally, should "methodize and correct" the opinions and sentiments of vulgar theism. But Hume thinks this is unlikely. The rationale of fear locked into vulgar theism may be expected to overwhelm the philosophical love of truth: "Philosophy will soon find herself very unequally yoaked with her new associate; and instead of regulating each principle, as they advance together, she is at every turn perverted to serve the purposes of superstition" (*NHR*, 65).

But it is not only that vulgar theism may pervert philosophy into being her handmaiden; philosophy itself may transform vulgar theism into something worse than it is. It is easy to overlook this possibility because of the tendency to speak of philosophy and religion as substances and to treat Hume as an Enlightenment thinker engaged in a Manichean battle between philosophy (as light) and religion (as darkness). But Hume made a critical distinction between true and false philosophical criticism; and, as noted in the previous chapter, Hume thinks that false philosophy generates an order of superstition peculiar to itself. Out of autonomous reason, false philosophy may transform whatever the items of its experience might be (and these can be theistic as well other items) into a world of its own making and at the service of its own dominion. In this way a theistic "system becomes more absurd in the end, merely from its being reasonable and philosophical in the beginning" (*NHR*, 66).

And there is another possibility which the Enlightenment overlooked, but Hume did not. Philosophy does not need religion for its perversion. Philosophy can pervert itself. That is, false philosophy can subvert the true. Hume teaches that religion, though natural to man, was not necessary. The essence of religion is fear. The three original principles of transcendence, *prosopopeia,* and systematic thinking gave rise to religion only because mankind found itself in a terrifying world. The same being, in a world that was not terrifying, would not have developed religion but would have developed philosophy, for philosophy did in fact, in Hume's account, arise from conditions of security and leisure. But is there any reason to think that the philosophy that emerged would be the true rather than the false? In Hume's narrative it was indeed the false that first emerged. Hume taught that popular religion had been the bane of human life and that the fear-motivated superstition internal to it is the only part of human life that might be thought of as unqualifiedly bad (*D*, 223 n). But is there any reason to think that, in a world without religion, false philosophy, with its own peculiar forms of superstition, alienation, and self-deception, and these pushed to their limits by the principles of ultimacy, autonomy, and dominion, would not be as oppressive as religion or even worse? This is a question that began to surface in Hume's mind as he observed, later in his career, the waning influence of religion in political life and the rising influence of philosophy. I shall turn to it later when discussing Hume's views on how philosophy has appeared in the practices and institutions of culture and what its proper role in culture is.

In the meantime, it is important to observe that the highest achievement of philosophical reflection is philosophical theism. "What a noble privilege," Hume writes, "is it of human reason to attain the knowledge of the supreme being; and, from the visible works of nature, be enabled to infer as sublime a principle as its supreme Creator" (*NHR*, 94). The philosophical idea of God is experienced with feelings of awe and wonder but without fear. Indeed, it is experienced more as a gift than as an achievement which is an occasion for pride. Accordingly the philosopher thinks of the idea "as a kind of mark or stamp, which the divine workman has set upon his work" (*NHR*, 93). The sentiments generated by this idea ennoble its possessor: "The good, the great, the sublime, the ravishing are found eminently in the genuine principles of theism" (*NHR*, 93).

But the thesis of *The Natural History of Religion* is that the best things suffer the worst corruption. Though it should serve to "dignify mankind," the image of divinity as it has actually appeared in the world is to be regarded more as "sick men's dreams" or "the playsome whimsies of monkeys in human shape, than the serious, positive, dogmatical asseverations of a being, who dignifies himself with the name of rational" (*NHR*, 94). It is worth remarking that Hume did not employ the "conspiracy of the priests" explanation of the cause of religious oppression so popular among freethinkers of his time: "the artifices of men aggravate our natural infirmities and follies of this kind, but never originally beget them. Their root strikes deeper into the mind, and springs from the essential and universal properties of human nature" (*NHR*, 92). The only antidote to this disorder in human affairs is philosophy, which has a different origin from religion and a different rationale. *The Natural History of Religion* and the *Dialogues* are works of true philosophy in that they attempt to "methodize and correct" our idea of divinity in the direction of the sublime and ennobling idea of philosophical theism. It is for this reason that Hume's cousin the Reverend John Home, to whom the *Natural History* is dedicated, could describe it as one of the most pious works in that it attempts to rescue the corrupted and disfigured image of divinity.[3]

But it is misleading to say that philosophy is the only antidote to religion. Philosophical theism is the work not simply of philosophy but of *true* philosophy. And true philosophy is extremely rare. The errors of false philosophy can be as perverse and dangerous as those of religion. And it is a central teaching of the *Natural History* that when men seek to engage the real, whether through religion (fear) or philosophy (speculative curiosity), the mind falls into incoherences which even the most rigorous reflection and the calmest passions find invincible. And when the two forms of experience merge, as in history they often have, the incoherence is worse. Hume traced the origin of philosophical theism to Anaxagoras. It was cultivated by Socrates, Plato, Aristotle, and the Stoics but existed as such an amalgam of philosophical and religious superstition that Hume could identify it only as, at most, a precursor of the refined theism he defends. He mentions Xenophon, that "great captain and philosopher, the disciple of Socrates, and one who has delivered some of the most refined sentiments with regard to a deity" as "incontestable proof of . . . the incoherences, in all ages, of men's opinions in religious matters" (*NHR,* 78 n). Though a philosophical theist, Xenophon was still in the grip of auguries, sacrifices, oracles, and beliefs such as that sneezing is a luck omen. The same was true of most other pagan philosophical theists such as Socrates and Hume's own hero Cicero (*NHR,* 73). The Stoics were especially remarkable for blending philosophical theism with pagan superstition: "The force of their mind, being all turned to the side of morals, unbent itself in that of religion" (*NHR,* 77). Marcus Aurelius "received many admonitions from the gods in his sleep," and Panaetius "was the only Stoic, amongst the Greeks, who so much as doubted with regard to augeries and divinations" (*NHR,* 77). Epictetus believed in the "language of rooks and ravens" (*NHR,* 77). And so Hume concluded,

> For my part, I can scarce allow the principles even of *Marcus Aurelius, Plutarch,* and some other *Stoics* and *Academics,* tho' infinitely more refined than the pagan superstition, to be worthy of the honourable denomination of theism. For if the mythology of the heathens resemble the antient *European* system of spiritual beings, excluding God and angels, and leaving only fairies and sprights; the creed of these philosophers [though pretending otherwise] may justly be said to exclude a deity, and to leave only angels and fairies. (*NHR,* 45)

Turning to modern philosophical theists, Hume observes, "I maintain, that Newton, Locke, Clarke, etc. being Arians or Socianians, were very sincere in the creed they profest: And I always oppose this argument to some libertines, who will needs have it, that it was impossible, but that these great philosophers must have been hypocrites" (*NHR,* 79). Indeed, the philosophical libertines themselves may not know what they really believe. They may accept the tenets of philosophical theism and many of the tenets of vulgar theism while denying them. And so "might seem determined infidels, and enemies to the established religion, without being so in reality; or at least, without knowing their own minds in that particular" (*NHR,* 74). And the "greatest and truest zeal gives us no security against hypocrisy: The most open impiety is attended with a secret dread and compunction" (*NHR,* 94). But if it is that difficult for both the religious and the irreligious minds to know themselves, what, we may ask, of Hume's own mind in respect to religious sentiments? And in particular what does he mean by "true religion"?

True religion is, first of all, an order of sentiments which naturally arise when the philosopher achieves the thought that what is experienced ("the visible system") constitutes a systematic whole. Just as the experience of constant conjunction prompts the belief in invisible causal power, so the idea of the whole of reality prompts the belief that experience is the result of purposive intelligence and that this intelligence is "single and undivided." "A purpose, an intention, a design is evident in every thing," and this thought about the whole produces in the philosopher a sense of awe and wonder. These sentiments naturally lead to the conception of the Deity as the perfection of reason and goodness: "The good, the great, the sublime, the ravishing are found eminently in the genuine principles of theism." The philosophical response to the thought of the Deity is that of awe and gratitude but not fear. "What a noble privilege is it of human reason to attain the knowledge of the supreme being; and from the visible work of nature, be enabled to infer so sublime a principle as its supreme Creator" (*NHR,* 92–94).

Fear and ignorance motivate vulgar theism, whereas the sentiments of "true theism" are impressions of reflection consequent upon contemplating the thought of the whole of reality, and this thought has its source in the unrelenting pursuit of truth and in the greatness of mind inseparable from that pursuit. "Genuine theism" is the discovery of the "true philosopher." It is "that speculative tenet of theism, which . . . is a species of philosophy;" and it is religion of the "philosophical and rational kind" (*D,* 220, 223, 225). No one of "good understanding" can reject it because it *spontaneously* arises from contemplating reality as a systematic whole, and to be incapable of this idea of the whole is not to be one of "good understanding" (*NHR,* 92). Hume in a number of places doubts that there are any real atheists, though he acknowledges there are a few who claim to be (*NHR,* 25–26; *D,* 142, 214–18). Mossner has given an account of how Holbach's circle in Paris ridiculed Hume for his view that there were no genuine atheists and for his own theism. Years later Hume could recall how Lord Marischal and Helvétius "used to laugh at me for my narrow way of thinking in these particulars." And

Sir James Macdonald, writing from Paris to a friend in England, could speak of "poor Hume who on your side of the water was thought to have too little religion, is here thought to have too much."[4]

When Hume says that it is a privilege to "infer" a supreme Creator from the visible system and Philo in the *Dialogues* declares that the "existence of a Deity is plainly ascertained by reason," the "inference" in question is neither *a priori* nor causal inference (*NHR*, 25, 92; *D*, 142, 217). Hume is clear that there is no *a priori* argument for the existence of anything and that no causal inference from a part of reality can legitimate an inference about the origin of the whole. Hume's use of "reason" and "inference" here reflects that deeper notion whereby reason is said to be "nothing but a wonderful and unintelligible instinct in our souls" (*T*, 179). This primordial sense of reason is the "cement of the universe" which enables us to move from experience of constant conjunctions to belief in invisible causal power; it enables us to move from a miscellaneous assortment of regularities to the belief that they are part of a systematic whole and thence to appropriate sentiments about the origin of the whole in purposive intelligence.

Beliefs about the causally connected parts of reality as well as about the whole have their origin not in the "application" of rules for *a priori* or causal reasoning but in the soul. For this reason Hume can say that the contemplation of the Deity is experienced not so much as the achievement of an inference but "as a kind of mark or stamp, which the divine workman has set upon his work; and nothing surely can more dignify mankind than to bear the image or impression of the universal Creator" (*NHR*, 93).

Here as elsewhere, human beliefs are the result of poetic acts of the imagination. The attributes of the Deity are supreme reason, goodness, knowledge, and power. We ascribe to the Deity what is highest and most noble in our own nature, but these are only symbols which point to what we cannot fully grasp (*D*, 142). To think we possess an adequate conception of the Deity is impious because it always degrades divinity to the level of the human or even lower and is at the service of the dominion and barbarism that usually attend theological theorizing. And to claim to know the goodness and rationality of the Creator (independent of any prior conception of that goodness and rationality) merely by calculating the goods and evils in the world, as effects on the basis of which an empirical inference can be drawn regarding the character of the Creator, leads to the devastating arguments of Philo in the *Dialogues* that the Deity must be conceived as either evil or incompetent or perhaps both (*D*, 203–13). The thought of the whole and its origins cannot be arrived at by the ordinary canons of empirical inference; rather it is the idea of the whole as a coherent system that guides empirical inquiry (*D*, 214–16).

But this inadequacy in our conception of the Deity is not peculiar to that idea and cannot in itself subvert theistic belief. For Hume, all beliefs about the real are metaphorical and point to more than we can picture. We have no adequate idea of causal power, but belief in causal power is the source of all causal reasoning. Hume has no difficulty with beliefs which (from the point of view of an artificial reflection purged of all human sentiment) are incomprehensible. All of our fundamental beliefs are of this sort.

Since it is an order of sentiments, true religion can motivate. What difference does it make in the life of the true philosopher? Religious sentiments are not the same as moral sentiments, though much of the influence of true religion is displayed in moral conduct. Moral sentiments stain and color a part of experience transforming it into a moral reality. Religious sentiments stain and color the *whole* of experience transforming it into an expression of divine intelligence. The philosopher believes and feels himself to be a participant in a general but mysterious providence. This providential order is known through direct participation; no reason can be given "for our most general and most refined principles, beside our experience of their reality" (*T*, xviii). And the fundamental categories of this experience are a causally ordered world, self, society, and the divine.

Participating in a general (not a particular) providence reinforces the true philosopher's disposition to inquiry (contemplation) and to virtue. Since the world is rationally ordered, the relentless pursuit of truth makes sense. And conceiving of himself as a *creature* participating in a general providence, the true philosopher must defer and submit to that order as he finds it in experience. This fundamental act of deference reinforces the dialectic of true and false philosophy and suppresses the hubristic disposition of the philosopher to conceive of himself as a self-determining pagan god in pursuit of dominion and self-display. The Nietzschean will to power makes no appearance in the scene opened up by Hume's conception of "genuine theism."

The "standard" of morality arises "from the internal frame and constitution of animals" and is "ultimately derived from that Supreme Will, which bestowed on each being its peculiar nature, and arranged the several classes and orders of existence" (*EM*, 294). Philosophical theism strengthens the disposition to virtue, for as we ascribe to the Deity the highest qualities we know (in an act of adoration, not an act of ordinary epistemological inference), we are inclined to order our own souls in accord with these qualities (*D,* 142). A mixed life of contemplation and virtue is the highest life possible for man; and in it are "united whatever can distinguish human nature, or elevate mortal man to a resemblance with the divinity" (*E,* 153).

Vulgar religion is motivated by fear, which is manipulated by priests for the sake of dominion. Priests compete with each other for followers by multiplying doctrines and rituals which purport to placate the terror of the Deity. These doctrines and rituals, far from strengthening moral dispositions, are often in conflict with them. In contrast true religion imposes no special religious duties to gain divine favor. True religion affirms man's place in the universe as a creature endowed with the capacity for contemplation and virtue. It demands only that we live according to the highest of which we are capable. It issues in "a manly steddy virtue," the "calm sunshine of the mind" which repels "these spectres of false divinity" (*NHR,* 91).

True religion is not a characteristic of philosophy as such but only of true philosophy, and as the latter is rare, so is true religion. Its "proper office" is "to regulate the heart of men, humanize their conduct, infuse the spirit of temperance, order, and obedience, and as its operation is silent, and only enforces the motives of morality and justice, it is in danger of being overlooked, and confounded with these other motives. When it distinguishes itself, and acts as a separate principle over men, it has departed from its proper sphere and has become only a cover to faction and ambition" (*D,* 220). Religious sentiments and moral sentiments, though mutually reinforcing, are not the same. When religious sentiments are detached from common life and become an object of reflection, they become the plaything of philosophical theorizing and issue in antinomic theologies which, in becoming institutionalized, generate civil strife.

It is for this reason that Hume doubts that there could ever be an institutionalized form of true religion. Such a religion must present itself as the absolute and final form of religion. Philosophical parties would immediately arise in dispute over its true character, and new duties, spawned by reflection alone, would arise to usurp and displace its proper content. "Nay, if we should suppose, what seldom happens, that a popular religion were found, in which it was expressly declared, that nothing but morality could gain the divine favor . . . yet so inveterate are the people's prejudices, that for want of some other superstition, they would make the very attendance on these sermons the essentials of religion, rather than place them in virtue and good morals" (*NHR,*

87–88). Contemporary Enlightenment ideologies such as liberalism and Marxism, though typically atheistic, resemble religions of the kind Hume imagines in being devoted to moral ideals such as liberty, equality, and humanity. From the terror of the French Revolution carried out in the name of the rights of man to the egalitarianism of totalitarian Marxist regimes, two world wars, and the cold war, these humanistic ideologies have produced a greater scene of devastation and terror than was ever wrought by the popular religions Hume criticizes.

If it is unlikely that true religion can be institutionalized, how does it appear in the world? The struggle between true and false religion and between true and false philosophy are variations on the general struggle between nature and reflection. The conflict is permanent and can never be resolved. The most that can be done is to moderate it by exposing the errors of false religion and false philosophy and to cultivate in one's own soul, through thoughtful participation in common life, the philosophical character of true religion.

But even this cannot fully satisfy the restlessness of philosophical speculation once it has achieved belief in an intelligent Creator of the universe. Just as vulgar theism becomes restless when contemplating an abstract conception of divine perfections and has recourse to intermediate beings which can enter common life, so the philosopher, having given "philosophical assent" to propositions about the Deity and having experienced the "astonishment" of the religious sentiments that "the greatness of the object" produces, will naturally desire a more concrete grasp of the Deity—one that can enter the flow of common life. Philosophical theism now plunges into "melancholy" and even displays "some contempt of human reason" which, having brought it this far, "can give no solution more satisfying with regard to so extraordinary and magnificent a question" (*D*, 227).

Hume (speaking through Philo) says that "the natural sentiment" felt at this moment in the progress of philosophical theism is a "longing desire and expectation" that the Deity has revealed himself in a tradition which provides concrete images of the nature, attributes, and operation of the Deity. And so the true philosopher, having followed the path up to and through philosophical theism, will be open to participation in a tradition of revealed religion. But this return to the concrete is different from the return of vulgar theism to the worship of intermediary beings. That move has its source in ignorance and fear, whereas the return that Philo describes has its source in a *philosophical* inclination and is similar to the return (in the dialectic of true and false philosophy) of reflection to common life. This inclination presupposes the achievement of philosophical theism and so flows from a "well disposed mind," one "seasoned with a just sense of the imperfections of natural reason" (*D*, 227). That is, it is conceived as a natural and final move in the true philosopher's dialectical encounter with divinity. And so Philo concludes that "to be a philosophical sceptic is, in a man of letters, the first and most essential step towards being a sound, believing Christian" (*D*, 228). There are, of course, vulgar reasons (fear) to participate in the Christian tradition, but these are not worthy of the "man of letters." The only thoughtful avenue to Christianity is the philosophical path to true theism and the skepticism internal to it.

This passage has puzzled many who have taken Philo to speak for Hume (as I think he generally does). Given Philo's devastating arguments against natural theology, it has been thought that the conclusion of the *Dialogues* must be either atheism or a total suspense of judgment. But Hume is a theist, not an atheist. And the dialectic of nature and reflection, in all its forms in Hume's writings, always ends in *belief,* not suspense of judgment. In the dialectic, belief emerges through an experience of total doubt, the point of which is to expose a specious but false source of belief and to call attention to the true source. The dialectic always ends in what Hume calls a "sceptical solution" to doubt. For Hume man is a believing animal, and a main objective of his philosophy is to moderate, not subvert, the inclination to beliefs about the real.

What Philo has exposed is a defensible philosophical path whereby the philosopher can return to a revealed religious tradition. But again it is not just any kind of philosopher who can take this path but only one who is a "philosophic sceptic," that is, a true philosopher. Here, as elsewhere, the enemy is false philosophy, "the haughty dogmatist, [Cleanthes and Demea] persuaded that he can erect a complete system of theology by the mere help of philosophy" (*D*, 227).

Philo does not argue that a philosophical theist *must* participate in a revealed tradition but only that there is a justifiable philosophical inclination to do so. But we may suppose that the philosopher who takes this path will retain the dispositions of true religion and so will be a critic of the tendency of a revealed tradition to fall into the corruptions of popular religion—especially the tendency to ossification by constructing theological theories and by treating belief in these as worship of the Deity. We may recall here Hume's teaching in the *Natural History of Religion* that the more rational a religion becomes, the more absurd are its doctrines. A philosophical skeptic participating in a revealed religion would have a noble vocation and a humanizing influence, ideally bringing popular religion in line with the demands of true religion. This is not a vocation that Philo undertook, but he recommends it as a goal in the education of Cleanthes' pupil Pamphilus: that he become a participant in the Christian tradition by acquiring the disposition of a philosophical skeptic.

But the mature Pamphilus, who relates the conversation between Philo, Cleanthes, and Demea, took a different route. He viewed the whole conversation as merely an occasion for evaluating the merits of abstract arguments, and he concludes with the judgment that "Philo's principles are more probable than Demea's; but . . . those of Cleanthes approach still nearer to the truth" (*D*, 228). Pamphilus follows Cleanthes as a rationalist in religion who thinks that religion can be founded on reflection alone. The Humean dialectic, displayed by Philo, that sought to penetrate to the source of religious beliefs in human nature and from thence to their correction, made no impression at all.

CHAPTER FOUR

The Ancient Philosophy

The Idea of a History of Philosophy

Although Hume did not write a history of philosophy, his philosophic and historical writings are filled with critical reflections on the work of his philosophical ancestors. These occur in many forms. There are topical sketches which capture a mode or tradition of philosophizing, such as what he calls the ancient philosophy, the philosophy of the Schoolmen, and modern philosophy. Schools of philosophy such as Epicureanism, Stoicism, Platonism, the Cynics, Skepticism, and the Peripatetics are identified and compared as exemplifications of certain possibilities immanent in philosophizing and in human nature. Hume finds cycles recurring in the history of philosophy. And he has much to say about the evolution of the arts and sciences and of philosophy's role in this evolution; of how philosophy has been influenced by the wider culture in which it has found itself, and how it has in turn shaped culture; how it has, at one time, captured religion and shaped it to its own ends, only at a later time to be dominated by religion and seduced into serving her purposes; and how philosophy has sought to guide politics and at other times has been content to be guided by it.

Hume observes that philosophy in its true form has ennobled human nature beyond all other activities and in its false forms has utterly corrupted it, and these forms dance in and out of philosophy's history, weaving the tapestry of a philosophical bestiary. Hume judges philosophers in respect of their greatness. He compares himself with philosophers such as Socrates and thinks of himself as reenacting dramatic episodes in the history of philosophy such as the trial of Socrates before the Athenians. He uses dialogue form to express his thoughts through voices from philosophy's past which are and are not his own.

Collected together, this rich display of judgment may be viewed as notes and sketches of a history of philosophy which Hume never wrote but which is required by his conception of philosophy. On what principles are these sketches ordered? Did he think of his own philosophical insights as timeless and related to the history of philosophy conceived only as the history of error? Or did he think of the history of philosophy as the story of progress leading up to modern philosophy and even more narrowly to Hume himself? Or did he conceive of it as the story of decline and of himself as recovering an ancient philosophical wisdom for modern times? A tradition is an order of beliefs and sentiments. To understand a tradition requires the making of a narrative, and it is a peculiarity of narratives of traditions that they contain implicit idealizations of the subject narrated. A narrative of the Christian tradition presupposes some judgment about what true Christianity is. A narrative of the American tradition of constitutional law presupposes some idealization of the true American polity. And so a narrative understanding of the philosophical tradition presupposes an ideal conception of what philosophy is and ought to be. Just as Hume's anthropology of philosophy presupposes the dialectical distinction between true and false philosophy, so his understanding of the philosophical tradition is guided by the same ideal distinction.

It is no accident that Hume's first reflections on the philosophical tradition occur in part 4 of book 1 of the *Treatise,* where the dialectic of true and false philosophy is first presented. In working out the dialectic, Hume had his eye on the philosophical tradition. The dialectic is used to illuminate the tradition, and the tradition is shown to exemplify the dialectic. This occurs as follows. In section 2, part 4 of book 1, Hume charts the struggles of the mind as it seeks a coherent understanding of what it means to perceive a public world. A dialectical drama is carried out between the senses, the imagination, and reason. Hume shows how a certain order of philosophical theories arises naturally from propensities original to the mind. All of these theories have one thing in common: they all claim to have rejected vulgar realism in favor of a higher degree of philosophical self-understanding. What Hume shows is that none of the theories have in fact rejected vulgar realism, nor could they reject it. The demonstration that vulgar realism is in fact believed and presupposed by any theory of perception that purports to replace it is an insight of true philosophy. It represents the highest degree of philosophical understanding on the question of perception; that is, those who recognize the necessity of vulgar realism in our thinking about perceiving the world have a higher degree of philosophical self-understanding than those who think they have emancipated themselves from vulgar realism. But this insight is not itself another theory of perception. Hume does not argue that vulgar realism is true, but only that it is believed and presupposed. Theories of perception are theories about the world, whereas Hume's insight is a thesis about self-knowledge. Philosophers who do not recognize the necessity of vulgar realism in their own thinking do not understand the nature of their own thinking. But there is more.

At the end of section 2, Hume lays it down as a thesis of true philosophy that there is (or rather that we suppose there is) "both an external and internal world," however difficult it might be to explain what these are. And he goes on to say that in the following sections of part 4, he intends to examine a number of philosophical theories that have been offered of both (*T,* 218). It is important to see that the internal and external worlds of which Hume speaks are structures of experience known through participation and brought to explicit self-consciousness through the dialectical reflections of section 2. Again Hume's affirmation of an internal and an external world is not a theory of objects in the world, but rather is the recognition, through dialectical self-reflection, of a necessary mode of participation in common life.[1]

The theories examined later in section 2 are presented as incoherent accounts of what, through philosophical reflection, is known to be a structure of participation in common life: that it necessarily has the structure of "inner" and "outer." But what is most important for the present argument is that these theories are also taken by Hume as representations of different modes of philosophizing in the Western tradition. Section 3 is entitled "Of the Antient Philosophy" and section 4 is entitled "Of the Modern Philosophy." Hume deftly sketches out what he considers to be essential to these traditions. Both are forms of false philosophical consciousness; that is, they spring from the natural operations of the mind which are distorted by philosophical reflection into alienating forms of experience. "Of the Antient Philosophy" and "Of the Modern Philosophy" are exercises in philosophical pathology.

The great discovery of the ancients was *being,* conceived as substance. The great discovery of the moderns was *mind,* or consciousness, and the recognition that mind influences our conception of being. The ancients directed their theorizing to the "outer" world. It was the genius of the moderns to have attended to the "inner" world and to have understood that the mind makes its own contribution to our experience of the world. Hume's criticism of modern philosophizing about the internal world appears in "Of the Modern Philosophy," "Of the Immateriality of the Soul," and "Of Personal Identity." But I turn first to his criticism of the ancients.

"Of the Antient Philosophy"

Hume compares his pathology of the ancient philosophers to the method of certain "moralists" who say we should rigorously examine our dreams upon arising as a clue to our character. Our true character is often hidden in waking life by "artifice, fear, and policy." In the transparent medium of dreams, "men can neither be hypocrites with themselves nor others" (*T,* 219). In this model, we are to see ancient philosophy as a dream in which our own philosophical character is mirrored. Hume uses "we" for both. The mind of the ancient philosophers is our own mind. Their errors are our errors, as are "the means by which we endeavour to conceal them" (*T,* 219). A clear understanding of the errors of ancient philosophy is a way of unmasking our own philosophical self-deceptions and hypocrisy.

The governing idea of ancient philosophy is the metaphysics of substance, which Hume takes to include Platonic forms and Aristotelian substances, as well as Scholastic theories of substance, essences, accidents, and occult qualities. All of substance metaphysics derives from an error in philosophical reflection having to do with a simple and natural operation of the mind, whereby distinct but similar perceptions are viewed as unities. "Hence, the colour, taste, figure, solidity, and other qualities, combin'd in a peach or melon, are conceiv'd to form *one thing*" (*T,* 221). But this naive notion of substance is soon exploded by reflection, which shows that all the above qualities are "different, and distinguishable, and separable from each other" (*T,* 221). Thus reflection subverts our "primary and more natural notions" of substance. In the light of this knowledge, we see that the vulgar notion of substance is a poetic or metaphorical one. That is, the notion of substance is a unity structured by a false identity; numerically distinct qualities which change are thought of as one quality which does not change.

The dialectic here is the same as that in section 2 concerning our conception of perceiving a public world. Once the poetic unities of the imagination are brought to the light of reflection, they are seen as an embarrassment and are disowned by reflection as childish. Yet they are taken seriously enough to force reason to suppose that there *is* a unity which is now conceived by the understanding as "something unknown and invisible, which it supposes the same under all these variations; and this unintelligible something it calls a *substance, or original and first mat-*

ter" (*T*, 220). The rationale of this move in the dialectic is the same as that in section 2 which resulted in the doctrine of "double existence" (*T*, 215). Reflection, though arrogantly pretending emancipation from vulgar opinion, cannot bear the trauma of separation and is unknowingly guided by vulgar opinion to create its ghostly image, which is then ontologized as the reality behind appearance.

Conceiving substance as "original," the imagination soon invests substance with causal properties and treats observable qualities as dependent upon substance and as modifications or accidents of it. To understand how these sensory qualities behave as they do, the mind launches into a hopeless inquiry to discover invisible qualities of substance which generate observable qualities. These invisible qualities are necessarily occult because the substance itself is a metaphor which the mind tries to treat as nonmetaphorical, that is, as an object of rational insight purged of all the poetic workings of the imagination. Hume compares this unhappy consciousness with the condition "the poets have given us but a faint notion of in their descriptions of the punishment of *Sisyphus* and *Tantalus*." For what is more "tormenting, than to seek with eagerness, what for ever flies us; and seek for it in a place, where 'tis impossible it can ever exist?" (*T*, 223).

But nature has provided philosophers with a "consolation amid all their disappointments and afflictions" with the invention of the terms *faculty* and *occult quality*. The ritualistic use of language hides the absurdity and impossibility of the philosophical task of treating as nonmetaphorical what is in fact a metaphorical object. Hume's point is not the positivist one that terms not replaceable by empirical terms are meaningless; rather it is that the fictions by which we order the world are, and must be, metaphorical and that this is denied by philosophers (including positivistic empiricists) who seek emancipation from the imagination and hypocritically construct devices to hide the workings of the imagination in what they are pleased to call the work of reason. It matters little whether reason is conceived in the rationalist sense or in the inductive empiricist sense: for both, reason is the domain of the literal, the clear and distinct, and not the metaphorical. Hume's point, however, is that the metaphorical has dominion over the literal. The deeper notion of reason recognizes that fact about human thought. The rationalistic and positivistic notions of reason then are shallow in that they lack self-knowledge. Neither understands the proper relation between critical reflection and primordial (metaphorical) vulgar thought.

That Hume thought he was developing a deeper and more discriminating notion of reason is clear from a memorable passage of this section quoted previously: "In considering this subject we may observe a gradation of three opinions, that rise above each other, according as the persons, who form them, acquire *new degrees of reason and knowledge* . . . that of the vulgar, that of a false philosophy, and that of the true; where we shall find upon enquiry, that the true philosophy approaches nearer to the sentiments of the vulgar, than to those of a mistaken knowledge" (*T,* 222–23; italics mine). The vulgar error is that the poetic notion of substance is conceived so that there is a "perceivable connexion betwixt the several sensible qualities and actions of matter" (*T,* 223). Philosophy in the moment of heroic reflection explodes this as metaphorical. But instead of concluding "that we have no idea of power or agency separate from the mind," (i.e., the metaphorical imagination), the false philosopher searches for the qualities of agency in objects, and not finding them in what is perceivable, looks for them in an invisible metaphysical realm to which the name "matter or causes" is given. Entirely cut off and emancipated from the imagination, the false philosophers are necessarily "displeased with every system which their reason suggests to them" (*T,* 223). The failure of self-knowledge of the false philosopher is exhibited in that act whereby the mind constructs objects and connections and then looks for them in a metaphysical realm and not in its own activity.

What renders the Sisyphean labor especially absurd is that it is the poetic work of the imagination that prompts the naive belief in substance in the first place, and the force of this belief is so strong that even when exploded by reflection, the mind seeks its ghost in the notion of substance. Reflection can strip the metaphorical notion of substance of content but cannot eliminate belief in its ghost as a metaphysical entity to which the mind hopelessly seeks to give content. Substance metaphysics, as guided by the imagination, is seen not only in the belief in a metaphorical realm of substance but also in the metaphorical way that realm is understood, that is, by reference to "sympathies, antipathies, and horrors of a vacuum" (*T,* 224). Thus the "remarkable inclination in human nature, to bestow on external objects the same emotions, which it observes in itself" takes place in "children, poets, and the antient philosophers" (*T,* 224; *NHR,* 34). It is the primordial poetic imagination that first brings order into experience. As observed in chapter 3, the first *system* of thought (and hence the origin of all science) was polytheism, in which the metaphorical act of *prosopopeia* brought into being the experience of a world of gods. Hume describes polytheism as a "true poetical religion" (*NHR,* 75). Out of this poetical system, philosophy gradually emerged in the form of substance metaphysics, which both disowned the act of *prosopopeia* and at the same time instantiated it in the form of "these fictions of sympathy and antipathy" (*T,* 225). The primordial inclination to read the mind's affections into the world can be "suppres'd by a little reflection" (*T,* 224). The inclination cannot, of course, be eliminated, but it can be recognized for what it is and, in relation to other inclinations and beliefs, "methodized and corrected." The philosophical self-deception and hypocrisy of ancient philosophy, then, is that it indulged this inclination while at the same time claiming emancipation from it.

Morals and Eloquence

Although Hume considered the ancient philosophers to be children in metaphysics, he judged them adults in their understanding of morals, and even superior to the moderns. The "ancient moralists," he wrote, are still "the best models" (*EM,* 318). The ancients are superior because they drew morals from the well of sentiment and not from the abstractions of reason. "The ancient philosophers, though they often affirm, that virtue is nothing but conformity to reason, yet, in general, seem to consider morals as deriving their existence from taste and sentiment. On the other hand, our modern enquirers, though they also talk much of the beauty of virtue, and deformity of vice, yet have commonly endeavoured to account for these distinctions by metaphysical reasonings, and by deductions from the most abstract principles of the understanding" (*EM,* 170).

Modern ethics is not only rationalistic, it is also legalistic and is greatly concerned with following rules. The modern sees ethics as primarily a matter of establishing "the relation of actions to the rule of right" (*EM,* 288). By contrast, the ancients for the most part saw ethics as a study of the virtues necessary for happiness. The moderns too have a system of virtues, but these are restricted to a small range of virtues deemed necessary to bring action in accord with whatever abstract reason has determined to be "the rule of right." Since this rule is to determine the will, the only qualities that can count as virtues are those within our control. Hume follows the "ancient moralists," however, by including within human excellence qualities beyond our control, such as natural endowments, place of origin, family and inherited status, and even the goods of fortune. Indeed Hume defines a virtue as any quality of character useful and agreeable to ourselves or others. With this formula, he intends to recover the wisdom of the ancient moralists for his own time.

In saying that the ancients had a better understanding of *the nature of morals,* Hume does not mean that they were in all respects superior in moral practice. As will be discussed more fully later, he thinks the moderns are superior in a number of respects, for example, humanity, clemency, liberty, and political stability (*EM,* 256–57). But there is one virtue in which the ancients are clearly superior to the moderns, and that is eloquence. Moreover, it is the mastery of this art that, in part, explains their superior grasp of the nature of morals. I argued in chapter 2 that eloquence is a virtue of the true philosopher. The world of common life is a social world constituted by the communication of sentiments through sympathy. Eloquence is the art of discriminating among sentiments and communicating them. Since the true philosopher is a critical participant in custom, he must develop the art of eloquence. But the very nature of philosophical reflection is a barrier to the development of this art among philosophers. The tendency of philosophical reflection is to its false forms rather than the true. False philosophy seeks emancipation from custom and sentiment into an abstract, conceptual world of its own making. Instead of being receptive to the spontaneous order of sentiments, and educating them according to patterns of excellence, the false philosopher seeks to transmute these through philosophical "chymistry" into substances of his own making. Thus his speech, when heard in common life, tends to be that of paradox, not eloquence.

Hume taught that the beauties of eloquence are more stable and enduring than philosophical systems. Being self-contained and abstract, it is easy to enter into a discarded philosophical system no matter how absurd it might be. "There needs but a certain turn of thought or imagination to make us enter into all the opinions, which then prevailed, and relish the sentiments or conclusions derived from them" (*E,* 246–47). Philosophical systems come and go, and "nothing has been experienced more liable to the revolutions of chance and fashion than these pretended decisions of science" (*E,* 242). But the case is otherwise with "the beauties of eloquence and poetry." "Just expressions of passion and nature are sure, after a little time, to gain public applause, which they maintain for ever. Aristotle, and Plato, and Epicurus, and Descartes, may successively yield to each other: But Terence and Virgil maintain an universal undisputed empire over the minds of men. The abstract philosophy of Cicero has lost its credit. The vehemence of his oratory is still the object of our admiration" (*E,* 242–43). So although a civilized people may long "be mistaken in the choice of their admired philosopher, they never have been found long to err, in their affection for a favourite epic or tragic author" (*E*, 243). Hume makes the same judgment regarding oratory. People may for a time be satisfied with an orator "and know not in what he is defective: Yet, whenever the true genius arises, *he* draws to him the attention of everyone, and immediately appears superior to his rival" (*E*, 107). The reason for Hume's confidence here is his belief that "The principles of every passion, and of every sentiment, are in every man; and when touched properly, they rise to life, and warm the heart, and convey that satisfaction, by which a work of genius is distinguished from the adulterate beauties of a capricious wit and fancy. And if this observation be true, with regard to all the liberal arts, it must be peculiarly so, with regard to eloquence" (*E*, 107).

The power of eloquence to explore, discriminate, and make manifest the passions constitutive of common life affords the most important sort of self-knowledge and gives eloquent speech its divine character. "Can it possibly be doubted, that this talent itself of poets, to move the passions, this pathetic and sublime of sentiment, is a very considerable merit; and being enhanced by its extreme rarity, may exalt the person possessed of it, above every character of the age in which he lives? . . . Augustus, adorned with all the splendour of his noble birth and imperial crown, render him but an unequal competitor for fame with Virgil, who lays nothing into the opposite scale but the divine beauties of his poetical genius" (*EM*, 260). Hume remarks with some approval the opinion of "eminent writers" of antiquity that no work of genius required greater capacity than the eloquence of oratory and that even the talents "of a great poet or philosopher, [were] of an inferior nature to those which are requisite for such an undertaking" (*E*, 98). Even the greatest of the ancient orators, Demosthenes and Cicero, thought "they were far from reaching the perfection of their art, which was infinite, and not only exceeded human force to attain, but human imagination to conceive" (*E*, 98). Cicero said that his ears yearned for "something vast and boundless" (*E*, 98 n).

How are we to understand Hume's conception of the sublime and divine character of eloquence? It may be helpful to begin with a distinction Hume makes between the "abstruser studies of logic and metaphysics" and the "practical and more intelligible sciences of politics and morals" (*EM*, 214). Why are the human sciences more intelligible than "logic and metaphysics"? The latter, which for Hume includes the natural sciences, infers from "circumstances known or supposed . . . to the discovery of the concealed and unknown" (*EM*, 294). But in all moral decisions, "all the circumstances and relations must be previously known; and the mind, from the contemplation of the whole, feels some new impression of affection or disgust, esteem or contempt, approbation or blame" (*EM,* 290). Likewise for "all decisions of taste or external beauty," we pronounce "from the contemplation of the whole" a new sentiment of blame or approbation (*EM,* 291–93). The human sciences are more intelligible than the natural sciences because the former consist in understanding parts internally related to a whole produced by the imagination. It is this "productive faculty" that constitutes the whole within which and in response to which judgment moves. This whole is the topic, or common place, the tacit dimension, which gives point and force to the making of rules and provides the context without which their applicability is empty or arbitrary. In a court of law, one is sworn to tell the truth, the whole truth, and nothing but the truth. Here the "whole truth" is not a set of true propositions but the relevant truth, the truth that makes sense relative to the whole or the topic at hand. Vico, who, like Hume, was profoundly influenced by the Ciceronian humanistic tradition in philosophy, taught that truth or wisdom is the whole and that eloquence is wisdom speaking.[2]

Hume teaches that eloquence must be both "sublime and pathetic" (*E,* 104). That eloquence is the speech of the whole renders it sublime; but it must also be pathetic; that is, it must be a genuine communication of the sentiments that constitutes a whole of common life. And Hume is even prepared to insist that the bold poetic devices of *apostrophe* and *prosopopeia,* employed by the ancients, should be revived in modern oratory, though he will not go so far as to recommend the "*supplosio pedis,* or stamping with the foot" (*E,* 101). Recall that it was acts of poetic thought such as apostrophe and prosopopeia that generated the polytheistic cosmology, that "true poetical religion" for which Hume betrays some nostalgia. And it was poetic thought, incoherently combined with propositional thought, that produced the fantasy of substance metaphysics among the ancient philosophers, with the attendant torments of Tantalus and Sisyphus. Although out of place in metaphysics, poetical tropes which generate the "sublime and pathetic" can and must be used in the speech of the true philosopher about the unities of common life. Hume's philosophic speech (as he seeks to understand the whole of human nature, "the science of man") is rich in these devices, and a study of Humean eloquence as a constituent of true philosophical criticism is yet to be done.[3]

Though its power is to persuade, eloquence is not propaganda or manipulation. There is true and false eloquence as there is true and false philosophy. True eloquence is speech in contemplation of the whole. Since, for Hume, the thought and passion which constitutes the moral unities of common life are internally connected in “the contemplation of the whole,” no speech is truly eloquent which confines itself to abstract argument. It is a false speech, because in ignoring the passions, it is not a speech of the whole. This is precisely the error of what Hume calls modern eloquence. “Now banish the pathetic from public discourses, and you reduce the speakers merely to modern eloquence; that is, to good sense, delivered in proper expression” (*E,* 104). And Hume concludes that “ancient eloquence, that is, the sublime and passionate, is of a much juster taste than the modern, or the argumentative and rational; and if properly executed, will always have more command and authority over mankind” (*E,* 108).

The moderns think that “the decline of eloquence is owing to the superior good sense of the moderns, who reject with disdain all those rhetorical tricks, employed to seduce the judges, and will admit of nothing but solid argument in any debate of deliberation” (*E,* 103–4). But in this they are deceived. Whatever superior “good sense” the moderns might have is and must be compatible with eloquence. They should “redouble their art, not abandon it entirely” (*E,* 104). Hume distinguishes between the Roman and Attic eloquence, of which Cicero and Demosthenes are, respectively, the exemplars. Though both contain the pathetic and sublime, Hume thinks Attic eloquence is more akin to modern tastes and the best model for imitation. It is a form of eloquence that is “chaste and austere,” “calm, elegant, and subtile”; it “instructed the reason more than affected the passions, and never raised its tone above argument or common discourse” (*E,* 105, 108).

Eloquence is not the province of experts and technicians. It is speech directed to mankind in common life. Hume is clear on this. Eloquence is made for the “public, and for men of the world” and so “cannot, with any pretence of reason, appeal from the people to more refined judges; but must submit to the public verdict, without reserve or limitation. Whoever, upon comparison, is deemed by a common audience the greatest orator, ought most certainly to be pronounced such, by men of science and erudition” (*E,* 107). The great Demosthenes had to submit to the “lowest vulgar of Athens” as “his sovereigns, and the arbiters of his eloquence” (*E,* 105). Here again we have an instance of the true philosopher’s tie to and rootedness in common life and custom. It appears first in the “Advertisement” to books 1 and 2 of the *Treatise,* where Hume says, “The approbation of the public I consider as the greatest reward of my labours; but am determin’d to regard its judgment, whatever it be, as my best instruction.” It appears again in “Of Essay Writing,” where Hume pictures himself as an “ambassador” between the worlds of "abstruse learning" and the everyday world of "conversation." The "manufacturing" of truths belongs to learning, but the "materials" for truth come from the world of conversation, and the truths made must speak to the world of conversation. The same theme appears in the first *Enquiry* in the distinction between the "abstruse" philosophy and the "easy and humane," where the former is required to submit to the latter (*EU,* 9, 16).

In none of this is Hume saying that the vulgar, the public, the world of conversation contains infallible truths to which the learned or abstruse must conform. His point is that the relation between the two domains is a social one, requiring mutual deference. Truths are made by reflection from the materials of common life, but the materials constitute a limit as to what can be made. So although the great Demosthenes had to submit to the judgment of the "lowest vulgar," he, in turn, formed the nature of that judgment. "The orators formed the taste of the ATHENIAN people, not the people of the orators" (*E,* 105 n, 105). The speech of true philosophy is the speech of common life, refined by reflection and for the sake of common life. The true philosopher must somehow reconcile the common to the abstruse in such a way that the common may recognize itself in the abstruse. Philosophical eloquence is an art whose aspirations, as Hume said of the ancient orators, are "vast and boundless" and which exceed not only "human force to attain, but human imagination to conceive" (*E,* 98).

The Heroes of Philosophy

Although Hume thought the ancients superior in eloquence and their moralists the best models in ethics, he did not think they were superior in philosophy. The tendency of philosophy is always to its false forms, though this tendency can be, in some measure, sublimated by a more critical reflection and a deeper self-knowledge. Philosophy necessarily first appeared in the ancient world in its false forms. The fundamental error of false philosophy is what I have called the Midas touch: the magical transformation of the whole of experience into one of its parts. The paradoxes generated by false philosophy invert experience and give the philosopher a title to an esoteric and superior wisdom and dominion. The paradoxes generated by philosophy are at odds with the opinions of the unreflective vulgar, and so the question arises as to how this strange form of thinking ever gained a hold, much less spread, as it did, throughout the ancient world. Hume offers several reasons for the success of philosophy among the ancients.

First, he taught that polytheism, of all religions, is the most tolerant. And it was in polytheistic republics that philosophy first made its appearance. One must admire the "good fortune of philosophy, which, as it requires entire liberty above all other privileges, and chiefly flourishes from the free opposition of sentiments and argumentation, received its first birth in an age and country of freedom and toleration, and was never cramped, even in its most extravagant principles, by any creeds, concessions, or penal statutes" (*EU,* 132). Hume thinks the matter would have been otherwise had philosophy first appeared in a theistic culture, even a civilized one such as modern Europe. "Except the banishment of Protagoras, and the death of Socrates, which last event proceeded partly from other motives, there are scarcely any instances to be met with, in ancient history, of this bigoted jealousy, with which the present age is so much infested. Epicurus lived in Athens to an advanced age, in peace and tranquillity: Epicureans were even admitted to receive the sacerdotal character, and to officiate at the altar, in the most sacred rites of the established religion" (*EU,* 132–33). There could be a conflict between theism and philosophy because both make a claim about ultimate reality, and consequently both make an ultimate claim on the life of the individual and the state. The free play of the autonomy principle in philosophy makes it a permanent source of impiety and heresy and so threatens to undermine the social and political order which makes a community of theistic life possible. Polytheism was tolerant because it was poetic thought in its philosophical innocence. It was entirely devoid of the ultimacy principle and was founded on "traditional tales and fictions" which were spontaneously embraced by "the prince, as well as peasant" (*E,* 62, 61). These stories were poetic reflections on a part of human experience. They made no claim about the whole. Without the idea of ultimate reality, polytheism did not and could not have seen philosophy as a competitor. And so "religion had, in ancient times, very little influence on common life, and . . . after men had performed their duty in sacrifices and prayers at the temple, they thought, that the gods left the rest of their conduct to themselves, and were little pleased or offended with those virtues or vices, which only affected the peace and happiness of human society" (*EM,* 341).

But with the world-inverting paradoxes of philosophy, a new and demanding guide to life appeared, a guide that made a claim on the totality of one's existence. As long as the civil order of the polytheistic republics was not threatened, philosophy peacefully coexisted with polytheism. "After the first alarm, therefore, was over, which arose from the new paradoxes and principles of the philosophers; these teachers seem ever after, during the ages of antiquity, to have lived in great harmony with the established superstition, and to have made a fair partition of mankind between them; the former claiming all the learned and wise, the latter possessing all the vulgar and illiterate" (*EU,* 133).

Once established, philosophy proved to be a hardy plant, answering to the original human inclinations to autonomy and curiosity. But what chiefly gave rise to the spread of philosophy was not the noble search for truth, nor even the desire for independence of thought, but the less worthy desire of dominion over others. "In those ages, it was the business [not of religion but] of philosophy *alone* to regulate men's ordinary behaviour and deportment; and accordingly, we may observe, that this being the sole principle, by which a man could elevate himself above his fellows, it acquired a mighty ascendant over many, and produced great singularities of maxims and conduct" (*EM,* 341; italics mine). From the very first, philosophers sought dominion.

In the *Treatise* Hume explained how the human desire for dominion along with the fascination with novelty naturally augments the number of philosophers and their disciples.

> Whatever has the air of a paradox, and is contrary to the first and most unprejudic'd notions of mankind is often greedily embrac'd by philosophers, as shewing the superiority of their science, which cou'd discover opinions so remote from vulgar conception. On the other hand, any thing propos'd to us, which causes surprise and admiration, gives such a satisfaction to the mind, that it indulges itself in those agreeable emotions, and will never be perswaded that its pleasure is entirely without foundation. From these dispositions in philosophers and their disciples arises that mutual complaisance betwixt them; while the former furnish such plenty of strange and unaccountable opinions, and the latter so readily believe them. (*T,* 26)

The world-inverting paradoxes of philosophy keep the vulgar in a state of awe. This was easy in the ancient world because philosophy had no competition. The stories of polytheism were numberless, and "no one could believe or know the whole." The traditions of different cities were often contrary, and "no reason could be found for preferring one to the other." Finally, polytheism was not principled or systematic. "The gradation was insensible, from the most fundamental articles of faith, to those loose and precarious fictions." And so the "pagan religion . . . seemed to vanish like a cloud, whenever one approached to it, and examined it piecemeal" (*NHR,* 75). This of course did not convert the generality of people away from polytheism, but "it made them falter and hesitate" and produced dispositions of mind "which had the appearance of determined infidelity" (*NHR*, 75). So philosophy not only coexisted with polytheism, it tended to subvert it.

Ancient philosophy was philosophy at play producing great "singularities of maxims and conduct" (*EM*, 341). The autonomy principle operated in a "vacuum," and by the Midas touch generated a spiritual zoo of theoretical inversions, each making a claim to ultimacy and each holding a self-professed title to dominion (*EM*, 343). The insistent triad of ultimacy, autonomy, and dominion placed the ancient philosophers in implacable opposition to each other. And so a form of fanaticism and bigotry emerged which was peculiar to philosophy itself and which was in sharp contrast to the toleration of polytheism. "Sects of philosophy, in the ancient world, were more zealous than parties of religion" (*E*, 63). These fanatical philosophical sects were not dangerous, however, because they were confined to the private sphere. The ancient philosophers acquiesced in the authority of the polytheistic magistrate. Indeed, the tendency of ancient philosophy was to withdraw from the public world into contemplation. For the most part, ancient philosophy was philosophy in the *ascetic* mode of the dialectic rather than its revolutionary mode. It was an inversion of Marx's maxim that the point of philosophy is not to understand the world but to change it. The ancient philosophers sought radical independence in contemplation, but it was a form of contemplation the object of which was to gain the self-mastery necessary to secure their own happiness. For the ancients, the autonomy principle meant not merely the self-knowledge involved in seeing for one's self that something is true, but imposing upon the self a rule of conduct in accord with what is thought to be the real.

In Hume's view, this attempt by the ancients to understand human happiness resulted in insights which render the ancient moralists superior to the moderns. But the inquiry had a dark side insofar as it was captured by the distortions of false philosophy. Indeed Hume taught that these world-inverting distortions are worse when turned inward on the question of human happiness. "The passion for philosophy . . . by imprudent management" not only magically transforms a part of experience into the whole but in this case transforms a dominant passion into the whole of happiness thereby distorting and constricting life. This "infirmity of philosophers" is worse "in their reasonings concerning human life, and the methods of attaining happiness. In that case, they are led astray, not only by the narrowness of their understandings, but by that also of their passions" (*E*, 160). The principle of dominion internal to philosophy gives a title to rule not only to the beliefs of the understanding but to the passions as well. Philosophers not only necessarily deny the authority of contrary systems of thought, but also of contrary ways of life. "Almost every one has a predominant inclination, to which his other desires and affections submit, and which governs him, though, perhaps, with some intervals, through the whole course of his life. It is difficult for him to apprehend, that any thing, which appears totally indifferent to him, can ever give enjoyment to any person, or can possess charms, which altogether escape his observation" (*E,* 160).

The nature of philosophy to claim total dominion over the metaphysical beliefs of others is now turned on the philosopher himself, whose passions must undergo the transmutation of philosophical alchemy, yielding a contorted and compressed life which the philosopher yet declares to be the greatest happiness. "It is certain that, while we aspire to the magnanimous firmness of the philosophic sage, and endeavour to confine our pleasures altogether within our own minds, we may, at last, render our philosophy like that of *Epictetus,* and other *Stoics,* only a more refined system of selfishness, and reason ourselves out of all virtue as well as social enjoyment" (*EU,* 40). Here, through his own autonomous reason, the philosopher plays the tyrant to himself. Through philosophical alchemy, virtues are transformed into vices and vices into virtues. "While we study with attention the vanity of human life, and turn all our thoughts towards the empty and transitory nature of riches and honours, we are, perhaps, all the while flattering our natural indolence, which hating the bustle of the world, and drudgery of business seeks a pretence of reason to give itself a full and uncontrolled indulgence" (*EU,* 40). More generally, the totalizing character of false philosophy cannot distinguish the subtle ordering of virtue and vice in the soul. "Another defect of those refined reflections, which philosophers suggest to us, is, that commonly they cannot diminish or extinguish our vicious passions, without diminishing or extinguishing such as are virtuous, and rendering the mind totally indifferent and unactive. They are, for the most part, general, and are applicable to *all* our affections. In vain do we hope to direct their influence only to one side" (*E,* 173; italics mine).

A life generated entirely by autonomous reason Hume calls an "artificial" life. It is a life framed not in the open air of custom but in the "vacuum" of philosophical autonomy. It is not limited by deference to and negotiation with the social world. In the vacuum of false philosophy *any* life is possible. "When men depart from the maxims of common reason, and affect these *artificial* lives . . . no one can answer for what will please or displease them. They are in a different element from the rest of mankind; and the natural principles of their mind play not with the same regularity, as if left to themselves, free from the illusions of . . . philosophical enthusiasm" (*EM,* 343).

If false philosophy is at its worst when reflecting on the nature of human happiness, then the ancient philosophers, for whom this was the central object of inquiry and who were the most rigorous in taking their own autonomy seriously, provide the best examples of the pathology and misanthropy of which false philosophy is capable. Hume gives a number of examples of this error among the ancients. "There is another Humour, which may be observ'd in some Pretenders to Wisdom," which has "a very bad Effect on those who indulge it. I mean that grave philosophic Endeavour after Perfection, which, under Pretext of reforming Prejudices and Errors, strikes at all the most endearing Sentiments of the Heart, and all the most useful Byasses and Instincts, which can govern a human Creature. The *Stoics* were remarkable for this Folly among the Antients" (*E,* 539). Heroic philosophic existence in the ascetic mode takes over at the expense of the virtuous prejudices of common life. "The virtuous and tender Sentiments, or Prejudices, if you will, have suffer'd mightily by these Reflections; while a certain sullen Pride or Contempt of Mankind has prevail'd in their Stead" (*E,* 539). Hume gives the example of Statilius who "being solicited by *Brutus* to make one of that noble Band . . . refus'd to accompany them, saying, *That all Men were Fools or Mad, and did not deserve that a wise Man should trouble his Head about them*" (*E,* 539). An "ancient" philosopher, whom Hume does not name, would not be reconciled to his brother. "He was too much a Philosopher to think, that the Connexion of having sprung from the same Parent, ought to have any Influence on a reasonable Mind" (*E,* 539–40). One may "counterfeit a Sympathy" with a friend under affliction if it gives him relief, advised Epictetus, but "take Care not to allow any Compassion to sink into your Heart, or disturb that Tranquillity, which is the Perfection of Wisdom" (*E,* 540). Diogenes, when asked by his friends what to do with his body after his death, commanded that it be thrown into the fields to be devoured by the birds and beasts. Of this spirited contempt for the human convention of burial, Hume observes, "I know none of the Sayings of that Philosopher, which shews more evidently both the Liveliness and Ferocity of his Temper" (*E,* 540). Stoicism and Cynicism are ascetic modes of the heroic moment of philosophical reflection and are consequently fertile breeding grounds for hypocrisy, and so Hume observes that "the perpetual cant of the *Stoics* and *Cynics* concerning *virtue,* their magnificent professions and slender performances, bred a disgust in mankind; and Lucian . . . cannot sometimes talk of virtue, so much boasted, without betraying symptoms of spleen and irony" (*EM,* 242).

Hume recognized that the philosophical search for human excellence, which he takes to be the high watermark of ancient philosophy, has through custom and tradition become a part of the philosophical heritage shaping his own mind and that of his contemporaries. In the remarkable quartet of essays "The Epicurean," "The Stoic," "The Platonist," and "The Sceptic," the main schools of ancient philosophy are treated as philosophical archetypes that spontaneously occur in the world when men philosophize about the good life. Hume has given to each archetype "the name of the philosophical sect, to which it bears the greatest affinity" (*E,* 138). What were hard-won paths of thought and life carved out by the "heroes of philosophy" have over time become part of the general cultural heritage and so can be thought of as moments of consciousness (or as Hume says "sentiments") in the mind of one who has inherited that culture. When Hume says that these "sentiments . . . naturally form themselves in the world," he does not mean that men everywhere and at all times instantiate them. Platonism, for instance, is theistic, and Hume taught that theism could not have preceded polytheism, so a culture without the idea of theism would be incapable of Platonism. More generally, early polytheists had no idea of philosophical reflection of any kind and so could not think of their unsettled state as one to which philosophy could provide an answer. But given the appearance of philosophy and its incorporation in culture, we may think of human happiness as a philosophical problem and pass through a dialectical pattern of thinking in which there are Epicurean, Stoical, Platonic, and Sceptical moments of reflection.

The dialectical pattern of the quartet reflects the dialectic of the *Treatise.* The first three forms of thought (the Epicurean, the Stoic, and the Platonist) are exhibited hierarchically as the thinker acquires "new degrees of reason and knowledge" (*T,* 222). All three contain some truth but in the end are forms of false philosophy. The higher "degrees of reason and knowledge" do not occur until one instantiates the fourth stage of thought, "The Sceptic," which is the perspective of true philosophy. It is this perspective that comprehends the whole of the topic (what *philosophy* can and cannot say about the good life), and so it is this perspective alone that is capable of eloquent speech, that is, a speech that is complete. Strictly speaking, the position of true philosophy is not a "perspective." It is a grasp of the whole, not of the part, as are the other three. In respect to philosophical self-knowledge there is no position outside its true form. The speech of the "Sceptic" is not merely another speech about happiness. It is also and primarily a speech about the limits of philosophical theories of happiness. It is, philosophically, a higher form of self-knowledge than the other forms. And truth in philosophy is simply the highest form of self-knowledge relative to the topic at hand. The Epicurean, the Stoic, and the Platonist each have some distinct object of happiness as the sole object of thought. Each assumes philosophy to be a transparent medium through which the object is known, and this knowledge to be the source of virtuous conduct. It is the "Sceptic" alone who takes philosophy itself to be problematic and who gives a speech about happiness mediated through a philosophical criticism of philosophical conceptions of happiness. In respect to philosophical self-knowledge, we may say, if we like, that the speech of the Sceptic is delivered from an absolute perspective. So much is suggested by Hume's distinction between philosophy that is false and that which is *true.* Considering philosophical self-knowledge itself, there is no perspective outside the true. This is not to say, of course, that the claims of true philosophy are infallible (as Descartes thought), for Hume makes clear that they are not (*T,* 273–74), but only that they are fallible claims about *the whole of philosophy* and will, if successful, be found "satisfactory to the human mind" (*T,* 272).

Epicureanism is the ethic of youth. It fixes on the innocence of natural pleasures. By the Midas touch, the good of pleasure is transformed into the whole of life, yielding the egocentric and antisocial aesthete. But since man is a social being, the Epicurean harbors within him a secret loneliness, guilt, and self-disgust (*E,* 156). To find a more satisfactory state, thought moves on to the position of the Stoic, who is a man of action, not a passive recipient of pleasure. Since action must display itself in the social world, the Stoic affirms the social order as the metaphor of the real. Reality is the *polis,* a realm of action, and the Stoic eventually broadens this metaphor so as to consider himself a citizen of the universe. The Platonist now appears observing that what we really admire are not actions but the mind behind them, and not merely the human minds behind particular actions but the divine mind that brought all into being. The search for divinity is the secret longing of the Epicurean and the Stoic. This is the theistic moment in philosophical reflection and has been a part of philosophy since the evolution from philosophical atheism to philosophical theism. Hume takes Plato to be the exemplar of this rationalistic love of God because "the ancient Platonists . . . were the most religious and devout of all the pagan philosophers" (*D,* 156). The Platonic sentiment is, in many ways, the most dangerous because it is an attitude of contempt for the world and an infinite longing for the Divine essence. "The ancient Platonists . . . particularly Plotinus, expressly declare, that intellect or understanding is not to be ascribed to the Deity, and that our most perfect worship of him consists, not in acts of veneration, reverence, gratitude or love; but in a certain mysterious self-annihilation or total extinction of all our faculties" (*D*, 156). Hume pictures the Platonic divinity, that "immensity of perfection," as an ocean and human minds as streams which arise from it but can never rest until they return to it. "When checked in this natural course, by vice or folly, they become furious and enraged; and swelling to a torrent, do then spread horror and devastation on the neighbouring plains" (*E*, 156). In this way the Platonist whose thought is not disciplined by an original affirmation of the world of common life may become a threat to the peace and stability of society. I shall have occasion later to examine Hume's understanding of the different historical forms that the enraged Platonist has taken in the evolution of culture.

Philosophical thought about happiness begins with an affirmation of *nature* (Epicureanism); through self-disgust it moves to the realm of *action* (Stoicism). Action, made coherent, leads to the divine mind from which nature and the realm of action are generated (Platonism). But the Platonic affirmation of mind is made at the expense of nature. And so the dialectical search for happiness which begins with the Epicurean affirmation of the physical and the Stoic affirmation of the social ends in the annihilation of both. It is the "Sceptic" alone who understands this dialectic and can mark out the true position from which to think about human happiness.

It is significant that, except for "The Sceptic," the title of each speech about happiness is given a subtitle. The Epicurean is "the man of elegance and pleasure." The Stoic is "the man of action and virtue." The Platonist is "the man of contemplation, and *philosophical* devotion" (Hume's italics). These subtitles suggest that the false philosophical speeches are merely perspectives on the good life. They are speeches about the part which are mistakenly thought to be about the whole. Each speech is philosophically naive in that it does not recognize the problematic character of its own philosophical thinking. That is, it cannot see that the philosophical construction of the object of happiness is itself a problem to be pondered. This recognition is reserved to the "Sceptic," who, because of his superior philosophical self-knowledge, is not presented as occupying a perspective. In keeping his eye on the nature of philosophy as a whole and in recognizing its problematic character, he alone is entitled to give a speech about the whole that is a true act of philosophical self-knowledge. In the Sceptic's speech, the philosopher is not lost in the man, nor the man in the philosopher. But both, insofar as reflection can determine the matter, are brought into their true relationship.

To sum up, ancient philosophy was the youth of philosophy. Flourishing in a polytheistic culture, too naive to understand it, but tolerant and even respectful, the autonomy of philosophy was given free reign. Trying its powers everywhere, it was jealous of its autonomy and boldly imposed its own self-determining order on the world, though ignorant that this was what was being done. In metaphysics, the ancients, captured by a false understanding of the idea of substance, suffered the torments of Sisyphus and Tantalus. Their greatest achievement was the inquiry into human happiness. The insights achieved were considerable and have become part and parcel of the philosophical characters that were to follow. They not only forged new forms of thought about human happiness, but courageously tried to live them out. "Among the ancients, the heroes of philosophy . . . have a grandeur and force of sentiment, which astonishes our narrow souls, and is rashly rejected as extravagant and supernatural" (*EM,* 256). But just as the heroic moment in the dialectic cannot sustain itself, so neither could the heroic existence of the ancient philosophers. The inquiry into happiness degenerated into schools with rigid dogmas and systems, and so autonomy hardened into a new sentiment: philosophical bigotry. Consider, Hume says, "the blind submission of the ancient philosophers to the several masters in each school, and you will be convinced, that little good could be expected from a hundred centuries of such servile philosophy. Even the ECLECTICS, who arose about the age of AUGUSTUS, notwithstanding their professing to chuse freely what pleased them from every different sect, were yet, in the main, as slavish and dependent as any of their bretheren; since they sought for truth not in nature, but in the *several schools;* where they supposed she must necessarily be found, though not united in a body, yet dispersed in parts" (*E,* 123; my italics). Thus ancient philosophy degenerated from its heroic moment into *scholasticism,* where the instruments of reflection, the "doctrine," the "system," take on a life of their own and are finally confused with reality itself. This tendency of philosophy to barbarize itself into scholasticism is permanent and, as I shall show, takes on different historical forms as Hume's story of the evolution of culture unfolds. Meanwhile, it is worth observing that in the scholastic twilight of ancient philosophy, the philosophical hypocrisy of false philosophy (mingled now with the new sentiment of bigotry) flourished in an astonishing act of self-deception. Philosophical autonomy collapsed into servility, into what Hume called the "servile philosophy" of the Hellenic period, while still boasting its freedom and independence of custom. But custom was no longer philosophically innocent; it now contained within itself the habits, prejudices, and traditions of centuries of philosophical thinking.

The total dominion demanded by false philosophy was a potential threat to the state, but ancient philosophers, for the most part, deferred to the authority of the polytheistic magistrate, and the errors of philosophy were suffered only by the philosophical sects themselves. That philosophy did not pose a threat to the peace, stability, and happiness of ancient society was due to contingent historical circumstances. That philosophy could be such a threat is clear from the dialectic. The triad of ultimacy, autonomy, and dominion is a dynamo from which a great variety of destructive forms of consciousness might be generated. The self-determining quality of philosophy to invert experience and to demand that its autonomous reason have total dominion is a source of power only waiting to be unleashed. Traces of it could be seen in the peculiar historical shapes philosophy assumed in the ancient world. The cynical "ferocity" of Diogenes' thought and the willingness of the enraged Platonist to "spread horror and devestation on the neighbouring plains" (*E,* 540, 156) in the name of virtue exhibit the threat that purely philosophic thought could be to society under historical circumstances different from the polytheistic culture in which it was born. At the end of the pagan world, circumstances did in fact change. Philosophy took on a radically new historical form, one that, in Hume's view, constrained her virtues more than her vices. I turn now to Hume's account of this change.

CHAPTER FIVE

Philosophy and Christendom

The Union of Philosophy and Christianity

Hume taught that philosophy was a novelty in the ancient world. The principles of ultimacy, autonomy, and dominion introduced a new and demanding guide to life unlike anything the polytheists had known. Philosophy in the name of reason claimed total dominion over the life of the thinker, the sect, and in principle over all men. Polytheistic culture eventually came to admire its philosopher; and philosophy, with its title to dominion, became "the sole principle, by which a man could elevate himself above his fellows," and so it "acquired a mighty ascendant over many, and produced great singularities of maxims and conduct" (*EM,* 341). It was in this setting that Christianity appeared.

Christianity also claimed total dominion over its members but for reasons different from those of philosophy. Christianity is a form of vulgar theism which ultimately evolved, through the logic of fear, from a polytheistic source. Christianity and the Jewish religion, from which it originated, were founded not on philosophical theory but on sacred stories about the relation of God to the Jewish people. Yet when confronted with Hellenistic philosophy, Christianity immediately began recasting itself into philosophical terms. "As philosophy was widely spread over the world, at the time when Christianity arose, the teachers of the new sect were obliged to form a system of speculative opinions; to divide, with some accuracy, their articles of faith; and to explain, comment, and defend with all the subtilty of argument and science" (*E,* 62). Indeed, so great was the prestige of philosophy that before the appearance of Christianity, the Jewish thinker, Philo of Alexandria, had read Greek philosophy back into the Jewish tradition, arguing that Moses was the first philosopher. Henceforth theism would have philosophical form, and to be religious would be largely a question of which theological *theory* to accept.

Another reason for the union of philosophy and theism is that both contain the idea of a perfect being, though they reach that idea by different routes. Philosophy reaches it by the love of truth. But the "sublime ideas suggested by Moses and the inspired writers" were generated by fear: they were "guided to that notion, not by reason, of which they are in a great measure incapable, but by the adulation and fears of the most vulgar superstition" (*NHR*, 52). In this way the idea of a perfect being in vulgar theism "coincides, by chance, with the principles of reason and true philosophy" (*NHR*, 53, 52). Largely because of this conceptual overlap, philosophy and theism have a natural affinity. "Where theism forms the fundamental principle of any popular religion, that tenet is so conformable to sound reason, that philosophy is apt to incorporate itself with such a system of theology" (*NHR*, 65).

This union of philosophy and Christianity had a number of consequences. First, vulgar theism is intolerant and when in power tends to persecution. "The intolerance of almost all religions, which have maintained the unity of god, is as remarkable as the contrary principle in polytheists" (*NHR*, 60). But philosophy, especially in its false forms, generates a form of intolerance that is peculiarly its own. Philosophical disagreements are ultimate disagreements, and we have observed Hume's view that philosophical sects in the ancient world were more fanatical than religious sects. So the usual tendency of theistic Christianity to intolerance was reinforced by the same tendency in philosophy. But the rationale of intolerance in each is different. In theism it is sacred obligation. In philosophy it is what a self-congratulatory autonomous reason has determined to be theoretically correct. The union in Christianity of sacred obligation with theoretical correctness ("theological theories") generates the new passions of *bigotry* and *zeal* which, Hume thinks, have poisoned the culture of Christendom. Bigotry is not simply jealousy about one's obligation to God, it is jealousy about one's theoretical interpretation of God. Such a passion is not possible without a blending of vulgar theism and philosophy.

Second, it is the nature of false philosophy to break up into a variety of sects each with a self-proclaimed title to dominion. Because of its philosophical character, Christianity tended to shatter into innumerable sects. As a philosophical religion Christianity both spawned these sects and had to suppress them. This painful dialectic was made worse by a persecuting spirit which informed Christianity at its beginning but which was due not so much to its theistic nature as to the peculiar historical circumstances of its origin. Hume tells this story. In polytheistic culture religion was sacred tradition, and the "magistrate embraced the religion of the people, and entering cordially into the care of sacred matters, naturally acquired an authority in them, and united the ecclesiastical with the civil power" (*E*, 61). This union of church and state was a principle Hume defended throughout his writings. In the ancient world it enabled the state both to extend freedom to philosophers and to control them. In modern times, Hume hoped it would enable the state to control a philosophically structured Christianity and extend freedom to true philosophers. But Christianity appeared at a time when "principles directly opposite to it were firmly established in the polite part of the world, who despised the nation that first broached this novelty; no wonder, that, in such circumstances, it was but little countenanced by the civil magistrate, and that the priesthood was allowed to engross all the authority in the new sect" (*E*, 61). The priests, operating in a "vacuum" cut off from the affairs of the world, generated a sect of those "artificial lives" Hume mentions in "A Dialogue" at the end of the second *Enquiry* which arise from "the illusions of religious superstition or philosophical enthusiasm" and for which "no one can answer for what will please or displease them" (*EM*, 343). The priests drove their sects with zeal and without regard to common prudence. "So bad a use did they make of this power, even in those early times, that the primitive persecutions may, perhaps, *in part*, be ascribed to the violence instilled by them into their followers" (*E*, 62). After Christianity became the established religion, the habit of bigotry continued. "The same principles of priestly government continuing, after Christianity became the established religion, they have engendered a spirit of persecution, which has ever since been the poison of human society, and the source of the most inveterate factions in every government" (*E*, 62).

Third, theism demands one system, one creed, and so one philosophical framework. Eventually Christianity settled on Aristotelianism and entered its scholastic phase. "After the ROMAN *christian* or *catholic* church had spread itself over the civilized world, and had engrossed all the learning of the times; being really one large state within itself, and united under one head; this variety of sects [philosophical sects in the ancient world] immediately disappeared, and the PERIPATETIC philosophy was alone admitted into all the schools, to the utter depravation of every kind of learning" (*E*, 121). Learning was carried on in the vacuum of the schools cut off from common life and conversation. The case was much the same as "the blind submission of the ancient philosophers to the several masters in each school" in the decadent phase of pagan philosophy, except that the ancients had several schools to choose from, and the Christians had only different sects of one school.

In a union of philosophy and theism, philosophy still retains her title to dominion, and takes on the task of guiding and correcting theism. But philosophy soon found "herself very unequally yoaked with her new associate; and instead of regulating each principle, as they advance together, she is at every turn perverted to serve the purposes of superstition" (*NHR,* 65). The two are supposed to "advance together" but cannot. The subjugation of philosophy occurs naturally because the tendency of philosophy is to its false forms. And false philosophy contains its own special forms of self-deceit and hypocrisy, which render it easily seduced by a theism which has established itself in the passions of a community in which the philosopher participates. And so philosophy became the handmaiden of the theology not only of Christendom but of Islam and of the Jews as well.

Scholastic "Refinement"

But it was not simply that scholastic theology had "perverted" philosophy to its ends; false philosophy had also twisted theology to *its* ends. And so Hume could observe of scholastic theology that it "becomes more absurd in the end, merely from its being reasonable and philosophical in the beginning" (*NHR,* 66). What is the special absurdity and corruption that philosophy brings to theism? We may begin with the following remark. A scholastic system "has a kind of appetite for absurdity and contradiction. If that theology went not beyond reason and common sense, her doctrines would appear too easy and familiar. Amazement must of necessity be raised: Mystery affected: Darkness and obscurity sought after: And a foundation of merit afforded the devout votaries, who desire an opportunity of subduing their rebellious reason, by the belief of the most unintelligible sophisms" (*NHR,* 65).

But this appetite for absurdity is precisely what appears in the heroic moment of the dialectic of true and false philosophy, where everything grasped by the mind of the false philosopher is endowed with the quality of a superstition, and always at the expense of common life. In the first *Enquiry* Hume again refers to a force which seeks to subdue "rebellious reason," but this time it is philosophy, not religion. "No priestly *dogmas,* invented on purpose to tame and subdue the rebellious reason of mankind, ever shocked common sense more than the doctrine of the infinitive divisibility of extension, with its consequences; as they are pompously displayed by all geometricians and metaphysicians, with a kind of triumph and exultation" (*EU,* 156). More generally, whatever has "the air of a paradox, and is contrary to the first and most unprejud-ic'd notions of mankind is often greedily embrac'd by philosophers" as showing their superiority from vulgar conception (*T,* 26). And Hume gives the instance in the *Treatise* of how purely philosophical thought can yield absurdities the equal to any in religion. "The Cynics are an extraordinary instance of philosophers, who from reasonings purely philosophical ran into as great extravagancies of conduct as any *Monk* or *Dervise* that ever was in the world" (*T,* 272).

A theistic religion without philosophy would be free of the twisted postures of false philosophy. The devotees of this religion would follow the precepts of sacred story without much reasoning or reflection. Theism would still tend to intolerance, but it would not be made worse by the appetite for absurdity that philosophy, in its false form, brings to whatever it engages. But though one can imagine theism without philosophy, such a state of affairs is not likely. Once rooted in human culture, philosophy is a hardy plant. And once theism becomes aware of philosophy, it naturally seeks its legitimacy in a philosophical theory or system. Moreover, since theism better satisfies the human disposition to find unity in the parts of its experience, polytheism is no longer credible. So the teaching of the *Natural History of Religion* is that we are faced with a permanent and melancholy spectacle in human affairs: a religious culture driven by theistic zeal but shaped and guided by philosophical paradox.

It is for this reason that Hume evinces sympathy for a "mythological religion" that makes no pretence of being philosophical. "The greatest and most observable differences betwixt a *traditional, mythological* religion, and a systematical, scholastic one, are two: The former is often more reasonable, as consisting of a multitude of stories, which, however groundless, imply no express absurdity and demonstrative contradiction; and sits so easy and light on men's minds, that tho' it may be as universally received, it makes no such deep impression on the affections and understanding" (*NHR,* 80–81). By "deep impression" Hume means that a traditional religion based merely on sacred stories does not and cannot even conceive of making the strong claim to dominion over all thought, action, and sentiment that a philosophical religion does. Whatever other absurdities it may contain, it will be free of the self-deceptions and distortions of experience that a corrupt philosophical theorizing in the form of theology always brings with it.

Hume interprets the heresies of Christianity as instances of the prejudices of common life in rebellion against the dominion of philosophical paradox that informs the interpretation of Christianity's sacred story. He suggests the hypothesis that when a controversy is started in Christianity, one can predict at the outset that the position most in line with the prejudices of common life will be declared the heresy. "Any one . . . that has but learning enough of this kind to know the definition of Arian, Pelagian, Erastian, Socinian, Sabellian, Eutychian, Nestorian, Monothelite, etc. not to mention Protestant, whose fate is yet uncertain, will be convinced of the truth of this observation." And Hume makes it clear that this absurdity follows merely from the attempt of sacred story to become "philosophical" (*NHR*, 65–66).

By contrast the sacred stories of prephilosophical polytheism are a natural reflection of the human world. "Where is the difficulty of conceiving, that the same powers or principles, whatever they were, which formed this visible world, men and animals, produced also a species of intelligent creatures, of more refined substance and greater authority than the rest? That these creatures may be capricious, revengeful, passionate, voluptuous, is easily conceived" (*NHR*, 64). And he goes so far as to conclude that "the whole mythological system is so natural, that, in the vast variety of planets and worlds . . . it seems more than probable, that, somewhere or other, it is really carried into execution" (*NHR*, 64). Hume is not suggesting here a return to polytheism. The theme of the *Natural History of Religion* is that "the corruption of the best things begets the worst." Philosophy and true theism are noble and sublime achievements, but their corruption brings on the worst. Theism degenerates into "sick men's dreams" and "the playsome whimsies of monkeys in human shape" (*NHR*, 94). Philosophy degenerates into the "furious and enraged" Platonist, the "ferocity" of Diogenes, and the "sullen Pride or Contempt of mankind" of some of the Stoic moralists. Both in their different ways seek to tame the "rebellious reason of mankind." What is this mutinous reason? It is the reason won by the dialectic of true philosophy which represents the party of common life. But that voice can scarcely be heard amid the massive corruption of philosophy and of theism in popular theistic culture.

Contemplating this state of corruption in human thought, the true philosopher reflects back to a time of mythological existence when there was neither theism nor philosophy. The mythological world of the ancients becomes a symbol for the world of common life exposed by the dialectic of true philosophy—a fantasy world governed by custom and sacred tradition. And so, for Hume, a true understanding of our corrupt state requires a recognition of the truth of mythological existence. *The Natural History of Religion* offers no suggestions for reform but only the consolations of true philosophy. The corruption is vast and too well established. That mankind should corrupt what is noble and sublime and not even recognize it as corruption leaves little hope for reform. And to attempt a rational penetration of the corruption is to confront "a riddle, an aenigma, an inexplicable mystery." All we can do is "enlarge our view" and "make our escape, into the calm, tho' obscure regions of philosophy" (*NHR*, 95).

The scholastic and systematic philosophy of Christendom followed the natural course of false philosophy in the direction of what Hume calls "refinement." This notion was touched on earlier, but it is worthwhile to recall that refinement is not the elegant reshaping of the "gross earthy mixture" of common life but the distillation of it into what is abstract, sterile, and even poisonous. Alcohol is "refined" from grain. In Humean "refinement," the abstraction, the principle, the rule, the abridgement, the theory, the system becomes the real, and common life is transformed into the "vacuum" of false philosophy, where only an "artificial" life is possible. Scholasticism follows this natural process of refinement, issuing finally in the absurdities of the "relaxed casuists" (*EM,* 200 n). But the decadence of Scholasticism is not due to a moral failure. It proceeded rather from a corruption natural to philosophical theorizing itself: it proceeded "as much from the habit of scholastic refinement as from any corruption of the heart" (*EM,* 200 n).

With the Renaissance and the Reformation, the relation of philosophy to theism changes. A growing demand appears for greater autonomy of thought as well as greater personal and political liberty. Hume sees this change as a move away from philosophical "refinement" to something he calls "nature" and "experience." We should not think of these in terms of a Newtonian model of a mechanical nature or of the sense observation of mechanical relations. There is a place in Hume's philosophy for mechanism and the observation of it, but his deepest conception of nature is human nature, since all of the sciences, including physics, fall under human nature and are shaped by it. So the question is how are we to study human nature, and Hume's answer is "experience," and by that he means not the passive sense observations of a spectator but participation in the pyramid of customs and conventions that constitute common life. We must "glean up our experiments" from "the common course of the world, by men's behaviour in company, in affairs, and in their pleasures" (*T,* xix). And our primary way of "experiencing" this world is through what he calls "conversation," and it is for this reason that eloquence is a constituent of true philosophy. Hume's model of "nature" and "experience" is more that of Cicero than of Newton. In a letter to Hutcheson regarding the *Treatise,* Hume says that it was Cicero's *Offices* that he had "in my Eye in all my Reasonings" (*L,* 1: 34).

Keeping this view of nature in mind, we may think of Hume's conception of modernity as a rebellion against Scholastic refinement in the name of nature and as a reenactment of the dialectic of the *Treatise,* where the prejudices of common life, the "rebellious reason of mankind," reasserts its authority in the face of the oppression of false philosophy. This is indeed the central theme of Hume's philosophy, that philosophical reflection once cut loose from the prejudices of common life will naturally refine itself into a state of abstract barbarism against which human nature will eventually rebel. The "revival of learning" and the attack on Scholasticism is just such a rebellion.

I have suggested that the barbarism of Scholasticism is parallel to the last and decadent stage of classical philosophy. For, lost in philosophical refinement, the ancients too "sought for truth not in nature, but in the several schools; where they supposed she must necessarily be found" (*E,* 123). The low point of this corruption were the "ECLECTICS, who arose about the age of AUGUSTUS," for this was a school of thought not about nature, but a school of thought about the schools. The Eclectics were the Scholastics of ancient philosophy, an instance of the tendency of hubristic philosophical reflection to barbarize itself into abstract refinement.

Once free of the yoke of Scholasticism, the early moderns returned for inspiration to the ancient philosophers, but they did not begin where the ancients had left off. That is, they did not convert to one of the ancient schools of thought. Being liberated from Scholasticism, they were able to keep some distance from the "Schoolmen" of pagan philosophy and to look with some diffidence on the post-Scholastic schools that were beginning to form: the ancient "sects of STOICS and EPICUREANS, PLATONISTS and PYTHAGOREANS could never regain any credit or authority; and, at the same time, by the example of their fall, kept men from submitting, with such blind deference, to those new sects, which have attempted to gain an ascendant over them" (*E,* 123).

Hume did not have our idea of the Renaissance as primarily an Italian affair. Hume refers to the transition from Scholasticism to modern thought as simply "the revival of learning," and he treats it as a European phenomenon. Scholasticism did not contain "learning" because it was "shut up in Colleges and Cells" and did not consult nature or experience. "Philosophy went to Wrack by this moaping recluse Method of Study, and became as chimerical in her Conclusions as she was unintelligible in her Stile and Manner of Delivery" (*E*, 534–35). The return to the ancient philosophers was for inspiration, not imitation. But in respect to literary style, eloquence, and models of human excellence, the ancients were worthy of imitation as well as inspiration. For Hume, the pagan philosophers are symbols of a time when philosophical reflection, however confused, was closer to nature and less distracted by systems of theology. Just as there is a truth to "mythological religion" (prior to theism and philosophy) as being symbolic of the primordial and unreflective part of common life, so there is a truth to pagan philosophy as symbolic of man's rational autonomy. In contrast, Biblical theism is founded on revelation and a doctrine of obedience to it. Since it is the nature of philosophy to be autonomous, the revival of pagan philosophy is a revival of philosophy as such.

We may think of Hume's understanding of Christian Scholasticism as a chemical product of two atomic elements, each with characteristics distinct from the product of their union and each of which can be recovered by analysis. And we may think of the product as unstable: the philosophical element demanding autonomy, and the vulgar theistic element demanding obedience to revelation. Under certain conditions the elements of the product may be expected to fly apart. And this is just what began to happen upon the "revival of learning." The process of separation was well under way in Hume's time, and that meant that philosophy and religion would be ambiguous experiences. It was only later that a philosopher such as Nietzsche could celebrate the total emancipation of philosophy from theism, and a philosopher such as Kierkegaard could celebrate the emancipation of revelation from the oppressive grip of philosophy. This must be kept in mind in trying to understand the Enlightenment criticism of religion. This criticism sets up a Manichean drama where religion is darkness and philosophy is light, and where light struggles to overcome darkness. Hume sometimes writes in this way, but his understanding of the relation between philosophy and religion in modern times is more subtle.

He views philosophy and religion as cultural forms of experience having different origins in human nature and different histories, and sees that the nature of both has changed over time. It is worthwhile to briefly review these features. Philosophy originates from the love of truth, religion from fear. Philosophy begins as atheistic, but its perfection is philosophical theism. Though motivated by the love of truth, philosophy is liable to a corruption of its own making (as exhibited in the dialectic), and so its true form must be distinguished from the false. Vulgar theism grows out of polytheism but is never free of its pull. It reaches its full development in the idea of a perfect being, but this idea is too refined to give the imagination any satisfaction, and so thought sinks back in the direction of polytheism, and theism becomes corrupted with forms of idolatry. In Christendom, philosophy, with its dialectic of true and false forms, and religion, with its dialectic of theism and polytheism, unite to form a dynamic and unique form of experience. It was this form of experience that Hume inherited and about which he sought to gain self-knowledge. What he discovered is that, in Christian culture, philosophy could not be said to be in opposition to religion because philosophy is a constituent of religion. Without philosophy, Christendom would not be what it is. So the battle between philosophy and religion in Christendom may be viewed as a battle of philosophy with itself; or to put it another way, as a battle between philosophy in its true and false forms. That false philosophy has taken on religious form does not destroy its identity as philosophy.

Religion, of course, need not be philosophical. Polytheism was a prephilosophical religion, and vulgar theism existed prior to philosophy. But Christianity is a philosophical religion, and in modern times the philosophical element in that unstable compound has become restless. Christianity now claims philosophical legitimacy not only for natural theology but also for revealed theology. Hume wrote section 11 of the first *Enquiry* and the *Dialogues Concerning Natural Religion* to rebut the former and section 10 of the *Enquiry* to rebut the latter.

Superstition and Enthusiasm

The tension caused in Christianity by the insistence of its philosophical element (that is, the demand for more autonomy) Hume describes as the tension between "superstition" and "enthusiasm." These are best understood as sociological terms used by Hume to describe a wide range of social phenomena which includes much more than religion.

The origin of superstition is the same as that of the first religion: fear, ignorance, and impotence regarding the unknown powers that govern life. The powers are placated by rituals under the authority of priests who are thought to embody special powers from the Divine. Here there is no autonomy, and thought moves within a world of external "forms, ceremonies, and traditions" (*E*, 75). As discussed earlier, Hume is prepared to stretch the use of *superstition* to include any ritual in common life that is thought to constitute a reality. This includes not only rituals that constitute the authority of priests but also the entire hierarchy of social and political order: marriage, contracts, social status, property, law, and justice are all constituted by the "performative" use of language in rituals. Hume was also able to appreciate the humanizing influence of high liturgy in the Catholic and Anglican churches, and he criticizes the Protestants for their unthinking ridicule and blanket rejection of these practices. He recognized that a society respectful of the authority of ritual would tend to support an established clergy and monarchy which produce a fertile soil for the flourishing of "manners" and the arts, though not of commerce.

Conceived in this general and neutral way, Hume treats "superstition" as a primordial mode of being in the great flow of culture which has many aspects and has appeared in many forms. Like all that is deep in human nature, the true philosopher is not concerned to reject it out of hand but to "methodize and correct" it with whatever critical principles are available at the time. Mythological memories of man's polytheistic past survive in the rituals and liturgy of Christian theism; in the attraction men have for an established priesthood and monarchy; in the rituals that constitute social and political order, even in a republic; and finally in that disposition of the true philosopher to regard the prejudices of common life, considered as a totality, as sacred, that is, as having an original authority independent of autonomous reason. From the point of view of false philosophy (autonomous reason purged of all custom), all of these may appear as "superstition."

Underlying and prior to all of them is the work of the metaphorical imagination which, taking one thing to be another, generates the identities that make up the world of common life. This poetic act occurs at the deepest level, where the imagination, in taking its similar but discrete perceptions to be the same, creates a unity which is experienced as a physical object. From the point of view of false philosophy, all ritual acts are "superstition" in the pejorative sense. To counter this *total criticism* of the authority of ritual in human life, Hume is prepared to stretch the use of the term *superstition* to the point of irony, making justice and the whole of common life a kind of superstition.

The true philosopher knows that there are true and false forms of ritual, or, if one likes, superstition, and it is to describe the false form that Hume most often uses the term *superstition* in its pejorative sense. Superstition sets up a barrier to the improvement of causal judgment and so alienates men from the main source of knowledge about themselves and the world. Hume taught that the goods and ills of life come mixed with their opposites except perhaps in the case of superstition (*D*, 223 n), which prevents true causal judgment but brings with it no redeeming good. Finally, there are the superstitions that flow from false philosophical reflection—the "magic or witchcraft" displayed in the philosophical inversions of common life (*E,* 161). These too are presumably unmixed ills; and they are worse, for religious superstition is largely due to ignorance, whereas false philosophy is a sin against reason by reason.

Enthusiasm is contrary to superstition and originates not in a mind captured by ignorance, fear, and impotence but "from prosperous success, from luxuriant health, from strong spirits, or from a bold and confident disposition" (*E,* 74). The mind in this state "swells with great and confused conceptions" which transcend the totality of common life, and "everything mortal and perishable vanishes as unworthy of attention" (*E,* 74). It is worth noticing that the material origins of enthusiasm and philosophy are the same. Religious superstition arose when mankind was a "necessitous animal" roaming the forests and fields. Philosophy arose under conditions of "security and good government" and had to await the evolution of that knowledge which is required to build and maintain cities. Presumably enthusiasm also requires such background knowledge and security. Another similarity to philosophy is that the enthusiastic mode of thought resembles radical philosophical autonomy. In both cases what is grasped as truth is due to the mind's own self-certification, independent of the totality of custom. As in the heroic moment of philosophical reflection, truth is achieved "by way of contemplation and inward converse" (*E,* 76), and the "soul is at liberty to indulge itself in every imagination" (*E,* 74). And as the thought of the heroic philosopher is self-subverting, so in the case of enthusiasm the "soul [is] active to its own prejudice" (*E,* 73–74). Both are instances of a "presumptuous pride and confidence," and both issue in a "contempt for the common rules of reason, morality, and prudence" (*E,* 76, 77). Finally, Hume uses the term *enthusiasm* to refer indifferently to a religious or a philosophical state of mind (*EM,* 343). The heroic philosopher whose thought is framed in the "vacuum" of radical autonomy and who leads, or tries to lead, an artificial life is an "enthusiast." Most of the ancient "heroes of philosophy" are enthusiasts. But the primary meaning of the term is religious, not philosophical. When used to describe the latter experience, it is qualified as "philosophical" enthusiasm (*EM,* 343; *NHR,* 77).

The differences are also important. The elevated conceptions of both are "unaccountable" by the ordinary maxims of the world. The religious enthusiast accounts for these as the work of Divinity and comes to view himself as favored by the Divine and superior to the rest of mankind. The philosophical enthusiast accounts for his elevated conceptions as the work of his own reason which alone is able to penetrate into the ultimate nature of reality. His superiority is due to self-congratulatory pride and to the servile applause of his followers. In like manner, the enthusiast "consecrates himself" (*E,* 76). Although they are different forms of mind, religious and philosophical enthusiasm may, under certain historical circumstances, mutually reinforce each other and even combine to form novel philosophic-religious experiences as in the case of the modern philosopher Pascal and in the case of the Platonists, "the most devout of the ancient philosophers," or the "Stoics," who "join a philosophical enthusiasm to a religious superstition" (*EM,* 342; *NHR,* 77).

The same modes of experience (philosophical enthusiasm and religious superstition) that had informed Stoicism come together in the quite different historical context of modern Europe to form Protestantism and especially Puritanism, which is the most philosophical, as well as enthusiastic, of the Protestant sects. Hume is very clear about this. Protestantism, he says, "being chiefly spiritual, resembles more a system of metaphysics" than a religion (*H,* 4: 14). The more "enthusiastic" a religion becomes, the more philosophical it becomes. And the less enthusiasm a religion has, the more inclined it is to "superstition," that is, to the dictates of sacred tradition and to the commands of priests. If Protestantism is the most philosophical of modern religions, Judaism and Catholicism are the most superstitious. "Modern Judaism and Popery, especially the latter, being the most barbarous and absurd Superstitions that have yet been known in the World, are the most enslav'd by their Priests" (*E,* 617).

Protestantism, and especially the more radical sects such as the Puritans, represent the unstable philosophical element in the molecular union of religion and philosophy. Protestantism is the philosophical element seeking autonomy. Whether Catholic or Protestant, however, the religion of Christendom is virtually a philosophical system; thus it is best to view Hume's criticism of religion, not in the Enlightenment and Manichean manner of philosophy as light and religion as darkness, but as a battle of true philosophy with a false philosophy that has taken on religious form.

It is for this reason that Hume can speak ambiguously about the identity of religion and philosophy. He inveighs against the "speculative doctrines, or the metaphysics of religion" (*H,* 3, chap. 35: 385). The attack on modern religion is an attack on "an abstruse philosophy, which seems to have hitherto served only as a shelter to superstition, and a cover to absurdity and error" (*EU,* 16). The "passion for philosophy, like that for religion," can lead to the same inversions of experience (*EU,* 40). And again the inversions of experience brought on by "the illusions of religious superstition or philosophical enthusiasm" are taken to be the same (*EM,* 343). Philosophers and Divines are treated as different aspects of the same activity. He observes that "divines, and some philosophers" have distorted our conception of morals (*EM,* 279). "Philosophers, or rather divines under that disguise," have treated morals on the model of civil laws (*EM,* 322). Finally Hume is prepared to treat religion as a mere species of philosophy. "All the philosophy, therefore, in the world, and all the religion, which is nothing but a species of philosophy," are impotent to find a grounding for morals beyond the prejudices of common life (*EU,* 146).

Modern Religion

When Hume speaks of religion, he most often means what he calls "modern religion," which is, in effect, a philosophical system. At other times, however, he thinks of religion as those prephilosophical religions of antiquity whose authority rests entirely on sacred tradition. Hume has some sympathy for religion in this sense, as indicated by his indulgent remarks on polytheism, his recognition of the humanizing value of ceremony and ritual in the Anglican and Catholic churches, and his philosophical teaching about the importance of ritual in common life generally. His attack on "religion," then, is primarily an attack on the "religious philosophers" and not against religion as sacred story and tradition. And this raises the question of whether modern religion could be purged of its philosophical content so as to yield a religion which could have a place in the economy of true philosophy. Hume gives some hints in this direction which are worth considering.

In the first *Enquiry,* Hume constructs a dialogue in which an Epicurean defends his philosophy and that of his school against the charge of impiety and subversion before the Athenian people. Just before the speech, the character playing the Epicurean observes that the complaint of some philosophers in modern times about religious bigotry requires qualification insofar as it is religious philosophy, not religion as sacred tradition, that is the problem. "This pertinacious bigotry, of which you complain, as so fatal to philosophy, is really her offspring, who, after allying with superstition, separates himself entirely from the interest of his parent, and becomes her most inveterate enemy and persecutor" (*EU,* 133). It is not sacred tradition but the "speculative dogmas of religion" that are the "occasions of such furious dispute." Such disputes were impossible in prephilosophical "ages of the world, when mankind . . . composed their sacred tenets of such tales chiefly as were the objects of traditional belief, more than of argument or disputation" (*EU*, 133). The Epicurean has no difficulty in accepting the sacred tradition; the problem arises when religion begins to seek philosophical legitimacy, for then the logic of false philosophy comes into play, generating a source of inversions and implacable hostility which is endless. "The religious philosophers, not satisfied with the tradition of your forefathers, and doctrine of your priests (in which I willingly acquiesce), indulge a rash curiosity, in trying how far they can establish religion upon the principles of reason, and they thereby excite, instead of satisfying, the doubts, which naturally arise from a diligent and scrutinous enquiry" (*EU*, 135). The Epicurean is prepared to hear "with attention and with reverence" a teaching rooted in sacred tradition. "But when philosophers, who pretend to neglect authority, and to cultivate reason, hold the same discourse, I pay them not, I own, the same obsequious submission and pious deference" (*EU*, 138).

Hume appears to be saying that religion, viewed as sacred story and tradition, is acceptable to a true philosopher as long as it is disentangled from its speculative philosophical content. If so, this suggests that Hume could accept a Biblical form of Christianity purged of its claim to philosophical legitimacy.

That Christianity could be purged of its claim to philosophical legitimacy, leaving only the authority of Biblical tradition, is a possibility that follows from Hume's distinction between philosophical and nonphilosophical religions. But it is not pursued as a matter of practical reform. What he calls "modern religion" is so bound up with philosophy as to be virtually inconceivable without it—and even if stripped of philosophical content and transformed into sacred tradition, Christianity would still be a theistic religion containing the idea of a perfect being. That idea is "so conformable to sound reason, that philosophy is apt to incorporate itself with such a system of theology" (*NHR*, 65). But given Hume's teaching that once philosophy appears in the world, it is a hardy plant that can scarcely be eliminated entirely, and given the deep roots it has in modern culture (due in part to Christianity itself), the temptation of a nonphilosophical Christianity to seek philosophical legitimacy would be overwhelming. The union of theism and philosophy would spontaneously occur to the corruption of both: theism would twist philosophy to its own ends, and philosophy would corrupt the sacred character of tradition. In a Humean framework this could be prevented only if a reform could occur *within* philosophy, purging it of its false forms and leaving only true philosophy as the representative of philosophy in culture. Since true philosophy presumes all custom innocent unless proven otherwise, theistic sacred tradition would be as legitimate as the rest of custom. All of them, of course, would have to be "methodized and corrected" in light of the others for the sake of stability and coherence, but there is no reason why theistic traditions could not have a voice in this debate as well as any other.

But the idea that philosophy could so reform itself as to leave only its true form is as utopian (and largely for the same reasons) as the idea of Christianity emptying itself of its philosophical content. Modern religion is heavily infused with that insistent philosophical triad of ultimacy, autonomy, and dominion. And it is this philosophical aspect, in corrupt form, that endows modern religion with the quality of total control. Hume taught that in ancient times, "it was the business of philosophy alone to regulate men's ordinary behaviour and deportment." That is, it was philosophy alone that claimed total dominion over every dimension of thought and existence and for this reason "acquired a mighty ascendant over many, and produced great singularities of maxims and conduct" (*EM,* 341). Mythical religion, not having the aspect of a philosophical system, had no concept of total dominion and so laid claim only to that part of one's existence that had to do with the public order. But modern religion, being a corrupt union of theism and philosophy, now performs the same task of total regulation as that of ancient philosophy, and with the same oppressive results. "Its place is now supplied by the modern religion, which inspects our whole conduct, and prescribes an universal rule to our actions, to our words, to our very thoughts and inclinations" (*EM,* 342).

In ancient times false philosophical consciousness was not a threat to the public, but oppressed only the thinker himself and the sect to which he belonged. With the appearance of Christianity, however, the oppression of the corrupt philosophical act was incorporated into the nature of Christian theism. This union has ever since been "the poison of society" and the main source of the religious wars that have disturbed Christendom. This union of philosophy and Christian theism has evolved up to Hume's time into the form of what he called "the modern religion" which, like the false philosophy of the pagan world, claims total dominion over the acts, words, and inclinations of the thinker. Here, as elsewhere, the task of the true philosopher is to gain self-knowledge by understanding the customs and traditions in which he participates. In this case what is required is a history of the union and evolution of philosophy and Christian theism. In the light of this history it is possible to see that the task of the philosopher in modern times is fundamentally different from that in ancient times.

The pagan philosopher is heroic, and the heroic moment of the dialectic is the time of ancient philosophy. The task of the pagan philosopher is to emancipate reflective thought from the world of custom and inclination and to assert its autonomy and title to dominion. Ancient philosophy is philosophy in its youth trying out its speculative powers in radical freedom, a freedom ending in the corruption of the Hellenic schools, where thought sought to rest in a world entirely of its own making. This progressive alienation from custom and nature reached its end in the "refinement" of Eclecticism: an abstraction from abstractions. But the philosopher in modern times is in an entirely different position. He has inherited layer upon layer of bewildering speculation. His task is not that of freeing the abstract from unreflective custom but of preserving his humanity in a world of abstractions. Unlike ancient speculation, which was more or less free of the religious impulse, the modern inheritance of philosophical speculation is inexorably bound up with the specifically religious interests of theism. The modern thinker is not born into a heroic world of philosophical thought but into a philosophically decadent world of abstractions and systems. If the task of the ancient was to found the abstraction and to assert its worth, the task of the modern is to sift through the clutter of abstractions that *is* his mind in order to recover the truth of nature and custom.

Born in the culture of modern religion, the true philosopher has the task of exposing the false philosophical content of "the religious philosophers." Ideally this would result in the reduction of Christianity to sacred tradition. This ideal is in turn a reenactment of the ancient solution to the problem of religion and philosophy, namely, "a fair partition of mankind" between "the learned and wise" and "the vulgar and illiterate" (*EU,* 133). But Hume saw a problem even with this solution, for what if the learned, purged of the religious impulse, became false philosophers? Those in the "vacuum" of false philosophy have no title to dominion, except what is self-imposed. And this leads to the second task of the philosopher in modern times. He must emancipate himself not only from "the modern religion" but also from what Hume calls "the modern philosophy," a form of philosophy he considers to be false. The philosopher in modern times has inherited not only a corruption of philosophy in the union of philosophy and theism but also a corrupt form of philosophy that is not enslaved by the religious impulse and has no one but itself to blame. Hume's criticism of this philosophy is the subject of the next chapter.

CHAPTER SIX

The Modern Philosophy

There is a distinction in Hume's writings between modern philosophy and modern culture, or what he calls "modern times" or "manners" (*E*, 94). Modern philosophy is a certain sort of self-understanding of speculative activity. Modern culture is a certain order of practices, prejudices, and customs beginning about the fifteenth century and more or less established in the Europe of Hume's time. The practices that render modern culture superior to ancient culture are largely moral and political. The moderns are the first to explore philosophically the nature of commerce and the means for achieving material prosperity. The moderns have a superior understanding of political order, the administration of government, the rule of law, and consequently of liberty. Modern regimes are stronger in authority and liberty and so are more stable. But most important, the moderns are superior in the practice of "humanity," "benevolence," "clemency," and "other social virtues" (*E*, 416; *EM*, 256–57).

The "Abstract Theory of Morals"

But if Hume affirms modern culture, he rejects "modern philosophy." What did he consider this philosophy to be? His first discussion of it occurs in part 4, section 4 of book 1 of the *Treatise*, entitled "Of the Modern Philosophy," and he treats it as a pathological state of the intellect. Section 4 follows a critique of the doctrine of substance which captures the essentials of what he calls "the antient philosophy." The ancient philosopher boldly projected metaphorical identities into the world without realizing that he was doing so. These ideal identities were treated as the real, and in an attempt to understand this reality, the ancient philosopher was launched on the hopeless task of Sisyphus and Tantalus (*T,* 223).

Modern philosophy appears as the unmasking of ancient philosophy, where the latter is perceived as the thought of "children" or "poets" (*T,* 225). Modern philosophy pretends to be entirely emancipated from the metaphorical imagination and is determined to base its conclusions on empirically determined cause-effect reasoning. This yields the "fundamental principle of that philosophy," namely, that secondary qualities such as "colours, tastes, smells, heat and cold" are nothing but "impressions in the mind, deriv'd from the operation of external objects, and without any resemblance to the qualities of the objects" (*T,* 226). This leaves us with the "primary qualities" of "extension and solidity, with their different mixtures and modifications; figure, motion, gravity, and cohesion" as "the only *real* ones, of which we have any adequate notion" (*T,* 227). Hume argues that instead of explaining the operations of external objects, the modern philosopher "utterly annihilates all these objects" (*T,* 228). The reason is that we can form no idea of primary qualities devoid of the secondary qualities. Thus if the latter are not continuous and independent existences, then neither are the former: "When we exclude these sensible qualities there remains nothing in the universe, which has such an existence" (*T,* 231). The "fundamental principle" of modern philosophy, if consistently carried out, yields nihilism about public objects.

Ancient and modern philosophy are false forms of the philosophical act. Both in their own way seek, by reflection, to emancipate thought from the dictates of the metaphorical imagination—but in vain. Though he describes them as poets and children, Hume has more sympathy with the ancients than with the moderns. There is something innocent and world-affirming about the ancient philosophers as they give considerable reign to the imagination and extend their own poetic substance into the world, something which, in the end, we must do in any case. The moderns, however, in their attempt to be more rigorous and to purge thought of what they are pleased to consider as the distorting influence of the imagination, turn inward, by a false reflection, and subvert their own substance, disowning as unreal the secondary qualities without which there is no experience of public objects.

The moderns, of course, are not reduced to nihilism about public objects, nor are the ancients reduced to the torments of Tantalus and Sisyphus, because the same imagination that constitutes a public world makes it such that philosophers in common life cannot (except verbally) take their own theories seriously (though there are those such as Diogenes and the ancient "heroes of philosophy" who come close to doing so). Philosophers typically, but unknowingly, preserve some favorite prejudice of the imagination which gives content to and covers over what reflection has entirely eviscerated. This false self-knowledge and hypocrisy is the "consolation" that *nature* has afforded philosophers "amid all their disappointments and afflictions" (*T,* 224).

The nihilism about physical objects which follows from modern philosophy is due to the arrogance of reflection, which denies any authority to the sensory imagination in constituting physical objects. The nature and existence of the physical world is to be determined by self-certifying reflection alone. But there is a parallel nihilism in morals, where modern philosophers attempt to purge ethics of sentiment and the workings of the moral imagination. Here is another act of philosophical "refinement" by which morals are reduced to abstract "rapports" and "relations" known only through abstract reflection. Hume observes a sharp distinction between ancient and modern philosophers: "The ancient philosophers, though they often affirm, that virtue is nothing but conformity to reason, yet, in general, seem to consider morals as deriving their existence from taste and sentiment. On the other hand, our modern enquirers, though they also talk much of the beauty of virtue, and deformity of vice, yet have commonly endeavoured to account for these distinctions by metaphysical reasonings, and by deductions from the most abstract reasonings of the understanding" (*EM,* 170).

Hume gives several examples of this misplaced philosophical distillery in ethics and traces its origin up to its Cartesian roots in Malebranche. Of Montesquieu, he observes that this "illustrious writer, however, sets out with a different theory, and supposes all right to be founded on certain *rapports* and relations; which is a system, that, in my opinion, never will be reconciled with true philosophy. Father Malebranche, as far as I can learn, was the first that started this abstract theory of morals, which was afterwards adopted by Cudworth, Clarke, and others; and as it excludes all sentiment, and pretends to found everything on reason, it has not wanted followers in this philosophic age" (*EM,* 197 n). By "this philosophic age," Hume means the modern self-understanding of philosophy, and the expression is used pointedly as one of disapprobation. In doing so, Hume is not insisting that an age in which philosophical reflection exists is to be disapproved of. He is not and never does advocate philistinism.

Hume often uses the term *philosophy* and related terms such as *reason* and *reflection* to refer not to philosophy, as such, but to a kind of philosophical reflection that is false. Since so much philosophy is false, the term *philosophy* has acquired a bad reputation. In this very passage Hume contrasts what he calls "true philosophy" with the false sort of philosophizing that those in "this philosophic age" are inclined to follow.

At the end of the passage, Hume refers the reader to appendix 1, section 1 of the second *Enquiry,* where he explores further the absurdities and attractions of false philosophical reflection in morals. Philosophers find it extremely difficult to grasp a kind of critical thinking that takes the particular seriously both as the object of criticism and as a restriction upon it. The preferred method is "where a general abstract principle is first established, and is afterwards branched out into a variety of inferences and conclusions," but this "is a common source of illusion and mistake in this [morals] as well as in other subjects" (*EM,* 174). The moderns are especially guilty of inverting the proper relation between the principle, rule, or ideal and the practice, which is always particular and has a history. For Hume the principle is merely an abridgement of the practice. As abstract principle, it does not constitute the practice and does not "guide" it. Insofar as principles are useful at all in ordering practice, they must themselves be interpreted, not by another abstract rule, but by participants skilled in the practice itself. A principle, being an abstraction from or aspect of a practice, cannot in any particular case illuminate a practice without considering its relation to other aspects of the practice which may be relevant to the issue at hand. And this knowledge is not and cannot be contained in the principle itself.

Again we have the familiar Humean point that knowledge by philosophically unreflective participation is prior to knowledge by reflection. Understanding this is difficult for the false philosopher, who inevitably tends to think that the object of reflection is the original source of belief and conduct. The error is due to the misplaced pride which attends the act of autonomous philosophical reflection. Once lost in the error, however, it is difficult to find one's way out: "It is easy for a false hypothesis to maintain some appearance of truth, while it keeps wholly in generals, makes use of undefined terms, and employs comparisons, instead of instances. This is particularly remarkable in that philosophy, which ascribes the discernment of all moral distinctions to reason alone, without concurrence of sentiment" (*EM,* 287).

The moral rationalism Hume attacks is that of Cudworth, Wollaston, Clarke, Montesquieu, and Malebranche, but his criticism applies equally to moral rationalists such as Kant and the long line of contemporary moral critics and moralists who have followed Kant's lead. In words that could be addressed to Kant, Hume remarks: "No, say you, the morality consists in *the relation to the rule of right;* and they are denominated good or ill, according as they agree or disagree with it. What then is this rule of right? In what does it consist? How is it determined? By reason you say, which examines the moral relations of actions. So that moral relations are determined by the comparison of action to a rule. And that rule is determined by considering the moral relations of objects. Is not this fine reasoning?" (*EM,* 289; italics mine). Hume compares moral qualities to color qualities. They are subjective in the same way: their being depends upon our consciousness of them. But they are also objective in the same way: our consciousness of them is what it is because of a certain order of objects in the world related to a certain order in human psychology. What Hume calls "taste" is "a productive faculty, and gilding or staining all natural objects with the colours, borrowed from internal sentiment, raises in a manner a new creation" (*EM,* 294). In like manner our sensory consciousness stains the light waves we receive with the colors and hues of sensibility. Color order and moral order are "in a manner a new creation," but they are nonetheless objective and real orders in the world of human experience—painters and dye makers as well as men of virtue are sought after as much as physicians and chemists.

Hume compares scientific judgments about the physical world with moral judgments about human actions. Science moves from "circumstances and relations, known or supposed . . . to the discovery of the concealed and unknown." Moral judgment, however, requires an act of imagination whereby circumstances are arranged into a moral *whole:* "After all circumstances and relations are laid before us, the latter makes us feel from the whole a new sentiment of blame or approbation" (*EM,* 294). Immediately after this passage Hume stains and colors moral qualities themselves with the sentiments of philosophical theism as a way of driving home the point that moral qualities are real orders in the nature of things: "The standard of the one [scientific judgments], being founded on the nature of things, is eternal and inflexible, even by the will of the Supreme Being: the standard of the other [moral judgments], arising from the eternal frame and constitution of animals, is ultimately derived from that Supreme Will, which bestowed on each being its particular nature, and arranged the several classes and orders of existence" (*EM,* 294).

Just as there arc standard, "normal" conditions, involving both the order of the physical world and human psychology, for arriving at sound beliefs about causal relations, and standard conditions for making correct color judgments, so there are standard conditions for making sound moral judgments. In each case the judgments, though not possible without sentiments, are not *about* sentiments but are about "the nature of things" or "the several classes and orders of existence." Since there are a number of excellent discussions of what Hume considers the standard and normal conditions for making causal and moral judgments to be, they need not be considered here; our problem is Hume's conception of the nature of sound *philosophical* judgment whatever its object might be.[1]

Philosophical Alchemy

I have examined Hume's conception of how the modern moral rationalist inverts the proper relation of a principle to a practice, treating the former as autonomous and having dominion over the practice. We have now to consider a case of philosophical alchemy in morals, where the practice is inverted into its opposite, a case parallel to nihilism about physical objects which Hume discovered in his discussion of "the modern philosophy" in the *Treatise*. In appendix 2 of the second *Enquiry* and in other places, Hume explores the doctrine that morality, as generally understood, is an illusion because there is no such thing as benevolence; and that is so because what is called benevolence is really self-love. Hume mentions Epicurus, Atticus, and Horace as ancient examples of "the selfish system" and Hobbes and Locke as modern examples (*EM*, 296). This doctrine is a typical act of the false philosopher, who takes a favorite part of experience and through the Midas touch transforms the part into the whole. In this case the entire domain of human affections is magically transmuted into one of its parts: "Yes: All is self-love" (*E*, 85).

In its cruder forms the doctrine entails a project of "unmasking" the hypocrisy of the common understanding of morals: "This principle is, that all *benevolence* is mere hypocrisy, friendship a cheat, public spirit a farce, fidelity a snare to procure trust and confidence; and that while all of us, at bottom, pursue only our private interest, we wear these fair disguises, in order to put others off their guard, and expose them the more to our wiles and machinations" (*EM*, 295). There are more modest forms of the doctrine: "An Epicurean or a Hobbist readily allows, that there is such a thing as a friendship in the world, without hypocrisy or disguise; though he may attempt, by a philosophical chymistry, to resolve the elements of this passion, if I may so speak, into those of another, and explain every affection to be self-love, twisted and moulded, by a particular turn of imagination, into a variety of appearances" (*EM,* 296–97).

Hume stresses that even if such doctrine were accepted, it would not necessarily be the threat to morals that many think. Proponents of the selfish system can lead and have led "irreproachable lives" (*E,* 296). But this is a contingent matter. The selfish system is a form of philosophical self-understanding and "is certainly of consequence in the speculative science of human nature, and is a proper object of curiosity and enquiry" (*EM,* 297–98). It is an all-pervasive teaching of Hume's that philosophical self-understanding can influence morals and indeed the whole of life, claiming as it does a dominion over the whole of life. What Hume calls "philosophical enthusiasm" can capture a life, as it did in the case of the "heroes of philosophy," as much as religious enthusiasm can. Hume employs, in his refutation of the selfish system, the maxim of true philosophy that the customs, prejudices, and appearances of common life are presumed true unless shown otherwise: "The most obvious objection to the selfish hypothesis is, that, as it is contrary to common feeling and our most unprejudiced notions, there is required the highest stretch of philosophy to establish so extraordinary a paradox." Such "dispositions as benevolence and generosity; such affections as love, friendship, compassion, gratitude" are sentiments which "have their causes, effects, objects, and operations, marked by common language and observation, and plainly distinguished from those of the selfish passions. And as this is the obvious appearance of things, it must be admitted, till some hypothesis be discovered, which by penetrating deeper into human nature, may prove the former affections to be nothing but modifications of the latter" (*EM,* 298). Hume observes that all such systems have failed, but he goes further and argues from the very "nature of the subject" (that is, from the very nature of philosophical theorizing in the human sciences) that no "system will ever, for the future, be invented" which can "reduce all the various emotions of the human mind to a perfect simplicity" (*EM,* 298–99).

To make his case, Hume distinguishes between theorizing in the human sciences and theorizing in the physical sciences: "The case is not the same in this species of philosophy [the human sciences] as in physics. Many an hypothesis in nature, contrary to first appearances, has been found, on more accurate scrutiny, solid and satisfactory" (*EM,* 299). Indeed Hume follows the witticism of Fontenelle that if there be more than one way in which a phenomenon can be explained, there is a "general presumption for its arising from the causes which are the least obvious and familiar. But *the presumption always lies on the other side,* in all enquiries concerning the origin of our passions, and of the internal operations of the human mind. The simplest and most obvious cause which can there be assigned for any phenomenon, is probably the true one" (*EM,* 299; italics mine). This presumption is simply an instance of the principle of the autonomy of custom, the rational ground of which is worked out in the dialectic of true and false philosophy first laid out in book 1, part 4 of the *Treatise.* Failure to reason within this presumption leads to the alienation from and distortions of common life that characterize a false philosophical consciousness. Theorizing in the physical sciences does not contain this presumption because we know the physical world through speculation, not through social participation in common life. The physical world is a strange and alien environment of constant conjunctions which can be understood only externally by the observations of a spectator. The human world, however, can be grasped from the inside through the self-understanding of role-playing participants.

This, of course, is not to say that one motive may not mask another and that the surface understanding of things is always the right one. Hume goes out of his way to insist that "our predominant motive or intention is, indeed, frequently concealed from ourselves when it is mingled and confounded with other motives which the mind, from vanity or self-conceit, is desirous of supposing more prevalent: but there is no instance that a concealment of this nature has ever arisen from the abstruseness and intricacy of the motive" (*EM,* 299). Hypocrisy and self-delusion can be discovered within the ordinary and surface understanding of the passions without recourse to the philosophic superstition of total theoretical inversion. Hume gives an example: "A man that has lost a friend and patron may flatter himself that all his grief arises from generous sentiments, without any mixture of narrow or interested considerations: but a man that grieves for a valuable friend, who needed his patronage and protection; how can we suppose, that his passionate tenderness arises from some metaphysical regards to a self-interest, which has no foundation or reality" (*EM,* 299–300)? Hume returns to the alchemy metaphor of transmuting base metals into gold, insisting that selfishness and benevolence are "in practice pretty durable and untransmutable. And I find not in this more than in other subjects, that the natural sentiments arising from the general appearances of things are easily destroyed by subtle reflections concerning the minute origin of these appearances" (*EM,* 297). In theoretical physics the surface must be penetrated to discover the alien reality below it. But in the world of common life, which is known through participation, the surface is the reality; and so of the independence of benevolence, Hume is prepared to say, "I assume it as real, from general experience, without any other proof" (*EM,* 298 n).

The attempt to change benevolence alchemically into self-love proceeds not only from the illegitimate transfer into common life of a pattern of theorizing proper to physics, but most importantly "from that love of *simplicity* which has been the source of much false reasoning in philosophy" (*EM,* 298). This false simplicity is merely a feature of the heroic moment of the dialectic which is characteristic of all false philosophical consciousness. Hume argues that, on a deeper understanding of the matter, "a disinterested benevolence, distinct from self-love, has really more *simplicity* in it, and is more conformable to the analogy of nature" (*EM,* 301). There are passions for objects such as power and vengeance which are pursued directly without regard to self-interest. If it is true of the darker passions of "enmity," "resentment," and "vengeance" that we may pursue them without regard to either safety or self-interest and seek to "infuse our very souls into the wounds we give an enemy," why not allow the same independent status to "humanity and friendship"? Once again we see the dark side of a false philosophical consciousness: its hubristic and arbitrary theoretical inversions, its drive for dominion, and its misanthropy. Hume describes the selfish system not merely with the morally neutral term *false* but as the expression of a corrupt philosophical consciousness. It is "a malignant philosophy"—the result of a self-imposed distortion. And "such a philosophy is more like a satyr than a true delineation or description of human nature" (*EM,* 302).

Another instance of philosophic superstition in modern moral philosophy that Hume explores is the contract theory of government. In this view, the legitimacy of government consists in the keeping of a contract made explicitly or implicitly by the people. Hume agrees that government by consent is the ideal, "the best and most sacred of any" (*E,* 474). But government, as we experience it, is a human institution, and a distinction must be made between the legitimate regime and the ideal regime. The contract theory collapses this distinction, investing the idea of the legitimate with the implacable logic of the ideal. To the extent that the contract theory is taken seriously and rigorously applied, with no concession being made to custom and tradition, it is easy to show that no government has ever been legitimate. If so, the contract theory is not a deep and radical form of criticism, as it appears to be, but no form of criticism at all. For a true theory of legitimacy would enable us to distinguish, within the world of custom, between legitimate and illegitimate regimes. It would necessarily presume that *some* regimes had been legitimate.

Contract theorists such as Locke typically do not claim that no regime has been legitimate. In the manner of all false philosophy, such theorists are always able, through self-deception or through the manipulation of concepts, to protect their favorite regime from slipping into the void of illegitimacy. Locke thought that the English regime under the Glorious Revolution of 1688 was founded on a contract. Hume had no difficulty in showing that it was not (*E,* 472–73). But Locke does claim that no form of absolute monarchy is or can be legitimate since it is "inconsistent with Civil Society, and so can be no Form of Civil Government at all."[2] Likewise, Algernon Sidney writes, "Whatever . . . proceeds not from the consent of the people, must be 'de facto' only, that is, void of all right."[3] Again, the claim of modern contract theory is not that consent is an ideal and that absolute monarchy is far down on the scale of perfection. Rather the claim is the nihilistic one that absolute monarchy is no form of civil government at all. Modern philosophy annihilates it as, in its metaphysics, it annihilates the physical world. Subjects in an absolute monarchy who construct their experience of the political order through the lens of this false philosophical consciousness will be able to "unmask" the pretence of the regime to legitimacy. Such a frame of mind must smolder, not with true resentment, but with that philosophically contrived resentment which always attends the guilty and revolutionary modes of false philosophical existence. In an individual of heroic spirit, such philosophically contrived resentment, if resolutely pursued, leads naturally to the fantasy of root-and-branch revolution.

In criticizing the contract theory, Hume again uses the metaphor of chemical refinement. The contract theory is too "refined and philosophical a system" (*E,* 470). Those captured by "these refined ideas" are "delirious" and have difficulty penetrating this philosophically imposed hallucination to understand what a true investigation of the origins of government and the conditions of authority would be (*E,* 470). Rather they are "so in love with a philosophical origin to government, as to imagine all others monstrous and irregular" (*E,* 472). The poison distilled in the philosophical refinery is confused with the original substance and viewed as its essence. But the pure alcohol that can be distilled from wine is not the essence of the wine. The wine has its own properties, which can be understood only by attentive discrimination within the concrete whole of experience, shaped by the imagination, and in the experience of tasting and comparing different wines. And so it is with a true philosophical investigation of that mode of participation known as political authority. We begin with concrete wholes of authority known through participation and, through discrimination and comparison, seek to determine their postulates or rationales.

The error of the contract theory follows the pattern of all false philosophy. A part of common life is seized upon as especially significant (that men form contracts); the rest is then refined away, leaving contract as the whole of political authority. The absurdity, as Hume observes, is that the notion of a contract is the notion of something enforced by the authority of government. Since contract presupposes authority, it cannot be used to explain the nature of authority.

But aside from being intrinsically absurd, the contract theory, like all false philosophy, fosters passions (philosophical enthusiasm) which block true inquiry into the nature of political practice. Hume carried on a running polemic throughout his career with English Whig nationalism. The contract theory was part of this nationalist ideology, and the absolute monarchy of France was regularly described as a "Turkish" despotism, and the people of France as unthinking slaves. Hume argued that liberty (understood mainly as the rule of law and protection of property) was not an achievement unique to the English. The rule of law and protection of property was part of a civilizing process at work in Europe since about the fifteenth century. It was stronger in some places than in others and was especially strong in England. But it also existed in a high degree in France, despite the claim of the monarchy to absolutism. Hume also argued that the French regime needed reform, and he considered what institutions within the French political tradition could be rallied to effect reform (*E,* 95; for anticipation of a revolution in France see *L,* 2: 242). But none of this could be seen through the distorting lens of the English contract theorist. The virtues and vices of the French regime, not to mention their subtle interconnection, simply do not appear within the field of vision. All but the contract is refined away. But, with the inexhaustible ingenuity of a corrupt philosophical consciousness, the fires kindled for the regime of France can, with equal facility, be set under *any* particular regime, even one classed as representative democracy. For when the principle of the autonomy of custom is abandoned, there is no regime "but what may, with facility, be refined away, if we indulge a false philosophy in sifting and scrutinizing it, by every captious rule of logic, in every light or position, in which it may be placed" (*E,* 482).

The New Vulgar Philosophers

A number of themes having to do with the emancipated rationalism of modern theorizing about morals are highlighted in the essay "Of Moral Prejudices" (1742). Here the selfish system makes its appearance again along with the cynicism of philosophical unmasking: "There is a Set of Men lately sprung up amongst us, who endeavour to distinguish themselves by ridiculing every Thing, that has hitherto appear'd sacred and venerable in the Eyes of Mankind. Reason, Sobriety, Honour, Friendship, Marriage, are the perpetual Subjects of their insipid Raillery: And even public Spirit, and a Regard to our Country, are treated as chimerical and romantic" (*E,* 538). There are two things to be said about this popular new breed of men. First, their alienation from moral sentiments established in custom is not due to the spontaneous exercise of self-interest and greed. Rather, their self-interest and greed is legitimated by a corrupt philosophical self-understanding which is boldly displayed as superior to vulgar understanding. Hume speaks of their "Schemes" and describes them as "Anti-reformers" (*E,* 538). That is, they are not concerned to *reform* moral experience but to totally invert it. And *total* inversions are always the mark of the philosophical act.

Second, though informed by philosophical reflection, those belonging to this new group are not members of philosophical sects seeking self-perfection in the manner of the eudaemonistic sects of antiquity. They are modern men from all walks of life, owing allegiance to no sect or institution. Among them are the modern libertine and the dilettante. Something of the drift of their thought was captured in the clear-eyed reflections of the Marquise de Sade.

They are reflective, but Hume cannot quite dignify them with the name of philosopher. He calls them "Pretenders to Wisdom" (*E,* 539). Yet their thought bears the unmistakable imprint of the philosophical act. Another exploration of this new popular philosophy appears in Berkeley's *Alciphron.* He called them "minute philosophers"; that is, shallow thinkers or thinkers of small or low mind. In the name of rational autonomy and superior understanding, the minute philosopher unmasks this or that custom or prejudice and in the end the whole of custom. Indeed, he transcends all interests but his own. And as we learn from Hume that extensive benevolence and greatness of mind are dispositions of the true philosopher, so we may learn from Berkeley that the egoism of the minute philosopher is the unabsorbed residue in all false philosophy. With these men philosophy becomes vulgar and popular, and assumes a peculiarly modern cultural shape unknown to the ancients and the medievals. Hume's new set of men who are "pretenders to wisdom" and Berkeley's "minute philosophers" have vastly increased in numbers and repertoire since the eighteenth century, and I shall have more to say about them later. It is important here only to record Hume's awareness of their appearance.

Hume contrasts these with another group of modern thinkers who have the dignity worthy of the name of philosophy but are stuck in various modes of the heroic moment of philosophical reflection. They are philosophers of the false form. Hume introduces them by reference to examples from antiquity: Statilius, Epictetus, and Diogenes. The modern group is a reflection of these ancient forms of false philosophy that have appeared in "latter Times" (*E*, 539). Heroic philosophy, instead of correcting errors against the background of custom in the manner of true philosophy, subverts or inverts the entire domain of moral custom and prejudice. "I mean that grave philosophic Endeavour after Perfection, which, under Pretext of reforming Prejudices and Errors, strikes at all the most endearing Sentiments of the Heart, and all the most useful Byasses and Instincts, which can govern a human Creature" (*E*, 539).

The essay "Of Moral Prejudices" is, as its title suggests, a defense of "prejudice." Such a defense is necessary only because of a massive infusion of false philosophical consciousness in modern culture, not only in the form of the new vulgar "philosophers" but in the theorizing of moral rationalists such as Malebranche, Hobbes, Locke, Montesquieu, Clarke, Cudworth, and so on. If moral order really is an abstract order of "rapports and relations" known by radically autonomous reason, then the sentiments framed in custom have no original authority to command judgment. Custom is merely what must submit to the grim measuring rod of rational principle; it has no influence of its own in shaping that principle. Therefore terms such as *custom, prejudice, convention,* and *tradition* not only lose their moral authority, but take on an invidious connotation. In modern moral speech, custom, as such, is seen as a barrier to moral rectitude.

This, of course, is the central rhetorical problem of Hume's philosophy: How can we argue that custom is a constituent of critical reason in a world of discourse in which custom is perceived as in opposition to reason? How can we reconstruct a false conception of reason when those lost in it must perceive the reconstruction as an attack on reason itself? How can we invert the inversion, and how can we unmask the unmasker? For this project discursive argument alone is not sufficient, for it cannot penetrate the seamless whole of a corrupt philosophical consciousness. We have reached the limits of discursive thought and are probing into that tacit dimension of prejudice, sentiment, and thought from which all discursive thought arises, against which it is displayed, and without which it has no authority. In its deepest sense this is what Hume is getting at with the notion of the force and vivacity of impressions and ideas. It is only by tapping into the tacit dimension that one can hope to penetrate and shatter the seamless and self-protecting discursive whole that is a false philosophical self-determination. For this project the art of eloquence is necessary; and, as I have argued, it is this art, above all others, that the true philosopher in modern times must develop. Modern rationalism has subverted eloquence as a constituent of critical thinking and so has denied the poetic character of common life. Not only is this a false conception of rational criticism, but eloquence is the only art capable of keeping the "man" from being lost in the "philosopher." The subsequent history of modern ethics shows that Hume's own attempt to prevent this was not successful.

The modern vulgar philosophers are "pernicious" to society. In contrast, the modern reconstitution of ancient Epicurean, Stoical, and Cynical perfection is not a public nuisance, but it nevertheless "has a very bad Effect on those who indulge it" and those close to them. The casualties of both are "the virtuous and tender Sentiments, or Prejudices, if you will, [which] have suffer'd mightily by these Reflections" (*E*, 539). Hume tells two stories to illustrate the proper relationship between reflection and prejudice.

The first is about an intelligent and spirited young woman of good birth and fortune who is jealous of her autonomy and has resolved never to marry. She desires, however, to have a son whose education will be the main concern of her life. To this end she selects a young man whom she thinks would be a good breeder; forms a friendship, and upon perceiving him to be of worthy character reveals her plans. He agrees to sign a contract to produce a child over which he renounces any claim. After the birth of the child, the mother severs the relationship. The young man, however, has come to love the woman and the child and will not be put off. She reminds him of the contract, but to no avail. The story ends with the two going to court: he claims the child and the right to educate him according to the usual maxims of the law, and she claims the child by right of contract. How to resolve the case "puzzles all the Lawyers, as much as it does the Philosophers" (*E*, 544).

Hume presents the error of the young woman as an error in philosophical self-understanding. He describes her as "our Philosophical Heroine" and as "an Instance of a Philosophic Spirit" which yields the lesson "not to depart too far from the receiv'd Maxims of Conduct and Behavior, by a refin'd Search after Happiness or Perfection" (*E*, 542). The moral sentiments framed in custom and hammered out over time which bear on the question of how children are to enter the world are ruled out *a priori* by the young woman. She has reasoned herself out of the moral world by too "refin'd" a reflection. Through philosophical alchemy she has transmuted the moral world into one of its aspects: autonomous agents engaged in contracts and stripped of the rich wardrobe of an inherited moral tradition. Hobbes and Locke had refined political authority away into the alien residue of contract. The young woman does the same for the moral world. Like a good Kantian, she is governed by self-interest and supposes everyone else to be, but she can *respect* others as persons, which she does in the contract with the young man.

Being bemused by an abstraction, however, she has passed through the moral world without seeing it. The peculiar woodenness and innocence she betrays is not due to nature but is self-imposed by the dictates of philosophical reflection. She evokes neither pity nor contempt. Indeed, there is something noble about her, as there is in all heroic philosophical reflection. In the natural progress of the dialectic, however, the heroic philosopher who gains true philosophical self-knowledge knows himself to be "a strange uncouth monster," and knows also that the monstrosity is of his own making. And being of generous mind, as the true philosopher must be, he "will be the first to join in the laugh against himself" (*EU*, 160). But such a discovery, in the adventure of philosophical self-knowledge, is not to be expected of the philosophical heroine. She cannot laugh at herself, but is entirely lost in heroic philosophical existence. On her countenance is to be found that "grave philosophic Endeavour after Perfection" which poisons the heart with a "Sullen Pride or Contempt of Mankind" (*E*, 539).

The selfishness or self-centeredness of the young woman is again of a peculiar kind and is shaped by the philosophical act. Heroic philosophical reflection purports to transcend all custom. Its language is always that of liberation, emancipation, and enlightenment. But it transcends everything except itself. Radical self-determination is never transcended, and its disposition is to be unaffected by the "other." The young woman wishes to determine her own life by her own choices. She is quite content to mind her own business and to allow others to mind theirs. But Hume's point is that this cannot be done without being influenced and shaped by the sentiments of others. The "minds of men," he says, "are mirrors to one another" (*T*, 365). It is one of Hume's central doctrines that the self gains its identity through engagement with others (*T,* 340). Emancipated philosophical existence is at war with this authority of other participants in custom to shape the self. Thus the philosophical heroine will not allow herself to be modified by the sentiments of the young man or by custom. This would be a "Weakness," and so she is "oblig'd" to put a "Violence upon herself" (*E,* 543). Nor is any consideration given to what the child's sentiments might be about his manner of appearance in the world. He exists for the sake of her own self-fulfillment.

Hume contrasts the philosophical heroine with Eugenius (meaning nobly born or born of generous spirit), who represents the true philosopher. "In his Youth he apply'd himself, with the most unwearied Labour, to the Study of Philosophy; and nothing was ever able to draw him from it, except when an Opportunity offer'd of serving his Friends, or doing a Pleasure to some Man of Merit" (*E,* 540). Like the young woman, he preferred a single life devoted to philosophical pursuits. But he was the last branch of an ancient family that would have died out had he not married; out of duty to his family, therefore, he marries Emira, a beautiful and virtuous woman who bears him several children. Eventually he forms a deep attachment to his wife, and after her untimely death he continues to celebrate her birthday with the same joy and festivity as when she was alive. He finds some consolation in his children and especially in one of his daughters, whose countenance, manners, and voice recall the person of his wife. He is to be buried with his wife and has ordered a monument to be placed over their grave on which he has composed an epitaph to celebrate their love and happiness. Eugenius embodies the social virtues of benevolence and greatness of mind. These are "the most endearing Sentiments of the Heart and . . . the most useful Byasses and Instincts, which can govern a human Creature" (*E,* 539). And it is these "Prejudices, if you will," which "have suffer'd mightily by these [corrupt philosophical] Reflections" (*E,* 539). Of his essentially social nature, Hume observes that Eugenius is not "so affectedly Philosophical, as . . . to call it by the Name of *Weakness*" (*E,* 541).

Eugenius is an example of the life of the true philosopher whose sentiments and philosophical reflections are in harmony. Here the philosopher is unashamedly embedded in a social world to which he is loyal. Philosophical reflection may lead to "reforming Prejudices and Errors," but such correction must always be piecemeal; the world itself cannot be transcended. It is the new vulgar "philosophers" and the philosophical heroine who, in thought at least, purport to transcend the social world, and Hume properly describes them as "Anti-reformers" (*E,* 538). All true criticism is reformist and is internal to an order of participation in custom.

Hume's philosophical heroine is a type of which there have been many and varied instances since his time. One may see in her the image of Kantian autonomy with its division of human motivation into self-interest and respect for other self-interested agents whose maxims are not in conflict. But one may also see in her, if with less clarity, the radical-choice ethics of Kierkegaard, Nietzsche, and Sartre. For all of these thinkers, but for different reasons, Eugenius is an unacceptable character. It is true that both he and the young woman make a fundamental choice, but the meaning of the choice is different in each case.

The philosophical heroine's choice is one of radical self-determination in a world of "others" who are treated with respect but are not engaged in such a way that the self is modified by them. Eugenius's choice is made out of piety for his ancestors. Piety is not and cannot be a serious form of moral determination for Kant, Kierkegaard, Nietzsche, and Sartre because it requires an act of submission to the other. One might argue, as Sartre does, that in submitting, one has chosen to do so, and consequently has engaged in an act of radical freedom. There is a trivial sense in which this is true. One's choice is one's own. But more than this commonplace is needed to explain the heady issues that are supposed to be at stake in the radical-choice ethics of the above thinkers, and more is needed to explain the "forelorn solitude" (*T*, 264) of the characters who pass through the pages of Kierkegaard, Nietzsche, and Sartre.

There is a clear sense in which Eugenius's act is not an act of radical self-determination but an act of deference to his family. In performing it he is honoring their will, not his. This conception of the act for Kant is a case of heteronomy, and for Sartre a case of bad faith. For Hume it is a simple act of piety untransmutable by philosophical alchemy. Is there a philosophical justification for this act of submission? The answer is to be found in the dialectic of true and false philosophy which generates the principle of the autonomy of custom. Given this principle, Eugenius need give no reason for his decision to marry other than piety to ancestors. It is the philosophical grounding of this principle by the dialectic that enables Hume to engage the false philosopher on his own ground. Piety is not heteronomy and bad faith; rather, what in this instance is called heteronomy and bad faith is really piety. The dialectic of true and false philosophy here as elsewhere enables Hume to invert the inversion and to unmask the unmasker.

Hume as Classical Moralist

Why, Hume asks, have "modern philosophers . . . often followed a course in their moral enquiries so different from that of the ancients?" (*EM,* 322). How did the moderns come to think of morals as abstract "rapports or relations" formulated into moral rules for the purpose of guiding choices? His answer has to do with that union of philosophy and theism in Christendom discussed in chapter 5. That peculiar mixture of philosophy and theism which has produced "modern religion" has also produced modern ethics: "In later times, philosophy of all kinds, especially ethics, have been more closely united with theology than ever they were observed to be among the heathens. . . . Philosophers, or rather divines under that disguise, treating all morals as on a like footing with civil laws, guarded by the sanctions of reward and punishment, were necessarily led to render this circumstance, of *voluntary* or *involuntary,* the foundation of their whole theory" (*EM,* 322).

Hume's observation here is insightful. First, religious philosophers used secular civil law as the model for the whole of the moral order. Morality is a matter of obeying divine commands. Modern philosophers, seeking emancipation from theology, attempted to give an account of divine law which would satisfy the demands of autonomous reason, independent of a divine lawgiver, but which would be consistent with the existence of one. As secularization continued, confidence in the importance of divinity to morality began to wane, but the form of moral discourse remained the same. Morality is a matter of following a rule (that is in some way lawlike) designed to answer the question, What ought I to do? Self-conscious choice is central. Kant is a good example of a modern moral philosopher in transition. He saw morality as a matter of obeying a supreme moral law certified by reason alone but presupposing God, immortality, and a radical notion of freedom. And in this he was right, for God, immortality, and freedom were presupposed in the philosophical-religious moral culture that Kant and Hume inherited.

But it would not be long before Kierkegaard, in *Either/Or,* would argue that the moral order itself is merely one order among others to be chosen or not by an act of will more radical and primordial than even Kant supposed. Nietzsche and Sartre would go further and argue that the moral order, whatever it might be, is not chosen so much as *constituted* by radical freedom. And with this move "the modern philosophy," in its latter-day refinement, utterly barbarizes the moral life as, in Hume's time, it had barbarized morals into rapports and relations and had annihilated physical objects (*T,* 231).

Hume rejected entirely modern *theorizing* about ethics. But although he thought of himself as a classical moralist, he accepted modern moral prejudices: personal liberty, political liberty, the rule of law, and a more extensive benevolence. He thought of himself as a classical moralist in a modern culture.[4] Classical ethics is virtue ethics, and its main question is not What ought I to do, but What should I be? The former question has been the favorite of moral rationalists, in Hume's time and later, who seek to found morality on "the rule of right" (*EM,* 288). Ethics is a matter of making choices about particular acts, and the main problem of ethical theorizing is to determine a supreme moral rule for making choices. Mill went so far as to say that without such a rule, ethics has no foundation.[5] He thought, of course, that he had discovered it. Ethics conceived in this way makes of a human life a mere sequence of actions each of which is covered by the supreme rule or lower-level rules which are determined by it.

Those who conceive of ethics under the latter question (What should I be?) think of actions not as a sequence but against the background notion of a whole life. The task of ethics is to construct a model of the good life and to display an order of dispositions or virtues which make this life possible. In this view there is no supreme rule to govern actions conceived as discrete entities. There are rules, but they have a different character. They are essentially rules of prudence in a life of self-perfection guided by a model of human excellence.

What is Hume's conception of human excellence? His most sustained discussion is in the quartet of essays "The Epicurean," "The Stoic," "The Platonist," and "The Sceptic." Hume discusses four views of human excellence that naturally occur in the world and which may be roughly identified with historical sects. The first three views are given subtitles. The Epicurean is "the man of elegance and pleasure"; the Stoic is "the man of action and virtue"; and the Platonist is "the man of contemplation, and *philosophical* devotion." The last essay, "The Sceptic," does not have a subtitle and indeed displays a concrete ideal of the good life in only an oblique way. The Sceptic explores what it means even to ask the question about the good life and how far, if at all, philosophical reflection can be a source of human conduct. In short, "The Sceptic" is concerned with the philosophically self-reflective task of distinguishing between true and false forms of philosophical reflection on the question of the good life. And what the Sceptic exposes are the absurdities and illusions that a corrupt philosophical consciousness generates in answering the question.

Hume's own view of human excellence is expressed in "The Stoic," who is "the man of action and virtue" (*E*, 146–54; 167–68). The task of the Sceptic is to disentangle the speech of the Stoic from the false philosophy in which it is embedded. This may seem strange, for Hume often presents Stoics such as Seneca and Epictetus as especially clear examples of corrupt philosophical consciousness (*E*, 172 and 173–76). But these should now be seen as false forms of Stoicism. They are false because they presume that philosophical autonomy can be the source of human conduct and because they seek to use philosophical reflection to harden the heart against the social affections. Hume's Stoic, however, is thoroughly rooted in, and largely defined by, the social and political world. There is a progress in human excellence from the savage to the citizen and to the philosopher. "As the wildest savage is inferior to the polished citizen, who, under the protection of laws, enjoys every convenience which industry has invented; so much is this citizen himself inferior to the man of virtue, and the true philosopher, who governs his appetites, subdues his passions, and has learned, from reason, to set a just value on every pursuit and enjoyment" (*E*, 148). When "we have fixed all the rules of conduct, we are *philosophers:* When we have reduced these rules to practice, we are *sages*" (*E*, 149).

Hume's ideal Stoic embodies two master virtues: one is greatness of mind, which was discovered and cultivated by the ancients, and the other is benevolence, which has been more finely cultivated by the moderns. The Humean sage affirms himself and takes pride in the knowledge of who he is. He refrains from doing wrong not because doing so would violate a rule (he is not a Kantian whose spring of conduct is mere respect for law as such) but because the action would be *unworthy of him.* The sage or true philosopher occupies the "temple of wisdom" which "is seated on a rock, above the rage of the fighting elements, and inaccessible to all the malice of man. . . . The sage, while he breathes that serene air, looks down with pleasure, mixed with compassion, on the errors of mistaken mortals, who blindly seek for the true path of life, and pursue riches, nobility, honour, or power, for genuine felicity" (*E*, 150–51). But the sage does not "constantly indulge this severe wisdom, which, by pretending to elevate him above human accidents, does in reality harden his heart, and render him careless of the interest of mankind, and of society" (*E*, 151). The true sage knows this heroic state of mind to be merely a "sullen *Apathy*" in which "neither true wisdom nor true happiness can be found" (*E*, 151). So greatness of mind must be modified by benevolence, or what Hume calls "the social affections" or "the generous dispositions."

The social passions have a natural history of perfection. "As harmonious colours mutually give and receive a lustre by their friendly union; so do these ennobling sentiments of the human mind" in parental affection and "in the harmony of minds . . . in friendship founded on mutual esteem and gratitude" (*E*, 152). But the social passions include more than friendship. The sage finds satisfaction in "relieving the distressed, in comforting the afflicted, in raising the fallen, and in stopping the career of cruel fortune, or of more cruel man, in their insults over the good and virtuous" and by victories over vice "where by virtuous example or wise exhortation, our fellow creatures are taught to govern their passions, reform their vices, and subdue their worst enemies, which inhabit within their own bosoms" (*E*, 152). But the sage does not stop here, for his mind "being of celestial origin, swells with the divinest and most enlarged affections." It goes beyond kindred and acquaintance and "extends its benevolent wishes to the most distant posterity." It recognizes "liberty and laws as the source of human happiness, and devotes itself, with the utmost alacrity, to their guardianship and protection" (*E*, 152–53).

The sage, being the true philosopher in affirming the social passions, ends by being a guardian of law and liberty and so necessarily a patriot. And Hume concludes with a formula of human excellence: "In the true sage and patriot are united whatever can distinguish human nature, or elevate mortal man to a resemblance with the divinity" (*E*, 153). Human excellence is extensive benevolence modified by greatness of mind. In this Hume thinks he is combining the most noble virtue of classical experience with the most noble virtue of modern experience. Greatness of mind has a progress; it is first of all heroic pride in the knowledge of who one is in the social order. One who has this pride can transcend adverse circumstances, and may maintain heroic dignity even in defeat after one's social order has collapsed. But the most sublime form of greatness of mind is found in the philosopher. The philosopher's heroic sense of worth derives not from his social place so much as from his experience of autonomy and his thought of the whole of reality. But greatness of mind in philosophy may quickly degenerate into a barbarous form which not only distinguishes between the philosopher's dignity and his social place but counts the social place as having no authority. This is the error of the "heroes of philosophy" examined previously. Hume both admires and condemns them. Aside from Diogenes, some of the worst offenders are the Stoics. Hence Hume's use of "Stoic" as the name of the best life, though eccentric, is an attempt to place at the center of the good life the pagan virtue of greatness of mind.

But the ancient philosophers corrupted greatness of mind by cutting it off from the social order. In respect to the social order, heroic philosophical existence degenerated into a "sullen Apathy" or even hostility. This error has, in effect, been corrected by the moderns, who hold benevolence and the social affections in higher regard. This is not to say, of course, that the ancients knew nothing of benevolence; since it is a universal human disposition, they could not help but experience it. But a disposition may be explored and cultivated more deeply by some people than by others. It was the Christian tradition that first focused on charity as the central feature of the moral life. For centuries Christian Europeans had explored and pondered the intimations of this disposition and, by the beginning of modern times, charity had long been established in European sentiments and habits. For Hume the moral life springs not from an autonomous mind which, guided by ideals and principles, seeks to conduct itself in the world but from a settled way of life. A moral tradition or way of life may, of course, be modified by reflection, but reflection cannot itself be the source of human conduct. The priority of moral habit over philosophically reflective precept is asserted by Hume in the case of charity itself: "That people, who invented the word *charity,* and used it in a good sense, inculcated more clearly and much more efficaciously, the precept *be charitable,* than any pretended legislator or prophet, who should insert such a *maxim* in his writings" (*E,* 229). Hume goes so far as to say that whoever "recommends any moral virtues, really does no more than is implied in the terms themselves" (*E,* 229). That is, moral language is internal to a way of life, and to know the idiom of a moral language is to know the idiom of a way of life.

Hume explores the classical pagan-philosophical way of life that generated the virtue of greatness of mind, but he never mentions the Christian tradition as the way of life that spread the sentiment of benevolence throughout European culture: "that people, who invented the word *charity,* and used it in a good sense." When Hume thinks of Christianity, he does not tend to think of a way of life that springs from a disposition of charity and sets for itself the ideal of strengthening that disposition. Rather he thinks first of *theology,* which is vulgar theism shaped by philosophical theory, and second of clericalism, the highly artificial life of the "monkish virtues" which is presented as the image of human excellence. The practices of celibacy, fasting, penance, and mortification prevent the establishment of greatness of mind. Hume is implacably opposed both to Christian theology (as a form of false philosophy) and to Christian ethics (understood as the monkish virtues). That he could see no more than this in the Christian moral tradition is understandable but is, nonetheless, an unfortunate lapse into Enlightenment that should be noted in passing.

Hume said that he took his list of virtues from Cicero's *Offices.* Since one may think of Cicero as being in the Stoic tradition, this judgment is consistent with Hume's identification of human excellence with Stoicism. Extensive benevolence, however, is not a feature of Cicero's nor of pagan Stoic ethics generally, but this does not bother Hume, who has taught all along that the character of human life is poetic. In this case the imagination is forging a metaphorical identity between the unacknowledged Christian virtue of charity and the classical pagan virtue of greatness of mind. A pagan name is given to this vision of the moral life to quarantine it as far as possible from the corruptions of Christendom with which Hume imagines himself surrounded.

The model of human excellence as extensive benevolence modified by greatness of mind first appears in the *Treatise* (*T,* 592–605). These qualities have their source respectively in the primordial and distinct human dispositions of love of others and love of self. The cultivation of these dispositions, in the many ways in which culture, reflection, and circumstances have made possible, constitutes the natural virtues, which are in turn the source of the artificial virtues. The history of morals is essentially the adventure of cultivating the natural virtues, though the cultural conditions for displaying these may vary enormously (*EM,* 324–43). The ideal of benevolence united to greatness of mind appears in the concluding section of the second *Enquiry,* where the character of a young man is sketched of which Hume says that "a philosopher might select this character as a model of perfect virtue" (*EM,* 270). His character is a balance of "honor" and "humanity." Hume gives the name of Cleanthes, a Stoic name, to the young man. The "philosophical heroine" in "Of Moral Prejudices" exemplifies a corrupt form of Stoicism (greatness of mind dominates extensive benevolence) as Eugenius exemplifies the true form. The noble characters in *The History of England* exemplify the model in varying degrees. In his autobiography, *My Own Life,* Hume narrates his own life as one embodying the same virtues that are to be found in the true Stoic, Cleanthes, and Eugenius. When considered as ideal types, greatness of mind and extensive benevolence contain a natural progress that gravitates to extremes and renders them warring opposites. The one leads to the arrogance of aristocratic pride, the other to a bankruptcy of the self for the sake of others. The task of the true philosopher is to moderate these forms of experience and, through a poetic act of the imagination, to unite what reflection must consider to be contraries into one amiable character.

CHAPTER SEVEN

True Philosophy and the Skeptical Tradition

Philosophical-Historical Images

In separating himself from "the antient philosophy," the "religious philosophers" of Christendom, and "the modern philosophy," it might appear that Hume, like Descartes, imagines himself outside the entire Western tradition, forging an entirely new philosophical position out of his own autonomous reason—which would violate a stricture of true philosophy that there is no view from nowhere from which to criticize an order of custom or tradition. This suspicion is partly correct and partly mistaken. First, Hume never denied the autonomy of philosophy. Indeed, the dialectical distinction between true and false philosophy presupposes it. He sought only to reform the traditional understanding of philosophical autonomy by recognizing the autonomy of custom, that is, by demonstrating that custom is an original and authoritative constituent of speculative thought. The true philosopher stands within and without the flow of custom and tradition he is criticizing, and this goes for the philosophical tradition as well as any other.

The philosopher first engages the philosophical tradition through the mode of participation. One learns the moves, the idiom, the style of philosophical activity and becomes skillful in the art of speculation as one becomes skillful in any other activity by apprenticeship, emulation, and practice. But eventually the thinker must ask what his participation in the philosophical tradition means, and he must make a judgment about the nature and worth of his own philosophical activity and that of his philosophical ancestors.

This is not an empirical question, nor can it be answered by a simple appeal to the tradition itself. It is a dialectical question of self-inquiry to be answered *a priori* by an act of speculative thought whereby philosophy inquires into its own nature and worth, discovers its own essence, and in the light of this discovery distinguishes between true and false forms of its own activity. Whatever the answer to this speculative and normative question might be, it will express the paradoxical character of the philosopher as both rooted in the philosophical tradition and as transcending it. He transcends it insofar as an answer to the question will be seen as having authority to decide what is important and what is unimportant in the tradition. But he exists within the tradition insofar as the very ability to ask philosophical questions and to discriminate among answers is a disposition of one skilled in the practice of an inherited philosophical tradition. Consequently, true philosophical self-knowledge must acknowledge both the independence of the assessment of the philosophical tradition, on the one hand, and the rootedness of the assessment in the tradition on the other. The philosopher becomes aware of and engages the philosophical tradition in an act of philosophical-historical self-knowledge.

The paradoxical character of the philosopher as existing within and without the philosophical tradition requires metaphor for its understanding. That is, in understanding his relation to the philosophical tradition, the philosopher must construct metaphorical identities that allow him to identify with the tradition and at the same time to preserve his critical independence from it. I have argued that the speculative metaphorical understanding of the world is central to Hume's account of what it means to understand. The metaphorical imagination (Hume's theory of the association of ideas) is, for us, not only "the cement of the Universe"; it is also what binds philosophical autonomy to the philosophical tradition.

Hume's image of "the Stoic" as exemplifying the true ideal of human excellence is a good example of a philosophical-historical metaphor that unites the transcendence of the philosopher with his embeddedness in a tradition. As a philosopher Hume must raise the timeless Socratic question, "What is human excellence?" His answer is extensive benevolence united with greatness of mind. But in explaining this formula, Hume acknowledges his participation in both the classical and modern traditions. The formula is not an ideal that could have been available to the pagan Stoics, for they had no experience of the extensive benevolence manifest in "modern manners." Nor had they any experience of the Christian ideal of charity without which modern manners would not be what they are.

The essay "The Stoic," then, is a poetic work of the philosophical-historical imagination as it seeks to ground an answer to the timeless question, "What is human excellence?" both in the philosophical tradition and in the speculation of the contemporary philosopher. In this act the philosopher has not only inherited a tradition, he has shaped it into a form of his own. Hume does the same for the question, "What is the nature and worth of philosophy?" His answer is grounded in a metaphorical identification with the skeptical tradition. What form does this identification take, and why did Hume choose the skeptical tradition to illuminate philosophy?

Skepticism in the *Treatise*, *Abstract*, and *Letter from a Gentleman*

In book 1, part 4 of the *Treatise*, Hume works out what I have called the dialectic of true and false philosophy. The title of part 4 is "Of the Sceptical and Other Systems of Philosophy." The dialectical pattern of criticism exhibiting the nature of true philosophy is called the "sceptical" system of philosophy. False forms of philosophy are the "other systems of philosophy." But nowhere in the *Treatise* does Hume explain the meaning of the terms *scepticism, sceptic,* and *sceptical system* by reference to historical figures or to historical schools of thought. These expressions get their meaning in the *Treatise* from their use in the dialectic of true and false philosophy exhibited in the eighty-three-page adventure of part 4. The speculative distinction between true and false philosophy would be the same even if the language of "scepticism" had not been used.

The only ancient historical figure with whom Hume identifies in the *Treatise* is Socrates, and he does this not to illuminate skepticism in the *Treatise* but to distinguish it as a work in the moral sciences as distinct from the natural sciences. The former sciences, he says, are relatively new and unexplored, and his writing suggests that there is a natural progress in the development of the sciences, which is of a piece with the accounts of the origin of philosophy given in *The Natural History of Religion* and in "Of the Rise and Progress of the Arts and Sciences." Thought, in its barbarous state, first gains some mastery of the physical world; builds cities in which some measure of security is achieved; and, having leisure, begins to reflect on its own works and seeks to determine the nature of its own activity. There must first have been a Thales (natural philosophy) before there could have been a Socrates (moral philosophy). With the collapse of classical civilization, the natural sciences were lost. When they reappear, the same pattern repeats itself. Hume identifies Bacon (as Bacon identified himself) with Thales and the pre-Socratics, and he identifies himself with Socrates. Even the interval of time it took the ancients to move from the natural to the moral sciences is the same as that played out in the modern reenactment. "That reckoning from THALES to SOCRATES, the space of time is nearly equal to that betwixt my Lord Bacon and some late philosophers in *England,* who have begun to put the science of man on a new footing, and have engaged the attention, and excited the curiosity of the public" (*T,* xvi–xvii). Hume mentions, as falling under the Socratic image, "Mr. Locke, my Lord Shaftsbury, Dr. Mandeville, Mr. Hutchinson, Dr. Butler, etc." (*T,* xvii n). But they are not mentioned to clarify what "scepticism" as true philosophy means but only as coexplorers in the new territory of the science of man.

The Humean reenactment of Socratic moral philosophy appears in quite different historical circumstances from those of Socrates, however. The ancient Socratic problem was to find a space for philosophical self-inquiry in a polytheistic world in which philosophical speculation was a novelty. The Humean problem is to distinguish true philosophy from its corrupt forms in a culture all too disposed to philosophical-religious speculation. Socratic philosophy is philosophy in its youth, boldly trying its powers. Humean philosophy appears at a time of philosophical decadence and must struggle, not with pre-philosophical ignorance, but with a mode of its own activity, namely, theological bigotry, which "is really her [philosophy's] offspring" (*EU,* 133).

The dialectic of true and false philosophy in book 1, part 4 is Hume's own achievement and can be understood apart from the skeptical tradition. In later writings, however, Hume endows the drama of philosophical self-knowledge in part 4 with historical significance.

This first occurs in the *Abstract* of the *Treatise,* which Hume published anonymously in 1740 to promote his first work and to remove misunderstandings. There he says that "the philosophy contain'd in this book is very sceptical, and tends to give us a notion of the imperfections and narrow limits of human understanding" (*T,* 657). Human understanding is limited in that the primal source of all beliefs about the world is custom and not reflection: "We assent to our faculties, and employ our reason only because we cannot help it" (*T,* 657). He adds that "philosophy wou'd render us entirely Pyrrhonian were not nature too strong for it." But, of course, this insight into the limits of critical reflection is not itself determined by custom but is an achievement of philosophical speculation. It is that moment in the dialectic where the true philosopher recognizes that the attempt of philosophical reflection to emancipate itself totally from custom ends in *total doubt.* And in the *Abstract* this total doubt is identified, for the first time, with the historical school of Pyrrhonism. Looking back, we may now identify Pyrrhonism with "the arguments of that fantastic sect" in section 1, part 4, book 1 of the *Treatise,* which ends in "total scepticism," and with the "few extravagant sceptics" in section 2 who are brought to total doubt that we experience an external world (*T,* 183, 214).

In *A Letter from a Gentleman to His Friend in Edinburgh* (1745), Hume undertook to defend himself against the charge that the *Treatise* teaches a nihilistic sort of skepticism. Again skepticism is identified with "the Doctrine of the Pyrrhonian or Scepticks," and Pyrrhonism (as in the *Abstract* and by implication in the *Treatise*) is taken as an act of total doubt. Hume is at pains to show that this act of doubt is not directed to natural beliefs about the world but to higher-order acts of autonomous philosophical reflection which pretend to be totally emancipated from custom. Total doubt, then, is presented as a moment in the dialectical drama of philosophical self-knowledge designed to undermine a false view of philosophical autonomy and to restore the thinker to the autonomy of custom. "'Tis evident, that so extravagant a Doubt as that which Scepticism may seem to recommend, by destroying *every Thing,* really affects nothing . . . but was meant as a mere Philosophical Amusement, or Trial of *wit* and *Subtilty*" (*LG,* 20).

Hume's accusers in *A Letter from a Gentleman* have confused a moment in the dialectic with Hume's final position. Hume's subtle phenomenology of the mind of the false philosopher (what I have called the ascetic, revolutionary, and guilty modes of philosophical thought) are taken to be expressions of Hume's own mind. "And all those Principles, cited in the *Specimen* as Proofs of his Scepticism, are positively renounced in a few Pages afterwards, and called the Effects of Philosophical Melancholy and Delusion. These are his very Words; and his Accuser's overlooking them . . . is a Degree of Unfairness which appears to me altogether astonishing" (*LG,* 20). Hume's accusers may have been unfair, but many readers, otherwise sympathetic to Hume, by not understanding the dialectic of part 4, book 1 as an engagement of philosophy with its own nature, have made the same error of confusing a moment in the dialectic with its final result.

One result of skepticism is to shape the moral character of the true philosopher. The point of the Pyrrhonian moment in the dialectic is "to abate the Pride of *mere human Reasoners,* by showing them, that even with regard to Principles which seem the clearest, and which they are necessitated from the strongest Instincts of Nature to embrace, they are not able to attain a full Confidence and absolute Certainty. Modesty then, and Humility, with regard to the operations of our Natural Faculties, is the Result of Scepticism" (*LG,* 19). Along with the virtues of modesty and humility, the true philosopher has the virtue of *pietas.* In recognizing that "this boasted Reason . . . is not able fully to satisfy itself with regard to its own Operations, and must in some Measure fall into a Kind of implicite Faith, even in the most obvious and familiar Principles," the true philosopher realizes that his own reason does not, at the deepest level, determine judgment but that he must rely upon and is a participant in a general providence. Hume criticized belief in a particular providence; however, as a philosophical theist, he always held to belief in a general providence. Radical Pyrrhonian doubt makes this belief possible by reducing to naught the radical autonomy of philosophical reflection. The result of the dialectic is not only rational insight into the necessity of the autonomy of custom as a constituent of speculative thought, but an attitude of piety and affirmation toward the domain of custom taken as a whole.

As examples of the philosophical piety that only learned ignorance can bring, Hume mentions "Socrates the wisest and most religious of the Greek Philosophers, as well as Cicero among the Romans, who both of them carried their Philosophical Doubts to the highest Degree of Scepticism" (*LG,* 21). The fideistic tradition of the Christian Church also cultivated the skeptical attitude. "All the antient Fathers, as well as our first Reformers, are copious in representing the Weakness and Uncertainty of mere *human* Reason. And Monsieur *Huet* the learned Bishop of *Avaranches* . . . wrote also a Book on this very Topick [defense of Christian doctrine] wherein he endeavours to revive all the Doctrines of the ancient *Scepticks* or *Pyrrhonians*" (*LG,* 21).

This remark has seemed disingenuous to many, but the fact is that the philosophy of the *Treatise* (as Johann Hamann understood) is compatible with fideism.[1] What true philosophy shows is that our simplest and most natural beliefs, such as that we perceive substances, a public world, and causal connections, are founded on metaphorical identities. Consequently, "the great Mysteries of the Trinity and Incarnation" viewed under the aspect of philosophical autonomy, that is, independent of all custom and tradition, are not less intelligible than "the most obvious and familiar Principles," for example, that there is a public world, that there are causal connections, and so on (*LG,* 21). Speaking of himself, Hume considers it "ridiculous to assert that our Author denies the Principles of Religion, when he looks upon them as equally certain with the Objects of his Senses. If I be as much assured of these Principles, as that this Table at which I now write is before me; Can any Thing further be desired by the most rigorous Antagonist?" (*LG,* 20). To philosophical reflection, *independent of custom,* all beliefs about the real are equally mysterious.

Once reconciled to custom, we just find ourselves participating in a world of public objects, society, and the Divine. It is *within* the domain of custom that serious conflicts of belief occur, and it is within this domain that Hume criticizes religious beliefs. The general structure of Hume's criticism can be stated briefly. Causal judgments are founded on custom, and these conflict with certain religious beliefs, such as testimony that miracles have occurred, which are also founded on custom. How are we to choose? Hume observes that causal beliefs are unavoidable and are necessary to survival. This, of course, does not mean that custom, as causal judgment, reveals the truth about reality; it may be that miracles have occurred, but they are incompatible with a consistent application of the causal principle, and if there is to be any science at all, it must be consistent.

If it could be shown that religious beliefs were compatible with a consistent application of causal judgment, Hume could have no logical objection. And indeed he has no difficulty with and even affirms philosophical theism and the doctrine of a general providence. There is no inconsistency here because belief in philosophical theism is not itself the result of a particular causal judgment *within* the totality of the visible system. It is rather a religious sentiment prompted by a reflection on the *totality* of the visible system viewed as the result of purposive activity.

At the close of the *Dialogues,* Philo's confession of belief in a supreme author of the universe is coupled with frustration that speculation reveals so little about the nature of God. There naturally arises "some contempt of human reason, that it can give no solution more satisfactory with regard to so extraordinary and magnificent a question." And he adds that

> the most natural sentiment, which a well-disposed mind will feel on this occasion, is a longing desire and expectation, that Heaven would be pleased to dissipate, at least alleviate, this profound ignorance, by affording some more particular revelation to mankind, and making discoveries of the nature, attributes, and operations of the divine object of our Faith. A person, seasoned with a just sense of the imperfections of natural reason, will fly to revealed truth with the greatest avidity: While the haughty dogmatist, persuaded that he can erect a complete system of theology by the *mere help of philosophy,* disdains any farther aid, and rejects this adventitious instructor. To be a philosophical sceptic is, in a man of letters, the first and most essential step towards being a sound, believing Christian; a proposition which I would willingly recommend to the attention of Pamphilus: And I hope Cleanthes will forgive me

> for interposing so far in the education and instruction of his pupil. (*D*, 227–28; italics mine)

Just as the sublime thought of the visible system as a whole prompts the religious sentiment of philosophical theism, so "the most natural sentiment, which a well-disposed mind will feel" upon the contemplation of philosophical theism and a recognition of the limits of reason is "a longing desire and expectation" that the Divine will reveal itself in a more particular fashion. Philo does not himself affirm revelation, but he recognizes it as a demand of human nature and of a "well-disposed mind." Although true philosophy may criticize the world of culture that these deep demands generate, the principle of the autonomy of custom demands that they be respected. Accordingly, the self-confessed, philosophical theist Philo has no difficulty in recommending that Pamphilus be educated in a tradition which purports to contain revealed truth. And had he secured the position in moral philosophy at the University of Edinburgh, Hume would have been, and was prepared to be, an educator in just such a tradition.

Hume's most searching criticism of the doctrine of revelation is presented in the first *Enquiry*. In section 10 he attacks the doctrine of miracles and in section 11 the doctrine of a particular providence and of a future state. But these are not attacks on revelation in the sense required by the fideist. Rather Hume's attack is of the same sort launched by Philo in the *Dialogues*, namely a criticism of religious *philosophers* who attempt to establish religious doctrines using the ordinary principles of inductive reasoning. If this could be done, it would show that people who reject religious doctrines do so in violation of ordinary inductive canons. It is this claim that Hume attempts to refute.

But none of this rules out the fideistic alternative, which is that belief in miracles is an act of faith, or a gift of faith, which does subvert or at least suspend the ordinary canons of inductive reason; and so Hume concludes the criticism of miracles, as he concludes the *Dialogues*, on a fideistic note. Belief in miracles is itself a miracle in that it is contrary to ordinary inductive canons. "We may conclude, that the Christian Religion not only was at first attended with miracles, but even at this day cannot be believed by any reasonable person without one. Mere reason is insufficient to convince us of its veracity: And whoever is moved by Faith to assent to it, is conscious of a continued miracle in his own person, which subverts all the principles of his understanding, and gives him a determination to believe what is most contrary to custom and experience" (*EU*, 131). Fideism is the only way Christianity can be "reasonable."

Hume is right that belief in miracles is not and cannot be founded on testimony and the ordinary canons of induction. Belief in miracles presupposes a metaphysical background belief about the significance of the visible system as a whole. Let us call this metaphysical belief revelatory theism, the view that God created the visible system according to law but that such law may be suspended on particular occasions in acts of revelation. Revelatory theism contrasts with Hume's philosophical theism, which is the belief that the visible system is the result of purposive intelligence and thus lawlike, but that Divine providence is mysterious and can be understood only by a consistent and rigorous application of the causal principle. But both revelatory theism and philosophical theism are *metaphysical beliefs;* neither, in Hume's view, can be justified by *a priori* or *a posteriori* arguments. Both are metaphorical identities framed by poetic acts of the imagination and arise upon contemplation of the visible system as a whole. Both serve as ultimate control beliefs for interpreting particular events within the visible system. The philosophical theist *never* interprets any event as revelatory. The revelatory theist interprets some events as particular acts of God, but only if they are coherent with prior acts of revelation in a sacred tradition. Since both are ultimate metaphysical beliefs, neither admit of demonstration from anything more fundamental. When ultimate metaphysical beliefs clash, it is difficult to launch a criticism of the one from the other without begging the question. And indeed it is the charge of begging the question that is most often made by critics of Hume's argument against miracles in the *Enquiry.* But I think Hume is aware of this problem, and it is significant that in every place where he criticizes revelation, he is careful to direct the argument in such a way as to leave open the fideistic alternative.

How are we to understand the significance of this? In the *Treatise* Hume says that "if my philosophy, therefore, makes no addition to the arguments for religion, I have at least the satisfaction to think it takes nothing from them, but that every thing remains precisely as before" (*T,* 250–51). Hume's quarrel with religion goes on *within* the domain of custom which true philosophy has the authority to methodize and correct. Independent of custom, revelatory theism is as reasonable as philosophical theism. But within that domain it exhibits strains with other deeply established prejudices. First, revealed religion is incompatible with a consistent application of the causal principle, without which there can be no empirical science. Second, given the historic union of revealed religion and philosophy, much of revealed religion is an instance of a false philosophical consciousness. Hume attacks especially the pretensions of religion to a rational foundation. This massive philosophical self-deception enables the religious mind both to claim the authority of ordinary causal judgment and to subvert it when its interests so demand. Third, Hume attacks religious morality, which both participates in ordinary human morality (and necessarily so) and yet is in conflict with it. Fourth, Hume argues that revealed religion originates not in the love of truth but in fear. The logic of fear in revealed religious culture tends to produce a servile and crippled character which is unworthy of the greatness of mind admired in ordinary human morality and required of a true philosopher.

A fideistic revealed religion that abandoned philosophical pretenses and had a satisfactory reply to the above objections could enter Hume's world of custom alongside philosophical theism. That this is possible at all is due to the *pietas* inseparable from the principle of the autonomy of custom. Custom conceived as a totality has a sacred character for true philosophy, and this character receives its complete philosophical expression in the sentiment of philosophical theism, the view that the totality of custom is the work of a general providence. It is in this way that Hume's skeptical philosophy, in respect to religion, may be said to leave everything "precisely as before."

In this regard Hume's criticism of religion is radically different from a great variety of latter-day Enlightenment criticisms which, refusing to acknowledge the humility of creatures embedded in custom, seek in the name of radical philosophical autonomy to purge human consciousness of the sentiment of the sacred. *Pietas* is no part of the criticism of religion launched by such philosophers as Nietzsche, Marx, and Sartre, all of whom must, from a Humean view, be lost in corrupt forms of the philosophical act. Religion is one of the deeply established prejudices of common life and is presumed innocent until proven otherwise. That Hume found much that could be proven otherwise does not change the character of this presumption.

To sum up. The skepticism of the *Treatise* is presented in its own terms and is not identified with any philosophical tradition. It is only when Hume is forced to defend the *Treatise* in the *Abstract* and in the *Letter from a Gentleman* that he identifies his thought with the Pyrrhonian philosophical tradition. The *Letter* was written as a last-ditch attempt to secure a position at the University of Edinburgh by showing that the skepticism of the *Treatise* is not incompatible with the religious tradition Hume himself would have to participate in as professor of moral philosophy. He does this by identifying with the Pyrrhonian tradition but stressing that he is using it as a mode of reflection designed to "abate the Pride of mere human Reasoners" and that this is compatible with the fideism of the Church Fathers, the Reformers, and later Christian Pyrrhonists. I have argued that Hume is not disingenuous here and that Christian Pyrrhonism is a path open to a Humean true philosopher. But to say that Hume's critique of philosophy in the *Treatise* is compatible with Christian Pyrrhonism is, of course, not to say that it is a path Hume himself could take. And it is clear enough that he did not take it.

Skepticism in the *Enquiry Concerning Human Understanding*

The *Letter from a Gentleman* was written to defend Hume's candidacy for a position at the University of Edinburgh. The first *Enquiry* was written to pass judgment on the Edinburgh authorities who had unjustly denied him that position. The *Enquiry* is a modern reenactment of Socrates' apology before the Athenians—but there are important differences. Hume's defense is in reality a counteroffensive. Socrates knows that his speech is delivered to authorities who are philosophically unreflective, and since he has piety for his city and its laws, he accepts their judgment. The injury done to him was done out of ignorance and can be appreciated only by philosophers. But Hume pictures the Edinburgh authorities as "religious philosophers," and so the battle is not between philosophy and the vulgar; rather it is a conflict within philosophy itself. The struggle is between "true metaphysics" and the "false and adulterate" (*EU,* 12). This struggle is of a different order from that in which Socrates was engaged. The false philosopher cannot appeal, as the Athenians did, to the authority of custom, and the injury done to true philosophy by a corrupt philosophical consciousness cannot be accepted with pious deference. The war within philosophical consciousness is and must be a protracted conflict.

The deferential Pyrrhonian tone of the *Letter from a Gentleman,* which describes natural beliefs, such as belief in a public world, as a philosophical mystery on the same footing with belief in the Trinity, vanishes in the *Enquiry.* The same deference is found in the *Treatise,* where Hume observes that though his philosophy adds nothing to the arguments of religion, "it takes nothing from them" (*T,* 250–51). In the *Enquiry* nothing is to remain as before. In the first section he openly declares his intention of "carrying the war into the most secret recesses of the enemy" who lie in wait "to break in upon every unguarded avenue of the mind" (*EU,* 12, 11). And in the last section, using an image from the Inquisition, he consigns the books of the religious philosophers to the flames.

This reading of the *Enquiry* as a modern parallel to Plato's *Apology* receives added confirmation from an anonymous writer who published "A Short but Impartial Account of the Life and Character of the late David Hume" shortly after Hume's death, 25 August 1776, in Edinburgh's *Weekly Magazine.* The author judges that Hume's work in philosophy and history "has placed him on equality with the most celebrated names either in antient or modern story." He grants that Hume's philosophy is skeptical, but it is not the sort of skepticism that is incompatible with religion. The anticlerical strain in his thought was a reaction to the religious barriers which prevented him in 1745 from being appointed to the chair in moral philosophy at the University of Edinburgh. "It was from this period that he declared open and irreconcileable war, not only against the presbytery of Edinburgh, but against the whole body of the clergy."

Hume dedicated *The Natural History of Religion* to his cousin, Reverend John Home. In doing so he claimed to be reviving the practice of the ancients who, out of a love of liberty, dedicated their books not to the great but to friends and equals as expressions of genuine esteem and affection. And he follows the example of the ancient skeptics who did not allow disagreements about abstract principle to poison friendship and who were resolved "never to quarrel about principles, while they agreed in inclinations and manners. Science was often the subject of disputation, never of animosity. Cicero, an Academic, addressed his philosophical treatises, sometimes to Brutus, a stoic; sometimes to Atticus, an epicurean" (*NHR,* 19), and so Hume, "the true sceptic," dedicates *The Natural History of Religion* to John Home, a Christian minister. The cement of this friendship was "a common passion for science and letters," and Hume observed, "I still admired your genius, even when I imagined, that you lay under the influence of prejudice; and you sometimes told me, that you excused my errors, on account of the candor and sincerity, which, you thought, accompanied them" (*NHR,* 20). Hume exemplifies here that diffidence which, in the *Treatise,* he said a true skeptic will have in regard to his own speculative beliefs and doubts. Common life is an order of affection and loyalty, not of speculative principle.

But if Hume could find in Home a true philosopher despite his theology, Home found in Hume a true Christian without theology. Late in his life Home wrote "A Sketch of the Character of Mr. Hume and Diary of a Journey from Morpeth to Bath 23 April–1 May, 1776" in which he observes that "so general was the respect to his Candor and merit that even good natured believers said of him . . . that he was the best Christian in the world without knowing it."[2] Home judged *The Natural History of Religion* to be Hume's "capital production" and thought that even the essay "Of Miracles," viewed as "a vindication of the order of nature and a defense of divine Providence against Imposters and Enthusiasts," may "be regarded as the most pious of all human compositions."

It may well have been Home who published anonymously a long and remarkable poem on the front page of Edinburgh's leading newspaper *The Caledonian Mercury,* on 6 September 1769, welcoming Hume back to Edinburgh after an absence of some six years.[3] A part of the poem is worth quoting as a recognition of Hume's philosophical theism and the perception of his character as a true philosopher.

> O thou to Albion's deathless honour born,
> Whom worth, wit, wisdom, eloquence, adorn;
> To whom the gods their richest gifts impart,
> The soundest judgment and the soundest heart:
> O first of sages! whose immortal page
> In spite of bigot zeal and party rage,
> Illumes the lamp of reason in the mind,
> And holds a faithful mirror to mankind;
> No gaudy nothings in the works reside;
> No air-built systems, flatt'ring human pride;
> No venal incense burnt at Fortune's shrine;
> To pamper malice no invective thine.
> From Virtue's basis, by no passions hurl'd,
> You walk innoxious through a noxious world;
> In silence hear its furious spleen and spite,
> And trust posterity to do you right.
> Whate'er thy modest disquisitions scan,
> (Always the friend of truth and friend of man)
> You take the truly philosophic road
> "That Leads through nature up to nature's God."

All the virtues embodied in Hume's conception of the true philosopher are present here. "The soundest judgment and the soundest heart" echo Hume's teaching that the order of affection is prior to the order of reflection. In another passage the author finds true piety in Hume and not in the ideological enthusiasms of a warring Christendom that had plagued Scotland for centuries:

> Long civil discord vast confusion spread,
> Her sons were furies, and the Muses fled;
> Yet the pretence to piety so nice,

> Learning was held profane, and genius vice;
> As your immortal annals well disclose,
> Your patriot-bosom weeping o'er her woes.

In the "weeping" patriot, there is an image of Hume's true Stoic, "the true sage and patriot," who can hold together both tears and greatness of mind. "The softest benevolence, the most undaunted resolution, the tenderest sentiments, the most sublime love of virtue, all these animate successively his transported bosom" (*E,* 153).

In the *Treatise,* Hume had shown that custom, or the order of affection, is prior to the order of reflection. Custom, considered as an order entirely independent of reflection, is a philosophical idealization just as is the idea of reflection considered entirely independent of custom. In concrete experience the two are internally connected. General rules inform custom and, indeed, are "able to impose on the very senses" (*T,* 374). This allows him to speak of the senses as being the same as the imagination: "my senses, or rather imagination" (*T,* 217).

Custom and reflection, then, are not Cartesian substances but dialectically related concepts. Because they are internally connected, their ideal characters can be distinguished only through what Hume called a "distinction of reason," and in this case the ideal distinction emerges only by working through the dialectic of true and false philosophy in part 4 of book 1. What is discovered is that, although they are internally connected, reason presupposes the authority of custom. But what happens when this truth of true philosophy is violated, not by this or that individual but by an entire culture? What happens when reflection seeks to dominate and pretends, in effect, to have the authority of custom? Something like this had happened, Hume thought, in Christian Europe where religious philosophy had sought to impose its dominion over the whole of life. In this case pious deference to custom was not possible, and true philosophy had no recourse but to expose the corrupt philosophical consciousness that informs the usurpation. The Hume of the *Treatise* and the *Letter from a Gentleman* was prepared to reach an accommodation with the Christian piety and the sacred stories of his native city. What he confronted instead was the fury of the "religious philosophers." With that there could be no accommodation, for it is the nature of true philosophy to do battle with the false, which is its dialectical other.

One charge against Hume's skeptical philosophy, which he had to contend with throughout his career, is that it tends to undermine the moral and political order of society. William Warburton wrote of

Hume's thought that "there are vices of the mind as well as the body: and I think a wickeder mind, and more obstinately bent on public mischief, I never knew."[4] The charge was still being made in 1770 when James Beattie published *An Essay on the Nature and Immutability of Truth in Opposition to Sophistry and Scepticism,* which was an attempt to refute Hume and was enormously popular, going through eleven editions in the first decade after its publication. Beattie observes that "Mr. Hume, more subtle, or less reserved, than any of his predecessors, hath gone to still greater lengths in the demolition of common sense."[5] And in 1773 Edinburgh's *Weekly Magazine* published an article entitled "Character of the Works of David Hume, Esq." in which the anonymous author wonders if Hume's picture of human nature is not "the worst portrait that ever was drawn." Hume's conception of morals is utterly nihilistic, abandoning virtue entirely "to the sport of human passions and customs." But the author concludes with the comforting thought that "this monster of learning, so treacherous to the peace of mankind, has been combated and subdued by more than one antagonist."[6]

The parallelism of Hume's ordeal with Edinburgh and Socrates' ordeal with Athens is most clearly seen in section 11 of the *Enquiry,* entitled "Of a Particular Providence and of a Future State." This section is a dialogue between two friends, one of whom nominally stands for Hume, but both express views that may plausibly be attributed to Hume. The dialogue is the embryo of what will later become *The Dialogues Concerning Natural Religion,* and it is worth noting that the dialogue begins with an observation that the persecution of philosophy is greater in modern times than in ancient. The "banishment of Protagoras" and "the death of Socrates" are exceptions. For the most part, philosophy, however extravagant, existed in harmony with the civic religion. In what is difficult not to see as an oblique reference to his own banishment, Hume drives home the point that even "Epicurus lived at Athens to an advanced age, in peace and tranquillity: Epicureans were even admitted to receive the sacerdotal character, and to officiate at the alter, in the most sacred rites of the established religion: And the public encouragement of pensions and salaries was afforded equally, by the wisest of all the Roman emperors, to the professors of every sect of philosophy" (*EU,* 132–33).

Roger Emerson has argued that the religious conflict between Hume and the Edinburgh authorities was not as great as has been supposed and that it is possible to think that Hume was genuinely surprised at the charge of impiety. Behind the religious and philosophical reasons was a battle over patronage that Hume's friends were too weak to carry. Had he been accepted for a professorship at either Edinburgh or Glasgow, he would have had to sign the Westminster Confession; he would have been required to attend church, and at Glasgow to lead students in prayer. Hume was known by his supporters, and they thought his character sufficiently religious to carry out these duties.[7] We must be careful to avoid the fallacy of premature secularization when interpreting eighteenth-century thinkers. Few in the eighteenth century were post-Nietzschean atheists. But whatever Hume's religious views may have been, he was prepared, like the Epicurean, to fully participate in the sacred rites and teachings of the established religion.

Ancient religion was tolerant because it was sacred tradition devoid of philosophical interests. Modern religion, however, has been captured by those with a corrupt philosophical consciousness, who exhibit a "bigotted jealousy" against philosophical opponents who would engage them in fair debate. The real threat to the peace of society comes not from sacred tradition or secular philosophy but from religious philosophy. One of the characters in the dialogue assumes the form of Epicurus, who must defend himself against the charge of subversion and impiety before the Athenians. Hume is careful to point out that the speech is directed not to "the mob of Athens" but to "the more philosophical part" of the audience, namely the "religious philosophers" (*EU,* 134–35).

It is these who have transmuted a sacred tradition into a philosophical system. "The religious philosophers, not satisfied with the tradition of your forefathers, and doctrine of your priests (in which I willingly acquiesce), indulge a rash curiosity, in trying how far they can establish religion upon the principles of reason," but "they thereby excite, instead of satisfying, the doubts, which naturally arise from a diligent and scrutinous inquiry" (*EU,* 135). Philosophical disputes governed by the principles of ultimacy, autonomy, and dominion are both implacable and endless. Thus it is the religious philosophers who disturb the peace of society and the security of government. In contrast, "When priests and poets, supported by your authority, O Athenians, talk of a golden or silver age, which preceded the present state of vice and misery, I hear them with attention and with reverence. But when philosophers, who pretend to neglect authority, and to cultivate reason, hold the same discourse, I pay them not, I own, the same obsequious submission and pious deference" (*EU,* 138).

Hume concludes that "the state ought to tolerate every principle of philosophy; nor is there an instance, that any government has suffered in its political interests by such indulgence. There is no enthusiasm among philosophers" (*EU,* 147). This conclusion must be read with some qualification. First, religious philosophy is *philosophy,* albeit of a false form, and there is enthusiasm among religious philosophers. Second, Hume recognizes enthusiasm in purely *secular* philosophy in the *Treatise,* second *Enquiry,* and in the *Essays* (*T,* 272; *EM,* 341–43; *E,* 60–62, 465–66). What Hume means here is that, in the case of secular philosophy, there is no enthusiasm among philosophers that could pose a threat to society or government, but only because philosophical reflection is confined to a few and because its "doctrines are not very alluring to the people" (*EU,* 147). Therefore mass ideological movements based on purely secular philosophical doctrine are not likely. As I shall show in a later chapter, however, Hume came to see, by actually confronting one, that mass ideological movements of a corrupt secular philosophy are indeed possible.

The other argument for toleration is that philosophical reflection is internal to the sciences, which are beneficial to the state. Any restriction on philosophical reflection made for the sake of purging it of "philosophical enthusiasm," though worthy in itself, would have bad consequences for the sciences and for the state. So false philosophy, as well as the true, should be tolerated. But that form of false philosophy which is religious poses a special problem precisely because of its popularity. Here Hume inverts the image of the Inquisition and casts the books of the religious philosophers into the flames. As Plato purged the city of the poets, Hume purges it of religious philosophers. But he does not eliminate religion in the sense of sacred tradition. For this the clergy are retained, but not the priests. "By *Priests* I understand only the Pretenders to Power and Dominion, and to a superior Sanctity of Character, distinct from Virtue and good Morals. These are very different from Clergymen, who are set apart [Hume added "by the laws" in 1742, making clear that the clergy are subject to civil authority] to the care of sacred Matters, and the conducting our public Devotions with greater Decency and Order. There is no Rank of Men more to be respected than the latter" (*E,* 617 n). Priests are those agents through whom the speculative doctrines of the religious philosophers are imposed upon the philosophically unreflective vulgar and are made popular. Priests are the instruments through which the principle of dominion in a corrupt philosophical consciousness that has taken on the form of religious philosophy seeks total control in the world.

With this Hume has inverted the inversion of the Edinburgh authorities. It is not secular philosophy (true or false) that is a threat to the state but religious philosophy, and it alone is not to be tolerated. But why should not all forms of philosophy be tolerated, religious as well as secular? The reason is that the speculative doctrines of religious philosophers are Midas-touch transformations of vulgar sacred tradition and, being reworked by the priests for popular consumption, *are* "very alluring to the people," and so can generate mass ideological movements. It is to suppress and control such movements in the name of the public interest that true philosophy entertains the fantasy of burning the books of the religious philosophers and banishing their retainers, the priests. Although this was only a fantasy spawned by reflecting on the ideality of things, there is a truth in the fantasy about which Hume was serious and which took on a more practical form in his "Idea of a Perfect Commonwealth" (1752), where a state religion is proposed that could monitor and suppress the formation of mass ideological religious movements. In this model republic the "Presbyterian government is established," and there are six councils of state, one of which is the "council of religion and learning," which "inspects the universities and clergy" (*E,* 520, 519).

The dialectic of part 4, book 1 of the *Treatise,* which first opened up the distinction between true and false philosophy, is recast in shorter form in the *Enquiry* as section 12, entitled "Of the Academical or Sceptical Philosophy." Here Pyrrhonism appears not as a historical school but as a philosophical-historical image representing a necessary moment in the dialectic: One must be "thoroughly convinced of the force of the Pyrrhonian doubt, and of the impossibility, that anything, but the strong power of natural instinct, could free us from it" (*EU,* 162). Pyrrhonism is the natural result of a consistent philosophy that seeks to purge itself of custom, and no thought is philosophical thought unless it has, in one moment of its natural history, sought to do just that. It is for this reason that the Pyrrhonian moment in the dialectic is necessary. The impossibility of total emancipation from custom is experienced, not merely as a formal relation, but as total despair and melancholy which drives thought back to the once-rejected domain of custom. It is only in this domain that recovery can occur. Looking back, the thinker sees his former alienation from custom as a dream from which the Pyrrhonian shock has liberated him.

But the dialectic leading to the Pyrrhonian moment is not entirely a dream, for it contains an insight from which the philosopher cannot escape and in the light of which he can never be the same. The true philosopher, rooted now in custom, has seen through to what he did not expect to see when he first undertook the "voyage" of philosophical reflection, namely, the "strange infirmities of human understanding, even in its most perfect state, and when most accurate and cautious in its determinations" (*EU,* 161). By virtue of the principles of autonomy and dominion, the philosopher had set himself against the "other," those lost in custom: the masses, the many, the vulgar, the middle class, the unraised consciousness of those who participate in a customary way of life. These are all antagonists invented by the false philosopher to make philosophical unmasking possible, which is the only path to philosophical dominion.

Philosophical laughter was at the expense of this other. But having awakened from his dream, the philosopher sees that the joke is on him, and he is now "the first to join in the laugh against himself" (*EU,* 160). The Pyrrhonian "shows . . . his own and our weakness" (*EU,* 159). I have shown that, as the object of his own joke, the Humean true philosopher assumes the role of the fool—and folly, so conceived, is the beginning of wisdom. The principle of dominion had relegated the vulgar to the status of subordination and "deformity" (*T,* 264), but in the mode of philosophical folly they are now seen as one's "fellows" and as equals. Of false philosophers Hume says that "Pyrrhonism might abate their pride, by showing them, that the few advantages, which they may have obtained over their fellows, are but inconsiderable, if compared with the universal perplexity and confusion, which is inherent in human nature" (*EU,* 161).

Hume, then, finds truth in the Pyrrhonian tradition, but the recognition of this truth is made possible by the dialectic of true and false philosophy first worked out in the *Treatise,* which made no reference to the Pyrrhonian or any other particular tradition of skepticism. Pyrrhonism appears in the dialectic as a true and necessary moment in the act of philosophical self-knowledge, but it is not the whole truth of that act. Pagan Pyrrhonism sought to suppress beliefs about the ultimate while refusing to argue that such beliefs could not possibly be known to be true (that would be a negative form of dogmatism). The Pyrrhonians sought a furtive peace of mind in custom while remaining vulnerable to any philosophical claim about the ultimate that had not been brought into suspense of judgment. For Hume, however, man is a believing animal: "The *imagination* of man is naturally sublime" (*EU,* 162). Happiness is not achieved by suppressing beliefs about the ultimate, but by methodizing and correcting them in the light of the whole of common life.

In section 12 of the *Enquiry,* Hume for the first time gives a name, taken from the philosophical tradition, to what he had described in the

Treatise as "true philosophy." He now calls it "*mitigated* scepticism" and identifies it with a particular tradition: "*academical* philosophy" (*EU,* 161). Academic skepticism is said to be "the result of this Pyrrhonism, or *excessive* scepticism, when its undistinguished doubts are, in some measure corrected by common sense and reflection" (*EU,* 161). To say that Academic skepticism is the "result" of Pyrrhonism is just to say that it is the final moment of the dialectic where philosophical reflection finally reaches a true understanding of its own nature. In the *Enquiry* Hume does not mention any historical figure who exemplifies what he means by "Academic scepticism." And, strictly speaking, there is no one; for no one prior to Hume had worked out the dialectic of true and false philosophy. There were, of course, intimations in the philosophical tradition of that reasoning which leads to true philosophy, and Hume's view appears to be that, in its attempt to fix beliefs about the real, the Academic skeptical tradition anticipates in some fashion his own philosophy. But the source richest in intimations which Hume saw himself as developing was Cicero, who may be identified with the Academic tradition, and Hume so identifies him (*NHR,* 19). But it was not Cicero's speculative philosophy that inspired Hume. "The abstract philosophy of Cicero has lost its credit" (*E,* 243). What Hume admired in Cicero was his eloquence, the style and idiom of his thought: the Ciceronian way of life and being that contains those dispositions which make up a good part of the character of Hume's true Stoic.

Hume taught that the only antidote to false philosophy (especially in its religious form) is true philosophy (*T,* 271; *EU,* 12). And William Cullen reported that Hume maintained on his deathbed "that he had not yet finished the great work" of freeing his countrymen "from the Christian Superstition."[8] Hume finds anticipations of his own struggle with the religious philosophers in the Academic skeptical tradition. He observed in the *Natural History of Religion* that philosophers of antiquity, like their modern counterparts, were not entirely free of religious superstition. Of the ancient philosophers he says that though "some parts of the national religion hung loose upon the minds of men, other parts adhered more closely to them: And it was the great business of the sceptical philosophers to show, that there was no more foundation for one than for the other" (*NHR,* 80). Hume mentions the arguments of Cotta in Cicero's *On the Nature of the Gods,* who defends the Academic philosophy against the Epicurean and Stoic, and his teacher Carneades, who "had employed the same method of reasoning" (*NHR,* 80). Hume sees himself and the Academic skeptical tradition as both engaged in the same "great business."

The common project takes on universal meaning in the *Dialogues,* which were modeled on Cicero's *On the Nature of the Gods.* Philo, the skeptic, recommends a total suspension of judgment on "all religious Systems," observing that "if every attack . . . and no Defence, among Theologians, is successful; how compleat must be *his* Victory, who remains always, with all Mankind, on the Offensive, and has himself no fixt Station or abiding City, which he is ever, on any Occasion, oblig'd to defend" (*D,* 187). By *mankind* Hume does not mean men as they exist in the world, for they believe in the systems of the religious philosophers. Mankind here is an idealization of true philosophy and is identified with what Hume refers to throughout his writings as "common life" and in the *Enquiry* as the "*party* of humankind" (*EM,* 275), that is, mankind as it would be if purged of a false philosophical and religious consciousness, which is the residue left after the skeptic has done his work.

The dialectic enables Hume to distinguish between true and false forms of skepticism among both the ancients and moderns. Hume aspires in the *Treatise* to be a "true sceptic" (*T,* 273), but skepticism, like any other philosophy, can get lost in the heroic moment of philosophical reflection. Pyrrhonism is a false form of skepticism because total suspension of judgment cannot be the path to human well-being. We can no more refrain from beliefs about the real than we can refrain from breathing. There is, of course, a truth in Pyrrhonism, but it can be appreciated only after it is detoxified of its corrupt aspects and given its proper place in the dialectic.

Modern instances of false skepticism appear in the first *Enquiry* in two forms: "Antecedent Scepticism" and "Consequent Scepticism." Hume presents Descartes as the best example of the former and Berkeley as the best example of the latter. Both are heroic forms of philosophical reflection.

Antecedent skepticism, in an attempt to free the mind of prejudice, proposes a universal doubt concerning not only all former beliefs but also our very faculties until these can be certified by some original principle about which we cannot be mistaken. Hume argues that there is no such principle, nor, if there were, could a science be founded upon it without presupposing some of the very beliefs and faculties which are still methodologically suppressed. There are, of course, principles about which we are strongly convinced, but this is only because of the unacknowledged influence of prejudice, and none of these "has a prerogative above others, that are self-evident and convincing" (*EU,* 150). Here we have that "monstrous offspring" which emerged in one moment of the dialectic in the *Treatise,* where the attempt to escape prejudice ends in hiding a prejudice behind the mask of autonomous reason (*T,* 215). This is a form of philosophical self-deception that is virtually invincible, for how can "reason" be prejudice?

Consequent skepticism assumes the validity of our faculties but discovers upon inquiry that they are either fallacious or incapable of reaching a fixed belief on any subject. The example Hume gives of this sort of skepticism is the failure of modern philosophers to provide a rational account of what it means to perceive a public world. He reworks, in shorter form, the dialectic of the senses, imagination, and reason, which he had explored in "Of Scepticism with Regard to the Senses" and "Of the Modern Philosophy" in the *Treatise.* Here again, as in the *Treatise,* the modern conception of primary and secondary qualities, instead of explaining our conception of a public world, leads to its annihilation. He finds in the philosophy of "Dr. Berkeley" the "best lessons of scepticism, which are to be found either among the ancient or modern philosophers, Bayle not excepted" (*EU,* 155 n). Hume is aware that Berkeley's intention is to refute skeptics, atheists, and freethinkers. Nevertheless, "that all his arguments, though otherwise intended, are, in reality, merely sceptical, appears from this, *that they admit of no answer and produce no conviction.* Their only effect is to cause that momentary amazement and irresolution and confusion, which is the result of scepticism" (*EU,* 155 n).

Here skepticism is presented in its negative moment as false philosophy. (Berkeley's philosophy is "merely sceptical.") It is false because it works to block conviction and to alienate from common life; the search for truth and the establishment of belief are goals of true philosophy. Other terms Hume uses to describe this false form of skepticism are "extravagant scepticism," "*total* scepticism," "*excessive* scepticism," and "Pyrrhonism or the excessive principles of scepticism" (*T,* 183, 214; *EU,* 158–59). All of these are cases of philosophical thought in its heroic form. But the important point to make here about skepticism as false philosophy, which Hume goes out of his way to make about Berkeley, is that it is not the intentionality of an argument that makes it skeptical in this nihilistic sense. Any argument that subverts a domain of common life (such as belief in a public world), transforming one of its parts or aspects into the whole, is nihilistic in that it causes that "momentary amazement and irresolution and confusion, which is the result of scepticism." This is what Berkeley did in the paradoxical maxim, "To be is to be perceived." The result is an act of philosophical dominion that leaves participants in common life dazzled and confused.

From this confusion there are only two avenues of escape. One is to believe in the reality of the transmutation and to fall under the dominion of a "philosophical enthusiasm." The other is to push on with the dialectic to the end and to arrive at a true understanding of the nature of critical reflection. Hume's view of the philosophical tradition is that it is the former path that is most often taken.

Skepticism in this extended and admittedly unhistorical sense, which Hume applies to Berkeley, is just another name for false philosophy in all its forms: ascetic, revolutionary, and guilty. The expressions "true philosophy" and "false philosophy" are interchangeable with "true scepticism" and "false skepticism." Thus in the *Enquiry,* as in the *Treatise,* "scepticism" gets its meaning not from identification with any school of thought, but by reference to Hume's own dialectic of true and false philosophy.

Hume's complicated use of the term *skepticism* has been confusing to his readers from the first. It was paradoxical of Hume to call the new science of human nature "the sceptical philosophy" and in the *Enquiry* to talk of "sceptical solutions" to problems when "scepticism" meant to his readers (and to Hume also in one of its modes) doubt, confusion, and something nihilistic. The attempt to distinguish between true and false forms of skepticism only made matters worse.

But if the *topos* of Hume's philosophy is, as I have argued, a critique of philosophy by itself; if its central feature is the dialectic of true and false philosophy, then the whole of that philosophy could be stated without any reference to skepticism at all. The similar critiques of philosophy offered by Hegel, Nietzsche, and Heidegger are not cast in the idiom of skepticism. Why then did Hume choose to cast his philosophy in that form?

One reason is suggested by the nature of Pyrrhonism in contrast to the other philosophical sects of antiquity. Philosophical reflection was engaged in by these sects for the sake of achieving happiness or eudaemonia. But reflection spoke in many contrary voices: Platonism, Stoicism, Epicureanism, Cynicism, Eclecticism, and so forth. It was the genius of Pyrrhonism to raise the question of whether philosophical reflection itself is not the main barrier to eudaemonia. This is, of course, a paradoxical question, for it is a *philosophical* question that throws the worth of philosophy itself into question. But however paradoxical the question, it was an advance in the history of philosophy. Prior to the Pyrrhonians, philosophy was a transparent medium through which thought could view and have dominion over the whole of life. Insofar as it examined itself, philosophy confirmed this unique position of sovereign spectator. But the Pyrrhonians opened up another possibility, namely, that philosophical reflection, if consistently pursued, is not self-certifying but self-subverting. In subverting itself philosophy reveals the authority of its other: the philosophically unreflective domain of custom, which henceforth must be taken seriously in *its* own terms.

If the mark of philosophical profundity is to have achieved a higher form of self-knowledge, then there is a sense in which the Pyrrhonians were the most profound of the ancient philosophers, for they alone succeeded in forcing philosophy into a radical examination of itself. Since a radical critique of philosophy is the foundation of Hume's own philosophy, it is not surprising that he should take inspiration from the Pyrrhonian tradition.

Why then does Hume identify true philosophy with the Academic skeptical tradition and not the Pyrrhonian? A number of commentators have suggested that Hume's own philosophy is more in accord with the Pyrrhonian tradition. There is much to be said for that view. One good reason Hume may have had for not identifying with the Pyrrhonians is the traditional image of Pyrrho as an absurd figure whose suspension of judgment made him vulnerable to walking off cliffs and the like. This is exactly the picture Hume draws of Pyrrhonism in the *Enquiry.* Were suspension of judgment "universally and steadily to prevail," all "discourse, all action would immediately cease, and men remain in a total lethargy till the necessities of nature, unsatisfied, put an end to their miserable existence" (*EU,* 160).

The view of Pyrrhonism presented by Sextus Empiricus in *The Outlines of Pyrrhonism* is quite different. There a practical criterion is offered to guide judgment and action: instinct, natural inclination, piety for the customs and traditions of one's country, and the instruction of the arts. And this appears very like Hume's view of philosophy as reflections upon common life methodized and corrected. But even in Sextus Empiricus it is possible to detect an *obsession* with suspension of judgment as a way of life. On one way of reading Sextus Empiricus, judgments afforded by the practical criterion are not about reality but about appearance. One must not say that "honey is sweet" but that "it appears that honey is sweet." Judgment must be kept strictly on the appearance side of the line dividing the categories of appearance and reality. The Pyrrhonian does not claim that reality cannot be known; that would be dogmatism. He leaves the question open and is willing to consider any claim about the real, but experience has taught him that peace of mind does not come from theorizing about the real, and so the point of his inquiry is always to bring theorizing to bay by showing that the contrary of whatever theory is seized upon is as well supported as that theory. As a way of life, therefore, the point of Pyrrhonism is the melancholy one of having to stay as much as possible on the appearance side of the dividing line between appearance and reality while at the same time being constantly distracted by the possibility of having to cross it.

This is a plausible reading of Sextus Empiricus, and Hume may well have read him this way. His own view was that it is natural and unavoidable for human beings to make judgments about the real, and the attempt to block this inclination leads not to peace of mind but to anxiety. The task of true philosophy is not to suppress speculative beliefs about the real but to understand what it means to make them and to moderate them. It is perhaps worth noting that in his account of how the Pyrrhonian is shaken out of his suspension of judgment by "the first and most trivial event in life," Hume says that he is left "the same, in every point of action and *speculation, with the philosophers of every other sect* or with those who never concerned themselves in any philosophical researches" (*EU,* 160; italics mine).

The tradition of Academic skepticism afforded Hume an image of philosophy as being content with making probable judgments, whether or not they are true of the real. But perhaps the most compelling reason for identification with the Academic tradition was Cicero, whose civic humanism, eloquence, and style of life and thought were greatly admired by the learned world of the eighteenth century.

My concern in this chapter has not been to determine whether Hume's understanding of past thinkers is correct nor to determine the historical sources of his thought; it has been, rather, to understand how the dialectic of true and false philosophy was used to construct a philosophical tradition that, in turn, became part of Hume's own philosophical self-understanding. That tradition is the skeptical tradition, which Hume takes to be historically the deepest development of philosophy and, when methodized and corrected, the perfection of philosophy. In the *Treatise* the "true sceptic" and the "true philosopher" are the same, and the skeptical tradition appears as an idealization having virtually no historical content. In later writings, however, when Hume is forced to defend the *Treatise,* a group of skeptical heroes and villains begins to emerge: Socrates, Cicero, Cotta, pagan Pyrrhonists, Christian Pyrrhonists, the Church Fathers, Bishop Huet and Bishop Avaranches, the Academic skeptics, and modern skeptics such as Montaigne, Bayle, Descartes, and Berkeley. In Hume's hands these historical beings are transformed into philosophical-historical images that represent necessary moments in the dialectic of true and false philosophy. With a little imagination, one could order Hume's use of these images into necessary moments of the dialectic: a Socratic moment, a Cartesian moment, a Berklean moment, a pagan Pyrrhonian moment, a Christian Pyrrhonian moment, an Academic moment, and so forth.

Skepticism in the *Essays*

Another place where the skeptic appears as a philosophical-historical image and as a moment in a dialectical pattern of thought is in the quartet of essays "The Epicurean," "The Stoic," "The Platonist," and "The Sceptic," which explore the question of the good life. Here skepticism appears not only in the mode of theoretical wisdom but also in the mode of practical wisdom. I have argued that these essays are arranged in a dialectical pattern that resembles the dialectical structure of "Scepticism with Regard to the Senses" in book 1, part 4 of the *Treatise.* In both cases various positions are offered on a first-order question. Proponents of these positions assume that the philosophical reflection engaged in is unproblematic. Philosophical reflection is like light and needs only to be properly aimed at its object. The skeptic, however, knows that there are true and false forms of reflection and an inherent tendency in all philosophical reflection to corruption and self-deceit.

The skeptic, or true philosopher, cannot immediately give a speech on the nature of the good life but must first make a critical judgment about the philosophical medium that stains and colors its object (*E*, 159). Only after that judgment, and in the light of it, can he give his own speech on the human good. Hume's Sceptic accepts the Stoic's speech on what human excellence is, the life of "action and virtue" (*E*, 168). But the intervening meditation on the limits of philosophy transforms the Stoic's speech into the skeptical mode of theoretical and practical wisdom.

The assumption behind the speeches of the Epicurean, Stoic, and Platonist is that philosophy is the "*medicine of the mind,*" that it can determine what human happiness is, reduce it to rules, and then apply them to practice (*E*, 169). To this the skeptic has two objections. First, there is a difference between human happiness and human excellence. Hume may have in mind Shaftesbury and Hutcheson, who taught that Providence has arranged things so that happiness and excellence coincide. The Sceptic does not deny that there is a standard of human excellence, and he agrees with what the Stoic says it is, but he argues that such a life does not necessarily lead to happiness nor a failure to unhappiness.

Second, the Sceptic rejects an assumption made by the three orations on the good life, namely that philosophical reflection can be the source of conduct. All assume that we can, through theorizing, know what the good life is, and that, through the formulation and application of rules, virtuous and happy conduct can flow from that knowledge. But to believe that is to come to the "philosopher as to a *cunning man,* to learn something by magic or witchcraft" (*E,* 161). The primary source of conduct is not reflection but custom. Happiness, as well as love of excellence, depends upon the dispositions we are born with and the dispositions shaped by inherited moral traditions. There are rules of prudence ("common prudence and discretion") which may be helpful in attempts to order this mix into a pattern of excellence and happiness. Philosophers may bring them to attention, refine them, and systematize them, but none of this can be effective unless there is a character shaped by nature and inherited moral traditions disposed to receive them. And on the original formation of character, philosophy is and must be silent. Hume's diffidence here about the value of formulating rules for leading the good life is of a piece with that expressed in the *Treatise* about forming rules for making causal judgments (*T,* 175).

To say that reflection is not the primary source of human conduct is not to say that it has no influence. Hume taught that man is a reflective being as well as a being of custom. True philosophy can point out those authors whose writings have a tendency to tranquilize and humanize the dispositions of those whose sentiments are antecedently disposed to receive them. The contemplation of a certain kind of literature by long study and habit can strengthen those virtues necessary for the life of human excellence. What authors did Hume recommend for improving the character of the true philosopher? We must speak of Hume and not the Sceptic, for he interrupts with a long footnote, distinguishing himself from the Sceptic on this point and arguing that philosophical reflection has a stronger influence in perfecting and strengthening character than the Sceptic has allowed. Hume's advice is this:

> Assist yourself by a frequent perusal of the entertaining moralists: Have recourse to the learning of PLUTARCH, the imagination of LUCIAN, the eloquence of CICERO, the wit of SENECA, the gaiety of MONTAIGNE, the sublimity of SHAFTESBURY. Moral precepts, so couched, strike deep, and fortify the mind against the illusions of passion. But trust not altogether to external aid: By habit and study acquire that philosophical temper which both *gives force to reflec-*

> *tion,* and by rendering a great part of your happiness independent, takes off the edge from all disorderly passions, and tranquilizes the mind. Despise not these helps; but confide not too much in them neither; unless nature has been favourable in the temper, with which she has endowed you. (*E,* 179 n; italics mine)

Two comments must be made about this passage. First, Hume here appropriates and transforms the Skeptical and Stoical traditions, unifying them into a philosophical-historical image that governs his understanding of true philosophy as practical wisdom. Lucian is an ancient skeptic; Montaigne a modern Christian Pyrrhonist; Cicero, Plutarch, and Seneca are ancient Stoics; Shaftesbury is an instance of Hume's own modern Stoicism that unites greatness of mind with extensive benevolence. Together they form a poetic whole in which we may find represented those virtues that constitute the character of Hume's true philosopher: philosophical humility, piety, folly, eloquence, greatness of mind, and extensive benevolence.

Second, none of the six authors are valued because of their theorizing, nor because of the propositional content of their teachings. T. S. Eliot once said that a thing can be communicated before it is understood. What gives these authors the power to influence conduct is the style and eloquence of their writing: they are "entertaining moralists." And it is not moral precepts as such but precepts "so couched" that they "strike deep, and fortify the mind." Here again eloquence is essential to Humean true philosophy.

Hume took the skeptical tradition to be the highest development of that disposition in human beings to inquire—what he called "curiosity" or "the love of truth" (*T,* 448). Skepticism is the purest expression of philosophical inquiry because "every passion is mortified by it, except the love of truth; and that passion never is nor can be carried to too high a degree" (*EU,* 41). And it is because false philosophers stop short at some point in the dialectic in the pursuit of truth that they fail to discover the corruptions of the philosophical intellect. In the character of the true philosopher, the passion for truth has come to a reconciliation with the social world of custom and is determined to pursue its quest for understanding the real in and through that world. As a loyal participant in common life, the speech of the true philosopher must necessarily combine the love of truth with eloquence and prudence, yielding the triad of Ciceronian humanistic philosophy: *sapientia, eloquentia,* and *prudentia.* Therefore it is not and could not be theoretical philosophical literature that Hume recommends to educate the passions (including the philosophical passions) but the eloquent literature of the great skeptic and stoic moralists. It is perhaps worthwhile to mention here John Home's judgment that Hume is a superior philosopher to Aristotle because the latter was "void of elegance as a writer, and if we mistake not wanted taste: for the taste which he discovers is that which arises from *reason* and *reflection,* not that which flows from an internal sense" (italics mine).[9] The "internal sense" is the educated sentiment of a skillful, loyal, and critical participant in common life. This is a quality that the anonymous poet (perhaps John Home), in the *Caledonian Mercury,* found expressed in Hume's philosophy: "O first of Sages," "The soundest judgment and the soundest heart." And this was the quality Hume had in mind when he said of the character of the true philosopher that "sound Understandings and delicate Affections . . . are inseparable" (*E,* 536).

Regarding that literature which helps to form and strengthen the character of the philosopher, special mention should be made of history. When Hume speaks of the "learning" of Plutarch in the above passage, he means Plutarch as historian (compare with *E,* 564, 566). In "Of the Study of History," Hume argues that the contemplation of history has three benefits: "It amuses the fancy," "improves the understanding," and "strengthens virtue" (*E,* 565). It is the last of these that is of interest here, and Hume teaches that, in promoting virtue, history is superior to poetry or philosophy. Poetry may paint virtue in vivid colors, but as it speaks to the passions, it as easily "becomes an advocate for vice." The tendency of philosophical theorizing is to be false, and so philosophy is as likely to corrupt our understanding of morals as to improve it. "Philosophers are apt to bewilder themselves in the subtility of their speculations; and . . . deny the reality of all moral distinctions" (*E,* 567). But "historians have been, almost without exception, the true friends of virtue, and have always represented it in its proper colours, however they may have erred in their judgments of particular persons" (*E,* 567). Hume mentions Machiavelli as a telling example. As a philosophical theorist, he considers "poisoning, assassination, and perjury, as lawful arts of power," but "when he speaks as an *Historian,* in his particular narrations, he shows so keen an indignation against vice, and so warm an approbation of virtue," that Hume cannot forebear applying to him the "remark of Horace, That if you chace away nature, tho' with ever so great indignity, she will always return upon you" (*E,* 567). The connoisseur's contemplation of particulars in concrete human affairs, free of the distortions of false philosophical theorizing, is the true scene of moral thought; and history is its proper medium.

But the study and contemplation of history has an even wider significance for Hume than simply that of strengthening moral virtue. The true philosopher understands that he must think about the real in and through the limiting conditions of custom. For this he needs, and knows he needs, not only speculative skills but historical skills as well. As a participant in custom, he must know custom in its concreteness and in its particularity; otherwise he may fall into the error of false philosophers who "bewilder themselves in the subtility of their speculations" and become alienated from their own participation. Thus the study of history not only promotes moral virtue, it strengthens the *intellectual* virtues required to keep speculation rooted in common life and within its proper bounds. Nor is common life to be thought of as confined to the present; it extends to the remote past to include a tradition in which the thinker understands himself to be a participant. It is "an unpardonable ignorance," Hume wrote, "in persons of whatever sex or condition, not to be acquainted with the history of their own country, together with the histories of ancient GREECE and ROME" (*E,* 566). True philosophy requires not only speculative self-understanding but historical self-understanding as well. This follows from the paradoxical position of the true philosopher, who exists within and without the world of common life.

CHAPTER EIGHT

True Philosophy and Civilization

The Philosopher as Patriot

The true philosopher unites in one life the qualities of "the true sage and patriot" in which are manifest "whatever can distinguish human nature, or elevate mortal man to a resemblance with the divinity" (*E*, 153). The sage is philosophy in its aspect of *speculation*. The patriot is philosophy in its aspect of *action* in the social and political arena. In previous chapters philosophy was explored largely under the *topos* of the sage: the dialectical self-examination of philosophy issuing in the normative distinction between true and false philosophy; Hume's anthropology of philosophy; and Hume's understanding of his relation to the philosophical tradition. This and the remaining chapters explore Hume's conception of philosophy under the *topos* of the patriot.

What is the sphere of action of the philosopher as patriot? He is characterized first of all as embodying the social virtue of benevolence, "the generous passion" (*E*, 152). This passion first appears as family affection and loyalty, but the orbit is enlarged to include friendships "founded on mutual esteem and gratitude" and acts of charity to anyone near us in trouble: "What satisfaction in relieving the distressed, in comforting the afflicted, in raising the fallen, and in stopping the career of cruel fortune, or of more cruel man, in their insults over the good and virtuous" (*E*, 152). But affection for those in the circle of acquaintance is still too limited for the human mind which "swells with the divinest and most enlarged affections, and carrying its . . . benevolent wishes to the most distant posterity, . . . views liberty and laws as the source of human happiness, and devotes itself, with the utmost alacrity, to their guardianship and protection. Toils, dangers, and death itself carry their charms, when we brave them for the public good, and ennoble that being, which we generously sacrifice for the interests of our country" (*E,* 153). In another essay Hume taught that "a man, who is only susceptible of friendship, without public spirit, or a regard to the community, is deficient in the most material part of virtue" (*E,* 27). The teaching that the "most material part of virtue" is a regard to the community places Hume in the civic humanist tradition, where man is considered as an essentially social creature and where morality has an irreducibly communitarian element. This teaching is in stark contrast to the view of Hume as a radical individualist in the liberal tradition whose highest conception of moral order is that which makes possible market exchanges for mutual profit and benefit. A classical statement of this view is C. B. MacPherson's *Possessive Individualism* (1962). But what MacPherson describes as possessive individualism is just what Hume called "the selfish system" of Locke, Hobbes, and Mandeville, against which he leveled some of his most spirited criticisms.

There is a doctrine of individualism in Hume, but it is a doctrine of the individual as structured by custom and the social. Here, as always, it is important to keep in mind that Hume lived and thought in a preindustrial age. His support of free trade, a market economy, personal liberty, and political liberty enable one to view him as part of the classical liberal tradition. But these "liberal" values take on a special coloring because they are firmly constrained by an agrarian economy, substantial moral and religious traditions, and a social and political world still largely structured by a hierarchy of families. To be sure, changes were occurring within this order, but large-scale industrialization—which went hand-in-hand with the increase of governmental power and its concentration in large unitary states, the resulting destruction of smaller social and political orders, the weakening of all sense of community, and the anomie of rootless individuals—had not yet occurred.

In "Of Parties in General," Hume celebrates "LEGISLATORS and founders of states" as the most memorable of human beings. What they achieve is more important than the work of speculative philosophy because, although the latter improves the mind, it is confined to the few who have the leisure to pursue it. The "practical arts, which encrease the commodities and enjoyments of life," are worthless without the peace and security necessary to enjoy them, and that is the work of "good government." Even "general virtue and good morals in a state, which are so requisite to happiness, . . . must proceed entirely from the virtuous education of youth, the effect of wise laws and institutions" (*E,* 55).

Legislators and founders of states lift man from a barbarous to a civilized state. Hume once described himself as a "citizen of the world," aligning himself again with Stoic *humanitas*, but also suggesting that the sphere of the true patriot goes beyond the political order of his own country to include the whole of civilization. That is, he knows that as a participant in his own country he is also participating in the larger sphere of human civilization.

Civilization is the story of the development and cultivation of the human mind. Central to this development is "liberty and laws," which are "the source of all human happiness." Liberty was the central theme of political speech in Hume's time, but especially in England. Hume's monumental *History of England* (1754–62) is essentially the story of the rise of civilization in Britain, with special emphasis on the nature and origin of modern liberty. The same theme of the origin of civilization and modern liberty dominates the *Essays Moral, Political, and Literary.* If we may think of the *Treatise,* the two *Enquiries,* the *Dialogues,* and *The Natural History of Religion* as largely the speculative speech of the true sage, then the *History* and the *Essays* are largely the practical speech of the true patriot. That speech is about liberty as the perfection of civilization.

A Theory of Liberty?

The first and most important thing to appreciate is that Hume's understanding of liberty is not presented in the form of an abstract speculative theory of liberty. There is, for instance, nothing in Hume comparable to Mill's discussion in *Of Liberty* of a "simple" theoretical principle which could distinguish the liberty of the individual from the liberty of the state. Liberty is not presented as a natural right or as a deduction from natural law. It is not an abstract principle deduced from a theorem in game theory, as it is for Rawls and for contemporary liberal philosophers too numerous to name. Hume's thought about liberty is about certain sorts of human dispositions both natural and acquired. It is about liberty as a historically evolving practice. His main concern is to understand, as a participant, the origin and rationale of the practice of liberty, to determine the conditions that sustain liberty and the values it makes possible as well as the conditions that threaten to undermine it. In addition to these acts of historical self-knowledge, Hume exposes the conflicts and ambiguities that exist with the practice of liberty (the evils that attend it as well as the goods it drives out), and he explores what the practice intimates about the direction of its own reform. Hume always supposes liberty to be something with which his readers are familiar and which needs no philosophical definition or justification.

Consequently, Hume's writing on liberty is more rhetorical than theoretical, and to many this will mean that Hume can have nothing of philosophical importance to say about liberty. Mill, for instance, seems to have regarded all of Hume's work as merely "rhetorical." He wrote, "Hume possessed powers of a very high order; but regard for truth formed no part of his character. . . . His mind, too, was completely enslaved by a taste for literature . . . that literature which without regard for truth or utility, seeks only to excite emotion."[1] But this is profoundly mistaken. As was discussed in chapter 2, eloquence is a virtue of the true philosopher. Properly understood, rhetoric is a bearer of truth, not a barrier to it. And there is no abstract speculative theory of liberty in Hume, not because he failed to present one, but because his conception of true philosophy rules it out as of little importance and even as destructive.

Such theories tend to mislead because abstract philosophical theories encourage the already dominant disposition of philosophy to fall into its corrupt forms. When that happens the theory becomes an obsession, and we enter the laboratory of the philosophical alchemist. But if the tendency to philosophical obsession is suppressed and the theory is taken for what it is, then it is of minor importance, for it is at most an abridgement or stylization of a political way of life which is and must have been constituted by custom and not by reflection independent of custom.

Mill is a good example of what Hume called a "grave" philosopher who is confused about the importance of abstract theorizing. In *Utilitarianism* he declares it to be a scandal that philosophers have not yet established a supreme moral rule to guide action and that failure to have such a guide places morality itself in jeopardy. Not only is there no supreme moral rule to guide action, but even if there were one, it could not be a source of moral conduct. Morals flow from the dispositions of one's character as shaped by nature and custom. Morals do not rest upon the "refined precepts of philosophy, or even the severest injunctions of religion" but "proceed entirely from the virtuous education of youth, the effect of wise laws and institutions" (*E*, 55). And wise institutions are the result not of a philosophical spectator applying the abstract and necessarily antinomic rule of utility but of a loyal participant methodizing and correcting the inherited practices of a way of life.

Philosophical theories of liberty are typically framed in an ahistorical framework and purport to be timeless and universal. Mill's "simple" theoretical principle, for instance, specifies timeless conditions of liberty for an abstract entity called the "individual" and one called the "state." Likewise, in all contract theories, principles of liberty are constructed in a timeless order in abstraction from the established norms of any actual social and political order. These abstract principles are then applied as stern measuring rods for guiding and criticizing the practices of actual societies. This way of thinking is so well established in both political philosophy and political science that we are apt to demand such theories from Hume and to be disappointed.

But if we are to reject *a priori* philosophical theories of political conceptions such as liberty, how is critical reflection to proceed? The traditional model of critical reflection for philosophy and political science is the spectator model of false philosophy. This is as true of "empirical" as of rationalistic theories. On this model the thinker must, at some methodological point, step out of any existing political order for the purpose of critically surveying it. In this moment the existing regimes of the world are viewed as alien objects having no normative authority for the spectator. The critical spectator conceptually ceases to be a *participant* in any regime whatsoever.

In contrast, Hume proposed a participation model of critical reflection. The thinker originally finds himself to be a loyal participant in some practice whose principles he may not have conceptualized (*T*, xviii). The principles of a practice are preconceptually internal to the practice. Practices may and often do conflict. The task of critical reflection is to conceptualize the principles internal to a practice, distinguish between the deep and variable principles, systematize them with principles of other practices, and critically adjust principles to each other to avoid conflicts. The Humean critical thinker begins in the established practices of common life, and, although practices may be modified by reflection informed by custom, he ends there too. At no time does he become an outside spectator of the practices, and at no time do these become alien objects of theoretical reflection.

Such a model of critical thinking requires historical investigation into the evolution and rationale of original practices. But such a historical inquiry is not "theoretical" in the sense in which Marxist and liberal historical inquiry is; if it were, it would view the practice as an alien object. Humean historical inquiry into practice is by and for participants who must be able to recognize themselves in it, whatever the critical results of their inquiry. The practice must be illuminated from within. For this project, the art of eloquence is essential. The reason is that original participation in a practice is preconceptual. The process of conceptualizing the principles immanent in the practice (that is, of bringing them to consciousness) requires a critical act of thought which can test the purported conceptualization against the primordial, preconceptual practice. This critical act is in fact an eloquent speech in which we are called upon to recognize who we are as participants in the practice, and so we are able to recognize ourselves in the conceptualization. The arts of eloquence and history are essential to the participation model of critical inquiry; they are irrelevant to the spectator model. The spectator model has proved successful in the natural sciences, where the object of reflection is an alien object; it has been a disaster in the human sciences. In what follows I shall piece together Hume's conception of liberty from the philosophical, rhetorical, and historical structures in which it is embedded.

What Liberty Is

There is no timeless object called liberty or freedom about which a philosophical spectator can devise a theory. Liberty is a practice that has evolved over time. In its most differentiated form, it is a British experience, though less differentiated forms of it can be found throughout Europe. This European experience that has evolved is modern, and although analogues may be found in antiquity, they must not be confused with it. Consequently, Hume's understanding of liberty is not presented through a speculative theory but through *narratives* of the evolution of the experience of liberty as shaped by the conventions of a common European life. The task of theorizing is to methodize and correct the practices illuminated by these narratives. The stories are presented with rhetorical force to those who are participants in the conventions, reminding them of who they are and where they came from. Nearly everything Hume wrote on liberty can be viewed as a speech addressed to the dominant Whig literary and political establishment of his time, whose members claimed to be the spokesmen for and guardians of British liberty. Although the Whig establishment participated in the experience of liberty, it seemed to Hume that its thought about that experience was confused. Distorted thinking about an experience, if extreme, can so alienate one from it that one loses one's grip on the experience itself and may come to subvert it. As Hume's career developed, he became increasingly alarmed that the distorted thinking of the dominant Whig literary and political establishment about liberty threatened to destroy the newly emerged practice of liberty.

Liberty appeared to Hume and his contemporaries primarily as something in opposition to slavery. The feudal distinction between the free man and the serf was still a vivid part of eighteenth-century cultural memory. The slave cannot determine his life by his own plans and decisions but is coerced to act by the arbitrary will of another. The stress is on *arbitrary,* since the free man may be under many restraints from moral and political custom which, as a participant, he does not view as arbitrary. Legal constraints are not arbitrary if they are publicly known and equally applicable to all. It was liberty in this sense of the equal rule of law that the Glorious Revolution of 1688 had secured and which made British political order the wonder and envy of eighteenth-century Europe. Throughout most of the seventeenth century, Britain was a weak, politically chaotic country with less than half the population of France. But by the first quarter of the eighteenth century, Britain appeared as a rich, powerful, and populous nation. It was generally agreed that this success was due entirely to her constitution of liberty, which had unleashed the productive powers and ambitions of the populace.

Bernard Bailyn observes that "it would be difficult to exaggerate the keenness of eighteenth-century Britons' sense of their multifarious accomplishments and world eminence and their distinctiveness in the achievement of liberty. From the end of the war in 1713 until the crisis over America a half-century later, the triumph of Britain in warfare, in commerce, and in statecraft was the constant theme not only of formal state pronouncements and of political essays, tracts, and orations but of belles-lettres as well. There was a general paean of praise to the steady increase in wealth, refinement, and security, and to the apparent perfection of government."[2] Hume complained bitterly about the Whig panegyric literature that had dominated British letters since the late seventeenth century and throughout his lifetime. In 1769 he confessed that "it has been my Misfortune to write in the language of the most stupid and factious Barbarians in the world" (*L,* 2: 209). The charge of Whig barbarism occurs often in letters written during the last decade of Hume's life. In the next chapter I examine the sense in which the Whig establishment is barbarous. In the meantime it is important to observe that Hume's attack on the Whig *interpretation* of the British experience of liberty is not an attack on the experience itself. No Whig panegyrist ever surpassed Hume (except in excess) in praise either of liberty or of the British constitution. The following passages exhibit the depth of Hume's commitment to a free political order.

Liberty is an original demand of human nature. "The heart of man delights in liberty: the very image of constraint is grievous to it"

(*E,* 187). Hume roundly condemned the "remains . . . of domestic slavery in the American colonies, and among some European nations" not only because slavery is intrinsically odious, but because it corrupts the humanity of the slaveholder. "The little humanity commonly observed in persons accustomed, from their infancy, to exercise so great authority over their fellow-creatures, and to trample upon human nature, were sufficient alone to disgust us with that unbounded dominion" (*E,* 383–84). As he rejected the institution of domestic slavery as incompatible with extensive benevolence, so he recognized the rational autonomy of the mass of mankind. "It has been found as the experience of mankind increases, that the *people* are no such dangerous monsters as they have been represented, and it is in every respect better to guide them like rational creatures than to lead or drive them like brute beasts" (*E,* 604–5). It was this recognition of the rationality of human nature that led Hume to present freedom of the press as a demand of human nature. "But I would fain go a step further, and assert, that this liberty is attended with so few inconveniences, that it may be claimed as the *common right of mankind,* and ought to be indulged them almost in every government except the ecclesiastical, to which, indeed, it would be fatal" (*E,* 604; italics mine). More generally, Hume could say, "For my part, I esteem liberty so invaluable a blessing in society, that whatever favours its progress and security, can scarce be too fondly cherished by every one who is a lover of human kind" (*E,* 646).

Hume agreed with the Whig panegyrists about the intrinsic worth and valuable consequences of the British constitution of liberty. "During these last sixty years," Hume could write at the middle of the eighteenth century, "public liberty, with internal peace and order, has flourished . . . trade and manufactures, and agriculture, have increased: the arts, and sciences, and philosophy have been cultivated. Even religious parties have been necessitated to lay aside their mutual rancour; And the glory of the nation has spread itself all over Europe; derived equally from our progress in the arts of peace, and from valour and success in war. So long and so glorious a period no nation almost can boast of: Nor is there another instance in the whole history of mankind, that so many millions of people have, during such a space of time, been held together, in a manner so free, so rational, and so suitable to the dignity of human nature" (*E,* 508). Hume recognized and affirmed the great variety of customs, manners, and characters that a constitution of liberty necessarily produces, and he observed that British society had developed a pluralistic tone which distinguished it from the more uniform national characteristics of other nations. "The great liberty and independency, which every man enjoys, allows him to display the manners peculiar to him. Hence the English, of any people in the universe, have the least of a national character, unless this very singularity may pass for such" (*E*, 207). The increase in trade and manufacturing that liberty makes possible has resulted in wealth being "dispersed among multitudes," satisfying another demand of human nature. "Every person, if possible, ought to enjoy the fruits of his labour, in a full possession of all the necessaries, and many of the conveniences of life. No one can doubt but such an equality is most suitable to human nature and diminishes much less from the *happiness* of the rich, than it adds to that of the poor" (*E*, 265).

Like his Whig contemporaries, Hume was "alarmed by the danger of universal monarchy" from the authoritarian regimes of the Continent. The Emperor Charles had tried and failed to establish Europe under one monarch. The new and more formidable threat was the absolute monarchy of France. "Europe has now, for above a century, remained on the defensive against the greatest force that ever, perhaps, was formed by the civil or political combination of mankind" (*E*, 634). In the struggle to achieve a balance of power against "this ambitious power," Hume saw Britain as playing a world historical role. British liberty serves as a model to Europe, and British power serves to protect the liberties of Europe. And so Hume could describe Britain's role philosophically as "the guardian of the general liberties of Europe, and patron of mankind." (*E*, 635).

Hume is often thought of as a Tory and (given the violent reaction, as expressed in the letters of the last decade of his life, to an extension of republican institutions in Britain) as a reactionary. Caroline Robbins, in her magisterial study of the Whig tradition, does not include Hume on the grounds that he was a Tory and so not part of that tradition.[3] Yet the preceding passages and many similar ones present a different picture. They suggest that Hume viewed liberty as a demand of human nature which, ideally, should be extended as much as possible to all men. They suggest a view of society as an order of productive equals and self-directing individuals, and imply that the task of society is not to constrain personality but to allow it expression so that, as in the liberal order of eighteenth-century Britain, each may "display the manners peculiar to him" (*E*, 207). Yet these passages do not tell us exactly what Hume meant by the term *liberty*, and it is to this question that I now turn.

Hume uses the term *liberty* in three main senses. The first, and by far the most important, is the one we have already mentioned. The free man is not a slave. He can determine his life by his own thought and decisions uncoerced by the arbitrary will of another. The institution which men have contrived to secure liberty in this sense is government. The coercion of government is not arbitrary if it is in accord with law. Hume adopts here the classical Whig expression: "a government of Laws, not of Men" (*E*, 94). In such a government, whatever its form, law is conceived to precede the statutes enacted by the sovereign power. Hume affirms the classical checks to arbitrary power embodied in the traditional notion of "the rule of law." Law must be known, regular, and predictable; the rules of justice must be applied equally to all; imprisonment or confiscation of property must not occur without due process of law; and there must be an independent judiciary capable of reviewing the statues of the sovereign and their administration by magistrates.

The primary sense of liberty in Hume's thought is unoriginal. It is simply the familiar Whig notion of liberty as the rule of law. What is original with Hume is the historical, dialectical, and evolutionary context in which he places the concept. This context is discussed later; in the meantime I turn to Hume's second sense of liberty. In the primary conception of liberty, coercion, by virtue of the concept of law, is not only compatible with liberty, it is internal to it. The presence of coercion in the concept of liberty logically implies a weaker sense of the term according to which liberty is the absence of any constraint. Hume uses the term in this way when discussing the traditional problem of free will in the *Treatise* and the *Enquiry* on understanding. There a person is said to have "liberty" of the will when his actions flow from his character and are independent of any external constraint. Liberty, so conceived, is morally neutral. Whether it is good that anyone possess liberty in this second sense is a contingent question. Liberty in the first sense (as the rule of law) is presumed good. I say "presumed" because Hume thinks reasons of public interest may arise for suspending the rule of law.

Although liberty in the second sense is morally neutral, Hume often uses it in political contexts where it can be confused with the morally favorable connotations of liberty in the first sense. For example, religious liberty, the freedom to philosophize, and liberty of the press are ornaments of political society that may be "indulged" under certain conditions.

Liberty in this second and weaker sense is also used to describe the liberty of the state of nature and conditions of society approximating it. Liberty in such contexts is usually a bad thing. For instance, "the abject Britons," upon being free from the coercion of Roman rule, "regarded this present liberty as fatal to them" (*H,* 1: 13). In opposition to the popular Whig belief that the British constitution can be traced back to the Saxon forests, Hume sarcastically remarks, "The same picture of a fierce and bold liberty, which is drawn by the masterly pencil of Tacitus, will suit those founders of the English government." And of the liberty of the feudal order, Hume writes, "The pretended liberty of the times was only an incapacity of submitting to government" (*H,* 1: 161; 2: 521).

Hume's third use of the term is for that form of government which he calls "free" and which he defines as follows: "The government, which, in common appellation, receives the appellation of free, is that which admits of a partition of power among several members, whose united authority is no less, or is commonly greater, than that of any monarch; but who, in the usual course of administration, must act by general and equal laws, that are previously known to all the members, and to all their subjects" (*E,* 40–41). Free governments contain a division of sovereign powers and are either republics or, as in Britain, limited monarchies. Liberty, as the rule of law, usually attends free government but is not confined to it, since Hume thinks that civilized absolute monarchies can embody the rule of law to a degree equal to or even higher than that in republics and limited monarchies. Hume uses the term *liberty* in this third sense when attacking the demand for greater representation in government, which found expression in the Wilkes and Liberty affair. In October, 1769, he wrote: "So much Liberty is incompatible with human Society: And it will be happy, if we can escape from it, without falling into a military Government, such as Algiers or Tunis" (*L,* 2: 210). Hume does not mean here "too much liberty" in the sense of the rule of law. He means rather that the "free government" of Britain is "too free," that is, the "partition of power" is such that the monarchical part of the government is too weak to punish displays of disrespect, and this, he fears, will subvert the rule of law. Free governments are not presumed by Hume to be good. Indeed, the freest are the worst. The freest government would be a democratic republic where the partition of power would be not between independent social authorities but between individuals, and where the majority would rule directly, as in the "Athenian Democracy." There the "whole collective body of the people voted in every law, without any limitation of property, without any distinction of rank, without controul from any magistracy or senate; and consequently, without regard to order, justice, or prudence" (*E,* 368–69).

Hume rejected the main thesis of the individualistic Whig tradition as taught by such thinkers as Sidney and Locke, and followers such as Price and Macaulay, who forged a conceptual connection between representative government and liberty. For Hume, it is a contingent question whether representative governments embody liberty to a greater degree than absolute monarchies. Locke had argued that absolute monarchy is "*inconsistent with Civil society,* and so can be no Form of Government at all."[4] In contrast, Hume taught that "human nature, in general, really enjoys more liberty at present, in the most arbitrary government of Europe, than it ever did during the most flourishing period of ancient times" (*E,* 383). Hume includes here the Roman and Spartan republics, so much admired by popular Whig ideology. He argued also that the free government of Britain (the limited monarchy), given its peculiar historical conditions, most likely would and should develop into a civilized absolute monarchy. "Absolute monarchy, therefore, is the easiest death, the true *Euthanasia* of the British constitution" (*E,* 53).

To sum up, the primary sense of liberty for Hume is the rule of law: action uncoerced by the arbitrary will of the sovereign power. The other two senses of liberty (freedom from external constraint and free government) are subordinate to liberty as the rule of law. Having examined the substance of liberty, we may ask about its relation to governmental *authority.* It might appear that liberty, as the rule of law, is essential to legitimate government. But this is not Hume's view. For instance, the monarch in a free government must abide by the rule of law; that is, he "must act by general and equal laws, that are previously known to all. . . . In this sense, it must be owned, that liberty is the perfection of civil society" (*E,* 41). This passage suggests that liberty is a perfection of government but not essential to it. Consider also the following passage, where Hume distinguishes his own reading of the political conflict during the reign of the Stuarts from the dominant Whig interpretation: "Forgetting that a regard to liberty, though a laudable passion, ought commonly to be subordinate to a reverence for established government, the prevailing faction has celebrated only the partisans of the former, who pursued as their object the perfection of civil society, and has extolled them at the expense of their antagonists, who maintained those maxims that are essential to its very existence" (*H,* 6: 533). The liberty here that is a nonessential perfection of society is not liberty either from constraint or free government, but liberty as the rule of law. For one charge against the Stuarts was that they had violated some of those checks traditionally thought to be essential to the rule of law.

No check to arbitrary power is more important than *habeas corpus,* a rule which Hume fully celebrates, but he does not construe it as an absolute limit to governmental authority. "It must, however, be confessed, that there is some difficulty to reconcile with such extreme liberty the full security and the regular police of a state, especially the police of great cities" (*H,* 6: 367). Hume mentions other checks essential to the rule of law which have been secured in the limited monarchy of Britain. These checks are designed "to remove all discretionary powers, and to secure every one's life and fortune by general and inflexible laws. No action must be deemed a crime but what the law has plainly determined to be such: no crime must be imputed to a man but from a legal proof before his judges; and even these judges must be his fellow-subjects, who are obliged, by their own interest, to have a watchful eye over the encroachments and violence of the ministers" (*E,* 12). But Hume's praise of these checks against arbitrary power is qualified. "From these causes it proceeds, that there is as much liberty, and even perhaps licentiousness, in Great Britain, as there were formerly slavery and tyranny in Rome" (*E,* 12). *Habeas corpus* is described as "extreme liberty": the checks just mentioned yield "licentiousness" as well as liberty.

Clearly Hume does not conceive of the traditional checks internal to the rule of law as absolute limits to government authority. His own view of the relation between liberty and authority is a dialectical one with an ambiguity at the core that can never be eliminated. "In all governments, there is a perpetual intestine struggle, open or secret, between Authority and Liberty; and neither of them can ever absolutely prevail in the contest" (*E,* 40). Since authority is essential to government, it takes precedence over liberty. But it can never be detached from it. "A great sacrifice of liberty must necessarily be made in every government; yet even the authority, which confines liberty, can never, and perhaps ought never, in any constitution, to become quite entire and uncontroulable" (*E,* 40).

But what form will this control take? And, if not identical to, how close is it to those controls known as the rule of law? To answer these questions we must look briefly at Hume's conception of the rationale of government. Government exists to interpret and to enforce the rules of justice: the stability of possession, its transference by consent, and the performance of promises. Government that violates the reason for its existence loses it authority and may be overthrown by violence. There is, then, a minimum "rule of law" that government must satisfy, namely, the laws of justice. No rule can be given as to when revolution is justified except to say that the circumstances must be extraordinary and desperate and must be so recognized by the public. "I must confess," Hume writes, "that I shall always incline to their side, who draw the bond of allegiance very close, and consider an infringement of it, as the last refuge in desperate cases, when the public is in the highest danger from violence and tyranny" (*E,* 490).

This, of course, is vague. The contract theory, in contrast, appears to provide a clear rule: Revolution is justified whenever the terms of the contract have been broken by government. From Hume's point of view the apparent rational superiority of the contract theory is illusory. The theory assumes that since government is constituted by self-consciously imposed rules, there must be such rules for dissolving it. But Hume holds that government is established not by the imposition of rules but spontaneously; its dissolution likewise must be spontaneous. There is a Humean metaphorical notion of consent involved in the formation of government, but it is not the consent of a self-reflective, self-assertive individual. Rather, it is the sort of consent implied in Humean social conventions. The "consent" is of the sort, for example, without which language would be impossible. It is deeply social and not self-assertive. Nor is the Humean consent that founds and dissolves government the numerical majority of individual wills, as in contemporary democratic theory. For Hume the political individual is always the individual rooted in an actual historical community whose will cannot be detached from the prejudices, traditions, and bonds of affection that hold the community together.

One reason, then, why no rule can be given *a priori* as to how the laws of justice are to be interpreted or when revolution is justified is that the content of the laws is historically relative to the customs and prejudices of the people. Since, for Hume, the authority of government is based not on contract but on opinion, authoritarian regimes that would appear arbitrary and oppressive to those accustomed to the formal notion of the rule of law would appear just to those who share the prejudices of the order. For example, the reign of Elizabeth I was considered, at the time, a regime in which the laws of justice were instantiated. Yet Hume observes that there were many institutions which violated the rule of law as understood in eighteenth-century Britain, the most notorious being the Star Chamber, "which possessed an unlimited discretionary authority of fining, imprisoning, and inflicting corporal punishment." The members were not subject to judicial review and held office at the Queen's pleasure. Hume adds that such an institution was needed as much then as it would be oppressive now. Generally the prejudices which support an authoritarian regime contain checks to that authority which are peculiar to the order and which are considered satisfactory. "The sultan is master of the life and fortune of any individual; but will not be permitted to impose new taxes on his subjects: a French monarch can impose taxes at pleasure; but would find it dangerous to attempt the lives and fortunes of individuals. Religion also . . . is commonly found to be a very intractable principle; and other principles or prejudices frequently resist all the authority of the civil magistrate; whose power, being founded on opinion, can never subvert other opinions equally rooted with that of his title to dominion" (*E,* 40).

In the usual course of affairs, therefore, authority and liberty (liberty conceived now as the "irregular" checks necessary to secure the laws of justice) will be established spontaneously. Since it is the habits, customs, and traditions of the people that ultimately constitute authority and, at the same time, are the basic rules for interpreting the laws of justice, these same prejudices (and not the empty and arbitrary reasonings of contract philosophers) will dictate when authority has failed to establish the laws of justice. The formal reasoning of contract theory is empty because the contract is framed in a hypothetical state uncontaminated by any prejudice or custom of an actual social and political order. It is arbitrary because, being purely formal, any arrangement in the world may appear to satisfy the contract or no arrangement may appear to satisfy it. The contract can serve as a guide for political action only if given some content by the very prejudices that were methodologically eliminated in the first place. And there can be no formal way to choose which prejudices should fill the contract with content, for the choice must be made either by another prejudice or by a principle free of all prejudice. If the latter, we are back to another formal principle which is empty; if the former, we have abandoned the whole point of contract theory. The apparent superiority of the contractarian criterion for when revolution is justified as opposed to Hume's criterion of public prejudice is an illusion.

A final point should be observed on the question of when revolution is justified. Hume thinks of governmental authority as something we are born into, roughly in the way we are born into parental authority. In both cases we enter in a vulnerable state and feel the effects of both authority and benevolence. Over time these feelings generate a sense of loyalty as one identifies with the authority. In the way in which children are loath to leave their natural parents, even when abusive, for artificial and morally improved substitutes, so citizens and subjects of long-established authority are loath to overthrow the constitution of that authority for an improved instrument.

And this brings up another way in which government, for Hume, is like a family. A family does not think of itself as an instrument designed to serve some goal other than the natural associations provided by the family itself. A family, like a friendship, is an end in itself. Families and friendships may serve temporary goals, but the bonds that constitute them do not dissolve upon achieving the goals or upon failure to achieve them. Likewise, Hume does not think of government as an instrument for achieving some end other than the need for civil association (peace and stability) out of which government was spontaneously generated in the first place. Government, therefore, is not a teleological instrument for bringing into being an external goal such as a Christian polity, the rights of man, the classless society, or freedom.

In these theories revolution is a forward-looking idea: If a better instrument can be devised for accomplishing the external ends of government, there is no reason, in principle, why a new instrument should not replace the old. For Hume the idea of a just revolution is an essentially present and backward-looking notion: rebellion appears reasonable in the face of a present and serious usurpation of deeply established opinion and entitlements.

By "the rule of law," I have meant those formal checks to arbitrary power, equal laws known to all, *habeas corpus,* judicial review, and so on usually associated with the expression. But there is a wider and weaker sense that can be given to the expression, for we may now include the establishment of the laws of justice done in the "irregular" way (whether or not they conform to the traditional formal checks to arbitrary power) as a minimum condition of lawlikeness in government. The rule of law in this weak and informal sense is internal to authority and cannot be separated from it. The formal notion of "the rule of law" is not a feature of government as such but of what Hume calls *civilized* government as opposed to barbarous government. But it is internal to the concept of governmental authority, whether civilized or barbarous, that it be limited by the laws of justice, although these limits can take many forms depending on the established prejudices and opinions of the people. In barbarous ages the checks to encroachment are "irregular," eclectic, and short-lived. Hume, for instance, describes the government of pre-Tudor England as "limited," but it was limited not by the formal convention of the rule of law but only in that the prince was, at point of sword, "restrained by the barons" (*H,* 5: 550). More generally Hume says that throughout the barbarous ages of English history the monarch was never absolute. But again the "limit" was barbarous, being dependent not on the "legal and determinate liberty" of the rule of law, but on the personalities and power of individuals.

The story of civilization is largely the story of how the checks to arbitrary power framed in the modern notion of the rule of law have gradually become established. Of Elizabeth's reign, which was emerging out of barbarism, Hume observes that "the jealousy of Liberty, though rouzed, was not yet thoroughly enlightened" (*H,* 5: 550). What does it mean to be enlightened? It is to understand the rationale of government in human nature, and to bring to conscious awareness and make regular those checks to arbitrary authority of which even barbarians, being "novices . . . in the principles of liberty," had some dim understanding. This disposition to follow "the maxim of adhering strictly to law," Hume makes clear, is a modern phenomenon emerging around the seventeenth century. "It was not till this age, when the spirit of liberty was universally diffused, when the principles of government were nearly reduced to a system, when the tempers of men, more civilized, seemed less to require those violent exertions of prerogative" (*H,* 5: 179).

Hume is especially concerned in the *History* to discourage the tendency of Whigs to read the maxim of the rule of law back into earlier periods as a standard for moral judgment. Though a partisan of the maxim himself, Hume insists that mankind has managed without it until modern times. Writing about the attempt of Parliament to remove the court of the Star Chamber during the reign of Charles I, Hume observes: "No government, at that time, appeared in the world, nor is perhaps to be found in the records of any history, which subsisted without the mixture of some arbitrary authority, committed to some magistrate; and it might reasonably, *beforehand,* appear doubtful, whether human society could ever reach that state of perfection, as to support itself with no other controul than the general and rigid maxims of law and equity" (*H,* 5: 329; italics mine). Retrospectively, as lovers of liberty, we must praise the initiative and energy of Parliament but recognize at the same time that to a thoughtful person the ideal of the rule of law could have appeared dangerous at the time. Nor do we understand all of the ramifications of this ideal now. Thus what Hume finally celebrates is the gradual establishment through "repeated contests" of that "noble, though dangerous, principle" (*H,* 5: 330).

Hume does not use the expression "the rule of law." His own expressions are "the maxims of rigid law and liberty" and "the line of rigid law and severe principles," suggesting something of the novelty of this modern disposition and perhaps also its tendency to be captured by rationalistic superstition (*H,* 5: 291, 313).

The disposition to the rule of law has gradually, to some degree or other, become established in all the countries of civilized Europe. It is established to a high degree in republics such as Holland and in absolute monarchies such as France. But it has reached its highest development in the limited monarchy of Britain. "We in this island have ever since [the Revolution of 1688] enjoyed, if not the best system of government, at least the most entire system of liberty, that ever was known amongst mankind" (*H,* 6: 531).

As men become, through time and experience, more self-conscious about the advantages of the rule of law, and as their institutions evolve into "free governments," with publicly acknowledged constitutions, their rights become more explicit and are more jealously guarded. Particular violations of the constitution then become publicly obvious, as when one branch of the government usurps the rights of another. Paradoxically, the conditions for rebellion are clearer and easier to justify the more civilized and constitutional a regime becomes. Of a prince who would encroach on "other parts of the constitution" in a civilized regime, Hume says "it is allowable to resist and dethrone him; tho' such resistance and violence may, in the general tenor of the laws, be deem'd unlawful and rebellious" (*T,* 564). It was in this way that Hume justified the dethroning of James II even though, unlike Nero, he was not guilty of "enormous tyranny and oppression." Such resistance is justified because it can be viewed as an act of conservative reform motivated by respect for the constitution rather than by the self-assertive desire to innovate. In this Hume affirmed the classical republican wisdom of "Machiavel" that the founding of a state is good and that "a government . . . must often be brought back to its original principles" (*E,* 516).

Liberty, Tradition, and Civilization

Hume's conception of convention exposes a peculiar sort of order which cannot be thought of as the product of human design and need not be thought of as the product of Divine design but is the unintended result of man's attempt to satisfy human needs. The total set of these historically evolving conventions (language, law, art, religion, etc.) Hume calls the moral world. To the degree that men become *aware* of the evolutionary process of the moral world and gain some measure of control over it, they become to that degree *civilized.* Civilization, then, is not merely a matter of acting according to certain principles; it is a form of the most important self-knowledge, and so (philosophy being the most developed form of self-knowledge) there is a close connection between Hume's conception of civilization and philosophy. The civilized man plays the role in Hume's philosophy that the sage or wise man played in the eudaemonistic philosophies of the ancients. For Hume the true philosopher and the truly civilized man are the same. I want now to explore Hume's conception of civilization further and show how two conceptions are essential to it: tradition and liberty.

The story of civilization is the story of the improvements of the human mind. This seems to imply a standard of goodness which is the aim of civilization. But Hume rejected the Aristotelian *telos* that lures men on to self-realization. Hume's conception of good can be inferred from his conception of moral virtue. Personal virtue consists in qualities of character useful or agreeable to ourselves and others. Social virtue consists in qualities of institutions that are useful or agreeable to ourselves and others. The good is not conceived as an *a priori* form, as in Plato and Aristotle, to which men are driven by eros; nor is it the forward-looking "species being" of Marx from which man is alienated by class struggle. For Hume the good is, as it were, present and backward-looking; it is what has been hammered out over time through a largely unreflective process of trial and error, lived through, enjoyed, and upon reflection approved.

Civilization is an evolving order of custom and sentiment with a life of its own independent of reflection. This is not to say that the civilizing process cannot be modified by reflection; indeed, as civilization develops it becomes more subject to modification by reflection. But its source is not reflection, it is not constituted by reflection, and it is not in any substantial way guided by reflection. Here, as elsewhere, reflection is subordinate to custom. Concerning the relationship between reflection and civilization, we may apply what Hume said in another context regarding moral virtue, namely, that civilization is substantially the work of "the blind, but sure testimony of taste and sentiment . . . left by nature to baffle all the pride of philosophy, and make her sensible of her narrow boundaries and slender acquisitions" (*EM*, 267). One may say that the civilizing process is blind, but it is only so (to use an image of Oakeshott's) in being "blind as a bat."

The good is what is housed in the deeply established prejudices, customs, and traditions that make up the substance of the moral world. These prejudices constitute the moral world not because they are known to be good by some theoretical grasp of the good independent of the prejudices; rather, they are known to be good because they are the deeply established prejudices which have been lived through and tested, and which constitute one's participation in the moral world. Custom and tradition, then, are the great guides of life in the radical sense that there is no standard of goodness independent of tradition that can either certify or criticize them. Of course, in the manner of true philosophy, one custom may be used as a standard to criticize another custom; and abstract standards, ideals, and models can be constructed to criticize or affirm particular customs. But such standards are themselves abridgments of existing customs and cannot be applied in a nonarbitrary way to the world without the mediation and interpretation of existing custom.

Two features of Hume's conception of tradition must be mentioned. First, tradition is *dynamic* and *open-ended.* Tradition originates in ignorance and issues in ignorance. No one knows the ultimate ground of the qualities of virtue framed in traditions. One just finds oneself living through, tasting, and approving these goods as internal to one's existence. Some goods are deep and common to all traditions (such as benevolence and justice), and some vary with the "manners" of the age, but all are stained and colored with a historical dimension, formed as they are by the interplay of human propensities, needs, and historical events. What qualities will be established as virtues cannot be known beforehand, nor can any established set of qualities preclude the emergence of new qualities unthought of by participants in the tradition. Hume stresses that human nature, as manifest in the world of custom and tradition, is in constant change: to be "inconstant and irregular . . . is, in a manner, the constant character of human nature" (*EU,* 88). Just as the ancients could not have known what modifications would be made in virtue today, so no one can know what changes in virtue may appear in the future. "It is not fully known, what degree of refinement, either in virtue or vice, human nature is susceptible of, nor what may be expected of mankind from any great revolution in their education, customs or principles" (*E,* 87–88).

The second feature of tradition is that it is *dialectical* and *ingenious.* Tradition is not only in constant change; it is in conflict with itself. The new goods that emerge in a tradition will typically be in conflict with the old, and a painful process of adjustment will ensue in which new and old goods are mutually selected, modified, and rejected. The process of grafting new, conflicting goods onto established goods follows no rational prescription. It is carried out largely in ignorance; it is the work of judgment, and it can be critically understood only after the new goods are settled into common life. A tradition such as Christianity, for instance, is able to bring into some sort of unity the conflicting Hebrew, Greek, and Roman traditions. Hume, in the *History,* sought to forge a new national unity out of the warring Puritan and Royalist traditions and the current Hanoverian regime. Here again the poetic imagination, as custom, consolidates what clear and distinct principles of reflection could not establish.

Tradition, as a form of thought that brings opposites into unity, is simply an expression of the workings of the imagination in the moral world. In the *Treatise* Hume had shown how rational analysis of our experience of physical objects, causal connections, ourselves, and others renders these experiences incoherent. All are viewed by reflection as structured by inconsistent elements which cannot be reconciled but which are nonetheless believed. The mind must somehow come to terms with "principles, which are contrary to each other, which are both at once embrac'd by the mind, and which are unable mutually to destroy each other" (*T,* 215). Reason dissolves; the poetic imagination unifies, reconciles, and constructs even with elements that are logical contraries. Reason reveals that man "is . . . but a heap of contradictions" (*E,* 188). But "the heart of man is made to reconcile contradictions" (*E,* 71). In Hume's famous account of causation, the orderly, perceptible world of causally connected objects is the expression of the reconciling "fictions" of the imagination. To call these "fictions" is not to say that they are false but to call attention to the poetic character of all deep beliefs about the real. The poetic unities of the imagination are not barriers to understanding reality but our only means of understanding it. Far from being illusionary, Hume calls these fictions "the cement of the universe," the universe needing cement only because of the conceptual dissolution that rational reflection always brings in its wake. The contrarieties reconciled in the moral and political traditions of common life are expressions of the same imagination at work.

Hume often makes a special point of showing how apparently rationally ordered structures such as the British constitution are, in fact, fragile instruments containing the most jarring and discordant elements. One example is his analysis of what the opposition called "court corruption," that is, the patronage system following upon the crown's right to appoint magistrates and to grant titles. The charge was that the crown had used this power to corrupt the integrity of Parliament and so to undermine the constitution. Hume granted that such power could be abused but observed that the famous "balance" of the constitution which all affirmed was not possible without the patronage system. The crown had been so reduced in formal powers and revenue that Parliament was virtually supreme. Cry as moralists might against corruption, court patronage was the only means left to ensure some independence to the crown and thus the only way of securing an independent executive and judiciary, so important to the traditional concept of the rule of law.

Hume devoted an entire essay, "Of Some Remarkable Customs," to this subject. One of these customs is the arbitrary pressing of seamen in violation of the rights of "English subjects." Hume shows the bizarre way this violation of the rule of law serves the interests of liberty and for that reason is tolerated. "Authority, in times of full internal peace and concord, is armed against law. . . . Liberty, in a country of the highest liberty, is left entirely to its own defense, without any countenance or protection. The wild state of nature is renewed in one of the most civilized societies of mankind" (*E*, 375–76). What is true here of the British Constitution, that its unity is an uneasy tension of contrary elements, is true of all the Humean conventions and traditions that make up the moral world.

Hume often describes the process of civilization as one of experimentation where men, through trial and error, discover new and successful ways of living. There are three models of "experimentation" that can be confused with the process Hume picks out. One is the Darwinian model of natural selection where, out of a life-and-death struggle, successful traits are genetically communicated to succeeding generations. Another is the abstract model of classical economics, where an unintended order, for example, the market price and wage, arises spontaneously in a condition of free competition. Finally, there is the model of scientific or technological experimentation, which has been applied to social reality by utilitarians such as Bentham and pragmatists such as Dewey.

Hume's model differs from the Darwinian in that the new traits are transmitted not genetically but by sympathetic communication and emulation, and they are established not by their survival value but by *opinion* as being qualities useful and agreeable to ourselves and others. Nor is the model of unrestrained competition in a free market generating an unintended market price especially helpful. Hume shares with the model the notion that free transactions among individuals yield unintended public orders. But the market, in this model, is conceived as a timeless order of rational individuals, free of traditional constraints, seeking to maximize their gains and minimize their losses. By contrast, the Humean model of "experimentation" requires agents who are fully social and historical and not fully rational in the sense of self-interested prudence. One should recall that, for Hume, public spirit is "the most material part of virtue" (*E,* 27). The very thoughts and motives of Humean individuals are clothed with the restraints woven historically into the prejudices, customs, and traditions of their order (*T,* 303, 363, 365).

Finally, the Humean model has little affinity with the model of technological experimentation. This model too conceives of individuals and groups in a timeless manner, whereas Humean individuals and groups are conceived as being internal to a unique historical order. Most important, however, the technological model implies a degree of self-conscious control which is entirely absent from the Humean model. The conventions of the moral world, though the result of trial-and-error-experience over many generations, were not intended by any individual or group. "It is not with forms of government, as with other artificial contrivances, where an old engine may be rejected, if we can discover another more accurate and commodious, or where trials may safely be made, even though the success be doubtful" (*E,* 512). Technological experiments can be "called off." An historically developed "experiment" such as the British Constitution cannot be called off.

Hume stresses so strongly the authority of custom and tradition that one is apt to overlook the remarks he makes on behalf of novelty and invention. "I have sometimes been inclined to think, that interruptions in the periods of learning, were they not attended with such a destruction of ancient books, and the records of history, would be rather favourable to the arts and sciences, by breaking the progress of authority, and dethroning the tyrannical usurpers over human reason" (*E,* 123). In the *History* he entertained the notion that "governments too steady and uniform, as they are seldom free, so are they, in the judgment of some attended with another sensible inconvenience: They abate the active powers of man; depress courage, invention, and genius; and produce an universal lethargy in the people" (*H,* 6: 530–31). Hume grants that "this opinion may be just." His only dissent is that the value of novelty cannot be used to justify such radical changes as were attempted during the reigns of James I and Charles I. That "spirit of innovation with which the age was generally seized" was too radical and violent for safety.

One value of liberty, as the rule of law, is that it provides an orderly and secure framework in which emerging novelties may be tested, modified, and peacefully incorporated into the fabric of tradition. In this way institutions of liberty bring to conscious awareness (to some degree) and make rational the process of "experimentation" that had more or less blindly characterized the historical process.

Civilization as True Philosophy

Civilization, then, is a process whereby the conventions of common life are raised to the level of critical self-consciousness. The difference between the barbarous man and the civilized man is not marked by a difference in political regimes, for any regime may be barbarous. The difference is a *cognitive* one. The barbarous man is lost in the conventions of common life; the civilized man has some critical understanding of them. The barbarous man successfully speaks a language, but he has no conception of its grammar, its phonetics, and he cannot symbolize or write it. The civilized man has reflected upon the practice he is engaged in, abstracted its rules, and is in a position to make critical judgments about it. The self-knowledge of the civilized man is identical to that of the true philosopher, since Hume holds that philosophical decisions are simply reflections on common life methodized and corrected (*EU,* 162). Philosophical understanding, for Hume, is a social act. The more civilized a people become, the more reflective they become, and consequently the more philosophical they become. But it is not philosophical reflection that is the source of civilization; it is civilization that is the source of philosophical reflection. The security and stability of good government is not an idea discovered by philosophers and applied to the world; rather, it was in the security and stability provided by the first barbarous republics that philosophy had its origins. Philosophical reflection has a role in criticizing civilization, but (unless it is to degenerate into false philosophy) it can criticize only what is a mode of its own participation.

There is a doctrine of the sociology of knowledge to be found in Hume, for not only is philosophy a social act, it is internally connected to all the other conventions that make up the moral world. "Industry, knowledge, and humanity, are linked together, by an indissoluble chain, and are found, from experience as well as reason, to be peculiar to the more polished, and, what are commonly denominated, the more luxurious ages" (*E,* 271). "We cannot reasonably expect, that a piece of woollen cloth will be wrought to perfection in a nation, which is ignorant of astronomy, or where ethics are neglected" (*E,* 270–71), nor "can we expect, that a government will be well modelled by a people, who know not how to make a spinning-wheel, or to employ a loom to advantage"

(*E*, 273). For this reason Hume could say, in the first *Enquiry*, that the cultivation of philosophy in modern times had led to a better understanding of the rule of law and, consequently, to the stability of government, and why he could hope that the cultivation of philosophy would lead to further political improvements (*EU*, 10). In the next chapter I show how Hume began to have second thoughts about the beneficent influence of philosophical reflection. In the meantime it is important to observe that the perfection of civilization is philosophy, that is, a finely cultivated science of man which can provide historical understanding of, and critical norms for, the spontaneously evolving conventions of the arts, sciences, morals, and government.

Liberty is essential to the process of civilization viewed as a social, philosophical act. Just as liberty of thought and expression are necessary for the perfection of philosophy and science, so liberty of *action*, under the rule of law, is necessary for the perfection of civilization generally. For, as we have seen, the rule of law provides a secure and orderly framework through which novelties may emerge and be tested for inclusion in the conventions of common life. If the perfection of civilization is the achievement of philosophical self-knowledge, as expressed in the arts and sciences, then the original instrument of this perfection is *republican* government. "It is impossible for the arts and sciences to arise, at first, among any people, unless that people enjoy the blessing of a free government" (*E*, 115). By a "free" government, Hume means here a republic. Liberty as the rule of law may flourish in a *civilized* monarchy but not in a barbarous one. Before "science were known in the world," it is impossible to suppose a barbarous monarch to be a "legislator, and govern his people by law, not by the arbitrary will of their fellow-subjects" (*E*, 117). But a republic, though barbarous, "necessarily, by an infallible operation, gives rise to law, even before mankind have made any considerable advances in the other sciences. From law arises security; from security curiosity; And from curiosity knowledge. The later steps of this progress may be more accidental; but the former are altogether necessary. A republic without laws can never have any duration" (*E*, 118).

Hume links liberty, as the rule of law, to free government by a historical, causal bond, not, as Locke does, by a logical one. For Locke, government that is not free cannot contain the rule of law. For Hume, such governments can and do operate by law. The primacy of republican government for Hume is its *causal* power to generate something of the practice of the rule of law, even under barbarous conditions before men have self-consciously come to understand the nature of law. But republican forms, especially when barbarous, are not sufficient to secure liberty in the full sense. The rule of law must be settled deeply in the habits, prejudices, and traditions of mankind, and this process takes time and is the work of countless generations. "No human genius, however comprehensive, is able, by the mere dint of reason and reflection, to effect it. The judgments of many must unite in this work: Experience must guide their labour: Time must bring it to perfection: And the feeling of inconveniences must correct the mistakes, which they inevitably fall into, in their first trials and experiments" (*E,* 124).

In this way, law, like language or any other profound Humean convention, evolves spontaneously, guided by custom and tradition. It is not due to the insights of speculative philosophers and the craft of constitution makers. Civilization and its fundamental institutions are not "brilliant ideas" worked up by the reflections of men of genius and acted out in the world. The heroes of civilization were all skillful participants in an inherited order of custom and tradition. Critical reflection had its place, but it was the reflection of a craftsman and limited by what skill could accomplish. Hume does celebrate the founders of states and considers them among the most memorable of men (*E,* 54). But what the founders establish is what many generations have prepared men to approve of. "In vain, are we asked in what records this charter of our liberties is registered. It was not written on parchment, nor yet on leaves or barks of trees. It preceded the use of writing, and all the other civilized arts of life" (*E,* 468). But most important, who the founders are is not a decision that can be made by the founders themselves nor by their contemporaries; it must be left exclusively to *future* generations (*T,* 566). The heroic project of being a founder is encouraged by the modern cults of rationalism, creativity, and genius. But if Hume is right about the nature of critical thinking, it is a hubristic project that cannot be coherently undertaken.

The rule of law is the source of "all security and happiness" that civilization can afford, and although it is the spontaneous, "slow product of order and of liberty, it is not preserved with the same difficulty, with which it is produced; but when it has once taken root, is a hardy plant, which will scarcely ever perish through the ill culture of men, or the rigour of the seasons" (*E,* 124). Through sympathy and emulation, the rule of law is, to some degree, communicated from republics to monarchies, bringing the latter into the process of civilization. "From these causes proceed civilized monarchies; where the arts of government, first invented in free states, are preserved to the mutual advantage and security of sovereign and subject" (*E,* 125). Once civilized by the rule of law, monarchies may even surpass republics in the perfection of art, science, and government; but this is only because of the "republican" elements contained within the larger sphere of prejudice and tradition of which the monarchy is a part. Civilized monarchy "owes all its perfection to the republican" (*E,* 125). The rule of law, and hence the process of civilization, has its primal scene in the barbarous republic. Hume salutes these in the *History* when discussing the evolution of the British constitution from the Saxon forests. The British owe the advantages of liberty "chiefly to the seeds implanted by those generous barbarians" (*H,* 1: 161).

The True Commonwealth

Hume held not only that civilization originates in republics but that the most perfect form of civilized government would be a republic—albeit a republic of a special kind. In "Idea of a Perfect Commonwealth" (1752), he argued for "the falsehood of the common opinion, that no large state, such as France or Great Britain, could ever be modelled into a commonwealth, but that such a form of government can only take place in a city or small territory" (*E,* 527). Indeed, Hume went so far as to argue that "the contrary seems probable. Though it is more difficult to form a republican government in an extensive country than in a city, there is more facility, when once it is formed, of preserving it steady and uniform, without tumult and faction" (*E,* 527). Hume then laid out a federal hierarchy of electoral bodies ordered from the local to the national level where each local unit is "a kind of republic within itself," having a certain degree of autonomy and the power to elect representatives to the higher levels (*E,* 520). At the top would be a chamber of magistrates who would have the legislative power and a chamber of senators who would, among themselves, constitute an executive branch with a presiding chief executive. The higher magistrates would be indirectly elected by the people through their elected representatives. Such government could claim consent of the people and so could command popular loyalty and authority.

Hume's perfect commonwealth is not presented as a utopia but takes men as they are. "All plans of government, which suppose great reformations in the manners of mankind, are plainly imaginary" (*E,* 514). As I have argued, Humean theorizing must both transcend and bear the imprint of actual practice. As an indication of its concrete character, Hume compared his model of government to Huygen's model of a ship the most commodious for the practice of sailing. But if the ideal is concrete, why did he choose the counterintuitive model of a large republic for the ideal constitution in the face of the traditional view that republics must be small and the fact that no such republic had ever existed?

The answer is that Hume's ideal commonwealth can claim to solve a number of problems of political order which neither ancient nor modern philosophers could resolve and in some cases did not even perceive. And it is, further, an ideal already intimated in the cultural and political practices of Europe, roughly in the way in which Huygen's ideal ship may be said to have been intimated in the practice of sailing. To appreciate how this is so, we must examine more closely Hume's views of republicanism, monarchies, and commerce. I have said that Hume identified with the classical republican tradition. To identify with this tradition is to be a partisan of liberty. "Passionate admirers of the ancients" are "zealous partizans of civil liberty, (for these sentiments, as they are, both of them, in the main, extremely just, are found to be almost inseparable)" (*E,* 383). The republican humanistic tradition held that liberty is possible only in a small territory and where there is not great disparity of wealth among citizens. The economy of a republic is largely agrarian, and the citizens are independent farmers. The source of the moral life is the family and the community of families that make up the small republic. Its military force is a militia of public-spirited farmers, and it considers a standing army in the pay of the state to be a threat to liberty. It allows commerce but is suspicious of its growth, and considers the accumulation of great wealth to be a source of corruption. It is especially hostile to that modern form of commerce financed by public credit. Hume accepted much of this picture of the political order necessary for human well-being. "Where each man had his little house and field to himself, and each county had its capital, free and independent; what a happy situation of mankind! How favorable to industry and agriculture; to marriage and propagation. . . . And nothing surely can give it more liberty, than such small commonwealths, and such an equality of fortune among the citizens" (*E,* 401). Where Hume parted ways with the republican humanistic tradition, both ancient and modern, was in rejecting the claim that extensive commerce and economic growth were corrupt. Hume argued, to the contrary, that extensive commerce in a state actually promotes republican virtue.

The first thing to appreciate is that commerce has not been well understood by philosophers. "Trade was never esteemed an affair of state till the last century; and there scarcely is any ancient writer on politics, who has made mention of it" (*E,* 88). It was the example of the maritime powers of England and Holland that "seem first to have instructed mankind in the importance of an extensive commerce" (*E,* 89). Here again it is practice that "instructs," not theory; though theory is necessary to refine our understanding of practice. Aristotle taught that some men are slaves by nature, and this doctrine survived into modern discussions about how to manage those whom Hume called "the slaving poor." It was thought by many that the poor were incapable of achievement and self-direction and consequently could not be expected to behave rationally. Since their labor was necessary, they had to be managed by severe measures. Hume agreed that the poor did not exhibit the virtues of the "middling rank," which he considered the "Station of Life, that . . . is more favourable to the acquiring of *Wisdom* and *Ability,* as well as *Virtue,*" and for this reason "is more favourable to *Happiness*" (*E,* 547, 551). This rank, because of its critical involvement with the everyday world, "has a better Chance for attaining a Knowledge both of Men and Things, than those of a more elevated Station" (*E,* 547). Consequently, it is to this rank that true philosophy must speak. "These form the most numerous Rank of Men, that can be suppos'd susceptible of Philosophy; and therefore, all Discourses of Morality ought principally to be address'd to them. The Great are too much immers'd in Pleasure; and the Poor too much occupy'd in providing the Necessities of Life, to hearken to the calm Voice of Reason" (*E,* 546).

Hume did not think, however, that the poor need remain in this condition. I quoted earlier Hume's remark that "the *people* are no such dangerous monsters as they have been represented, and it is in every respect better to guide them, like rational creatures, than to lead them like brute beasts" (*E,* 604–5). Hume argued that experience has shown that the disposition to achieve among the poor is equal to that of the middling rank. What they need is the opportunity, and this can only be provided by free trade and an expanding commerce. Hume taught that the best life for man is one of action and contemplation, and action is prior to contemplation. "There is no craving or demand of the human mind more constant and insatiable than that for exercise and employment; and this desire seems the foundation of most of our passions and pursuits" (*E,* 300). The world of culture is "purchased by labor; and our passions are the only causes of labor" (*E,* 261). Men originally labor out of necessity but eventually learn to enjoy the activity itself and take pleasure in the excellence of achievement. The slaving poor working for low wages have no incentive to improve their condition, but "if the employment you give him be lucrative, especially if the profit be attached to every particular exertion of industry, he has gain so often in his eye, that he acquires, by degrees, a passion for it, and knows no such pleasure as that of seeing the daily encrease of his fortune" (*E*, 301). And the promise of a better livelihood raises in "them a desire for a more splendid way of life" (*E*, 264). In this way the poor may eventually enter the middle rank and learn to desire to hear "the calm Voice of Reason."

Recognizing an original disposition in the poor to achievement would encourage them to improve their condition and consequently that of the public. "The encrease and consumption of all the commodities, which serve to the ornament and pleasure of life, are advantageous to society; because, at the same time they multiply those innocent gratifications to individuals, they are a kind of *storehouse* of labour, which, in the exigencies of state, may be turned to public service. In a nation, where there is no demand for such superfluities, men sink into indolence, lose all enjoyment and are useless to the public" (*E*, 272). Thus an extensive commerce serves to bring about that near equality of wealth and independence so cherished by classical republican doctrine and, at the same time, to provide the republic with a revenue to be used when the public interest requires it.

But, according to the classical republican tradition, these advantages did not outweigh the intrinsically corrupting effect that economic growth had on morals. Virtue demanded that the state be rich and the people frugal. The code word in the modern republican tradition for this source of corruption was *luxury*. It was luxury and all that it brought in its wake that caused the collapse of the Roman republic and later of the Roman empire. That luxury necessarily corrupts was challenged in "Of Refinement of the Arts." Hume defined luxury as "great refinement in the gratification of the senses; and any degree of it may be innocent or blameable, according to the age, or country, or condition of the person" (*E*, 268). Luxury becomes a vice only when it is at the expense of "some virtue, as liberality or charity" (*E*, 269). When innocent, luxury is not only not a vice but is a positive good, being a natural expression of the human dispositions to achievement and contemplation which are the twofold sources of human happiness. I mentioned above Hume's view that the skills and excellence required to perfect the contemplative arts are internally connected to those required for the mechanical arts that produce commodities. The latter cannot be "carried to perfection, without being accompanied, in some degree, with the [former]. The same age, which produces great philosophers and politicians, renowned generals and poets, usually abounds with skillful weavers, and ship-carpenters" (*E*, 270). It is only through the mutual cultivation of the mechanical and contemplative arts that "profound ignorance is totally banished, and men enjoy the privilege of rational creatures, to think as well as to act, to cultivate the pleasures of the mind as well as those of the body" (*E*, 271).

As both arts develop, men become more sociable. "Nor is it possible, that, when enriched with science and . . . conversation, they should be contented to remain in solitude, or live with their fellow citizens in that distant manner, which is peculiar to ignorant and barbarous nations. They flock into cities; love to receive and communicate knowledge; to show their wit or their breeding; their taste in conversation or living, in clothes or furniture. Curiosity allures the wise; vanity the foolish; and pleasure both. Particular clubs and societies are everywhere formed: Both sexes meet in an easy and sociable manner: and the tempers of men, as well as their behavior, refine apace. So that, beside the improvements which they receive from knowledge and the liberal arts, it is impossible but they must feel an encrease of humanity, from the very habit of conversing together, and contributing to each other's pleasure and entertainment" (*E*, 271).

Hume was at pains to argue against those who defended luxury within the framework of the "selfish system" such as Mandeville, who argued that private vices provide work for others and so yield public virtues. To this Hume tersely replied, "To say, that, without a vicious luxury, the labour would not have been employed at all, is only to say, that there is some other defect in human nature, such as indolence, selfishness, inattention to others, for which luxury, in some measure, provides a remedy; as one poison may be an antidote to another" (*E*, 279). The most Hume will admit is that by banishing vicious luxury, without curing sloth or indifference towards others, you simply diminish industry without adding anything to charity or generosity. But language and the reality of things must be kept clear. "Let us never pronounce vice in itself advantageous. . . . And indeed it seems upon any system of morality, little less than a contradiction in terms, to talk of a vice, which is in general beneficial to society" (*E*, 280).

To the charge that luxury corrupts liberty and martial virtue, Hume replied that experience shows clearly that the martial virtue of modern England and France is equal to anything the ancient republican armies could display. As to liberty, "The liberties of England, so far from decaying since the improvements in the arts, have never flourished so much as during that period" (*E*, 277). And more generally, a growing economy and "progress in the arts is rather favourable to liberty, and has a natural tendency to preserve, if not produce a free government" (*E*, 277). It has this tendency because "where luxury nourishes commerce and industry, the peasants, by a proper cultivation of the land, become rich and independent; while the tradesmen and merchants acquire a share of the property." This leads to an increase in "that middling rank of men, who are the best and firmest basis of public liberty. These submit not to slavery, like the peasants, from poverty and meanness of spirit; and having no hopes of tyrannizing over others, like the barons, they are not tempted, for the sake of that gratification, to submit to the tyranny of their sovereign. They covet equal laws, which may secure their property, and preserve them from monarchical, as well as aristocratical tyranny" (*E,* 277–78). Hume reminds those "old Whigs" who hanker after the lost virtue of the ancient republics that the House of Commons "is the support of our popular government; and all the world acknowledges, that it owed its chief influence and consideration to the encrease of commerce, which threw such a balance of property into the hands of the commons. How inconsistent, then, is it to blame so violently a refinement in the arts, and to represent it as the bane of liberty and public spirit" (*E,* 278).

I discussed in chapter 4 Hume's teaching that the ancient moralists were superior to modern moral theorizing but inferior to "modern manners." Hume admired the ancients for their love of liberty and their meditation on the good life or human excellence. But the ancients were deficient in two respects. First, they did not understand very well either the source of liberty or the means of its preservation. "These people were extremely fond of liberty; but seem not to have understood it very well" (*E,* 408). Second, they were limited in their experience of "the generous passion," that is, extensive benevolence or humanity. The ancients had thought deeply about human excellence and had cultivated the virtue of greatness of mind, but their experience of benevolence was constricted. There was no motivation to discover the instruments which could extend the blessings of the good life to all men. Both deficiencies were due largely to the failure to understand the links between liberty, the rule of law, commerce, industriousness, and humanity. It is the insight into these links gained through long experience that makes modern political science superior to ancient.

Hume taught that the Roman republic and the Roman empire fell not because of any corruption due to "luxury," but because of "an ill-modelled government, and the unlimited extent of conquests" (*E,* 276). The one is an intellectual failure, the other a moral one. But what is a well-modeled government? And what is the image of a regime that can embody the insights of the moderns into the nature of liberty, commerce, industry, and humanity? Hume does not think of this as a question about abstract forms of government independent of the context of custom. That is the path of false philosophy and must yield conclusions that are antinomic. The true path is to explore the intimations of a concrete practice through the contemplative art of true philosophy, which includes the historical and rhetorical arts. Hume did think that forms of government shape practice (*E*, 14–31), and that there is an ideal form of government for Europeans engaged in the practice of liberty. But forms of government are embedded in even deeper practices which influence their concrete shape. For Hume, the civilizing process is a deeper notion than forms of government. The deep question is not whether republican government is superior to monarchical (as false philosophers such as Locke had thought) but whether a government, whatever its form, embodies to a high degree the qualities of civilization.

Hume taught that ancient republics were unstable, factious, provincial, and cruel. They were, however, preferable to ancient monarchies which were quite intolerable. But "all kinds of government, free and absolute, seem to have undergone, in modern times, a great change for the better, with regard both to foreign and domestic management" (*E*, 93). Ancient republics had difficulty establishing an aristocracy with sufficient authority to restrain factions among the people, but in modern times "there is not one republic in Europe . . . that is not remarkable for justice, lenity, and stability, equal to, or even beyond Marseilles, Rhodes, or the most celebrated in antiquity. Almost all of them are well-tempered Aristocracies" (*E*, 416).

But the form of government that is most improved is monarchy. "Monarchical government seems to have made the greatest advances towards perfection. It may now be affirmed of civilized monarchies, what was formerly said in praise of republics alone, that they are a government of laws, not of Men. They are found susceptible of order, method, and constancy, to a surprizing degree. Property is there secure; industry encouraged; the arts flourish; and the prince lives among his subjects, like a father among his children" (*E*, 94). Hume calculates that during the last two centuries there had been approximately two hundred "absolute princes, great and small" in Europe. Yet "of these there has not been one, not even Philip II of Spain, so bad as Tiberius, Caligula, Nero, or Domitian, who were four in twelve amongst the Roman emperors" (*E*, 94). Though ancient republics were superior to ancient monarchies, modern monarchies are superior to ancient republics. Here again forms of government become objects of philosophic superstition when abstracted from the larger whole of common life of which they are merely a part.

Hume credits the superiority of modern government in respect to stability, liberty, and humanity to the reciprocal evolution of the mechanical and contemplative arts, and he explicitly acknowledges the contribution that philosophical reflection has played in this process. "The stability of modern governments above the ancient, and the accuracy of modern philosophy, have improved, and probably will still improve, by similar gradations" (*EU,* 10). I mentioned above Hume's observation that the mechanical arts and commerce flourish in the absolute governments and principalities of Europe; the same is true of the contemplative arts. "The most eminent instance of the flourishing of learning in absolute governments, is that of France, which scarcely ever enjoyed any established liberty, [i.e., formal acknowledgement of the rule of law] and yet has carried the arts and sciences as near perfection as any other nation" (*E,* 91).

And Hume is concerned to subvert another Whig myth, namely, that creation of wealth "is an infallible result of liberty." "Liberty," he says, "must be attended with particular accidents, and a certain turn of thinking, in order to produce that effect" (*E,* 265). That peculiar "turn of thinking" is the spirit of industriousness and individual achievement that is peculiarly modern and European and which opened the era of "modern manners" (*E,* 273). But the wealth of a nation is not significantly increased until it is recognized that the spirit of achievement is a disposition of laborers as well as those of rank and education. I discussed above Hume's insistence that laborers are achieving equals and that they should be given an incentive to improve their condition. That laborers are so endowed is an insight into human nature gained by a largely English experience. "England above any nation at present in the world, or that appears in the records of any story" has provided the laboring class with opportunities to increase their wealth. This has led to high wages which, Hume grants, has led to something of an imbalance in foreign trade, but "as foreign trade is not the most material circumstance, it is not to be put in competition with the happiness of so many millions" (*E,* 265). That the prosperity of the common people in England is not due entirely to its present "free government" and to civil liberty, Hume infers from Bacon who accounted for the advantages obtained by the English in their wars with France by the "superior ease and plenty of the common people amongst the former." Yet absolute monarchy was the form of government of both kingdoms at the time (*E,* 266–67). This peculiar English practice is one of those "particular accidents" that over time generates a practice or a "turn of thinking" which, upon critical reflection, reveals dispositions in human nature hitherto unrecognized. Here, as elsewhere, impressions of reflection are prior to ideas of reflection. Only after we have lived through a practice and tasted it can we have its idea.

Though civilized absolute monarchies are superior in many respects to republics, ancient and modern, they are inferior to modern republics in respect to "gentleness and stability." Hume observes that "our modern education and customs instill more humanity and moderation than the ancient; but have not as yet been able to overcome entirely the disadvantages of that form of government" (*E,* 94). Hume believes, however, that there is a source of improvement in modern monarchies and a source of degeneracy in free governments that "will bring these species of civil polity still nearer an equality." A modern absolute monarchy such as that of France does not have higher or more taxes than what are encountered in "free countries," but they are expensive, unequal, and arbitrary and are so contrived that "the industry of the poor, especially of the peasants and farmers, is, in a great measure, discouraged, and agriculture rendered a beggarly and slavish employment" (*E,* 95). This system is to no one's advantage except the tax collectors, "a race of men rather odious to the nobility and the whole kingdom." A wise prince or minister might easily remedy this abuse, in which case "the difference between that absolute government and our free one, would not appear so considerable as at present" (*E,* 95).

The source of degeneracy in free governments is the practice of "contracting debt, and mortgaging the public revenues, by which taxes may, in time, become altogether intolerable, and all the property of the state be brought into the hands of the public." Should this happen or come close to happening, a free state could become more oppressive than a civilized absolute monarchy. This is an "inconvenience, which nearly threatens all free governments," and the freer the government, the greater the threat (*E,* 95–96; and "Of Public Credit").

Hume's suggestion that modern monarchies and free governments will eventually approach each other in form does not imply that a true form of government will emerge which solves the problems of the original forms. What would emerge in the case of free government would be something still tainted with corruption, and the improved monarchy would still contain the weakness of that form of government, namely, its tendency to impoverish the lower orders. Though superior to the ancients, modern political order contains conflicting, discordant, and even destructive elements, and so is in need of being "methodized and corrected." Here, as always in Hume's philosophy, the source of correction is intimated in the practices themselves. The quality of human life is poetic. The Humean imagination is a "productive faculty" which connects what reflection shows to be separable, which unites what is different, and which reconciles what is in opposition. Imagination requires the concrete knowledge of a loyal but critical participant in the practice; one who is skilled in the style and idiom of the practice and who possesses good judgment, or what Hume calls "taste." Here the idiom illuminates, and not the concept; the judgment, and not the proposition; and the whole of common life guides interpretation, not an abstract system. So the question of true philosophy must be, What solution to modern political conflicts is intimated in the prejudices, customs, and manners of modern political practice? The essay "Idea of a Perfect Commonwealth" is Hume's answer to that question.

Hume discerns a dialectic between republican and monarchical government, each of which expresses a truth about human dispositions but neither of which expresses the whole truth. One truth of republicanism is that participation in a community is a demand of human nature. The central teaching of Hume's science of man is that man is a social being through and through. Whereas liberal theorizing about government begins with an image of abstract individuals contracting to form political society in a state of nature, behind the veil of ignorance, or on spaceship earth, Hume begins with an image of social development. "Man, born in a family, is compelled to maintain society, from necessity, from natural inclination, and from habit" (*E,* 37). The whole of Hume's moral and political philosophy can be viewed as a meditation on this sentence. The source of the moral life is to be found in the sentiments of dependence, affection, authority, and loyalty first experienced in the family and community. Though modified, these sentiments survive in the larger sphere of political society. Justice and interest require a larger sphere, but it must not become so large and abstract as to subvert the moral life. Hence the necessity of small republics of the City-State size, where face-to-face knowledge is possible.

A gross index of whether a form of government answers the demands of human nature is whether it makes possible a flourishing and growing population. Hume is quite insistent about the importance of size to the moral life. "Extended governments," he says, "soon become absolute," and a "large government is accustomed by degrees to tyranny" (*E,* 119). "Enormous monarchies are, probably, destructive to human nature; in their progress, in their continuance, and even in their downfall, which never can be very distant from their establishment" (*E,* 340–41). The same threat to the moral life is posed by large cities. "Enormous cities are, besides, destructive to society, beget vice and disorder of all kinds, starve the remoter provinces, and even starve themselves, by the prices to which they raise all provisions" (*E*, 401). Small republics encourage liberty and equality of fortune. "All small states naturally produce equality of fortune, because they afford no opportunities of great encrease; but small commonwealths much more, by that division of power and authority which is essential to them" (*E*, 401). Though inferior in wealth, there is not the great distance between rich and poor in small republics that is inevitable in extended governments. Each citizen has "a small fortune, secure and independent," which is conducive to propagation (*E*, 401). Hume thought affairs in modern times were not as happy. "It must be owned, that the situation of affairs in modern times, with regard to civil liberty, as well as equality of fortune, is not near so favorable, either to the propagation or happiness of mankind." The reason is that "Europe is shared out mostly into great monarchies" and even "small territories, are commonly governed by absolute princes, who ruin their people by a mimicry of the greatest monarchs in the splendor of their court and number of their forces" (*E*, 402). Only Switzerland and Holland "resemble the ancient republics," and of the former Hume observes that although "far from possessing any advantage either of soil, climate, or commerce, yet the number of people, with which it abounds, notwithstanding their enlisting themselves into every service in Europe, prove sufficiently the advantages of their political institutions" (*E*, 403).

Small republics, however, are susceptible to invasion by larger powers, and the high incidence of monarchies in history is due largely to the security that is provided by a central authority governing a large territory. Another advantage of monarchy when civilized is that a uniform system of laws prevails over all subjects, and in a wise prince this can lead to a flourishing economy within a large territory free of the inevitable tariffs and wars that trade among nations inevitably brings. China is just such a political order; Hume presents it "as one of the most flourishing empires in the world; though it has very little commerce beyond its own territories" (*E*, 264). Hume finds China to be an interesting case of an order that combines vast empire, monarchy, and republican elements. The people have always been governed by a monarch and "can scarcely form an idea of a free government," yet commerce flourishes in "that industrious nation," and the people enjoy the liberty and stability associated with the rule of law without the explicit recognition of it. Hume's explanation for this is that the Chinese have few threatening neighbors; consequently there is no incentive to maintain and discipline a large standing army. The armed forces of China are militia that receive little discipline and so are unfit to suppress the rebellions that might be expected to occur in so vast and populous a territory. In this way the "sword . . . may properly be said to be always in the hands of the people, which is a sufficient restraint upon the monarch, and obliges him to lay his *mandarins* or governors of provinces under the restraint of general laws, in order to prevent those rebellions, which we learn from history to have been so frequent and dangerous in that government" (*E*, 122 n). Without a philosophy to guide them, the Chinese have, through trial and error over a long stretch of time, developed a form of government which answers to fundamental demands of human nature: the communitarian imperative, security, the rule of law, and the surplus of wealth required for a contemplative culture which is possible only where industriousness and commerce are encouraged and protected. And so Hume discerns within the Chinese experience an order that suggests the ideal form of government. "Perhaps, a pure monarchy of this kind, were it fitted for defence against foreign enemies, would be the best of all governments, as having the tranquillity attending kingly power, and the moderation and liberty of popular assemblies" (*E*, 122 n).

But it is not clear how this could be achieved, for it is the military weakness of the monarch along with "a peculiarity in the situation of that country" that makes possible "the happiness, riches, and good police of the Chinese" (*E*, 122 n). Were the monarch to have a force large enough to protect so vast an empire, it could be used also to oppress the provinces. It would appear, then, that the best regime would be an extensive republic with equal rights for the provinces, and this for four reasons.

First, the communitarian principle requires that family and community be given independent status because these are the sources of the moral life. This status is best protected in small republics where people can know each other and be known. Second, small republics are vulnerable to invasion and themselves need the protection of a larger polity. Third, extensive commerce is required for human flourishing not only in that a surplus of wealth ("luxury") can be transformed into culture but because the skills required to produce such wealth encourage the virtues of liberty, knowledge, industriousness, and humanity. Extensive commerce requires some sort of political regulation over a large territory. Fourth, republics encourage the ideals of liberty, equality, and the rule of law which are necessary for the human good. How does Hume's ideal commonwealth exemplify these conditions?

Hume imagines the extensive republic to be divided into one hundred counties and the counties into one hundred parishes. The citizens are county freeholders of twenty pounds a year and town householders of five hundred pounds. These meet annually in the "parish church" and elect a county representative. These meet in the county capital and elect one senator and ten county magistrates. Since each senator has the authority of a county magistrate, each county will have eleven magistrates. The senate holds the executive power, and the county representatives hold the legislative power. Law originates in the senate but must be ratified by a majority of the counties. This can be done either by sending the law down to the county representatives themselves or, as would be more convenient, to their magistrates. If the latter, any five county representatives can, if they desire, take the law out of the hands of the magistrates and place it before the county representatives for a vote. Further, the county representatives or magistrates may give to the senator of the county a law to be proposed to the senate. Should the senate refuse the law, five counties are sufficient to bring the law for a decision before the county magistrates or representatives.

Twenty counties are sufficient to throw any man out of office for a year, and thirty counties for three years. The senate may expel any of its members for a year, not to be reelected for that year, but it can never expel twice in a year the senator of the same county.

Each county "is a kind of republic within itself" and can make its own laws. All crimes are tried in the county by its magistrates and a jury, but the senate can stop any trial and bring it before themselves. Any county law can be annulled by another county or by the senate. This protects against the formation of a special interest. Should the matter be contested, no county could decide for itself but would have to submit the matter to the whole, which can best determine what agrees with the general interest.

Hume observes that all free governments consist of a greater and a lower house, "a senate and people." Hume accepts Harrington's maxim that the people without a senate would lack wisdom, and a senate without the people would lack honesty. Wisdom in the people is maintained by the rules of citizenship and the mechanics of election. First, although Hume considered the "slaving poor" to be achieving equals, he did not think of them as social and political equals. Politics requires good judgment, and the source of judgment is not some abstract reason that all men may be said to possess but *educated sentiment,* which requires a virtuous education in a political tradition. The skill required to achieve and maintain property and a household is a rough index of the skill required to manage a state. A market economy can serve to elevate the poor to this condition, but elevation there must be before political participation is possible. Second, democracy requires the assembly of great numbers of people to debate, and such assemblies are susceptible to mass enthusiasms. The problem then is that if the people debate, all is confusion; if they are not allowed to debate, the senate carves for them. Hume's remedy is to divide the people into small bodies. "Separate this great body; and though every member be only of middling sense, it is not probable, that any thing but reason can prevail over the whole" (*E*, 523).

Honesty is maintained in the senate by a number of checks, the most remarkable of which is "the court of competitors." Any candidate for the senate having more than a third of the vote but not elected is incapable for one year of holding any public office, but he takes his seat in the court of competitors. The court may have as much as a hundred members or none. The court has no power in the commonwealth, but it has the right to inspect public accounts and to bring accusation against any person before the senate. If the senate acquit him, the court may appeal to the people, either in the form of their magistrates or representatives. Upon that appeal the people must elect three persons from each county to the number of three hundred who meet in the capital and bring the accused to a new trial. The court may propose any law to the senate and if refused may appeal to the people. Any senator thrown out of office by the court of competitors takes his seat in the court.

In addition to this check of the great upon the great, the senate is further restrained by annual elections, by the small number of offices at its disposal, by the requirement that those holding such offices must be reelected annually by the senate, and by the right of the counties to throw any person out of office (twenty counties for one year, thirty for three years).

The magistrates could also form a special interest, but this is prevented in part by the vast territory of the commonwealth, by "the separation of places and interests." Should that fail, the county representatives may resume the power of the magistrates whenever any five of a hundred demand it.

Hume's ideal commonwealth is not a utopia but an imaginative insight into an ideal that reconciles several conflicting demands of human nature: first, the communitarian principle, which is the source of the moral life and which requires liberty, equality, and the government of a small republic; second, the need for security against invasion, which requires a strong central government over a vast territory, the solution to which has typically been a monarchical empire with a necessary loss of liberty and equality; third, the deep human need for achievement and the creation of a contemplative culture. The material condition for these spiritual values is extensive commerce, which encourages the development of knowledge, industriousness, responsibility, liberty, and humanity. Such commerce demands a polity larger than a small republic.

What must be stressed, especially in view of the still-popular misconception of Hume as a Tory, is the democratic-republican character of the ideal commonwealth. *Democracy* was largely a term of abuse in Hume's time and implied anarchy. "Democracies are turbulent," he wrote, and in "Of Some Remarkable Customs," he described the Athenian democracy as "a tumultuous government as we can scarcely form a notion of in the present age of the world" (*E,* 368–69). The traditional solution to this problem is aristocracies, which are better adapted for peace and order, and "accordingly were most admired by ancient writers," although "they are jealous and oppressive" (*E,* 528). Though they possess greatness of mind, and consequently love of liberty, aristocracies lack the virtue of "extensive benevolence." The aristocrat tends not to think of the people as equals in their desire to achieve or as having the same potential for self-development. The mechanism for arousing this potential is a flourishing market economy in an extensive territory under the rule of law. It was this mechanism that by the eighteenth century had been able "to confound all ranks of men" (*H,* 5: 132).

Hume did not think the people were "monsters," but neither did he believe in the innate virtue of the people in the mass. The source of political judgment is not reflection; it is not a set of abstract rules, methods, or self-evident truths that anyone of even minimal intelligence can understand and apply. It is not what Thomas Paine described in *Common Sense.* The sources of political judgment are skills and virtuous dispositions. At the level of the lowest common denominator, these dispositions are communicated through families who are skilled in the management of property. But this is only a necessary condition; the best political judgment requires skill in the contemplative arts of civilization and especially of true philosophy. Hume's stress on the importance of families in educating sentiment implies that two or more generations are necessary to cultivate political judgment. This must be a hard saying for modern political theorists who conceive of political philosophy as a matter of discerning abstract "rapports and relations" that all rational individuals can understand and for modern political ideologies that think of political practice as a matter of applying such abstractions. In respect to political judgment, there is no rationalistic bypassing of "the virtuous education of youth" through families practiced in a political tradition.

Hume is not opposed to democracy in principle; indeed his philosophy of common life and moral sentiments could not rule it out. But a democracy that is acceptable must at least have a virtuous citizenry. Democracy must be "refined" by virtue, and this is what Hume's ideal commonwealth purports to do. "In a large government, which is modelled with masterly skill, there is compass and room enough to refine the democracy, from the lower people, who may be admitted into the first elections or first concoction of the commonwealth, to the higher magistrates, who direct all the movements" (*E,* 528).

Democracy in its purest form appears in the parochial assemblies of the small parish republics, which are a division of the country into something very like Thomas Jefferson's "ward republics." These provincial settings are not only the original source of the moral life; they are the contexts in which knowledge of character is intimate and deep. Here even the rustic vulgar can be expected to make good judgments. "The lower sort of people and small proprietors are good judges enough of one not very distant from them in rank or habitation; and therefore, in their parochial meetings, will probably chuse the best, or nearly the best representative," but they are unfit "for electing into the higher offices of the republic. Their ignorance gives the grandees an opportunity of deceiving them" (*E,* 522).

There is an evident concern in Hume's commonwealth to protect the liberty and the moral life of the small republics. National legislation is decided not by a one-man, one-vote referendum, but by the majority vote of the republics, each deciding according to its own laws. The republics are further protected by the constitutional right of any republic to nullify the laws of any other republic which threatens its interest and, in the case of persistent conflict, to place the matter before the republics as a whole for a decision. Annual elections and the many barriers Hume has erected to corruption and faction give a republic ample opportunity to make its grievance known and ample opportunity to persuade. If all else fails, each republic has its own militia, "in imitation of that of Swisserland," which requires that all able-bodied males receive regular military training. The threat of civil war is a strong inducement for the republics to reach agreement.

The entire system is designed to secure liberty and to ensure that a free and open consensus is reached and that abuses are known and can be quickly remedied. Indeed, Hume is so solicitous about securing these values of the rule of law and in preventing the abuse of power that the most obvious criticism to make of the ideal regime is that there may not be sufficient continuity in the legislative and administrative offices to govern effectively. But if there is an error here, then within that eternal dialectic between liberty and authority that Hume says is internal to all political order, the error is on the side of liberty, not authority.

The idiom of Hume's political thought is deeply rooted in the ancient and modern republican humanistic tradition, though methodized and corrected as any Humean participation in tradition must be. Hume may be thought of as an Old Whig detoxified; that is, purged of the corrupt philosophical consciousness that had distorted and alienated the political theorizing of Locke, Sidney, Harrington, and other "Old," "Real," or "True" Whig heroes. Hume described the difference between Whig and Tory as follows: "A TORY, therefore, since the *revolution,* [the Glorious Revolution of 1688] may be defined in a few words, to be *a lover of monarchy, though without abandoning liberty; and a partizan of the family of* STUART. As a WHIG may be defined to be *a lover of liberty though without renouncing monarchy; and a friend of the settlement in the* PROTESTANT *line*" (*E,* 71). In a letter of 1756, written shortly after publishing the volume on the Stuarts, Hume wrote, "My views of *things* are more conformable to Whig principles; my representations of *persons* to Tory prejudices. Nothing can so much prove that men commonly regard more persons than things, as to find that I am commonly numbered among the Tories" (*L,* 1: 237). Hume's view of things (what is and ought to be in the political order) follows Whig *principle;* his view of persons (the evaluation of character) follows Tory *prejudices.* The corrupt philosophical consciousness informing much of Whig thinking about the English Civil War led to a distorted view of the character and conduct of the Stuarts, picturing them as forces of oppression in a story of liberation. Hume's correction of this distortion led to a more sympathetic picture of the Stuarts, one that elicits moral sentiment. Another name for this in Hume's lexicon is "moral prejudice." But to conform to Tory moral prejudices is not to conform to Tory political principles. Hume "shed a generous tear for the fate of Charles I, and the earl of Strafford," but he was not a "partizan" of the house of Stuart (*H,* 1: xxx).

But Hume's republicanism is set in a context of philosophical theorizing which carries it quite beyond the political debate between Whigs and Tories in eighteenth-century Britain. Hume taught that civilization began and had to begin in barbarous republics where the first obscure efforts at the rule of law appeared. Republics answer to something deep in human nature: the demand for community (equality) and the rule of law (liberty). Once established, republics remain as a standard which political thought can never entirely abandon. Civilized monarchies can be and have been superior to republics, but this is only because they participate in a political tradition containing republican dispositions. These dispositions may be obscured by monarchical forms, but it is republican dispositions and these alone that civilize monarchy. Europeans received republican dispositions in part from their classical education. Nearly all of the learned of Europe admired the ancient republican moralists, however critical they were of them in this or that respect. This was as true of the courtiers of the absolute monarchy of France as of the citizens of Geneva. Republican prejudices would, of course, sit uneasily with other prejudices—monarchical, aristocratic, or clerical—and with the modern desire for a more commodious life. But it is precisely the task of the Humean imagination, through a poetic act, to reconcile these contrary prejudices into one amiable character. There is no way to know beforehand what form such reconciliation will take either in the individual soul or in that of a nation. A central task of the *Essays* and the *History* is to explore how contrary prejudices have come to receive some measure of reconciliation in the British constitution of liberty and to explore its intimations. The poetic act of the imagination in forming identities yields wisdom but does not follow a rational method, and so Hume can speak of "the wisdom of the English constitution, or rather the concurrence of accidents" (*H,* 5: 569). The wisdom of the British constitution is part of a wider civilizing process at work throughout Europe. It was in exploring the intimations of that process that Hume discovered the ideal of a perfect commonwealth.

The civilizing process proper began in the republics of pagan antiquity. The ancient republics established, if only obscurely, some notions of law, liberty, and equality. From these arise the mechanical and contemplative arts. Philosophy arises late in the civilizing process, but the ideal history of philosophy and the ideal history of republics are internally connected. I have argued that, in Hume's thought, the true philosopher and the civilized man are the same. The true philosopher is the sage and patriot, and his story is the story of civilization. In that story, as narrated so far, his true home is in the order illuminated by Hume's idea of a perfect commonwealth.

CHAPTER NINE

False Philosophy and Barbarism

The Barbarism of Refinement

Barbarism is a frequently used term in Hume's moral vocabulary. It is a term used in dialectical opposition to *civilization.* The process of civilization is driven by labor and the passion for achievement. The character of the civilized man is marked by the qualities of "*industry, knowledge, and humanity*" (*E,* 271). The opposites of these qualities, sloth, inhumanity, and ignorance, characterize man in his original barbarous state, a condition almost entirely devoid of the mechanical and contemplative arts. Civilization comes in degrees. A people having achieved some degree of civilization may be inferior to another people who have achieved a higher degree, and in relation to them, may be thought of as barbarous. Thus any unusual display of sloth, ignorance, or inhumanity among a people who are otherwise civilized counts for Hume as barbarism. The medieval English parliament was composed of "barbarians" (*H,* 5: 556 n). The seventeenth-century English were civilized, but Cromwell was "a barbarian," as were the theological factions that plunged the nation into civil war and regicide (*H,* 6: 149, 15, 25), and the modern Irish are often thought of as sunk in sloth, ignorance, and barbarism (*H,* 5: 335, 425).

Although knowledge, industry, and humanity are "linked together by an indissoluble chain," knowledge has priority. The source of barbarism is ignorance and fear. Man begins his career as "a necessitous animal," born in ignorance and fear. Emancipation from this condition is possible only through knowledge. The knowledge that cures, however, is not the work of reflection, which discovers abstract principles and applies them; rather, it is the slow work of many generations linked together by common traditions and customs.

A failure to have these qualities (knowledge, industry, and humanity) may drive a civilized people back into barbarism. Roman civilization collapsed due to an "ill-modelled government" and "unlimited conquests," that is, to a failure in knowledge and humanity. Such failures may be viewed as the persistence of those original qualities of ignorance, fear, scarce goods, and limited benevolence which were the original condition of mankind. And this gives rise to the thought that these imperfections could be overcome by the evolution of knowledge, industry, and humanity, with knowledge leading the way. Hume's friend Turgot and later his follower Condorcet would develop this suggestion into a theory of inevitable moral progress through knowledge.[1] Hume explicitly rejected the theory of inevitable progress, but he accepted the ideal of "improvement" through critical judgment (*L*, 2: 180). The cultivation of philosophy in modern times had led to a better understanding of political order and of commerce. Because of this, modern regimes are superior to ancient regimes in stability, liberty, material prosperity, and morals.

Viewing matters this way suggests that the main threat to civilization is ignorance, which can be overcome by the cultivation of critical reflection. As men become more civilized, they necessarily become more reflective, and an increase in critical reflection yields an increase in civilization. This does not mean that progress is inevitable, but it does suggest that the ever-expanding order of critical reflection itself poses no threat to civilization. That the source of civilization is critical reflection was the faith of the Enlightenment and all forms of progressive thought, liberal and Marxist, that have taken inspiration from it. But it is just here that the Humean understanding of civilization diverges from the progressive faith, for there is to be found in Hume the suggestion that the civilizing process itself contains the seeds of its own corruption.

We may stylize the account as follows. The original source of all action and belief, and consequently of civilization, is custom. Reflection can understand the customs in which it is embedded. Working within the domain of custom, reflection can discern conflicts and suggest reforms to correct them. But reflection does not constitute custom, nor can it emancipate itself from it, nor can it in any deep way guide it. Again, it is civilization that produces reason, not reason that produces civilization. But as men become more civilized, they necessarily become more reflective. The most developed form of critical reflection is philosophy. As Hume's dialectic shows, however, philosophy may appear in a true or corrupt form. A true philosophical consciousness knows custom to be the source of its own critical activity. A false philosophical consciousness attempts to disown the authority of custom and to make reflection itself the source of critical activity.

The tendency of philosophy in human affairs is always to its false forms. In disowning the authority of custom the false philosopher rebels against the source of his own being and that of civilization. In generating this form of reflection, civilization falls into conflict with itself. This in turn yields a new form of barbarism—a form possible only in an advanced stage of civilization.

An act of false philosophy cuts the thinker off from custom, which is the source of all belief and action. John Rawls, in his own instantiation of this act, has rightly called it "the veil of ignorance."[2] The ignorance that arises from suspending the authority of common life is a self-imposed ignorance fostered by a reflection that is determined to find the source of belief and conduct within itself. The source of man's original barbarism is ignorance and fear. But we have now to consider two types of ignorance: the ignorance and blindness of man's original condition, emancipation from which is achieved by the process of civilization, and the self-imposed ignorance and blindness of a corrupt form of the philosophical act, which is possible only in an advanced stage of civilization. The ignorance of the one is coupled with fear and generates a servile obedience to a world of gods and vulgar theism. The self-imposed ignorance of the other is coupled with resentment (the sentiment that one may have been "taken in" by custom) and generates the hostile and antisocial modes of ascetic, revolutionary, and guilty philosophical existence. The term Hume most often uses to characterize this new sort of barbarism is *refinement.* As mentioned earlier, Hume often uses this term in the sense of a chemical refinement whereby the bouquet, color, and body of wine is refined away, leaving the poison of pure alcohol. In a philosophic age no domain of custom is able to protect itself against the world-inverting violence of philosophical refinement. There is no custom or way of life, Hume says, "but what, may, with facility, be refined away, if we indulge a false philosophy, in sifting and scrutinizing it, by every captious rule of logic, in every light or position, in which it may be placed" (*E*, 482). Hume gives as an instance the contract theory of government, in which a richly endowed political order, the work of time and memory, is refined away, leaving only the contract and abstract contractors. This abstract system is favored as the essence of legitimate government merely because it is the creation of reflection, and reflection delights, and can only delight, in its own constructions.

The barbarism of refinement occurs not only in philosophical interpretations of reality but in literature as well. Hume recommends Addison's "definition of fine writing," which "consists of sentiments which are natural, without being obvious" (*E,* 191). The task of literature is to give form to feeling so as to render it intelligible and agreeable. Writing that succeeds in doing this possesses what Hume calls the character of "simplicity." But simplicity is not merely a faithful copy of nature; it requires interesting form for its expression, and this act of informing sentiment Hume calls "refinement." Two extremes can be discerned in writing. The extreme of simplicity would be nature presented devoid of interesting form: "the chit-chat of the tea-table, copied faithfully and at a full length" (*E,* 191–92). The extreme of refinement would be writing that had become obsessed with form itself. Here form is not in the service of rendering sentiment intelligible and agreeable but has itself become the main object of attention. As in refinement in philosophy, the mind ceases to engage nature; it becomes aware of its own power to impose form on sentiment, becomes fascinated with that form, and begins to treat it as the reality.

Simplicity carried to extremes ends in boredom; refinement carried to extremes ends in self-absorption. Hume lays it down that although both extremes are to be avoided, "we ought to be more on our guard against the excess of refinement than that of simplicity; and that because the former excess is both less *beautiful,* and more *dangerous* than the latter" (*E,* 194). Simplicity even in its crude forms keeps thought tied to sentiment, which is the source of all belief and action. The excess of refinement cuts thought loose from this source and leaves it wandering in an abstract world of its own making. There is a parallel here between false literary refinement and the "vacuum" created by false philosophy, in which the philosopher seeks to live an "artificial life," where no one can answer for what will please or displease him (*E,* 343). Hume is clear that this stricture on refinement applies to philosophical writing as well as to any other. "The case is the same with orators, philosophers, critics, or any author" (*E,* 192), and "no criticism can be instructive, which descends not to particulars, and is not full of examples and illustrations" (*E,* 194).

The excess of refinement is more likely in a highly civilized age with a reflective culture than in an earlier stage of civilization where thought is more engaged with nature. Consequently, "the excess of refinement is now more to be guarded against than ever; because it is the extreme, which men are the most apt to fall into, after learning has made some progress, and after eminent writers have appeared in every species of composition. The endeavour to please by novelty leads men wide of simplicity and nature, and fills their writing with affectation and conceit" (*E,* 196). Hume explains how the simplicity of Greek writing and eloquence gave way to the overly reflective and refined style of the Roman writers. He includes Ovid, Seneca, Lucan, Martial, the Plinys, and even Cicero, and he thinks he sees "some symptoms of a like degeneracy of taste, in France as well as in England" (*E,* 196).

Hume thinks there is a natural history of the arts whereby literature moves from an admirable simplicity to ever-increasing refinement and finally to the complete barbarization of style and the total elimination of natural sentiment in writing. Hume seems to think that the height of simplicity occurs at the origins of a literature. The first literature "whatever rudeness may sometimes attend it, is so fitted to express the genuine movements of nature and passion, that the compositions possessed of it must ever appear valuable to the discerning part of mankind." The barbarism that seeks to find the source of literature in reflection alone, the "glaring figures of discourse, the pointed antithesis, the unnatural conceit, the jingle of words . . . were not employed by early writers; not because they were rejected, but because they scarcely ever occurred to them" (*H,* 5: 149). But as writing becomes more self-reflective and critical, more attention is given to the writing itself. Play with forms becomes a substitute for making sentiment intelligible and agreeable. In this play, wit is matched against wit, and each bid for novelty is met by a higher bid. These barbarisms of refinement "multiply every day more and more in the fashionable compositions: Nature and good sense are neglected. . . . And a total degeneracy of style and language prepares the way for barbarism and ignorance" (*H,* 5: 149–50).

The barbarism and ignorance of which Hume speaks here are possible only among those who have acquired the habit of critical reflection. The ignorance which now restricts human life is not an ignorance of nature and cannot plead innocence as its excuse. It is entirely self-imposed and is strongest in the "fashionable compositions." What one becomes ignorant of is sentiment as shaped by custom, and to be ignorant of this domain is to be ignorant of the source of all belief and action. In this way, through the barbarism of refinement, civilized mankind comes to reenact something like the original ignorance of the precivilized state.

The dialectic of simplicity and refinement, like that of liberty and authority, and the dialectic of true and false philosophy create a tension internal to human existence. Through this ideal identity, one can discern when literature is moving to a state of corruption and make corrections. Hume thought that the cultivation of the arts and sciences had been going on for about two hundred years (*E,* 135). Upon the revival of the arts, the ignorant Europeans were attracted not to the simplicity of Attic Greek eloquence but to the gaudy refinements of the Latin and Hellenic writers. Thus learning at its revival "was attired in the same unnatural garb, which it wore at the time of its decay among the Greeks and Romans." An instance of this error is Waller, who "was the first *refiner* of English poetry" (italics mine). His works contain but "feeble and superficial beauties. Gaiety, wit, and ingenuity are their ruling character: They aspire not to the sublime; still less to the pathetic. They treat of love, without making us feel any tenderness; and abound in panegyric, without exciting admiration" (*H,* 6: 152). But eventually this error in European letters of delighting in form over nature was detected, and "observation and reflection gave rise to a more natural turn of thought and composition" (*H,* 5: 150).

But by 1742 Hume thought there were "some symptoms" of a "degeneracy of taste" in the direction of a false refinement. By the late 1760s and throughout the remainder of his life, he thought that English literature had been thoroughly corrupted. He complained to his publisher Strahan in 1769 that it had been his "misfortune to write in the language of the most stupid and factious Barbarians in the World" (*L,* 2: 209), and in 1773 he told Strahan that finding an English author of merit would be unlikely: "For as to any Englishman, that Nation is so sunk in Stupidity and Barbarism and Faction that you may as well think of Lapland for an Author" (*L,* 2: 269). Three decades after his observation that there were symptoms of a degeneracy of taste in English literature, he could say that the best book written by an "Englishman these thirty years (for Dr Franklyn is an American) is Tristram Shandy, bad as it is" (*L,* 2: 269). Three years later Hume expressed his surprise to Gibbon, upon receiving a copy of his *Decline and Fall,* that such a work could have come from an Englishman. "You may smile at this Sentiment; but as it seems to me that your Countrymen, for almost a whole Generation, have given themselves up to barbarous and absurd Faction, and have totally neglected all polite letters, I no longer expected any valuable Production ever to come from them" (*L,* 2: 310).

Hume thought that a decline in literature was an indicator of a fundamental weakening of the arts of civilized life. Writing to Thomas Percy in 1773, he observed, "I am only sorry to see, that the great Decline, if we ought not rather to say, the total Extinction of Literature in England, prognosticates a very short Duration of all our other improvements, and threatens a new and a sudden Inroad of Ignorance, Superstition, and Barbarism" (*NHL,* 199). Two years later in the letter to Gibbon mentioned above, Hume intimated that "the Fall of Philosophy and Decay of Taste" go hand in hand (*L*, 2: 310). The reason is that the dialectic of simplicity and refinement is of a piece with the dialectic of true and false philosophy. Both are forms of critical reflection. Barbarism in both consists in "refinement," that is, in taking the order of reflection as the source of critical thinking and not sentiment and custom. And given Hume's principle that the parts of culture constitute a unity and mutually affect each other, one would expect that a widespread corruption of philosophical reflection would yield a like corruption of literature and vice versa. But the philosophical refinement of false philosophy is, as it were, the ultimate refinement. The barbarism of refinement in literature is a retreat from the serious task of comprehending sentiment in favor of "the pointed antithesis, the unnatural conceit, the jingle of words," but refinement in philosophy involves the alchemy of world-inversion issuing in "artificial lives" framed in the "vacuum" of philosophical autonomy. The literature of these inverted beings necessarily instantiates the barbarism of refinement.

Did Hume think that the decline of literature in his own time was due to the influence of corrupt philosophical reflection? The answer might appear to be that he did not, for what he most often cites as the cause of the decline is religious fanaticism and political factionalism—especially the latter (*L*, 2: 233). One might ask what these experiences have to do with the philosophical act. Surely religion and politics can be carried on without being informed by the philosophical act. But what Hume discovered is that in modern times religion and politics *are* so informed. His understanding of this peculiarity of modern culture deepened as his career developed.

At the beginning of his career Hume wrote in the *Treatise* that "generally speaking, the errors in religion are dangerous; those in philosophy only ridiculous" (*T*, 272). However, the dialectic of true and false philosophy shows that philosophy is capable of alienation and distortion equal to anything in religion. And even in the context of the passage just quoted from the *Treatise*, Hume makes it clear that philosophy alone can subvert experience in as absurd a way as religion. "The Cynics are an extraordinary instance of philosophers, who from reasoning purely philosophical ran into as great extravagancies of conduct as any *Monk* or *Dervise* that ever was in the world" (272). Whether the philosophical act can disturb society is entirely an empirical question. In the first *Enquiry* Hume offers reasons why philosophy, even when corrupt, is not likely to be a threat: only a few do philosophy, and their doctrines, being general and abstract, "are not very alluring to the people" (*EU*, 147). But this state of affairs could change and in fact was changing during Hume's lifetime. The sheer number of people instantiating the philosophical act had greatly increased, generating a popular philosophical consciousness (the new vulgar philosophers discussed in chapter 6). This popular philosophical mind occupied itself with topics of morals and politics—topics very "alluring to the people." Hume's awareness of this change is registered in the *Essays* and especially in the letters of the last ten years of his life (1766–1776), which record his judgments on Rousseau, the Wilkes and Liberty affair, and the American crisis. During this period Hume was made aware of a phenomenon unprecedented in history: the emergence of philosophical passions on a popular level and of a purely secular sort.

This new vulgar philosophical consciousness was typically of the false sort, and so the alienated and resentful modes of false philosophical existence, the ascetic, the revolutionary, and the guilty, could be acted out in the public arena. The errors of philosophy would now be not merely ridiculous but dangerous as well. What Hume had feared, and what he thought the decline of literature in England prognosticated, namely, "a new and sudden Inroad of Ignorance, Superstition, and Barbarism," had come to pass. But here barbarism and ignorance were not due to nature but were self-imposed. They were not the result of a lack of civilization but a consequence of its development.

This is a hard saying and one to which the *philosophes* were deaf. Enlightenment liberalism viewed religion and tradition as barriers to progress in civilization. Religion and tradition are darkness; philosophy is light. The light should remove the darkness. But philosophy is the province of a few. What is needed is to create a philosophical public opinion. Diderot issued the call to action. "Let us hasten to make philosophy popular. If we want the philosophers to march on before, let us approach the people at the point where the philosophers are."[3]

For Hume the matter was much more complicated. First, as heir to the Pyrrhonian tradition, he had made a distinction *within* philosophy between its true and corrupt forms. The latter were capable of absurdity and destruction equal to anything religion had produced. Second, Hume's analysis of Christendom showed that it is the union of two distinct forms of experience: vulgar theism and philosophy. Hume goes so far as to say that modern religion is nothing but a species of philosophy (*EU,* 146). Modern religion is made worse by the philosophical consciousness internal to it. The bigotry usually attending prephilosophical vulgar theism is qualitatively transformed and made worse by the original bigotry that a corrupt philosophical consciousness brings to whatever it touches.

The Enlightenment hoped to replace religion with critical philosophical reflection as the dominant form of culture. Hume was sympathetic to this project, but he recognized more clearly than his Enlightenment colleagues that ritualistic anticlericalism was not enough. Everything depended on whether the philosophical reflection informing the new culture would be of the true or the false form. A culture informed by a corrupt philosophical consciousness would suffer the barbarism of refinement on a massive scale. No such culture had ever existed, and Hume did not speculate as to what one would be like. Near the end of his life, however, he caught a glimpse of such a culture emerging, and he compared it unfavorably to a form of barbarism he knew quite well because he had written the history of it, namely, the barbarism which led to the English Civil War, the overthrow of the monarchy, and the establishment of the Puritan republic under the dictatorship of Oliver Cromwell. The Puritan republic was not a secular society informed by a philosophical consciousness. It claimed to be a religious society, but as an instance of the union of vulgar theism and philosophical theorizing characteristic of all Christendom, Puritanism had a philosophical content. The philosophical act is the same whether it takes the sacred or the secular as its object of reflection. The difference between Puritan totalitarianism and later secular forms of totalitarianism is that the former uses the idiom of the sacred, whereas the latter uses the language of secular theorizing: the rights of man, the class struggle, race struggle, gender struggle, or whatever the philosophical act in its corrupt form has seized upon for its obsession.

The Gloomy Enthusiasm of the Parliamentary Party

Hume taught that "Sects of philosophy, in the ancient world, were more zealous than parties of religion" (*E,* 63). The reason is that philosophy—being informed by the principles of ultimacy, autonomy, and dominion—is necessarily intolerant, and unless restrained by the dialectic of true and false philosophy is sure to appear in fanaticism of some form or other. Polytheism was a prephilosophical religion and, not making a claim about one system of ultimate reality, tended to be tolerant to the point of allowing philosophy itself to flourish. Philosophers were not a threat to society because they were under the watchful eye of the polytheistic magistrate and because they were content to remain within the realm of private sects. Philosophical animosity was among sects and was largely contained within the private sphere.

But Hume thought that in modern times sects of religion were more zealous than sects of philosophy. He gave three reasons for this. First, modern religion is theistic, and theism tends to be more intolerant than polytheism. Second, Christianity first appeared as a form of vulgar theism; that is, it was a prephilosophical religion grounded not in theory but in the sacred tradition of the Jews. It consisted in little more than belief in a person, expectation of an event, and an ethic of love.[4] The community was held together by a ritualistic feast. But Christianity had to defend itself in a Hellenic world in which philosophy was widespread. By this time philosophy had barbarized itself into the "refinement" of Electicism, a school of the schools (*E,* 123). As in the barbarization of literature, philosophy had long since lost its engagement with nature, had turned inward to become fascinated with its own symbols and forms. It was philosophy in the decadence of refinement that first captured Christianity. Henceforth Christianity would lose much of its character as a way of life in a sacred tradition and would take on the character of life according to a theory. A sacred ritual, such as the Eucharist, would take on the absurd character of a science. "As philosophy was widely spread over the world, at the time when Christianity arose, the teachers of the new sect were obliged to form a system of speculative opinions; to divide, with some accuracy, their articles of faith; and to explain, comment, confute, and defend with all the subtilty of argument and science" (*E,* 62). When speculative philosophy undisciplined by the dialectic of true and false philosophy mingles itself with any domain of custom (sacred or secular), it generates endless sects, each, through the Midas touch, seizing upon some fragment of custom and transforming it into the whole, and each in implacable opposition.

Third, Christianity very early took on the form of "priestly government," and this government eventually gained considerable control over the state. The "mutual hatred and antipathy" that usually attends speculative disputes about the real was manipulated by the priests for their own interests. Such ideological conflicts have "ever since been the poison of human society, and the source of the most inveterate factions in every government" (*E,* 62).

For the first time in history, through the union of vulgar theism and philosophy in Christendom and its control of the state, a mass speculative consciousness appeared. Christendom evolved into philosophical Scholasticism and "the refinements of casuistry." The Protestant Reformation yielded a form of Christianity in which the autonomy which is an essential part of philosophical consciousness began to assert itself. Intimations of philosophical autonomy were always a part of Christendom and were responsible for its divisions into sects. Catholic tradition, however, had been able to hold these together, but once the authority of tradition was subverted by the Protestant demand to interpret the tradition for oneself, theological sects multiplied, and Protestantism itself went through a reformation in which one vestige after another of tradition was subverted in favor of autonomy. Presbyterianism gave way to Puritanism, which gave way to the Independents and the more austere sects of Quakers, Millenarians, Fifth Monarchists, and so forth.

The form of autonomy that drives this subversion of tradition Hume calls "enthusiasm." The enthusiast practices philosophy under the constraints of vulgar theism. The enthusiast does not exemplify the autonomy of philosophy in its pure form, but then, as Hume has shown, there is no such thing as pure philosophical autonomy except in that moment of the dialectic which only true philosophers achieve, when philosophy, seeking to determine thought entirely out of its own reflection, ends in total skepticism (*EU,* 162). Philosophical autonomy as it appears in the world is always guided by some unacknowledged custom and prejudice, and it matters little whether this prejudice is sacred or secular. The philosopher acts in the name of something he calls reason; the enthusiast acts in the name of Divine inspiration. Both speak in many voices and generate endless sects. The philosopher's reason is radically self-determining. Similarly, the enthusiast "consecrates himself, and bestows on his own person a sacred character" (*E,* 76). Both are instances of a radical act of self-certification.

Hume teaches that there is a natural history to enthusiasm that will serve to illuminate further the parallel between philosophical autonomy and enthusiasm. A life guided by pure inspiration cannot be sustained, anymore than can a life of pure philosophical autonomy. In the end thought must repair to custom and the sensory. It is for this reason that vulgar theism, having reached the sublime notion of a perfect being who transcends the world, could not found a religion on the mere contemplation of it and so necessarily returns in the direction of polytheism to connect divinity in some fashion to the concrete. Vulgar theism has required a doctrine of historical revelation in addition to a rational contemplation of God. Similarly, the "Platonist" who seeks to live the life of "*philosophical* devotion" must fail.

Another similarity between enthusiasm and philosophy is that both are opposed to superstition and priestly government. The sources of superstition are "Weakness, fear, melancholy, together with ignorance" (*E,* 74). The infinite anxiety and guilt of the superstitious mind finds some relief in ceremonies, mortifications, observances, or "in any practice, however absurd or frivolous, which either folly or knavery recommends to a blind and terrified credulity." The sources of enthusiasm are "hope, pride, presumption, a warm imagination, together with ignorance" (*E,* 74). The philosopher and the enthusiast display the dispositions of self-worth and independence. Both are loath to surrender their autonomy to the dictates of tradition and priestly government. Indeed, enthusiasm is "not less or rather more contrary to it, than sound reason and philosophy" (*E,* 75). The qualification is necessary because the true philosopher is prepared to see some value in the rituals of priestly religion. In the *History* Hume criticizes "protestant historians" for ridiculing the veneration of relics (*H,* 3: 252–53) and those of a "philosophical mind" who ridicule "pious ceremonies" (*H,* 5: 459). Hume was sympathetic to the "humane and inoffensive liturgy" introduced by Bishop Laud and defended by Charles I against the Puritans, and he observed that "during a very religious age, no institutions can be more advantageous to the rude multitude, and tend more to mollify that fierce and gloomy spirit of devotion to which they are subject." Indeed, although Laud had "corrected the error of the first reformers," he had perhaps not gone far enough. "Even the English church, though it had retained a share of popish ceremonies, may justly be thought too naked and unadorned, and still to approach too near the abstract and spiritual religion of the puritans." Unable to sustain any grasp of the "divine and mysterious essence, so superior to the narrow capacities of mankind," the devotee becomes melancholy and violent. This energy is better employed in liturgical religion, where the mind can "relax itself in the contemplation of pictures, postures, vestments, buildings, and all the fine arts, which minister to religion" (*H,* 5: 459–60).

The enthusiast is more zealous and revolutionary than one under the dominion of priestly government, but Hume compares this zeal to a thunderstorm which, once spent, leaves the air "more calm and serene than before." After the first fury of enthusiasm is spent, there being no priestly order, tradition, or ritual to preserve the sacred principles, they sink into oblivion. In time the descendants of the puritan sects "become very free reasoners; and the *quakers* seem to approach nearly the only regular body of *deists* in the universe, the *literati,* or the disciples of Confucius in China" (*E,* 78). Freethinkers instantiate philosophical autonomy, and the autonomy that emerges once enthusiasm has run its course is what was intimated and sublimated in Christendom from the beginning with its union of philosophy and vulgar theism.

Finally, enthusiasm, like philosophy, being the result of "bold and ambitious tempers," is naturally attended with "a spirit of liberty," whereas priestly government "renders men tame and abject, and fits them for slavery." Hume points out that during the English Civil War the radical Protestant sects, though differing in religious principles, were all passionate for a commonwealth. Indeed, the most radical group of sects, the Independents, went so far as to support religious toleration "during its prosperity, as well as its adversity" (*H,* 5: 443). Their "mind, set afloat in the wide sea of inspiration, could confine itself within no certain limits; and the same variations, in which an enthusiast indulged himself, he was apt, by a natural train of thinking, to permit in others" (*H,* 5: 443). Hume judged it to be remarkable "that so reasonable a doctrine owed its origin, not to reasoning, but to the height of extravagance and fanaticism" (*H,* 5: 443). That is, the principle of toleration supported by the Independents arose not out of the positive judgment that toleration is good for mankind, but merely from the negation of all established religious authority. The entire landscape of religious tradition had to be destroyed and replaced by "the wide sea of inspiration." The wide and empty sea of the enthusiast arises from the same disposition as the "vacuum" in which a corrupt philosophical consciousness seeks to live an "artificial life" and which Hume pointedly described as "philosophical enthusiasm" (*EM,* 343).

All in Christendom carry within them the sublimated intimations of a philosophical consciousness. In Protestantism, and especially in its more radical forms, the disposition of philosophical autonomy began to be insistent. The Puritan religion was "abstract and spiritual," and Hume compares it unfavorably with "the Catholic religion," which, adapting itself to the senses and enjoining observances which enter into the "common train of life," is less alienated from common life, is less abstract, partakes less of the barbarism of refinement than Puritanism, and is consequently more reasonable. Hume thinks that a philosophical consciousness is internal to Puritanism, which "being chiefly spiritual, resembles more a system of metaphysics" (*H,* 4: 14). In the Puritan enthusiast one finds an echo of Hume's "enraged" Platonist, and the Puritans may also be compared to the Stoics, who grafted "a philosophical enthusiasm" onto their religion (*NHR,* 77). The difference is that the Stoics express the religious disposition philosophically; the Puritans express the philosophical disposition in religious terms. But when enthusiasm runs its course, something very like pure philosophy tends to emerge.

Hume laid it down as a principle that in human affairs we are to look for the moral causes of actions rather than hidden and unconscious forces. A moral cause operates on the mind as a motive or reason for action and requires reference to the agent's intentions and beliefs about the world and his conception of his situation. Accordingly, he argued that the main cause of the English Civil War was religious enthusiasm. He speaks of the "fire of puritanism" which consumed the nation, and he is able to discern in the debates of the House of Commons, at the very beginning of the conflict, "some sparks of that enthusiastic fire, which afterwards set the whole nation in combustion" (*H,* 5: 241, 213). Of course there were other factors, such as changing economic, social, and political conditions, but these were transmuted by a religious-philosophical mode of reflection into ideological objects that could not be handled by the natural principles of prudence. This corrupt mode of reflection Hume describes in the usual way as a false "refinement." He writes, "The confusions, which overspread England after the murder of Charles I proceeded as well from the spirit of *refinement* and innovation, which agitated the ruling party, as from the dissolution of all that authority, both civil and ecclesiastical, by which the nation had ever been accustomed to be governed" (*H,* 6: 3; italics mine).

It was very much an age addicted to abstract speculative principles and not merely those of philosophers such as Descartes. James I had "established within his own mind a speculative system of absolute government" which he was zealous to defend in his disputes with Parliament and before the nation (*H,* 5: 19). The divine right of kings had not been questioned until His Majesty began to transmute the prejudice into the form of philosophical theory. In the meantime, great changes were occurring which would necessarily force the House of Commons into a new role and would limit the power of the monarchy. Hume observes, for instance, that at about this time the property represented by the House of Commons was about three times that of the House of Lords. Neither King nor Commons understood these changes very well, but the latter began to feel their power and the former began to perceive a threat. In opposition to this threat James had only a speculative theory about absolute monarchy to offer. This theory showed no understanding of the origin of political authority in human sentiment and opinion and no understanding of the changing historical conditions which necessarily give a particular twist to the form that political authority must take at any particular time. A speculative proposition founded on reason naturally generates its contrary. And it would not be long before another speculative theory of political authority equally oblivious to the workings of the world would be placed in opposition to the theory of absolute government, namely, the contract theory. And so, the "King having . . . torn off that sacred veil, which had hitherto covered the English constitution, and which threw an obscurity upon it so advantageous to royal prerogative, every man began to indulge himself in political reasonings and inquiries; and the same factions which commenced in parliament, were propagated throughout the nation" (*H,* 5: 93).

By the time of Charles I, political disputes had moved further from the domain of custom, where they could be settled by prudence, into the realm of metaphysical speculation, where they necessarily became implacable. A metaphysical conflict ensued between Charles and Parliament involving not only disagreement over speculative tenets of church doctrine but disagreements about the ultimate foundation of political order. Metaphysical doctrines such as fatalism and free-will, "being strongly interwoven both with philosophy and theology," were debated in Parliament. Hume comments that to "impartial spectators surely, if any such had been at that time in England, it must have given great entertainment, to see a popular assembly, enflamed with faction and enthusiasm, pretend to discuss questions, to which the greatest philosophers, in the tranquillity of retreat, had never hitherto been able to find any satisfactory solution" (*H,* 5: 211–12). Practical issues of everyday politics which should have been settled by prudence were transmuted by the Midas touch into unappeasable metaphysical oppositions.

Speculative philosophical and theological debate soon spilled out of Parliament, and through the medium of the pulpit spread to the people, whose minds, being the product of Christendom, already contained the rudiments of a speculative philosophical consciousness. Hume describes the theologians of the Reformation as the bearers of a corrupt form of reflection: these "wretched composers of metaphysical polemics" worked tirelessly to instill their "speculative and abstract principles" into the unguarded minds of the credulous multitude (*H,* 3: 224). The barbarism of refinement had now gripped the entire nation and had entirely supplanted politics. London became that "furious vortex" of speculative "opinions and principles, which had transported the capital" (*H,* 5: 378). The incommensurable oppositions that false philosophy always generates would now be violently acted out in the world. But first, the "war of the pen preceded that of the sword, and daily sharpened the humours of the opposite parties. . . . The king and parliament themselves carried on the controversy by messages, remonstrances, and declarations; where the nation was really the party, to whom all arguments were addressed" (*H,* 5: 380).

Hume taught in *The Natural History of Religion* that a religion becomes more absurd by becoming more philosophical. The absurdities of false religion are multiplied when informed by a system of false philosophy. Absurdity that takes on the form of reason and science is the ultimate absurdity. "Learning itself, which tends so much to enlarge the mind, and humanize the temper, rather served on this occasion to exalt that epidemical frenzy which prevailed. Rude as yet, and imperfect, it supplied the dismal fanaticism with a variety of views, founded it on some coherency of system, enriched it with different figures of elocution; advantages with which a people, totally ignorant and barbarous, had been *happily unacquainted*" (*H*, 5: 348–49; italics mine). Critical reflection, when of the false sort, is worse than the uncritical state it seeks to displace. The struggle was over ideological principle. "Never was there a people less corrupted by vice, and more actuated by principle, than the English during that period: Never were there individuals who possessed more capacity, more courage, more public spirit, more disinterested zeal." But "the infusion of one ingredient, in too large a proportion, had corrupted all these noble principles, and converted them into the most virulent poison" (*H*, 5: 380). The natural interests of civil society, the natural dictates of morals, all were eclipsed by ideological principle. "When principles are so absurd and so destructive of human society, it may safely be averred, that, the more sincere and the more disinterested they are, they only become the more ridiculous and more odious" (*H*, 5: 527). More generally, to seek to guide the domain of custom by principle, framed independent of custom, is to subvert morality. "The more principle any person possesses, the more apt is he, on such occasions, to neglect and abandon his domestic duties" (*H*, 6: 513).

Once the domain of common life is totally captured by a corrupt reflection, questions of prudence and reform become impossible. Since custom, as a whole, has lost its authority, no reforms within the domain of custom will be taken as authoritative. Nothing less than a total transformation of the world is necessary. Hume shows that for every demand made by Parliament to restrict the power of the Crown to which Charles conceded, Parliament had a new one to make (*H*, 5: 454–56). In the end the demand was made to abolish the monarchy itself. The Crown, accordingly, could do nothing to placate "the endless demands of certain insatiable and turbulent spirits, whom nothing less will content than a total subversion of the ancient constitution" (*H*, 5: 321). Though it was not so at first, in the end the intention of the Commons came to be "to subvert the whole system of the constitution" (*H*, 5: 355). As the conflict progressed, "The bands of society were everywhere loosened, and the irregular passions of men were encouraged by speculative principles, still more unsocial and irregular" (*H*, 6: 4). Guided by the principles of ultimacy, autonomy, and dominion, a false philosophical reflection totally transforms common life, and we enter an inverted world where, by the Midas touch, everything appears other than what it is. Property is theft, immodesty is true modesty, injustice is justice, revolution is restoration, and so on. Once liberated by a false philosophical reflection from the domain of custom, the usual judgments of right and wrong lose their authority. The Puritans, accordingly, thought themselves "dispensed from all the ordinary rules of morality, by which inferior mortals must allow themselves to be governed" (*H*, 5: 514). To a false reflection, speculative principle must appear "superior to the beggarly elements of justice and humanity" which can be known only through participation in the customs of common life.

Hume writes that "all orders of men had drunk deep of the intoxicating poison" which a disordered reflection had generated. Speculative principle informed "all business" and "every discourse or conversation" (*H*, 5: 348). "Every man had framed the model of a republic; and, however new it was, or fantastical, he was eager in recommending it to his fellow citizens, or even imposing it by force upon them" (*H*, 6: 3). The barbarism of refinement continually raised the ante, and unrestrained by the authority of custom, "nothing remained to confine the wild projects of zeal and ambition. And every successive revolution became a precedent for that which followed it" (*H*, 5: 492). A Quaker woman walks into Cromwell's presence naked because clothing is no longer necessary among the elect (*H*, 6: 145). The irregularities of pleasure were considered worse than the most odious crimes (*H*, 5: 288). Christ having descended into the hearts of the elect, some thought that ministers, magistrates, and the Bible itself were to be abolished (*H*, 6: 546). Hume observes that "it became pretty common doctrine at that time, that it was unworthy of a Christian man to pay rent to his fellow creatures," and extraordinary means had to be taken with those "whose conscience was scrupulous" (*H*, 6: 547). One party "inveighed against the law and its professors; and, on pretence of rendering more simple the distribution of justice, were desirous of abolishing the whole system of English jurisprudence, which seemed interwoven with monarchical government" (*H*, 6: 4).

Even names were changed in order to be politically correct. Old Testament names were considered "more sanctified and godly," and sometimes a whole sentence was adopted as a name. Hume records the names of a jury of eighteen people enclosed in the county of Sussex, all of whom had sentence-names such as "Fight the good Fight of Faith,

White of Emer," "Be Faithful, Joiner of Britling," "Kill Sin, Pimple of Witham," "Make Peace, Heaton of Hare," "Fly Debate, Roberts of Britling." A member of Parliament, known for his harangues, was named "Praise-God Barebone." The assembly in which he was a member came to be known as the Barebone Parliament. Hume mentions that his brother had the incredible name of "If Christ had not died for you, you had been damned Barebone," and he dryly observes that people grew tired of this long, politically correct name and commonly gave him the simpler appellation of "Damn'd Barebone" (*H,* 6: 62, 62 n).

It all ended in the murder of Charles I and the establishment of a Puritan republic under the military dictatorship of Oliver Cromwell. The Puritan revolutionaries exemplify the revolutionary mode of false philosophical existence that I argued is intimated in the dialectic of true and false philosophy in the *Treatise.* First there is a total criticism of common life projected by an act of self-certifying autonomy independent of custom. In the case of Puritanism, autonomy takes the form of self-consecrating enthusiasm. In the moment of total criticism the thinker finds himself in an inverted world and cannot bear "to mix with such deformity" (*T,* 264). Reform is out of the question, and nothing can satisfy thought but a total destruction and transformation of the existing order. In a passage quoted earlier Marx declared, "We are not interested in a change in private property but only in its annihilation, not in conciliation of class antagonisms but in the abolition of classes, not in reforms of present society but in the foundation of a new one."[5] Total criticism, which is a uniquely philosophical act, whether expressed in a secular or scared idiom, seeks total destruction, total transformation, and, in the end, total dominion—and always in the philosophical language of inverted existence. After the murder of Charles, the House of Commons ordered a new seal on which was engraved "On The First Year Of Freedom, By God's Blessing, *Restored,* 1648 (italics mine)." The form of public business was changed from the king's name to that of "the keepers of the liberties of England" (*H,* 5: 546). Revolution is restoration, and tyranny is liberty.

The Puritans ruled behind the mask of God and liberty, but they secretly pursued the "sweets of dominion" (*H,* 5: 513). Juries were abolished in treason trials. Though government was declared to be founded on the "agreement of the people," parliamentary elections were long postponed, and when they finally came, the sovereignty of Parliament proved imaginary. The real power still resided in Cromwell's army. But the loss of public liberty was not the whole of it; the Puritans sought to transform the social and moral world as well. Hume describes them as "sanctified robbers . . . who, under pretence of superior illuminations, would soon extirpate, if possible, all private morality, as they had already done all public law and justice, from the British dominions" (*H,* 6: 120). All was to be regulated by principle, even down to recreation. "Parliament appointed the second Tuesday of every month for play and recreation," but as Hume sardonically remarked, "The people were resolved to be merry when they themselves pleased, not when the parliament should prescribe it to them" (*H,* 5: 452–53 n). The theoretical inversions first spawned by a corrupt critical reflection were acted out to the bitter end, and Hume concludes with pointed irony that "never, in this island, was known a more severe and arbitrary government, than was generally exercised, by the patrons of liberty in both kingdoms" (*H,* 5: 528).

Hume described Sir Harry Vane as the "perfect enthusiast." The revolution began with Vane's prosecution of Strafford, which ended in his execution. Hume thought it fitting that the effusion of blood finally ended with the prosecution and execution of Vane. The revolution had devoured its own substance. Hume viewed Vane as an icon of the revolution. Though a man of great ability, he was entirely captured by enthusiasm and emerged as a paradox of learned and brilliant absurdity. "A strange paradox! did we not know, that men of the greatest genius, where they *relinquish by principle* the use of their reason, are only enabled, by their vigour of mind, to work themselves the deeper into error and absurdity" (*H,* 6: 181–82; italics mine). Here we have another instance of the barbarism of refinement. Vane's absurdity was self-imposed "by principle." An act of critical reflection of a corrupt sort obscures and eventually extinguishes critical reflection of the true sort.

Lambert, the other great remaining Puritan leader, was also condemned but was given a reprieve and confined to the Isle of Guernesey, where he lived in contentment for thirty years. Hume records, ironically, that he converted to Roman Catholicism, the greatest horror of the Puritan. The fires of enthusiasm were spent.

After the "fumes of enthusiasm" had dissipated, the people of the nation spontaneously and with eagerness returned to their traditional ways. Hume warmly records this triumph of the social passions, untainted by false philosophy or enthusiasm, when it became clear that a restoration of the monarchy was possible. "This was one of those popular torrents, where the most indifferent, or even the most averse, are transported with the general passion, and zealously adopt the sentiments of the community, to which they belong. The enthusiasts themselves seemed to be disarmed of their fury" (*H,* 6: 135). When the restoration was declared, the people experienced "unmixt effusions of joy; and displayed a social triumph and exultation, which *no private prosperity, even the greatest,* is ever able fully to inspire. Traditions remain of men, particularly of Oughtred, the mathematician, who died of pleasure, when informed of this happy and surprising event" (*H,* 6: 138; italics mine).

Hume thought the English Civil War was unique in history and had a special philosophical significance. For the first time, a mass speculative consciousness had generated mass speculative passions which had the power to overthrow an established political order and which eventually sought to destroy not only the political order but the moral and social order as well, and to replace it with a new one. The barbarism of refinement had actually taken place. But it was not the work merely of philosopher kings or philosopher priests; the people themselves were in the grip of speculative passions. Hume stresses that the war was not the result of any manifest injustice on the King's part. Changes had occurred which neither King nor Parliament fully understood, and reforms were necessary. But enthusiasm, by the Midas touch, had transformed every object of negotiation into a superstition. In this dark and magical world, prudence and reform, which are and must be tied to custom, were driven out. Ultimacy, autonomy, and dominion held sway. I have argued that enthusiasm is simply the autonomy of false philosophy in its religious aspect. If so, the fundamental lessons of volumes 5 and 6 of the *History* and of the dialectic of true and false philosophy in the *Treatise* are the same, namely, that philosophical autonomy cut free of the domain of custom entirely subverts itself. It is this insight of true philosophy, first broached in the *Treatise,* that Hume brought to the interpretation of the English Civil War as an ideological struggle and which led him to conclude that "the gloomy enthusiasm, which prevailed among the parliamentary party, is surely the most curious spectacle presented by any history; and the most instructive, as well as entertaining, to a philosophical mind" (*H,* 6: 142).

The New Vulgar Philosophers

As wars typically do, the English Civil War brought about many changes that neither side intended. One of these was a tendency towards secularization. Hume had argued that the natural history of enthusiasm was to change into a more philosophical style of religion that values civil liberty. Liberty had been a battle cry at the very beginning of the conflict between Charles I and Parliament—but liberty was shaped and limited by the forces of enthusiasm. Hume gives this formula for understanding the forces that formed the early stages of the conflict: "In short, fanaticism mingling with faction, private interest with the spirit of liberty, symptoms appeared, on all hands, of the most dangerous insurrection and disorder" (*H,* 5: 256–57). The army was the force through which Cromwell seized and maintained power, and it was heavily infused with the republican spirit. "The camp, in many respects, carried more the appearance of civil liberty than of military obedience. The troops themselves were formed into a kind of republic; and the plans of imaginary republics, for the settlement of the state, were every day, the topics of conversation among these armed legislators" (*H,* 5: 513). The Levellers were one of the more radical parties to this conversation. They taught that royalty and nobility had to be abolished, "all ranks of men be levelled; and an universal equality of property, as well as of power, be introduced among citizens" (*H,* 5: 513). By the time of the restoration Hume could discern "a material difference" in the contending parties. The usual cry against popery was heard, "but it proceeded less from religious than from party zeal" (*H,* 6: 377). The focus of attention was now on political order, not religious order. "And instead of denominating themselves the *godly* party, the appellation affected at the beginning of the civil wars, the present patriots were content with calling themselves the *good* and the *honest* party: A sure prognostic, that their measures were not to be so furious, nor their pretensions so exorbitant" (*H,* 6: 377). The people began to "dread lest the zeal for liberty should engraft itself on fanaticism, and should once more kindle a civil war in the kingdom" (*H,* 6: 377).

Attention also began to focus on commerce. Hume criticized the ancient philosophers for neglecting commerce (*E,* 88), and he credits the Puritan Parliament as the place where "the nature of commerce began now to be understood" (*H,* 5: 307 n). The "democratical principles" which prevailed during the Puritan regime encouraged "the country gentlemen to bind their sons apprentices to merchants; and commerce has ever since been more honourable in England than in any other European kingdom" (*H,* 6: 148).

Commerce and civil liberty are mutually reinforcing. Their cultivation was the driving force of a secularizing trend that subverted not only religious enthusiasm but had begun to put religion as such on the defensive. By 1741 Hume could describe the progress of secularization as follows: "Now, there has been a sudden and sensible change in the opinions of men within these last fifty years, by the progress of learning and of liberty. Most people, in this island, have divested themselves of all superstitious reverence to names and authority: The clergy have much lost their credit: Their pretensions and doctrines have been ridiculed; and even religion can scarcely support itself in the world. The mere name of *king* commands little respect; and to talk of a king as GOD's vicegerent on earth, or to give him any of those magnificent titles, which formerly dazzled mankind, would but excite laughter in every one" (*E*, 51).

Two points are worth stressing with regard to this passage. First, the new secular consciousness is not merely the experience of elites but is instantiated on a popular level. Second, this consciousness is due to the progress of "learning" and "liberty," and this meant the secularization of philosophy. By 1741 Hume thought that philosophical consciousness had more or less freed itself from its union with vulgar theism. Indeed, philosophy had not only asserted its autonomy, but religion itself had been driven to seek legitimacy in philosophical argument. Revelation had not been abandoned, but among the liberal and learned, religion had to conform to the authority of secular philosophical argument.

The new secular philosophical consciousness had its ancestry in the Independents, the Levellers, and other Puritan sects which discovered their autonomy during the English Civil War. The Parliament not only engaged in philosophical debates concerning such topics as free will and fatalism, they debated the question of the ultimate origin of government and invoked the contract theory to legitimate the trial and execution of Charles I. The emergence of the contract theory is significant. There are two images of how philosophical autonomy may be related to political order. One is that of the philosopher king, which supposes a distinction between those capable of philosophical autonomy and the vulgar, who are not. The other is the contract theory, which supposes that all are capable of autonomy, and this suggests that all the contractors are endowed with the rudiments of a philosophical consciousness. Centuries of cultivating the union of philosophy and vulgar theism in Christendom had prepared men for just this condition. The contract theory may be viewed as the philosophical reflection of this condition. Hume thought that the contract theory was a uniquely modern theory and, moreover, a theory to which the English were particularly addicted. What we may entertain as an explanation of why it emerged as a particularly powerful force in modern times is that its appearance presupposes the experience of autonomy on a fairly large scale, such as occurred during the English Civil War and in the secularizing disposition that followed. In one form or another it has been the favorite image of political order for modern philosophers ranging from Hobbes, Locke, Rousseau, Kant, and Rawls to Habermas. Even the Marxist notion of the dictatorship of the proletariat is conceived as a temporary measure to be eliminated when the vulgar satisfy the conditions for autonomy.

Hume considered the contract theory to be a philosophic superstition whereby political authority, as it is actually experienced by human beings, is "refined away" by a "false philosophy" (*E*, 482). And his account of the evolution of philosophy in the culture of Christendom suggests that its emergence and influence in modern times reflects a growing philosophical consciousness in the public. The philosophical fantasy could now be entertained that the public, not having achieved the "forelorn solitude" of philosophical autonomy, should now do so. To put the matter another way, the contract theory represents the insistence by philosophers that philosophical existence should be the dominant form of society. Indeed this, we may say, was the ideological project of the *Encyclopedia:* to make rationalism available to the people.

Hume recognized that this new vulgar philosophical consciousness had begun to inform the political parties of his time. In "Of Parties in General," he classified political parties into three kinds: parties of interest, affection, and principle. Although Hume recognized that parties are necessary and could even be taken to represent a flourishing condition of the state, he also thought they tended to faction and, hence, were in constant need of control. The most reasonable parties are those of interest, such as the division between "the landed and trading part of the nation," and those of affection, such as attachment to the claims and dignity of a noble or royal family. The most unreasonable parties are those of "principle, especially abstract speculative principle" (*E*, 60). The former are reasonable because they consider interests and affections of common life, the demands of which can be known and negotiated. Even parties of principle can be reasonable if the conditions for satisfying the principles can be known in common life. But the problem with parties of principle is that the principle tends to take on philosophical shape and to be transformed into the implacable demands of ultimacy, autonomy, and dominion. When the principle enters the "vacuum" of a corrupt philosophical reflection, no one can tell what in common life can satisfy it. Hume puts it this way: "Where different principles beget a contrariety of conduct, which is the case with all different political principles, the matter may be more easily explained. . . . But where the difference of principle is attended with no contrariety of action . . . what madness, what fury, can beget such unhappy and such fatal divisions?" (*E,* 60).

But though political parties of abstract speculative principle are necessarily absurd and destructive, Hume recognized that they are a permanent feature of modern politics. "No party, in the present age, can well support itself, without a philosophical or speculative system of principles, annexed to its political or practical one; we accordingly find, that each of the factions, into which this nation is divided, has reared up a fabric of the former kind, in order to protect and cover that scheme of actions, which it pursues" (*E,* 465). The most one can do is render such parties as harmless as possible, the first step being to recognize that they are destructive and why.

In a remarkable passage Hume points out that parties of abstract speculative principle are unique to modern times and signal some great transformation in human affairs. "Parties from *principle,* especially abstract speculative principle, are known only to modern times, and are, perhaps, the most extraordinary and unaccountable *phenomenon,* that has yet appeared in human affairs" (*E,* 60). The great transformation is precisely the appearance of a mass philosophical consciousness in the world.

What he refers to above as "the present age" in which philosophical parties occur, he disdainfully described in a passage of the second *Enquiry* as "this philosophic age" (*EM,* 197 n). By this he meant an age caught in the grip of corrupt forms of the philosophical act—an age, for instance, that ritualistically accepts the rationalist "abstract theory of morals," which "excludes all sentiment, and pretends to found everything on reason." He refers here to Montesquieu, Malebranche, "Cudworth, Clarke, and others," who seek to ground morality on abstract "*rapports* or relations" of reflection. Here again we have the barbarism of refinement, that higher sort of self-imposed ignorance of which only a philosophical intellect is capable. Hume realized that he was living in the first "philosophic age," an age in which philosophy would no longer be the province of elites but would inform the activity of the vulgar as well.

Hume uses two metaphors to describe the thought of the false philosopher which appear to be opposites: the refined and the crude. The philosopher is said to exist where the air is too fine to breath, or even to exist in a vacuum. The philosopher is composed of refined "fiery particles" as opposed to men in common life, who are made up of a "gross earthy mixture" (*T,* 272). In all of this the philosopher, though false, is a refined and rarified being, and common life is crude. From another perspective, however, common life, as the work of nature and custom, is highly complicated, nuanced, subtle, and fragile. Against this background the philosopher appears as a crude "uncouth monster" who not only does not know how to conduct himself but to whom no one knows, or can know, how to respond (*T,* 264). What had been viewed as rarified is now seen as crude and clumsy, and for the same reason, namely, "that love of *simplicity* which has been the source of much false reasoning in philosophy" (*EM,* 298).

The moral rationalism of Montesquieu and the other philosophers mentioned above is crude and monstrous. Hume inveighs against the attempt of philosophy to "impose its crude dictates and principles on mankind" (*EU,* 15). In a letter, Hume again has occasion to criticize Montesquieu's rationalism, mingling the metaphors of the refined and the crude. Though he otherwise admired Montesquieu, he was compelled to call attention to the "false Refinements" of his thought and to its "rash and crude Positions" (*L,* 2: 133). But Montesquieu's rationalism is not crude in the sense of being vulgar. The crudity of the vulgar is a crudity of innocence, whereas Montesquieu's crudity is the work of reflection and is self-imposed. It is a higher sort of crudity, made even worse because the philosopher, acting in the name of reason, is virtually incapable of recognizing his own clumsiness.

When the vulgar begin to be philosophers, they mingle in a strange way the crudity of innocence with that of reflection. The vulgar, like philosophers, seize onto a few slogans with which to explain everything, but they are less critical. The people, Hume says, "always take opinions in the lump, the whole system and all the principles" (*H,* 5: 178). Being new to the work and constrained by their former selves, vulgar philosophers cannot be expected to exhibit much skill in speculative activity. The new scene of thought for the new vulgar philosophers is politics. They are the ones who formed those political parties of speculative principle which Hume says are unique to modern times. Writing of their work in erecting ideologies that are to guide political life, he says, "The people being commonly very rude builders, especially in this speculative way, and more especially still, when actuated by party-zeal; it is natural to imagine, that their workmanship must be a little unshapely, and discover evident marks of that violence and hurry, in which it was raised" (*E,* 466). Vulgar speculative political parties are crude in both senses of the term.

Two philosophical theories were especially alluring to the new vulgar philosophers: the egoistic theory of morals, which Hume called "the selfish system," and the contract theory of political authority. Both flatter the vanity of philosophical autonomy, and both exhibit that hypocritical character of the false philosopher in pretending to have accomplished what ordinary mortals cannot do, namely, to have transcended the prejudices of common life in favor of a rational space untainted by custom. What most often happens, however, is that the philosopher succeeds in transcending everything but his own interests. Philosophical hypocrisy bears comparison with what Hume said about the hypocrisy of speculative enthusiasm during the English Civil War. "The religious hypocrisy, it may be remarked, is of a peculiar nature; and being generally unknown to the person himself, though more dangerous, it implies less falsehood than other species of insincerity" (*H,* 6: 142). Similarly, philosophers actually believe they have instantiated a position of pure rational autonomy. Speculative hypocrisy is structurally the same whether it is due to the self-consecration of enthusiasm or the self-certification of a supposed rational autonomy. In neither case is total emancipation from custom possible. Speculative hypocrisy can grip an entire nation, and one of the many things Hume finds interesting about the English Civil War is that hypocrisy of this sort was instantiated on a vast and unprecedented scale. "Though the English nation be naturally candid and sincere, hypocrisy prevailed among them beyond any example in ancient or modern times" (*H,* 6: 142).

The new vulgar philosophers are the secular descendants of the Puritan enthusiasts, having undergone a century of evolution. They have "seen through" and "unmasked" the moral conventions of society. The vulgar philosophers are not to be "taken in" by the world of custom. They know that men are and can only be motivated by self-interest and that what is called morality is simply a power play. Their moral ideal is egoism, and their political protection is the contract theory of government. Berkeley described this as the "minute philosophy" and inveighed against it in *Alciphron.* Hume referred to it as "philosophical chymistry" and as the "malignant philosophy" (*EM,* 297, 302). But there was no doubt about its popularity among "thinking" people. Hume described its popular manifestation in "Of Moral Prejudices." The new vulgar philosophers unmask everything that "has hitherto appear'd sacred and venerable in the Eyes of Mankind. Reason, Sobriety, Honour, Friendship, Marriage are the perpetual Subjects of their insipid Raillery: And even public Spirit, and a Regard to our Country, are treated as chimerical and romantic" (*E,* 538). Included in this new breed, and the subject of the essay, is the philosophical "heroine" discussed in chapter 6.

Here we have an early manifestation, and on a popular level, of that favorite activity of philosophical modernity, namely, unmasking and consciousness-raising. Hume significantly describes this new "Set of men" as "Anti-reformers" (*E,* 538). Reform goes on within the constraints of common life. The radical individualism and unmasking of the vulgar philosophers is at the service, not of reform, but of philosophical alchemy and is an instance of the world-inversion that always attends the Midas touch of false philosophy. The many bizarre forms of philosophical existence generated by the ascetic, revolutionary, and guilty modes of false philosophical consciousness, instead of being confined to the philosopher's closet or contained, as in the ancient world, in private sects, would now be acted out in the public sphere.

Diderot's call "to make philosophy popular" was coming to pass with little assistance needed. The Humean maxim that the tendency of philosophy is to its false forms meant that the new popular philosophical consciousness would be of the corrupt sort. A century or so later Marx could write that "philosophy has become secularized, and the striking proof thereof is that the philosophical consciousness itself has been pulled into the torment of struggle not only externally but internally."[6] The endless world-inversions generated by corrupt forms of the philosophical act could now be packaged and sold to the people. In an age of Puritan enthusiasm this packaging was done in the pulpits, each of which contained a "ghostly practitioner" who worked tirelessly to instill "speculative and abstract principles" into the minds of the credulous multitude. In an age of "philosophical enthusiasm," this role would be played by a new breed whom Hume compares to robbers in the forest who "lie in wait to break in upon every unguarded avenue of the mind" and "to impose [their] crude dictates and principles on mankind" (*EU,* 11, 15). In the first philosophic age it would be necessary to warn the people that if they are to be philosophers, they must take care also to be men, and that to consume the "gross earthy mixture" of common life in the flames of "those fiery particles" that are a false philosophical consciousness is to plunge into the barbarism of refinement, which, to the degree that it is taken seriously, is worse than the philosophically innocent barbarism of nature. As philosophy is "the only catholic remedy" for the errors of religion, so true philosophy is the only remedy for false philosophy. But since the people take systems in the "lump," it is unlikely that they would, or even could, follow the subtle and mortifying dialectic of true and false philosophy in order to understand the nature and limits of critical reflection. True philosophy would be drowned out as nihilistic skepticism and as a threat to reason itself.

The history of philosophy shows that philosophers themselves, who have had ample leisure and an interest in truth, have been insufficiently critical and have allowed the mind a full indulgence to its "supine indolence . . . its rash arrogance, its lofty pretensions, and its superstitious credulity" (*EU,* 41). If philosophers have not been very successful in restraining their own intellects—if they have rarely gotten beyond that level of the dialectic which Hume calls false philosophy or a "mistaken knowledge"—what is to be thought of the new vulgar philosophers who, not having the leisure or interest to seek truth, must throw up their "rude" and "unshapely" speculative systems in "violence and hurry" (*E,* 466)? A new epoch in the story of the relation of philosophy to society had begun.

Rousseau

Although Hume recognized that the emergence of purely secular philosophical modes of reflection and existence on a popular level was unique to modern times, and by informing political parties was a source of barbarism in society, the full range of the threat was not impressed upon him until the last decade of his life. This period, from 1766 until his death on 25 August 1776, included his encounter with Rousseau and a constitutional crisis manifest in a long period of ministerial instability, the weakness of the Crown, the three-year-long Wilkes and Liberty riots, and the crisis of American secession. Except for releasing his correspondence with Rousseau in an attempt to vindicate his character against Rousseau's accusations, Hume published nothing on these topics, but his letters of this period are filled with bold and philosophically suggestive judgments about them. These letters constitute a proper source for understanding Hume's thought on the relation of philosophy to society in modern times, and they are the main source for the account given in the remainder of this chapter and in the next.

By the mid-eighteenth century philosophers had become public figures and objects of general conversation. Newton, Voltaire, and Hume himself are cases in point. The *Encyclopedia* was making philosophy popular, and Hume had taken up essay writing in an attempt to reach this broader philosophical audience. But the Encyclopediasts and Hume as essayist had different goals. The former sought to bring the vulgar up to the level of vanguard philosophers, and their work was heavily laced with the world-inverting project of consciousness-raising and unmasking. In contrast, Hume pictured the vulgar and the philosophers as possessing different but complementary forms of wisdom, the former possessing the wisdom of common life, namely, knowledge through participation, and the latter possessing the wisdom of speculation, or knowledge through reflection. The wisdom of common life is thoroughly social and can be known only through *conversation.* The wisdom of reflection is gained in the solitude of the study. Hume pictures the true philosopher, as essayist, as an "Ambassador from the Dominions of Learning to those of Conversation; and [I] shall think it my constant Duty to promote a good Correspondence betwixt these two States, which have so great a Dependence on each other" (*E,* 535).

Here again we have the central truth of the dialectic that the source of belief and conduct is not reflection but custom. Critical reflection may be carried out within the domain of custom but cannot go beyond it. "The Materials of this Commerce must chiefly be furnish'd by Conversation and common Life: The manufacturing of them alone belongs to Learning" (*E,* 535). The error of "the last Age" was that philosophy became "shut up in Colleges and Cells, and secluded from the World and good Company" (*E,* 534). Hume describes this as a "moaping recluse Method of Study" which "became totally barbarous." Here the barbarism of refinement appears as a failure to consult experience as the source of critical thought. But by "experience" Hume does not mean the sense-data epistemology of modern empiricism with which he is unhappily still identified. That abstract notion of experience is itself a barbarism of refinement. Experience for Hume is the enjoyment through conversation of the deeply established customs and conventions of a way of life. "And indeed, what cou'd be expected from Men who never consulted Experience in any of their Reasonings, or who never search'd for that Experience, *where alone it is to be found, in common Life and Conversation*" (*E,* 535; italics mine). Hume also stresses that the participation of women is essential to achieving the sort of humane self-knowledge that the conversation of common life makes possible.

The image of the moping and reclusive philosopher depicts false philosophy in its ascetic mode. The new image was of the philosopher involved in the affairs of common life. It is indeed remarkable that the great early modern philosophers, with the exception of Kant, did not have lifelong careers in the university. Montaigne, Bacon, Hobbes, Descartes, Spinoza, Locke, Leibniz, Pascal, Berkeley, Hume, Montesquieu, and Rousseau made their way in the world philosophizing as they could while carrying out such occupations as lens grinder, librarian, gentleman, statesman, secretary, and bishop. All of them were men of affairs. The philosopher had become public.

But Rousseau was what we may call the first "philosophic personality." Hume thought that he was the most talked about man in Europe.

"By his genius, his singularities, his quackery, his misfortunes, and his adventures, [he has] become more the subject of general conversation in Europe (for I venture again on the word) than any person in it. I do not even except Voltaire, much less the King of Prussia and Mr. Pitt" (*L,* 2: 108).

It was not simply that people had read Rousseau and found his works interesting; he had become the embodiment of something. People were interested in stories about his life, his clothes, his dog, and his manners. A young friend of Hume's, Robert Liston, had waited an hour or two for a peep at Rousseau. He declined Hume's invitation to introduce him, desiring only to "stare in full Liberty." Hume insisted, and upon meeting him Liston was dazzled and remarked how "his sharp black Eyes promise every thing he has shown himself possessed of."[7] It is remarkable that one of the first modern idols was a philosopher, extravagantly loved by some, hated to an equal degree by others, and to still others an object of curiosity. Hume distinguished between the "enthusiasm" of Paris and the "curiosity" of London, a distinction which, in regard to philosophical matters, has ever since been more or less applicable. Rousseau was a peripatetic icon of philosophy in one of its modes, but he could not have had this status at all unless there had been a secular philosophical consciousness diffused throughout Europe to constitute him. Hume observed of this "imaginary being" that "he is the man who has acquired the most enthusiastic and most passionate Admirers. I have seen many extraordinary Scenes of this Nature" (*L,* 1: 529–30; 2: 27).

Hume's personal encounter with Rousseau has been narrated by Mossner and need not be examined here except in outline. The gist of the story is that Hume sought to be of assistance to Rousseau as a persecuted man of letters. By some effort he arranged a retreat for him in the English countryside, but not far removed from the booksellers in London. He also secured, with Rousseau's approval, a pension from the King. Rousseau, who was not only persecuted but tended to imagine himself to be so when he was not, came to think that Hume was part of an international conspiracy to ridicule him and had brought him to England for that purpose. He said as much publicly, and Hume was forced to publish an account of the affair and the letters that had passed between them. Hume reacted to Rousseau's accusations first with bewilderment, then with pointed anger, and finally with pity as he came to recognize that Rousseau was mad.

What did Hume think of Rousseau as a philosopher? He distinguished between the eloquence of Rousseau's writings and their speculative content. He had great praise for the former, but only contempt for the latter. Concerning their eloquence, Hume wrote to Madame de Boufflers that Rousseau's writings bore "the stamp of a great genius; and, what enhances [their] beauty, the stamp of a very particular genius." He admired the "noble pride and spleen and indignation" which "bursts out with freedom in a hundred places, and serves fully to characterize the lofty spirit of the man" (*L,* 1: 374). Rousseau had given to "the French tongue an energy, which it scarce seems to have reached in other hands" (*L,* 1: 373). Earlier Hume had conveyed these sentiments to Rousseau himself. "Of all men of Letters in Europe, since the death of President Montesquieu, you are the Person whom I most revere, both for the Force of your Genius and the Greatness of your Mind" (*L,* 1: 364). This was written before Hume had come to know Rousseau and was one of those extravagant effusions of praise that he would later regret with equal extravagance. "I am heartily asham'd of any thing I ever wrote in his Favour" (*L,* 2: 57). But even at his most effusive, Hume never praised Rousseau for anything other than the eloquence of his writings—an eloquence at the service of greatness of mind, which for Hume is only part, though a necessary part, of human excellence.

Writing to Turgot after he had taken the full measure of the man, he said, "You know, that I always esteemed his Writings for their Eloquence alone and that I looked on them, at the bottom, as full of Extravagance and of Sophistry. I found many good Judges in France and all in England, of a like Opinion" (*L,* 2: 91). When Hume speaks of "extravagance" in philosophy, he means that error peculiar to the philosophical intellect alone, namely, the world-inverting paradoxes which he called "philosophical chymistry" and of which the Cynics were presented as the best examples (*EM,* 342; *T,* 272). Before he had met Rousseau, Hume wrote to Madame de Boufflers that with the "domineering force of genius" that is Rousseau's eloquence there "is always intermingled some degree of extravagance." And he went so far as to judge that Rousseau did not have that love of truth that characterizes true philosophy. "He chooses his topics less from persuasion, than from the pleasure of showing his invention, and surprizing the reader by his paradoxes" (*L,* 1: 373). But this is just an exemplification of that barbarism of refinement by which reflection conceives itself to be the source of thought and action, and can issue in nothing but world-inverting paradox. Writing of Rousseau's "Treatise of Education" (presumably *Emile*), Hume found it deplorable that "even in so serious a subject" and indeed in all "his other performances" Rousseau "indulges his love of the marvelous" (*L,* 1: 373–74).

Rousseau was a strange mixture of the new secular philosophical autonomy and of Protestant enthusiasm; both are alienated from common life and the ordinary paths to learning, and both proceed from some inner, self-certifying sentiment. This meant that Rousseau would suffer that "forelorn solitude" which is one of the moments of false philosophical existence. Before the rupture in their friendship had occurred, Hume gave Hugh Blair this telling sketch of Rousseau as a thinker: "He has read very little during the Course of his Life, and has now totally renounc'd all Reading: He has seen very little, and has no manner of Curiosity to see or remark: He has reflected, properly speaking, and study'd very little; and has not indeed much Knowledge: He has only felt, during the whole Course of his Life; and in this Respect, his Sensibility rises to a Pitch beyond what I have seen any Example of: But it still gives him a more acute Feeling of Pain than of Pleasure" (*L,* 2: 29).

Hume told Blair about a conversation in which Rousseau expressed disgust at his writings. Hume insisted that the style and eloquence must be pleasing to him, to which Rousseau is said to have replied, "I am not displeased with myself in that particular: But I still dread, that my Writings are good for nothing at the bottom, and that all my Theories are full of Extravagance" (*L,* 2: 31, 103–4). Hume took this to be a telling and courageous remark, for here Rousseau was "judging himself with the utmost Severity, and censuring his Writings on the Side where they are most expos'd to Criticism" (*L,* 2: 31).

Hume did not interpret Rousseau's madness as a misfortune that had suddenly befallen him, but as the advanced stage of a condition he had always been in and one which was self-imposed. Replying to Turgot, who had written him in Rousseau's defense, Hume said, "I agree heartily with you, My Dear Sir, that M. Rousseau is a Madman and I shall add, if you please, that he always was so; but this will, by no means, excuse him, or save him from more black Imputations. On the contrary it is by means of his Madness that his other bad Qualities appear in their full Light" (*L,* 2: 88). These qualities exhibited in his writings are the expression of that philosophical melancholy and delirium which a false philosophical reflection imposes upon itself. Hume saw in Rousseau's character the self-deception and hypocrisy that inevitably attend a determined attempt to live out a corrupt philosophical existence. Rousseau, for instance, pretended to seek solitude and to abhor public attention, but was unforgiving when the slightest attention was not paid to him. He resented and said that he resented being under obligation. "This Prodigy of Pride and Ferocity interprets every Favour into an Injury" (*L,* 2: 89). These and other self-deceptions, including the great distance between the motto with which Rousseau sealed every letter, "Vitam impendere vero," and his practice, forced Hume to the conclusion that "the Life of such a Man is to be regarded as one continu'd Lye and imposture" (*L,* 2: 90). Rousseau's specifically philosophical hypocrisy he described as "Falsehood and Quackery" (*L,* 2: 88, 108), as in "Quacking like a Physician" (*L,* 2: 184).

Rousseau's madness, Hume thought, threw new light on the quackery of his writings, which had been obscured by the "domineering genius" of his eloquence. From the first, Hume had thought that his writings were filled with "philosophical" madness, that is, the world-inversions that false philosophy brings to whatever it touches. Rousseau began to doubt the value of these world-inversions when, upon reflection, he confessed to Hume that his "Theories" might be entirely empty.

It is worth quoting at length what Edmund Burke learned from Hume about Rousseau's philosophical writings. Surveying the wreckage of the French Revolution, which had conjured with Rousseau as a spiritual precursor, Burke wrote,

> Mr. Hume told me that he had from Rousseau himself the secret of his principles of composition. That acute though eccentric observer had perceived that to strike and interest the public the marvelous must be produced; that the marvelous of the heathen mythology had long since lost its effect; that giants, magicians, fairies, and heroes of romance which succeeded had exhausted the portion of credulity which belonged to their age; that now nothing was left to the writer but that species of the marvelous which might still be produced, and with as great an effect as ever, though in another way; that is, the marvelous in life, in manners, in characters, and in extraordinary situations, giving rise to new and unlooked-for strokes in politics and morals. I believe that were Rousseau alive . . . he would be shocked at the practical frenzy of his scholars, who in their paradoxes are servile imitators, and even in their incredulity discover an implicite faith.[8] (See also *L,* 2: 32).

The superstitions of mythology are to give way to the world-inverting superstitions of secular philosophers. Here we may recall Hume's observation that superstition is nearly the only thing in human affairs that is an evil almost entirely unmixed with good.

Hume disagreed with Turgot that it was a misfortune that the rupture with Rousseau should come to the attention of the public. "I think rather that nothing can be more fortunate than the Detection of such a Mountebank: For I am willing to soften my Epithets, in Complaisance to you. I wish, that all other Cheats and Impostors in all Professions were as fairly exposed. You know, that I always esteemed his Writings for their Eloquence alone and that I looked on them, at the bottom, as full of Extravagance and Sophystry. . . . Is there any Harm that the public in general shou'd adopt the same Sentiments, and shou'd appreciate at their just Value Compositions whose general Tendency is surely rather to do hurt than Service to Mankind?" (*L,* 2: 91). But the tendency to harm here is contained in all false philosophy. Hume described the world-inversions of the "selfish system" of Epicurus, Hobbes, and others as the "malignant philosophy."

Rousseau begins the *Social Contract* with the following world-inverting paradox: "Man is born free but everywhere he is in chains." The rhetorical power of the statement consists in the implication that there is a prior state of freedom relative to which civil society is, in some way, enslaving. The paradox conveys the sense that one's own has been taken away and so generates a philosophically contrived resentment, directed not against this or that ill in civil society but against civil society as a whole. Alienated from the constraints of common life, reflection is free to feed upon and to indulge this resentment guided only by itself.

Compare this with Hume's theorizing about the origins of civil society. He begins not with a world-inverting paradox but with a commonplace. The first sentence of "Of the Origin of Government" reads, "Man, born in a family, is compelled to maintain society, from necessity, from natural inclination, and from habit." Here Hume reminds us of, and even celebrates, our common condition and theorizes from there. There is no hint of a freedom we have lost, no suggestion that civil society is enslaving. Far from being born free, man is born helpless and is entirely dependent upon the benevolence and interests of parents and society. Likewise, the original condition of mankind in general was not a freedom since lost, but the condition of a "necessitous animal" in a world of scarce goods and limited benevolence. What freedom there is results from the long and painful evolution of civil society, whereby mankind has come to understand better the nature of government, commerce, and the rule of law. Man is not born free; but with a political constitution informed by the rule of law, he may become so.

In the first philosophic age the marvelous is the province not of poets, priests, soothsayers, and old wives but of secular philosophers acting in the name of something called "reason." Hume's use of the term *marvelous* carries the connotation of the monstrous, as in the marvels of a circus freak show, where the expectation of the commonplace is subverted by the two-headed calf or the bearded lady. The world-inversions of philosophy are what Hume called the "monstrous offspring" of imagination and a false reflection; when exhibited, they draw great crowds from among the new vulgar philosophical public. There was a vast market for the philosophical monstrosities Rousseau created. But he not only produced the marvelous, he became the embodiment of it and was constantly on public exhibit. And Hume himself was caught up in the circus.

In the early stages of their association, Hume was more than happy to play the role of exhibiting Rousseau to the public. He took some pains to have Rousseau seated in a box opposite the King and Queen at a playhouse. Rousseau was enraptured and leaned so far out of the box that a generous lady next to him held his coat during the performance to keep him from falling. Hume glowingly observed "their Majestys to look at him, more than at the Players" (*L*, 2: 8). So popular was Rousseau in Paris that Hume was asked by friends to warn them before the two were to take a walk. Hume speculated, "Were the Public to be informed, he coud not fail to have many thousand Spectators. . . . no Person ever so much engag'd their Attention as Rousseau. Voltaire and every body else, are quite eclipsed by him. . . . Even his Maid, La Vasseur, who is very homely and very awkward, is more talkd of than the Princess of Monaco or the Countess of Egmont. . . . His very Dog, who is no better than a Coly, has a Name and Reputation in the World" (*L*, 1: 529–30).

Hume had ignored the warning of d'Holbach and others about Rousseau's character. What he saw in Rousseau was "persecuted merit," a fellow victim in the republic of letters persecuted by the bigotry of the religious establishment. Hume enjoyed the notoriety attaching to his association with Rousseau. "I am sensible," he wrote to Hugh Blair, "that my Connexions with him, add to my Importance at present" (*L*, 1: 529). By exhibiting Rousseau at the circus, Hume was indulging his own fascination with the marvelous as well as playing the vicarious role of persecuted man of letters and benefactor. It was not an attractive sight. Defying the advice of his friends, who knew Rousseau, Hume gushed to the Marquise de Barbentane, "For my part, I think I could pass all my life in his company, without any danger of our quarrelling" (*L*, 2: 14), and he wrote his brother, "I shoud desire no better Fortune than to have the Privilege of showing him to all I please" (*L*, 2: 8). In exhibiting Rousseau, Hume was exhibiting himself.

It was remarkable that princes should humble themselves and make a path to Rousseau's door. "The hereditary Prince payd him a Visit a few days ago; and I imagine the Duke of York calld on him one Evening when he was abroad. I love him very much and shall separate from him with much Regreat" (*L,* 2: 8). And all of this was not for a religious or political figure, but for a secular philosopher guided entirely by radical philosophical autonomy. For a parallel, one must go back to pagan antiquity and consider Alexander the Great going out of his way to visit Diogenes in his hovel. We have seen that Hume considered Diogenes the best case of "extravagant" philosophy and the equal in absurdity to any "Monk or Dervise" (*T,* 272). Eventually Hume would form the same judgment of Rousseau. To Turgot he wrote, "I really believe him one of the worst and most depraved of Men" (*L,* 2: 90). And it is remarkable that Hume should characterize Rousseau with the same epithet he had marked out for Diogenes, namely, "Ferocity" (*L,* 2: 89, 90; *E,* 540).

But there is this difference between Diogenes and Rousseau as images of the philosopher in the world. Diogenes presented himself as an example of philosophical greatness of mind with the task of unmasking and seeing through the hypocrisy of convention. Rousseau also presented himself in this role, and it was the greatness of mind displayed in his eloquence that Hume first admired. But Rousseau also exhibited himself as *victim* and was courted as victim. It was this incongruous combination of greatness of mind and victimhood that Hume came to describe as "quackery." One who possesses radical philosophical greatness of mind finds his worth in the autonomy of his own reflection, which is emancipated from the ordinary standards of custom. The philosopher in this ascetic mode of existence has and must have a "certain sullen Pride or Contempt of Mankind" (*E,* 539). One in this condition cannot play the role of victim, for to do so would be to participate in custom, claiming victimhood under its rules while at the same time pretending to transcend it with contempt. The Diogenes of legend lived a life of ascetic and cynical independence. Diogenes was not a victim, nor did he present himself as such. Alexander the Great paid homage to Diogenes' greatness of mind, not to his status as victim. Rousseau's theoretical inversions, however, enabled the thinker to see himself as endowed with a kind of freedom suppressed by society. This inversion necessarily spawns resentment and guilt—resentment when attending to one's freedom, and guilt when attending to one's inevitable role as a participant in society, and hence, as an oppressor. In the end *everyone* in Rousseau's inverted world is a victim and an oppressor.

Rousseau's philosophy is an instance of that moment of the dialectic I have called the guilty philosophical consciousness. This corrupt mode of philosophizing has provided the *topos* for emancipation and liberation philosophies, which have since multiplied victims and oppressors beyond necessity. Much of philosophy in the last two centuries has explored the themes of guilt, resentment, oppression, and liberation which flow from the false philosophy of Rousseau's inverted world. For the most part these themes are philosophically self-imposed; they are housed in the vacuum of false philosophy and are unrestrained by the moral criteria of an established way of life. In this story of the victim, or "hermeneutics of suspicion," the pagan philosophical virtue of greatness of mind is entirely lost. Likewise, among the classical philosophers the modern themes of guilt and resentment are missing.

One reason for this difference, suggested by Nietzsche, is the insensible influence that Christian guilt has exercised on modern philosophy. Even if we grant this influence, however, it should not be overplayed. The source of Christian guilt is original sin, and that does not carry with it the notion of resentment. Original sin is not so much a condition of society as it is a condition of each soul, and what must happen is not the transformation of society in the direction of radical freedom so that one can live only under rules that are self-imposed, but a miraculous transformation of the soul in the direction of God's will. Whatever causal influence Christian themes may have had on the formation of the modern philosophical themes of guilt, resentment, oppression, and liberation, the *form* the doctrines take arises entirely from the philosophical intellect itself and is sufficiently explained as that necessary moment in the dialectic where a false philosophical consciousness finds itself theorizing in the mode of guilt and resentment.

The superficial similarity between Christian and modern themes would mean that many in Christendom would be attracted to Rousseau's inverted world of guilt and resentment. The first philosophical personality in the first philosophic age displayed himself as a victim and imposed guilt, not upon this or that evil in society, but upon society as a whole. Alexander the Great paid homage to Diogenes; he could not have paid homage to Rousseau. But Christian princes could and did.

Another, and the deepest, explanation of Rousseau's grip on the public is that the public itself had taken on the form of the philosophical act. Why are people attracted to the absurd inversions of false philosophy? Hume's answer in the *Treatise* was *dominion.* Philosophy appears to give one power over others. Philosophical inversions seem deep, and since they invert ordinary conceptions, those in possession of them appear to be more profound than the philosophically unreflective vulgar. But philosophy can have this influence only if it is respected in society. In a prephilosophic age where the philosophical act first appears, custom has too strong a hold, and philosophical inversions are laughed at. As respect for philosophy grows, however, people have an interest in being counted among those who are reflective and profound. A gulf is opened up between the philosophers and the vulgar. Philosophical inversions are "greedily embrac'd by philosophers, as shewing the superiority of their science, which cou'd discover opinions so remote from vulgar conception" (*T,* 26). It was just this self-professed title to rule that made philosophy in the ancient world more fanatical than religion (*E,* 63).

Philosophy could have and seek this power in large part because it was a "novelty" (*EM,* 341). In the ancient world it was the business not of religion but "of philosophy alone to regulate men's ordinary behaviour and deportment; and accordingly . . . this being the sole principle, by which a man could elevate himself above his fellows, it acquired a mighty ascendant over many, and produced great singularities of maxims and conduct" (*EM,* 341). Hume adds that in modern times "philosophy has lost the allurement of novelty," and religion has taken its place in ruling over men's lives. Philosophy, he says, "seems to confine itself mostly to speculations in the closet; in the same manner, as the ancient religion was limited to sacrifices in the temple" (*EM,* 342). These words are spoken by a character in "A Dialogue" who speaks, we may presume, for Hume. Two qualifications are needed, however. First, Hume has not forgotten his teaching that Christendom is the union of philosophy and vulgar theism. The subjects of Christendom have inherited layer upon layer of "religious philosophy," from the intricate systems of Scholasticism to the campfire inquiries into the ultimate foundations of government by the soldiers of Cromwell's army. This religious philosophy was not confined to speculations in the closet but was very much a part of public life, and Hume thinks its influence has been disastrous. Second, the philosophy of the closet is secular philosophy, and Hume's character says that it "seems" to be so confined. But when Hume wrote these words, he had already recognized that purely secular philosophy had begun to exert an influence on public life. It was the spectacular phenomenon of Rousseau that perhaps first impressed upon him the extent of the influence that secular philosophizing had on the public.

Philosophy, therefore, was not a novelty in modern Europe; the subjects of Christendom had long been familiar with it. What was novel was the emergence of purely secular philosophy as the guide of public life. This philosophy resembled that of the ancients in reenacting the principles of ultimacy, autonomy, and dominion, but its style and tone were entirely different. Hume characterized ancient philosophy as philosophy in its childhood, trying out its powers in a great variety of play, but still attached to the authority of poets and priests. Thus we may view modern secular philosophy as philosophy in its adolescence, rebelling against its parents (the autonomy of custom) and determined to live only in a world of its own making. From Bacon's dictum that knowledge is power to Marx's dictum that the task of philosophy is not to understand the world but to transform it, much of modern philosophizing would be associated with power and at the service of vast social transformation and revolutions guided by the theoretical inversions of false philosophy.

The entrance of false philosophy in common life would bring with it a form of madness that Hume had explored in the English Civil War and which he had attributed to the pernicious influence of religious philosophy. He recognized the power of purely secular philosophy in the new metaphysical political parties, which he argued were unique to modern times. In Rousseau he encountered a *peripatetic icon* of purely philosophical madness courted by the public. He called him the "Philosopher of this Age" (*L*, 2: 13). And perhaps part of the intensity of Hume's outrage was that as a philosopher, who should have known better, he was seduced like all the others. After disentangling himself from the first philosophical personality, Hume retired to Edinburgh, finished with all literary ambition, and content to live out his remaining years in the enjoyment of his native city and friends. No sooner was he established than fresh instances of the force of vulgar philosophical reflection in public affairs occurred: the Wilkes and Liberty affair and the American crisis. These events had for Hume not only a political significance but a philosophical one as well. They exemplified on a mass level the new, secular philosophical consciousness that was about to replace religion as the dominant form of culture. Hume now saw more clearly what had been intimated in the emergence of metaphysical political parties and in the phenomenon of Rousseau. Philosophy was no longer confined mainly to "speculations in the closet" but was in the strcets with the power to mobilize men and armies and to act out the moments in the dialectic of a false philosophical consciousness. I turn now to an account of how the Wilkes and Liberty affair and the American crisis could have this philosophical significance for Hume.

CHAPTER TEN

English Barbarism: "Wilkes and Liberty"

English Barbarism

Three months after Hume's death, his publisher and friend, William Strahan, wrote to Adam Smith suggesting that he publish a small volume containing Hume's "My Own Life," Smith's account of his last days and character, and "some of his Letters to me on political subjects." Strahan goes on to say that Gibbon and some other "very good Judges" think the letters would do honor to Hume and that Smith should be able to augment the collection with selections from his own correspondence and from letters in the possession of John Home, William Robertson, and other mutual friends of Hume and Smith.[1] The letters on politics, which Strahan mentions, no doubt refer to Hume's remarks on the political events of the last decade of his life, which include the Wilkes and Liberty affair and the threat that a number of the American colonies might secede from the British empire. Prior to that period, Hume's letters seldom mention political issues, and when they do, they rarely reveal any interesting interpretation or even much passion concerning political events. But from the Stamp Act crisis in 1765 until his death, the case is quite otherwise.

Smith rejected Strahan's proposal, deferring to Hume's wish that his letters not be published and, indeed, that they be destroyed. It is regrettable that Strahan's little volume of letters on the politics of this period was never published. But enough of the letters survive to give us some idea of what Strahan found interesting in them. The concern here, however, is not to examine Hume's views on political issues per se but to explore what those views suggest about the nature of *philosophy* and its relation to politics.

Ever since the Enlightenment, the great theme of history has been the mythical story of individual and political freedom. The content of this myth has varied, but its form has remained the same. The favorite conception of freedom is taken from the critic's present. The standards of this freedom are then retrospectively read back into the past to inform the motives, institutions, criteria of rationality, and morality of an age for whom these later standards not only were not recognized but might have been scarcely even conceivable. In this way an order of heroes and villains is generated in a Manichaean morality tale. The Whig historical critic discovers a long tradition of struggle leading directly up to his own self-congratulatory existence, or to his revolutionary vision, or both. Thus Martin Luther opened up freedom of conscience for Europe; the War between the American States was fought to free slaves; Charles I sought to subvert English freedom; the history of women is the story of male oppression; and more generally all history is the story of class struggle.

Historical agents are categorically viewed as being either precursors of this freedom, victims to whom it was denied, or oppressors who sought to block the work of the precursors. What falls within these three categories is historically real; what falls without is no part of history. In a classic analysis and criticism, Herbert Butterfield has dubbed this the "whig interpretation of history," by which he meant a *topos,* or common theme, around which a number of family-resembling, "progressive" story lines congregate, which include not only eighteenth- and nineteenth-century Whiggism but twentieth-century liberal and Marxist historiographies as well.[2] Marxism may perhaps be viewed as simply radical Whiggism with a theory of the causal mechanism of history.

Hume wrote the *History of England* largely to subvert the Whig interpretation of British political history. But so strong is the Whig *topos* that it is difficult for any modern thinker to be entirely free from it. As his understanding of British history deepened and as he revised and corrected new editions of the *History,* he came to see how strongly "the plaguy Prejudices of Whiggism" had distorted his historical writing. Hume was mortified at this discovery and confessed to Gilbert Eliot, "As I began the History with these two Reigns [those of James I and Charles I], I now find that they, above all the rest, have been corrupted with Whig Rancour, and that I really deserv'd the Name of a party Writer, and boasted without any Foundation of my Impartiality" (*NHL,* 69, 70). Hume's *History* is the first scientific attempt to subvert the progressive "Whig" interpretation of history and may itself be taken as a standard around which subversions of later liberal and Marxist forms of the error may rally.

The Wilkes and Liberty movement, which occupied the public off and on from 1763 to 1772, and the American crisis are typically viewed through the eyes of the Whig *topos* as "liberating" and "progressive" events. Assuming the Whig interpretation of history, we may pose a paradox: Hume strongly supported independence for the colonies but was just as strongly opposed to the Wilkes and Liberty movement. From the progressive point of view this must appear contradictory, for how could one support one liberating event and not the other, especially since the two movements were mutually supportive. This was just the perplexity of Hume's biographer, J. Y. T. Greig. "How could the same man, and at the same time, be both, Edmund Burke and George III? How could he defend the colonists in North America for their resistance to the arbitrary power of king, ministers, and a venal House of Commons and yet attack the old Whigs, Patriots, and Wilkites, and the democratic radicals of every sort for trying to resist the same agencies at home?"[3]

But there is no inconsistency in Hume's political views on these topics. The paradox is generated from the "whig interpretation of history," which views, retrospectively, the American crisis and the Wilkes and Liberty affair as "liberating" events in a master story of human emancipation. Although, as Hume pointed out, it is difficult to escape the "plaguy Prejudices of Whiggism," it is possible to do so and to see that Hume was neither Edmund Burke nor George III. His reading of the political events during the last decade of his life is his own and flows from a comprehensive philosophical and historical interpretation of British social and political order, which began with the *Treatise* and is most forcefully displayed in the *Essays* and in the *History.* The sage was from the very beginning united with the patriot. The letters that Strahan had hoped to publish (or what remain of them) are an extension of that interpretation applied to the momentous political events Hume was living through in his last years.

Hume brought to these events a sophisticated historical and philosophical understanding, cultivated over a lifetime, which neither Edmund Burke nor George III could match. The concern here, however, is not to see what the letters suggest about Hume's political philosophy but to see what they suggest about his conception of philosophy, and in particular what they suggest about the emergence of a new mass philosophical consciousness in political life. For this purpose it is best to begin with the topic of the last chapter, namely, the theme of barbarism. Throughout the letters Hume's remarks on political issues are made against the background claim that English culture has become barbaric. In nearly every letter having to do with political issues, English culture is described as barbarous or in similar terms. Hume inveighs against the "Madness and Wickedness of the English," who are "sunk in Stupidity and Barbarism and Faction" (*L,* 1: 417, 517; 2: 226, 269). Again, the English are a "deluded People," a "pernicious People," who have "given themselves up to barbarous and absurd Faction" (*L,* 2: 215, 208, 310).

Some of this is a reaction to anti-Scottish prejudice, strong in England at this time. Its sting can be felt in Adam Smith's remark about "the whole wise English nation, who will love to mortify a Scotchman,"[4] and in Hume's reply to Gilbert Elliot's refusal to take seriously his plan of leaving England permanently for France: "Can you seriously talk of my continuing an Englishman? . . . Will they allow us to be so? Do they not treat with Derision our Pretensions to that Name, and with Hatred our just pretensions to surpass and to govern them?" (*L,* 1: 470). But there is more to Hume's ascription of barbarism to the English than a provincial's injured merit. *Barbarism,* for Hume, is a descriptive term, and in the letters of this period it points to something specific: political faction. The English are barbarous because they are a "stupid, factious Nation," who have been "corrupted by above a Century of Licentiousness" (*L,* 2: 269, 216). And its most civilized part was the worst: "the factious barbarians of London" (*L,* 1: 417, 517).

Hume taught that "Faction, next to Fanaticism, is, of all passions, the most destructive of Morality" (*L,* 2: 286). The kind of factions Hume had in mind in this case were not the theological-political factions that had inflamed England during the Civil War, but political factions of an entirely secular sort. Writing to Strahan in 1771, Hume observed that "[political] factious prejudices are more prevalent in England than religious ones" (*L,* 2: 233). In "Of Parties in General," he distinguished three sorts of political faction: those of affection, interest, and principle. Each is a menace to the public good, but the first two are the most excusable because they pursue a limited good that is empirically identifiable and, consequently, can be the object of judgment and negotiation. But parties of "principle, especially abstract speculative principle," are singled out as being highly toxic and as an evil "known only to modern times" (*E,* 60). The English are barbarous because their factions are of this speculative sort, and consequently their politics is informed by a corrupt philosophical consciousness which distorts, constricts, and alienates people from political reality. This is another instance of the barbarism of refinement, discussed in the last chapter, which is possible only in an advanced stage of civilization where a *philosophical* culture has been developed and where the habit of philosophical reflection has become a widespread phenomenon. I turn now to an examination of the rather complicated ideology that Hume thinks has corrupted British politics and rendered it barbarous.

Revolution Ideology

Bernard Bailyn observes that "it would be difficult to exaggerate the keenness of eighteenth-century Britons' sense of their multifarious accomplishments and world eminence and their distinctiveness in the achievement of liberty." Liberty, by unleashing the energies of the British people, had generated great wealth, population, and power. France had two and one-half times the population of Britain during the Seven Years' War (1756–63) but could hardly raise 12 million pounds, whereas Britain easily raised over 13 million.[5] There was a theory as to how this remarkable achievement had come to pass, which had both a historical and a philosophical dimension. Briefly stated it was as follows.

The greatness of Britain is due to her constitution, the end of which is liberty. The constitution is a balance of three estates, King, Lords, and Commons, representing in Parliament the three classical forms of government (monarchy, aristocracy, and democracy) as well as the three functions of government (executive, judicial, and legislative). In balancing these estates, functions, and forms of government (all of which are rooted in human nature), the constitution is the perfection of political rationality. Moreover, the constitution has its origin in English national character and can be traced back to the Anglo-Saxon forests. It existed in greater perfection prior to the Norman conquest, and English history has been largely the story of preserving the balance of the constitution from encroachment by wicked kings and other unpatriotic factions. In modern times, the authoritarian Scottish kings of the house of Stuart have posed the greatest threat. But in the Glorious Revolution of 1688, the papist James II was thrown out. The English nation asserted its ancient rights and restored a liberty-loving Protestant family to the throne. It is this restoration of the ancient constitution that accounts for Britain's present greatness.

There was also a philosophical theory, namely, the theory of natural rights, according to which all legitimate government is based on consent of the people either directly or by their representatives. This philosophical truth is expressed in Locke's contract theory of government, but its historical exemplification is the British constitution.

Together the historical and philosophical theories constitute what can be called Revolution ideology because they were used to justify the Glorious Revolution of 1688. Like the Revolution itself, this ideology was accepted in some form by nearly everyone—George III as well as the Whig establishment. But it was an ideology that generated an unreal, conspiratorial style in politics. If the constitution is a perfect balance of estates, functions, and forms of government, any great stress in government must be the result of some dark faction seeking to undo the balance for its own interests. Thus the Whig opposition writer Catharine Macaulay could darkly write that "a faction has ever existed in this state, from the earliest period of our constitution" to "remove the limitations necessary to render monarchy consistent with liberty."[6] On the other side, George III could think that there was a faction in the House of Commons and ministry bent on making it impossible for him to carry out his constitutional responsibilities as executive. Eighteenth-century British politics was very much a matter of discovering and guarding against *conspiracies.*

Hume accepted much of this Revolution panegyric and even made his own contribution: "During these last sixty years," he wrote in 1752, "public liberty, with internal peace and order, has flourished. . . . Trade and manufactures, and agriculture have increased; the arts, and sciences, and philosophy, have been cultivated," and there is not "another instance in the whole history of mankind, that so many millions of people have, during such a space of time, been held together, in a manner so free, so rational, and so suitable to the dignity of human nature" (*E*, 508). Hume's explanation, however, of how this wonder had come to be was quite different from that of Revolution ideology.

To begin with, Hume did not think of the constitution as ancient. For Hume the human world is an order of evolving conventions which are not the result of a contract or of any conscious planning. Like a natural language, they evolve spontaneously over time to satisfy human needs. The moral and legal rules of a political constitution are like the rules of English grammar: a formal expression of a practice that evolved unreflectively over time and is open to still further evolution. From this position Hume argued that the English constitution is not a reenactment of an ancient constitution that has been successfully handed down despite attacks by unpatriotic factions. In the *History* he showed that the constitution has been in constant flux and that there have been four discernible constitutions in English history. And so Hume could speak dryly of the "wisdom of the constitution or rather the concurrence of accidents" (*H,* 5: 569).[7]

A true understanding of the historicity of conventions subverts the philosophical part of the theory, for given the spontaneous and evolutionary character of all constitutions, it follows that the legitimacy of government is not founded on anything that could be called a contract. It is an absurdity to think of a natural language as being founded on a contract, and it is equally absurd to think of government as being so founded. However, to a rationalistic mind given to individualism, the idea is a compelling one, and if taken seriously, as it was in Revolution ideology, it powerfully distorts and constricts political experience. Since its appearance in the seventeenth century, the contract theory, through the medium of Revolution ideology, had become a part of English political consciousness on a popular level. It was difficult for anyone to escape it, and Hume noticed that his own writings were "too full of those foolish English prejudices [the contract theory], which all Nations and all Ages disavow" (*L,* 2: 216). This theory, he thought, is a quirk of the English and is rejected "in every place but this single kingdom" (*E,* 487).

Revolution ideology, whether employed by the Whig opposition or by George III, construed the political world in moralistic and legalistic terms. All issues were issues of "rights" and conspiracies against rights. But by viewing rights as the formal expression of moral practices in evolving conventions, Hume was able to achieve a deeper and more comprehensive understanding of how the constitution actually functioned. Much was made by the Whig opposition of how the Crown, by virtue of its right to fill and create offices, was corrupting the independence of Parliament by the power of patronage and, hence, undoing the balance of the constitution. Hume replied to this in "Of the Independency of Parliament." He argued that the Revolution settlement of 1688 had left Parliament virtually all-powerful. If, according to Revolution ideology, the Crown was to "balance" the Commons and Lords, and to carry out the executive function, some "influence" in Parliament was necessary. More generally, Hume saw that the doctrine of three independent estates corresponding to three separate functions of government was a distortion which could only breed misunderstanding and conspiratorial attitudes. The interests, property, and constitutional functions of each intertwined in a subtle way that could be understood only by careful historical and causal analysis of how the convention of the constitution had evolved and what utilities it served. It was Montesquieu who, under the influence of Revolution ideology, had made popular a picture of the English constitution as having separated the executive, legislative, and judicial functions of government. Hume considered Montesquieu's theory one of those "false Refinements" of reflection which distorts and alienates people from political practice, making it impossible to understand the practice and, hence, to reform it when reform becomes necessary (*L,* 2: 133).

Although Hume agreed that the English enjoy "the most entire system of liberty, that ever was known amongst mankind" (*H,* 6: 531), he did not think this was due to an ancient balanced and perfect constitution that was the unique possession of the English and an expression of their national character. This was central to the ritual of Revolution ideology and, for Hume, one of its most absurdly provincial aspects. Viewed as a historical process, liberty (as the rule of law) is not unique to the English but is part of a larger civilizing process of moral, economic, and social forces at work in Europe. These civilizing forces ("modern manners") have established, to some degree, the ideal and much of the practice of civil liberty even in absolute monarchies (*E,* 92–93).

The English chauvinism in Revolution ideology helps to explain anti-Scottish attitudes about which Hume bitterly complained in the letters. The union of Scottish and English Parliaments occurred in 1707, completing the union of Great Britain. But the liberty celebrated in Revolution ideology was English not British. In more vulgar versions of the ideology, the Scots were viewed as having an authoritarian cast of mind like the French, with whom they had formed alliances for centuries. In support of this, one could point to two abortive Jacobite uprisings in 1708 and 1719, and to two full-fledged Jacobite rebellions in 1715 and 1745, all of which received moral and, in some cases, military support from the French.

Revolution chauvinism not only prevented the English from seeing their own enjoyment of liberty as the tip of the iceberg of a larger civilizing process going on in Europe, it also prevented an adequate appreciation of the superior cultural achievements of France. The French were regularly described as "Turkish slaves" and their culture as corrupting and effeminate. Catharine Macaulay thought that the fascination of French and Italian culture for English youth is "the finishing stroke that renders them useless to all the good purposes of preserving the birthright of an Englishman." Hume had no patience with this English republican chauvinism. Though subjects of an absolute monarchy, the French had "carried the arts and sciences as near perfection as any other nation." He granted that the English are "perhaps, greater philosophers"; the Italians better "painters and musicians"; the Romans "greater orators"; but "the French are the only people, except the Greeks, who have been at once philosophers, poets, orators, historians, painters, architects, sculptors, and musicians." They have even excelled the Greeks and the English in the theater, but most important, "in common life, they have, in a great measure, perfected that art, the most useful and agreeable of any, l'Art de Vivre, the *art of society and conversation*" (*E*, 91; italics mine).

There has been occasion throughout this study to point out the central place that conversation has in Hume's conception of true philosophy. While considering the theme of English barbarism, it might be worthwhile to note a distinction that Henry Mackenzie made in *An Account of the Life and Writings of John Home, Esq.* (1822) between the genial, playful wit of the Edinburgh literary circle of Hume's time and "that prize-fighting of wit" characteristic of its London counterpart. "There all ease of intercourse was changed for the pride of victory; and the victors, like some savage combatants, gave no quarter to the vanquished." Mackenzie's explanation of this difference is important: "The literary circle of London was a sort of sect, a *caste* separate from the ordinary professions and habits of common life. They were traders in talent and learning, and brought, like other traders, samples of their goods into company, with a jealousy of competition which prevented their enjoying, as much as otherwise they might, any excellence in their competitors."[8] Wit and learning are no longer at the service of making the sentiment of common life intelligible but of ideological self-display and competition; alienated from the poetic character of common life ("the ordinary professions and habits"), the artifacts of reflection turn into instruments of power. This is another instance of that self-displaying barbarism of refinement, discussed in the last chapter, which Hume claims had captured literature and politics in England.

The dominant form of this barbarism was Revolution ideology itself, which, owing to the Whig establishment, had thoroughly politicized literature. Hume complained that throughout his life "the Whig party were in possession of bestowing all places, both in the state and in literature" (*E*, xxxviii). From this position of power, Whig Revolution ideology was hammered into the national consciousness over a period of some sixty years. Hume's judgment is corroborated by Bernard Bailyn, who observes that from "the end of the war in 1713 until the crisis over America," the triumph of Britain in commerce, war, and liberty "was the constant theme not only of formal state pronouncements and of political essays, tracts, and orations but of belles-lettres as well."[9] In a letter to Tobias Smollett (1768), Hume remarks on "the indifference of ministers towards literature, which has been long, and indeed always, the case in England" (*L,* 2: 186). John Home records that Hume talked frequently about "the design [in England] to ruin him as an author, by the people that were ministers, at the first publication of his history; and called themselves Whigs, who, he said, were determined not to suffer truth to be told in Britain."[10]

The truth that could not be told was what contradicted Revolution ideology, particularly the doctrine of the ancient constitution. In "My Own Life," Hume remained unrepentant and even took a parting shot at the Whig establishment, pointing out that of over a hundred changes that had been made in the histories of the first two Stuarts, "I have made all of them invariably to the Tory side. It is ridiculous to consider the English constitution before that period as a regular plan of liberty" (*E,* xxxviii). Part of Hume's bitterness is due to the unreal and alienated character of Whig ideology. The Whig speaks of nothing but liberty, yet does not have the liberty of thought to consider the truth of history. Once again reflection usurps practice, and an ideology of liberty takes on a reality of its own. When this happens, liberty can be suppressed in the name of liberty and the absurdity never recognized. It was this sort of ideological distortion that led Thomas Jefferson, the great advocate of free speech, to ban Hume's *History* from the University of Virginia in favor of Baxter's politically correct version, which was simply Hume's *History* "republicanized."[11]

Throughout his writings Hume complains about the ideological politicization of English literature. "The elegance and propriety of style have been very much neglected among us. We have no dictionary of our language, and scarcely a tolerable grammar. The first polite prose we have, was writ by a man who is still alive [Swift]" (*E,* 91). He lamented to his fellow Scot, William Strahan, that it had been his "Misfortune to write in the Language of the most stupid and factious barbarians in the world" (*L,* 2: 209). He wrote to Gibbon praising his *Decline and Fall of Rome* but added that "as it seems to me that your Countrymen, for almost a whole Generation, have given themselves up to barbarous and absurd Faction, and have totally neglected all polite letters, I no longer expected any valuable Production ever to come from them" (*L,* 2: 310).

That Hume's opinion had some substance is corroborated by J. H. Plumb's judgment on the state of English letters in Georgian England. "Here and there Gibbon—and perhaps Hume there—is a writer of European stature, but the general level of achievement in philosophy, history, and literature is mediocre. . . . In many ways England in the eighteenth century in its attitude to things European was similar to . . . Rome in the first century [in its attitude] to Greece or [to] America in the late nineteenth [in its attitude] to Europe—too conscious both of its own riches and its own rawness."[12] But the wealth and rawness was richly dressed in Revolution ideology, for although the British had neglected polite letters, they had cultivated those forms of thought that encourage ideological factions. "Men, in this country, have been so much occupied in the great disputes of *Religion, Politics,* and *Philosophy,* that they had no relish for the seemingly minute observations of grammar and criticism" (*E,* 92).

The politicization of literature was, for Hume, a serious matter. It meant that a corrupt reflection would usurp sentiment and custom and take on a life of its own. Literature would no longer have the task of making sentiment intelligible but would be at the service of false philosophical reflection and, hence, of barbarism. He wrote Thomas Percy in 1773 that "the great Decline, if we ought not rather to say, the total Extinction of Literature in England, prognosticates a very short Duration of all our other improvements, and threatens a new and a sudden inroad of Ignorance, Superstition, and Barbarism." He adds that there "cannot be a stronger Symptom of this miserable Degeneracy, than the Treatment which I have met with for telling them Truth in these particulars" (*NHL,* 199).

Again the "truth" is Hume's criticism of Revolution ideology, and the ignorance, superstition, and barbarism that is now feared has its source not in the self-distorting philosophical reflections of religion but in those of secular politics. The barbarism of refinement (possible only in an age that has developed a philosophical culture) yields philosophically self-imposed inversions and the paradoxes that ignorance can be the achievement of scholarship; superstition can be the achievement of theory; and barbarism can proceed under the name of liberty. Hume thought that a "sudden inroad" of barbarism and ignorance had occurred with the Wilkes and Liberty riots which flared up throughout the nation, and indeed the Empire, during the late 1760s and early 1770s and which were continuous with the war that erupted in the American colonies during the spring of 1775.

"Wilkes and Liberty"

Hume's criticism of the Wilkes and Liberty movement is internally connected to a wider criticism of British political order that includes Pitt's imperial policies, free trade, a Scots militia, public debt, ritualistic

Whig ideology, and the status of the colonies. Any one of these would be an interesting study in itself. Here they are touched on only insofar as they illuminate our topic of philosophy in politics.

Very early in his career, Pitt had formed the idea of a British mercantile empire that would dominate world trade through sea power. This policy required war with France, with the ultimate goal of sweeping the French fleet from the seas. Pitt had thoroughly absorbed Revolution ideology, and he was a man of great eloquence whose speeches in Parliament were able to impart to this vision of a commercial empire an ineffable sense of moral grandeur and greatness. According to Revolution ideology, Britain was the last bastion of liberty in a modern world of creeping authoritarianism, the most formidable instance of which was the "Turkish" regime of France. Liberty, patriotism, empire, and commercial wealth went hand in hand. It was a bold vision which required a bellicose stance in relation to France and, in the end, a war which would have to be fought simultaneously around the world. This would require the coordination of land and sea forces on a scale which, given the difficulties in communication, was difficult to imagine. It was Hume's view that Pitt and others had plotted to jockey the nation into the Seven Years' War contrary to the intentions of the "two Kings" and the "two Ministries" (*NHL,* 235). But if Pitt's vision was not embraced by the King and the Whig magnates, it was a vision with great appeal to the trading classes of London, the colonies of North America, the West Indies, and those involved in the India trade. Consequently, Pitt built a constituency not in the Court but among the people, that is, among merchants, manufacturers, craftsmen, and others who saw their interests in an expanding commercial empire. He became known as "the great Commoner."

This new, aggressive, commercial class which Pitt represented was just beginning to exercise its power, but it was not well understood by the King, by the Whig magnates, or indeed by its own partisans. Pitt built up an extra-Parliamentary constituency centered in London, which was the hub of a great commercial empire. For the first time, an extra-Parliamentary power began to assert its will in government. Eventually George III, against his own wishes, was forced to appoint Pitt to the ministry, prompting Samuel Johnson's remark that whereas Walpole was a minister given by the King to the people, Pitt was a minister given by the people to the King. Pitt's speeches in Parliament echoed throughout the empire, and while toasts were drunk to him in London and Bristol, glasses were also being raised in Carolina, New York, Jamaica, and India.

Pitt conceived and engineered the Seven Years' War (1756–63), which secured Canada and dealt a blow to French naval power from which it never recovered. But despite the astonishing success of the war, the King lacked Pitt's vision and grew weary of the struggle. Pitt was forced to resign at the height of success and when he thought there was still much to be done. The King and his advisor, the Scottish Lord Bute, sought and secured peace with France on what Pitt thought were absurdly generous terms. John Wilkes was a protégé of Pitt's and established (anonymously) the *North Briton,* a journal designed to undermine the King's peace policy with France and to restore Pitt to power on a new wave of national enthusiasm.

In an age in which the obscene was familiar, Wilkes had acquired a reputation for profligacy. He loved to shock and outrage the very polite society to which he desperately wished to belong. But however outrageous he might become, there was a certain cheerfulness, sociability, integrity, and personal warmth that over time could win over even such a formidable enemy as Samuel Johnson. Wilkes was also a man of courage and honor and fought several duels. Though unattractive (he had a large, jutting jaw, his teeth were ajar, and his eyes were crossed), he had a voracious appetite for women and was not disappointed by their reception. He boasted that he could talk away his face in half an hour. This outrageous but good-humored man would have lived out his life comfortably placed in the opposition Whig establishment and dallying with his mistresses were it not for circumstances which called forth deeper resources in his character and, indeed, those of the English political public. What Hume said of Cromwell is true of Wilkes as well, namely, that he was suited to his age and to that alone.

Anti-Scottish prejudice was strong in London during the beginning of George III's reign, and it became focused on the Scottish Lord Bute, who was rumored to be having an affair with the young King's widowed mother and who was imagined to be the force behind the King's policy of establishing peace with France. The very title of Wilkes's journal, the *North Briton,* symbolized Bute and the grip that a supposedly French-loving Scotland had on England. Wilkes's attack on the government was not only merciless, it became increasingly scandalous. In what was to be the famous issue number 45, he finally went too far, and the ministry issued a general warrant to arrest the printer and publisher of the *North Briton* for seditious libel. Wilkes goaded and defied the ministry, and in the Court of Common Pleas won the judgment that General Warrants were unconstitutional except in cases of treason. (A General Warrant gave the government the authority to seize unnamed persons and their property; Pitt issued three during the Seven Years' War.)

Thousands attended Wilkes's trial, and it was here that he heard for the first time the shouts of "Wilkes and Liberty." The judgment of seditious libel against number 45 of the *North Briton* still stood, but there was no proof that Wilkes was the publisher. In utter contempt of the ministry's judgment, Wilkes set up a press in his own house to print the entire collection of the *North Briton* and an *Essay on Woman*, a pornographic parody of Pope's *Essay on Man*, in which Bishop Warburton and others were given pornographic roles and handled without mercy. The House of Commons declared that number 45 of the *North Briton* was a seditious libel against King and Parliament. Wilkes was expelled from the House on 20 January 1764.

In the meantime Wilkes had fled to France, both to recover from a wound received in a duel and to escape the judgment of a court friendly to the ministry. He was tried on 17 February *in absentia* and convicted on both counts of libel, not as author but as printer. Since he did not appear, he was declared an outlaw.

Wilkes remained an exile for five years, during which time his debts mounted and his friends faded away. The loss of Pitt was a special blow. Pitt believed in a strong, united Britain; he had no sympathy for Wilkes's disruptive tactics and his anti-Scottish invective. (Pitt had great plans for the use of Highland valor in future mercantile wars.) Wilkes's only hope for advancement lay in exploiting Revolution ideology that had now become part of English middle-class identity. Wilkes had previously shown no interest in the middle and lower middle class. He was kept up by and served the interests of the large Whig magnates who, at the moment, were in opposition. He turned now to raising Revolution ideological consciousness among the people. Nor was this entirely opportunistic. Wilkes had undergone a sudden but genuine conversion to the interests of the rising middle class, the same people who had supported Pitt but were now turning away, since "the great Commoner" had been bought off by accepting the title of Lord Chatham. Wilkes waited until the time was right. The winter of 1768 was severe: bad harvests the year before had sent food prices soaring, taxes had been increased to pay for the Seven Years' War, wages dropped, and England was in a profound state of social unrest. Wilkes made his move and returned on 6 February 1768.

Though an outlaw, Wilkes (only a month after he arrived) had the audacity to stand as a member of Parliament from London. He was defeated but immediately stood for the London county of Middlesex and was elected. Middlesex was a borough with one of the most liberal franchises in the country and an electorate that included the lower middle class. The demonstrations for Wilkes were astonishing in their spontaneity, size, and energy. They were also ominous. There was a great deal of seditious republican talk, and along with the cry of "Wilkes and Liberty," there was the cry, "Wilkes and no King." Within less than two months, Wilkes, a penniless outlaw, had become a challenge to the King. The government was paralyzed, neither able to pardon Wilkes nor to arrest him. On 20 April Wilkes submitted to the charge of outlawry, after having failed to receive a pardon from the King, and was placed in prison to await trial. The government vacillated into the summer. Finally on 18 June 1768, Wilkes was sentenced to twenty-two months in the King's Bench Prison and fined £1,000. The House of Commons expelled Wilkes in February of 1769. The county of Middlesex reelected him on 16 February. The House expelled him the next day. The next day he was a candidate again and was elected on 16 March. He was again expelled. On 13 April he was reelected once more. The next day the House declared the election void and admitted the candidate who had run against Wilkes. A year after this farce, Wilkes, having served his time, was released in April of 1770. Shortly before leaving prison, he was elected Alderman for London. He was elected Lord Mayor of London on 8 October 1774 and was returned to Parliament later in the same month.

Wilkes's election as Mayor marked the end of the Wilkes and Liberty movement. For a decade London had resounded, off and on, with the cry of "Wilkes and Liberty," sending shock waves of enthusiasm throughout the nation and empire. Riots and demonstrations occurred frequently throughout this period. The Wilkite "mob" was middle and lower middle class, but it could not always be distinguished from those involved in the embryonic industrial unrest that was beginning to appear. The coal-heavers, sailors, dock workers, weavers, and other wage earners began to organize and to riot for higher wages.[13] These demonstrations were often vicious and even murderous. This was also the period in which American unrest was evolving in the direction of secession. All of these forces were more or less informed by Revolution ideology and could conveniently fix on the Wilkes and Liberty movement as the symbol of their discontents, however different and even contradictory they might be.

The Wilkes riots were spectacular. Thousands attended his first trial, and his supporters grew more numerous and more ominous as the decade wore on. On each victory over the government, the mob demanded that fires be lit and houses illuminated or suffer broken windows. London was often ablaze with lights. Franklin estimated that in two nights of illumination the city had paid out £50,000 on candles alone, not to mention the cost of broken windows.[14] William Strahan wrote to Hume in disgust about how even the great submitted to the mob: "You will not easily believe it, but it is true, that the Duke of Grafton and Northumberland, and many others of the first Nobility, nay some of the Royal family itself . . . were mean enough to submit to illuminate their Windows upon this infamous occasion in obedience to the orders of a paltry Mob, which a dozen of their Footmen might easily have dispersed." Franklin reported in May of 1768 that for fifteen miles out of town there was scarce a door or window shutter without number 45 painted on it. Crowds halted passing carriages, painted 45 on them, and forced the passengers to hail "Wilkes and Liberty."[15]

The enthusiasm spread through England but not to Scotland. Wilkes's anti-Scottish *North Briton* had poisoned his relations with the Scots and also with Hume, who was attacked in numbers 47, 61, and 73. One polite writer to Edinburgh's *Caledonian Mercury* observed in April of 1769: "Mr. W——s, by playing on the passions of people, and by his invidious, not to say, highly unjust reactions on the Scotch, has created a misunderstanding and breach between them and the English, that will require years to heal." Wilkes was hanged in effigy in Edinburgh on the Grassmarket execution ground.[16] Hume was in London a little over a year and a half from the time Wilkes arrived from France early in 1768. During that time he witnessed the second and more furious round of the Wilkes and Liberty movement. Writing from London to William Robertson, he reflected, "I think every day more seriously of retiring to Edinburgh for Life. Every Event here fills me with Indignation, which I cannot command and care not to conceal; and yet to a Philosopher & Historian the Madness and imbecillity & Wickedness of Mankind ought to appear ordinary Events" (*NHL*, 186). Hume did in fact leave for Edinburgh to retire in August, 1769. Upon returning he was greeted by a long anonymous poem published in the *Caledonian Mercury* welcoming him to his native city. Part of the poem compares Edinburgh's conception of liberty under law with London's conception of liberty under English chauvinism, bellicose mercantilism, and philosophical enthusiasm:

> What tho' Londona's over-weening pride,
> Fond of her race, and just to few beside,
> Refuse the Europe's wits proclaim,
> And sicken at the sounding of your name;
> What tho' barbarians on the banks of Thames,
> Their genius sunk in Lucre's sordid flames,

Despise the Scot, and hate the letter'd sage,
Your fame, my son, shall stretch from age to age;
Like some great stream, indignant, burst each mound,
While sallow envy prostrate bites the ground,
Let then Londona still with greatness dwell,
Let courts and commerce all her triumphs swell;
With Wilkes and Liberty, and Green and Horne,
And P——t, and Beck——d, ring from morn to morn;
Let patriot worthies, in her own guildhall,
Teach Monarchs wisdom, and be all in all:
For joys so turbulent I ne'er shall pine,
Nor e'er shall envy, while a HUME is mine.

What Hume called "the frenzy of liberty" which had seized the English found a sympathetic response on the continent. Hume's friend D'Alembert (not knowing his man) regretted that he could not be in England with Hume to hail "Wilkes and Liberty."[17] The cause of Wilkes, D'Alembert thought, was the cause of Enlightenment. The enthusiasm quickly spread from London throughout the arteries of the empire. Glasses were raised in Boston, Charleston, Pittsburgh (the western frontier of empire, named after William Pitt), the West Indies, and in India. While Wilkes was in the King's Bench Prison, gifts poured in from Britain and the empire on a spectacular scale. The colony of South Carolina voted a gift of £1,500. "The Sons of Liberty" (including John Adams) assembled to the good number of forty-five at the Whig Tavern in Boston and sent a gift of live turtles, one of which weighed forty-five pounds. They addressed Wilkes as "*one* of those incorruptible *honest men* reserved by heaven to bless and perhaps save a tottering Empire." And one of their members, William Palfrey, wrote to Wilkes in February, 1769, that "the fate of Wilkes and America must stand or fall together."[18] From Maryland he received 45 hogsheads of tobacco to be smoked in 45 months, taking 45 pipes a day and 45 whiffs to every pipe. If this could not be managed, the tobacco was to be divided among the prisoners of the King's Bench. Children, towns, and counties in America were named after Wilkes: for example, Wilkesborough, North Carolina, and Wilkes-Barre, Pennsylvania (co-named with Isaac Barré, another friend of liberty and also a friend of Hume's). Wilkes's fame even drifted to China.[19]

Between demonstrations, a kind of Wilkes worship reigned in England. It was said that half the mantlepieces of London displayed busts of Wilkes in marble, bronze, or china. Articles of his clothing were sold as sacred relics. His portrait was prominently displayed in shops, and many taverns hung out the Wilkes head as their sign. Shops were filled with plates, mugs, snuff boxes, and other trinkets bearing his portrait. These were eagerly bought up by admirers and tourists. The ritualistic use of the number 45 was exploited in every possible direction. Wilkes had a surprising number of admirers among the English clergy. Prayers were offered for the preservation of English liberty and the restoration of Wilkes. Sermons played with endless Biblical allusions to the number 45.[20] When Wilkes was released from prison, demonstrations and illuminations occurred throughout the empire. The town of Bradford may be taken as an instance:

> The morning was ushered in with the ringing of bells, which continued till ten at night, and in the evening were illuminations, and the following, we hear, was given at the sole expence of Mr. Richard Shackleton, at the Bull's Head, *viz.* A bonfire of 45 of coals: a curious representation of the figures 45, composed of 45 candles, under which was wrote in large characters, Wilkes at Liberty; also a supper to the sons of Liberty, which consisted of 45 lbs. of roast beef; legs of mutton and tongues 45 lb.; three hams 45 lb.; 45 fowls; a lamb 45 lbs.; of bread 45; 45 lb. of vegetables; 45 gallons of ale and 45 bowls of punch.[21]

A young woman in Bath curled her hair in the shape of 45 and married a man of 45. A stiff and haughty Austrian ambassador was dragged out of his coach and hoisted upside down by a good-humored Wilkite mob so that 45 could be painted on the soles of his shoes.[22]

But the Wilkes demonstrations also wore an ominous face. From the beginning, revolution and civil war were in the air. The city of London had, on a number of occasions, goaded and defied King and Parliament. The city sent several insulting Remonstrances to the King demanding that he dissolve Parliament and dismiss evil ministers. On one occasion he was grimly warned that Parliament had engaged in illegal acts more serious than the levying of ship money by Charles I.[23] Dark comparisons with the Civil War were frequent. When in 1771 London Alderman Richard Oliver was thrown into prison for committing a messenger of Parliament to jail, toasts were drunk to "Oliver the second." Poems referred to "Cromwell Wilkes." And the fantasy was indulged of a new Puritan revolution in the name of liberty: "A rumour is spread about town, that many of the majority have seen the ghost of Cromwell, dressed in full armour, which has filled them with terrible apprehensions and grievances."[24] The Wilkes and Liberty movement was identified (by both sides) with Puritan heroes and especially with John Lilburne, the leader of the Leveller movement, whom even Cromwell was forced to discipline. John Hampden was Wilkes's own hero.[25]

County meetings grew larger and more fanatical; petitions and remonstrances began pouring in to the King. There were demands to impeach the King's mother, and Horace Walpole thought that her life was in danger. The King's ministers were assaulted (Lord North on one occasion barely escaped with his life), and the King himself was openly insulted by the public. The *Caledonian Mercury*, 3 April 1771, estimated that "no fewer than 500 constables and peace officers attended his Majesty on Thursday last, at his going to the House of Peers." While the King was in the House of Lords, the crowd smashed the windows of the House of Commons. It took two hundred constables to protect the speaker of the House as he entered.

In its remonstrances and defiance of King and Parliament, the city of London appeared to be acting like an independent republic. There was a lot of seditious talk (and at the highest level, e.g., by Pitt) of resisting tyranny. Pitt praised American resistance to tyranny and corruption and encouraged the same resistance at home. As the King was leaving the House of Lords (at a time when the liberty of the mayor was in danger) a gentleman cried out, "No Lord Mayor, no King!"[26] He was brought to the justice of the peace but insisted that he was a "citizen of London" and would not retract what he had said.

The government was manifestly weak, and it was not clear that English troops would have the loyalty necessary to put down a rebellion of English "patriots." Scottish troops had been used before to control a Wilkite mob, with unhappy results. Goaded by anti-Scottish prejudices, the troops went berserk, killing half a dozen persons and wounding a dozen or so more. Some were bayoneted. Several innocent bystanders were killed, including a pregnant woman and a girl carrying a basket of fruit. It became known as the massacre of St. George's Field.

The King had resolved to punish the city but was persuaded otherwise by the peace-loving Lord North. Had the Lord Mayor, the sheriffs, and the city members been thrown in prison, a large part of the opposition would have been out in the streets. One could imagine a vast mob filled with the resentments of Revolution ideology at the head of which would have been Pitt, Wilkes, Beckford, and other Whig leaders; shots fired by hated Scots troops on Englishmen; the unbinding determination of George III to fight if revolt should occur—all of these were real possibilities and ingredients for civil war. It seemed to many that some great constitutional crisis was coming to a head and that revolution was imminent. Horace Walpole wrote in 1769 that England "approached by fast strides to some great crisis, and to me never wore so serious an air, except in the Rebellion" (*L,* 2: 209 n). A writer to the *Caledonian Mercury* predicted: "From the present prospect of things, it is expected, that the aera 1771, will be productive of more political phenomena, than has arose since 1648 [the year Charles I was executed]." Writing to Strahan a little over a year earlier, Hume worried whether English troops would be loyal in case of rebellion: "I wish only the Army may be faithful and the Militia quiet: Woud to God we had a Scotch Militia at present. This Country is almost unanimous" (*L,* 2: 211–12).[27]

As it turned out, civil war did occur, but it was confined to a battle between the King's army and the American Wilkites abroad. The feared revolution in England did not occur, in part because those who could have led it (Wilkes and Pitt) were not revolutionaries. Being loyal to Revolution ideology, they did not desire another revolution. But there were wild rumors in distant parts of the empire that Wilkes had been made King.[28] After his release from prison, success in office improved Wilkes. He changed from an outrageous opportunistic libertine who delighted in poking a stick in the lion's ear to a thoughtful and loyal critic of British political order. He supported a number of reforms expanding the sphere of individual liberty which were not popular even with the opposition, and he was one of the strongest supporters of the American cause.

The Gordon riots occurred in 1780 and lasted ten days, paralyzing much of London. The cry was "No popery," but the cause of Protestantism was identified also with the "progressive" cause of radicalism. William Blake was a sympathizer. This was the same sort of mob Wilkes had engineered. Indeed, many wore the blue Wilkes cockade and identified with the older movement, but the Gordon riots were more radical and violent. The mob turned to arson, and by the fifth day eleven great fires were blazing in London. Newgate prison was destroyed, and some three hundred prisoners released, the political significance of which can be appreciated by comparing it with the mythical storming of the Bastille, which contained only seven prisoners, none of whom were political. Newgate was said to have contained some political prisoners, but since no revolution followed, the "storming of Newgate" never entered the mythology of the progressive mind as a liberating event.

During the riots the mayor dithered and refused to call out troops. Wilkes (though only an alderman) took matters into his own hands; he organized an armed band and went after the rioters. A number of ironies followed. Wilkes fired on rioters and killed them, ignoring the outrage that he and others had felt when the government had fired into a Wilkite mob. He dispersed a crowd gathered at the printing shop of one William Moore. Wilkes seized papers and arrested Moore who, as it turned out, had been a printer for the *North Briton!*[29] He appears also to have issued some "general warrants." Wilkes had come a long way.

In his handling of the Gordon riots, Wilkes displayed courage and public spirit. The duty of preserving public peace was the mayor's, not his. The mayor's refusal to act had its source in the same timidity before a popular enthusiasm that had made King and Parliament incompetent before the Wilkes and Liberty riots. The suppression of his own supporters and those associated with them marked the end of Wilkes as an ideological symbol. Over a decade later an aged woman recognized Wilkes in his carriage and hailed him with the old cry of "Wilkes and Liberty!" He is said to have replied, in a good humored way, "Be quiet, you old fool that was all over long ago."[30]

The Philosophical Meaning of "Wilkes and Liberty"

Hume taught that self-consecrating religious enthusiasm alienated from common life cannot sustain itself but must, after running its wild course, return chastened to common life. Likewise, the self-certifying philosophical enthusiasm internal to the Wilkes and Liberty movement had run its course. Mingling opportunism with Revolution ideology, Wilkes had finally found a place for himself. He eventually became reconciled with former enemies such as Samuel Johnson and George III. He had, in his own terms, become an "exhausted volcano." The ideological meaning of the movement, as reflected in the old lady's ingratiating and cheerful enthusiasm, was empty and embarrassing.

Hume appears to have been surprised at the violence of his own reaction to the Wilkes and Liberty movement. Writing from Edinburgh to Gilbert Elliot in 1770, he said, "As I had renounced the World, I did not think it had been possible for any public Business to have interested me so much as I am against the success of those Banditti" (*NHL,* 189). What is the explanation of what we may properly describe as Hume's rage? There were four main elements. First, anti-Scottish bigotry exploited by the movement, which made it difficult for Scots to enjoy the fruits of the union for which they had given up their sovereignty in 1707. Hume had, from the first of his career, supported the union because it would bring an increase in prosperity and civility to Scotland. Hume abandoned much of his own heritage and encouraged young

Scots to do the same in order to participate in the more universal sphere of London. He was even prepared to describe this as an "English" rather than a "British" sphere, and notwithstanding his thick Scots brogue (which he confessed was desperate and irreclaimable), he tried the experiment of thinking and speaking of himself as an Englishman. It was a bitter pill to have conformed so far and still to have one's self and people rejected. It is worth observing that most of Hume's years were spent in Scotland and France, and it was only in these two countries that he thought seriously of retiring. He never felt at home in London and throughout his life stayed there intermittently for a total of only about five years, about the same amount of time he spent in France.

Second, English chauvinistic nationalism, based on a false historical theory of the origin and nature of the English constitution, yielded the absurd idea that modern liberty was a unique trait of English national character and that England was the last bastion of freedom in the world. Hume viewed liberty as a European achievement. Third, the bellicose mercantilism behind the movement, based on a false theory of political economy, had forced the nation into one useless war after another, vastly expanding the public debt and bringing the nation close to the point of bankruptcy. He explained the matter to William Strahan in 1771, dissenting from Strahan's optimistic picture of the future:

> But when I reflect, that, from 1740 to 1761, during the Course of no more than 21 Years, while a pacific Monarch sat on the Throne of France, the Nation ran in Debt about a hundred Millions; that the wise and virtuous Minister, Pitt, could contract more Incumbrances, in six months of an unnecessary War, than we have been able to discharge during eight Years of Peace; and that we persevere in the same frantic Maxims; I can forsee nothing but certain and speedy Ruin either to the Nation or to the public Creditors. The last, tho' a great Calamity, would be a small one in comparison; but I cannot see how it can be brought about, while these Creditors fill all the chief Offices and are the Men of greatest Authority in the Nation. (*L*, 2: 237)

Fourth, there was the seditious republican strain in the movement deriving largely from the contract theory, the popular acceptance of which Hume considered to be a philosophical parochialism of the English, "those foolish English Prejudices, which all Nations and all Ages disavow" (*L*, 2: 216). But if contractarian republicanism was largely a philosophical superstition of the English, something like it had spread to Scotland, and in a letter written in December, 1773, Hume found it necessary to warn his young nephew who was in danger of being seduced by the radical republicanism of John Millar. Hume agreed that republican regimes are in theory the best regimes, but he found it necessary to give young David a lesson on the nature of true philosophical criticism, namely, that speculation cannot be carried out in alienation from the prejudices of common life. "An established Government cannot without the most criminal imputation, be disjointed from any Speculation" (*L,* 2: 306). A patient historical and rhetorical examination of British political experience shows that the sentiments and institutions are not available to support a change to republicanism. And Hume asks whether Mr. Millar is prepared to "tell us, what is that form of a Republic which we must aspire to? Or will the Revolution be afterward decided by the Sword? One great Advantage of a Commonwealth over our mixt Monarchy is, that it would considerably abridge our liberty, which is growing to such an Extreme, as to be incompatible with all Government. Such Fools are they, who perpetually cry out Liberty: and think to augment it, by shaking off the Monarchy" (*L,* 2: 306).

All of these reasons for opposition to the Wilkes and Liberty movement, with the exception of the first (which relates to English bigotry about Scottish national character), have to do with false theorizing in history, economics, and political philosophy. These theories have blinded the nation to the true origin and nature of commerce and liberty. Material prosperity is being threatened by a false theory of political economy, and civil liberty is being subverted by a corrupt philosophical theory of liberty.

The Wilkes and Liberty movement was complicated, and Hume's response to it was also complicated. Here, however, I wish to stress only one aspect of it, namely, the sense in which the movement outraged him not as a Scotsman, nor as an advocate of the union, nor as a supporter of free trade, nor as a constitutional monarchist, nor as an anti-imperialist, but as a *philosopher.* All of these were involved, but Hume also understood that in the Wilkes and Liberty movement he was witnessing something new: a mass movement fueled not by religious ideology but by purely secular ideology complete with its own rituals. Heretofore, Hume had taught that although a corrupt philosophical consciousness could be as dangerous to the peace and order of society as religion, experience had not as yet provided any instance of its being so: "Generally speaking," he wrote in the *Treatise,* "the errors in religion are dangerous; those in philosophy only ridiculous" (*T,* 272). Although Wilkes had surprisingly large support among the clergy, there was no religious theme whatsoever associated with the movement. Philosophical errors alone were generating mass passions and hysteria. Hume's recognition of the novelty of the movement and its contrast with religious enthusiasm is revealed in a letter to Hugh Blair (1769): "This Madness about Wilkes . . . exceeds the Absurdity of Titus Oates and the popish Plot; and is so much more disgraceful to the Nation, as the former Folly, being derivd from Religion, flow'd from a Source, which has, from uniform Prescription, acquird a Right to impose Nonsense on all Nations & all Ages: But the present Extravagance is peculiar to Ourselves, and quite risible. However, I am afraid my Mirth will soon be spoilt, and Affairs become quite serious" (*L*, 2: 197).

The popish plot was an hysteria of the Restoration period which Hume explored at some length in the volume of the *History* covering the reigns of Charles II and James II. He observed that it was during this period that secular political passions began to dominate over religious passions. By 1771 that domination would be complete, and Hume could declare that political "factious prejudices are more prevelant in England than religious ones" (*L*, 2: 233). But during the Restoration period the religious idiom was very much alive, and political interests often appeared in religious garb. Conspiracy theories about a Catholic takeover were believed by the masses and were indulged and manipulated for political purposes by their leaders. Protestants, it was thought, were to be murdered in their sleep. A mass hysteria had gripped the nation. A market was generated for testimony to these conspiracies, and rewards were given for them. Trials were held on the basis of contradictory and even perjured testimony. Hume treats this period as the nadir of absurdity and folly in English political history. It was worse than the Puritan enthusiasm, for the Puritans at least believed their speculative tenets and were willing to sacrifice their interests and lives for them. The popish plot, however, was largely a cover for political interests. Its show trials were cynically manipulative and tawdry.

But Hume judged the Wilkes and Liberty movement to be even worse because it derived not from the authority of religion, the master disposition of which is fear, but from the authority of philosophy, the master disposition of which should be the love of truth. Religion had acquired a prescriptive right "to impose nonsense on all nations," but philosophy, which had existed only in the practice of elites and whose errors had been largely confined to the closets of elites, had acquired no such right. Now, entirely free from religion, it was claiming that right.

It is the unprecedented phenomenon of mass passions spiritualized by a corrupt philosophical reflection about liberty that explains the peculiar rage expressed in the letters of the last decade of Hume's life. His outrage is that of the philosophical connoisseur who is able to recognize a corrupt philosophical mind where others cannot see it and who now recognizes that the Enlightenment hope of achieving peace, prosperity, and humanity by cultivating philosophy may not succeed. Heretofore, the problem had been religion, the antidote of which was philosophy. Religion is darkness, philosophy is light. Henceforth, in a secular age, the battle would occur *within* philosophy between its true and its corrupt forms.

Earlier I discussed Hume's view that the source of reform is to come not from the "slaving poor" (as Marx would teach) nor from the grandees but from what he called the "middling rank." It is this class that forms "the most numerous Rank of Men, that can be suppos'd susceptible of Philosophy; and therefore, all Discourses of Morality ought principally to be address'd to them." It is this class that is most likely "to hearken to the calm Voice of Reason" (*E*, 546). But it was precisely this middling rank that made up the Wilkes "mob." Hume is very clear on this: "For do not say, the Scum of London" (*L*, 2: 226). Hume was not alone in perceiving this change. Mrs. Montague spoke of a wicked mob and a foolish ministry. "It was better in the old times," she wrote, "when the Ministry was wicked and the mob foolish. Ministers, however wicked, do not pull down houses, nor ignorant mobs pull down governments. A mob that can read, and a Ministry that cannot think, are sadly matched."[31] A mob that could read was a philosophical mob; something quite new and, if informed by a corrupt philosophical consciousness, something quite dangerous.

Diderot's call to "make philosophy popular" was being heard. It would not be long before Thomas Paine would be peddling simplified versions of Lockean and Hobbesian individualism for the people. And the mob that had sung "God Save Great Wilkes our King" would some years later adapt the song to "God Save Great Thomas Paine."[32] In France a mob that could read would initiate not reform but the philosophical alchemy of a total revolution. It would be consumed in a terror of its own making and placed in the service of a Cromwell-style "new model army" to spread with a writ of fire and sword not the Puritan faith but the Rights of Man across Europe. And in 1843 Marx, himself a child of the middling rank, could write to Ruge that "philosophy has become secularized, and the striking proof thereof is that the philosophical consciousness itself has been pulled into the torment of struggle. . . . What we must accomplish is the ruthless criticism of all that exists."[33] Here we have false philosophy in what I have called its revolutionary mode, which if not restrained by the prejudices of common life logically leads to total criticism, total revolution, and totalitarian power.

But this carries us to a world which, though intimated in Hume's critique of philosophy, is beyond his experience. What he did confront and reject was the ritualistic Enlightenment belief that an increase in knowledge and liberty was the formula for inevitable progress. This was the faith of his friend Turgot. In a letter written to Turgot in 1768, Hume firmly rejected it, presenting the Wilkes and Liberty affair as his reason. England, he thought, was the most philosophical country in Europe and had more liberty than any other nation in history (*E*, 91, 508). Yet the increase in philosophical knowledge led to a new return of "Barbarism and Ignorance," where false philosophy was subverting the true. Caught in the grip of corrupt and alienating theories of liberty (and with no understanding of the historical origins of the practice of liberty), the people seemed bent on subverting the liberty they actually enjoyed in the name of liberty (*L*, 2: 180).

The experience of the Wilkes and Liberty movement left its mark on Hume's writings. Although he undertook no substantial literary project during the last decade of his life, he took the opportunity to correct and change new editions of his works in order to address the issues of that period. First, over and over in the letters Hume says that the English are self-obsessed with their liberty, that they have too much liberty, and that they have a disposition to extend it without proper regard to authority. Liberty, for Hume, is always ordered liberty. And what that order of authority is and how susceptible it is to change is determined not by *a priori* speculation but by a careful and patient understanding of established practice. In the letter to Turgot mentioned above, where Hume presents the Wilkes and Liberty movement as a counterexample to Turgot's thesis that an increase in knowledge and liberty is the formula for inevitable progress, he insists that it is the surfeit of liberty and its abuse that are responsible for barbarism in England, and he singles out "the Liberty of the Press" as the main cause (*L*, 2: 180).

In 1741 at the beginning of his career, Hume published "Of the Liberty of the Press" in which he criticized the ancient philosophers for their judgment about the folly and credulity of the multitude. It has been found "as the experience of mankind increases, that the *people* are no such dangerous monster as they have been represented, and that it is in every respect better to guide them, like rational creatures, than to lead or drive them like brute beasts" (*E*, 604–5). Hume then judged that the abuse of the press would not likely ever be dangerous: "The liberty of the press, therefore, however abused, can scarce ever excite popular tumults or rebellion." And he praised England for setting an "example of civil liberty; and though this liberty seems to occasion some small ferment at present, it has not as yet produced any pernicious effects; and it is to be hoped, that men, being every day more accustomed to the free discussion of public affairs, *will improve in the judgment of them*" (*E,* 605; italics mine). The two paragraphs containing these sanguine views of the press were dropped in the editions of 1771 and the last edition of 1777. In this edition Hume added the following melancholic statement for future statesmen to ponder: "It must however be allowed, that the unbounded liberty of the press, though it be difficult, perhaps impossible, to propose a suitable remedy for it, is one of the evils, attending those mixt forms of government" (*E,* 13). The freedom of the press now appears as a necessary evil, and the true philosopher's relation to it is not that of adolescent Enlightenment celebration but of adult circumspection.

Second, in the first edition of "Idea of a Perfect Commonwealth," Hume had allowed voting rights to all freeholders in the county republics and all householders in the towns who pay taxes. By 1753 and in all editions through 1768, he limited voting rights to freeholders worth ten pounds a year and householders in the towns worth two hundred pounds. But in the 1770 edition, at the height of the Wilkes and Liberty affair, he raised the qualification to a twenty-pound freehold in the counties and a very stiff five-hundred-pound household in the towns. This would have disenfranchised much of the Middlesex electorate on which Wilkes depended.

Third, Hume wrote Strahan in 1772 asking him to restore the words "and happy," which he had dropped from his description of the English constitution in previous editions as "singular and happy." His old theme of excessive liberty is sounded; but upon reflection Hume had to admit (especially as the Wilkes and Liberty affair had cooled a bit by 1772) that "as the English Government is certainly happy, though probably not calculated for Duration, by reasons of its excessive Liberty, I believe it will be as well to restore them: But if that Sheet be already printed, it is not worth while to attend to the matter. I am as well pleas'd that this Instance of Spleen and Indignation shoud remain" (*L,* 2: 261).

Finally, in the last revisions of his account of Elizabeth's reign, Hume took a final shot at Pitt and the huge public debt brought on by mercantile wars: "The minister [Pitt], in the war began in 1754, was, in some periods, allowed to lavish in two months as great a sum as was granted by parliament to queen Elizabeth in forty-five years. The extreme frivilous object of the late war, [the Seven Years' War] and the great importance of hers, set this matter in still a stronger light." Hume continues, making again the point that the new secular ideological superstitions are the equal of any absurdity in religion. This time the comparison is made not with the popish plot but with the crusades: "Our late delusions have much *exceeded any thing known in history,* not even excepting those of the crusades. For, I suppose, there is no mathematical, still less an arithmetical demonstration, that the road to the Holy Land was not the road to Paradise, as there is, that the endless encrease of national debts is the direct road to national ruin. . . . It will be found in the present year, 1776, that all the revenues of this island, north of Trent and west of Reading, are mortgaged or anticipated for ever" (*H,* 4: 373 n; italics mine).

Hume's response to the Wilkes and Liberty movement has usually been thought of as "conservative" or even as "reactionary" (e.g., Greig's judgment that Hume was George III). Recently, however, John Stewart has argued forcefully that Hume's response reveals a liberal progressive spirit.[34] Stewart views Wilkes not as the leader of a reform movement concerned to strengthen personal liberty by eliminating general warrants, securing the freedom of the press, reforming the franchise, and securing the rights of electors to determine their own representatives. Rather, he sees the Wilkes and Liberty affair as a symbol of English chauvinism, anti-Scottish bigotry, and bellicose mercantilism.

But the language of "progressives" and "conservatives" was not applicable until after the French Revolution, when a self-professed conservative movement arose to combat Enlightenment total criticism, and after the Industrial Revolution, which by providing a self-augmenting machinery, gave some empirical substance to dreams of perpetual progress.[35] To read these essentially nineteenth-century terms into Hume is to appropriate him for present political purposes by seeking intimations in his thought of later experiences. There is nothing wrong with this political mode of understanding Hume if it is adequately supported by the text. Narrative understanding of the past is, in the end, always a matter of finding heroes. And there are sufficient aspects to Hume's thought in which progressives and conservatives can find, up to a point, intimations of their own experiences. But to think in this way is to engage a *political* mode of understanding, whereas the purpose of this study is to explore the philosophical mode of understanding. What I have tried to bring out is the sense in which the mass movement for Wilkes and Liberty exhibited, in part, the force of a vulgar philosophical consciousness in politics. What is of interest here is the philosophical or ideological form of the movement. For that purpose it matters little whether the content of the movement is viewed retrospectively as progressive or conservative, whatever those terms might mean.

But there are special reasons why it is difficult to read Hume's response to the Wilkes and Liberty affair in purely political terms. To determine that his response was "progressive" or "conservative," one would have to examine the demands for reform internal to the Wilkes and Liberty movement, what Hume's views were on these questions, and what the political context could reasonably allow in reform, and then judge all of this by "conservative" or "progressive" standards. What is interesting about Hume's response, however, is that he never takes up the issues of reform that progressives have found essential to the Wilkes and Liberty movement. He is aware of them, but what he criticizes is the ideological frenzy about liberty, which is a maelstrom capable of sweeping together into an indiscriminate mass legitimate demands for reform, political ambition, personal and regional grievance, fear, suspicion, and that special form of hatred which only philosophical opposition can generate and to which Hume had called attention at the beginning of his career in "Of Parties in General" (1741).

What he focused on was the *form* of the maelstrom—that peculiar feature that held and blurred the parts together and gave the movement its driving force in quite different contexts throughout the empire. That peculiar feature was an ideological enthusiasm about "liberty" constituting a philosophical whole which was the result of the habit of a rude form of philosophical theorizing among the vulgar. Or we may put it another way: Given Hume's distinction between the legitimate political parties of affection and interest and the illegitimate ones of speculative principle, we may say of the Wilkes and Liberty movement that though it contained affection for such leaders as Wilkes and Pitt and interests such as the mercantile interests of the commercial centers of the empire, all of these were spiritualized into a philosophical whole that was greater than the parts and made dynamic by something called "Liberty." The ritualistic incantation of "liberty" was an effect of those parties of speculative principle which Hume found to be unique to modern times and, unfortunately, was required of all modern political parties (*E,* 465).

Hume's perception of the Wilkes and Liberty movement was similar to his treatment of the English Civil War. That war was not a "progressive" event as the Whig and "liberal" mentality has been fond of picturing it. It was not fought because reasonable demands for reform were rejected by a recalcitrant king; nor was it fought because the king invaded the clearly established rights of Parliament. Questions of reform and prerogative were involved, but these were transformed by a religious-philosophical enthusiasm into a dynamic whole with a life of its own, which eventually carried *everything* in its path. The ordinary rules of morals, law, and politics were deconstructed and their parts carried up into the maelstrom. An obscure, moderately dissenting member of the House of Commons who would have lived out his life in that style was magically transformed into a militant peripatetic icon of Puritan enthusiasm. Dispositions were drawn forth from Oliver Cromwell which would have lain dormant. Cromwell eventually embodied the storm and was even able to guide it, but when he died, it died with him.

It was the added dimension of a totalizing religious-philosophical principle, peculiar to the Puritan mind, that made the war a total revolution and carried it quite beyond the ordinary categories of good and evil internal to common life. Hume wrote the *History* of the Stuarts in large part to explode the dominant Whig interpretation, which had pictured the Puritans as patriots and defenders of English liberty. Hume was concerned to stress the historicity of ideal conceptions such as liberty and to show that once the concept of liberty is cut loose from its historical roots in practice and is transformed by speculation into a totalizing ideal, political life becomes absurd. Hume expresses this by saying that the nation lost its liberty by "the too eager pursuit of liberty." The result was a philosophical inversion of liberty into tyranny. "Never in this island, was known a more severe and arbitrary government than was generally exercised by the patrons of liberty" (*H,* 5: 528).

By the time of the Restoration, there had insensibly developed a distinct prejudice against speculative enthusiasms: the people were afraid that "the zeal for liberty [would] engraft itself on fanaticism, and [would] once more kindle a civil war in the kingdom" (*H,* 6: 377). Hume thought this very engrafting of liberty onto speculative fanaticism was happening in the Wilkes and Liberty movement. Looking back, it is easy to say that Wilkes and Pitt did not have the characters of totalizing revolutionaries, but then neither had Cromwell betrayed any such qualities in his character prior to the Civil War. Hume knew and had demonstrated that the totalizing consciousness of speculative reason, whether in religious or secular form, is capable of alchemical transformations in the moral world. Under the right conditions Wilkes or Pitt could perhaps have become a Danton or Robespierre, or more likely, some obscure Cromwell could have arisen to sweep away both and carry out a root-and-branch republican revolution in the name of "Liberty."

Hume's insight into the Wilkes and Liberty movement carries us beyond the political categories of "progressive" and "conservative." His trained eye discerned the philosophical dimension of the movement, and his rage was prompted by the fact that the parties of speculative principle acting out before his eyes were infused by a secular philosophical consciousness and not a religious one. It was now not the errors of religion but those of philosophy that were proving dangerous. And his fear was not the result of pessimism or Tory reaction; it was reasonable. He had seen something very like this before in the Puritan revolution.

Modern total revolutions, provided they speak in a progressive political idiom, always appear initially to be reform movements and are ritualistically supported by the Whiggish or progressive mind, which is not philosophically sophisticated enough to discern the larger spiritual totalities that inform and can perversely transmute ordinary political issues into superstitions. Hume noticed that the speculative enthusiasm of the Puritan mind spiritualized and distorted everything it touched. "Enquiries and debates concerning tonnage and poundage went hand in hand with these theological or metaphysical controversies" (*H,* 5: 214). But a reforming mind and a mind captured by philosophical enthusiasm are quite different.

Consider the French Revolution. That, too, has been identified as a liberating movement, in a narrative of universal human emancipation, designed to establish the rights of man. But it was disastrous in its consequences, resulting in the first secular totalitarian regime, the Reign of Terror, and the imperialism of Napoleon, all of which were carried out in the name of liberty and human rights. The first totalitarian regime was not the work of "fascists" or "Marxists" but of liberals, and liberalism, throughout its history, has revealed a tendency to totalism that has been restrained only by the contingent circumstance of substantial, inherited moral traditions that hedge it in, but whose authority cannot be acknowledged.

In the beginning, the French Revolution was eagerly embraced by Whig progressives. Burke estimated that two-thirds of the clergy of the Church of England supported it initially. Richard Price, one of the more thoughtful of the Old Whigs and a dissenting minister, was transported by the new secular ideology of liberty, which he could nevertheless chant in a religious tone. "What an eventful period is this! I am thankful that I have lived to it; and I could almost say, Lord, now lettest thou thy servant depart in peace, for mine eyes have seen thy salvation. . . . I have lived to see the rights of men better understood than ever; and nations panting for liberty, which seemed to have lost the idea of it. . . . After sharing in the benefits of one Revolution [the Glorious Revolution of 1688], I have been spared to be a witness to two other

Revolutions, both glorious."[36] The French Revolution, however, had just begun, and even as Price wrote, it was turning into something barbarous, not glorious. But knowledge of the actual circumstances of France was not necessary. All that Price needed to spark his enthusiasm was to know that the movement was informed by a politically correct idiom (the rights of man). The presumption that deeply established institutions such as the nobility, monarchy, church, the Parliaments, and the States-Provincial should be reformed rather than swept away and that a patient moral and empirical inquiry into the nature of those institutions would be necessary to see what reforms were possible were not considerations that restrained Price's enthusiasms. Price was ecstatic that he had inherited one, seen a second, and was now living through a third revolution. The more the better, and like his Puritan ancestors and progressive posterity since, Price listened to the auguries of history: His truth is marching on.

Price's superficial rationalism and superstitious providentialism prevented him from understanding how the French Revolution differed from the Glorious Revolution of 1688 and the American Revolution. The latter two were reformist in character. In neither was there an attempt to totally transform the social and political order. In each case, those who made the revolution lived to govern afterwards. The French Revolution devoured its makers. Burke perceived a fundamental difference between the three revolutions, even before the French Revolution had run its course. He saw that the French Revolution was informed by the language, not of reform, but of total criticism. In the *Reflections* he explored instances of this language used by "those within and without the Assembly, who direct the operations of the machine now at work in France." He gave as an instance a speech of a leading member of the National Assembly calling for the destruction of "all the establishments in France" and total transformation. "Their ideas, their laws, their customs must be changed . . . men changed, things changed, words changed . . . destroy everything; yes destroy everything; then everything is to be recreated."[37] It would be hard to find a better example of what Hume called "philosophical enthusiasm" and of corrupt philosophical existence in its revolutionary mode.

Price, on the other hand, is a good example of what I have called false philosophy in its guilty mode. This sort of mentality has sufficient philosophical enthusiasm to be transported by the language of total criticism, total destruction, and total renewal but Price lacks the courage to risk his own position or to draw the knife himself in order to see the revolutionary project through. Price does not have what Sartre praised as "dirty hands."[38] He is, however, at least in reflection, the fellow traveler (as Sartre himself was) of those who do have such courage. And even if the revolution turns barbarous, he is ready with some sort of apologetic and a disposition to be transported again when the next liberation movement appears.

It is common to think of Burke as "reacting" to the French Revolution and of Price as "progressive," and to think of the latter as rational and the former as unthinking. But if the mark of rationality is the ability to discriminate among differences and to perceive identities, then Burke was the more rational, for he was able to distinguish between political action carried out in the idiom of reform and that carried out in the idiom of total criticism, whereas Price could not. Price's judgment was ritualistic; it was not discriminating, and it was not insightful. Price was, to use Adam Smith's memorable description, one of those "men of system" who were partisans of the revolution but were blinded by the abstract system of the rights of man from perceiving what was likely to happen in France and, indeed, what was happening before their eyes. Burke recognized that not all that passes for criticism in the name of liberty, equality, or humanity is worthy of respect. He understood the point Hume made in "Of Moral Prejudices" that many of the new vulgar philosophers, though they spoke the language of reform and freedom, were in fact inverted "Anti-reformers" (*E*, 538).

Although Burke's predictions about the French Revolution came true, we are not to think of him as a prophet. Burke was endowed with something of the timeless disposition of the Humean true philosopher. The true philosopher is prohibited from playing with a national constitution like a "quack with a sickly patient" (*E*, 509). It is not enough for him to grasp a few superficial aspects of a political order that correspond with politically correct abstractions; he must have the connoisseur's eye for affairs and must seek to grasp the social and political order as a poetic whole.

The true philosopher also knows that the vast amount of knowledge and virtue contained in that whole is implicit and locked into established customs and traditions. Only a fraction of this knowledge can be brought to the level of explicit awareness. The true philosopher will defer to this totality, correcting this or that part of it, but only after a patient, careful, and generous attempt to understand the whole. Burke attempted this in the *Reflections;* whether he entirely succeeded may be questioned, but his critique of the total criticism of the French Revolutionaries exemplified the timeless wisdom of true philosophy. And the counsel would have been no less wise and prudent had the revolution not barbarized itself. The same is true of Hume's criticism of the Wilkes and Liberty affair as the enactment of a vulgar and corrupt philosophical enthusiasm.

Fortunately, not all the ingredients for revolution were present in the Wilkes and Liberty movement. But Hume, the philosophical connoisseur, knew that something new had entered the world, the nature and consequences of which he did not and could not fully understand. Hume the historian was impatient to know the end of the story. The scene that was unfolding (the Wilkes and Liberty movement and the American crisis) contained, he thought, "the true ingredients for making a fine Narrative in History" (*L,* 2: 208). He knew that the historian cannot now know the end of the story he is living through: "I dare not," he wrote, "venture to play the Prophet" (*L,* 2: 210). Yet he could not forbear to conjecture in 1770 that "we shall have curious Scenes coming, worthy the Pen of the greatest Historian," and he confessed to being "tird and disgusted with Conjecture" (*L,* 2: 214). In the end, Hume was content merely to envy "the Lot of that Historian, who is to transmit to Posterity an account of these mad abandon'd times" (*NHL,* 189). He knew that something strange had flown over, which he hastily compared to the worst thing he had known (religious-philosophical fanaticism in politics as exhibited in the religious wars and revolutions of Europe), but he did not know exactly what it was. He had caught an intimation of the emerging age of mass secular philosophical enthusiasms.

CHAPTER ELEVEN

English Barbarism: "The Poor Infatuated Americans"

Hume's Support of American Secession

If Hume was not George III in his reaction to the Wilkes and Liberty affair, neither was he Edmund Burke in his reaction to the American crisis. Hume's position on America was much more radical than Burke's. As early as 1768 Hume argued for complete independence of the colonies from Great Britain—something few Americans at that time had even contemplated. Burke was one of the "friends of America" who supported reform short of outright independence. These included Shelburne, Barré, Rockingham, Fox, Dartmouth, Pitt, and, of course, Wilkes. Pitt especially was an "America man," as control of North American and West Indian trade was the cornerstone of his vision of a blue-water commercial empire. Pitt was prepared to make almost any concession to keep the empire together, and he was the only person of ministerial capacity who could reconcile the Americans. But none of these men advocated total independence. Even after the capture of Burgoyne's forces at Saratoga in 1777, most hoped for at least some sort of commonwealth arrangement under the Crown. Hume, however, advocated independence and sovereignty for the colonies.

But if the causes of the Wilkes and Liberty movement and of America were of a piece, as John Adams and many Americans thought they were, how is it that Hume could make so sharp a distinction between the two? The short answer is that the source of his rejection of the former was the same as his support for the latter. There were four considerations that went into Hume's support for the Americans.

In "That Politics May be Reduced to a Science," published in 1741, Hume laid it down as a maxim that republican empires are more oppressive to their colonies than those of absolute monarchies. It is in the interest of monarchs to view their colonial subjects as having the same status as those of the home country, but "a free state necessarily makes a great distinction . . . and will be sure to contrive matters, by restrictions on trade, and by taxes, so as to draw some private, as well as public, advantage from [its] conquests. Provincial governors have also a better chance, in a republic, to escape with their plunder, by means of bribery or intrigue; and their fellow-citizens, . . . enriched by the spoils of the subject provinces, will be the more inclined to tolerate such abuses" (*E*, 19; italics mine). England has a "free government" and is treated in the essay as being, in all but name, a republic. Hume mentions the oppressive treatment of Ireland by England in contrast to the more liberal treatment extended by France to her colonies. And Corsica fares much better under the absolute monarchy of France than it did under the republic of Genoa. As if to confirm this thesis that monarchy is a better office for preserving the corporate liberty of provinces in an empire, Hume pointed out to Strahan in 1772 that the idea of a Parliamentary inquiry into the activities of the East India Company "did not originally proceed from the Ministry, but from the King himself, who was shocked with the Accounts he received of the Oppressions exercised over the poor Natives, and demanded a Remedy. I wish it may be possible to provide any, that will be durable" (*L*, 2: 260).

It is perhaps worth noting that the Americans at first appealed to the Crown for protection, arguing that they were subjects of the King, not of the House of Commons. Even after war broke out in 1775, George Washington described his opponent as "the ministerial army." But this colonial appeal made little sense within the structure of Revolution ideology, as interpreted in England, for it implied compromising the independence of Parliament to tax. And it made no sense at all when it became clear that the King was in full support of coercion. After the Stamp Act and the emergence of Grenville's model of empire as a system of orbiting satellites serving the interests of the center, Hume, like the Americans, saw the colonies as swept out of the protection of monarchy into the oppression of a mercantile republican empire governed by London.

Second, though Hume thought monarchical empires better than republican ones, he was opposed to empire generally. His own vision of macropolitical order was of independent states connected by free trade and a policy of the balance of power. Commercial empires mean constant war and, under modern conditions, a constant increase in public debt and a massive transfer of the nation's resources to the central government. In "Of Public Credit," he argued that one pernicious effect of public debt is that it leads to a steady transfer of revenue from the provinces to the capital. Although Hume argued that modern commercial life has revealed new dimensions of human excellence unknown to the ancients, he always thought of commerce as rooted in the virtuous life, which is fostered mainly in the provinces, where ties of kinship and community are strong. The virtues that extensive commerce made possible required an urban setting for their display, but Hume thought that cities could become too large, too artificial, and too abstract. Under such conditions, the barbarism of refinement sets in, and men tend to lose contact with the source of moral sentiment.

Hume took London as an example: the "immense greatness" of that city, "under a government which admits not of discretionary power, renders the people factious, mutinous, seditious, and even perhaps rebellious" (*E*, 355). These remarks were published in 1752 before the conclusion of the Seven Years' War in 1763. The nation was left with an unprecedented national debt and a vast mercantile empire to protect against a humiliated and vengeful France, which meant further wars and more debt. All of this had increased the power of London beyond what Hume had imagined in 1752 when he judged that "the head is undoubtedly too large for the body." The Stamp Act was passed to help pay for the Seven Years' War and to protect the empire. The colonists had accepted their status as providing commerce for the mother country, and they had long accepted the regulation of their commerce for the advantage of England. But treating them as a source of revenue for the imperial projects of London was another matter. Hume, like the colonists, saw London as a remote and arbitrary power draining the provinces in Britain and the colonies of their wealth. Hume observed in 1766, after the repeal of the Stamp Act, that its repeal would not be enough. A transformation had occurred. Deep in debt as it was and as it would continue to be, the government in London would have to treat the colonies as a source not only of commerce but of revenue as well.

Third, in "Of the Balance of Trade" and "Of the Jealousy of Trade," Hume had defended the principles of free trade. These principles were presupposed in his attack on Pitt's mercantile policies, which had united war and commerce: "that wicked madman Pitt" (*L*, 2: 300–301). Consequently, Hume was prepared to argue that loss of the colonies would have no serious effect on British commerce. Writing to Strahan in 1775, he pointed out that a "forced and every day more precarious Monopoly of about 6 or 700,000 Pounds a year of Manufactures, was not worth contending for" and "that we should preserve the greater part of this Trade even if the Ports of America were open to all Nations" (*L,* 2: 300).

In a letter to Gilbert Elliot of 22 July 1768, when the second round of the Wilkes and Liberty movement was just beginning, Hume indulged a fantasy which tied together the themes discussed above of the wickedness of English republican imperialism, the inordinate growth of London through mercantile wars and public credit, and its consequent republicanization. "These are fine doings in America. O! how I long to see America and the East Indies revolted totally & finally, the Revenue reduc'd to half, public Credit fully discredited by Bankruptcy, the third of London in Ruins, and the rascally Mob subdu'd" (*L,* 2: 184). The same fantasy appears over a year later in a letter to Strahan. "Notwithstanding my Age, I hope to see a public Bankruptcy, the total Revolt of America, the Expulsion of the English from the East Indies, the Diminution of London to less than a half, and the Restoration of the Government to the King, Nobility, and Gentry of this Realm. To adorn the Scene, I hope also that some hundreds of Patriots will make their Exit at Tyburn, and improve English eloquence by their dying speeches" (*L,* 2: 210). In this fantasy Hume was able to include his old criticism of English barbarism as a scene from which eloquence and good literature had been banished by philosophical and political enthusiasms.

Fourth, Hume argued that the government in its present state could not win a war against the colonies and that a defeat might shatter its already weakened authority, resulting in a civil war at home. For a decade after the Seven Years' War the government was unstable. Resignations from the ministry were frequent, and it was during this period, when government was at its weakest, that Wilkes, a person of no importance, had without intending to do so, come close to toppling the Crown. This same government, already loaded with debt from the Seven Years' War, was now preparing to launch a long war that could not be won. After defeat, what could it expect its credit with the people to be?

Hume had little respect for the ability of those who were to conduct the war. His friends Lord Home and Baron Mure had asked him to write a loyal address to the King asking for strong measures against the Americans; Hume with some awkwardness had refused. To Baron Mure he flatly declared in October 1775,

> Besides, I am an American in my Principles, and wish we woud let them alone to govern or misgovern themselves as they think

> proper: The affair is of no Consequence, or of little Consequence to us. If the County of Renfrew think it indispensably necessary for them to interpose in public Matters, I wish they wou'd advise the King first to punish those insolent Rascals in London and Middlesex [the Wilkes crowd], who daily insult him and the whole Legislature, before he think of America. Ask him, how he can expect, that a form of Government will maintain an Authority at 3,000 Miles distance when it cannot make itself be respected or even treated with common Decency at home. Tell him, that Lord North, tho in appearance a worthy Gentleman, has not a head for these great Operations, and that if fifty thousand Men, and twenty Millions of Money were entrusted to such a lukewarm Coward as Gage, they never coud produce any Effect. These are Objects worthy of the respectable County of Renfrew, not mauling the poor infatuated Americans in the other Hemisphere. (*L*, 2: 303)

Lord North and General Gage were not the only ones who lacked the energy and capacities necessary to coordinate, under the severe restrictions of eighteenth-century communication, the land and sea forces necessary for so vast an undertaking as the subjugation of the American colonies. Lord Sandwich, who, as first Lord of the Admiralty from 1771 to 1782, presided over the American disaster, was even worse. Writing to Strahan on 10 May 1776, Hume, the historian, painted a memorable image of the disaster awaiting Britain from the character of such as Sandwich, a character which he took to be emblematic of the regime. Returning very ill from Bath in a last attempt to restore his health, Hume encountered a member of the company of Lord Sandwich, a notorious womanizer, who with some prostitutes and friends was in the midst of a three-weeks' stay in the country to enjoy the trouting season. As the war was moving into its second year, Hume reflected, "I do not remember in all my little or great Knowledge of History (according as you and Dr. Johnson can settle between you the Degrees of my Knowledge) such another Instance; and I am sure such a one does not exist: That the First Lord of the Admiralty, who is absolute and uncontrouled Master in his Department, shou'd at a time when the Fate of the British Empire is in dependance, and in dependance on him, find so much Leizure, Tranquillity, Presence of Mind and Magnanimity, as to have Amusement in trouting during three Weeks near sixty Miles from the scene of Business, and during the most critical Season of the Year. There needs but this single Fact to decide the Fate of the Nation. What an Ornament would it be in a future History to open the glorious Events of the ensuing Year with the Narrative of so singular an Incident" (*L*, 2: 319).

Total War as a Philosophical Refinement

Hume's good friend John Home had published a pamphlet calling for war against the Americans to which Hume responded in February 1776: "I make no doubt, since you sound the trumpet for war against the Americans, that you have a plan ready for governing them, after they are subdued; but you will not subdue them, unless they break in pieces among themselves—an event very probable. It is a wonder it has not happened sooner" (*L*, 2: 307–8). Hume's friend Strahan was very much for war. He wrote Hume in October 1775, "I am entirely for coercive Methods with those obstinate madmen: and why should we despair of success" (*L*, 2: 301 n)? Hume replied: "I am sorry, that I cannot agree with you, in your hopes of subduing and what is more difficult, of governing America. Think only of the great Kingdom of France which is within a days sailing of the small Island of Corsica; yet has not been able, in eight or nine Years, to subdue and govern it, contrary to the Sentiments of the Inhabitants. But the worst Effect of the Loss of America, will not be the Detriment to our Manufactures, which will be a mere trifle, or to our Navigation, which will not be considerable; but to the Credit and Reputation of Government, which has already but too little Authority. You will probably see a Scene of Anarchy and Confusion open'd at home, the best Consequence of which is a settled Plan of arbitrary Power; the worst, total Ruin and Destruction" (*L*, 2: 305).

Even if the colonies were conquered, however, they could not be governed without destroying their social and political institutions and their republican way of life. To enforce such an act of barbarism would require not only a massive military presence but also a determination that a free government such as that of Britain could not long sustain. "Arbitrary Power can extend its oppressive Arm to the Antipodes; but a limited Government can never long be upheld at a distance, even where no Disgusts have interven'd: Much less, where such violent Animosities have taken place." Nothing less than total war would be required. "We must, therefore, annul all the Charters; abolish every democratical Power in every Colony; repeal the Habeas Corpus Act with regard to them; invest every Governor with full discretionary or arbitrary Powers; confiscate the Estates of all the chief Planters; and hang three-fourths of their Clergy. To execute such Acts of destructive Violence twenty thousand Men will not be sufficient; nor thirty thousand to maintain them, in so wide and disjointed a Territory." And who is to pay for so great an Army? The colonists could not in "such a State of Desolation"; nor could Britain in her "over-loaded or rather over-whelm'd" state of finances. Hume's recommendation was that Britain should display an act of greatness of mind and magnanimity. "Let us, therefore, lay aside all Anger; shake hands, and part Friends. Or if we retain anger, let it only be against ourselves for our past Folly; and against that wicked Madman, Pitt; who has reduced us to our present Condition" (*L,* 2: 300–301).

Although Hume presented the specter of total war directed against the civilian population as a reduction to absurdity of British policy on both moral and practical grounds, his good friend Allan Ramsay embraced it as the only way to win the war. But what is most important about Ramsay's proposal is the moral justification he offered for it. Allan Ramsay was court painter to George III and one of the finest portrait painters of his day. He was also a political theorist of some merit and wrote a number of pamphlets on political topics, including "A Succinct Review of the American Contest" (1778) published under the pen name of Zero. Ramsay argues that the war is being lost because the British have not followed a proper strategy. The war must be turned against the civilian population.

Ramsay proposes that a garrison be established in New York large enough to be safe from attack and to serve as the rendezvous point for all British operations. Ten thousand troops are then to embark on transports to any province that is vulnerable and important. The troops are to carry away all "that may be useful to the public service" and then "burn and destroy the houses, magazines, and plantations, as far as they are conveniently within their reach; sparing the lives of all the persons who do not attempt by arms to prevent them." The troops are then to embark for some other province "where the like may be repeated."[1]

Washington's army could not match the mobility of the British navy, and one could expect the colonial army to melt away as men returned to their devastated provinces to assist their families. Should the people remain obstinate, their scorched and impoverished land could be occupied by loyal immigrants. Ramsay recognized that "such a scheme for securing the public, at the expence of private people altogether innocent" would be rejected as barbarous by "the more humane, and more respectable part of the community."[2] But to this he had an ingenious reply. He observed that in the last war with France the British had landed with a force of six thousand and could have burned Cherbourg and the surrounding area before troops could have dislodged them. Why then did they not do so? Because, Ramsay argues, it would have been an act of cruelty not acceptable under the rules of just warfare. What then is the difference between the American and the French case?

Ramsay explains that the British were at war with the army of the French sovereign, namely, the King. The French people are subjects of the king who alone is sovereign, whereas the American people claim to be sovereign; thus the people themselves are in a state of war with the King's forces. The French people are not to be compared with "the inhabitants of America; for they, with the express purpose of making war upon England, have formed themselves into a Government, the most popular imaginable, in which every man, is, as it were, a Counsellor of state; as there every man by himself, or his representative in Congress, grants money for carrying on war, and orders the mode in which this money is to be expended; where every man may be said, in his own individual person, to have bid defiance to the King of Great Britain; so that he must thank his own folly and temerity, if, at any time, he should come off short from so unequal a contest."[3]

We have here the germ of the twentieth-century rationale for total war: war aimed at the people of a nation, scorched-earth strategy, the bombing of civilian populations, massive deportations of peoples, and the enslavement of the vanquished. Total war is not unique to the twentieth century, nor is it due to "technology," which has merely made its implementation more practicable and terrible. But neither is modern total war to be seen as simply a reversion to the primitive warfare of precivilized times, where one tribe seeks to exterminate another. Modern total war is possible only among "civilized" nations. It is shaped and legitimated by an act of reflection, a way of thinking about the world whereby an entire people becomes the enemy. This requires a prior act of total criticism, which is the characteristic mark of the philosophical act. Something like this had happened in the religious wars of Europe fueled by (or, better perhaps, exploited by) speculative religious enthusiasms. One-third of the population of Central Europe perished in the Thirty Years' War from violence, starvation, and disease.[4] This massive destruction was accomplished not by the availability of advanced technology but by the persistence of speculative opinion. Cardinal Richelieu with an army of eight thousand and limited technological means was able to inflict a million casualties on the civilian population. For more than a generation after the war, one-third of the arable land in North Germany remained uncultivated. Emperor Ferdinand got the desert he said he would rather rule over than a country populated with heretics.[5]

One great achievement of "modern manners" was the attempt to purge warfare of its unconditional philosophical character and to conceive of it as directed to limited goals. The concept of civilized warfare is unique to Europe and lasted about two centuries, roughly from the beginning of the eighteenth century until World War I. Civilized war was to be between combatants only and could not be directed against civilians as part of a strategy for victory. It was war devoid of all speculative philosophical and religious content. As Clausewitz famously put it, war is political policy by other means, and where politics is understood to be the pursuit of a limited object that can be the subject of negotiation such as territory or trade. The rules of civilized warfare were codified by the Swiss jurist Emmeric de Vattel in *The Law of Nations, or the Principles of Natural Law as Applied to the Administration of National Affairs and of Sovereigns* (1758). The most important part of this system consisted of the rules for ending a war and establishing an equitable peace. The vanquished were to be treated with respect. Compensation to the victor was not to be conceived as punishment but as the cost of defeat in an honorable contest of arms. The idea of demanding unconditional surrender was out of the question. Such a demand denies the right of a nation to exist and so would destroy the principle of the comity of nations. In 1770 the Comte de Guibert could boast, "Today the whole of Europe is civilized. Wars have become less cruel. Save in combat no blood is shed; prisoners are respected; towns are no more destroyed; the countryside is no more ravaged; conquered peoples are only obliged to pay some sort of contributions which are often less than the taxes they pay to their own sovereign."[6]

The distinguished military historian B. H. Liddell Hart judged that the first break in the system came not from Europe but from America, when Lincoln shocked European opinion by directing war against the civilian population of the eleven American states that in state conventions (the same legal instrument that had authorized the state's entrance into the union) had voted to withdraw from the federation and form a union of their own.[7] Lincoln's scorched-earth policy and demand for unconditional surrender exhibited a new frame of mind that only eighty years later would reveal itself again in the terror-bombing of Dresden and Hiroshima. Perhaps the most barbarous event of the Thirty Years' War was the massacre of some 25,000 during the sack of Magdeburg in 1631; yet it has been estimated that more than 135,000 perished in the British and American bombing of Dresden carried out within three months of the end of the war, when the defeat of Germany was certain. Dresden was a city of no military value and known to be packed with refugees, mostly women and children fleeing from the Soviet armies in the east.[8]

This new and unexpected lapse into barbarism from America in the middle of the nineteenth century and those that would follow it in Europe were legitimated in part by entirely secular philosophical enthusiasms. World War I began as the usual limited European war to be won quickly and settled quickly. It was greeted with almost sporting enthusiasm on both sides. But after the first year a stalemate was reached, and casualties had risen beyond what anyone could have imagined. Rather than reach a negotiated settlement, it was thought that there had to be an ultimate meaning to such losses. America entered the war. Social progressives now spiritualized the war into a holy crusade to restructure all of Europe, to abolish autocracy, and to establish universal democracy. The war was transformed by the language of totality. It was now the war to make the world safe for democracy, and the war to end all wars. The concept of the final war, the philosophically reflexive war, is perhaps the ultimate in the barbarism of refinement.

Prior to its entrance into the war, Germany imported a third of its food. The Allied blockade of Germany was so effective that the government was forced to a choice between continuing the war and mass starvation. The Armistice was signed on 11 November 1918. Article 26 specified that Germany would be supplied with food as necessary. Yet the blockade was retained for nearly a year in an effort to insure compliance with the impossible demands of the Versailles Treaty, some of which were held up because of logistical difficulties. The blockade resulted in nearly a million deaths from starvation, mostly of women and children, to which must be added the millions of children who suffered the physical and mental deformities that attend malnourishment in the formative years.[9] Here was an act of violence directed against civilians with no pretense of military valuc.

During the 1920s a debate arose among military leaders as to whether the new instrument of an air force should be thought of as merely an extension of army artillery and so limited to combatants or whether it should be developed as a strategic weapon for crippling a nation. Air Marshal Sir Hugh Trenchard, Chief of the British Air Staff put the point succinctly. "The Army policy was to defeat the enemy army; our policy was to defeat the enemy nation."[10] Allan Ramsay's theory that war could be directed against the people of a nation had become policy. Once this path was crossed, and given that wars would be informed by secular ideological hatred, it would be virtually impossible to exclude the bombing of civilians as part of a war effort. The reversion to the ideological barbarism of the religious wars of the seventeenth century was complete, but now the philosophical enthusiasm was entirely secular. Yet the imagery from the religious wars of the past was still available. In a letter written in May 1942, Air Minister Sir Archibald Sinclair defended terror bombing, declaring that he was "all for the bombing of working-class areas in German cities. I am a Cromwellian—I believe in 'slaying in the name of the Lord.'"[11]

This is not the place for a jeremiad against modern total war. Such wars were extremely complex events, and there is no pretense here to have given an adequate moral account of them. What should not be controversial is that total war did in fact appear, beginning with the American Civil War, and has been the form of war in the twentieth century. Moreover, such wars emerged in a culture which has assumed the moral posture of being the most civilized and humane culture in history. What is of interest here is the spectacular destruction wrought by modern wars and the philosophical self-conceptions and self-deceptions that, in part, inform our understanding of them—"refined" conceptions of the sort that appeared in Allan Ramsay's argument for total war against the seceding American colonies. In military casualties alone, World War I resulted in 8 million dead and 6 million mutilated. This was more than were killed in all wars fought in Europe during the two-century period of "civilized" warfare, including the Napoleonic wars.[12] Here was a massacre on a scale that dwarfed the religious wars of the seventeenth century, but was now conducted by Enlightenment liberal regimes in the service of secular philosophical ideals. And it was a barbarism of refinement, for despite all of the legitimating philosophical enthusiasm about "democracy" and "self-determination of nations," Germany, Britain, France, and the United States were both empires and liberal progressive regimes. The totalizing war to make the world safe for democracy was the first step in a secular ideological conflict that would lead to World War II and the Cold War. World War II resulted in some fifty million battle and civilian deaths, and more than that were mutilated and displaced.[13] Vattel's rules distinguishing between combatants and civilians and his counsel against demanding unconditional surrender had been entirely abandoned.

Happily the rules were still in force for Lord North and George III, who did not follow Ramsay's advice to wage total war against the colonies. The complete domination of reflection over moral sentiment, which is the mark of the barbarism of refinement, had not yet occurred. It would not be until the twentieth century that the barbarism of refinement would become, as it were, second nature. One could then speak normally and without embarrassment of total war, unconditional surrender, total revolution, and total reconstruction. And this language of the absolute would shape the intellects not only of the children of darkness (authoritarianism and fascism) but also of the children of light (democracy, liberalism, and Marxism).

Although Hume was no pacifist and admired military virtues as a species of greatness of mind, he had no sympathy for wars fought to establish empire, glory, national honor, or ideological goals. The only legitimate war was a defense against attack or military intervention to maintain the balance of power in Europe against the threat of a universal European monarchy. He was bitterly opposed to the popular wars Britain had recently fought over trade, empire, and national glory. He argued that free trade is mutually beneficial and yields more in prosperity than can be achieved by war. John Home records a conversation with Hume on this topic four months before his death during the trip they took to Bath for Hume's health. Hume began by imagining how he would manage his kingdom if John Home and Adam Ferguson were princes of the adjacent states.

> He knew very well, he said, (having often disputed the point with us,) the great opinion we had of military virtues as essential to every state; that from these sentiments rooted in us, he was certain he would be attacked and interrupted in his projects of cultivating, improving, and civilizing mankind by the arts of peace; that he comforted himself with reflecting, that from our want of economy and order in our affairs, we should be continually in want of money [due to mortaging future revenues to pay for wars of national glory]; whilst he would have his finances in excellent condition, his magazines well filled, and naval stores in abundance; but that his final stroke of policy, upon which he depended, was to give one of us a large subsidy to fall upon the other, which would infallibly secure to him peace and quiet, and after a long war, would probably terminate in his being master of all the three kingdoms. At this sally, so like David's manner of playing with his friends, I fell into a fit of laughing, in which David joined; and the people that passed us certainly thought we were very merry travellers.[14]

"I Am an American in My Principles"

Hume's support for American independence had a deeper source than the principles of anti-imperialism, free trade, and his belief that war would be barbarous, would necessarily fail, and could lead to civil war and despotism at home. In addition to these reasons, Hume seems to have had a genuine regard for the American colonies and the republican way of life that had evolved there. Hume, a lifelong republican in his principles, thought it wicked to destroy the "democratical Power" that had developed in the colonies and which would have to be destroyed if the government were to pursue the sort of war that could really subdue the colonies.

The Spanish colonization was driven by "avidity" in pursuit of gold and jewels and led to "depopulation" of their own country as well as of the countries they conquered. The Spanish enterprise added to the vice of avidity those of "sloth" and "barbarity." In contrast the English colonies were planted under the notions of liberty and achievement: what "chiefly renders the reign of James memorable, is the commencement of the English colonies in America; colonies established on the noblest footing that has been known in any age or nation" (*H,* 5: 146). What was noble about the English settlements was that they were populated by "the necessitous and indigent," who increased neither the wealth nor the population of their mother country. In America, however, these people had ample scope for achievement and for the development of their own capacities. In doing so they not only improved themselves but "encouraged the industry, and even perhaps multiplied the inhabitants of their mother country." On the grand scheme of history, Hume viewed the colonies as the far westward expression of that spirit of personal liberty that had been growing in Europe since the thirteenth century. Its growth in America had the dynamic effect of stimulating its growth in England: "The spirit of Independency, which was reviving in England, here shone forth in its full lustre, and received new accession from the aspiring character of those, who, being discontented with the established church and monarchy, had sought for freedom amidst those savage desarts" (*H,* 5: 147). America was a symbol of the dynamic character of the new civilization of liberty.

There were those during the reign of James I who predicted that establishing the colonies was foolish; that it would drain England of wealth and people who would then set up "an independent government in America." But the theorist of moral sentiments who preached the providential imperative of extensive benevolence was happy to show that "the views entertained by those who encouraged such generous undertakings, were more just and solid" than the niggardly and confined views of those who were afraid to let people out of England. Just how severe the judgments of providence can be Hume illustrates with an episode from the reign of Charles I. The King had resolved to prevent the immigration of Puritans to America, fearing the establishment of "so disaffected a colony." Eight ships lying in the Thames and ready to sail were prevented from doing so by order of the King. In these were the future Puritan leaders Sir Arthur Hazelrig, John Hambden, John Pym, and Oliver Cromwell. Hume dryly observes that the "king had afterwards full leisure to repent this exercise of his authority" (*H,* 5: 242). The "generous" policy has born fruit for America and England, and Hume can observe in the late 1750s that "more than a fourth of the English shipping is at present computed to be employed in carrying on the traffic with the American settlements" (*H,* 5: 148). This happy arrangement has been the result of a "mild government" and a great naval force, and Hume thinks that these "may still preserve during some time, the dominion of England over her colonies" (*H,* 5: 148). But everything depended on the continued exercise of limited and mild government.

These words were published in 1757 at the beginning of the Seven Years' War. After the war the relation of England to her colonies would change substantially. Government would cease to be "mild" and, instead of being content to regulate trade in the interest of the mother country, would exploit the colonies as a source of revenue to pay for a vast empire stretching from India to Canada. London would, henceforth, be viewed as the scene of a remote and arbitrary power. On this point, if not on the Wilkes and Liberty issue, Hume and the colonists were in agreement. I remarked earlier on Hume's belief that imperial wars and public credit were draining the "provinces" in Britain and aggrandizing the capital. The same drain was now to be felt by the colonies.

Hume thought that the American colonies were conceived in the spirit of freedom and independence and that from the very first, the dominion of England depended on the frank recognition of that spirit. Dominion could take many forms, but its hold had to be gentle and in accord with a connoisseur's understanding of the American spirit. As Hume records, this spirit was first established in Virginia. Later the Puritans in New England would lay "the foundations of a government, which possessed all the liberty, both civil and religious, of which they found themselves bereaved in their native country" (*H,* 5: 241). Hume had read Thomas Hutchinson's *History of Massachusetts's Bay,* Mather's

History of New England, and other authors on America and would have been aware of the acts of virtual sovereignty claimed by the colonies from the very beginning.[15] A New England confederacy was formed on 19 May 1643, and shortly after that a coinage of silver money was ordered at Boston, stamped with the name of the colony and a tree symbolizing its vigor and growth. The right to coin money is one of the prerogatives of sovereignty. The formation of a self-governing confederacy with its own coinage was a considerable step towards independence. Similar moves were made by other colonies in the early period of their formation. Hume's earliest remark on America is to be found in a set of notes on various topics written between 1729 and 1740, during the time he was doing the reading and writing for the *Treatise.* There he says that "the Charter Governments in America are almost entirely independent of England."[16]

The earliest record of Hume's belief that the colonies should be granted complete independence is in a letter quoted above, written on 22 July 1768. Although there is no evidence that Hume supported complete independence earlier than 1768, he certainly thought from the earliest period of his career that the colonies were virtually independent and had to be treated with respect and good judgment. Writing to Lord Hertford in February 1766, he described the Stamp Act (1765) as "an invidious law," and writing to him again in May 1766 he remarked, "It does not seem probable that the Repeal alone of the Stamp Act will suffice" (*L,* 2: 43, 20–21). Having sent Hume a volume on Pennsylvania, Franklin wrote on 27 September 1760, "I am not a little pleas'd to hear of your change of Sentiments in some particulars relating to America; because I think it of Importance to our general Welfare that the People of this Nation should have right notions of us, and I know of no one that has it more in his Power to rectify their notions, than Mr. Hume." It is not clear what change Franklin is referring to, but whatever it was, Hume came to see some aspect of the American outlook in a more favorable light. Franklin goes on to praise Hume's essay "Of the Jealousy of Trade" as promoting "the Interest of Humanity," and he hopes that its argument might serve to abate "the Jealousy that reigns here of the Commerce of the colonies, at least so far as such Abatement may be reasonable."[17]

Hume foresaw that the colonies would one day become a great empire and a flourishing culture. Gibbon had sent Hume a manuscript beginning a *History of the Swiss Revolution* written in French. Hume praised the manuscript but advised Gibbon to write in English even though the French language was "much more generally diffused" than

English. He recalled the advice Horace had given to the Romans to write in Latin rather than Greek. Though Greek was the language of the learned world, Latin, through the Roman empire, was destined to become the more widely diffused language. Likewise, English will eventually become more important than French, not because of the influence of the literature of England but because of the expansion of the colonies. "Let the French, therefore, triumph in the present diffusion of their tongue. Our solid and increasing establishments in America, where we need less dread the inundation of Barbarians, promise a superior stability and duration to the English language" (*L,* 2: 171). One should keep in mind that young Scotsmen in the early eighteenth century approached English as virtually a foreign language. Hume had none of the native Englishman's attachment and affection for the language, and Samuel Johnson thought he wrote it like a Frenchman. Hume treats English here with some distance as a cosmopolitan instrument to be made good in the future by the American colonies. One casualty of the philosophical and political factionalism that had plagued the English was literature. He wrote Strahan in 1773 that the best work produced by an Englishman in the past thirty years was *Tristram Shandy,* "bad as it is." The best writers were Scottish, but Hume also included Franklin, whom he refused to consider an English author, "for Dr. Franklin is an American" (*L,* 2: 269). Writing to Franklin in February 1772, Hume complained of his treatment by the English literary and political establishment and remarked, "I fancy that I must have recourse to America for justice." He reminded him of the intention the Americans had expressed of producing an edition of his writings, and he urged Franklin's good offices in the enterprise.

Hume's interest in America as the scene of a new culture may have been enlivened by the stake some of his close friends had in developing it. In 1769 Benjamin Franklin and some London financiers petitioned the King to purchase some 2,400,000 acres between the Ohio and the Alleghanies. The petition was eventually granted. Hume's publisher, William Strahan, and his benefactor, Lord Hertford, were keen on acquiring somc of the new territory. Strahan placed the project before Hertford as the noble one of "no less than the forming a new government on the Ohio" (*L,* 2: 233 n). Hume wished them success in their project, but the whole scheme (as well as the Franklin-sponsored American edition of Hume's works) went up in smoke when thirteen of some thirty British Colonies seceded from the empire. Upon the beginning of hostilities, Franklin penned these harsh words to Strahan: "You are a Member of Parliament, and one of that Majority which has doomed my Country to Destruction. You have begun to burn our Towns, and murder our People: Look upon your Hands! They are stained with the Blood of your Relations! You and I were long Friends: You are now my Enemy and I am, Yours."[18] Had the war not occurred, Strahan might well have produced an American edition of the works of his most popular author. Hume's writings were admirably suited to serve as civilizing texts for Strahan's new government on the Ohio.

To sum up, Hume saw the colonies as an emerging empire of republican and "democratical" regimes which had long enjoyed the experience of virtual independence and self-government. Considered as such, they were a continuation of the practice of personal and political liberty that began to emerge in Europe at the close of the medieval period and had reached its most self-conscious development in England. Hume thought that this self-consciousness among the English had been captured by a false philosophical reflection and was becoming progressively self-indulgent, self-alienating, and xenophobic. The barbarism of refinement over liberty was in danger of destroying the actual practice of liberty (an order of sentiments, dispositions, customs, prejudices, and practices rooted in time and place, which can be known and evaluated only by the philosophical connoisseur) in the name of a corrupt form of theorizing (Revolution ideology and the contract theory), which was being confused with the reality of the practice. But though Hume pointed out the dangers of the philosophically neurotic English self-consciousness about liberty, he cherished the historic practice of liberty as the discovery of new virtues which were immanent in human nature and which required a rethinking of the classical and Christian conceptions of human excellence. These virtues had been planted in the woods of America, an entirely different context from that of Europe, where the democratic and republican dispositions to self-government celebrated by Hume in "Idea of a Perfect Commonwealth" were flourishing.

Hume framed an image of these dispositions, ordering them into principles which he identified as "American." It was painful for him to have to turn down Baron Mure, who "was among the oldest and best Friends I had in the World" and who had asked him to write a loyal address to the King requesting that strong measures be taken against the colonies. But Hume did turn him down, explaining that "I am an American in my Principles, and wish we woud let them alone to govern or misgovern themselves as they think proper: The affair is of no Consequence, or of little Consequence to us" (*L*, 2: 312, 303). This position is entirely consistent with Hume's observation at the time of writing the *Treatise* that the "Charter Governments" of America were "almost entirely independent of England" (*HEM*, 504), with the federation of self-governing republics argued for in "Idea of a Perfect Commonwealth," and with the lifelong republicanism running throughout his writings but constrained in a European context, as it had to be, by the deeply established practice of monarchy.

The Philosophical Meaning of Hume's Support for American Independence

On the issue of the American crisis, the Edinburgh literati, and Scotland generally, were strongly pro-government. Hume's good friend Hugh Blair prayed against the Americans not only as chaplain of the 71st Foot, which was engaged in the war, but also as minister from his pulpit in the High Church.[19] Hume's friends John Home, Adam Ferguson, Allan Ramsay, and Thomas Blacklock wrote pamphlets against the Americans. William Strahan was stunned by Hume's position on America: "I am really surprised you are of a different opinion" (*L*, 2: 301 n). The Scots were inclined to a strong pro-government position on the American question for the same reason they were opposed to the Wilkes and Liberty movement. One must keep in mind that the North American colonies were planted by the English before the union of the Scottish and English Parliaments. By the time of the American crisis, the colonies had the form of an English culture; the Scots were newcomers and were as resented in the English colonies as they were in London. This attitude is well expressed in a letter from New York published in the *Caledonian Mercury*, 13 August 1776:

> All America is exasperated against Scotland. All letters from England confirm us in the opinion, that the Scots are hostile to us to a degree the most wicked and abandoned. It is universally believed here that the whole nation is against us. . . . The uncommon forwardness of the Scots in this unfortunate contest seems the more extraordinary, as they have no right to a connexion with America but what they were favored with by the union. America does not acknowledge Scotland as her mother country. We never heard of any original Caledonian settlement on this continent, but the one on the isthmus of Darien [Panama]. We heartily wish that all their subsequent emigrations had been confined to that spot. The middle colonies have within these few years been pestered with a number of them. Is it not surprising that these people, if they are determined to act at all, should not have modesty enough to content themselves with a secondary and subordinate part, but be so

> presumptuous as to be continually thrusting themselves forward in the most conspicuous manner.[20]

Thomas Jefferson, who was very much an "English" Whig, would later ban Hume's *History* from the University of Virginia because of its authoritarian cast of mind and the consequent threat to liberty it posed to the new republic. "Scotch mercenaries" almost made it into the Declaration of Independence as a ground for secession from the empire. John Adams, who had linked the cause of Wilkes and America, was also "English" in his conception of liberty, and so he could recommend the legal theory of Lord Kames as that of a "Scottish writer of great reputation, whose authority . . . ought to have more weight as his countrymen have not the most worthy ideas of liberty."[21] Liberty was apparently something a Scotsman had difficulty understanding.

But the Scots tended to be pro-government because they were pro-union. They had abandoned national self-government in 1707 and had entered the union in order to share in a wider sphere of economic activity and cultural achievement. The King was determined that the Scots should have the right to exercise their powers to the full in England and in America. In rejecting Wilkes and in supporting American independence, Hume's friends could view his position as not only incoherent but also as disloyal to the interests of his countrymen. The Scottish cosmopolitan notion of the union reached its most abstract expression in the thought of Adam Smith, who suggested that the empire be conceived as a commonwealth rather than as an English empire operated out of London. The American provinces would be represented in Parliament in proportion to the amount of tax revenue they generated. Rapid American growth would mean that American taxation would eventually outstrip the British contribution, at which point the seat of government would move to America. "The seat of the empire would then naturally remove itself to that part of the empire which contributed most to the general defence and support of the whole."[22] This was a philosophical view of the empire more easily taken by a Scotsman who had already alienated national self-government than by an Englishman who would tend to view the empire as "English" and London as its natural center.

Although Hume confessed himself to be an "American" in his principles in supporting self-determination for the colonies, he did not accept colonial *arguments* for secession from the British empire. The dispute between the colonies and the government was carried on within the framework of Revolution ideology. The conflict was a good example of the underdetermination of principles abstracted from the practices of common life and the eye of the philosophical connoisseur: with ingenuity, anything may be seen as satisfying or failing to satisfy them. Such quarrels become more acrimonious because both sides hold the same principles, and this leads to the view that one's opponent is being either obstinate or malicious. Such a posture (taking the principle to be the real) is the work of a corrupt philosophical consciousness and can have no other tendency than to "beget the fiercest animosities among men of the same nation, who ought to give mutual assistance and protection to each other" (*E*, 55). Argument within the arena marked out by false philosophy is and must be civil war by other means, and it is perhaps significant that Blacklock and Robertson described the conflict as a "civil war" within the British polity instead of a war of American "rebellion."

Hume rejected Revolution ideology as the work of the new vulgar philosophers and so rejected the terms in which both sides argued. Those terms were moralistic and legalistic, having to do with questions about applying abstract rights: the right of Parliament to tax, the right of the colonies to representation, and even natural rights. In this the American Whigs were as barbarous as their English counterparts. From the critical perspective of true philosophy, Hume spoke of the "poor infatuated Americans" and of the "frenzies of the people" (*L*, 2: 303, 308). Hume's friend Franklin was accused of obtaining letters relating to public affairs by immoral means and sending them to Boston. On the strength of these letters the Massachusetts Assembly petitioned the King to remove the Governor. For this Franklin lost his office as Deputy Postmaster General to the colonies. Hume was shocked and hoped that Franklin was not "guilty in the extreme Degree that is pretended," though he had to confess that "I always knew him to be a very factious man, and Faction, next to Fanaticism, is, of all passions, the most destructive of Morality" (*L*, 2: 286).

One speculative principle that the Americans eventually made much of and which Hume rejected was the principle of natural rights: individual rights which men hold and which are intelligible independent of the customs and conventions of common life. The American "Declaration of Independence" was published in Edinburgh five days before Hume's death. Since he was well enough to spend time reading during this period, he may have been aware of it.[23] If so, he would surely have rejected its doctrine that all men are endowed with natural rights to "life, liberty, and the pursuit of happiness" and that "to secure these rights governments are instituted among men." Hume taught that governments exist to provide authority, without which there is no peace or stability. His formula was that authority is essential to government but that liberty is merely its perfection. A government that does not secure political and individual liberty (though not the best) is not necessarily illegitimate. Consequently, government is not instituted merely to secure natural rights. That a theory of authority is central to Hume's political philosophy is not to be passed over without notice. The political philosophy of the liberal tradition has had little to say about the nature of authority. Like the Whigs of Hume's time, it has been obsessed with the exploration of "rights" while ignoring authority. A theory of authority, for instance, is not to be found in all of Rawls's large and influential *A Theory of Justice*. An exception is Michael Oakeshott, who grounds a theory of liberty in a Hobbesian conception of authority.[24]

To rest the legitimacy of government on the speculative principle of natural rights is to transform government from something that is known through participation in a common life into an object of corrupt philosophical reflection. Judgment now necessarily enters the vacuum where anything or nothing can be viewed as satisfying the demands of natural rights. Natural rights (though supposedly substantial and self-evidently known to all men) have been used both to legitimate *and* to criticize the French Revolution, the conservative Whig establishment in Britain, and the secession of the American colonies.

The true philosopher, of course, will be able to find some truth in the doctrine of natural rights as an abstraction from or as an abridgment of an established way of life. It was in this way that Hume found some truth in both the Divine Right theory of government and the Natural Right theory of government as contract, "though not in the sense, intended by the parties" (*E*, 466). Only the true philosopher, however, knows how to handle such philosophical fictions. The hubris of false philosophy will barbarize them and treat them not as abridgments of a way of life but as what might be called moral *substances* from which policies can be deduced. But the substantial doctrine of natural rights may be expected to suffer the punishments of Tantalus and Sisyphus which are reserved for all doctrines of substance (*T*, 223).

Hume appears to have avoided entirely thinking of the American conflict in the terms of Revolution ideology. His attention is focused on practices which he explores as a philosophical connoisseur seeking to make a wise judgment out of the contingent materials of common life. He discovered, first, that the colonies from the beginning were self-governing and virtually independent. Further, Hume taught that authority is grounded in opinion. The colonial opinion of self-government, firmly established in their own practice from the beginning, generates a title to self-government that Britain must take seriously. When people acquire the dispositions of self-government, it is prudent that they be recognized, especially by those who have themselves enjoyed the practice of liberty. Second, it is only a matter of time before the colonies assert their own independence. Third, it is in Britain's commercial and political interests to grant independence and connect herself with the Americans on the basis of free trade and the friendship of a common culture. Fourth, the war cannot be won; or if it can, the colonies cannot be governed without acts of barbarism odious in themselves, corrupting to Britain, and at a prohibitive cost.

Hume's conception of the American crisis went beyond the philosophically superstitious categories of ideological good and evil in favor of a causal analysis of human practices which takes the self-conception of men as it is. Something of this conception appears in the correspondence about American affairs and related matters he carried on with Sir John Pringle from at least 1772 to 1776. Writing from London in January 1773, Pringle disagreed with Hume on two points. "I consider as the main cause of the difference between our two opinions, to be the firm persuasion I have had that the Americans never wanted to separate from us, till we attempted to impose a tax upon them; but, that on the contrary, they considered themselves as a happy people, and took pride in being part of this great and flourishing empire. . . . Another point we differ in is with regard to the conquest of Canada by our troops in the late war. You are of opinion that it encouraged this revolt, whilst I imagine that it ought to have had quite the contrary effect."[25] And in March 1774, Pringle wrote to Hume, "I always thought you were in the wrong when you supposed those colonies wanted only a pretext to shake off their subjection to their mother country; I am persuaded they never would have entertained such a thought unless provoked to it by such measures as I apprehend are still carrying on against them."[26]

Pringle's analysis of the crisis is a moral one carried on within the traditional mercantile arrangement of colonies and mother country. The traditional arrangement was good, and the colonies were happy with it. The crisis arose because of the wickedness of the Stamp Act. Hume's analysis is largely causal. The colonies merely tolerated mercantilist control of their trade, and now they are strong enough to do something about it. The traditional arrangement must be "methodized and corrected," and in the present circumstances, that means independence for the colonies and free trade.

When traditional rights and duties are inconsistent with changed circumstances, an understanding of what must be done can often be achieved by returning to a primordial *topos* of common life. This Hume does by repairing to the image of a developing human being from infancy to adulthood. The colonies were once infants in need of authority, but now they are coming of age. Hume wrote to Strahan in March of 1774, "I remember, one day, at Lord Bathurst's, the Company, among whom was his Son, the present Chancellor, were speaking of American Affairs; and some of them mention'd former Acts of Authority exercisd over the Colonies. I observd to them, that Nations, as well as Individuals, had their different Ages, which challeng'd a different Treatment. For Instance, My Lord, said I to the old Peer, you have sometimes, no doubt, given your Son a Whipping; and I doubt not, but it was well merited and did him much good: Yet you will not think proper at present to employ the Birch: The Colonies are no longer in their Infancy" (*L*, 2: 287–88). It is this original scene, deeply rooted in pre-reflective prejudices of common life (and not abstract principles about "natural rights"), in which Hume's economic and political arguments for independence are rooted and from which they draw their vitality. A similar view is held by Francis Hutcheson, who argued that colonies naturally grow into independence.[27]

There was, of course, the question of just how mature the colonies were. Hume told Lord Bathurst that although not in their infancy, the colonies were "still in their Nonage; and Dr. Franklyn wishes to emancipate them too soon from their mother Country" (*L*, 2: 288). This letter was written in 1774, though the event it records occurred years before. When did Hume judge that the colonies had become mature enough for independence? We have seen that he supported independence as early as 1768, but that does not mean that he thought the colonies mature enough for self-government. The judgment of maturity in individuals, and even more so in nations, is an uncertain affair and cannot always be determined by outside observers. At some point in the 1760s, Hume judged that the colonies themselves should be allowed to decide whether they were capable of self-government and that it was in Britain's interest to allow the experiment. He wrote in October 1775 that they should be allowed "to govern or misgovern themselves as they think proper" (*L*, 2: 303). It was not clear that they would succeed. Hume wrote to John Home in February 1776 that Britain could not defeat the colonies "unless they break in pieces among themselves—an event very probable. It is a wonder it has not happened sooner. But no man can foretell how far these frenzies of the people may be carried" (*L*, 2: 307–8). Hume thought that the Americans suffered from the same

English barbarism against which he had inveighed since the late 1760s. Yet they had continued to hold together. How long they could do so would depend upon the depth of their civic character and how seriously they would take the philosophic superstitions in terms of which they were understanding themselves. That their civic character was unusually strong was recognized by a British writer whose history of the American crisis was published in Edinburgh's *Caledonian Mercury.* The following paragraph concerning affairs in Massachusetts appears in the same issue (20 August 1776) which published the American Declaration of Independence:

> The old constitution being taken away by act of parliament, and the new one being rejected by the people, and end was put to all forms of law and government in the province of Massachusetts's Bay, and the people were reduced to that state of anarchy, in which mankind are supposed to have existed in the earliest ages. The degree of order, however, which, by the general concurrence of the people, was preserved in this state of anarchy, will forever excite the astonishment of mankind, and continue amongst the strongest proofs of the efficacy of long established habits, and of a constant submission to laws. Excepting the general opposition to the new government and the excesses arising from it, in the outrages offered to particular persons, who were, upon that account, obnoxious to the people, no other very considerable marks appeared of the cessation of law or government.

If Hume had read this, he would have seen it as an exemplification of his master maxim that custom and tradition are the great teachers of mankind and not the philosophic superstitions of original contract and natural rights. Here also he could have found evidence that Americans had achieved the maturity necessary for self-government, because they were able to conduct themselves with propriety in a state without government.

PART TWO

HUMEAN INTIMATIONS

CHAPTER TWELVE

Hume and America

With the letters of the last decade of his life on the Wilkes and Liberty affair and the American crisis, Hume's own speech about philosophy and its place in the world ceases. Hume now enters the history of philosophy and becomes for us one of those historical philosophical icons, such as the Epicurean, the Stoic, the Hobbist, the Pyrrhonian, from which he had sought to acquire his own philosophical compass. We may now speak of a Humean idiom of thought or of a Humean understanding of things. To speak in this way is to engage in what Oakeshott called "the pursuit of intimations." This engagement is not the Collingwoodian project of rethinking past thoughts in the agent's own terms (though that is necessary) but the exploration of what that thought intimates for philosophers of a later time, and perhaps for all time. Such a project is necessarily retrospective, and the danger is that the interests of a later time may so color our interpretation of what the thinker says that our thesis about what those words imply will not be a feature of the thinker's own thought but a figure discerned in fanciful clouds of our own making. So any sound thesis about intimations must be grounded in a sound Collingwoodian understanding of past thoughts as the agent understood them.

In this and the remaining chapters, I explore four Humean intimations. The first finds inspiration in Hume as an intellectual source of the American regime. The second and third take a retrospective look at Hume in the light of the modern state. The fourth finds inspiration in Hume's conception of true philosophy as a guide to prudent conduct in the first philosophic age. I take these in turn, devoting a chapter to each.

Was Hume a Founding Father?

In 1957 Douglass Adair published a now famous essay in which he claimed to have discovered through Madison's *Tenth Federalist* an image of the American regime embedded in Hume's "Idea of a Perfect Commonwealth."[1] Since then Hume has been a figure to conjure with in attempts to understand the intellectual source of American political order. In 1981 Gary Wills published *Explaining America: The Federalist,* a book having to do with the influence of the Scottish Enlightenment on the Federalists, and each chapter is headed with a magisterial quote from Hume, leaving the rhetorical impression that the whole is a Humean speech. Hume has now become a virtual Founding Father.

There is no doubt that Hume was a presence in the thought of the founding generation. His works were available, and they were read. Adams said that Hume was a "mighty name" in American reflections on government. But the question of the nature and depth of Hume's influence on the Founders is not my concern here. Behind that question there is an assumption, rarely spelled out, about what it is that the Founders founded.

The nature of the American founding has been and continues to be a disputed question; nor could it be otherwise. Hume criticized the Royalists for treating the British Constitution as one of those substances of the Schoolmen. There is a historicity to constitutions that he thought was especially important for those in a free society to appreciate. In the *Treatise,* he observed that the very concept of a founder is a historically retrospective notion (*T,* 566–67). Who the Founders were and what they founded can only be determined retrospectively by later generations, and a later constitutional conflict will be mirrored in alternative theories of the founding.

From the very beginning, Americans have disagreed on what it was the Founders founded. If there are different and incompatible American self-conceptions of the founding, then the question of Hume's influence splinters and becomes ambiguous. We must now ask, Under what conception of the founding is Hume supposed to have had an influence? In what follows I explore two incompatible narratives that Americans have told themselves about the founding and, in the light of these, I raise the question of whether there are any significant structural similarities between Hume's political thought and these conceptions. Failure to appreciate the ambiguous nature of the founding can distort not only our understanding of the origin of the American regime (leading to a one-dimensional, Whig interpretation of the founding not unlike the Whig interpretation of the British Constitution that Hume criticized in the *History* and in the *Essays*) but, most important for this study, it can distort our understanding of Hume.

I shall call these contrary theories of the founding the compact theory and the nationalist theory. The compact theory holds that the Constitution is a compact between sovereign states which have delegated enumerated powers to a central government as their agent. The nationalist theory holds that the states were never sovereign. Upon breaking with Great Britain, the people of the various colonies descended into a state of nature from which emerged the American people as an aggregate. This people formed a central government called the Continental Congress that authorized the formation of states.[2]

The compact theory reflected the primordial self-understanding Americans had of their political order. From 1607 through the Revolution and Confederation eras, political life was organized around colonial and then state units. These units did not disappear, but were considerably strengthened in authority by secession from Britain in 1776. A form of the compact theory was ubiquitous from 1775 on. As an interpretation of the Constitution of 1789, the compact theory was first put forth and defended by Thomas Jefferson in the Kentucky Resolutions of 1798 and by James Madison in the Virginia Resolutions (1798) and the *Virginia Report* of 1799.[3] Although there were intimations of the nationalist theory in the thought of James Wilson and others, it was first put forth in systematic form by Joseph Story in 1833 in his *Commentaries on the Constitution.*[4] Daniel Webster had been a compact theorist and a New England secessionist prior to 1815 but became an eloquent defender of the nationalist theory from the 1830s until his death. It was not until after the Civil War that the fledgling nationalist theory began its awkward and unsteady flight. But success was slow in coming; it did not really take hold until the New Deal era of the 1930s and received a dramatic boost with World War II, the Cold War, and the Great Society of the 1960s. In his message to Congress on 4 July 1861, Lincoln justified his policy of coercing the southern states back into the Union with a firm statement of the nationalist theory of sovereignty: "The Union is older than any of the States, and, in fact, it created them as States." But the compact theory is by no means dead; over a century later, President Reagan in his first inaugural address (20 January 1981) found occasion to reassert it. "The Federal government," he declared, "did not create the states; the states created the Federal government."

What has held the American regime together has not been the coherence of its jurisprudence, which has been and continues to be antinomic. However the American Constitution may have evolved, a strong case can be made that the compact theory was dominant until the 1830s and continued to be widely believed and asserted in all sections of the Union up to the Civil War and even beyond. A brief look at the sort of case that can be made will be helpful in creating a context of thought in which Hume's "Idea of a Perfect Commonwealth" and the alternative theories of the American founding may be compared.

The compact theory can be stated simply. Sovereign states formed a compact creating a central government as their agent and endowing it with enumerated powers (having to do mainly with the areas of foreign treaties, defense, and interstate commerce) and reserving the vast domain of unenumerated powers to themselves. The states pledged to obey the laws of the central government as long as they were constitutional. The central government could create courts or in other ways determine whether actions *within its sphere* of enumerated powers were constitutional. But the central government (including its Supreme Court) did not have the final authority to decide whether or not it had wandered beyond the powers delegated to it and into the reserved powers of the states. It could not have this authority because it was the agent, and the states were the principals. As Jefferson put it in the Kentucky Resolutions, "As in all other cases of compact among parties having no common judge, each party has an equal right to judge for itself, as well of infraction, as of the mode and measure of redress."[5] The doctrine of Jefferson and Madison that a state, being sovereign, could "interpose" its authority to check an unconstitutional act of the central government did not go unchallenged. Nevertheless, throughout the antebellum period and in every section of the Union, from *Chisholm v. Georgia* to the nullification of fugitive slave laws, American states regularly interposed their authority to declare actions of the central government, including those of the Supreme Court, unconstitutional.[6]

Viewed in terms of the nationalist theory, this was anarchy; viewed in terms of the compact theory, state interposition and nullification were simply part of the system of checks and balances of American constitutionalism and the only way in which a genuine consensus could be reached between substantially different moral and political communities in a federal system of continental scale.

But if state intervention was a logical consequence of the compact theory that aimed to *preserve* the Union, there was another consequence that allowed for its dissolution. For if the parties to the compact were indeed sovereign states, then they could withdraw those powers they had delegated to the central government and secede from the Union.

Carl Swisher, in his study of American constitutional development, observes that "there seems never to have been a time in the early decades of American history under the Constitution when the secession of one section or another was not considered a real possibility." The first serious secession movements began not with the anti-Federalists, as one might suppose, but with New England Federalists. Secession was threatened over the Louisiana Purchase in 1803, the embargo in 1807–1808, and most dramatically, as John Quincy Adams records, at the Hartford Convention (1814) over the war of 1812.[7] Of these movements, Jefferson wrote in a letter to William Crawford (20 January 1816), "If any state in the Union will declare that it prefers separation . . . to continuance in the Union . . . I have no hesitation in saying, 'Let us separate.'"

From the 1830s until the Civil War, New England abolitionists would invoke the compact theory, arguing for the secession of the Northern states. The American Anti-Slavery Society declared in 1844, "Resolved, that the Abolitionists of this country should make it one of the primary objects of this agitation to dissolve the American Union."[8] One of the first studies of the Constitution was *A View of the Constitution,* by William Rawle, published in 1825. Rawle was a Pennsylvania Federalist, Washington's friend, and a leader of the Pennsylvania bar. He accepted the compact theory and laid out the legal conditions under which an American state could secede from the Union. Secession did not require the permission of any other state, since each state had ratified the Constitution for itself with no authority to bind another state. "The secession of a State from the Union depends on the will of the people of such State. The people alone . . . hold the power to alter their constitution." And again, "The States . . . may wholly withdraw from the Union." Charles Francis Adams records that Rawle's work was the text on Constitutional law at West Point from 1825 to 1840, after which it was replaced by Kent's *Commentaries.*[9] Kent also viewed the Constitution as a compact.

Rawle acknowledges that the right to secede was not written into the Constitution, but he claims that it was a right generally understood and indeed a matter of concern to all. This could be so because the states were sovereign and knew themselves to be so. By the laws of nations, sovereign states may withdraw from a compact having no precise period of duration. To make this clear, New York, Rhode Island, and Virginia wrote into their ordinances of ratification the right to secede and affirmed this right for all the other states. And later the republic of Texas, having seceded from Mexico and invoked the principles of the Declaration of Independence in doing so, would assert in its treaty of union with the United States the right to secede.[10]

Foreign writers who had studied the Constitution concluded that a state could secede from the compact. Tocqueville wrote, "The Union was formed by the voluntary agreement of the States; and in uniting together they have not forfeited their nationality, nor have they been reduced to the condition of one and the same people. If one of the States choose to withdraw from the compact, it would be difficult to disprove its right of doing so, and the Federal Government would have no means of maintaining its claims directly either by force or right."[11] Lord Brougham, in his magisterial, multivolume study of constitutions published in 1849, considered the Constitution as a compact from which a state could secede: "There is not, as with us, a government only and its subjects to be regarded; but a number of Governments, of States having each a separate and substantive, and even independent existence originally thirteen, now six and twenty and each having a legislature of its own, with laws differing from those of the other States. It is plainly impossible to consider the Constitution which professes to govern this Union, this Federacy of States, as any thing other than a treaty." He accordingly refers to the Union as the "Great League."[12]

John Quincy Adams, though devoted to the Union, nevertheless argued the Humean point that the only moral bond of the Union was common interest and sympathy: "not in the *right* but in the *heart*." Should that collapse, he declared in his speech of 1840 on the Jubilee of the Constitution, then "far better will it be for the people of the disunited States to part in friendship from each other than to be held together by constraint. Then will be the time for reverting to the precedents which occurred at the formation and adoption of the Constitution, to form again a more perfect union, by dissolving that which could no longer bind, and to leave the separated parts to be re-united by the law of political gravitation to the centre."[13] Four years later, in 1844, he signed a document along with other New England leaders declaring that the annexation of Texas would mean the dissolution of the Union.[14]

Finally, before South Carolina seceded there were numerous secession movements in the mid-Atlantic states, urged by state and national leaders in order to form what was called a Central Confederacy. In some scenarios this confederacy would include such states as Maryland, New

Jersey, Delaware, New York, Virginia, Kentucky, Tennessee, Ohio, Indiana, Pennsylvania, and Arkansas. It was argued that these states had common interests and moreover formed the moderate and conservative core of the Union. Isolating the fanaticism of both New England and the Deep South, a Central Confederacy could prevent war and provide a rallying point to which the disaffected states could, if they chose, eventually return.[15] Even after the Confederacy was formed, Horace Greeley, editor of the Republican *New York Tribune,* could declare on 23 February 1861, "We have repeatedly said . . . that the great principle embodied by Jefferson in the Declaration of Independence, that governments derive their powers from the consent of the governed, is sound and just. . . . Whenever it shall be clear that the great body of Southern people have become conclusively alienated from the Union, and anxious to escape from it, we will do our best to forward their views."

From the ratification of the Constitution until the Civil War, secession was a part of American political speech. That it could be so is due to widespread acceptance, in one form or another, of the compact theory. There were nods in the direction of the nationalist theory from the very beginning. Hamilton and Madison proposed nationalist constitutions at the Convention, but they were soundly defeated. The states were jealous of their sovereignty and were prepared to delegate to the central government only enumerated powers. Lincoln, in the light of a later emerging nationalism that was similar to the nationalisms that had been sweeping over Europe since the French Revolution, could say that the states had never been sovereign and that the constitution was not a compact. But this must be viewed as a Whiggish retrospective narrative legitimating a present policy in the pursuit of an imagined and wished-for constitution rather than an accurate description of the self-conception of the Founders themselves. For no counterfactual proposition about the founding is more certain than that if New York, Virginia, and Rhode Island (the three states that claimed the right of secession in their ordinances of ratification) had been told that they were not and had never been sovereign political societies and that once in the Union they could not withdraw, there would have been no Union.

There are then two narratives of the adventure of the American regime. One is a Lincolnian story of the unfolding of an organic nationalist founding, distracted from time to time by anarchical doctrines of state interposition, nullification, and secession. The other is a Jeffersonian story of the defeat of a dynamic democratic federalism of independent moral communities. The Lincolnian narrative is a nationalist story of political maturity and a passage through near anarchy. The Jeffersonian narrative is the story of the rejection of dynamic federalism in favor of increasing centralization, consolidation, and political ossification. Americans have told and continue to tell both stories about themselves, but it is the Lincolnian story that is most widely told. When we ask about the founding and the sources that influenced the founding, it is Lincoln's organic nationalist founding that guides the inquiry. It was some such presumption that enabled Douglass Adair to discover an image of the American regime in Hume's "Idea of a Perfect Commonwealth." I intend now to demonstrate that there is no such image.

The first thing to notice is that Hume's regime *is* a nationalist regime. It supposes a fairly homogeneous culture and even a national religion. Lincoln compared the states to counties in a consolidated nationalist regime. Likewise, Humean county republics are consolidated into a national political society. But this is not at all like the Constitution of 1789. That regime prohibited the establishment of a national religion. An established national church was a reserved right of the states, and Massachusetts maintained an established church until 1833. Furthermore, the doctrines of state interposition, nullification, and secession (doctrines that arose quite naturally in the American regime from the logic of the constitution as a compact) cannot arise in Hume's commonwealth. The county republics are entirely consolidated into a national political society.

Another difference between Hume's republic and the American counterpart has to do with the question of size and scale. Hume argued against the traditional view that republics had to be small. A republic could be larger than a city-state, but how much larger? Hume compares the ideal commonwealth to a country the size of Holland, Britain, or France. Hume's regime is extensive, but it is not an *empire* in the eighteenth-century sense of a government comprehending a vast territory that includes a number of political societies. The American regime *was* an empire, albeit republican and federal in form. In respect to scale, Hume's commonwealth resembles very much an American state such as Virginia or Massachusetts, but it does not at all resemble a federation of such states.

Hume's Conception of Macropolitical Order

There was, of course, an argument to be made for empire. It had been said that extended government over a vast territory, comprehending a number of political societies, reduces the amount of war in that territory, extends commerce, and provides better security from external threat. It is some such argument that sought to justify the project of "universal monarchy" in Europe as a rational and humane form of political order, a project that was said to have begun with Charlemagne and that was revived by Charles V, Philip II, and Louis XIV. In opposition to the theory of "universal monarchy," Hume argued that monarchical empires are conducive neither to peace nor stability: "Enormous monarchies are, probably, destructive to human nature; in their progress, in their continuance, and even in their downfall, which never can be very distant from their establishment" (*E,* 340–41).

But if monarchical empires are bad, empires constituted by republics or "free states" are even worse: "Though free governments have been commonly the most happy for those who partake of their freedom; yet are they the most ruinous and oppressive to their provinces" (*E,* 18–19). The reason is that (excepting a few friends or favorites) a monarch has an interest in treating his subjects equally. Consequently, he will tend to make no distinction among subjects "in his general laws." But "a free state necessarily makes a great distinction" between the conquered provinces and itself, "and will be sure to contrive matters, by restrictions on trade, and by taxes, so as to draw some private as well as public, advantage from [its] conquests." Hume observes that conquered provinces were treated better even under the worst of the Roman emperors than they were under the Roman Republic. Passing to modern times, he compares the oppressive treatment of Corsica when it was under the dominion of the republic of Genoa with the milder treatment it received after being conquered by the French monarchy. Closer to home is the oppression of Ireland by the free state of Britain. The oppression of Ireland is especially remarkable because, "being in good measure, peopled from England," one would expect it to receive "better treatment than that of a conquered province" (*E,* 21). Hume would make the same point about the American colonies in the letters of the last decade of his life.[16]

But if empire, both monarchical and republican, is to be rejected, what, might we ask, is Hume's vision of macropolitical order? An answer emerges if we compare the essay "Idea of a Perfect Commonwealth" with "Of the Rise and Progress of the Arts and Sciences," "Of the Jealousy of Trade," and "Of the Balance of Power." The model that emerges is that of "a number of neighbouring and independent states, connected together by commerce and policy" (*E,* 119). This, of course, is quite different from the federated empire the Americans founded in

1789, since it is neither an empire nor a federation. Hume's inspiration for this form of macropolitical order is the high level of culture attained in antiquity by the league of Greek city-states. And he observed that "Europe is at present a copy at large, of what Greece was formerly a pattern in miniature" (*E*, 121).

What reasons are there for preferring this model of macropolitical association over monarchical or republican empire, or over a federation having a central authority? Hume's answer stresses the matter of size and scale. The small size of the constituent states ("such limited territories") provides a check to the growth of "both . . . *power* and *authority*" (*E*, 119–20). "Extended governments," he says, "where a single person has great influence, soon become absolute; but small ones change naturally into commonwealths." A large government is accustomed by degrees to tyranny because oppression against a part is not easily perceived by the whole, and even when the whole is oppressed, it "may, by a little art, be kept in obedience; while each part, ignorant of the resolutions of the rest, is afraid to begin any commotion or insurrection" (*E*, 119). In "a small government," however, any act of oppression is immediately known throughout the whole.

When Hume says that Europe is a copy of what Greece was in miniature, he is talking about the order or scale in which the states are disposed, not their political form or size. The analogy would be nearly complete if the states of Europe were all republics. But they are not; and although it is natural for small principalities to evolve into republics, it is not obvious that large European monarchies will or can evolve into republics. John Stewart has argued persuasively that Hume's "Idea of a Perfect Commonwealth" was written to show that this could happen.[17] Further, Hume argued that the republican idiom of liberty is immanent in most European states. Property and the rule of law are about as secure in the absolute monarchy of France as in republics (*E*, 94). Viewed in this way, Hume's perfect commonwealth is a mirror in which an inarticulate republican mode of life, immanent in Europe, may come to recognize itself. Finally, although Hume recognized the legitimacy of monarchy and even thought that under certain considerations Britain would be better off as an absolute monarchy than as a republic, on the level of speculation he was always a republican. Of the Europe of his time he writes, "It must be owned, that the situation of affairs in modern times, with regard to civil liberty, as well as equality of fortune, is not near so favourable, either to the propagation or happiness of mankind." The reason is that "Europe is shared out mostly into great monarchies," which impoverish the people by the splendor of their court and the expenditure necessary to maintain a large military force (*E*, 402–3). The small principalities, rather than evolving into republics, exhaust their people by emulating the greater princes. In opposition to this, Hume presents Holland and Switzerland, the only European countries which resemble the ancient republics and which, notwithstanding their limited resources, are flourishing in respect to both population and civil liberty.

Hume's speculative vision of macropolitical order in Europe is, then, based on the Greek model, where each city-state expands to become an extensive European republic. What is excluded is the unification of these republics under a central authority, as in the American regime.

The second reason Hume gives for preferring the Greek model is the limit it places on authority. Independent moral and political societies with distinctive ways of life, connected by trade and common cultural interests, provide a fertile soil for competition, emulation, and criticism. A single prejudice cannot sweep a vast territory but is checked by the prejudices of a neighboring competitive republic, so that "nothing but nature and reason, or what bears them a strong resemblance, can force its way through all obstacles and unite the most rival nations into an esteem and admiration of it" (*E*, 120). Here we have a *moral argument* that the Greek model promotes not only liberty but the critical activity of "nature and reason" or "taste and reasoning" (*E*, 120).

Another component of Hume's idealized Greek model of large-scale political order is free trade. Hume taught that economic integration does not require political integration, but it was largely the desire for economic integration that led to abandonment of the Articles of Confederation, and it has been largely through the commerce clause of the Constitution that the American regime has evolved into the highly centralized and consolidated empire it is today. In Hume's model, Europe is economically integrated through free trade, but is politically integrated only through its great compacts, such as the Treaty of Utrecht, the Treaty of Paris, and later the Congress of Vienna.

Hume was probably aware of alternative schemes of European order which did require a degree of centralized authority and political integration (and, accordingly, bore some remote resemblance to the American system), namely, the visions of a European commonwealth explored by Montesquieu and Fletcher.[18] If so, he appears to have rejected them.

Some final reflections on the question of size are in order. Though Hume is prepared to argue that under modern conditions large republics are possible, there is still a strong moral presumption on behalf of small-scale political societies. In "Idea of a Perfect Commonwealth," he says that "a small commonwealth is the happiest government in the world within itself," but it lacks adequate means of defense, which a more extensive republic can remedy. It is perhaps significant that voting in Hume's commonwealth is by county, a system that bears some resemblance to Jefferson's system of ward republics. In addition, a moral argument for smallness derives from Hume's theory of moral sentiments. The original source of belief and conduct for Hume is not reflection but inherited custom, which is always particular and parochial. In the case of morals, reason appears as the methodizing and correcting of these sentiments in the direction of a more extensive benevolence. Thus Humean cosmopolitanism not only emerges from a parochial source, it continues to bear a parochial imprint. There is a moral imperative, then, that political association will both protect provincial life and also provide institutions for its correction. The Greek model of macropolitical order, in providing a check on power and authority, does both, and it is in this light, I think, that we must read Hume's criticism of the British commercial empire of Pitt. By spiritualizing the empire with a Whig idiom, Pitt was able to give it a certain moral grandeur. Hume, however, focused attention on its tendency to centralize and consolidate wealth and power in the capital. "Enormous cities are, besides, destructive to society, beget vice and disorder of all kinds, starve the remoter provinces, and even starve themselves by the prices to which they raise all provisions" (*E,* 401). Hume thought there were limits within the order of things that prevented a city from growing much beyond six or seven hundred thousand inhabitants (*E,* 447–48).

When the colonists resisted the trade policies of the British government, there were attempts by Americans and the "friends of America" in Britain (e.g., Burke, Isaac Barré, Pitt) to correct matters with schemes of imperial federalism that would place the dominions on a more equal footing. Hume was probably familiar with Franklin's Albany Plan. All of these bore some remote resemblance to the later American regime in having a central authority with enumerated powers governing a number of political societies. Hume, however, rejected them in favor of secession of the colonies and complete independence. This was a radical position, and among the "friends of America," Hume was the odd man out. Nevertheless, his position is consistent with his speculations on macropolitical order.

To conclude, we may state that there is no image of the American regime, conceived either under the compact theory or the nationalist theory, to be found in Hume's speculation about republican government and macropolitical order. Indeed, there is a presumption against it, insofar as it is incompatible with the vision of large-scale political order that Hume did defend, namely, the Greek model writ large as a European order of independent extensive republics integrated by free trade, cultural competition and emulation, and a policy of the balance of power.

Hume and the *Articles of Confederation*

Although there is no image of the American regime of 1789 to be found in Hume's writings, there is a Humean image of macropolitical order to be found in American political experience. Each American state is a Humean extensive republic: the order of these states that most resembles Hume's Greek model is the Continental Congress, and the constitution it framed styled the Articles of Confederation. Here political integration resembles the political integration Hume favored in the Greek model and in Europe: integration by compact between independent political societies. The Articles of Confederation are described in Article 3 as "a firm league of friendship" between states, each of which in Article 2 is said to retain "its Sovereignty, freedom, and independence."

We are inclined to view the Continental Congress, retrospectively, from the point of view of Lincoln's mid-nineteenth-century nationalism, as a *national* assembly. But the Congress was, in fact, a league of states as in the "Congress of Vienna." John Adams wrote of Massachusetts as "our country" and of the Massachusetts delegation to Congress as "our embassy." We are also inclined, in Whiggish fashion, to view the Continental Congress and the Articles of Confederation as a failure and the constitution of 1789 as the only alternative to chaos. But just because the Articles were replaced does not mean that they were either a failure or a success. This can be determined only by a thoughtful examination of the merits and defects of the Confederation period that is free of the Whiggish presumption that the Constitution of 1787 was the result of historic fate.

Aside from fighting and concluding a victorious war with Britain, the greatest political achievement of the Continental Congress was the settlement of disputes over claims to western territory, something that the Constitution of 1789 would not be able to accomplish without a civil war. And it could do this because it worked with a rule requiring unanimity of the states. The small state of Maryland was able to hold up the ratification of the Articles for three and a half years until major concessions were made by the large land-holding states. With a veto on major changes in the constitutional order, each state is more likely to preserve itself as a distinct moral and political society. This is certainly in the spirit, if not exactly to the letter, of Hume's Greek model of large-scale political association.

Finally, Hume's commonwealth is, in the language of the eighteenth century, a commonwealth of "preservation," whereas the regime of 1789 was a constitution of "increase." Hume argued that "extensive conquests . . . must be the ruin of every free government; and of the more perfect government sooner than of the imperfect" (*E*, 529). Hume's constitution imposes upon itself a law forbidding conquests, but he dryly adds that "republics have ambition as well as individuals" (*E*, 529). In fifty years the American regime, by conquest and purchase, would swell to some ten times its size. Territory would be acquired and disposed of, not by concurrent majority of the states as required by the Continental Congress, nor by a constitutional amendment requiring ratification of three-fourths of the states, but by a majority of Congress. This opened the door to rapid and destabilizing expansion. The Louisiana Purchase led to a secession movement in New England in 1803 with the argument that acquisition of territory required a constitutional amendment. Each new increase spawned secession movements in sections threatened by the expansion. In 1844 John Quincy Adams and other New England leaders threatened secession over the annexation of Texas.

Secession and annexation are destabilizing in the same way. Secession is destabilizing in that it suddenly creates new majorities and new minorities, but so does annexation. And, as Hume observed, the more perfect a free state is, the more vulnerable it becomes to the disorder of rapidly shifting majorities.

It is an irony worthy of a Humean historian that the other North American British colony, namely, Canada, the peaceable kingdom to the north of the United States, began as a highly centralized regime under monarchy and has evolved into a decentralized regime in which secession can be peacefully explored as a serious political option. A Canadian Province may also nullify acts of the central government in the area of civil rights by virtue of the "notwithstanding" clause of the Canadian Constitution. This is the very power that Jefferson said was a right of an American State under the Constitution viewed in terms of the compact theory. In contrast the American regime launched in 1789 began as a highly decentralized federation of republics with a central government that had only enumerated powers and was no more than a speck on the political landscape. As the regime expanded and its wars multiplied, the central government grew in size, becoming in time the largest centralization of military and financial power in history. We cannot know what judgment Hume would have made of this, for his thought was framed in a preindustrial age. But keeping his thought where it belongs in the eighteenth century, it is plausible to suggest that the man who defended the Greek model of macropolitical order, who proposed an extensive republic of preservation, who argued that republican empires were the worst sort of empires, and who argued for the secession of the American colonies and the dissolution of the mercantile empire spawned by the free state of Britain, would have taken very seriously the arguments of the anti-Federalists who opposed the constitution of 1787 on the ground that it would, in time, destroy the substantial moral communities of the states and lead to a consolidated republican empire worse in its tyranny than the British empire.

Indeed, Humean voices were heard in the debates over the Articles of Confederation. The small states feared being swallowed up by the large states if Congress was conceived as representing individuals on a national scale. Ignoring the inescapable fact of the sovereignty of the states (as Hamilton and Wilson would perversely do at the Convention of 1787), Benjamin Franklin presented the union of Scotland with England as proof that the fears of the small states were unfounded. John Witherspoon of Edinburgh replied to this sophism that the British Union was an "incorporation" under monarchy and that no one in America was contemplating an association of that kind. He then went on to make Hume's point that, on the scale of empire, the subjects of free states tend to be more oppressed than those of monarchy. A national Congress having authority over individuals would be just such an empire. "Every Colony," insisted Witherspoon, "is a distinct person."[19] Richard Henry Lee argued that the vast territory conquered by the republic of Virginia from Britain should be relinquished to the Confederation (as the small states had demanded) on the ground that Virginia could not both remain a republic and possess such extensive territory. This was just Hume's argument that the extensive republic is one of preservation and must restrain itself from conquest.

We cannot therefore properly view Hume as a mythical Founding Father of the regime of 1789, whether conceived under the nationalist theory or the compact theory. There is, however, a Humean image to be found in the macropolitical order of the Continental Congress and its Articles of Confederation. That regime was dissolved by an act of secession when nine states decided to form a new union in violation of their own rule that the Union was perpetual and could not be changed without unanimous consent of the states. Whether this dissolution reflected a manifest failure of the Articles, as Federalists maintained, or was an act of hubris and ambition on the part of the commercial centers of the east coast to institute an American version of regulated trade on the model of the British empire, as the anti-Federalists said it was, is a question to ponder.[20] Nevertheless, the Articles of Confederation are the closest thing to a Humean legacy in the adventure of American constitutionalism.

CHAPTER THIRTEEN

The Right of Resistance: A Humean Free State versus a Modern Consolidated Leviathan

Modern and Premodern Polities

Those who seek political intimations in Hume must take into account the great difference between the state as it was understood during the period of the *ancien régime* in which Hume lived and the quite different state that began to emerge after the French Revolution. I shall call the latter the "modern state," though with some diffidence, since some writers use the term *modern* to characterize a kind of state that began to emerge around the thirteenth century.[1] But a great change occurred in the style of politics after the French Revolution, and it is this change that I have in mind, whatever name is given to it. Political terms such as *authority, liberty, sovereignty, rights, allegiance, public, private, law,* and *justice* take on different meanings when embedded in the framework of the modern state as opposed to the premodern state of the *ancien régime.* My contention is that although nods in the direction of the modern state can be found in Hume's political vocabulary, most of it is shaped and constrained by his experience of the premodern state.

John Stewart has written perceptively about Hume's criticism of the political arrangements of his own time and sees him as a precursor of the liberalism that emerged in the nineteenth century; Hume's "Idea of a Perfect Commonwealth" and other writings certainly contain the lineaments of the "new Great Britain, the new France, and so forth."[2] Hume did imagine an order of extensive republics, and Europe has evolved into an order of extensive republics. But whether Hume conceived of these as having the form of what I have called the modern state may be questioned.

A full account of whether the modern state is intimated in Hume's political writings cannot be attempted here. Rather, in this and the next chapter, I examine Hume's political writings in the light of two doctrines essential to the identity of the modern state: the theory of sovereignty and the organic theory of the state. I conclude that there is no support in Hume's writings for either of these essential doctrines and that, consequently, there is a strong presumption in his political thought against the modern state.

The relevance of this exercise to a study of Hume's conception of philosophy will become apparent as the inquiry proceeds. But this much can be said: The modern state that emerges after the French Revolution is not just any kind of state; it is, among other things, a philosophically self-conscious state intent on legitimating itself in the world through the philosophical act. And whenever the philosophical act appears, a Humean critique is in order.

The first thing to notice about the modern state is its disposition to centralize and to consolidate smaller social and political units into a larger whole. At the time of William the Conqueror, Europe consisted of thousands of independent political units. As late as the end of the seventeenth century, Germany alone contained some 234 countries, 51 free cities, and 1,500 independent titled manors.[3] Today there are only a few dozen countries left, and there is a disposition to consolidate these into a European superstate.

Along with consolidation has come an increase in the state's power to command the resources, material and human, of a territory. The thought that there are "human resources" to be exploited is itself a creature of the modern state. One measure of this power—which points to a fundamental difference between the modern European state and its premodern counterpart—is the authority to impose an income tax and the authority to enact universal conscription. With these two powers the modern state has been able to carry out wars on a scale of destruction unprecedented in history.

Wars in the medieval and early modern period tended to be short engagements with relatively few casualties. The reason is that the state was divided into independent social authorities (the Church, nobility, Commons, free cities). The crown had to negotiate with these powerful independent orders for revenue and troops. They could refuse, as the Commons did when Charles I asked for revenue to build a navy, and in an attempt to bypass their authority, he lost his head. Since the upkeep of troops, not to mention their loss, was a direct cost to some proprietor, there was an economic interest in keeping military engagements few and short.

Monarchs, of course, chafed under such restrictions and sought to eliminate or at least to weaken the power of these independent social orders. The Crown typically accomplished this by presenting itself as the champion of those oppressed by this or that independent order. By the end of the medieval period the monarch had defeated the Church. By the eighteenth century the monarch was in contest with the nobility, and an ever-growing number of people began to look to the Crown for their security. Of this process (as it occurred in France), Lord Acton observed that "the development of absolute monarchy by the help of democracy is the one constant character of French history."[4] In time, popular assemblies would topple the monarchies of Europe and usher in the modern state.

By the eighteenth century absolute monarchy was something to contend with. It was most fully developed in France, and Hume judged in 1740 that it was only two reigns old (*T,* 557). Leaving aside its many ideological meanings, what absolute monarchy signified was a higher degree of centralization brought on by the progressive weakening of independent social orders and an administrative machinery that extended throughout the realm, along which a single will could flow that touched every individual. But the premodern idiom of government by negotiation among independent social orders, though weakened, had not collapsed under absolute monarchy. Frederick the Great could not impose an income tax on his people, nor could he enact universal conscription.

The fear that the existing limits to the growth of government would eventually fall away, and with them all independent social life, was a central theme of eighteenth-century European politics, but especially of British politics. It was a concern of the Old Whigs and of Hume as well. It is behind his support of a militia; his attack on public credit as a means of raising revenue; his opposition to the centralization required for mercantilism; his prejudice against "enormous" cities; his solicitude for provincial life; his praise of small states (while recognizing their limits); his proposal for a confederated Europe composed of independent states endowed with the right of secession; and his support of the secession of the American colonies, which were premodern in their refusal to be a source of revenue for an emerging, centralized British state. Finally, it appears even in his suggestion that absolute monarchy, bad as it is, would be preferable to republicanism in Britain. The former would be a better protection for independent social life than the latter, which could be expected to eliminate all independent social order, as the Puritan republic had attempted to do in England. Republicanism had resulted in and would again result in an even greater concentration of power at the center.

Events in France were soon to prove him right. The French Revolution swept away all independent social orders: Crown, nobility, Church, the states general, provincial authority, the parliaments. In their place was proclaimed a republic—one and indivisible—and a national assembly. One thing, however, remained intact: the *administrative machinery* invented by absolute monarchy. Now, however, it was run by "republicans," who greatly expanded its scope and grip on the people beyond anything a French monarch could have imagined.

For the first time, universal conscription could be ordered. Louis XVI had managed an army of around 180,000. Frederick the Great, carefully managing his resources, had an army of 190,000 and Austria's numbered 200,000. With universal conscription the French republic was suddenly able to throw into the field a million troops, which rolled back the frugal monarchies of Europe. Funded not by proprietors but by the "public," these troops were expendable in a way not previously possible. Napoleon developed aggressive tactics which brought high casualties but ensured success. By the time the French Revolution had run its course and Napoleon was finally brought to bay, the republic had raised some three million troops, the largest army that had ever been assembled.[5]

The whole ordeal of the French Revolution and its aftermath was a barbarism unprecedented in Europe. It was more destructive than the religious wars and the Inquisition of the previous age, and more disgraceful because legitimated in the name of Enlightenment and the philosophical doctrine of natural rights—but it was only a prelude to what was to come. To combat the centralized French republic, other states had to centralize, and so, by the early twentieth century, the modern state had vastly increased its control over the people and resources of a territory. Having now not only the device of public credit but also the revenue from an income tax and the authority to impose universal conscription, a state could mobilize a whole people for wars that would be global in scope and awesome in destructive power. The battle casualties of World War I were eight million killed and six million wounded. This was more than were killed in the nearly two centuries of "civilized warfare" introduced in Europe after the barbarism of the Thirty Years' War. The number of battle and civilian deaths in World War II has been estimated at around fifty million, not to mention those displaced and mutilated physically and mentally.[6]

But even the barbarism of its wars has been outmatched by the destructiveness of the modern state's attempts to totally transform society in accord with philosophical theories of human freedom and equality.

The countries of Eastern Europe, the former Soviet Union, China, Cambodia, and others have been laboratories for the practice of Marxist philosophical alchemy. The associated loss of life has been estimated conservatively at 100 million. To take just one example, in 1932–33, as part of its effort to establish collective agriculture, the Soviet government engaged in a policy of forced starvation in the area of the Ukraine and the Caucasus which left 14.5 million dead. In the purges of 1936–38, the Soviet government killed some 4 million of its own citizens. Russian textbooks today estimate that 20 million were killed under Stalin's administration and some 40 million consigned to forced labor.[7]

Such massive acts of terrorism could not have been accomplished had they met with resistance from Enlightenment liberal regimes similar to that directed against the policy of apartheid in South Africa. But the Western intelligentsia remained—throughout the 1930s and, to a remarkable extent, even later—in a state of denial. The shameful story of this ideologically self-imposed ignorance on the part of Western intellectuals has been told by Paul Hollander (*Political Pilgrims* [1981]), David Caute (*Fellow Travellers* [1988]), and Robert Conquest (*The Terror: A Reassessment* [1990]). As late as the mid-1980s some Soviet experts were still maintaining that in the terror of the 1930s only "thousands" were killed. Robert Conquest, who has spent his career in a scholarly study of the Soviet holocaust, has written, "The evidence was as complete and as consistent as it could conceivably be. It was widely rejected. Jean Paul Sartre even defended the proposition that the evidence about the Soviet forced labor camps should be ignored, even if true, on the grounds that otherwise the French proletariat might be thrown into despair."[8]

This corruption of the intellect for political purposes is akin to what Hume judged to be the nadir of British politics, symbolized in Titus Oates and the popish plot during the Restoration period. Although religious enthusiasm had run its course among elites, religion could still be used to inflame popular passions. Show trials were cynically held, imagined conspiracies uncovered, and false testimony eagerly accepted for political purposes (*H*, 6: 332–48).

There was a philosophical reason for Western acquiescence that fell short of Sartre's honest cynicism. Although liberalism and Marxism are distinct philosophies, they are both Enlightenment ideologies. At this philosophical level the liberal and the Marxist know and understand each other. Liberalism has its own history (beginning with the French Revolution) of destroying traditional societies in order to form the modern unitary state, legitimated by the philosophical theory of natural rights. The enemies of all Enlightenment ideologies are the same: religion, custom, traditional societies and hierarchies, and anything perceived to be "reactionary" or "unprogressive." Marxism, however barbarous its embodiment may have been, has always been clothed in the language of a progressive ideology, and the magic of this language has often called forth from the liberal a morally disarming respect that has prevented a clear grasp of moral reality. This is the inverted philosophical truth in the old saw that there are no enemies on the left.

It has been asked to what extent the Germans knew about the Nazi slaughter of the Jews and why no protest was made. But a similar question must be put to the Western intelligentsia who, enjoying a free press in liberal regimes during the 1930s, could not bring themselves to face the Soviet holocaust and to organize resistance to it. The case would have been otherwise had the slaughter been carried out by the Czars, or had it been racially motivated, for such acts would have offended liberal universalism in a way that action purportedly done in the name of class struggle for equality did not. "The scandal," Conquest writes, "is not that they justified the Soviet actions, but that they refused to hear about them; that they were not prepared to face the evidence."[9] There is no ignorance of nature as deep and as impenetrable as a philosophically self-imposed ignorance.

But I do not intend a jeremiad against the modern state. The point to be made is a limited one about the concentration of power, namely, that the massive destruction in war and the state terror brought on by the new centralized and consolidated form of the state that appeared with the French Revolution was not possible in the states of the *ancien régime*. It was impossible not because men were more virtuous or because the technology of destruction was inferior, but because no one, or no office, had the *authority* to command the total resources of a people and to order them put to such destructive use. Had Hitler or Stalin been installed as eighteenth-century absolute monarchs in Prussia or France, they could not have done what they did, because their authority would have been hedged in by powerful, independent social authorities whose titles were as good as their own and who could be expected to resist.

What this suggests is that the modern state itself has become an instrument of destruction. R. J. Rummel has sought to determine the number of people killed by modern governments for ideological reasons since 1900. He distinguishes what he calls "democide" from genocide; the latter is the destruction of a people having a common culture and identity; the former is the destruction of a great mass of people in the aggregate with or without a common identity. Using conservative statistical estimates, he concludes that the governments of modern states since 1900 have killed nearly four times as many people as the battle deaths in all wars, domestic and foreign. Battle deaths are estimated at approximately 35,700,000. The Soviet democide alone is estimated at 61,911,000 people, 7,142,000 of them foreigners, an unbelievable total. But as Rummel argues, "It is only the prudent, most probable tally."[10] When the other democides are added, it would appear that the greatest threat to human life in the twentieth century is not war (not even nuclear war) but the governments of unitary modern states which, being endowed with the authority to command the people and total resources of vast territories, have been able to carry out such destruction.

The barbarism of the nineteenth and twentieth centuries, then, is due primarily not to refinements in technology, or to triumphs of the wrong ideology, or to a lack of "democracy" so much as to a change in the form of political association: governments now have the *authority* to command the total resources (including human resources) of a territory. In this sense all modern states are "totalitarian"; they differ only in the degree to which and the way in which they exploit those resources. It was not totalitarian fascist or communist regimes that brought on the massive destruction of World War I and set the stage for World War II, but the liberal regimes of Germany, Britain, France, and the United States. The first totalitarian regime was the republic of the French Revolution, and its state terror was legitimated by the liberal doctrine of natural rights. And, as mentioned earlier, it was a liberal regime, the American Union, that according to Liddel Hart launched the first modern war, that is, total war against a civilian population in order to coerce eleven states back into a union from which they had voted to secede.

The modern state (especially in its liberal form) has accomplished much in the way of material prosperity, but we must recognize that it has also been an instrument of unprecedented barbarism in what prides itself as the most civilized of all ages. And we must raise the question of whether any office in human affairs can safely contain such a concentration of power. The suggestion, then, is that the modern state as such (independent of whether it wears the mask of liberalism, fascism, or Marxism) has a lot to answer for. It has been endowed with the authority to demand sacrifices that no eighteenth-century "absolute" monarch could have demanded or would even have dreamed of demanding. Had the destruction wrought by the modern state been carried out by a class of nobility or by a religion, judgment would have been unclouded, and it would have been severe, as indeed it has been against the crimes of the Church in the religious wars of Europe. The horror of religious bigotry is still that against which remnants of the Enlightenment define themselves. But the modern state is the work not of religion but of the Enlightenment and of rationalism; thus, moral judgment, in the first philosophic age, about the modern state itself has remained largely silent. Of this silence Bertrand De Jouvenel has written perceptively:

> From the twelfth to the eighteenth century governmental authority grew continuously. The process was understood by all who saw it happening; it stirred them to incessant protest and violent reaction. In later times its growth has continued at an accelerated pace. . . . And now we no longer understand the process, we no longer protest, we no longer react. This quiescence of ours is a new thing, for which Power has to thank the smoke-screen in which it has wrapped itself. . . . [M]asked in anonymity, it claims to have no existence of its own, and to be but the impersonal and passionless instrument of the general will.[11]

Part of this smoke screen is a liberal ideology of progress that views the destruction of independent social life and the concentration of power at the center as the only avenue of escape from the oppression of the *ancien régime* and its suppression of individual liberty. Liberalism typically assumes that liberalism is the only legitimate form of political association, a Whiggish theory that Hume rejected—though he affirmed the practice of liberty, which is quite a different thing.[12] He observed, with the eye of the philosophical connoisseur, that civil liberty was about as well established in the absolute monarchy of France as in Britain. Civil liberty was not incompatible with the practices of the *ancien régime;* indeed, it had its roots in those practices. The ideology of progress so deeply ingrained in modern thought hides from view the evils of the modern state and the virtues of the *ancien régime,* making a balanced moral judgment difficult. This ideology was recognizable in Hume's time, and he called it the "plaguy prejudices of whiggism" from which he sought to free himself.

The storming of the Bastille is a symbol of emancipation from monarchy, but the Bastille contained only seven inmates, none of whom were political prisoners. In contrast the terror instituted by the republic to secure the universal rights of man claimed half a million political prisoners and resulted in the execution after trial of 17,000 and of 12,000 without trial, and many died in prison.[13] Only a small fraction of these conformed to the image of the haughty grandees whose yoke was being thrown off.

But the stock image of an oppressive *ancien régime* is Tsarist Russia. The Czars were certainly authoritarian, but their power was limited, and they presided over the establishment of the practice of liberty in Russia. By 1907 Russia had become the world's fourth industrial power; its agriculture was flourishing; it was an exporter of grain and in good years accounted for 40 percent of world wheat exports. Education had improved, so that by 1915, 68 percent of all military conscripts were literate. During its last half century Tsarist Russia was a well-spring of cultural achievement in the arts and sciences.[14] In short, though an absolute monarchy, late Tsarist Russia was a flourishing civil society that compares favorably with regimes that exist today. John Gray has judged it "highly probable" that if the Russia of 1913 were to exist now, "it would come within the twenty states that are most liberal and least oppressive in today's world."[15]

The terror of the Soviet Union is often thought of as a continuation of the authoritarian tradition of the Czars, but the comparative study by Dziak presents a quite different picture. In the eighty years prior to the Revolution of 1905, the Czars executed an average of seventeen people a year. During the Soviet period, executions would be in the millions. The Czar's security forces in 1895, the Okhrana, amounted to 161 agents supported by less than 10,000 police. In contrast the Soviet Cheka in 1921 employed 240,400 agents, which had the resources of the Red Army, NKVD, and militiamen.[16]

Tsarist Russia, though authoritarian, did not embody the Asiatic despotism of liberal progressive fantasy, nor was Soviet terror an extension of that despotism. Soviet terror was legitimated by a *European progressive ideology* (what Hume called a philosophical enthusiasm), the very ideology that would corrupt the Western intelligentsia's initial, and to a great extent its continuing, moral assessment of the regime. The Soviet terror was the terror of the French Revolution writ large, and that revolution generated a republic which, in uprooting itself entirely from the *ancien régime,* became the first purely philosophical liberalism. Tsarist Russia collapsed not because of its oppression but because of its imprudent participation in World War I, a war that perhaps could have been settled after the stalemate of 1915, had it not been transformed into a holy progressive war to restructure Europe and make the *world* safe for democracy. What remained of the independent social authorities of the *ancien régime,* negotiation among which had been the soil in which the practice of liberty had taken root in Europe, was largely destroyed. The great revolutions of the modern age have not been against the oppressions of truly autocratic figures such as Henry VIII, Louis XIV, and Peter the Great but against conciliatory monarchs such as Charles I, Louis XVI, and Nicholas II. Ambition to rule, as much as genuine concern for oppression, has been the driving force behind modern revolutions, although it is usually masked by a sanitizing philosophical narrative about universal human emancipation.

The centralized and consolidated modern state is for us a historic fate, but it is not a natural fate. It is important to realize that it has not always existed, that its emergence was contingent, and, consequently, that it is not beyond criticism. We must therefore make an effort not to read the meaning of political terms appropriate to the scene of engagement that is the modern state back into the premodern political arrangements of Hume's time. Hume was one of those that De Jouvenel had in mind who witnessed and understood the relentless growth and centralization of government authority, and much of what he wrote was in opposition to it.

The suggestion that Hume's political thought is at home in the premodern regimes of eighteenth-century Europe will invite the criticism that such a view does not take into account Hume's "liberalism," or the "progressive" character of his thought, or that it gives us a "reactionary" Hume. But these are just the stock legitimating images of the modern state, which must view European history as the necessary unfolding of its own idea. One value of history, however, is that in entering another age, we gain a fresh perspective on our own. The spectacular destruction wrought almost continuously by the modern state since its beginning in the French Revolution must at least make us wonder whether its proponents are in any position to point a moral finger at the premodern regimes of Europe, inadequate in many respects as they no doubt were. But Hume's "liberalism" (or better his Whiggism, for the term *liberalism* gets its meaning only in the context of the modern state) is rooted in the world of the *ancien régime.* When Hume's Whiggism is transferred to the context of the modern state, much is lost in the translation. I want to call attention to what is lost.

The central feature of the modern state, whether legitimated by an ideology of liberalism, Marxism, fascism, or democracy, is its destruction or suppression of independent and traditional forms of corporate existence. Strong social orders that owe nothing to the state for their existence and which, in the premodern order, formed a buffer of authority between the crown and its subjects have gradually disappeared or have been marginalized by regulation. The idea of the modern state is that of a central authority acting directly on individuals. The idea of the premodern state is that of an order of independent social authorities united by compact and under the rule of law. The premodern state is federative in its tone and style even when it appears in its most modern unitary form: absolute monarchy. France under absolute monarchy was still highly decentralized and federative. Under the republic all historical, provincial, and corporate structures to which kings had been compelled to defer were annihilated. Benjamin Constant, who was a keen observer of the French Revolution and the state it generated, explained why. "The interests and memories which spring from local customs contain a germ of resistance which is so distasteful to authority that it hastens to uproot it. Authority finds private individuals easier game; its enormous weight can flatten them out effortlessly as if they were so much sand."[17]

Tocqueville was horrified at this deracinating process of centralization. "The old localized authorities disappear without either revival or replacement, and everywhere the central government succeeds them in the direction of affairs. The whole of Germany, even the whole of Europe, presents in this respect the same picture. Everywhere men are leaving behind the liberty of the Middle Ages, not to enter into a modern brand of liberty but to return to the ancient despotism; for centralization is nothing else than an up-to-date version of the administration seen in the Roman Empire."[18] Nor is this an exaggeration. Sieyès, who did as much as anyone to bring about the flattening of corporate life in France, is clear on the policy to be followed. "France must not be an assemblage of small nations each with its own democratic government. . . . She is a single whole, made up of integral parts; these parts must not have each a complete existence of its own, for they are not wholes joined in a mere federation but parts forming a single-whole. The difference is a big one, and one which is of vital importance to us. Everything is lost once we consent to regard the established municipalities, the districts, or the provinces as so many republics joined together only for the purposes of defence and common protection."[19]

This has ever since been the model of the unitary modern state and is in glaring contradiction to its claim, repeated over and over, to be grounded in popular sovereignty. The modern unitary state is government of the people and for the people, but it has difficulty tolerating government by the people, at least if the people are incorporated into substantial moral communities with strong regional, national, and religious identities. And this is as true of the modern state in its "liberal" form as in its communist or fascist form. Consequently the individual of a modern state is a progressively deracinated individual subject to the *anomie* that Durkheim observed and which, instead of being viewed as a moral disaster, is celebrated as emancipation from the provincial and the parochial. Deprived of the strong moral character that finds root only in substantial moral traditions and without the political protection that such traditions provide when incorporated into the state through a federative style of politics, the deracinated individual must turn to the central authority that commands all resources as the sole object of hope and fear.

What I have sketched out as the modern state and its premodern contrary (what Tocqueville called the "liberty of the Middle Ages," which he hoped could be preserved in a new "modern brand of liberty") are ideal identities which serve only as aids to reflection. They are not entities in the world but styles of political conduct, and although the modern style has come to dominate, the premodern idiom, however fragmented and distracted, continues to exist. Indeed, it sustains and gives stability to the modern state, which nevertheless cannot acknowledge its authority and is constantly at war with it.

The suppression of federative, premodern political order in favor of a unitary state marks a fundamental change in the conception of political authority. Hume taught that political authority is constituted not by power but by opinion. What were the changes in opinion that legitimated the modern state? Two of the most important were the emergence of the modern theory of sovereignty and the conception of the state as an organic whole.

The Modern Theory of Sovereignty

The modern theory of sovereignty is the doctrine that there must be lodged somewhere a supreme, indivisible will that regulates the affairs of men.[20] Two theories have been proposed of the source of sovereignty: God and the people. Hobbes held that God is sovereign but that He speaks through the mouth of the earthly sovereign. Rousseau located sovereignty in the people, not in their will as expressed in a vote (even one that is unanimous) but in what he called the General Will. The sovereign will, whether expressed through Hobbes' ruler or Rousseau's General Will, is indivisible and infallible. Such a theory conceptually eliminates any federative theory of sovereignty.

The modern theory of sovereignty can be made to sound like the medieval notion, but there is a great difference. Medieval sovereignty is also absolute, but not in the sense of a final and irresistible will that regulates the affairs of men; rather, it is absolute in the sense of being the highest in rank. And to say that the earthly sovereign is ordained by God is not to say, with Hobbes, that his authority is infallible and irresistible but that he is responsible to God and that God's will can be known through the independent social authority of the Church. It is the modern theory of sovereignty, not the medieval-federative notion, that logically rules out *legitimate* resistance *within* the polity. The modern theory allows only obedience or revolution (a return to the apolitical state of nature).

The premodern federative style of politics extended into Hume's time alongside intimations of the modern. It is clearly stated in Johannes Althusius's *Politica,* published in 1603, expanded in 1610, and revised in 1643. This well-received work was a systematic statement of the sort of theory of political authority that justified the provinces of the Netherlands in their resistance to the centralizing and consolidating policies of Philip of Spain and provided the philosophical justification for the federative constitution of the United Provinces. Hume greatly admired this constitution, describing it at one time as "one of the wisest and most renowned governments in the world" (*E,* 647). He said that his own "Idea of a Perfect Commonwealth" was modeled on it, with some changes in the direction of making it more democratic and strengthening its central authority (*E,* 526). Whether or not Hume read Althusius's *Politica,* it is a convenient place to begin in an attempt to understand the idea of political order that Hume admired in the federation of the Netherlands.

Althusius's constitution is a hierarchy of independent social and political authorities united by compact. At the bottom is the family and its extended relations of kinship. The family is a political society because it contains the relations of authority and subordination, and it is the oldest and most natural political society. Other social orders that naturally form in human affairs are the village composed of families; the city composed of families and collegia (corporations of all kinds: church, guild, university, and commercial); and the province composed of villages, cities, and family estates. The provinces unite to form the commonwealth.

Each social order has its own reason to be, something of its own to cultivate and to defend. Rights and duties are internal to the social order and are prescriptive, being rooted in secular and sacred traditions held together by memory and communicated through emulation. The idea of individuals endowed with natural rights independent of and in antinomic relation to established social order makes no appearance in Althusius's philosophy nor in Hume's. Individual rights are modifications of social rights, which are and must be primary. Accordingly, Althusius defines politics as "the art of associating men for the purpose of establishing, cultivating, and conserving social life among them. Whence it is called 'symbiotics.' The 'symbiotes' pledge themselves each to the other, by explicit or tacit agreement, to mutual communication of whatever is useful and necessary for the harmonious exercise of social life."[21]

Authority is delegated from the smaller social orders to the larger. Sovereignty exists only in the commonwealth but not in Hobbes's sense of a central authority having infallible and irresistible power. Sovereignty for Althusius is the symbiotic life of the social orders of the commonwealth in accord with the fundamental law of the realm. The commonwealth is not composed of individuals but of social orders (cities, provinces, families, and collegia). It is to these, when united together in communicating things, services, rights, and duties, that sovereignty properly belongs. To put it another way, sovereignty resides in the people, but by the "people" Althusius means the people as incorporated into symbiotic social life and not the people in the aggregate as conceived by modern democratic theory.

From a federative polity of this kind it follows that sovereignty is not indivisible, as in the modern theory, and that consequently Althusius's theory of resistance will also be different. In modern contract theory individuals transfer their natural rights to the sovereign for the advantage of entering political society. This transfer is not reversible. Once in political society, neither an individual nor a community can lawfully secede. Resistance to oppression is either unlawful and must be born patiently or is a return to the state of nature and so is not a political act.

Althusius, however, does not begin with individuals in a state of nature conceptually separated from political society by a Rawlsian, self-imposed veil of ignorance, but with people who are fully historical and already incorporated into social and political existence. Nothing has to be surrendered to enter this state because one is always and necessarily in such a state. And the compact that is the condition for symbiotic social existence is not a once-and-for-all affair; it is continuous. As encroachments on one's social order by other orders can be expected to occur frequently, so lawful resistance must occur with equal frequency.

As there are several kinds of sovereignty in Althusius, so there are several forms of resistance, but they all share a common idiom. They are defensive, and they typically take the form of secession or withdrawal. For example, an individual can secede from a collegium, village, city, or province and join another. Resistance, however, will most often come not from an individual but from one of the social orders, and a part of the realm having the size and dignity to do so (a city, province, estate) may secede from the commonwealth and declare itself independent or join itself to another commonwealth or principality. None of these are acts of "revolution" or a "return to a state of nature."[22]

In the modern theory such acts are acknowledged only when confronted with the egregious tyranny of Nero. But in Althusius's scheme various kinds of resistance are legitimate political acts that can be prompted by something less than a Nero. Indeed, a province or other significant part of the realm may peacefully secede if the "public and manifest welfare of this entire part altogether requires it."[23] Secession in such a case might be prompted not by oppression but by an opportunity to improve the conditions of the seceding part.

The idea of the commonwealth as a federative polity where individuals are viewed as incorporated into a historic social order endowed with inherited rights and obligations is assumed everywhere in Hume's political writings. It is in stark contrast to the modern theory of sovereignty and to the contract theory of government in which that theory is usually embedded. In the *Treatise* Hume says that the contract theory is "the foundation of our fashionable system of politics, and is in a manner the creed of a party amongst us" (*T,* 542). In rejecting it, he rejected by implication the modern theory of sovereignty.

But Hume went further and explicitly rejected the modern theory of sovereignty in "Of Some Remarkable Custom." There he challenged the modern theory of Bodin, Blackstone, and others that sovereignty cannot be divided. The idea that there could be an order of sovereignties within a commonwealth, or what Shaftesbury described as "wheels within wheels," or "one Empire within another" is rejected by the modern theory as "an absurdity in politics" (*E,* 370, 370 n). To refute this, Hume has the reader imagine a commonwealth with two distinct legislatures, "each of which possesses full and absolute authority within itself, and stands in no need of the other's assistance, in order to give validity to its acts." Moreover, the commonwealth, though divided into "two distinct factions, each of which predominated in a distinct legislature, . . . yet produced no clashing in these independent powers"; furthermore, the reader is told that this "disjointed, irregular government, was the most active, triumphant, and illustrious commonwealth, that ever yet appeared" (*E,* 370–71). Such a regime would be ruled out by modern political theory as "a political chimera . . . as absurd as any vision of priests or poets." But here the priests and poets prove wiser than the philosophers, for the regime described is the Roman republic, and the independent legislatures are the *comitia centuriata* and the *comitia tributa.* Hume then goes on to explain how such a system worked. Using the eye of the philosophical connoisseur, who is a master of the particular (and because of this, a master of the universal properly conceived), he brings to life what the false philosopher had declared to be an impossible form of political association. Armed with political power, as it was beginning to be in Hume's time ("the creed of a party amongst us") and would be later in full measure, the modern theory of sovereignty would not only deny the theoretical and practical possibility of sovereignties within sovereignties but would actively seek to destroy or suppress them, so that the only form of political association remaining would be that of the modern unitary state. To put it another way, it would be unable to recognize the reality of sovereignties within sovereignties but, through philosophical alchemy, would transmute these into anarchy, disorder, and threats to the natural rights of individuals.

In this essay we have again the familiar Humean point that the character of human life is poetic. Political association is not the result of applying rationalist propositions (such as the modern theory of sovereignty or natural rights), which are always arbitrarily selected parts or fragments of common life spiritualized as the whole. What reflection cannot establish or even recognize can be enjoyed as a *modus vivendi* of men knowing how to conduct themselves within the prescriptive order of an inherited way of life.

Another place where the federative character of Hume's conception of political association appears is in the definition of a free state given in "Of the Origin of Government." Government that "in common appellation, receives the appellation of free, is that which admits of a partition of power among several members, whose united authority is no less, or is commonly greater than that of any monarch; but who, in the usual course of administration, must act by general and equal laws, that are previously known to all the members and to all their subjects" (*E,* 40–41). This definition is broad enough to cover the Roman republic, the limited monarchy of Britain, the regime of the United Provinces, and the regime theorized by Althusius, but it cannot be extended to the modern state appearing after the French Revolution. The members of that state are individuals in the aggregate ruled directly by a sovereign office. In Hume's constitution the "members" are not individuals but great social orders and "their subjects." Hume is also clear that these social orders have something of their own to defend, an inherited order of rights and duties that are recognized in the association by a fundamental rule of law which restrains the civil magistrate. These orders owe nothing to the state for their existence, and their authority is rooted in the traditions and compacts that make up the rule of law and must be followed by the civil magistrate (whether appearing in the form of monarchical or republican administration). Hume calls these traditions and prescriptive rights "principles or prejudices" that "frequently resist all the authority of the civil magistrate; whose power, being founded on opinion, can never subvert other opinions, equally rooted with that of his title to dominion" (*E*, 40).

The government of a Humean "free" state is hedged in by powerful social orders whose authority is as well grounded as that of the chief magistrate. Such a magistrate cannot command the people and resources of a territory to the extent that they can be commanded by the modern state. This would require the flattening out of those intermediate social authorities which stand as a buffer between the individual and an all-powerful centralized and consolidated state. Should the attempt be made, Hume makes clear in the *Treatise* that these independent orders of social life, "the members of the constitution," have a "right of resistance."

By the right of resistance, Hume, like Althusius, means considerably more than the mere right of revolution and self-preservation in the face of insufferable tyranny. Even Hobbes allows resistance of this sort, though he considers it to be rare and not a political act. But for Hume, resistance is not only a political act, it can be expected to occur with some frequency in a "free" government: "Cases, wherein resistance is lawful, must occur much oftener, and greater indulgence be given to the subjects to defend themselves by force of arms, than in arbitrary governments" (*T*, 564). The reason is that in a free government "the supreme power is shar'd with the people," but by the "people" Hume does not mean the aggregate of deracinated individuals that constitutes the modern state but (in the manner of Althusius) the people as incorporated into great social orders and ways of life. Nor is it the resistance of individuals that he has in mind but the resistance of these social orders: "Every part or member of the constitution must have a right of self-defence, and of maintaining its antient bounds against the encroachment of every other authority" (*T*, 564). And as the forms of encroachment may be many and of varying degrees of seriousness, so the forms of resistance are many, ranging from remonstrance to "force of arms."

Here is a constitutional framework designed to preserve liberty by preserving the established prescriptive social orders in which individuals are incorporated, not by invoking the philosophic superstition of the natural rights of individuals, a doctrine which necessarily stands in antinomic relation to *any* established social order. The danger to which "free government" was a remedy is that the central authority will consolidate all power and destroy or suppress all independent social existence. "Absolute monarchy," or "arbitrary government," was an innovation of the late seventeenth century. What was fearful about absolute monarchy and what made it arbitrary was not its form as monarchy but what monarchy had created: a centralized administrative machinery through which a single will could reach throughout a vast territory and touch every individual. It would make little difference whether the will extended by this machinery was that of a monarch or that of a group of "republican" individuals acting in the name of Rousseau's infallible and irresistible General Will. What mattered was the mere existence of such an administrative system extending from a central office and unchecked by independent social life. The machinery was the thing, and it could be and would be detached from the monarchy that had created it. When American anti-Federalists opposed abandoning the Articles of Confederation for a constitution creating a central government having limited powers and accused their opponents of instituting monarchy, they did not mean a hereditary monarch, for that was not a serious possibility. Rather, they identified monarchy with consolidated government, and they meant that the central government, though limited on paper, would necessarily consolidate power to the center and eventually destroy the states that had created it, turning them into mere administrative units of itself. Time has proved them right, and it is no exaggeration to say that, from the perspective of Hume's understanding of free government, the unitary modern state could be described as "absolute monarchy" or "arbitrary government" without the monarch.

The Revolutionary Character of Public Credit

The modern theory of sovereignty and its concomitant doctrine of natural rights subverts the Humean doctrine of resistance. That doctrine presupposes a federative polity of independent social orders. But if sovereignty is found only in a single, indivisible will, a federative polity cannot be recognized. And if society is founded in an aggregate of individuals endowed with natural rights in abstraction from the inherited rights and duties of an established social order, then resistance by the latter cannot be recognized as having original authority. In the world of the false philosopher, natural rights will always defeat prescriptive rights because the former will be perceived as universal (whereas in fact they are empty or arbitrary) and the latter as particular and parochial. It was just this "fashionable" theory, Hume thought, that was being used by mercantile interests to legitimate the concentration of more power in London at the expense of the other "members" of the federative polity.

Though Hume defended the dignity of commerce, he was not (as he is sometimes seen) a booster of a "commercial society" of rootless consumers. Indeed, though there were nods in that direction in Hume's time, such a society was not really possible until the destruction of traditional social orders by the modern state and its management of the Industrial Revolution. Hume despised the new breed of rootless commercial men centered in London. These included the nabobs of India and sugar planters from the West Indies such as Beckford, who became mayor of London ("that insolent Fellow, Beckford, and the City of London"), and all of those living off the public debt and the mercantile wars of national glory funded by it. Their noble talk of republicanism and natural rights he saw as a mask for consolidating more and more power in London at the expense of the provinces, the colonies, and the "King, Nobility, and Gentry of this Realm" (*L,* 2: 210).

He opposed the republicanism being taught by John Millar to his nephew, not because he was a doctrinaire monarchist but because, given the circumstances of late-eighteenth-century British politics, he thought monarchy (weak as it was) a better instrument for preserving the social orders of Britain and for resisting more transfers of power to London (*L,* 2: 306–7). A republican Britain in the 1770s would be a mercantilist London writ large. And it would be English. Without monarchy, an independent Scottish social order would be in doubt. Hume was a proponent of the militia: "Without a militia, it is in vain to think that any free government will ever have security or stability" (*E,* 525). He lamented that London had disarmed the Scots and that they were not in a position to carry out the very sort of resistance justified in the *Treatise:* "Woud to God we had a Scotch Militia at present [the time of the Wilkes and Liberty riots, anti-Scottish invective, and wild republican talk in London]. This Country is almost unanimous" (*L,* 2: 212).

As David Raynor has observed, Hume was also strongly opposed to raising Highland regiments for use in imperial wars abroad.[24] He feared that an imperial England would be doing to Scotland what the Roman governors had done to the ancient Britons, namely, sending abroad, to perish in imperial wars, those best able to maintain the country's independence at home (*H,* 1: 13). But Highland regiments would be raised for the empire, and in greater numbers than Hume could have imagined. Winston Churchill wrote, with imperial pride, that "Pitt canalised the martial ardour of the Highland regiments into the service of his imperial dreams. Highland regiments brought glory to Scotland . . . and ever since have stood in the forefront of the British Army."[25]

Imperial mercantilism demanded centralization, national glory, and war as an instrument of commerce. War was financed by the policy of mortgaging future revenues, an invention of the modern state unknown to the ancients. Hume was strongly opposed to this innovation: "Either the nation must destroy public credit, or public credit will destroy the nation" (*E,* 360–61). Here is Hume in his least "modern" form. His rejection of public credit has been viewed by many as a surprising lack of economic imagination in a thinker otherwise astute in such matters. Forrest McDonald has compared Hume's understanding of public credit unfavorably with that of Alexander Hamilton. The system of public credit exploited by Walpole had certain social consequences (the elevation of a new class of paper-money men), which were loudly criticized by Bolingbroke and the republican opposition. But for Walpole public credit was not an instrument for changing society; it was merely a means of raising revenue. Hamilton, however, saw that public credit could be used to transform the social and political order of the United States from a decentralized federation of states with a hedged-in central government into a virtually unitary state with a strong central government able to establish its own glory in the world of nations.

"Hamilton's audacious mission in life," writes McDonald, "was to remake American society in accordance with his own values." Hamilton observed that "what distinguished the industrious minority from other Americans was that they measured worth and achievement in terms of money and worked to obtain money." To transform society "all that needed to be done was to monetize the whole—to rig the rules of the game so that money would be the universal measure of the value of things. For money is oblivious to class, status, color, and inherited social position; money is the ultimate, neutral, impersonal arbiter. Infused into an oligarchical, agrarian social order, money would be the leaven, the fermenting yeast, that would stimulate growth, change, prosperity, and national strength."[26]

This vision of the total commercialization of life and the subversion of a genuine federal order of states into a unitary state was vigorously opposed by Jeffersonian republicans with many of the same arguments that Bolingbroke and the English republicans had used against Walpole. Jeffersonian republicanism, especially strong in the southern states, more or less dominated the central government until the eve of the war of 1861–1865. Faced with an aggressive northern industrial regime bent on consolidating more power in the central government for its own interests and creating what amounted to a unitary state under its control, eleven contiguous southern states seceded in order to preserve a Jeffersonian republican order of decentralized federalism—the same sort of order that, in their view, had prompted secession from Britain in the first place. Hamiltonianism was Walpole writ large and transmuted into a philosophical doctrine. The complete Hamiltonization of American society would not be accomplished without resistance and war and would not be firmly rooted until the late nineteenth century.[27]

Hume understood quite well the economic benefits to commerce from the use of public credit. When he said that public credit would destroy the nation if the nation did not destroy it first, he did not mean that the debt could not be managed and that the nation would necessarily go bankrupt. He knew that the debt could be monetized and new taxes discovered and that both would spur industry. As McDonald has said of Hamilton's system, "The incentive to industry is powerful indeed when the choice is between paying one's debts and failure to survive."[28] What Hume found objectionable in the system was that these benefits were entirely outweighed by a transformation of "the body politic" that was *morally* unacceptable.

First, "national debts cause a mighty confluence of people and riches to the capital, by the great sums, levied in the provinces to pay the interest" and by "the advantages in trade . . . which they give the merchants in the capital above the rest of the kingdom" (*E,* 354). Second, a state that had mortgaged its revenues would have to "invent new ones." The new taxes would first fall on consumption leading to "vexation and ruin of the poor" (*E,* 356). Once these were mortgaged, taxes must fall on property, and the "proprietors of land" would become "stewards of the public," resulting in a more difficult life for their tenants. Third, with the impoverishment of the landed gentry and nobility, a traditional order rooted in land and place would collapse in favor of rule by a new rootless class of men, the "stockjobbers." "These are men, who have no connexions with the state, who can enjoy their revenue in any part of the globe in which they chuse to reside, who will naturally bury themselves in the capital or in great cities, and who will sink into the lethargy of a stupid and pampered luxury, without spirit, ambition, or enjoyment. Adieu to all ideas of nobility, gentry, and family" (*E,* 357–58).

As a moral sentiment theorist, Hume naturally valued strong social orders rooted in family traditions and place, for it is in these that moral sentiments first take root and flourish—though that is not the end of the matter, since cultivation in the larger scene of civil society is also necessary. Hume took pride in his own family and assisted his kinsman Alexander Home, who was doing research on the family, to be included in Robert Douglas's *Peerage of Scotland* (1764). Hume contrasted this *pietas* with the rootless commercial men of London: "I am not of the opinion of some, that these matters are altogether to be slighted. Though we should pretend to be wiser than our ancestors, yet it is arrogant to pretend that we are wiser than the other nations of Europe, who, all of them, *except perhaps the English,* make great account of their family descent. I doubt that our morals have not much improved since we began to think riches the sole thing worth regarding" (*L,* 1: 276; italics mine).

Since the national stocks can be traded instantly and are in a fluctuating state, they can scarcely hold together "three generations from father to son," and even if they remain in one family, "they convey no hereditary authority or credit." The result must be the destruction of those independent social authorities that are the work of a general providence and create a buffer between the individual and the centralized state. These "form a kind of *independent magistracy* in a state, instituted by the hand of nature" (italics mine). With their destruction, a federative style of polity disappears, to be replaced by a Hobbesian style in which "every man in authority derives his influence from the commission alone of the sovereign." The polity is now an aggregate of individuals. The militia disappears along with the social order in which it was rooted. The sovereign office takes command of a "mercenary" standing army. Independent social orders having been destroyed, "no expedient at all remains for resisting tyranny: Elections are swayed by bribery and corruption alone: And the middle power between king and people being totally removed, a grievous despotism must infallibly prevail. The landholders, despised for their poverty, and hated for their oppressions, will be utterly unable to make any opposition to it" (*E,* 358). This constitutional collapse would issue in something new, a centralized modern state commanding an aggregate of deracinated individuals, and consequently in "a degree of despotism, which no oriental monarchy has ever yet attained" (*E,* 359).

The engine driving the steady increase of the public debt was war. Hume supported a policy of limited intervention in Europe as Britain's duty in maintaining the balance of power against the threat of universal monarchy posed at one time by Spain and, early in his career, by France. In such an emergency a dose of public credit would be necessary. But after his stay in France in the 1760s, Hume no longer thought France harbored ambitions of universal monarchy. Britain herself had become the problem, pursuing wars of national glory and honor such as the Seven Years' War designed by Pitt to make the British blue-water mercantile system supreme. Hume described it as "that horrible, destructive, ruinous War; more pernicious to the Victors than to the Vanquished" (*NHL*, 235). Financing it had brought the debt close to the point that Hume thought would ruin the constitutional order. Seeking new taxes, the government viewed the colonies as a standing reserve of revenue to pay for an expanding empire. They resisted, and Hume lived to witness over a year of war with the Americans, and saw the debt rise even higher. It would nearly double by the end of the conflict.[29]

The dreaded concentration of power and the consequent destruction of independent provincial and social orders that Hume had predicted would follow from an ever-expanding public debt (see "Of Public Credit" [1752]) was beginning to come to pass in the last year of his life. He used the occasion of revising his *History* to leave a final warning to his countrymen: "It will be found in the present year, 1776, that all the revenues of this island north of Trent and west of Reading, are mortgaged or anticipated for ever. Could the small remainder be in a worse condition, were those provinces seized by Austria or Prussia? There is only this difference, that some event might happen in Europe which would oblige these great monarchs to disgorge their acquisitions. But no imagination can figure a situation which will induce our creditors to relinquish their claims, or the public to seize their revenues" (*H*, 4: 373 n). In 1752 he had imagined (as Bolingbroke had) that a "patriotic" government might have the courage to declare a bankruptcy, but by 1776 this was no longer possible. The new breed of monied men had become the government.

Here again is to be found Hume's solicitude for the provinces as real *places* where families have roots and are the soil of the moral life as opposed to the rootless and mobile creditors of the public debt working out of London or some other capital. The government itself is presented as virtually a foreign conqueror of the provinces, but more terrible because the new masters are not susceptible to the considerations which could induce a foreign monarch to relent. The outline of a new form of tyranny, worse in Hume's view than an oriental despotism, in which "the whole income of every individual in the state must lie entirely at the mercy of the sovereign" was beginning to emerge (*E*, 359).

It has been said that Hume was too pessimistic about public finance and that experience has proved him to be wrong. It is true that states have been able to manage public debts. But what such critics overlook is that the constitutional transformations required for such management have been precisely of the sort that Hume considered morally unacceptable. Hume's criticism of public credit was founded not in a failed understanding of its "economic" benefits, but in a moral judgment about the kind of society its unrestrained use would be likely to produce. That its use would be unrestrained he had no doubt, given the "nature of men and ministers" and the elimination of independent social authorities. His pessimism was deep and is to be found not only in the essay of 1752 but in the letters of the last decade of his life and in his revisions of the *History*. During the trip to Bath taken a few months before his death, John Home records that they talked often "of the state of the nation, which he continually laments," and that he "still maintains, that the national debt must be the ruin of Britain."[30] That history took the path of the consolidated unitary state and the commercialization of society, rather than the one Hume preferred does not mean that the former was inevitable, nor that it was the best. Nor does it mean that Hume's pessimism was unfounded.

Indeed, what he predicted (the emergence of a unitary monetized state; the commercialization of society and law; the destruction of independent social authorities, "the ranks of men, which form a kind of independent magistracy" and "middle power between king and people"; the unthinkable income tax; and the use of public credit to finance spectacular wars) has come to pass. That we have become reconciled to what Hume considered a new form of tyranny merely shows that we no longer value the notions of liberty and authority he defended. Whether we should do so is a moral question to ponder. But the constitutional collapse and destruction of independent social authorities that he predicted came first not in Britain but in France, bringing with it a despotism worse than any Europe had known, as well as a precedent for a new kind of state and a new kind of war.

The same tendency to consolidate power at the center that threatened the traditional social orders of Britain threatened also the traditional social and political orders in America. As Hume had noted early in his career, the colonies, under their charters, had been virtually self-governing polities. They had consented to have their trade regulated for the sake of the mother country, but after the Stamp Act they were to be treated as a standing source of revenue for the project of a consolidated empire. This was an innovation and an encroachment on their traditional liberties for no reason other than that of consolidating power, and they resisted (as Hume explained in the *Treatise* could lawfully be done) by refusing to pay taxes and, when that did not succeed, by the defensive and conservative act of secession.

Retrospectively, we can see that Britain was making the first moves toward becoming a modern consolidated Leviathan. In their arguments with the colonists, the British stressed again and again the doctrine that sovereignty is unitary, indivisible, and irresistible. In their response the Americans invoked a premodern idiom of resistance of just the sort that had been theorized by Althusius and Hume. This has been obscured by exaggerating the language of natural rights used by the colonists. Resistance was not by an aggregate of individuals invoking their natural rights (that would be a post–Civil War doctrine for late-nineteenth-century and twentieth-century American nationalists after the destruction of a federative polity in favor of a unitary state) but by social and political orders seeking to preserve an inheritance and way of life against encroachment. It was not individuals who seceded but thirteen distinct corporate entities (Virginia, New York, etc.), which had for over a century enjoyed the experience of self-government in what they considered to be a federative British polity of the sort that Hume had stylized "free government" as distinct from "absolute" or "arbitrary" government. In government of this sort with strong social authorities, resistance, as Hume said, was to be expected more frequently. And in the special case of the colonies, which were separated from the center of authority by an ocean, it naturally took the form of secession.

CHAPTER FOURTEEN

The Right of Resistance: Secession and the Modern State

What Secession Is

Hume's early support of the secession of the colonies put him at odds not only with his friends and public opinion in Britain but also with modern political philosophy. The great modern philosophers—Hobbes, Locke, Rousseau, Hegel, Mill, Marx—have been utterly silent on the question of whether it is ever morally legitimate for a people to secede from an established polity. The same is true of contemporary political philosophers. There is only one book in English by a philosopher on the morality of secession (Allen Buchanan, *Secession: The Morality of Political Divorce from Fort Sumter to Lithuania and Quebec,* [Boulder, CO and Oxford: Westview Press, 1991]). *The Philosopher's Index,* which includes references to all the articles in philosophy written in English, French, German, Italian, and Spanish from 1940 until today, lists only seven articles on the topic of secession, all of which were published after 1991. Two are on the secession of Quebec, and the others are responses to Buchanan's book. Economists, political scientists, and international jurists have had to consider secession because the idea is constantly encountered in the contemporary world. Among philosophers, however, secession is surely the most undertheorized concept in the repertoire of modern political philosophy.

Nor is this entirely surprising, for modern political philosophy has been very much engaged in theorizing and legitimating the modern unitary state. Marx was perhaps more correct than he knew in saying that Hobbes was the father of us all, for in Hobbes we have the clearest statement of the logic of the modern state. This is a state theorized out of individuals who in a state of nature contract with each other to submit to the indivisible, infallible, and irresistible will of a sovereign office.

The contract, once made, is irrevocable: a political marriage from which there is no divorce. This is as true for a "libertarian" such as Locke as it is for an "authoritarian" such as Hobbes. Though Locke allows revolution, secession is excluded. Modern sovereignty is one and indivisible and is internal to territory which is, consequently, also indivisible. Indeed, Locke does not even allow the right to freely exit. Once explicit consent is given, a citizen is forever bound to the state and cannot emigrate, much less take territory with him. Though Locke might have sympathized with the colonists' demands for representation, he could not, to be consistent with his theory of the state, have allowed secession any more than George III could.[1]

The term *secession* itself, as we understand it, is of recent origin. Prior to the nineteenth century it could be used to describe any act of withdrawal. The soul could be said to secede from the body, and one could secede from the drawing room to the library. Samuel Johnson limited the meaning to withdrawal of any human fellowship. But for us the term has exclusively political connotations, and these were worked out in an American context from 1790 to 1861 in the debate over whether an American state could legally secede from the Union. To say that a state could not secede was to think of the Union as a unitary state; to say that a state could secede was to think of the Union as a federative polity of sovereign States granting only enumerated powers to a central government. The same question is becoming a pressing one for the European Union today, and indeed for many states, especially after the peaceful secession of fifteen republics from the former Soviet Union. But although the question of whether secession is ever morally or legally justified is for us an intelligible one and, moreover, one which demands an answer in international law, it would have been unintelligible in the eighteenth century. It would have been like asking whether withdrawal is ever morally or legally justified. Secession does not appear as a uniquely political concept until the idea of the modern state is established, and then it becomes a conundrum, because the idea of the modern state contains an ethic of self-government (which may easily lead to a demand for secession) *and* a prohibition against secession—for a modern state is one and indivisible.

Hume did not work out a theory of secession, but his theory of the state as a federative polity of great social orders united and operating by concurrence, not majority will, and capable of frequent resistance to encroachment is logically compatible with secession, whereas secession is logically unthinkable in the framework of the modern state. It should not be surprising then that Hume entertained secession for the colonies as early as 1768, considerably before they were prepared to take that step.

The ubiquity of the theory of the modern state means not only that secession will be undertheorized but that any surviving premodern forms of political association cannot be recognized as political entities. Consequently, an act of secession will be systematically misdescribed as something that it is not by one whose vision of political reality is determined by the lens of the modern state. Nowhere is this more evident than in the confusion of *secession* with the terms *revolution* and *civil war.*

Three conceptions of revolution have dominated in modern political speech. The first is the Whig model that springs from the Glorious Revolution of 1688. This is revolution as restoration, and its image is the turning of a wheel. According to eighteenth-century Whiggism, the Glorious Revolution was a bloodless restoration of a liberty-loving Protestant regime that countered the attempted usurpation by the Catholic James II. The second is Lockean revolution. Here the majority of a sovereign people recall the powers they have delegated to a government that has violated its trust in protecting life, liberty, and property. The government is overthrown, and a new one instituted. The third form is Jacobin revolution. This is not Whiggish or Lockean revolution for the sake of preserving anything; rather, it is an attempt to subvert and to totally transform an entire social and political order in accord with an egalitarian philosophical theory. Whiggism and Lockean revolution leave the social order intact, whereas Jacobin revolution aims at a root-and-branch transformation. Marxist revolution is Jacobin revolution, as are many other forms of contemporary political criticism. Many forms of feminism, for instance, are not interested merely in reform for women but in the total transformation of the social and political order. Feminism so conceived is a form of Jacobin revolution.

Secession is quite distinct from these three conceptions of revolution. All presuppose the theory of sovereignty internal to the modern state and the absolute prohibition against dismembering its territory. Secession is not Whiggish revolution in the sense of the Glorious Revolution, because it is not the restoration of anything within the bounds of a modern state. It is the territorial dismemberment of a modern state in the name of self-government. Nor is it Lockean revolution. A seceding people need not claim that a government has violated its trust. And even if the claim is made, there is no attempt to overthrow the government and replace it with a better one. A seceding people merely wish to be left alone to govern themselves as they see fit. Finally, secession is not Jacobin revolution, because it does not seek a total transformation of the social and political order. Indeed, a seceding people typically seeks to preserve its social order through secession and self-government.

Revolution then is categorically distinct from secession. Revolution presupposes the integrity of the modern state and operates within that conceptual framework. Secession presupposes the premodern idiom of a federated polity. It does not accept the inviolability of the modern state and is prepared to dismember it. Revolution and secession proceed from entirely different conceptions of political reality.

If this is correct, then the so-called American Revolution was not a revolution in any of the senses mentioned above. It was certainly not Jacobin revolution, because it aimed to preserve the social order and most of the political order: the governing colonial classes that had ruled before secession would continue to rule afterwards. Nor was it Whiggish revolution. There were, to be sure, Whiggish themes from the ideology of 1688 about preserving the rights of Englishmen in America, and there were Lockean themes about self-government. But the colonists were not, in Whiggish fashion, seeking to restore anything within the British state; they sought to dismember that state and govern themselves. Nor, in Lockean fashion, were they attempting to overthrow a regime that had violated its trust. Commons, Lords, and Crown were to remain exactly as before. Indeed, many of the colonial leaders, such as Adams and Hamilton, greatly admired the British constitution and government, and sought to imitate its best features. They wished simply to limit its jurisdiction over the territory they occupied. This of course was a serious matter, but it was not revolution, and the moral considerations that would justify it are distinct from those required to justify revolution in any of the three senses mentioned above.

When Parliament looked at what the colonists were doing, they saw what the theory of the modern state determined that they would see: treason and subjects in rebellion. In short, they thought of the British polity as having the form of a unitary modern state, even though this form had not yet clearly emerged. Hume viewed the same polity as premodern and federated. He saw not treason but legitimate secession. Given their different philosophical presuppositions, Hume and Parliament perceived quite different realities.

Neither is secession to be confused with civil war. The primal scene described by this term is the English Civil War: a battle between two factions within a unitary state for the control of its government. To describe the conflict arising from an act of secession as a civil war begs every important moral question on behalf of the unitary modern state; it necessarily paints the seceding side with the brush of treason and hides from view whatever moral considerations may have legitimated secession. Next to the English case, the most famous use of the term *civil war* is that which describes the violent conflict in America from 1861 to 1865. But that conflict was not a civil war. Two factions were not fighting for control of the same government in a unitary state. It was a war of secession in which eleven contiguous American states in acts legally ratified by conventions of the people (the same conventions that authorized entrance into the union) withdrew from a federation of states to form a union of their own.[2]

The American case is especially interesting because it exhibits a clear contest between premodern and modern paradigms of political order and the conceptual confusions that result from not distinguishing the two. The secession of the American colonies from a would-be modern British state, the formation of Articles of Confederation, and later the formation of a central government to which the states had delegated only enumerated powers were acts in a premodern idiom. None of this was carried out by an aggregate of individuals contracting out of a state of nature to form a unitary state, but by historic social and political societies defending their prescriptive rights and acting in accord with their prescriptive duties. When Hume said that he was an "American" in his principles and wished "that we would let them alone to govern or misgovern themselves as they see fit," he was speaking in such an idiom and saying no more than that the conditions for resistance laid out in the *Treatise* had been satisfied, albeit, in this case, in the peculiar form of secession. In saying this he also put into language, perhaps for the first time, an ideology of "Americanism" cast in the premodern idiom of the corporate liberty of self-governing communities which still survives, although it contrasts sharply with another ideology of Americanism that emerged after the war of 1861–1865, which was rooted in the post–French Revolution idiom of the modern state and was expressed in terms of the radical individualism of natural rights. But more on this later.

What seceded from Britain (and was eventually recognized by the Crown and the world) was not a unitary state ruling over an aggregate of individuals but thirteen distinct sovereign states.[3] Each of these assumed the form of a modern state, but the central government they formed was not itself a modern state. It was an office to which the states, each acting in its corporate capacity and with no power to bind another state, had delegated only enumerated powers, reserving all other powers to themselves. To delegate powers is not to delegate sovereignty. Washington was not commonly described as the capital of a nation until after the war of 1861–1865. Prior to that, it was generally thought of as the "seat" of the central government, roughly in the way that Brussels and New York are the seats, respectively, of the European Union and the United Nations.

So the constitution authorized by the states in 1789 was a strange creature: a premodern federation of modern states authorizing the formation of a central government having only enumerated powers. Since each state thought of itself as sovereign, ease of entrance legitimated ease of exit. And, as I argued in the last chapter, secession was widely considered a lawful form of resistance available to an American state until after 1865.

Those such as Hamilton and Wilson who had wanted a unitary state on the model of the emerging modern British state and who were soundly defeated at the Constitutional Convention had rallied after the Constitution was ratified and began using the patronage of the central government to increase its power. Hamilton knew the Constitution he had received was a compact between states creating a central government having only enumerated powers, and he described it as a "frail and worthless fabric."[4] As finance minister, he sought to monetize the public debt and create a national bank, thereby generating a source of patronage in the central government. But this was only the first step in his long-term revolutionary goal of transforming a federation of states into a powerful unitary state. For Hamilton it was not enough to maintain an armed peace; a nation ought "to establish its reputation and glory,"[5] and this meant a consolidated state and a powerful military force with which to carve out a figure in the world of modern states. Opposed to this vision were Jeffersonian republicans, who defended the premodern federative style of polity rooted in respect for localism and the sovereignty of the states. We may say that the Jeffersonian vision was that America should be a kind of Switzerland writ large. Hamilton's vision was that it should be Britain writ large. Indeed, the Swiss Constitution of 1848 was written with the American Constitution in mind, conceived as a genuine federative polity endowed with the authority of state interposition. For seventy years American politics was a struggle between the Jeffersonian and Hamiltonian visions, until in 1861 Jefferson's beloved state of Virginia and ten other contiguous American states, alarmed by the growth of power in the central government, and armed with Jeffersonian constitutional arguments, recalled those powers they had delegated to the central government and seceded from the federation to form a union which could more perfectly preserve what they considered to be the original federal principles of the Constitution and which they considered to be morally superior to consolidation in a unitary state of continental scale.[6]

Lincoln gave in his first inaugural address the following reason for making war on the seceding states: "I hold that, in consideration of universal law and of the Constitution, the Union of these States is perpetual. Perpetuity is implied, if not expressed, in the fundamental law of all national governments. It is safe to assert that no government proper ever had a provision in its organic law for its own termination."[7] Lincoln's argument assumes that the American federation of states is a unitary state grounded in original contract theory. The theory runs as follows. In breaking with Britain, the people of the former colonies descended into a state of nature, becoming an aggregate of individuals. These individuals contracted with each other to form a central government, which in turn authorized the formation of states as administrative units of the general will. As with all original contract theory, once in a polity, there is no lawful exit. Secession from a modern state is not a contingently discernible good or evil but a conceptual impossibility.

Hume exploded all forms of original contract theory: No polity is or could be formed by a contract among individuals. A polity is a deep structure, like a natural language, spontaneously coordinating the work of many generations in a unity that no one intended or could have intended. A polity, so conceived, is the work of a general providence. But a federation of polities is the work of men and is founded on nothing but compact. And such was the American federation: the political societies of Massachusetts, Virginia, and the other former colonies continued to exist after seceding from Britain; each asserted its sovereignty, and each authorized the Constitution for itself with no authority to bind another state. Lincoln's theory that the American Constitution was authorized by the American people in the aggregate and not by the states acting in their corporate capacity is, despite the pious deference given to it, an American Whiggish absurdity as spectacular as any Whig myth Hume undertook to refute.[8]

Original contract theory is a corrupt form of the philosophical act: a fragment of experience (contractual relations) is spiritualized into the whole, thereby concealing real differentiations in common life. Lincoln was not preserving a modern unitary state from the anarchy of secession, as he said he was, for he had inherited no such state. Rather he was engaged in a latter-day episode of the revolutionary Hamiltonian act of transforming a federation of states into a modern unitary state. Nor was he alone in this, for he lived in an age of unabashed imperialism and consolidationism. Bismark in Germany, Garibaldi in Italy, and

Lenin in Russia attempted to forge modern unitary states by stamping out powerful, independent social and political orders, leaving in their wake millions of socially deracinated individuals to be gathered up into tighter consolidations later by Hitler, Mussolini, and Stalin. And the process of consolidating power at the center has continued throughout the world.

The dominion of the modern unitary state, especially in its form as liberal representative democracy, has led some to think that it is the final form of political association and that with its establishment, political history has come to an end. Politics henceforth will be an engagement carried out within the scene of the modern liberal state.[9] Is this an insight into the nature of political reality, or just another philosophic superstition? A Humean must plead the privilege of a skeptic, but it is worthwhile observing that the premodern idiom of the state as a federative polity has not been defeated and that resistance to the modern unitary state in the form of secession and devolution movements ranging in demand from increased autonomy to state sovereignty is a pressing problem throughout the world.

It has been estimated that not more than twenty-five members of the United Nations are free of secessionist and territorial disputes. An adequate political language for recognizing the moral merit of these pressures has not yet emerged, though international jurists have been compelled to try to frame one.[10] We still describe as revolution and civil war (begging every important moral question on behalf of the modern unitary state) what in fact are often legitimate acts of secession and self-determination. There was, however, no American Revolution, but the secession of thirteen self-proclaimed states, each refusing to be a source of revenue for a would-be unitary British state. There was no American Civil War, but a war to coerce eleven contiguous American states into a union only seventy years old in which secession had been considered by prominent leaders in every section as an option available to an American state. Moreover, it was a union which had swollen to some ten times its size in only fifty years and was racked by the instability and the clash of vital interests that necessarily attends the rapid shifting of majorities and minorities arising from the inclusion of new states by a simple majority of the legislature. There was no Nigerian civil war (1967–1970), but a war supported by Western powers to coerce the industrious Biafrans into a union merely seven years old which was nothing more than an artifact of the British empire and whose constitution had been disputed from the first.

There are, of course, both moral and legal difficulties with secession, but this is not the place to raise the question of when secession is morally justified. The point here is simply that philosophers have been strangely silent on the question. And perhaps enough has been said to question the reigning presumption that political consolidation into a unitary state is necessarily a good thing and secession necessarily a bad thing. The premodern conception of polity as federative is not absurd; though modified by time and circumstances, its voice can still be heard, and much of it is to be found in Hume. It is a view of polity that forms a strong presumption on behalf of natural social orders and smaller political units against ritualistic consolidation for the sake of material prosperity, human rights, a classless society, or whatever the consolidating ideology of individual rights or equality might be.

In his defense of the right of resistance to consolidation, Hume constructed an image that counters what might be called the centripetal model of the modern state: "As matter wou'd have been created in vain, were it derpriv'd of a power of resistance, without which no part of it cou'd preserve a distinct existence, and the whole might be crowded up into a single point: So 'tis a gross absurdity to suppose, in any government, a right without a remedy, or allow, that the supreme power is shar'd with the people, without allowing, that 'tis lawful for them to defend their share against every invader" (*T,* 564). As I have argued, the unit of resistance Hume has in mind is a *social order* "maintaining its antient bounds," not individuals asserting their natural rights. As consolidation by the modern state progressively tightens its grip, Hume suggests that divine providence has decreed that centrifugal forces will appear and must be taken seriously. Social life in the symbiotic shape of families, provinces, and regions, informed by natural languages, religion, and genuine national identities, is the work of a general providence. To labor so that "the whole might be crowded up into a single point" is to reenact the hubristic project of the tower of Babel.

The deep philosophical conflict underlying the contrary unitary and federative images of political reality is to be found in debates over the European Union. This, like most "unions" in the modern world (the United Kingdom, the United States, the former Union of Soviet Socialist Republics), was formed for the sake of economic prosperity and security and was entered into as a federative polity. There are those who view it this way, but there are others who, understandably, cannot but see it as a modern superstate or at least a modern superstate in the making (as Hamilton and Lincoln viewed the American federation). For them the powers delegated by the states to the central authority range over individuals in the aggregate and cannot be recalled by the states.

Once in, a state may not secede. This is far removed from Hume's vision of macropolitical order for Europe, which was a confederation with the right of secession. The compact formed by the American states in 1789 was one from which it was assumed that a state could secede, though the right of secession was not explicitly written into the Constitution itself. In like manner, the European Union has avoided confronting the question of secession. But a Humean voice can be heard in the argument of the Nobel laureate James Buchanan, who has urged that the constitution of the European Union include an explicit right of a member state to secede.[11] To those whose souls are attuned to federative polity, this suggestion will appear as a means of preserving liberty. To the devotee of the modern unitary state, however, it must appear (as it did to George III and to Lincoln in two different American contexts when confronted by secession) as an invitation to anarchy.

The Organic Theory of the State

Hume was well aware of the modern theory of sovereignty and confronted it directly. But the career of the theory that the state is an organic whole, though intimated in Hume's time, did not take off until the French Revolution and is largely a nineteenth- and twentieth-century affair. It is necessary to examine it, if only briefly, in a study of Hume's conception of philosophy, not only because it has been a powerful instrument for legitimating the consolidated modern state which Hume opposed but because it has been a powerful stimulus to the growth of an ideological style of politics which Hume considered to be the poison of modern society and to which he gave considerable attention.

The image of the state as organic is ancient, having roots in the Bible and in Plato, but in its modern form, it begins with Rousseau's theory of the General Will. The organic theory of the state presupposes the modern theory of sovereignty: There must be lodged somewhere a single will to regulate the affairs of men. For Rousseau this is not God's will as expressed through Church tradition, nor the will of Hobbes's ruler, but the will of the people themselves. The General Will (like all candidates for the sovereign will in the modern theory) is indivisible, irresistible, and infallible. Rousseau did not identify it with the empirical will of the people as registered in a vote, even one that is unanimous, because the empirical will can be mistaken. But he was never able to make clear how the General Will was to be recognized.[12] That there had to be such a will he had no doubt, because he accepted the modern theory of sovereignty. That it must somehow be lodged in the people he had no doubt, because he was a republican. Rousseau warded off criticism by simply announcing that all his ideas were consistent, but he could not present them all at once (the sort of thing Hume called his quackery). Whether consistent or not, the idea of the General Will would prove to be a potent one in the emerging democratic age, and the new vulgar philosophers as well as those of stature would exploit it.

Hegel provided a solution to the problem of the General Will. He theorized an ideal will immanent in a people and struggling to actualize itself. For Hegel the consciousness implicitly animating all consciousness is the philosophical act seeking a comprehensive self-determining experience. Thus the will animating the General Will is a philosophical will seeking dominion. History retrospectively ratifies the work of "world historical individuals" who knew what reason demanded in the circumstances even though it was comprehended by only a few and even resisted by many.

Hegel's theory may have been influenced by his experience of the French Revolution under a Rousseauistic understanding of it, and the modern state that emerged from the French Revolution certainly admits of a Hegelian reading. Some of the creators of this state had Rousseau's General Will in mind, and it has been used by others to legitimate later imitations of that state. Aside from Marx and Marxists, Rousseau was the only Western philosopher celebrated in the Cultural Revolution of Mao's China. It is doubtful that any of this would have been acceptable to Rousseau, whose political thought, like Hume's, was strongly premodern. He confines the General Will to a small polity with direct legislation by the people, and he considered the General Will impossible under conditions of representative democracy, even in a small polity.[13] What would he have said about a consolidated modern state comprehending tens and even hundreds of millions of people managed by a few hundred "representatives"? But ideas have consequences and outrun the management of their authors.

Prior to the French Revolution, what had constituted the unity of the people occupying the territory known as France was neither a common language, nor a common religion, nor a common culture, but simply allegiance to a common monarch. The many titles attending the monarch were not the result of vanity so much as an acknowledgment of the distinct peoples and corporate bodies that constituted the state. The "absolute monarchy" of France was a highly decentralized mosaic of powerful social orders whose titles were as good as that of the monarch and were internal to the same order. Each order was jealous of its liberty and had an interest in limiting monarchy and the growth of the central authority. But the Revolution sought not merely to limit monarchy but to sweep it away. And with it went all the great historic social orders of France: Church, Nobility, the Provinces, Parlements, the States General. There remained now only the "people" in the aggregate inhabiting a certain territory.

By what new principle could this aggregate be held together? The unifying principle had been the person of the monarch. This was now replaced by the personification of the nation. As the monarch had had a will, so now the "nation" could have a will. It would be through the person of France that Rousseau's General Will would speak. And as Hegel saw, it would be a *philosophical* speech, for the French "nation" was now endowed with a mission: to realize the philosophical principle of the rights of man. All the resources and all the people of the territory known as France could now be viewed as standing reserves for the actualization of this philosophical *telos.* The French Revolution introduced the first *philosophical nationalism.* Hume had taught that the unity of religion and philosophy in Christendom had produced a dynamic and virulent mixture, uniting religious fear with the philosophical impetus to dominion in the form of an aggressive and obsessive political theology. But a corrupt form of the philosophical act may seize on anything in common life as the object of its obsession and as the vehicle for its act of self-determination. In the case of the French Revolution, the notion of "nation" was captured and spiritualized by an act of philosophical alchemy into a philosophical mission seeking dominion.

Hume had seen something like this in the form of a totalizing Puritan revolution. The people and resources of England were conceived as instruments for perfecting and spreading the Puritan faith. But the nationality of England was pushed to the background of attention. The voice to be heard was that of God, not the English nation. There was perhaps a hint of what was to come in the Whiggish identification of philosophical conceptions of liberty (the contract theory and natural rights) with the "rights of Englishmen" ("those foolish English Prejudices, which all Nations and all Ages disavow," [*L,* 2: 216]). But this nationalism never quite took the full form of the philosophical act and was not (except in the case of a few radicals such as Price) spiritualized as the rights of man. Pitt's eloquent identification of liberty with English character and power, though possessing a philosophical component, appeared more chauvinistic than rationalistic or universalistic.

Hume had no notion of the national*isms* that were to come. His idea of "nation" was framed in the essay "Of National Characters." National character has no ideological structure and is of a piece with moral character: a set of dispositions, beliefs, and sentiments that form a pattern of conduct and a way of life. A national character is a flow of sympathy, a spontaneous growth, the work of many generations communicated by memory, affection, and emulation. It is a major constituent of common life and so is the work of a general providence, not the work of philosophical reflection. A national character is something inherited and to be enjoyed; its temporal reference is to past and present. It thinks of the future only when threatened and then out of anxiety to preserve itself from extinction. A national character is not about anything; it is not the unfolding of anything, and it has no mission. It is like a style of architecture to be judged by its aesthetic and practical merits. And it is also like a style of moral character to be evaluated in terms of its virtues and vices.

National character so conceived undergoes corruption when spiritualized by a corrupt form of the philosophical act and emerges as something incoherent: the parochial bearer of a rigid and implacable philosophical ideal. What had been the work of a general providence is now transmuted into a philosophic superstition. One of the first to understand the nature of this new and unexpected corruption of a part of common life by the philosophical act was Lord Acton. Writing in the mid-nineteenth century, Acton discerned three dominant ideologies: liberalism, socialism, and nationalism. Of these he argued that nationalism would have the most promising future. Liberalism and socialism are Enlightenment ideologies, the one being the inverted mirror image of the other. As acts of philosophical reflection, they are too abstract to be a source of human conduct. To gain purchase in the world, the philosophical act must attach itself to and transmute some part of common life into its own shape and interest. History has proved that Acton was right. All liberalisms have appeared as nationalisms, and all socialisms have been national socialisms.[14]

At first glance the "nation" appears an unlikely vehicle for a universalist philosophical *telos* because of its parochial character. But, as Hume taught, the imagination can unite what is conceptually incompatible. The prejudice and piety internal to genuine national character are dynamic qualities that can be and have been put to the service of a universalist ideology (as when, in a period of crisis, Stalin was able to invoke Holy Mother Russia to prop up the universalist Soviet regime threatened by German national socialists carrying out their own universalist project). But at the same time, this universalism (whether in its liberal or socialist forms) is at war with all genuine national character and has been a powerful force in destroying or suppressing the actual national characters that spontaneously arise in the world, while perversely acting in the name of nationality.

What emerged in Europe in the nineteenth century was not merely an order of Humean extensive republics, as John Stewart has correctly said was intimated in Hume's political writings, but an order of highly centralized philosophical nationalisms entirely at odds with the idiom and tone of Hume's political philosophy. There was now opened up a vast and unprecedented space in which the philosophical act could display itself in politics, and in which the new vulgar philosophers could throw up in "violence and hurry" those "unshapely" parties of metaphysical principle which Hume thought were unique to, and the bane of, the modern era. Misplaced national affection corrupted by a philosophical *telos* and at the command of a modern state controlling the total resources and people of a territory would be a virulent mixture indeed. The office of government could now be seen as an agent endowed with a mission in the world. The ideological wars fought by such leviathans would be spectacular barbarisms, but harmful also would be the effect of an ideological style of politics on the inherited moral traditions and ways of life of a polity.

For Hume these traditions are a communication of sympathy which constitute the moral core of society. The task of "free government" is to preserve them, to allow their cultivation, and to render their communication in society as harmonious as possible. A Humean free government is ordered by a fundamental rule of law, a set of procedures whose only purpose is to maintain the peaceful and harmonious arrangements of civil association. It is not a vast corporation with the mission of establishing in the world the philosophical ideal of the natural rights of individuals, or an egalitarian society, or a new universal order of some kind certified by the philosophical act. Nor is it a corporation in which the people and resources of a territory are marshaled for the pursuit of material prosperity. It is not a "capitalistic" society or a "consumer" society, nor is it an egalitarian socialist society. Hume explicitly rejected equality as a goal of the state (*EM,* 193–95).

In Oakeshott's terms a Humean free state is *nomocratic* (rule by law), not *teleocratic* (command in order to achieve a substantial goal).[15] The rule of law is a morality, an adverbial restraint on conduct, a set of procedures, not a command to achieve a substantial good. But this does not mean that a Humean free state is a "libertarian" state. Government in Hume's regime can be vigorous. It is not a "night watchman" state designed merely to protect the natural rights of property holders, as important as Hume thought these to be. The protection of private property and an ethic of individualism are internal to the very idea of civil association. But civil society is not itself founded on ahistorical natural rights because, in Hume's view, there are no such rights.

Civil society is itself a substantial moral tradition or way of life that values individual liberty and self-development, and like any other evolving Humean practice, it must be corrected by judgment in the light of the whole of common life. Its virtues, justice (in the special way Hume understands justice), and adherence to the law are artificial not natural virtues and are not to be overrated in their worth. Hume often presents justice as unattractive: "The cautious, jealous virtue of justice" (*EM,* 184). The artificial virtues are parasitic on the natural virtues for their *moral merit.* Antecedent to the artificial system of civil society is the order of natural virtue, which is the primal source of the social bond. From this source flow those inherited moral practices and forms of corporate existence in which moral character is shaped and which, in moral worth, precede justice and the rule of law, and color our interpretation of them.[16]

The doctrine of natural rights is a philosophic superstition because it is a case of the philosophical act seizing upon one aspect of common life (the notion of rights internal to the artificial virtues) and through an act of philosophical alchemy transforming the artificial into the natural. The rights that were necessary for the practice of civil society are spiritualized into the whole of the moral life. The practice of moral virtue (however conceived) as distinguishable from but connected to civil society is entirely obscured or, if it appears, can be seen as a threat to what is now an antinomic doctrine of natural rights. There is more than a nod in this direction in Hobbes, but the complete and clear-eyed transformation of the ethic of civil society into the whole of the moral life is to be found in Kant. Here morality is reduced to respect for the rule of law as such and respect for agency as such, conceived as independent of the excellence of the goals pursued. Virtue is transmuted into the cultivation of just those dispositions necessary to a moral life reduced to universalizing maxims. Kant's moral philosophy is a brilliant exposition of the ethic internal to civil association (the artificial virtues), but it cannot claim to have captured the whole of the moral life. Nor, if Hume is right, has it captured its most important part, for the moral merit of the artificial virtues has its source in the natural virtues. And these are displayed only in inherited moral practices and forms of corporate existence that have a local habitation and a name, and are quite different from civil society, which is a mode of association that can unite strangers and even enemies in the peaceful pursuit of their own ends. These background ways of social life color and give a certain tone and texture to any particular historical manifestation of civil association.

Thus, depending on its inherited moral traditions, a Humean civil society may authorize an established church, or it may be secular in regard to religion; it may be a bustling commercial society as the Netherlands were, or it may be content with a frugal agrarian existence as Switzerland was; it may be puritanical in its laws or hedonistic; it may impose few restraints on freedom of speech, the press, movement of property and persons, or these may be considerably constrained; civil association may flourish in an absolute monarchy or in a republic. All that is necessary for Humean civil association is the establishment of justice, the rule of law, and respect for inherited moral practices.

The Modern State as a Philosophic Superstition

What is incompatible with civil society of any kind is an organic conception of the state spiritualized by an ideological style of politics; for once society takes on the form of the philosophical act, then the substantial moral traditions which are the *sensus communis* presupposed by civil society become the playthings of antinomic philosophical reason. No inherited way of life can satisfy the implacable demands of the philosophical act. Whatever the philosophical ideal may be that is taken to legitimate political society, and however worthy it may appear (whether natural rights or the egalitarian ideal of socialism), no inherited tradition can conform to its demands. Whatever is done, it can always be argued that individual rights have not really been established, or that what are to count as the rights of individuals have been fundamentally misconceived, or that "true equality" has not been achieved. An ideological style of politics is a zero-sum game in which each sect alternately seeks to dominate and to escape the philosophical dominion of the other sect, and in which there is no limit as to what the issues are or in what ontological form they may appear. What had been innocent or even virtuous forms of association are now transmuted into exploitation; what had been shameful is now liberating. And as each expansion of the philosophical ideal encroaches further upon the inherited moral capital, an individual progressively loses the moral knowledge of how to behave.

Oakeshott has given a memorable description of a society in the grip of an ideological style of politics.

> Every moral ideal is potentially an obsession; the pursuit of moral ideals is an idolatry in which particular objects are recognized as 'gods.' This potentiality may be held in check by more profound reflection, by an intellectual grasp of the whole system which gives place and proportion to each moral ideal; but such a grasp is rarely achieved. Too often the excessive pursuit of one ideal leads to the exclusion of others, perhaps all others; in our eagerness to realize justice we come to forget charity, and a passion for righteousness has made many a man hard and merciless. There is, indeed, no ideal the pursuit of which will not lead to disillusion; *chagrin* waits at the end for all who take this path. Every admirable ideal has its opposite, no less admirable. Liberty or order, justice or charity, spontaneity or deliberateness, principle or circumstance, self or others, these are the kinds of dilemma[s] with which this form of the moral life is always confronting us, making us see double by directing our attention always to abstract extremes, none of which is wholly desirable.[17]

Such a society cut loose from inherited modes of conduct by the philosophical act is "on all occasions . . . called upon to seek virtue as the crow flies. It may even be said that the moral life, in this form, demands a hyperoptic moral vision and encourages intense moral emulation among those who enjoy it, the moral eccentric being recognized, not as a vicarious sufferer for the stability of a society, but as a leader and a guide. And the unhappy society, with an ear for every call, certain always about what it ought to *think* (though it will never for long be the same thing), in action shies and plunges like a distracted animal."[18]

False philosophy may be indulged by a moral eccentric such as Diogenes, whose self-display was protected by the common life of Athens. But what can be tolerated in an individual (and what may even be admirable) is fatal if engaged in by society as a whole. Happily, as Hume taught, nature is too strong for principle and hubristic reflection, and in the long run will assert her rights. At that time an ideological style of politics will be ridiculed retrospectively as the absurdity it always was. The long run, however, in which a society and its government are obsessed by a "philosophical enthusiasm," can be quite long. The people of the former Soviet Union endured some seventy years and the countries of eastern Europe some forty years before shaking off the Marxist philosophic superstition.

The unitary state constructed by the French Revolution conceived of itself as the result of philosophical reflection, owing nothing to an inherited and prescriptive *sensus communis.* It was a state dedicated to establishing the rights of man in the world and, along with the United States after the war of 1861–1865, has been a source of inspiration for a certain Jacobin strain of liberalism. It produced the first philosophical nationalism in history and began the hubristic project (imitated by modern states since) of "nation making." This was, among other things, the project of destroying the actual "national characters" (in Hume's sense) in a territory as a means of creating a solidarity for advancing a philosophical *telos.* Through mass public education and other centralizing devices, the modern state has sought to transform Gascons and Normans into Frenchmen, Prussians and Bavarians into Germans, and Florentines and Venetians into Italians. The project, greatly enhanced by the centralizing effects of two world wars, totalitarian revolutions, and the Cold War, has only partially succeeded. Though possessed of total power and even terror, the former Soviet Union was not able to create "socialist man" but has instead devolved power through secession to fifteen sovereign states. Metternich joked that Italy was a geographical expression; something that could be said of many would-be "nation states" today. As late as 1870 a survey of French schools showed that the majority of children could not correctly name France as the *nation* to which they belonged but mentioned instead their province or region. The children had a better grasp of true nationality than the rationalist educators in Paris.[19]

From a Humean perspective the project of "nation making" engaged in by modern states is another instance of a corrupt philosophical consciousness at war with nature. Few of the so-called nation states of Europe contain a genuine national character within their borders. States such as Spain, France, and Britain were the artifacts of monarchy held together only by allegiance to a crown but transmuted by an act of philosophical alchemy after the French Revolution into would-be nation-persons endowed with the philosophic superstition of Rousseau's General Will. But Britain is not a "nation state"; it is a united kingdom with at least four national characters held together by an unwritten constitution. Much the same could be said of most of the "nations" of Europe. As Oakeshott firmly put it, "No European state (let alone an imitation European state elsewhere in the world) has ever come within measurable distance of being a 'nation state.'"[20]

But if a philosophically imposed nationalism is absurd when applied to the boundaries of European polities, it has not seemed so in the case of the United States. America, it is said, is unique in being a nation that created itself out of reflection alone in accord with the philosophical idea of natural rights, and without the distortions of inherited cultures that plagued Europe. It is, in Lincoln's famous words, a polity "dedicated to the proposition that all men are created equal." It is a polity founded on ideas, principles, and ideals that arise from philosophical reflection alone and are deliberately applied to the world. It is said to be a "proposition country" or a "culture of rights." It is not grounded in the exploration and enjoyment of an inherited culture, nor is it a federative order of such cultures held together by the rule of law; it is a unitary state dedicated to establishing a philosophical *telos*.

This popular view has been forcefully stated by Allan Bloom: "America is actually nothing but a great stage on which theories have been played as tragedy and comedy. This is a regime founded by philosophers and their students. All the recalcitrant matter of the historical *is* gave way here before the practical and philosophical *ought to be,* as the raw and natural given of this wild continent meekly submitted to the yoke of theoretical science. Other people were autochthonous, deriving guidance from the gods of their various places. When they too decided to follow the principles we pioneered, they hobbled along awkwardly, unable to extricate themselves gracefully from their pasts."[21]

Here we have Hume's barbarism of refinement and the self-deception that accompanies it projected on a vast scale, and appearing in what is now, unhappily, a familiar form of American ideological arrogance. But there cannot be a philosophical nationalism, because philosophical reflection cut loose from an inherited culture cannot be the source of any belief or conduct at all. One may think that there is such a thing as philosophical nation-making, as Bloom and others do, and one may engage in politics under that description, as did the Jacobins of the French Revolution and the Soviets. But to make the attempt is both self-deceptive and corrupting: self-deceptive because reflection emancipated from tradition is empty or arbitrary, and corrupting because the claim to have done what is impossible always corrupts both those who make the claim and those who submit to it.

The Founders of the American polity were thoughtful men, but they were not Bloomian philosophers constructing a new state entirely out of philosophical reflection. What was most remarkable about them was not their intellectual display (the merit of which has been understandably exaggerated by nationalists) but their inherited moral character. It is rare that those who make a revolution live to govern afterwards. The Founders were men who knew how to conduct themselves with propriety, and they were men of this sort because they had inherited substantial moral and religious traditions from Britain which were transplanted in "places" such as Virginia and Massachusetts Bay, and which they were determined to preserve.

Contrary to Bloom, the Founders were *autochthonous.* They were overwhelmingly the descendants of Englishmen who brought with them not only their general culture but also the specific ideal of becoming *English freeholders.* And this meant that they were eager to originate a *place* and to be known as having come from someplace. By 1787, Virginia had long been spiritualized in song and story, and a Virginia gentleman was a genuine moral substance. George Washington represented the fourth generation of his American family, and he was called the "father" of his country not the "philosopher" of it. The most philosophical of the lot was Jefferson, who sometimes spoke in a rationalist idiom, but judging from his career as a whole, he appears (and wished to appear to posterity) to be more of a Virginia gentleman than a rationalist.[22]

To be sure, the Founders sometimes talked of their "natural rights," but what they usually meant by them was what Englishmen meant when they spoke of the inalienable rights of Englishmen, namely, rights that no truly English character could be deprived of without a fight. The philosophically universalist and antinomic meaning, capable of subverting *all* inherited ways of life, does not appear as a political force until the French Revolution, and it does not appear in America until after the defeat of the Confederacy in 1865 and the attempt to transform what had been a premodern, federative polity into a unitary state based on the model of the French Republic. The birth, after 1865, of a would-be unitary American state is the beginning of that ideological style of politics that Bloom proudly but foolishly celebrates as peculiar to the American regime. As an account of what contemporary American self-understanding has become, Bloom's picture is not far off the mark. The mistake is to have read this character into the constitutional origin.

By *inalienable rights,* the colonists meant concretely the rule of law: a set of procedures for conducting their political business which they had inherited as Englishmen, which were framed in their Charters, and which they had enjoyed in the new context of America for over a century. These rights would vanish if they were incorporated into an increasingly consolidated British state. Their resistance was on behalf of preserving a premodern polity having a self-governing federative structure.

They did not seek to transform the thirteen American polities according to a philosophical *telos* as the French Revolution did. Indeed, they engaged in the most conservative form of resistance possible: mere secession of distinct polities, now called states, each preserving its own inherited social and political order. The two constitutions they formed for themselves (the Articles of Confederation and the Constitution of 1789) were not the constitutions of forward-looking, modern unitary states capable of serving a philosophical *telos* but premodern federative polities designed, in the manner of Althusius, to preserve the symbiotic life of distinct social and political orders. As of 1860 the central government had been free of debt since the 1830s. It did not impose inland taxes, but lived off a tariff on imports and land sales. The philosophical projects favored by Bloom require consolidation, a vast revenue, and vigorous use of public credit. The Founders, however, aimed not at the ideal regime for human beings taken in the abstract (so important to rationalist philosophers such as Bloom) but at a *modus vivendi* in the manner of Humean true political philosophy.

In this their success was only temporary. They failed to make clear the boundary between the authority of the state governments and that of the central government. Nowhere can the incoherence resulting from this failure be seen better than in the spectacular inconsistency displayed in Madison's interpretation of the very constitution he did so much to create. At different times in his career, Madison defended both the view that the central government is sovereign, that it should have a veto power over the states, and the view that sovereignty resides in the states, that the powers of the central government are enumerated and delegated by the states and that the states are the final arbiters of those powers. The inconsistency is stark and has resisted all attempts to reconcile it in the direction of a nationalist interpretation.[23]

Madison has been called the "father" of the Constitution. But we must ask which Constitution, that of a federative polity or that of a unitary state? Madison was the last of the Founders. He died in 1836 with the foreboding that the Union could not last. In only twenty-five years, the American states would be at war with each other. He should not have been surprised, having forcefully argued for constitutional principles which could both legitimate the secession of an American state from the federation and legitimate the use of force by the central government to keep it in the Union against its will. He feared both the horrors of consolidationism (the reason for seceding from Britain in the first place) and the horrors of secession.

Madison aside, however, the premodern, federative style of polity lasted in America until 1861, when eleven southern states seceded, alarmed by the disposition of a northern industrial majority to create a unitary state. The constitution formed by the Confederate States of America sought to correct the ambiguity in the Constitution of 1789 by strengthening the central government in certain respects, but making clear that sovereignty resided in the states as parties to the compact. As in the secession of 1776, the Confederates imagined themselves not as revolutionaries, but as preserving an inherited constitutional order from being consolidated into a would-be unitary state. The Great Seal of the Confederacy bore an equestrian image of George Washington.[24]

Lord Acton is famous for his maxim that power tends to corrupt and that absolute power corrupts absolutely. What is not so well known is that the maxim flows from the idea of a federative polity. Acton considered federalism to be the best form of political association for reconciling the modern ethic of individualism with the independence of substantial moral communities. He thought the greatest threat to this sort of order, in his own time, was the ideology of the modern unitary state, especially in the form of ideological nationalism. Acton greatly admired the constitution of the Confederacy and lamented the South's tragic failure to heed the advice of Robert E. Lee and other Confederate leaders—until it was too late—to free slaves in exchange for military service and citizenship. Of the Confederacy as an exercise in American constitutionalism, he wrote in 1866, "History can show no instance of so great an effort made by Republicans to remedy the faults of that form of government. Had they adopted the means which would have ensured and justified success, had they called on the negroes to be partners with them in the perils of war and in the fruits of victory, I believe that generous resolution would have conferred in all future ages incalculable blessings on the human race."[25]

Acton also thought that the emergence of the new, aggressive, unitary American state would encourage the spread of a French Revolutionary style of philosophical nationalism, with the consequent destruction of those independent social authorities and substantial moral communities that alone give liberty and equality a human face and can exist only in a federative polity: "The cause that was to triumph comes forth from the conflict with renovated strength, and confirmed in the principles which must react dangerously on the other countries of the world. The spurious liberty of the United States is twice cursed, for it deceives those whom it attracts and those whom it repels. By exhibiting the spectacle of a people claiming to be free, but whose love of freedom means hatred of inequality, jealousy of limitations of power, and reliance on the State as an instrument to mould as well as to control society, it calls on its admirers to hate aristocracy and teaches its adversaries to fear the people. The North has used the doctrines of Democracy to destroy self-government. The South applied the principle of conditional federation to cure the evils and to correct the errors of a false interpretation of Democracy."[26]

What Acton refers to as "conditional federation" is a principle of premodern federation, namely, that consent is not a once-and-for-all affair, to be given up after entrance into a political union, but is continuous and can be withdrawn. What Acton admired in the Confederate Constitution was that it was the first constitution to provide the economic and moral benefits of large-scale political integration through a strong central government while preserving the corporate existence of its members through the right to secede. The next large-scale union to provide the right of secession to its members was that created by the Soviet Constitution, Article 17 of which declares that "the right freely to secede from the U.S.S.R. is reserved to every Union Republic." When by 1990 it was clear that the central government of the Soviet Union had failed, a peaceful and orderly secession by referendum was negotiated among the Union Republics. It is remarkable that in the two hundred years from 1790 to 1990, there appear to have been only three cases of successful peaceful secession (Belgium from the Netherlands, 1830; Norway from Sweden, 1905; and Singapore from Malaysia, 1965) but a vast number of consolidations through conquest and annexation, as well as brutal suppressions of attempts at secession. All of this is in sharp contrast to the number of secessions that occurred after 1990 in Europe, the former Soviet Union, and elsewhere.[27]

But though peaceful secession could occur in the last decade of the twentieth century among European states exhausted by eighty years of total wars and totalitarian regimes (forms of violence made possible by the enormous concentration of power in the modern state, which Hume portrayed as a new form of political association worse than an oriental despotism), such generous political conduct was not to be expected in mid-nineteenth-century America. That was very much the age of the modern theory of sovereignty, the theory of the organic state, philosophical nationalisms, industrialization, empire building, and consolidation. Whereas Acton could see the new, would-be unitary American state as a harbinger of bad tidings, other British thinkers such as Mill and Marx could see it as part of an inevitable progress. The editor of the liberal *Spectator* happily declared on 22 December 1866, "The American Revolution marches fast towards its goal—the change of a Federal Commonwealth into a Democratic Republic, one and indivisible. Congress, which only five years ago was little more powerful than a debating club, so weak that no journal in America has ever troubled itself to give either independent or full reports of its debates, has suddenly become the Sovereign power, begins even to be conscious that it is Sovereign."[28]

What has been called the American Civil War is perhaps better described as America's French Revolution. Lord Acton and other British commentators referred to it innocently as "the American Revolution" (conceiving of the break with Britain in 1776 as mere secession), and having in mind the model of the French Revolution: the movement from a premodern federative polity to that of a unitary modern state informed by Rousseau's General Will.[29] But what could be the principle of unity in a republic ruling over a vast aggregate of individuals on a continental scale? It could no longer be negotiations between independent political societies, for with the defeat of the Confederacy, the authority of these societies had been subverted. Unity must now come from an ideology, the source of which would be found in a rhetoric developed by Lincoln, who had transformed the Declaration of Independence from a legal brief presented in a forum of international law to justify the secession and claims to sovereignty of thirteen distinct political societies into a statement of an eschatological mission to establish the doctrine of natural rights throughout the world. What had been an eighteenth-century Whiggish secession to preserve the independent social and political authority of thirteen states was transformed into a mission in the style of the French Revolution to destroy or marginalize any independent social order that posed a threat to the natural rights of the individual. Since the doctrine flowed from reflection alone, independent of the particularities of custom, it was and is antinomic. Consequently, *any* inherited social authority whatsoever can be viewed as a threat to what must be an ever-increasing number of antinomic natural rights. What one proponent of natural rights might see as a restraining reason, another may easily see as a mere prejudice from which emancipation is demanded.

The modern state is for us a historic fate. Its achievement in material prosperity (Hobbes' commodious living) must be fully acknowledged. But the true philosopher will also see in it a spectacular act of philosophical hubris, self-deception, and destruction. Attending it from the first has been an ideological style of politics which has distorted and subverted the politics of a *sensus communis,* which alone (albeit in fragmented forms) gives the modern state whatever stability it has but which is everywhere disowned by corrupt forms of the philosophical act with which it is in constant conflict. The celebration of America as uniquely a nation of philosophers, as a "culture of rights," as a "proposition country" (without drawing Hume's mortifying distinction between true and false philosophy) provides no barrier to the impious political "projector" who can "tamper and play with a government and national constitution, like a quack with a sickly patient" (*E,* 509). The ideological style of politics, internal to the very idea of the modern unitary state, is a barbarism of refinement—but no one in the first philosophic age could fail to feel the power of its seduction.[30]

CHAPTER FIFTEEN

Preserving One's Humanity in the First Philosophic Age

"Be a philosopher; but, amidst all your philosophy, be still a man."

Hume and Vico

The passage from Hume quoted above frames the distinction explored in this study. True philosophy ennobles mankind; false philosophy distorts, corrupts, and dehumanizes. Hume's writings present us with a philosophical bestiary of spiritual forms generated by the undisciplined philosophical act as it promiscuously seizes upon any aspect of human experience as the object of its obsession. They pass before us in review: the philosopher as "strange uncouth monster," as "satyr," "as a cunning man," as a worker in "magic or witchcraft"; the misanthropy of Statilius; "the heroes of philosophy"; the "enraged" Platonist who spreads "horror and devastation on the neighbouring plains"; the torments of "Sisyphus and Tantalus" experienced by "the antient philosophy"; the "perpetual cant of the *Stoics* and *Cynics* concerning *Virtue,*" and their "sullen Pride or Contempt of mankind"; the heroic nihilism of the Pyrrhonians; the "ferocity" of Diogenes; "the servile philosophy of the Eclectics," the "moping recluse" philosophy of "Scholastic refinement"; the joining of "a philosophical enthusiasm to a religious superstition" in the character of the Stoic, and a modern reenactment of this character in Puritanism, which "being chiefly spiritual, resembles more a system of metaphysics" than a religion; "philosophical chymistry"; the inverted world of modern moral philosophy with its characters shaped by abstract "rapports or relations" or by "the malignant philosophy" (egoism); the "philosophical enthusiasm" informing political parties, a form of conduct "known only to modern times" and "the most extraordinary and unaccountable *phenomenon,* that has yet appeared in human affairs"; the "philosophical heroine"; and the "quackery" of Rousseau.

What this bestiary reveals is that philosophy is not necessarily a good thing. There is no philosophical innocence. Philosophy must always justify itself before the primordial speech of mankind. And even in its true form, which is extremely rare, it is only one human excellence among others and is not presented by Hume as the highest form of experience to which all others are inadequate approximations.

Cicero said that it was Socrates who brought philosophy down from the heavens and placed it in cities and homes. But the philosophical act in the pre-Christian, pagan world did not manage affairs. It danced lightly on the margins of traditional society, quarreling with the poets, priests, and the polis. It appeared as an eccentric, and its true home was the private sect, where it pointed to something beyond inherited practices. But with the union of philosophy and Christianity, the philosophical act (in the form of theology) began to manage the affairs of cities and homes. At length it cast off theology, appearing in the world as the unfettered philosophical act, and the thinkers of Christendom would recognize it as something with which they had, more or less, long been familiar. It pursued its old role of managing the affairs of men and was thrown into implacable opposition with its theological parent.

Its new scene of action would be politics, and its instrument of management would be the modern state. It would no longer quarrel with the small, traditional societies of the polis; it would eliminate them and command the good through the sovereign office of the modern state, a form of political association on a vast scale that could, in principle, place no limits on its size and expansion. Indeed, its logical outcome would be a global state or some approximation of a global state. Its politics would necessarily be an ideological style of politics in constant conflict with the remaining fragments of traditional societies and with the ideologies of other modern states pursuing their own universalizing projects.

As Plato had driven the poets out of the polis, so the philosophical act would drive the poets out of the modern state. Its own *universalist* language would be instituted, suppressing and obscuring the poetic character of human life, and rendering eloquence impossible. When Hume described his own age dryly as "this philosophic age," it was still an age in which a great variety of traditional forms of life were in place and in good working order. He could observe that there were in England "many honest gentlemen" who lived out their lives in the cultivation and enjoyment of an inherited culture. Of these he said, "They do well to keep themselves in their present situation; and instead of refining them into philosophers, I wish we cou'd communicate to our founders of systems, a share of this gross earthy mixture, as an ingredient, which they commonly stand much in need of, and which wou'd serve to temper those fiery particles, of which they are compos'd" (*T,* 272).

But the subversion of traditional societies by the philosophical act was already apparent to Hume by the end of his life and was rapidly increasing. DeMaistre fled to Russia in disgust over the ideological barbarism of the French Revolution, hoping to find a country not "scribbled on by philosophy." What he found instead was a lumpen intelligentsia eager to pattern itself after the *philosophes* of the French Revolution. Henceforth, there would be no country not scribbled on by philosophy. Every aspect of life would be spiritualized by the philosophical act.

Giambattista Vico has given a memorable account of how we might think of the first philosophic age. He presents the *sensus communis* that is the primordial source of all thought and conduct as passing through an "ideal eternal history." The first stage is grounded in the imaginative universal, an order of metaphorical identities in which mankind first differentiates itself from the divine. This is the age of the gods. The second is the age of heroes who found cities and states and whose force of character generates standards of excellence and a moral order of emulation. The last is the age of men, an age of egalitarianism and philosophical universalism in which men break free from the divine and from the heroic ethic of virtue in order to govern themselves by self-imposed rules. The abstract act of reflection is now taken to be the source of conduct and thought. The rule, the principle, the system are taken to be the real. But without a *sensus communis,* the rule is both indeterminate *and* authoritative. A scene of conflict necessarily follows in which each person's act of self-determination is seen as the violation of another's rights. In this final stage, free of divinity and virtue, men no longer know how to conduct themselves, and society collapses in violent conflict. Its fragments are gathered up by a general providence to confront again the primitive necessities of life and human association, from which springs a new instantiation of the ideal eternal history.

Vico's description of the age of men in the *New Science* is worth quoting at some length:

> For such peoples, like so many beasts, have fallen into the custom of each man thinking only of his own private interests and have reached the extreme of delicacy, or better of pride, in which like wild animals they bristle and lash out at the slightest displeasure. Thus no matter how great the throng and press of their bodies, they live like wild beasts in a deep solitude of spirit and will, scarcely any two being able to agree since each follows his own

> pleasure or caprice. By reason of all this, providence decrees that, through obstinate factions and desperate civil wars, they shall turn their cities into forests and the forests into dens and lairs of men. In this way, through long centuries of barbarism, rust will consume the misbegotten subtleties of malicious wits that have turned them into beasts made more inhuman by the barbarism of reflection than the first men had been made by the barbarism of sense. . . . And the few survivors in the midst of an abundance of the things necessary for life naturally become sociable and, returning to the primitive simplicity of the first world of peoples, are again religious, truthful, and faithful. Thus providence brings back among them the piety, faith, and truth which are the natural foundations of justice as well as the graces and beauties of the eternal order of God.[1]

There is more than a superficial similarity between Vico's "deep solitude of spirit and will" and Hume's "forelorn solitude," and between what Vico says about the "barbarism of reflection," "the barbarism of the intellect," and "reflective malice" and Hume's teaching about the barbarism of "refinement" and the corrupting effects of false philosophy.[2] Max Fisch, who has explored Vico's influence on European thought, was struck by the many structural similarities that exist not only between the philosophies of Vico and Hume, but between Vico and the entire Scottish Enlightenment.[3] John Gray has called attention to the importance the concept of barbarism had for the Scottish philosophers: "In the contemporary Western world, a self-denigrating guilt inhibits the discourse of civilization and barbarism that informed the Scottish Enlightenment (the only episode of enlightenment from which, if I am not mistaken, we have anything to learn)."[4]

Vico's ideas were available in Britain. He sent a copy of *The New Science* to Newton, and Fisch has speculated that Vico may have influenced Hume through his French connections or indirectly through Shaftesbury. But whether or not Hume read or discussed Vico, it is clear enough that their philosophies show a family resemblance in the traits of the Latin humanistic tradition of philosophy. Both were Ciceronian humanists. For both the source of thought and conduct is an inherited *sensus communis* (Hume's common life); for both the character of common life is poetic. Hume's teaching that the birth of a literature is its heroic moment, after which the barbarism of "refinement" and decline sets in, is Vichian; as is his rearguard attempt to preserve the remnants of eloquence in his age from the imperialistic universalism and abstractionism of modern speech. *The Natural History of Religion* contains many Vichian themes: that the first understanding of things came not from reason but the metaphorical identities of polytheism, which Hume called "a true poetical religion," and that polytheism necessarily evolves into theism, which seeks to emancipate itself from its poetic-mythical origin and become more rational. As it does so, however, a barbarism of refinement ensues; the idea of God becomes progressively abstract and antinomic, and as it becomes more rational, the practices of religion become more absurd and inhumane, until finally, unable to sustain such an abstract conception of God, the imagination returns to the primordial mythical understandings of the first religion, only to begin the movement again in the direction of the abstract and antinomic. This eternal dialectic of the religious mind, which Hume calls a "flux and reflux," sits easily alongside the *corsi e ricorsi* of Vico's ideal eternal history. Though this is not the place for a comparative study of Hume and Vico, it is important to place Hume's criticism of philosophy in the context of the Latin rhetorical tradition, where it is more at home than in the context of nineteenth- and twentieth-century forms of empiricism.

Hume and Hegel

This study may be viewed as an attempt to piece together from Hume's writings an imaginary *Natural History of Philosophical Consciousness* which would do for philosophy what *The Natural History of Religion* had done for religion, namely, to provide not only a complete speculative account of the nature of the philosophical act but also a counsel of prudent conduct in an age dominated by the philosophical act. The two great speculative accounts of philosophy in modern times were given by Hume and Hegel. Their accounts are inverted mirror images of each other, and they generate alternative paths that can be taken in the adventure of the first philosophic age.

Hegel actually wrote the natural history of philosophical consciousness that was intimated in Hume, namely, *The Phenomenology of Spirit* (1807). Both thinkers aim to give a complete account of experience. Hume describes himself in the *Treatise* as making a "voyage" in a "leaky weather-beaten vessel" with the intention of circumnavigating the globe of human experience. Hegel describes the *Phenomenology* as his "voyage of discovery" into the whole of experience. What he discovered is that all experiences (sensory, scientific, moral, political, religious, aesthetic, etc.) are, implicitly or explicitly, so many modes of the philosophical act. Each form implicitly claims to be a complete, self-determining account of the whole of experience, and each, through dialectical criticism, is shown to fail at being the absolutely coherent form of experience. Each fails because each takes a part of experience as the whole and eventually runs into conflict with other parts spiritualized by the philosophical act into the whole and equally insistent about their absolute character. Temporary resolutions are reached as subverted worlds are gathered up into greater wholes, only to discover once more their partial character.

What Hegel calls "absolute knowledge" is the philosophical insight that this is our condition: to seek an absolutely coherent and self-determining form of experience and always to fail. But in the process of this adventure in radical self-determination, numerous and varied spiritual forms emerge which constitute the rich tapestry of human culture. Hegel arranges the forms of experience in a hierarchy with sense experience at the bottom and the self-determining philosophical act at the top. Philosophy is superior to all the other forms in being the only form that knows what it is, namely the act of seeking an absolutely coherent, self-determining experience. But it is not superior in that it can replace the other forms or dictate their conduct. And it can understand the other forms only in the manner of the "owl of Minerva," when they have finished their work and are safely in the past.

There is much to be learned from a comparative study of Hume and Hegel.[5] Both are among those rare thinkers for whom philosophy itself is the fundamental problem of philosophy, and the solution they find shapes and colors what they have to say on every other topic. Both seek a rapprochement between philosophy and history, and both know that philosophy can be understood only dialectically. But the character of their respective dialectics is different. The fundamental difference turns on how they view the relation between philosophy and experience. For Hegel, philosophy is not grounded in experience, nor is it one experience among others; philosophy and experience are the same. This does not mean that in having something as simple as a sense experience, one is making a philosophical claim, but only that if one were to say what that experience is, one would be making a philosophical claim. And since the *telos* of philosophy is to achieve a self-determining, absolutely coherent form of experience, this must also be the *telos* of all experience. Each experience is an implicit form of the philosophical act waiting to be unfolded.

Viewing experience this way, it would be easy to conclude that the high incidence of the philosophical act in modern culture is not merely an increase in the aggregate of one kind of experience (philosophical) over what had existed previously, but an unfolding of experience toward its self-realization. Further, the emergence of the modern practice of civil society (rule of law; private property; civil liberties such as freedom of contract, conscience, movement; and the modern state as an instrument for maintaining civil society) is not to be viewed as another form of life incommensurably related to previous, objectively valuable ways of life (as Hume sees it), but as the necessary unfolding of institutions which, in the realm of practice, answer the speculative demand of experience to achieve a self-determining and absolutely coherent form of experience. In a word, modern political institutions are, for Hegel, the self-realization of the philosophical act.

Hume distinguished between "political whiggism" and what he sardonically called "religious whiggism." Had he been aware of the Hegelian doctrine that modern political institutions are the unfolding of the *telos* of experience and that the essence of experience is the philosophical act, he might well have dubbed it "metaphysical whiggism," for that doctrine is Whiggism writ as large as it could possibly be. And he would have viewed it as a spectacular case of philosophical alchemy and hubris. Hume teaches that philosophy is one form of experience among others. To treat the philosophical act as the essence of experience is just another instance of the stock error of false philosophy: spiritualizing a part of experience as the whole. The error is understandable, for Hegel did live in a culture increasingly dominated by forms of the philosophical act. From a Humean perspective, he may be said to have transmuted the true historicist thesis—that the philosophical act is the essence of the narrative substance I have called the first philosophic age—into the false speculative thesis that it is the essence of experience as such.

The Humean dialectic is a struggle between autonomous philosophical reason and the inherited, pre-reflective order of a *sensus communis.* The philosophical act seeks radical self-determination independent of the dictates of any common life, and necessarily fails. This failure is known through the despair of *absolute skepticism,* which is the fate that always awaits the philosophical act purged of every aspect of common life. Out of this despair the authoritative character of common life is noticed for the first time and is embraced by an act of philosophical deference and submission. The philosophy that proceeds after this act is carried out in the knowledge and memory of this deference. The full Humean account of philosophy unites true philosophy with true religion, viewing the whole of experience as the work of a general, though mysterious, providence. This order is known not through self-determining reason but through participation, memory, and critical reflection upon inherited practices. The lineaments of this order are easily discerned, though they are generic: a causally ordered world, self, society, and the divine; a generic human nature; a generic order of human passions; a generic outline of virtue (greatness of mind and extensive benevolence); and a philosophically certified generic theism. To say that these are generic is not to say that they are empty abstractions but only that they do not determine any specific way of life; they are both generic and substantial in the same way as are the primary colors or genres of architecture.

Although Hume is a virtue moralist, he rejects the virtue ethics of such thinkers as Aristotle and Aquinas who teach that there is only one form of human flourishing, in comparison to which all others must be viewed as failed approximations. Hume teaches that mankind is an inventive species; that *part* of life is shaped by self-imposed ideas (this is the partial truth that the philosophical act seeks to make absolute); and that within the constraints of a generic humanity, many forms of human flourishing are possible. Each of these is objectively valuable but may be incommensurable with others; and even when they are commensurable, it may be impossible to combine them into one life or even into one society. This is the meaning of Hume's parable about the customs and moral life of the imaginary country Fourli (*EM*, 324–43).

Hume's view on what reason can know about human flourishing is similar to, though not the same as, the objective pluralism to be found in a number of contemporary writers, notably Isaiah Berlin, Michael Oakeshott, and John Gray.[6] Just as there are forms of art that exhibit human excellences but are incommensurable not only across genres, but within a genre (Romanesque, Byzantine, Gothic, and Baroque are incommensurable styles within the genre of Christian church architecture), so there are objectively real and incommensurable forms of human flourishing within the constraints of a generic humanity.

In particular, that mode of human flourishing which Hume comprehends under the name of "liberty" is never thought of by him as the only form of human flourishing to which all societies must conform and in relation to which all previous societies must be viewed as failed approximations. This progressive view of history as the story of universal human emancipation shared by both liberalism and Marxism is simply a latter-day "refinement" of that Whiggism against which Hume carried on a lifelong struggle. Liberty for Hume is a contingent practice and is similar to what Oakeshott called the practice of "civil association."[7] This mode of political association was an artifact of European states, gradually introduced as a *modus vivendi* to establish order after the chaos of the religious wars of the sixteenth and seventeenth centuries. To say that liberty is a contingent practice is not only to say that its emergence was not necessary but also that the excellence it makes possible is unstable in at least four respects.

First, liberty is internally connected with evils which, if not managed, could destroy the practice; but neither can they be eliminated without destroying the practice. Hume thought that the evil necessarily attending a free press was one of these and that the sort of deracinated, egocentric character produced by commercialism, itself an evil attending a free market, was another.

Second, the practice of liberty generates goods which destroy other forms of human excellence. The engagement of civil society has uncovered a number of unexpected human excellences, the most important of which is an ethic of individualism and autonomy. Hume observes that this essentially European ethic has shown itself to be compatible with order and authority to a surprising degree; but he recognizes that an ethic of self-determination drives out those forms of human excellence rooted in forms of subordination that are not voluntary, such as family and traditional social hierarchies. Indeed, Hume considered it an absurdity peculiar to the modern ethic of autonomy that nothing could qualify as moral excellence unless it was the result of voluntary action, a view that is part of the common stock of most contemporary forms of liberalism (*EM,* 312–23).

Third, the practice of liberty tends to be hostile to all nonliberal goods and seeks to destroy or at least to marginalize them. But some of these are necessary for the practice of liberty itself; to destroy them is to subvert the practice. The most fundamental nonliberal good of this sort is authority. As was discussed earlier, the liberal tradition has had little to say about the nature of authority, notable exceptions being Hobbes, Hume, and Oakeshott. Without authority the rule of law and all other liberal practices are impossible. Authority is grounded in opinion and will have different forms depending on the historical, cultural context in which the practice of liberty occurs. Its source might be monarchy, an aristocratic class, patriarchy, or a religious tradition. Hume thought that the practice of liberty in Britain depended upon the authority of monarchy, a source quite different from the martial, patriarchal, agrarian order that was the source of liberty in Switzerland, and different in yet another way from what he was willing to recognize as the ground for an order of independent republics in America. The liberal ethic of self-determination is necessarily hostile to these nonliberal sources of authority and seeks to subvert them.

Finally, the practice of liberty appeared in a culture in which the art of philosophical reflection was highly cultivated. An ethic of self-determination (already in place) encouraged the rise of secular philosophy, and the latter not only reinforced the former but eventually transmuted it into a philosophic superstition. The nonliberal goods that were the sources of authority in the various practices of liberty in Europe were inverted by an act of philosophical alchemy into a liberal good by the doctrine that all legitimate authority is grounded in the consent of the people. Hume exploded this doctrine by arguing that no form of political association had ever instantiated it and that to do so, "consent" would have to be so diluted as to be compatible with the traditional, nonliberal forms of authority that had been rejected. The English under the Puritans and the French under the Jacobins lost liberty because they destroyed those traditional, nonliberal sources of authority that were the source of the practice of liberty. The practices, of course, were (as they always are) in need of reform, but to destroy a practice is not to reform it. In this way the practice of liberty generates forms of false philosophy that tend to subvert the practice while retaining the name and presenting an emancipatory narrative that masks the subversion and destruction.

The teaching that an ethic of self-determination is one contingent excellence among many, often incommensurable, excellences displayed by an inventive species rules out both the Hegelian notion that the ethic of autonomy framed in the institutions of modernity represents the actualization in practice of the *telos* of human experience and thus the highest form of human flourishing, as well as the radical Whig doctrine of natural rights, along with all of those latter-day versions of the same urged by Rawls, Nozick, Dworkin, and Gewirth that assume fundamental rights upon which political order can be grounded.[8] Rights for Hume are artifacts designed to preserve natural goods, namely, the many forms of excellence in which the natural virtues may display themselves. Because these goods are shaped by historical context and are contingent in the way described above, the rights that preserve them will also be contingent and come in a great variety of forms. To think that there are fundamental rights from which political order can flow is a spectacular case of philosophical alchemy: an inversion of the moral world that treats the *artificial* (rights) as the natural and the *natural* (goods of excellence) as the artificial.

To say that there are and have been many forms of human flourishing, that an ethic of self-determination is not absolutely privileged, and that there may be forms of human excellence that are unimaginable to those currently engaged in the practice of liberty is not to say that any form of human association is acceptable. Given the knowledge of a substantial but generic human nature, there may be general restraints that are necessary for any form of human flourishing. Being generic, however, they will not determine any specific form of human flourishing, nor will they be identical to those fundamental rights theorized by universalist and egalitarian liberalism, which are abridgments and stylizations of the parochial European practice of liberty that was being explored in Hume's time and which has hardened into a form of philosophical fundamentalism in our own.[9]

Generic conditions of human flourishing are to be found in Hume's theory of justice, which gives shape to property, political authority, chastity, and the law of nations. But these are artifacts designed to establish conditions of peace and stability, without which human flourishing is impossible; they are compatible with a wide range of human flourishing and do not privilege an ethic of self-determination. Hume's rules of property, "the laws of justice" (stability of possessions, their transference by consent, and the performance of promises) do not even determine a system of private property, which Hegel rightly argued is necessary for an ethic of self-determination. The stability of possessions demanded by the rules can be satisfied by a system of communal property or tribal property in a league of tribes where private ownership has not been dreamed of. Private property and an ethic of self-determination are, however, demanded by Hume's conception of the practice of liberty.

Hume does say that liberty is a hardy plant that once having taken root can be expected to flourish through harsh seasons and to propagate (*E*, 124). This suggests that the practice of liberty may be an excellence that other societies with traditional, nonliberal forms of political association may wish to emulate, but that is an empirical claim requiring the free judgment of those traditional societies. There is nothing in Hume to prevent the practice of liberty from becoming a global practice, but it is not necessitated either by morals or by what is known of human inclinations. And of course there is nothing to prevent its destruction. Indeed, Hume thought that the practice of liberty contained the seeds of its own destruction, notably the concentration of wealth at the center at the expense of the provinces and those independent social authorities necessary for "free government"; the inevitable abuse of public credit and the emergence of a new ruling class of monied men devoid of civic virtue; and the likely emergence of destructive, popular philosophical enthusiasms.

Further, the practice of liberty, as Hume understands it, is quite different from the universalist and egalitarian forms of fundamentalist liberalism that have been imposed on the world since the nineteenth century. For Hume, the self that has liberty can flourish in a traditional society with a division of roles and duties hierarchically ordered and not grounded in individual choice. Indeed, in his view the authority of individual choice presupposes traditional society. Liberty is always, for Hume, the delicate and finely tuned perfection of society; it is not essential to it, whereas authority is. His constant theme, during the last decade of his life, regarding the most cultivated example of liberty in history—Britain—is that it is balanced on the edge of "licentiousness" and despotism.

Any expansion of the practice of liberty around the globe that Hume could endorse would thus be hedged in by a careful consideration of the goods and evils intertwined in the practice and by the philosophical connoisseur's eye for the historical context, as well as by a frank recognition of the human excellences that would be obliterated if civil society and its ethic of self-determination were made universal.

Some latter-day Hegelians have argued that an ethic of self-determination has in fact spread around the globe, confirming Hegel's insight that autonomy is the *telos* of human experience and that liberal democracy in the modern unitary state is the final form of political association. The first philosophic age is, at the same time, the end of history.[10] But we must consider that the European practice of liberty was imposed largely by military force on traditional societies in the heyday of global imperialism. There was no question of these societies freely wishing to emulate a manifestly superior way of life. Indeed, they nearly everywhere resisted being assimilated. And the fact that, once it was established, many came to adopt the European practice does not at all mean that the excellences framed in traditional societies were inferior. The move may well have been, and in many cases was, a change from a superior form of life to an inferior one. This was the fate Hume thought had befallen the prosperous "stockjobbers" (holders of the public debt lounging in a "pampered and stupid luxury" made possible by the centralized modern state) in relation to the moral characters of their ancestors (*E*, 357; *L*, 1: 276). And when one considers the vast number and variety of the excellences framed in traditional societies around the globe, their destruction for the sake of what has become the increasingly uniform, banal, and abstract life of modernity must be accounted a spectacular loss. Nor is it obvious that the dispositions that produced these excellences are not deep in human nature and will not again reassert themselves.

But brute conquest was not the only form of subversion. The disposition of philosophers to philosophical alchemy is nowhere so strong as in "reasonings concerning human life, and the methods of attaining happiness." Here they are led astray not only by the usual "narrowness of their understandings, but by that also of their passions." When the philosopher surveys forms of human life, he typically and impiously makes "no account of that vast variety, which nature has so much affected in all her operations," but instead reduces these to failed approximations of one form of human flourishing by "the most violent and absurd reasoning" (*E,* 159–60). This error appears in modern philosophical ideologies—whether of the liberal or Marxist sort—which, in teaching doctrines of universal egalitarianism and human emancipation, have played their role in legitimating empire and the consolidated modern state, with the consequent destruction of traditional societies. Neither Marx nor Western liberals had any qualms about crushing traditional societies under the legitimating superstition of universal human emancipation.

The Human and the Divine in the First Philosophic Age

Because he does not hold the Hegelian doctrine that the philosophical act is the *telos* of experience, Hume does not view the forms of common life as failed forms of philosophy but as the manifestation of a general providence, deference to which alone makes speculative philosophy, insofar as we are capable of it, possible. For Hume there is no hierarchy of experience leading to the philosophical act at the top. Philosophy is the highest form of speculative thought, and true philosophy is superior to false philosophy, but it cannot intelligibly be said to be superior to the pre-reflective order of the *sensus communis,* because it presupposes that order as an inheritance to be critically cultivated and enjoyed. There is an "absolute moment" in Hume as in Hegel where the thinker's relation to the whole of experience is grasped. For Hegel it occurs at the moment of "absolute knowledge," where the philosopher grasps the whole of experience as a hierarchy animated by the philosophical act. For Hume it occurs at the moment of "absolute skepticism," where the emptiness of the project of radical self-determination becomes manifest and the primordial authority of common life is revealed.

Hegelian philosophical self-knowledge issues in an *ironic* mode of experience. Humean philosophical self-knowledge comprehends the distinction between true and false philosophy and, having passed through the despair of the Pyrrhonian doubt, issues not in irony but in humility, piety, folly, and the other philosophical virtues. Hume follows Cicero and the classical tradition in holding that philosophy is an attempt to grasp all things human and divine. But if the philosophical act of radical self-determination is the *telos* of all experience, as it is for Hegel, then it would appear that the distinction between the human and the divine collapses. The philosophical act becomes the divine. Just as the Aristotelian hierarchy of substantial forms leads to the divine activity of thought thinking thought, so the Hegelian hierarchy of spiritual forms leads to the philosophical act of thought determining itself.

The image of the divine in the Aristotelian and Hegelian accounts is just the radical freedom and aseity of a pagan Greek philosopher. There is and can be nothing outside the philosophical act. From the Humean perspective, this is not only philosophically absurd in that it fails to see that the philosophical act, if carried through consistently, yields absolute skepticism, from which something outside the domain of the philosophical act is recognized, namely, common life; it is also, from the position of Hume's theism, blasphemous. Moreover, in collapsing the distinction between the human and the divine into the philosophical act, the Hegelian philosophy loses not only the divine but the human as well.[11] Hume's maxim that in being a philosopher one should be still a man is not a maxim that naturally flows from Hegelian philosophy.

In dramatically transubstantiating the whole of experience into the philosophical act, Hegel stands as emblematic of the first philosophic age. From this source many forms of cultural criticism would flow, seeking radical self-determination. One main tributary would spring from Marx; another from Nietzsche. Neither could feel at home in any *sensus communis,* and in both the distinction between the human and the divine would collapse. Hume observed that the first philosophers were atheists out of innocence. He also taught that philosophers seldom know their own minds in this particular and that their professed atheism often presupposes the divine and even a "secret dread and compunction" (*NHR,* 94). This led him to the view that there might not be any true atheists. The impiety of Voltaire still supposes the divine. But the atheism of the first philosophic age would not be one of innocence; it would be self-imposed, in full knowledge of a theistic tradition, and it would be entirely emancipated from the divine. I quoted earlier Rorty's remark that an "enlightened," truly "liberal society . . . would be one in which no trace of divinity remained."[12]

This atheism, so essential to the first philosophic age, is in stark contrast to Hume's theism, which operates quietly in the background of thought (as he said it should) and is hardly noticed. This has led some to think that it serves no purpose whatsoever in his philosophy and is virtually the same as atheism by another name. But though Hume is primarily a philosopher of the human and not the divine, the divine is always in the background and is the horizon against which the human appears. And though there may be more to say about the divine than Hume allows, he does not think it can be said by philosophy. The importance of Hume's theism becomes apparent only when placed in contrast with the collapse of both the human and the divine in the first philosophic age.

Though Hume taught that philosophy could provide no support for revealed religion and the doctrine of a particular providence, it was compelled, he thought, to acknowledge the doctrine of a general providence. Nature as we experience it is not a construction of Nietzsche's will to power, nor the result of Sartre's radically free choice of essences, nor the result of an epistemology of power, as it is for Foucault, nor even a realm of odious necessity to be spiritualized by acts of self-determination, as it is for Marx. Nature is that which saves us from the absolute skepticism and nihilism to which autonomous reason inevitably leads. A general providence, as displayed in nature, is the source of all our deepest natural beliefs; it is the source of moral sentiments, aesthetic sentiments, and of the religious sentiments of true theism which the true philosopher views as the imprint of the divine on his creation.

None of this, of course, is Christianity (though, as Hume allowed, it is compatible with reformed versions of it, e.g., Fideism). It is perhaps closest to the divine of the ancient Stoics and modern reenactments such as that of Shaftesbury. It is far removed, however, from post-Hegelian atheism. Just how far can be seen by considering Nietzsche's remark in *The Twilight of the Idols:* "I fear we are not getting rid of God because we still believe in grammar." To think that language is somehow about reality implies that one mode of speech about it may be more adequate than another. In eliminating the category of the real, Nietzsche leaves us with a chaos of linguistic forms, none more adequate than another, to be ordered by the will to power. Commenting on this passage, Alasdair MacIntyre observes that, for Nietzsche, it "is not just that theism is in part false because it requires the truth of realism, but that realism is inherently theistic."[13] In this sense Hume believed not only in the grammar of language but in the "grammar" of much else besides: for example, of causal, moral, political, and aesthetic order. He could have these beliefs because of the background belief of theism.

The first philosophic age, including the postmodernism that is one of its modes, is said to be an age of "irony" and "disenchantment," and this is precisely because it has eliminated the category of the divine. Hume's philosophy is still one of enchantment. There is, of course, Humean irony in philosophy's self-conception as it works through the dialectic of true and false philosophy, but the beliefs and sentiments that issue from the dialectic are not ironic. Hume's writings are filled with the language of the divine: nature as a general providence known through participation in common life; the religious sentiments of the great and the good, which are impressions of reflection that supervene upon the philosophical contemplation of the whole; the sublime of Shaftesbury; the divine qualities of eloquence, poetry, and statecraft. Whatever we are to make of this language (and, of course, it can be read in more than one way), it is not the ironic, philosophically self-absorbed language of postmodernism.

In the first philosophic age the philosophical act is radically free of the divine and of the poetic character of *any* inherited *sensus communis.* Self-determining reflection alone is viewed as the source of thought and conduct. The corrupt modes of the philosophical act (the ascetic, the revolutionary, and the guilty) hitherto confined to the margins of society now become the forms of society. Whatever fragments of a *sensus communis* are left that could discipline radical self-determination and give it order are viewed as parochial and oppressive. Philosophical resentment necessarily ensues, spawning an endless stream of self-created victims. Someone's self-determination is met with the violent protest that someone else's rights have been violated. Ever more numerous rights are generated to protect ever more numerous desires. MacIntyre has observed that modern liberal societies, theoretically grounded in natural or human rights, are the first societies in history in which "I want" (without any further qualification) has become an argument of practical reason.[14] Foucault, through an act of philosophical alchemy, transmuted the social and cultural forms of moral and intellectual life into various forms of domination which result from a ceaseless struggle of wills for dominance. Unlike Marx, he did not think of this struggle as a struggle of classes, nor as a struggle of sexes, as feminists view it, but as a struggle of individuals, of "all against all. . . . Who fights against whom? We all fight each other."[15] This is exactly the condition described by Vico of men caught in the barbarism of reflection, and it is a version of what Hume characterized as the "selfish system." Foucault would have entered Hume's bestiary as the philosophical "satyr" (*EM*, 302). Thus a form of the Hobbesian state of nature is renewed in the most advanced civilization, and society is held together not by the enjoyment and cultivation of an inherited *sensus communis* but by *legalism* enforced by an increasingly consolidated and bureaucratic modern state. Consolidation must occur as power is transferred from dismantled, independent social authorities to the center in order to service an ever-increasing number of antinomic individual rights.

A world in which self-determining reflection alone is the source of thought and conduct would be one in which the philosophical act would take its own reflective artifacts as the real. It would be an age in which there could be such a thing as Kant's critical philosophy and such a thing as "analytic philosophy," where philosophical speech would not be about the real mediated by a common life "methodized and corrected" but about autonomous concepts and linguistic structures entirely emancipated from the contingencies of the inherited. And it would necessarily give rise to those dialectically opposed philosophies inspired by Nietzsche which rightly deconstruct such supposedly autonomous concepts but wrongly apply the same method to all of common life and even philosophy itself. This total deconstruction of language and philosophy, carried out in our time by such writers as Derrida and Deleuze, is a latter-day reenactment, in a linguistic mode, of Pyrrhonism.[16] Hume's challenge to Pyrrhonism can with equal force be directed to its twentieth-century reenactment, namely, "that no durable *good* can ever result from it; while it remains in its full force and vigour. We need only ask . . . *What his meaning is? And what he proposes by all these curious researches*" (*EU*, 159; italics mine). If an answer is forthcoming (as it was from the ancient Pyrrhonians, who were seeking *ataraxia*, but not from Hume's imaginary Pyrrhonian), then the deconstructionist has returned to common life, and his speech falls under the constraints of the general providence explored by true philosophy. If, on the other hand, the question itself is deconstructed, the thinker must be left to his prejudices, for no reply can be given to speech framed in the philosopher's "vacuum" (*EM*, 343). Such a thinker has abandoned entirely the question of the order of the real and of the human good—what "would be beneficial to society" (*EU*, 160). For the benefit of third parties, however, the Humean philosopher will locate such a thinker at the proper place in the dialectic of true and false philosophy, demonstrating that the deconstruction of common life both destroys and presupposes its providential order and so is absurd. In showing that the deconstructionist deconstructs everyone but himself and that he is the exception, a fresh instance of hubris, corruption, the love of dominion, and of false philosophy is revealed to all who are friends of the *sensus communis* and of inquiry into the real.

A world in which the artifacts of self-determining philosophical reflection were taken to be the real would be one in which "art" and "craft," would be severed from "taste." Cut loose from the human and the divine, art could become "conceptual art." A painting is wired to self-destruct. A work of sculpture is an aquarium containing three basketballs. In conceptual art, judgments of propriety or taste about the disposition of the sensuous are irrelevant. Conceptual art is not a craft in a tradition but the acting out of the heroic moment of the philosophical act in its ascetic, guilty, or revolutionary modes. Conceptual art, as "performance art," is a reenactment of the shocking display (public masturbation and fornication) of the Cynics. But whereas the Cynics pursued an ascetic ideal, living out the aseity of the pagan gods, contemporary performance art tends to pursue antinomic egalitarian universalisms. The task of art, the French feminist Orlan says, "is to change the world, that is its only justification." To do this, it must act out "philosophical" and "psychoanalytic theories." Orlan, who telecasts, live by satellite, surgical operations on herself in pursuit of male-generated standards of beauty which she *disowns,* and who (under local anesthetic) lectures and answers faxes during the operation, is typical at least of the *avant garde* in what she considers art to be: "It must challenge our *a prioris,* disrupt our thoughts; it is outside our norms, outside the law, against bourgeois order. . . . It is deviant." This is simply another instance of the heroic moment of the philosophical act in its condition of total negative transcendence. Her motto, "Je provocque donc j'existe," embodies the Cynic's wisdom and the wisdom of Foucault's "transgression of the limits."[17]

In sculpting her own flesh, Orlan is said to have achieved things of philosophical significance; she is said to have collapsed the distinction between subject and object and to have closed the gap between the artist and the medium. False philosophy always seeks to overcome the "gap" or the "limit," whatever it might be. No sort of order can withstand the act of heroic philosophical transcendence. But far from shocking the elites of bourgeois society, the *avant garde* greedily seize upon each act of transgressive art as showing the superiority of its understanding over vulgar conceptions (*T,* 26; *EM,* 342–43). In the first philosophic age, satire of the philosophical act is impossible.

The world of the self-determining, reflective artifact is the world of

Hume's "false refinements," Vico's "barbarism of reflection," and T. S. Eliot's "hollow men." The self-imposed inability to speak of the real; the condition of existing in the mode of irony in a hall of conceptual mirrors, far from being considered a disaster, would be, in the first philosophic age, celebrated as the "postmodern" condition. Umberto Eco in the *Postscript to The Name of the Rose* gives a touching description of this condition:

> I think of the postmodern attitude as that of a man who loves a very cultivated woman and knows he cannot say to her 'I love you madly,' because he knows that she knows (and that she knows that he knows) that these words have already been written by Barbara Cartland. Still, there is a solution. He can say, 'As Barbara Cartland would put it, I love you madly.' At this point, having avoided false innocence, having said clearly that it is no longer possible to speak innocently, he will nevertheless have said what he wanted to say to the woman: that he loves her, but he loves her in an age of lost innocence. If the woman goes along with this, she will have received a declaration of love all the same. Neither of the two speakers will feel innocent, both will have accepted the challenge of the past, of the already said, which cannot be eliminated, both will consciously and with pleasure play the game of irony. . . . But both will have succeeded, once again, in speaking of love.[18]

Here is reflective barbarism carried to a length Hume could not have imagined. Erotic love is transmuted into a mode of irony by a condition of corrupt reflection. Eco's celebration of a postmodern speech of love, from a Humean point of view, is simply another case of false philosophy reconciling itself to its self-imposed condition. To speak of the shadow of the shade of a human sentiment is not to speak of the sentiment. Nor is the postmodern condition of which Eco speaks the necessary condition of those in a highly refined culture, but only of those in a culture of a certain kind: one captured by the "false refinements" of philosophy and so cut off from the divine and any *sensus communis.* Eco's "very cultivated woman," in other ages of high culture, has inspired the speech of love undistracted by reflective irony. It is only in the first philosophic age that such speech seems and, indeed, is impossible for those whose characters have long been shaped by the habit of false philosophy. Authentic speech of love rooted in the radiant world of common life (Hume's impressions, i.e., the world of those things that impress themselves upon us and call forth a poetic response) vanishes in a world shaped by the philosophical act. Hume feared that eloquence in his own time would vanish in favor of abstract universalist speech; it never occurred to him that gallantry could vanish into a species of irony.

Philosophical Prudence

What can we learn from Hume about preserving one's humanity in the first philosophic age? The foundation of any Humean teaching on this question is the speculative thesis that a general providence will in the long run save mankind from the barbarism of false philosophy. The errors of philosophy are self-imposed. The sentiments of nature are a gift of providence and are always available. The philosopher is not always to be found in the man, but the man is always in the philosopher. True philosophy can gain only a generic understanding of the sentiments and dispositions that make up human nature. These sentiments and dispositions are given shape by the poetic imagination of an inventive species and are displayed in the world in a vast variety of forms. What is great and excellent in human nature is what has survived the test of time and conflict and to which mankind returns again and again. These are to be found, Hume thinks, more in works of poetry and in the memory of great moral characters preserved in literature than in the speculative systems of philosophy and theology. In these memorials what is great and substantial in human nature is preserved and can serve as objects of a "noble emulation" around which thought can rally in an age of barbarism, whether produced by the unrestrained use of the sword or by the unrestrained barbarism of refinement.

What Hume said of a literature in decline, discussed in an earlier chapter, can be said of the reflective barbarism of the first philosophic age: Though a whole people may lose perspective and incline to the false refinements of a decadent literature, the "jingle of words," the "false conceits," yet once the "true genius" appears who can speak eloquently about the human, he will draw all to himself. The role of the true genius in the first philosophic age would be to frame speech that can penetrate the cocoon of free-floating, reflective artifacts in which the philosophical character has enclosed itself so that the man within can hear. The difficulty is that philosophical ignorance is self-imposed, and so any such speech will be viewed as a threat to rationality and freedom: a threat to rationality because the philosophical act, no matter how corrupt, always views itself as the instantiation of rationality, and a threat to freedom because it is always self-determining. The speech of the human can be heard only by those in whom the seamless whole of a corrupt form of the philosophical act has been at least partially subverted. And it is just this act of subversion that Hume's dialectic of true and false philosophy was designed to accomplish.

Hume taught that the only remedy for false philosophy is the true. The dialectic of true and false philosophy, if presented with eloquence, is a potent weapon in the subversion of false philosophy, and the project of such subversion is permanent. For in that ideal identity I have called the first philosophic age, moral language is cut loose from the contingencies and practices of an inherited common life and is inverted by the alchemy of legitimating narratives of universal human emancipation. Consequently, terms such as *liberty, freedom, justice, emancipation, equality,* and *rights* must be presumed tainted until shown to be otherwise. In this world there is no innocent moral speech, because all moral speech is philosophic.

Eco's claim that the postmodern knows he can no longer speak the speech of innocence obscures from view the postmodern's self-conception, which in fact is one of complacency and self-imposed innocence. Nietzsche once declared that "atheism and a kind of *second innocence* belong together."[19] False philosophy always issues in self-imposed innocence. The speech arising from the Cartesian clear and distinct idea conceives itself to be the speech of innocence, as does that of the totalizing system. But the same is true of that tiresome tribe of unmasking genealogists inspired by Nietzsche whose task is to subvert the clear and distinct idea as well as the totalizing system and who have largely shaped the postmodern condition. However, in neither Cartesian self-certification nor in Nietzschean self-congratulatory unmasking is there the presence of a fundamental "opposite" or "other" of which the thinker must take account and over which he has no control. It is the presence of this other and a dialectical encounter with it, so essential to true philosophy, that renders impossible innocent philosophical speech. True philosophy is dialectical throughout, not just in its first moment. False philosophy is not. The Humean philosopher, by contrast, has passed through the self-mortifying fires of total Pyrrhonian doubt. Speculative thought was able to continue only by viewing itself as a participant in the contingently structured practices of common life, itself the work of a mysterious general providence. True philosophy is the adventure of thoughtfully participating in this domain. It is a philosophy permeated throughout with learned ignorance, providing only a partial and speculatively unsatisfying knowledge of the human and the divine. In it there is and can be no innocent philosophical speech.

The subversion of false philosophy by a Humean dialectic is not merely a formal affair of subverting "propositions." It is, in addition to this, speech directed to the man (or what is left of him) in the philosopher's character. It will employ, in addition to eloquence, the Shaftesburian art of ridicule as a technique for revealing truth. It will exhibit the "gaiety" of Montaigne and the "wit" of Lucian, both of which Hume argued were essential to a virtuous philosophical character. Lucian's *Sale of Philosophers* is not an argument, but it exposes the hubris of philosophy and points to its disowned and forgotten source in common life.[20]

Finally, one can imagine a Humean genealogy that would be the inversion of the Nietzschean genealogy. The possibility of such a narrative is grounded in the distinction Hume observed between Machiavelli as philosopher and Machiavelli as historian (*E,* 567–68). As a political philosopher, he was emancipated from the domain of virtue and vice, but when he wrote as a historian he was constrained by that domain. Nietzsche subverted all thought about the real by writing a narrative of it as a mask for unworthy motives. Nietzschean genealogy thereby clears the scene for a radical form of autonomous self-display. But this is just another instance of philosophical alchemy, the spiritualization of a part of common life (a class of unworthy motives) into the whole. The Humean countergenealogy would be a narrative of the genealogist as a character in the world (the world of Machiavelli's history) written from the point of view of common life and exposing the genealogist's own location in the very order he disowns. Hume's narrative of the "philosophical heroine" was just such a subverting genealogy (*E,* 538–44).

The Humean belief that a general providence will, in the long run, restore society from the barbarism of refinement to common life provides no hope for the restoration of a particular society. The long run can be quite long, and it may not be complete until, as in Vico's ideal eternal history, cities are turned into forests, and a new *sensus communis* is formed by a life pushed back into a necessitous condition. And since providence for Hume is general, not particular, there is nothing to prevent the barbarism of the first philosophic age from becoming more or less a permanent condition. Just as the dialectic of polytheism and vulgar theism is a permanent condition, so it might be with the dialectic of true and false philosophy as the structure of culture. Vulgar theism emerged out of polytheism but did not obliterate it. The vulgar theistic imagination continually swerves back to partially recover a lost polytheistic world which in reflection it disowns but in imagination it cannot live without. Hume considered the disappearance of the excellences of polytheism to be a great loss. And as theism (vulgar and philosophic, but inclining always to the vulgar side) supplanted polytheism, so philosophy (false and true, but inclining always to the false side) has supplanted theism as the dominant form of culture. The "flux and reflux" of the mind in this condition would be both to disown the *sensus communis,* which is the source of thought and conduct, and to long for its recovery.

This would be a world in which the characters of the philosophical bestiary would more or less populate society. The individuals in this society would be wrapped in a deep, self-imposed, philosophical solitude and would be strangers to one another. Such a society had already been provided for by Hobbes's notion of civil association, which allegedly did not require a *sensus communis* but only a sovereign office capable of conforming the wills not only of strangers but even of enemies to a condition of peace and cooperation. In this world the wisdom of true philosophy would be a form of Stoicism that could manifest itself in remarkable individuals who could intermittently illuminate society, but never for very long. Human hubris, ambition, love of dominion, and the tendency to spiritualize these by an ideological style of politics would ensure that false philosophy would more or less maintain its rule.

From this condition there can be no real escape, and the true philosopher will recognize it as a tragic condition. In the first philosophic age, there can be no life not scribbled on by false philosophy. Yet common life is still primordial. In Hume's view, nature will, in the end, assert her rights. Experience is not and cannot be autonomous philosophical interpretation "all the way down."

But neither should common life be thought of as a safe haven to which one can flee from the first philosophic age. Common life is not a substance from which self-evident rules can be abstracted for guiding life. It is not the "common sense" of Thomas Reid or Thomas Paine. Common life is a dialectical concept in eternal opposition with reflection, and neither can entirely triumph. The concept is properly grasped only by true philosophy and is revealed only obliquely through the encounter with philosophical error. Common life is the radiant horizon against which the hubristic absurdities of philosophy reveal their silhouettes.

As grasped by philosophy, common life is a generic notion. Yet every instance of it appears in a distinct and particular way of life. True philosophy can mark out the true dialectical order of common life and reflection, but the reforms needed to preserve a particular instance of humanity from the barbarism of refinement will require writing a history of the practices of a way of life that exhibits both their truth and their corruption by false philosophy. It would be the sort of history that

Hume wrote of the moral and philosophical weal and woe of the practice of liberty in Britain.

The first and most fundamental thing we learn from Hume concerns the condition of one placed in the first philosophic age. This is a condition in which the preservation of one's humanity is the first problem of true philosophy. This was not the problem of philosophy for Plato, who sought to secure a foothold for philosophy in a still largely mythological world. And it was not the problem of philosophy in its encounter with Christian theism at the collapse of the ancient world. But it is the problem of philosophy in its current posture.

The second thing to be learned from Hume is that since we are still living out the adventure of the practices of liberty narrated by Hume (practices in which the current condition of philosophy has its source), we may continue that narrative into our own time as its most fundamental story. Such a narrative written along Humean lines would unmask those seductive but incoherent philosophical narratives of universal human emancipation which have legitimated spectacular transfers of power to the modern state. This state, informed by an ideological style of politics, has been the most powerful instrument for destroying independent social authorities and that vast variety of forms of human flourishing that Hume celebrated, but which the principle of dominion internal to false philosophy cannot tolerate. A current Humean narrative would subvert these latter-day forms of philosophical Whiggism and, while recognizing the constructive achievements of the modern state, would also advocate the devolution of power away from the center as a move necessary to restore and strengthen those forms of *sensus communis* which alone make possible the flourishing of the natural virtues in a commercial world all too disposed to treat the artificial virtues (rights) as the whole of the moral life.

Beyond some such sketch we cannot go without writing an actual narrative of the practices of liberty and of their relation to "false refinements" and philosophic superstitions as we have experienced them so far. But just as Aristotle taught that the standard of conduct is what the good man would do, so for Hume the standard of conduct and reform, in the first philosophic age, can only be what the true philosopher—a character endowed with the philosophical virtues—would do. I have tried to show that this character is exhibited throughout Hume's philosophical and historical writings. But if we are looking for an abridgment, it can be found in the peculiar sort of Stoicism advocated by Hume in the essays "The Stoic" and "The Sceptic." And as Hume ended *The Natural History of Religion* with the admonition to leave warring religious factions to their strife and to escape into the "calm though obscure regions of philosophy," so the admonition at the end of a Humean *Natural History of Philosophical Consciousness* must be to leave the figures of the philosophical bestiary in struggle and to enter the calm though obscure regions of true philosophy. The theoretical limits of this life are marked out by "The Sceptic," but its soul is animated by the practical engagements of "The Stoic," whose character contains "whatever can distinguish human nature, or elevate mortal man to a resemblance with the divinity" (*E*, 153).

NOTES

Chapter One

1. See my discussion of the status of necessary propositions in the philosophy of Hume, in *Hume's Philosophy of Common Life* (Chicago: University of Chicago Press, 1984), 44–59.

2. A. J. Ayer, ed., *Logical Positivism* (Glencoe: The Free Press, 1959), 4.

3. Hiram Caton, *The Politics of Progress* (Gainesville: University of Florida Press, 1988), 369, 364.

4. Philip P. Hallie, ed., *Sextus Empiricus: Selections from the Major Writings on Skepticism, Man, and God* (Indianapolis: Hackett, 1985), 31–44.

5. For an in-depth discussion of the status of impressions and ideas in Hume, see my *Hume's Philosophy of Common Life,* chapters 1–5.

Chapter Two

1. Thomas Nagel, *The View from Nowhere* (Oxford: Oxford University Press, 1989).

2. René Descartes, *The Philosophical Works of Descartes,* trans. and ed. Elizabeth S. Haldane and G. R. T. Ross, 2 vols. (Cambridge: Cambridge University Press, 1969), 1: 313.

3. Edmund Burke, *Reflections on the Revolution in France* (Indianapolis: Bobbs-Merrill, 1955), 196 n.

4. Quoted in Eric Voegelin, "The Formation of the Marxian Revolutionary Idea," *The Review of Politics* 12: 301.

5. Quintilian, *Orat.* viii, pr. 15–16, Loeb Classical Library (Cambridge, MA: Harvard University Press; London: Heinemann, 1920).

6. Cicero, *De part. Orat.* 23.79, Loeb Classical Library (Cambridge, MA: Harvard University Press; London: Heinemann, 1948); and Giambattista Vico, *The Autobiography of Giambattista Vico,* trans. Max Harold Fisch and Thomas Goddard Bergin (1944; reprint, Ithaca: Cornell University Press, 1990), 199. See also Vico's, *On the Study Methods of Our Time,* trans. Elio Gianturco, to which is added "The Academies and the Relation between Philosophy and Eloquence," trans. Donald Phillip Verene (Ithaca and

London: Cornell University Press, 1994). For a study of Hume's conception of eloquence, see Adam Potkay, *The Fate of Eloquence in the Age of Hume* (Ithaca and London: Cornell University Press, 1994).

7. See Ernesto Grassi, *Rhetoric as Philosophy: The Humanist Tradition* (University Park, PA: Pennsylvania State University Press, 1980).

8. Giambattista Vico, *The New Science,* trans. Thomas Goddard Bergin and Max Harold Fisch (Ithaca: Cornell University Press, 1984), axiom 12, 142.

9. Richard Rorty, *Objectivity, Relativism, and Truth: Philosophical Papers,* vol. 1 (Cambridge: Cambridge University Press, 1991), 198–99.

10. Richard Rorty, *Contingency, Irony, and Solidarity* (Cambridge: Cambridge University Press, 1989), 44–45.

11. Alasdair MacIntyre, *Whose Justice? Which Rationality?* (Notre Dame: University of Notre Dame Press, 1988), chapters 15, 16.

Chapter Three

1. David Hume, "Of the Authenticity of Ossian's Poems," in *David Hume: The Philosophical Works,* ed. T. H. Green and T. H. Grose, 4 vols. (Reprint of new edition, London, 1886; Darmstadt: Scientia Verlag Aalen, 1964),), 4: 416; and David Raynor, "Hume and Ossian," in *Ossian Revisited,* ed. Howard Gaskill (Edinburgh University Press, 1991), 147–63.

2. Richard S. Westfall, "Isaac Newton's *Theologiae Gentilis Origines Philosophicae,*" in *The Secular Mind: Essays Presented to Franklin L. Baumer,* ed. Warren Wager (New York: Holmes & Meir, 1982), 25.

3. John Home, *A Sketch of the Character of Mr. Hume and Diary of a Journey from Morpeth to Bath, 23 April–1 May 1776, by John Home,* ed. David Fate Norton (Edinburgh: Tragara Press, 1976).

4. E. C. Mossner, *The Life of David Hume* (Oxford: Clarendon Press, 1970), 483–86.

Chapter Four

1. For a discussion of Hume's dialectical understanding of perceptions, see my *Hume's Philosophy of Common Life,* chapters 1–2.

2. Giambattista Vico, *The Autobiography of Giambattista Vico,* trans. Max Harold Fisch and Thomas Goddard Bergin (Ithaca: Cornell University Press, 1983), p. 199; Cicero, *De part. orat.* 23.79, Loeb Classical Library (Cambridge, MA: Harvard University Press; London: Heinemann, 1948). I am indebted to Donald Verene for this point about eloquence and wisdom in Vico.

3. Adam Potkay, *The Fate of Eloquence in the Age of Hume* (Ithaca and London: Cornell University Press, 1944). Potkay explores the tension between Hume's civic humanism, which gives a central place to eloquence, and his commitment to modernity. But the question of eloquence as a constituent of philosophy is not raised. For an important discussion of this question, see Ernesto Grassi, *Rhetoric as Philosophy: The Humanist Tradition* (University Park: Pennsylvania State University Press, 1980); and Donald Phillip Verene, *Vico's Science of Imagination* (Ithaca: Cornell University Press, 1981).

Chapter Six

1. See Galen Strawson, *The Secret Connexion* (Oxford: Clarendon Press, 1989), and my *Hume's Philosophy of Common Life,* especially chapters 6 and 7.

2. John Locke, *Two Treatises of Government* (New York: Mentor Books, 1963), 369.

3. Algernon Sidney, "Discourses Concerning Government," in *The Works of Algernon Sidney* (London, 1772), 446.

4. For a discussion of Hume as a moralist in the classical tradition of virtue ethics, see Marie Martin, "Hume on Human Excellence," in *Hume Studies* 18, no. 2 (November 1992): 383–99; "Hume as Classical Moralist," *International Philosophical Quarterly* 34, no. 3 (September 1994): 323–34; and "Hutcheson and Hume on Explaining the Nature of Morality: Why It Is Mistaken to Suppose Hume Even Raised the Is/Ought Question," *History of Philosophy Quarterly* 8, no. 3 (July 1991): 232–95. Donald Siebert discusses Hume's classical moralism from a literary point of view in *The Moral Animus of David Hume* (Newark: University of Delaware Press, 1990).

5. John Stuart Mill, *Utilitarianism* (New York: Macmillan, 1957), 3–8.

Chapter Seven

1. Isaiah Berlin, "Hume and the Sources of German Anti-Rationalism," in *David Hume, Bicentenary Papers,* ed. G. P. Morice (Austin: University of Texas Press, 1977), 93–116.

2. John Home, *A Sketch of the Character of Mr. Hume and Diary of a Journey from Morpeth to Bath, 23 April–1 May 1776, by John Home,* ed. David Fate Norton (Edinburgh: The Tragara Press, 1976), 11.

3. For the complete text of the poem, see Donald Livingston, "A Poem by Philocalos Celebrating Hume's Return to Edinburgh," *Studies in Scottish Literature* 24 (1990): 108–15.

4. William Warburton, *A Selection from Unpublished Works,* ed. Francis Kilvert (London, 1841), 309–10.

5. James Beattie, *An Essay on Truth,* (Edinburgh: A. Kincaid and J. Bell, 1770; reprint, New York: Garland, 1983), 228.

6. *Weekly Magazine,* vol. 22 (1773): 233–34.

7. Roger Emerson, "The 'affair' at Edinburgh and the 'project' at Glasgow: The politics of Hume's attempt to become a professor," in *Hume and Hume's Connexions,* ed. M. A. Stewart and John Wright (Edinburgh: Edinburgh University Press, 1994), 16. For a discussion of the religious and philosophical issues involved in denying Hume a professorship, see R. B. Sher, "Professors of Virtue," in *Studies in the Philosophy of the Scottish Enlightenment,* ed. M. A. Stewart (Oxford: Clarendon Press, 1990), 105–14; and J. Moore, "Hume and Hutcheson," in *Hume's Connexions,* ed. Stewart and Wright, 23–57.

8. Quoted in Peter Jones, *Hume's Sentiments: Their Ciceronian and French Context* (Edinburgh: University of Edinburgh Press, 1982), 2.

9. Home, *Journey from Morpeth,* 12.

Chapter Eight

1. John Stuart Mill, review of Brodie, *History of the British Empire,* in *Westminster Review* 2 (1824), 34.

2. Bernard Bailyn, *The Origins of American Politics* (New York: Knopf, 1968), 17–18.

3. Caroline Robbins, *The Eighteenth-Century Commonwealth Man* (Cambridge: Harvard University Press, 1959), 8.

4. John Locke, *Two Treatises of Government* (New York: Mentor Books, 1963), 369 nn.

Chapter Nine

1. A. R. J. Turgot, "A Philosophical Review of the Successive Advances of the Human Mind," in *Turgot on Progress, Sociology, and Economics,* trans. and ed. Ronald L. Meek (Cambridge: Cambridge University Press, 1973); and Marquis de Condorcet, *Esquisse d'un tableau historique des progrès de l'esprit humain,* 3rd ed. (Paris, 1797).

2. John Rawls, *A Theory of Justice* (Cambridge: Harvard University Press, 1971).

3. Denis Diderot, quoted in Ernst Cassirer, *The Philosophy of the Enlightenment,* trans. Fritz C. A. Koelin and James P. Pettegrove (Boston: Beacon Press, 1955), 268–69.

4. This prephilosophical characterization of Christianity is due to Michael Oakeshott, "The Tower of Babel," in *Rationalism in Politics* (Indianapolis: Liberty Press, 1991), 484. Here Oakeshott makes a point similar to the one Hume makes in "Of Parties in General" about the momentous consequences of the merger of vulgar theism and philosophy in Christianity.

5. Karl Marx, Quoted in Eric Voegelin, "The Formation of the Marxian Revolutionary Idea," *The Review of Politics* 12: 301.

6. Karl Marx, *Karl Marx on Revolution,* ed. and trans. Saul K. Padover, 13 vols. (New York: McGraw-Hill, 1971), 1: 516.

7. Liston Papers, Bundle I, in The National Library of Scotland.

8. Edmund Burke, *Reflections on the Revolution in France,* ed. Thomas H. D. Mahoney (Indianapolis: Bobbs-Merrill, 1955), 200.

Chapter Ten

1. E. C. Mossner and I. S. Ross, eds., *Correspondence of Adam Smith* (Indianapolis: Liberty Classics, 1987), 222.

2. Herbert Butterfield, *The Whig Interpretation of History* (London: G. Bell, 1968).

3. J. Y. T. Greig, *David Hume* (New York: Oxford University Press, 1931), 375–76.

4. Mossner and Ross, eds., *Correspondence of Adam Smith,* 113.

5. Stanley Ayling, *The Elder Pitt* (London: Collins, 1976), 240.

6. Catharine Macaulay, *The History of England* (London, 1763), xi.

7. For a good discussion of these constitutions, see Eugene Miller, "Hume on Liberty in the Successive English Constitutions," in *Liberty in Hume's History of England,* ed. Nicholas Capaldi and Donald Livingston (Dordrecht: Kluwer, 1990), 53–104.

8. Henry Mackenzie, *An Account of the Life and Writings of John Home, Esq.* (Edinburgh, 1822), 23.

9. Bernard Bailyn, *The Origins of American Politics* (New York: Knopf, 1968), 17–18.

10. John Home, *A Sketch of the Character of Mr. Hume and Diary of a Journey from Morpeth to Bath, 23 April–1 May 1776, by John Home,* ed. David Fate Norton (Edinburgh: Tragara Press, 1976), 20.

11. See Craig Walton, "Hume and Jefferson," in *Hume: A Re-Evaluation,* ed. Donald Livingston (New York: Fordham University Press, 1976).

12. J. H. Plumb, *The First Four Georges* (London: B. T. Batsford, 1956), 35.

13. Audrey Williamson, *Wilkes 'A Friend to Liberty'* (London: Allen and Unwin, 1974), 147.

14. Charles Chenevix Trench, *Portrait of a Patriot: A Biography of John Wilkes* (Edinburgh and London: William Blackwood & Sons, 1962), 218.

15. Letter to Sir Andrew Mitchell from Strahan, 1 April 1768 (Hume mss. no. 23158, p. 47, National Library of Scotland). On Franklin's report, see Trench, *Portrait,* 228.

16. Trench, *Portrait,* 229.

17. Laurence Bongie, *David Hume: Prophet of the Counter-Revolution* (Oxford: Clarendon Press, 1965), 30.

18. Williamson, *Wilkes,* 191.

19. Trench, *Portrait,* 229.

20. Trench, *Portrait,* 219; Williamson, *Wilkes,* 146.

21. Williamson, *Wilkes,* 152.

22. Trench, *Portrait,* 218.

23. Trench, *Portrait,* 263.

24. *Caledonian Mercury,* 6 April 1771.

25. Williamson, *Wilkes,* 67–68.

26. *Caledonian Mercury,* 3 April 1771.

27. Mackenzie records that he had seen among the "careless scraps of his earlier writings, which Mr. Hume had preserved, the beginning of a warm paper addressed to the landed gentlemen of Scotland, on the subject of the militia, ascribing to the want of it the early misfortunes of the Seven Years' War" (Mackenzie, *Life and Writings of John Home,* 28). That Hume had begun a piece on the militia provides some corroboration for David Raynor's thesis that Hume is the author of *Sister Peg,* which is traditionally attributed to Adam Ferguson. See *Sister Peg: A Pamphlet Hitherto Unknown, by David Hume,* ed. David Raynor (Cambridge: Cambridge University Press, 1982). This satirical work defends the revival of a Scots militia after the defeat of the Scottish Militia Bill in April, 1760. Hume's defense of an armed citizenry places him in the civic humanist tradition. A citizen's army also appears as a support of liberty in Hume's "Idea of a Perfect Commonwealth." See also John Robertson, *The Scottish Enlightenment and the Militia Issue* (Edinburgh: J. Donald, 1985).

28. Trench, *Portrait,* 266.

29. Trench, *Portrait,* 342.

30. Williamson, *Wilkes,* 227.

31. Trench, *Portrait,* 259.

32. Williamson, *Wilkes,* 138.

33. Karl Marx, *Karl Marx on Revolution,* ed. and trans. Saul K. Padover (New York: McGraw-Hill, 1971), 516.

34. John Stewart, *Opinion and Reform in Hume's Political Philosophy* (Princeton: Princeton University Press, 1992).

35. For a discussion of the philosophical meaning of conservatism, see my *Hume's Philosophy of Common Life,* chapter 12, and "On Hume's Conservatism," *Hume Studies* 21, no. 2: 151–64.

36. Richard Price, *A Discourse on the Laws of Our Country* (London, 1789), 49–51.

37. Edmund Burke, *Reflections on the Revolution in France* (Indianapolis: Bobbs-Merrill, 1955), 196 n.

38. Jean-Paul Sartre, *Les mains sales* (Paris: Gallimard, 1948).

Chapter Eleven

1. Allan Ramsay, "A Succinct Review of the American Contest," by Zero (1778), 23.

2. Ramsay, "American Contest," 28.

3. Ramsay, "American Contest," 28.

4. Estimates of the deaths caused by the Thirty Years' War range from 15 to 20 percent to two-thirds of the population of Central Europe, but one-third of the population seems to be the figure agreed upon by most historians. For the former figures, see Geoffrey Parker, *The Thirty Year's War* (London: Routledge and Paul, 1984), chapters 5–6; for the latter figures, see B. H. Liddell Hart, *The Revolution in Warfare* (Westport, CT: Greenwood Press, 1947), 45.

5. Fredrick J. P. Veale, *Advance to Barbarism: The Development of Total Warfare from Sarajevo to Hiroshima* (New York: Devin-Adair, 1968), 72–73.

6. Quoted in Veale, *Barbarism,* 14.

7. Consider Liddell Hart's judgment that the "large-scale landmark" in the collapse of civilized warfare "was created fifty years before 1914 in the American Civil War. This was in many ways the prototype of modern total war"; see Hart, *Warfare,* 72, and 72–79.

8. Francis Watson, *Wallenstein* (London: Chatto and Windus, 1939), 326; see also David Irving, *The Destruction of Dresden* (London: Kimber, 1963), 14; and Veale, *Barbarism,* 190–96.

9. See Paul C. Vincent, *The Politics of Hunger: The Allied Blockade of Germany* (Athens, OH: Ohio University Press, 1985).

10. Quoted in Veale, *Barbarism,* 193.

11. Sir Charles Webster and Noble Frankland, *The Strategic Air Offensive against Germany, 1939–1945* (London: H. M. Stationary Office, 1961), 115.

12. Leonard P. Ayres, *The War with Germany: A Statistical Survey* (Washington: Government Printing Office, 1919), 120.

13. Peter Young, ed., *The World Almanac of World War II* (Englewood Cliffs, NJ: Prentice-Hall, 1971), 614.

14. John Home, *A Sketch of the Character of Mr. Hume and Diary of a Journey from Morpeth to Bath, 23 April–1 May 1776, by John Home,* ed. David Fate Norton (Edinburgh: The Tragara Press, 1976), 24.

15. See the footnote on p. 241 of volume 5 of Hume's *History.*

16. Ernest C. Mossner, "Hume's Early Memoranda, 1729–1740: The Complete Text," *Journal of the History of Ideas* (October 1948): 504.

17. Letter from Franklin to Hume, 27 September 1760; manuscript 23155, National Library of Scotland.

18. William B. Willcox, ed., *The Papers of Benjamin Franklin,* 29 vols. (New Haven and London: Yale University Press, 1982), 22: 85.

19. Robert Morell Schmitz, *Hugh Blair* (New York: King's Crown Press, 1948), 80.

20. *Caledonian Mercury,* 13 August 1776, National Library of Scotland.

21. Quoted in Ian Ross, *Lord Kames and the Scotland of His Day* (Oxford: Clarendon Press, 1972), 218.

22. Adam Smith, *An Inquiry into the Nature and Causes of the Wealth of Nations,* ed. R. H. Campbell and A. S. Skinner 2 vols. (Indianapolis: Liberty Press, 1981), 2: 625–26.

23. Hume's doctor, Joseph Black, records that the immediate approach of death began in the early morning of 23 August (*L,* 2: 449). Prior to that, as Black wrote on 22 August, "He sits up, goes down stairs once a day, and amuses himself with reading, but seldom sees anybody. . . . He is quite free from anxiety . . . and passes his time very well with the assistance of amusing books"; see *The Correspondence of Adam Smith,* ed. Ernest Campbell Mossner and Ian Simpson Ross (Indianapolis: Liberty Classics, 1987), 220. Hume was able to write a farewell letter to Madame De Boufflers on 20 August.

24. See Michael Oakeshott, "Part Three, On Hobbes," in *Rationalism in Politics,* ed. Timothy Fuller (Indianapolis: Liberty Press, 1991), "The Rule of Law," in *On History and Other Essays* (Totowa, NJ: Barnes and Noble, 1983), and *On Human Conduct* (Oxford: Clarendon Press, 1975).

25. John Pringle to Hume, 26 January 1773; manuscript 23156, f. 88, National Library of Scotland.

26. John Pringle to Hume, 28 March 1774; manuscript 23156, f. 93, National Library of Scotland.

27. Francis Hutcheson, *A System of Moral Philosophy,* 2 vols. (London: A. Millar and T. Longman, 1755), 2: 306–9.

Chapter Twelve

1. Douglass Adair, "'That Politics May Be Reduced to a Science': David Hume, James Madison, and the *Tenth Federalist,*" *Huntington Library Quarterly* 20 (1957): 343–60.

2. For a recent statement of the nationalist theory, see Samuel H. Beer, *To Make a Nation: The Rediscovery of American Federalism* (Cambridge, MA: Harvard University Press, 1993).

3. James Madison, *The Virginia Report of 1799–1800, Touching the Alien and Sedition Laws; Together with the Virginia Resolutions of December 21, 1798, And Several Other Documents Illustrative of the Report and Resolutions* (Richmond, VA: J. W. Randolph, 1850). For an argument that the compact theory is primordial and the states were sovereign from the beginning, see Jack Greene, *Peripheries and Center: Constitutional Development in the Extended Polities of the British Empire and the United States, 1607–1788* (Athens, GA: University of Georgia Press, 1986); Merrill Jensen, *The Articles of Confederation* (Madison: University of Wisconsin Press, 1963); and H. Van Tyne "Sovereignty in the American Revolution: An Historical Study," in *The American Historical Review* 12 (April 1907): 529–45.

4. Joseph Story, *Commentaries on the Constitution of the United States,* 2 vols. (Boston: Hilliard Gray, 1833); see esp. vol. 1, chapter 3.

5. Madison, *Virginia Report,* 162.

6. James Jackson Kilpatrick, *The Sovereign States* (Chicago: Regnerey, 1957); see also H. Newcomb Morse, "The Foundations and Meaning of Secession," *Stetson Law Review* 15: 419–36.

7. Henry Adams, ed., *Documents Relating to New England Federalism, 1800–1815* (Boston: Little, Brown, 1877); see also Carl Swisher, *American Constitutional Development,* 2d ed. (Boston: Houghton Mifflin, 1954), 127

8. Quoted in Albert Taylor Bledsoe, *Is Davis a Traitor, or Was Secession a Constitutional Right Previous to the War of 1861?* (Richmond, VA: The Hermitage Press, 1907), chapter 16, 149.

9. William Rawle, *A View of the Constitution* (Philadelphia: H. Carey Lea, 1825), chapter 31; Charles Francis Adams, "The Constitutional Ethics of Secession" (Charleston, 1903). A new edition of Rawle's *View of the Constitution* is available, edited by Walter D. Kennedy and James R. Kennedy (Baton Rouge: Land and Land Publishing Division, 1993).

10. Jonathan Elliot, *The Debates of the Several State Constitutions on the Adoption of the Federal Constitution,* 4 vols. (Washington: Taylor and Maury, 1854) 1: 327–31, 333–37; and *The Constitutions of the Several States of the Union and United States,* (New York: A. S. Barnes & Co., 1852; and Cincinnati: H. W. Derby & Co., 1852), 491.

11. Alexis de Tocqueville, *Democracy in America,* trans. Henry Reeve, 2 vols. (New York: Alfred A. Knopf, 1945) 1: chapter 18, 403.

12. Henry Lord Brougham, *Political Philosophy,* 2d ed., 2 vols. (London: H. G. Bohn, 1849) 1: 336.

13. John Quincy Adams, *The Jubilee of the Constitution: A Discourse Delivered at the Request of the New York Historical Society* (New York: Samuel Coleman, 1839), 69.

14. John Quincy Adams, "Address to the People of the Free States of the Union," 3 March 1843, reprinted in Frederick W. Meek, *Slavery and the Annexation of Texas* (New York: Alfred A. Knopf, 1972), 205. I am indebted to Jefferey Hummel for this reference.

15. William C. Wright, *Secession Movement in the Middle Atlantic States* (Cranbury, NJ: Farleigh Dickinson, 1994).

16. Donald Livingston, "Hume, English Barbarism, and the American Crisis," in *Scotland and America in the Age of Enlightenment,* ed. Richard Sher and Jeffrey Smitten (Princeton: Princeton University Press, 1990).

17. John Stewart, *Opinion and Reform in Hume's Political Philosophy* (Princeton: Princeton University Press, 1992), 316.

18. See John Robertson's excellent discussion of these alternative schemes, "Universal Monarchy and the Liberties of Europe: David Hume's Critique of an English Whig Doctrine," in *Political Discourse in Early Modern Britain,* ed. Nicholas Phillipson and Quentin Skinner (Cambridge: Cambridge University Press, 1993).

19. Jensen, *Articles of Confederation,* 143, 162–69.

20. The so-called anti-Federalists, who were supporters of what I describe in chapters 13 and 14 as a federative polity as opposed to a unitary state, are casualties of American Whiggism. Their arguments against ratification of the proposed Constitution are worthy of respect and in some cases are retrospectively prophetic. See *The Complete Anti-Federalist,* ed. Herbert J. Storing, 7 vols. (Chicago: University of Chicago Press, 1981). The most powerful anti-Federalist speech is to be found in the essays by Brutus, 2: 358–452. See also Storing's essay, "What the Anti-Federalists Were *For,*" 1: 3–76. For an argument that the Union was not perpetual and was in fact dissolved by secession of nine states from The Articles of Confederation, see Kenneth M. Stamp, "The Concept of a Perpetual Union," *Journal of American History* 65 (1978): 5–33.

Chapter Thirteen

1. See, for example, Michael Oakeshott's account of the career of what he calls "a modern European state" in *On Human Conduct* (Oxford: Clarendon Press, 1991).

2. John Stewart, *Opinion and Reform in Hume's Political Philosophy* (Princeton: Princeton University Press, 1992), 316.

3. See Hans-Hermann Hoppe's excellent essay, "Nationalism and Secession," in *Chronicles of Culture* 17 (November 1993): 23–25.

4. John E. Acton, *Selected Writings of Lord Acton,* ed. Rufus Fears, 2 vols. (Indianapolis: Liberty Classics, 1985), 1: 417.

5. Samuel Dumas and K. O. Vedel-Petersen, *Losses of Life Caused by War* (Oxford: Clarendon Press, 1923), 28.

6. Peter Young, ed., *The World Almanac Book of World War II* (Englewood Cliffs, NJ: Prentice-Hall, 1981), 614; see also Leonard P. Ayres, *The War with Germany: A Statistical Survey* (Washington: Government Printing Office, 1919), 120.

7. Robert Conquest, *The Harvest of Sorrow: Soviet Collectivism and the Terror-Famine* (New York: Oxford University Press, 1986), 301, and *The Great Terror: A Reassessment* (New York: Oxford University Press, 1990).

8. Conquest, *The Great Terror,* 472.

9. Conquest, *Harvest of Sorrow,* 321.

10. See R. J. Rummel, *Lethal Politics: Soviet Genocide and Mass Murder Since 1917* (New Brunswick, NJ: Transaction, 1990), xi, 3; *Democide, Nazi Genocide, and Mass Murder* (New Brunswick, NJ: Transaction, 1992); *China's Bloody Century: Genocide and Mass Murder Since 1900* (New Brunswick, NJ: Transaction, 1991); and *Death by Government* (New Brunswick, NJ: Transaction, 1994).

11. Bertrand De Jouvenel, *On Power* (Indianapolis: Liberty Classics, 1993), 12–13. This is a brilliant study of the growth of the modern state and its disposition to concentrate power at the center. For an empirical study of the growth of the state, see Robert Higgs, *Crisis and Leviathan: Critical Episodes in the Growth of American Government* (New York & Oxford: Oxford University Press, 1987).

12. For a refutation of the doctrine that liberalism is the only legitimate form of political association, in relation to which all other forms must be viewed as failed approximations, see John Gray's *Liberalisms: Essays in Political Philosophy* (New York: Routledge, 1989). Gray's critique is philosophically in the spirit of Hume's criticism of Whiggism; see especially "Postscript: After Liberalism," 239–64. For Gray's attempt to recover the truth of liberalism detoxified, see *Post-Liberalism: Studies in Political Thought* (New York: Routledge, 1993), especially 283–328.

13. Samuel F. Scott and Barry Rothaus, eds., *Historical Dictionary of the French Revolution, 1789–1799* (Westport: Greenwood Press, 1985); see the article on the Terror. For a clear-eyed view of the French Revolution, see Rene Sedillot, *Le Cout de la Revolution* (Paris, 1987).

14. Gray, *Post-Liberalism,* 164–65. For a forceful argument that Soviet barbarism and totalitarianism are not the continuation of an authoritarian Russian mind-set but the result of Western political ideologies, see pp. 157–201. Totalitarianism has its roots in Enlightenment liberalism, and the first totalitarian state was the republic of the French Revolution. The Soviet Union was that state writ large.

15. Gray, *Post-Liberalism,* 168.

16. Gray, *Post-Liberalism,* 165–68, and John J. Dziak, *Chekisty: A History of the KGB* (Lexington, MA: Lexington Books, 1988).

17. Quoted in De Jouvenel, *On Power,* 253.

18. Quoted in De Jouvenel, *On Power,* 285 n.

19. Quoted in De Jouvenel, *On Power,* 286.

20. See De Jouvenel's discussion of modern and medieval theories of power, in *On*

Power, chapter 2; see also Michael Mendle, "Parliamentary Sovereignty: A Very English Absolutism," in *Political Discourse in Early Modern Britain,* ed. Nicholas Phillipson and Quentin Skinner (Cambridge: Cambridge University Press, 1993), 97–119.

21. Johannes Althusius, *Politica,* ed. Fredrick S. Carney (Indianapolis: Liberty Classics, 1995), 17.

22. Althusius, *Politica,* 197–98.

23. Althusius, *Politica.*

24. David Hume, *Sister Peg: A Pamphlet Hitherto Unknown, by Hume,* ed. David Raynor (Cambridge: Cambridge University Press, 1982), 123 n. 96.

25. Winston S. Churchill, *A History of the English-Speaking Peoples,* 6 vols. (New York: Dodd, Mead & Co., 1957), 3: 135.

26. Forrest McDonald, *Alexander Hamilton* (New York: W. W. Norton, 1982), 4.

27. The process of Hamiltonization, that is, of monetizing public debt and thereby transferring banking and currency into the hands of private interests, received a much-needed boost from the war of 1861–1865. The agrarian South had consistently vetoed Northern industrial interests, which required centralization and the use of public funds for private industrial development. The union of government and industrial commerce was not possible until the agrarian South was eliminated and the federative constitution replaced with that of a unitary state. An independent Southern confederacy could not be tolerated because Northern industrial interests required shutting out foreign manufactures. With the South out of the Union, the *average* tariff rate was raised in 1865 from a high rate of 18.84 percent to a prohibitive 47.56 percent and would not drop much below that for some seventy years. In contrast, the average rate of the Confederate tariff was 12 percent. The South had a flourishing export trade in staples in an unprotected world market, allowing it to fund some three-fourths of the federal revenue while it was in the Union. Ft. Sumter was a main port where the tariff was collected, which is why Lincoln was eager to control it. What neither Lincoln nor the Northern industrialists could accept was a low tariff zone on their southern border; see Charles Adams's chapter, "Was It Taxes or Slavery That Caused the Civil War?" in *For Good and Evil: The Impact of Taxes on the Course of Civilization* (New York: Madison Books, 1993), 323–37, and *Taxation in American History* (forthcoming). But with the South out of the Union, a new and unexpected path to Hamiltonization appeared. Its essence was sketched out in the famous "Hazard Circular," which was distributed to the wealthier classes of the North in 1862: "The great debt that capitalists will see to it is made out of the war, must be used as a means to control the volume of money. To accomplish this the bonds must be used as a banking basis. We are now waiting for the secretary of the treasury to make this recommendation to Congress. It will not do to allow the greenback . . . to circulate as money any length of time, as we cannot control that. But we can control the bonds and through them the bank issues" (quoted in Charles Lindbergh, *Banking and Currency and the Money Trust* [National Capitol Press, 1913], 101–4). The legislation that finally established the Hamiltonian system was the National Bank Acts of 1863 and 1864, the State Bank Note Acts of 1865 and 1866, and the Federal Reserve Act of 1913; see also Ludwell Johnson, *Division and Reunion: America, 1847–1877* (New York: John Wiley and Sons, 1978), 107–21. All of this and the massive corruption that followed the Civil War were right on schedule with what Hume had predicted regarding expanding republics and public credit.

28. McDonald, *Hamilton,* 227.

29. Istvon Hont, "The Rhapsody of Public Debt: David Hume and Voluntary State

Bankruptcy," in *Political Discourse in Early Modern Britain,* ed. Nicholas Phillipson and Quentin Skinner (Cambridge: Cambridge University Press, 1993), 344 n. This is an excellent discussion of Hume's worry about public debt.

30. John Home, *A Sketch of the Character of Mr. Hume and Diary of a Journey from Morpeth to Bath, 23 April–1 May 1776, by John Home,* ed. David Norton (Edinburgh: Tragara Press, 1976), 16, 22.

Chapter Fourteen

1. John Locke, *Two Treatises of Government,* ed. Peter Laslett (Cambridge: Cambridge University Press, 1988), 349.

2. The Confederates considered secession to be a legal act within the Constitutional framework considered as a compact between the states; it was not the appeal to heaven that the colonists made in seceding from Britain. For an argument that secession was a constitutional right of an American state, see H. Newcomb Morse, "The Foundations and Meaning of Secession," *Stetson Law Review* 15 (1986): 419–36. All the states called for elections of representatives to form a convention of the people to debate the question of secession. North Carolina, Virginia, Arkansas, and Tennessee initially voted to remain in the Union by large majorities. They reversed themselves only when Lincoln ordered troops to invade and coerce the seceding states back into the Union. President Buchanan had argued that the Constitution did not legitimate secession, nor did it authorize the central government to use force in preserving the Union. The matter was to be settled by political negotiations between the states. But Lincoln refused to receive Confederate commissioners and to negotiate a settlement. Jefferson had argued that because the Constitution was a compact between states, one could expect secession and that it should be allowed. But he also thought that the benefits of Union were so great that after a cooling off period (as in, as he put it, a lover's quarrel), the states would return to the Union with renewed and stronger affection (letter to R. Rush, 20 October 1820). This generous view echoes Hume's confession of being an "American in my principles" in supporting the secession of the colonies as well as the action of the Soviet Union in allowing peaceful secession of fifteen Soviet republics by referendum. All of this is in stark contrast to Lincoln's grim and uncompromising consolidationism and his willingness to carry out the bloodiest war of the nineteenth century in order to transform a federative polity into a unitary state.

3. King George III recognized the sovereignty of the states individually and by name in the Treaty of Paris, 3 September 1783: "His Britannic Majesty acknowledges the said United States, viz., New Hampshire, Massachusetts Bay, Rhode Island . . . and Georgia, to be free, sovereign, and independent States"; see Henry Steele Commager, ed., *Documents of American History,* 9th ed. (Englewood Cliffs: Prentice-Hall, 1988), 1: 117.

4. Quoted in Forrest McDonald, *Alexander Hamilton* (New York: W. W. Norton, 1982), 356.

5. McDonald, *Hamilton,* 56.

6. Allen Buchanan has suggested that Americans have not yet come to terms with the moral issue raised by Lincoln's insistence on war to suppress secession (*Secession: The Morality of Political Divorce from Fort Sumter to Lithuania and Quebec* [Boulder, CO and Oxford: Westview Press, 1991], x). It was the bloodiest war of the nineteenth century and left 1,500,000 dead, missing, and wounded. It met with massive resistance

in the North. To suppress this resistance, Lincoln suspended the writ of habeas corpus throughout the Union for the duration of the war, rounded up without trial tens of thousands of political prisoners, closed down some three hundred newspapers, defied the Supreme Court, and used the army to assure elections (see Ludwell Johnson, *Division and Reunion: America 1848–1877* [John Wiley and Sons, 1978]). The barbarism of suppressing secession has been obscured by the moral issue of slavery, but Lincoln was very clear that the war was being fought to preserve the Union and that he neither had the authority nor the inclination to interfere with slavery in the states where it was legal. When Lincoln sent troops to capture Ft. Sumter, there were more slave states in the Union than out of it, and slavery was protected in Union states throughout the war. He insisted only that the central government had the authority to prevent its extension to the territories. When the South seceded, the threat of slavery in the territories vanished. Indeed this was, in effect, what the abolitionists had worked to achieve: secession of the North from the South. Jeffrey Hummel has argued for the original hard abolitionist line that secession was the best way to achieve peaceful abolition of slavery in *Emancipating Slaves and Enslaving Freemen* (Chicago: Open Court, 1996).

What is missing from the American nationalist myth that the war between the states was fought to abolish slavery is the ugly fact of American racism. Nearly all Americans, including Lincoln and most abolitionists, believed that America was a white European polity, and that neither the aboriginal nor the African populations were to have full social and political participation. Northern states worked to rid themselves of the African population as they had done with the aboriginal population. To take only a few examples, the constitutions of Oregon (1857) and Indiana (1851) forebade the entrance of any free blacks or mulattos. Lincoln's state of Illinois forebade the entrance of any free blacks unless they could post a bond of one thousand dollars; see Franklin B. Hough, ed., *American Constitutions: Comprising the Constitution of Each State in the Union, and the United States, etc.*, 2 vols. (Albany: Weed, Parsons & Co., 1872), 2: 212; 1: 358; and Leon Litwack, *North of Slavery* (Chicago: University of Chicago Press, 1961). People who wrote such laws would not be inclined to wage war to emancipate a people they had sought to keep out of their territory. Lee was opposed to slavery and thought it was on the way to oblivion; he emancipated, at his own expense, the large number of slaves he had inherited by marrying into the family of George Washington. Only 10 percent of Southerners owned slaves. The Confederate Cabinet had agreed to abolish slavery within five years after the end of hostilities in exchange for recognition by Britain and France. With the exception of Haiti, all other countries in the Western hemisphere abolished slavery without war. When the moral issue of slavery as part of the war effort is subtracted from the equation, we are left with the question of whether Lincoln's war of coercion to suppress secession was morally justified. If all states west of the Mississippi should today secede, form a western confederacy, and agree to negotiate a treaty to apportion the national debt, would the eastern states be morally justified in launching a scorched-earth war to preserve the Union? Much less was such a war morally justified in 1861 in a Union only seventy years old, which had been born in secession and had expanded to some ten times its size in only fifty years, in which the states were perceived as sovereign political societies, and in which secession had been invoked by every section from the beginning. The cost of the war to the North alone, as Jeffrey Hummel has argued, would have paid for the emancipation of every slave as well as forty acres and a mule; see *Emancipating Slaves,* "Epilogue." The story of the enormous cost in human life and suffering of suppressing legitimate secession movements throughout the world over the last two centuries in order to create or maintain consolidated modern states has yet to be written. For a recent argument that the American Union, like the former Soviet Union, has become unworkable and that peaceful secession by referendum is the only remedy, see Thomas Naylor and William Willimon, *Downsizing the USA* (Grand Rapids, MI: Erdmans, 1997).

7. Carl Sandburg, ed., *Abraham Lincoln: The War Years* (New York: Harcourt, Brace, 1939), 128.

8. This nationalist constitution was what Hamilton had wished for, but he knew it was not the compact the states had ratified, which is why he called it a "worthless fabric." The first systematic statement of the nationalist theory did not appear until 1833, when Joseph Story's *Commentaries* were published. As has often happened in American constitutional jurisprudence, a wished-for Constitution was read back into the origin as what was founded and intended. A refutation of Story was published by Abel Upshur, a distinguished Virginia jurist and Secretary of State under Tyler, in *A Brief Enquiry into the True Nature and Character of Our Federal Government, Being a Review of Judge Story's Commentaries* (Petersburg, VA, 1840). But the first systematic refutation of the nationalist theory was given by Albert Taylor Bledsoe, *Is Davis a Traitor, or Was Secession a Constitutional Right Previous to the War of 1861?* (Baltimore, 1866). The Confederate Government had commissioned Bledsoe, a distinguished mathematician and theologian, to write a legal brief justifying the secession of the Southern states. The work was completed as the war ended. Bledsoe published it with the hope of saving the former president of the Confederacy from being hanged for treason, but the book is not about Davis's conduct. Its topic is simply the legal question of whether an American state can secede. Its argument was considered by many to be unanswerable, and Davis was not prosecuted. Bledsoe's work has been reprinted by Fletcher and Fletcher Publishers, North Charleston, SC, 1995. Upshur's work is forthcoming from the same press.

9. Francis Fukuyama, *The End of History and the Last Man* (New York: Free Press, 1992).

10. Milica Zarkovic Bookman, *The Economics of Secession* (New York: St. Martin's Press, 1992), 7. For attempts to establish a right of secession in international law, see Lee Buchheit, *Secession: The Legitimacy of Self-Determination* (New Haven, CT: Yale University Press, 1978).

11. I have discussed this on a number of occasions with Buchanan. He has argued in a number of speeches for the principle of legitimate secession and urged that the European Union frame a right to secede in its Constitution.

12. J. J. Rousseau, *Social Contract,* book 2, chapters 2–4.

13. Rousseau, *Social Contract,* book 3, chapter 4.

14. John E. Acton, *Selected Writings of Lord Acton,* ed. Rufus Fears, 2 vols. (Indianapolis: Liberty Classics, 1985); see the essay "Nationality" in vol. 1, 409–33.

15. Michael Oakeshott, *On Human Conduct* (Oxford: Oxford University Press, 1991). See also the essay "The Rule of Law" in *On History and Other Essays* (Totowa, NJ: Barnes & Noble, 1983).

16. Marie Martin, "Hume as Classical Moralist," *International Philosophical Quarterly* 34, no. 3 (September 1994), 323–33, and "Hume on Human Excellence," *Hume Studies* 18, no. 2 (November 1992), 383–99.

17. Michael Oakeshott, *Rationalism in Politics and Other Essays,* ed. Timothy Fuller (Indianapolis: Liberty Classics, 1991), 476.

18. Oakeshott, *Rationalism in Politics,* 475–76.

19. John Gray, *Post-Liberalism: Studies in Political Thought* (New York: Routledge, 1993), 263–64.

20. Oakeshott, *On Human Conduct,* 188.

21. Allan Bloom, "Sex and Separateness," in *Good Order: Right Answers to Contemporary Questions,* ed. Brad Miner (New York: Simon and Schuster, 1995).

22. See M. E. Bradford, *A Better Guide Than Reason* (New Brunswick: Transaction, 1994), especially the essay "Franklin and Jefferson: The Making and Binding of Self."

23. Kevin R. Gutzman, "A Troublesome Legacy: James Madison and 'The Principles of '98,'" *Journal of the Early Republic* 15, no. 4 (Winter 1995): 569–89.

24. It is a founding myth of American nationalism that the war between the states was fought to abolish slavery rather than for the morally dubious goal of coercing eleven states back into a union from which they had voted to withdraw. At most, this is a Platonic noble lie necessary to legitimate the violent transformation of a federation of states into a unitary state. The Southern states seceded over moral and legal issues having to do with the division of authority between the central and state governments. These issues are worthy of respect and have motivated other large-scale federative polities, as in the peaceful secession of Belgium from Holland in 1830 and of Norway from Sweden in 1905; in the decision of Western Australia to secede in 1935; and in the contemporary secession movement in Quebec. The extension of slavery into the territories was only one of these issues, and in seceding from the Union, the South abandoned any claim to those territories and so eliminated at least that problem. Another issue was economic exploitation. The central government was funded almost entirely by a tariff on imports. Since Southern staples accounted for the vast majority of exports, which were exchanged for manufactured imports, the South accounted for three-fourths of the federal revenue, which a Northern majority sought to use to improve its infrastructure. In addition to this transfer of wealth, the Northern industrial sector demanded a protective tariff which not only transferred wealth to the North but was undermining the Southern export economy. By 1865 the average tariff rate had climbed from 18.84 percent in 1861 to the spectacular high of 47.56 percent. This effectively shut out European manufactures that Southerners exchanged for agricultural staples. Upon being forced back into the union and having voted for the Thirteenth Amendment abolishing slavery, Southerners hoped the prohibitive tariff would be lifted. It was not. The tariff did not drop below 40 percent until 1914, except for two years when it was 38 percent, and after Wilson it rose again under Harding, Coolidge, and Hoover. Since the North could absorb only a small part of what the South was able to produce, the export trade dwindled, throwing the region into a condition of poverty that even Calhoun's pessimistic predictions could not imagine (see Johnson, *Division and Reunion,* 107–22).

Nineteenth-century historians, writing in the heyday of centralization, consolidation, gunboat diplomacy, and European and American imperialism, were honest about the reason for suppressing secession. In *The Footprints of Time: A Complete Analysis of Our American System of Government* (Burlington, IA: R. T. Root, 1875), Charles Bancroft wrote, "While so gigantic a war was an immense evil; to allow the right of peaceable secession would have been ruin to the enterprise and thrift of the industrious laborer, and keen-eyed business man of the North. It would have been the greatest calamity of the age. War was less to be feared" (p. 646). Forrest McDonald has shown that the Fourteenth Amendment, which has been manipulated by the courts to legitimate the policies of a unitary state, was never ratified by the states but was imposed by coercion shortly after the war; see "Was the Fourteenth Amendment Constitutionally Adopted?" *The Georgia Journal of Southern Legal History* 1, no. 1 (Spring/Summer 1991): 1–20. To this should be added the discriminatory economic policies imposed on the conquered provinces after the Civil War, which contributed to the poverty of the region and were not fully removed until World War II; see C. Vann Woodward, *Origins of the New South, 1877–1913* (Baton Rouge: Louisiana State University Press, 1971), chapter 11, "The Colonial Economy."

This was just the sort of economic exploitation that Hume said an *expanding republic* would impose on its conquered provinces. It was just such economic discrimination (and of a much milder form) that led the colonies to secede from Britain and that compelled agrarian Western Australia to secede from the eastern industrial part which, like the North, had imposed high tariffs at the expense of agriculture; see Gregory Craven, *Secession: The Ultimate States' Right* (Melbourne: University of Melbourne Press, 1986). There were other reasons for Southern secession, and the most eloquent statement of those reasons is to be found in the Confederate Constitution itself; see Johnson, *Division and Reunion,* pp. 72–74, and Marshall DeRosa, *The Confederate Constitution of 1861* (Columbia and London: University of Missouri Press, 1991). It is significant that the Confederate Constitution outlawed the slave trade and allowed the admission of non-slave-holding states. As Acton put it, "Slavery was not the cause of secession, but the reason for its failure," (*Selected Writings,* p. 277). The undertheorized character of secession, the ubiquitous prejudice on behalf of the modern state, and the deep need to legitimate a unitary American state are reasons why the moral and legal merits of Southern secession have not been appreciated and the barbarism of suppressing it confronted.

But there are exceptions; see Hummel's *Emancipating Slaves,* especially the epilogue, for a picture of the war to suppress secession as yet another act of violent consolidation in the formation of a modern unitary state. The article on Lincoln in Edmund Wilson's *Patriotic Gore* (New York: Farrar, Straus, and Giroux, 1977) presents Lincoln as engaged in the same project as Bismarck and Lenin: the violent destruction of federative polities in favor of unitary states. See also Ann Norton's *Alternative Americas* (Chicago: University of Chicago Press, 1986). For studies of Lincoln as a gnostic figure, see M. E. Bradford, "Dividing the House: The Gnosticism of Lincoln's Rhetoric," *Modern Age* 23 (1979): 10–24; "The Lincoln Legacy: A Long View," *Modern Age* 24 (1980): 355–63; *A Better Guide Than Reason: Studies in the American Revolution* (LaSalle, IL: Sherwood Sugden & Co., 1979), 29–57; and *The Reactionary Imperative* (Peru, IL: Sherwood Sugden & Co., 1990), 219–27. For a sympathetic view of the Southern political tradition and the war to suppress secession as a tragedy, see Eugene Genovese, *The Southern Tradition* (Cambridge, MA: Harvard University Press, 1994).

25. Acton, *Selected Writings,* 278.

26. Acton, *Selected Writings.*

27. For a study of thirty-seven of these secessionist movements, see Bookman, Economics of *Secession.*

28. *Spectator,* 22 December 1866, 1420.

29. See Acton, "Political Causes of the American Revolution," in *Selected Writings,* 216–62.

30. For a glimpse at the unique institutionalized form this barbarism has taken in the United States see William Quirk and R. Randall Bridwell, *Judicial Dictatorship* (New

Brunswick: Transaction Publishers, 1995) and Raoul Berger, *Government by Judiciary* (Indianapolis: Liberty Classics, 1997). The United States represents the first regime to be governed by legalism (i.e., determining social policy by the courts).

Chapter Fifteen

1. Giambattista Vico, *The New Science of Giambattista Vico,* ed. and trans. Thomas Goddard Bergin and Max Harold Fisch (Ithaca and London: Cornell University Press, 1968), para. 1106.

2. Vico, *New Science,* para. 159. The expression "reflective malice" is Donald Verene's, from whose writings and conversation I have learned much about Vico. See his *Vico's Science of Imagination* (Ithaca and London: Cornell University Press, 1981), 195, especially the chapter "Wisdom and Barbarism," and his *Philosophy and the Return to Self-Knowledge* (New Haven: Yale University Press, 1997).

3. Giambattista Vico, *The Autobiography of Giambattista Vico,* trans. Thomas Goddard Bergin and Max Harold Fisch (Ithaca: Cornell University Press, 1984), 72–99.

4. John Gray, *Post-Liberalism: Studies in Political Thought* (New York: Routledge, 1993), 328.

5. See Christopher Berry, *Hume, Hegel, and Human Nature* (The Hague: Nijhoff, 1982); and Leon Pompa, *Human Nature and Historical Knowledge: Hume, Hegel, and Vico* (Cambridge: Cambridge University Press, 1990).

6. Isaiah Berlin, *The Crooked Timber of Humanity* (London: Jon Murray, 1990); Michael Oakeshott, *Rationalism in Politics and Other Essays,* ed. Timothy Fuller (Indianapolis: Liberty Classics, 1991), and *On Human Conduct* (Oxford: Oxford University Press, 1991); and John Gray, *Liberalisms: Essays in Political Philosophy* (New York: Routledge, 1989), and *Post-Liberalism,* chapter 20.

7. Much can be learned from a comparative study of Hume and Oakeshott on the nature of "civil association"; see Oakeshott, *On Human Conduct.*

8. Robert Nozick, *Anarchy, State, and Utopia* (New York: Basic Books, 1974); John Rawls, *Theory of Justice* (Cambridge: Belknap Press, 1970); Alan Gewirth, *Reason and Morality* (Chicago: University of Chicago Press, 1978); Ronald Dworkin, *Taking Rights Seriously* (London: Duckworth, 1977).

9. I have taken from John Gray the happy expression "philosophical fundamentalism" to characterize the transformation of the practice of liberty into a philosophical superstition, an act that bears more than a superficial resemblance to religious fundamentalism; see *Post-Liberalism,* 283–328.

10. Francis Fukuyama, *The End of History and the Last Man* (New York: Free Press, 1992).

11. That Hegel's philosophy necessarily identifies the philosophical act with the divine has been argued by Emil Fackenheim, *The Religious Dimension in Hegel's Thought* (Boston: Beacon Press, 1967), 162, and Stanley Rosen, *G. W. F. Hegel: An Introduction to the Science of Wisdom* (New York: Yale University Press, 1974), 130. For a contrary view, see William Maker, "Hegel's Blasphemy?" *History of Philosophy Quarterly* 9, no. 1 (January 1992).

12. Richard Rorty, *Contingency, Irony, and Solidarity* (Cambridge: Cambridge University Press, 1989), 44–45.

13. Alasdair MacIntyre, *Three Rival Forms of Moral Enquiry* (Notre Dame: University of Notre Dame Press, 1990), 67.

14. Alasdair MacIntyre, *Whose Justice? Which Rationality?* (Notre Dame: University of Notre Dame Press, 1988), 338–39.

15. Foucault's reply to Jacque Alain Miller is quoted in MacIntyre, *Three Rival Forms of Moral Enquiry,* 53.

16. David Hiley explores this theme in *Philosophy in Question* (Chicago: University of Chicago Press, 1988).

17. The first two passages quoted are from Orlan's "Interventions," made while under surgery. They were circulated in private but are to be published; they were translated by Tanya Augsburg, Michel A. Moos, and Rachel Knecht, in April 1995. The last quotation appears in Eugenie Lemoine-Luccioni, *La Robe: Essai psychoanalytique sur le vetement* (Paris: Editions de Seuil, 1984), 139. For an account of the meaning of Orlan's performances, see Tanya Augsburg's dissertation, "Private Theaters Onstage: Hysteria and the Female Medical Subject from Baroque Theatricality to Contemporary Feminist Performance" (Emory University, 1996). On Foucault's transgression of the limits, see Hiley, *Philosophy in Question,* 105–10.

18. Umberto Eco, *Postscript to the Name of the Rose* (San Diego: Harcourt Brace Jovanovich, 1984), 67–68. I am grateful to Greg Johnson for calling this passage to my attention.

19. Friedrich Nietzsche, *On the Genealogy of Morals* and *Ecce Homo,* trans. Walter Kaufmann and R. J. Hollingdale (New York: Vintage Books, 1967), 91.

20. Lucian, "The Sale of Philosophers," in *Lucian: Selected Works,* trans. Bryan R. Reardon (Indianapolis: Bobbs-Merrill, 1965).

INDEX